Horizons

Mathematics 1

Teacher's Guide

by
Sareta A. Cummins

Edited by
David J. Korecki

Illustrated by
Tye A. Rausch

Editorial Staff
Christine A. Korecki
John P. Robinett

Alpha Omega Publications, Inc.
Rock Rapids, IA

Horizons Mathematics 1 Teacher's Guide
© MCMXCI by Alpha Omega Publications, Inc.® All rights reserved.
804 N. 2nd Ave. E., Rock Rapids, IA 51246-1759

Printed in the United States of America
ISBN 978-1-58095-931-5

Contents

Section One   **Page**

Introduction

Before You Start 1

Readiness Evaluation Part A 3

Readiness Evaluation Part B 6

Remedial Exercises 11

Preparing a Lesson 33

Scope & Sequence 38

Manipulatives 40

Where to Use Mathematics Worksheets 44

Appearance of Concepts 46

Development of Concepts 51

Section Two

Teacher's Lessons 53

Section Three

Answer Key (Lessons 1–160) 375

Section Four

Worksheets (1–80) 469

Section Five

Worksheets Answer Key 551

Introduction

Before You Start ...

THE CHALLENGE

Today's average high school graduate knows and can do less math than their counterpart of ten, fifteen, or twenty years ago. Basic math skills have deteriorated to the point that many wonder if this country can continue to be a leader in shaping the technology of the future. Unfortunately, the general trend of modern education of all types is downward. Students in private education, while they score higher overall than public school students, still do poorly in math computation skills.

THE GOAL

The goal of this curriculum is to provide the parent and teacher with a tool that will help them effectively combat this deterioration of math skills by raising the level of student performance. Research of the content and methods of other existing curriculums, the concepts evaluated by achievement tests, and typical courses of study resulted in selection of the *Scope and Sequence* starting on page 38. This curriculum was not planned around any particular group of students. Rather, it was determined that the material in this curriculum constituted a reasonable level of performance for first grade students who have successfully completed an academic kindergarten program. The curriculum is designed so that the teacher can adapt its use to student(s) of widely varying ability. In other words, the curriculum is a tool that is capable of performing well over a broad range of student ability to help them achieve a higher minimum level of proficiency. The two major components of the curriculum are the student text (in two volumes) and the *Teacher's Guide*. These are the absolute minimum components for accomplishing the objective of teaching the concepts in the *Scope and Sequence*. Since this guide was designed as an integral part of the curriculum, it is absolutely necessary to use the guide. The guide contains activities not found in the student texts that are essential to accomplishment of the curriculum objectives. As you will see in the following sections, this *Teacher's Guide* contains a significant number of suggestions and helps for the teacher. Some manipulatives are optional. The optional manipulatives are identified with *italics* so that the teacher may easily see what is optional and what is essential.

THE DESIGN

Take a moment to look at the chart entitled, *Development of Concepts*, on page 51. Take note of how the curriculum

1

concepts are developed. The first presentation is usually a brief familiarization. Then the basic teaching is accomplished as part of three to five lessons. The thoroughness of a presentation depends on how new and how important the concept is to the student's academic development.

The Development

Each concept will be reviewed for one week after the complete presentation. For the next two months the concept will be presented every two weeks as a part of two or three consecutive lessons. After a break in presentation of four weeks, the concept will be thoroughly reviewed as part of the lesson for three to five days. This will be followed by a period of two months where the concept will be reviewed every two weeks as part of two or three lessons. This progression continues until the student(s) have had the opportunity to thoroughly master the concept.

An Example

Some mathematics curriculums might teach *time* for three weeks and then not go back to it again. In this curriculum it will be introduced and practiced for two weeks. For the next two months, *time* will be presented every two weeks as a part of two or three lessons to give the student(s) continual practice to develop mastery of the concept. The third month will be considered a break

from presenting the concept and *time* will not be taught. In the fourth month, *time* will first be thoroughly reviewed and again practiced every two weeks as a part of two or three lessons. By having a series of practices every two weeks, the student(s) will retain what they have learned to a greater degree. Short periods of exposure done many times is much more effective than long periods with fewer exposures. Since *time* has three aspects at this level (hour, half hour, and quarter hour), each aspect is introduced at its own interval. The *hour* is taught at the introduction, *half hour* a month later (following the same progression), and *quarter hour* another month later. After each aspect has a break from its presentation, the three aspects are presented together for the remainder of the year. Review the chart on page 51 to see how the concepts are developed.

READINESS EVALUATION

There are two parts to the *Readiness Evaluation*. *Part A* evaluates the student in regard to the concepts of color, size, shapes, direction/position, matching/categorizing, and sets. *Part B* evaluates the student in regard to the concepts of numbers, counting, addition, subtraction, and number sequence. It is recommended that you give the two evaluations at different times rather than together at the same time.

Readiness Evaluation
Part A

WHY EVALUATE READINESS?

Teaching could be defined as the process of starting from what a student knows and guiding him to a knowledge of new material. While this may not be a dictionary definition of teaching, it is descriptive of the processes involved. Determining a student's readiness for first grade mathematics is the first step to successful teaching.

TYPES OF READINESS

True readiness has little to do with chronological age. Emotional maturity and mental preparation are the main components of academic readiness. The teacher who is dealing directly with the student is best able to determine a child's emotional maturity. An emotionally immature student may need special student training in their problem areas. It might be wise, in this case, to delay placing them in the first grade until the next year. A child's mental *preparation* can be more easily discerned with a simple diagnostic evaluation. Observing the child's attitude of confidence or insecurity while taking the evaluation may help you determine their emotional readiness.

DETERMINING READINESS

While administering *Part A* of the evaluation, keep in mind that each question has suggestions for proper remediation if the student should fail to demonstrate sufficient skill in a concept area.

If a student of any age is not able to listen and follow directions, complete an assigned task, or read and write well enough to communicate; they will experience great difficulty with this course. Likewise, if a student has not acquired the concepts of color, size, shapes, direction/position, matching/categorizing, sets, numbers, counting, addition, subtraction, and number sequence, they may fail from the beginning. In other words, if a student has missed the concepts taught in a formal kindergarten program, they need to acquire that knowledge before entering this course of study.

READINESS EVALUATION, PART A

(Tell the student this will be like a game to relax them. You will ask the question and they get to find the answer.)

1. Use a preformed set of shapes or make a simple set out of card stock. (It would be best if these were not colored since it could distract from the purpose of this part of the evaluation.)

   A. Lay out a circle, square, triangle, rectangle, oval, octagon, star, heart, and diamond in front of the student.

   B. Name one of the four basic shapes (circle, square, triangle, or rectangle) and ask the student to pick it up and to place it back. Then ask them to identify each of the remaining three basic shapes, one at a time. If the student makes any errors, ask if they want to try again (giving a chance for any nervousness to pass). If the student gets all four basic shapes correct, ask them to tell you if they know what any of the others are called. Work with the student until they have a grasp of the four basic shapes. Their knowing the four basic shapes and at least familiarization with some of the others is satisfactory.

2. Use construction paper or colored items with the following ten colors: red, blue, yellow, green, orange, purple, brown, pink, black, and white.

   Ask the student to show you the requested color (whether correct or not, say okay). Now ask them to replace the first color and show you another color that you will name. The student should identify seven to ten colors correctly or be asked if they want to try again. (Don't be surprised if a student identifies one object for two different colors.) A little drill will normally solve any deficiency with colors.

3. Use a set of objects that are different in size, height, and thickness to evaluate a student's ability to make comparisons.

   Ask the student to tell you which is bigger or littler, larger or smaller, taller or shorter, thicker or thinner, etc. Ask which of the objects is longest, tallest, or thinnest. Repeat this activity (if necessary) until the student demonstrates, to your satisfaction, that they comprehend the concept of comparisons.

4. Using a globe or large ball, ask the student a series of directional questions about where you place a ruler in relationship to the globe, like:

A. Place the ruler above the globe and ask, "If this is 'above,' where is this?" (placing the ruler under the globe). Be aware that the student might answer down or even under, and be correct. Your objective is to determine their comprehension of relative position, not their memorization of word associations.

B. Using your hands, indicate one direction (left or right, front or behind, up or down, etc.) and ask the student what the opposite is.

C. Positional questions can be asked about off or on, open or closed, first or next, first or last, etc.

The student only needs to show familiarization with directions and positions and know the most basic ones. Directions and positions can be a very confusing area. Drill or time will resolve most difficulties.

5. Use pairs of items (clothing, pictures, blocks, or cut-out shapes) to evaluate a child's ability to identify one-to-one correspondence, and differences.

A. Have the student match three or four pairs of socks or picture blocks from a mixed group.

B. Have the student select and show you a different sock or picture from one you select.

C. Have the student count out three similar items for you and three for himself. (These can be similar in type like socks or in color like a red sock, a red block, and red crayon.)

If the student doesn't do well on this section, a little personal drill should take care of the difficulty.

6. Create two sets of two objects each, two sets of three objects each, a set of five objects, and a set of ten objects (use toothpicks, blocks, or whatever you have available).

Ask the student to select the set with the least number of items, the greatest number, and two that are of equal number. A little drill should solve any confusion the student might have with the exercise.

If the student is unable to complete these activities successfully after some remedial drill, it would be wise to place the student in *Horizons Math K* so that he will receive all of the preparation needed to begin this first grade mathematics curriculum.

Readiness Evaluation Part B

PURPOSE
Readiness Evaluation, Part B helps the teacher to determine if student(s) are ready to begin study at the first grade level. It is designed specifically for the area of math concepts.

INSTRUCTIONS
Do this evaluation before school starts. If this is not possible, work with the student(s) on a one-to-one basis (before or after school, recess, or lunch time). The evaluation should take about ten minutes. It would be helpful to evaluate all of the students to determine what each student knows. However, you may want to evaluate only those student(s) who have not had a thorough kindergarten program. During the first week of school, you may find it necessary to evaluate some additional student(s) especially those who enroll later in the year or show considerable frustration with the curriculum.

This is an oral evaluation with the exception of activity 2 and 3 under **Numbers**. The student will need a clean sheet of paper for the written part of the evaluation. Record the student(s) response to each activity on the score sheet provided. Write "1" on the blank if the response is correct and "0" on the blank if the response is incorrect.

The first two sections (**Numbers** and **Counting**) are self explanatory. Have the student(s) orally answer the questions given for the last three concepts (**Addition**, **Subtraction**, and **Number Sequence**).

MINIMUM SCORES
The student must achieve certain minimum scores in the various sections in order to be ready for first grade. The minimum number of points for that section or numbered item is listed in parentheses after each section or numbered item.

In the first concept, **Numbers**, the student must have a total score of nine out of the twelve possible points on the score sheet. If the student does not get the minimum number of points, they must do remedial exercises to prepare them for this first grade curriculum. Note that item two, writing the numerals from 1 to 10, requires the student get eight of ten correct to get the one point on the score sheet.

In **Counting**, the student must have a total score of two of the four points on the score sheet. If the student does not get two of the four points on the score sheet, they must do remedial exercises. Note that in item one the student must get 16 of 20 correct in counting out loud to 20 to get the one point on the score sheet.

After completing the **Numbers** and **Counting** concepts, stop to total the student's scores. A student who does not attain the minimum score should not complete the rest of the evaluation. They must do all ten of the remedial exercises.

Below you will find a flow diagram that explains how to properly use the information obtained from the evaluation.

If the student does not achieve the minimum score:	If the student achieves the minimum score:
End the evaluation and have the student complete remedial exercises one through ten.	Continue the evaluation. In **Addition** and **Subtraction**, the student must get four of seven points for each of these concepts. If they do not, then they must do remedial exercise 10. In **Number Sequence**, the student needs to get five out of nine points. If they do not, they must do remedial exercise 10.

At this point, it is the teacher's responsibility to determine if the student should proceed with the first grade curriculum or be placed in *Horizons Math K*.

SCORING
NUMBERS
    1. 5 out of 6 (83%)
    2. 8 out of 10 (80%) for one point
    3. 3 out of 5 (60%)
COUNTING
    1. 16 out of 20 (80%) for one point
    2. 8 out of 10 on counting by 10's, 5's, or 2's (80%)
ADDITION
    4 out of 7 (57%)
SUBTRACTION
    4 out of 7 (57%)
NUMBER SEQUENCE
    5 out of 9 (56%)

Points on score sheet

NUMBERS (note that item two requires 8 of 10 correct to score one point on the score sheet)

(9 of 12)

1. Have the student tell you the following numbers as you point to them on the number chart: a. 6, b. 13, c. 45, d. 27, e. 89, and f. 30. *(5 of 6)*
2. Have the student write the numerals 1 to 10. *(8 of 10)*
3. Have the student write the following numbers as you say them with number chart visible to the student: a. 4, b. 15, c. 39, d. 51, and e. 80. *(3 of 5)*

COUNTING (note that item two requires 8 of 10 correct to score one point on the score sheet)

(2 of 4)

1. Have the student count from 1 to 20 out loud. *(16 of 20)*
2. Have the student count out loud: a. by 10's to 100, b. by 5's to 50, and c. by 2's to 20. *(8 of 10 on any of these three)*

ADDITION

(4 of 7)

1. When you put two numbers together are you adding or subtracting?
2. What is one more than 8?
3. What is one more than 13?
4. What is 27 plus 1?
5. What is 6 plus 0?
6. What is 15 plus 0?
7. What is 49 plus 0?

SUBTRACTION

(4 of 7)

1. When you take one number away from another are you adding or subtracting?
2. What is one taken away from 9?
3. What is one less than 18?
4. What is 52 minus 1?
5. What is 4 minus 0?
6. What is 12 minus 0?
7. What is 0 taken away from 33?

NUMBER SEQUENCE

Show the student flash cards of these numbers and ask the associated question.

(5 of 9)

1. This is a seven. What number comes after it?
2. This is a fourteen. What number comes after it?
3. This is a thirty-six. What number comes after it?
4. This is a five. What number comes before it?
5. This is a seventeen. What number comes before it?
6. This is a twenty-five. What number comes before it?
7. This is a four and this is a six. What number comes between them?
8. This is a forty-one and this is a forty-three. What number comes between them?
9. This is a fifty-nine and this is a sixty-one. What number comes between them?

READINESS EVALUATION, PART B: SCORE SHEET

Write "1" in the box if the response is correct and "0" in the box if the response is incorrect.
Reproduce this form as needed.

Student's name:

NUMBERS	1. a.	
	b.	
	c.	
	d.	
	e.	
	f.	
	2.	
	3. a.	
	b.	
	c.	
	d.	
	e.	
Concept Total (minimum of 9)		
COUNTING	1.	
	2. a.	
	b.	
	c.	
Concept Total (minimum of 2)		
ADDITION	1.	
	2.	
	3.	
	4.	
	5.	
	6.	
	7.	
Concept Total (minimum of 4)		
SUBTRACTION	1.	
	2.	
	3.	
	4.	
	5.	
	6.	
	7.	
Concept Total (minimum of 4)		
NUMBER SEQUENCE	1.	
	2.	
	3.	
	4.	
	5.	
	6.	
	7.	
	8.	
	9.	
Concept Total (minimum of 5)		

9

READINESS EVALUATION, PART B: SCORE SHEET

Write "1" in the box if the response is correct and "0" in the box if the response is incorrect.
Reproduce this form as needed.

Student's name:

NUMBERS	1. a.										
	b.										
	c.										
	d.										
	e.										
	f.										
	2.										
	3. a.										
	b.										
	c.										
	d.										
	e.										
Concept Total (minimum of 9)											
COUNTING	1.										
	2. a.										
	b.										
	c.										
Concept Total (minimum of 2)											
ADDITION	1.										
	2.										
	3.										
	4.										
	5.										
	6.										
	7.										
Concept Total (minimum of 4)											
SUBTRACTION	1.										
	2.										
	3.										
	4.										
	5.										
	6.										
	7.										
Concept Total (minimum of 4)											
NUMBER SEQUENCE	1.										
	2.										
	3.										
	4.										
	5.										
	6.										
	7.										
	8.										
	9.										
Concept Total (minimum of 5)											

Remedial Exercises

PURPOSE

The ten remedial exercises are designed to help the student(s) who need a refresher unit in writing the numerals (1–10); understanding number concepts (one to ten); and counting by ones, twos, fives, and tens to one hundred.

ACTIVITIES: EXERCISES 1–9

Each exercise consists of practice in tracing a number (1–10) several times and then writing the number. Guide the student(s) by pointing out the place to begin the strokes and the complete forming of each number. If additional practice in forming numerals is needed, use *Worksheet 1* given in the *Teacher's Guide*, which may be copied as many times as needed. Each exercise also has correspondence activities. For each of these activities, draw some objects on the chalk board and then draw lines to corresponding objects as examples for the student(s) to follow. When an exercise has an activity on sets, practice counting sets of objects either on the chalk board or flannel board, being careful that the student(s) say one number each time they point to an object. In Exercise 9, *Student Activity Five* you will need to dictate some numbers chosen at random to the students.

EXERCISE 10

Exercise 10 requires the guidance of the teacher for each activity. Carefully discuss the directions for *Student Activity One.* Discuss with the student(s) how counting by twos is the same thing as counting every two numbers, every other number, or every second number. Instruct the student(s) to circle the number "2." Then count over two and circle "4," count over two and circle "6," continuing until the student(s) can complete the chart on their own. Follow the same procedure for *Student Activity Two* (counting by tens) and *Three* (counting by fives). For *Student Activity Four*, *Five*, and *Six* discuss with the student(s) how the number that comes "after" is the same as one more than the number or adding one to the number. The number that comes "before" is the same as one less than the number or subtracting one from the number. Allow the student(s) to use the number chart in completing *Student Activity Four, Five,* and *Six*.

When the student(s) have completed these remedial exercises you must decide if the student(s) have demonstrated sufficient mastery of the material to be able to proceed with the first grade mathematics curriculum.

zero   0

0 boats

(1) Trace the number zero.

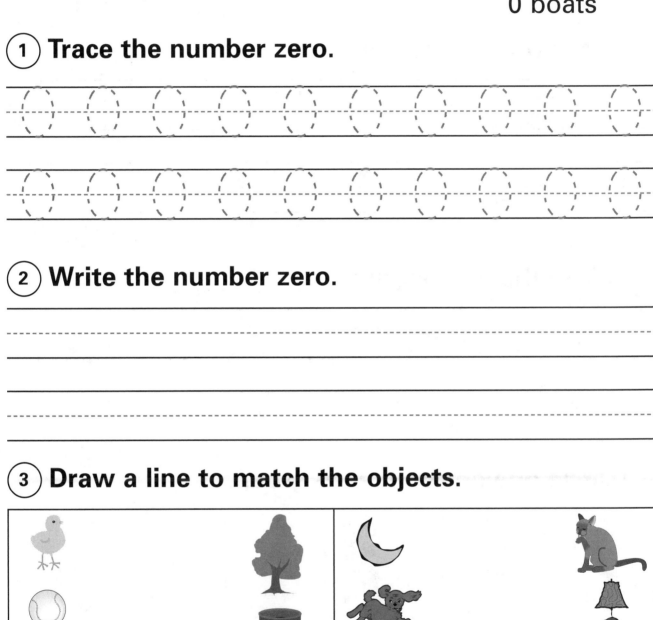

(2) Write the number zero.

(3) Draw a line to match the objects.

one　　1

1 boat

④ Trace the number one.

⑤ Write the number one.

⑥ Circle one object in each group.

two 2

2 boats

① **Trace the number two.**

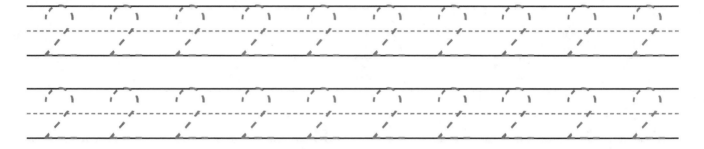

② **Write the number two.**

③ **Color two in each group.**

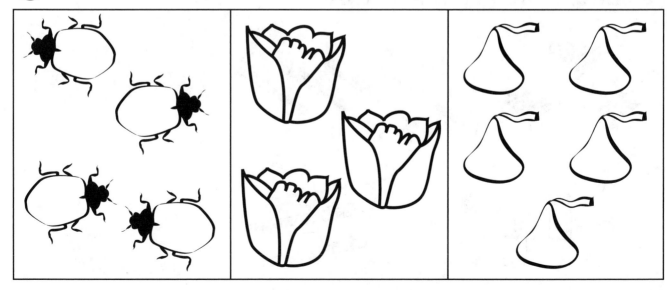

three   3

3 boats

④ **Trace the number three.**

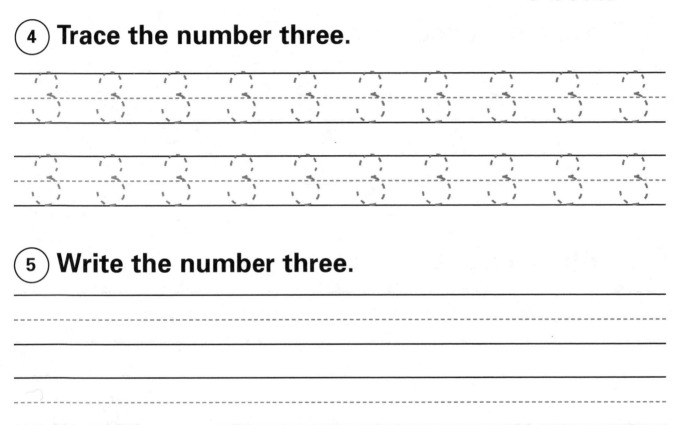

⑤ **Write the number three.**

⑥ **Circle the groups of three.**

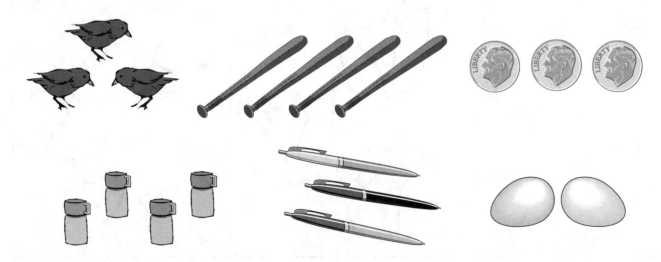

four 4

4 boats

(1) Trace the number four.

(2) Write the number four.

(3) Draw four legs for the table.

Draw four cookies on the plate.

five 5

5 boats

4 **Trace the number five.**

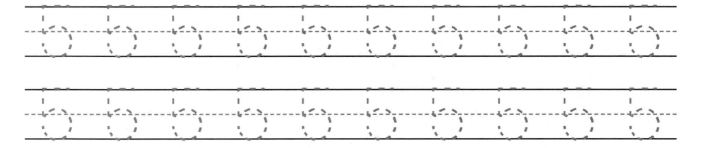

5 **Write the number five.**

6 **Circle the groups of five.**

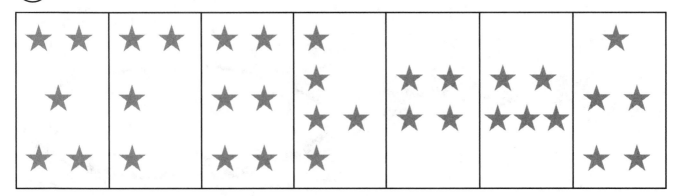

0 1 2 3 4 5

zero   one   two   three   four   five

(1) Trace the numbers to five.

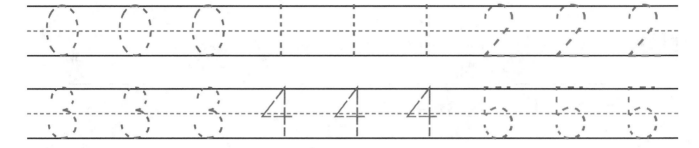

(2) Write the numbers to five.

(3) Draw a line to match the objects.

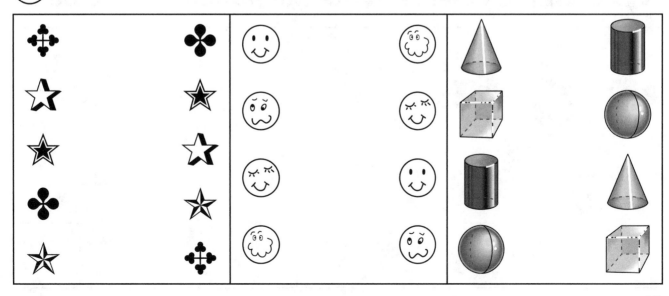

4 **Draw a line to match the objects.**

5 **Draw a line to match.**

four	1	☆ ☆	1
one	2	●●●●	2
five	3	■	3
three	4	▲▲ ▲▲▲	4
two	5	★ ★ ★	5

6 **Count the objects. Write the number in the box.**

six   6

6 boats

(1) **Trace the number six.**

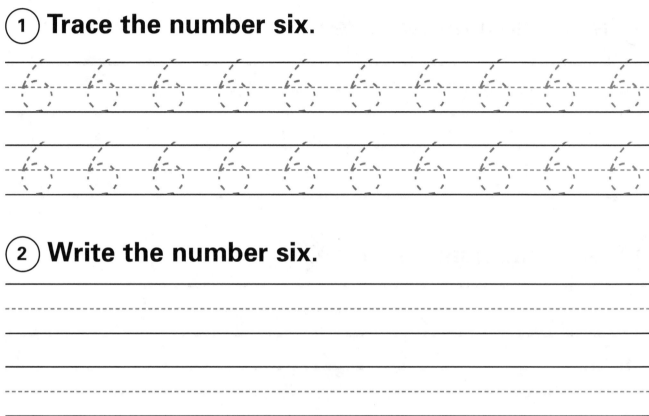

(2) **Write the number six.**

(3) **Put an X on the groups of six.**

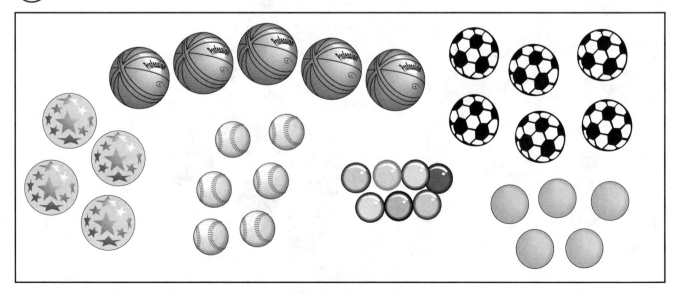

seven 7

7 boats

(4) **Trace the number seven.**

(5) **Write the number seven.**

(6) **Circle the groups of seven.**

eight 8

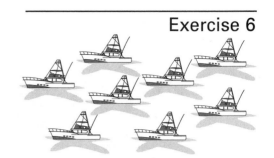

8 boats

① **Trace the number eight.**

② **Write the number eight.**

③ **Color eight in each group.**

nine 9

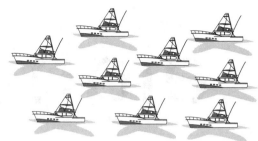

9 boats

4 **Trace the number nine.**

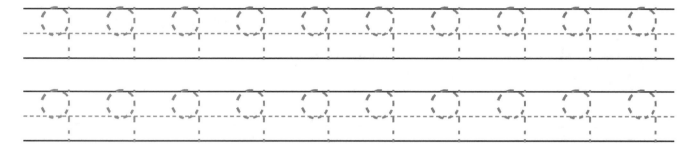

5 **Write the number nine.**

6 **Draw nine candles on the cake.**

Draw nine apples on the tree.

ten 10

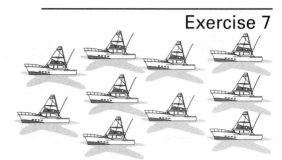

10 boats

(1) Trace the number ten.

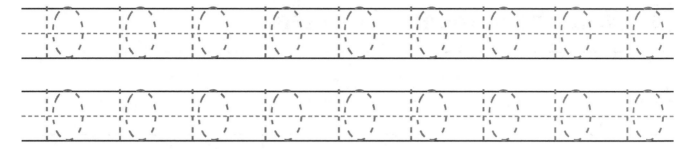

(2) Write the number ten.

(3) Color ten pencils.

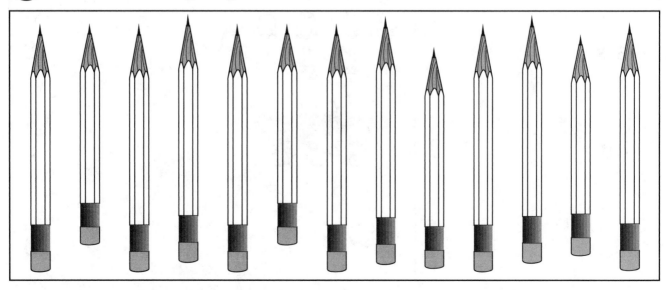

(4) **Trace the numbers six to ten.**

6 6 6 6 7 7 7 7 8 8

8 8 9 9 9 9 10 10 10 10

(5) **Write the numbers six to ten.**

(6) **Draw a line to match.**

seven	6		6
nine	7		7
six	8		8
ten	9		9
eight	10		10

numbers

(1) Trace the numbers to ten.

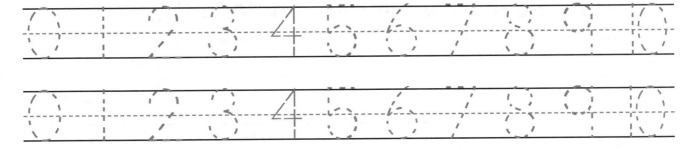

(2) Write the numbers to ten.

(3) Draw a line to match the objects.

4 **Trace the numbers ten to nineteen.**

10 11 12 13 14 15 16 17 18 19

10 11 12 13 14 15 16 17 18 19

5 **Write the numbers ten to nineteen.**

6 **Count the objects. Write the number in the box.**

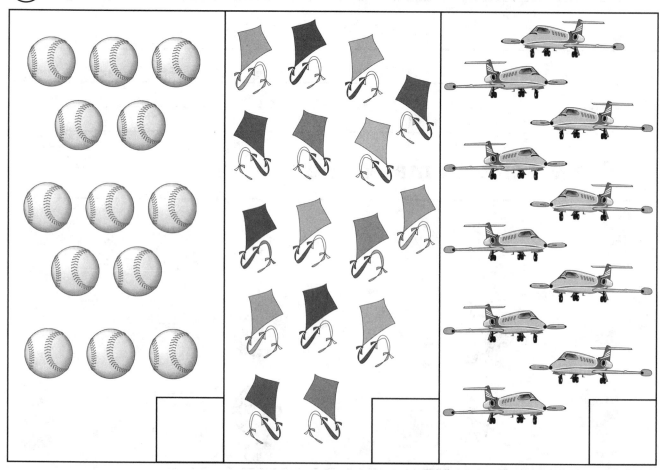

28

numbers

1 **Trace the numbers twenty to twenty-nine.**

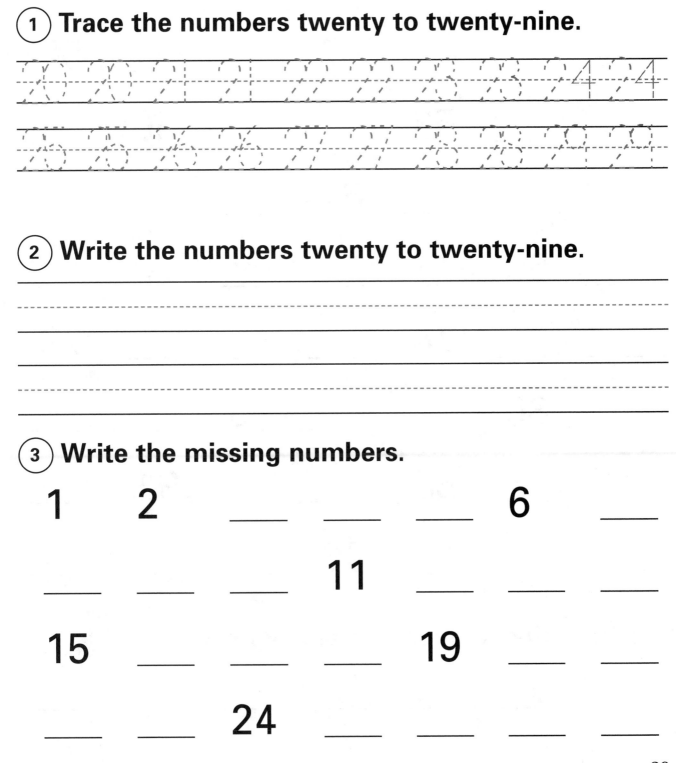

2 **Write the numbers twenty to twenty-nine.**

3 **Write the missing numbers.**

1	2	__	__	__	6	__
__	__	__	11	__	__	__
15	__	__	__	19	__	__
__	__	24	__	__	__	__

4 **Write the missing numbers.**

30   31   ___   ___   34   ___   36

___   ___   39   ___   ___   42   ___

44   ___   ___   47   ___   ___   50

___   ___   53   ___   ___   56   ___

___   ___   ___   61   ___   ___   ___

___   66   ___   ___   ___   70   ___

___   ___   74   ___   ___   ___   78

___   80   ___   83   ___   ___

___   ___   88   ___   ___   91   ___

___   ___   96   ___   ___

5 **Write the numbers the teacher says.**

___   ___   ___   ___   ___

counting

① Circle the numbers used in counting by twos.

② Color the numbers used in counting by tens.

③ X the numbers used in counting by fives.

0	1	2	3	4	5	6	7	8	9
10	11	12	13	14	15	16	17	18	19
20	21	22	23	24	25	26	27	28	29
30	31	32	33	34	35	36	37	38	39
40	41	42	43	44	45	46	47	48	49
50	51	52	53	54	55	56	57	58	59
60	61	62	63	64	65	66	67	68	69
70	71	72	73	74	75	76	77	78	79
80	81	82	83	84	85	86	87	88	89
90	91	92	93	94	95	96	97	98	99

(4) **Write the number that comes after.**

16 ___   61 ___   50 ___

5 ___   87 ___   42 ___

24 ___   38 ___   93 ___

(5) **Write the number that comes before.**

___ 8   ___ 67   ___ 23

___ 35   ___ 40   ___ 91

___ 14   ___ 52   ___ 76

(6) **Write the missing number that comes between.**

3 ___ 5   36 ___ 38   14 ___ 16

70 ___ 72   55 ___ 57   82 ___ 84

21 ___ 23   48 ___ 50   67 ___ 69

Preparing a Lesson

GENERAL INFORMATION

Although a guide is provided for writing the numerals in lesson one, please feel free to use the same writing style that you are teaching for handwriting and using in your other subjects. Also there is some room on the teacher lessons for you to write your own notes. The more you personalize your teacher guide in this way, the more useful it will be to you.

You will notice that there are 160 student lessons in the curriculum. This allows for the inevitable interruptions to the school year like holidays, test days, inclement weather days, and those unexpected interruptions. It also allows the teacher the opportunity to spend more time teaching any concept that the student(s) may have difficulty with. Or, you might wish to spend a day doing some of the fun activities mentioned in the Teaching Tips. If you find that the student(s) need extra drill, use the worksheets as extra lessons.

STUDENT'S LESSONS ORGANIZATION

Student lessons are designed to be completed in thirty to thirty-five minutes a day. If extra manipulatives or worksheets are utilized, you will need to allow more time for teaching. Each lesson consists of a major concept and practice of previously taught concepts. If the student(s) find the presence of four or five different activities in one lesson a little overwhelming at the beginning, start guiding the student(s) through each activity. By the end of two weeks, they should be able to work more independently as they adjust to the format. Mastery of a new concept is not necessary the first time it is presented. Complete understanding of a new concept will come as the concept is approached from different views using different methods at different intervals. Because of the way the curriculum is designed, *the student(s) need to do all the problems in every lesson every day*. Directions to the student(s) are given in black type and examples or explanations are presented in blue type. If you expect to have very many students, you will find it extremely helpful to remove all pages from the individual student books and file them (all of Lesson 1 in one file, all of Lesson 2 in another file, etc.) before school starts. This will keep the lessons from being damaged or lost in the students' desks.

Tests

Starting with Lesson 10, tests are included in every tenth lesson. They should require approximately fifteen minutes to administer. If your daily schedule time is a major factor, you may teach Lesson 10 on the following day. This will require efficient scheduling of the lessons throughout the year to complete the program by the end of the school year. Do not make the test a special lesson. Allow the student(s) to perceive the test as a regular lesson with no undue pressure. The purpose of testing is not just to measure student progress, although that is an important consideration. A test is also an important teaching tool. It should be returned to the student and any missed items discussed so that it is a true learning experience. For this reason, it is important to grade and return the tests as soon as possible while material is fresh in the student's mind. The test structure is such that the student(s) will have had sufficient practice with a concept to have learned it before being tested. Therefore, no concept is tested until the initial presentation has been completed. For example, test 2 in lesson 20 covers concepts completed in lessons 6–15. Test 8 in lesson 80 will cover lessons 66–75.

TEACHER'S LESSONS ORGANIZATION

Each lesson is organized into the following sections: *Concepts*; *Objectives*; *Teaching Tips*; *Materials, Supplies, and Equipment*; *Activities*; *Worksheets*; and occasionally a maxim or proverb. Each of the sections have a distinct symbol to help you locate them on the page of the teacher's lesson. To be a master teacher you will need to prepare each lesson well in advance.

Concepts

Concepts are listed at the beginning of each lesson in the following order: 1.) Concepts taught by the teacher from the activities in the *Teacher's Guide* that do not have a corresponding written activity in the student lesson 2.) New concepts 3.) Concepts that are practiced from previous lessons (listed in the order they appear in the student lesson). First grade math has seventeen major concepts. These are developed in a progression that is designed to give the student(s) a solid foundation in the basic math skills while providing enough variety to hold the student's interest. Definitions are given for new terms.

Objectives

The Objectives list criteria for the student's performance. They state what the student should be able to do at the completion of the lesson. You will find objectives helpful in determining the student's progress, the need for remedial work, and readiness for more advanced information. Objectives are stated in terms of measurable student performance so that the teacher has a fixed level of performance to be attained before the student(s) are ready to progress to the next level.

Teaching Tips

Each tip is related to one of the Activities in the lesson. Some Teaching Tips require the teacher to make a manipulative needed to complete the activity. Teaching Tips are optional activities that the teacher can do to enhance the teaching process. You will find them useful for helping the student who needs additional practice to master the concepts or for the student who needs to be challenged by extra work. The manipulatives needed only in the Teaching Tips are listed in *italics* to signify that they are optional.

Materials, Supplies, and Equipment

Materials, Supplies, and Equipment lists the things you'll need to find before you teach each lesson. Each item listed in *italics* is an optional item and will be referred to in *italics* in the Teaching Tips or Activities section. Sometimes you will also find instructions on how to make your own materials, supplies, and equipment. When "Number Chart" is listed, it is understood to refer to the chart for 0–99. The number chart for 100–199 will state "Number Chart 100–199." A complete list of all manipulatives and where they are used starts on page 40.

Activities

The Activities section is where the teacher will concentrate most of her time. Here the teacher will find step-by-step directions for teaching each lesson. All activities are designed to be teacher directed both in the student lesson and in the teacher's guide. You will need to use your own judgement concerning how much time is necessary to carry out the activities. Be sure, however, that the student(s) do every problem of every lesson. When the activity is part of the student lesson you will find it referred to as ***Student Activity One, Student Activity Two,*** etc. referring to the number in the circle on the student lesson. If the activity is not part of the student lesson there will be no bold face italic reference and the student will receive the activity from the teacher. Each activity is important to the over all scope of the lesson and must be completed. Do not omit any portion of the activities unless the student(s) have thoroughly mastered the concept being presented. Please do not put off looking at the activities in the lesson until you are actually teaching. Taking time to preview what you will be teaching is essential. Choose the manipulatives that fit your program best.

Worksheets

There is approximately one worksheet for every two lessons. If worksheets are suggested in a particular lesson you will find them listed in the Worksheets section. Each worksheet has a worksheet number and the number of the lesson with which it is associated. Note that some worksheets will be used over and over as resources, so you'll need to keep a master copy. The *Teacher's Guide* identifies where these resource worksheets are essential to the lessons. All addition and subtraction drill sheets are included in the worksheets. If the Worksheet symbol is on the page, there is a worksheet associated with that lesson. The worksheets will be handy for many purposes. You might use them for extra work for student(s) who demonstrate extra aptitude or ability or as remedial work for the student(s) who demonstrate a lack of aptitude or ability. You may also make your own worksheets and note where you would use them in the worksheet section on the teacher's lesson.

Maxims

In some lessons you will find a short maxim or proverb at the bottom of the right hand page.

These are intended for the teacher to share with the student and discuss. These maxims provide a collection of various wise and pithy sayings that deal with character. You will find many opportunities to challenge your student(s) in the day-to-day activities of life in these sayings. You may use or not use them as you wish.

Lesson Summary

The curriculum will work best when you prepare in the following manner. First, note that the teacher's lesson has items that pertain to an overview of the lesson on the left-hand page. The details are on the right-hand page. It is suggested that you first look at the Concepts involved in the lesson. Then study the Objectives to get an idea of the tasks that the student(s) will need to perform to complete the lesson. Next, look at the Activities to get an idea of the presentation of the lesson. If you would like to view the student lessons, the complete student curriculum is included in reduced format in the answer key section. This presentation will allow you to see the whole student lesson in one place as well as all the answers at the same time. You will need more preparation for some of the activities that aren't in the student lessons. Some of the activities will refer to a worksheet which you will find listed in the Worksheet section below the Activities section.

You might also want to check the Teaching Tips section for any additional ideas on presenting the lesson. Finally, check the Materials, Supplies, and Equipment for any resources that you may need before you begin the lesson.

ANSWER KEYS

The answer keys section of the *Teacher's Guide* provides answers (in red) to the student lessons (reduced so that there are four student pages on each answer key page and printed in black and white). It is suggested that you give the student(s) a grade for tests only. Daily work is to be a learning experience for the student, so do not put unnecessary pressure on them. You should correct every paper, but you should not grade every paper. This means that each lesson should be marked for correct and incorrect answers, but it is not necessary to record a letter or percentage grade on every lesson. The lessons should then be returned to the student(s) so that they have the opportunity to learn from their mistakes.

WORKSHEETS

The next section contains the worksheets. Note that some worksheets will be used over and over as resources, so you will need to keep a master copy. Worksheets are reproducible and may be copied freely. You will find a complete listing of worksheets, where they are used, and which worksheets are used more than once on pages 44 and 45. Separate packets of all the necessary worksheets for an individual student are also available.

WORKSHEET ANSWER KEYS

Answer keys to the worksheets are provided in the same manner as for the student lessons and reduced so that there are four worksheets on each page of the answer key. The multiple use worksheets do not have answer keys.

1. COUNTING 1–200
(Recognition)

By 1's, 10's, 5's, 2's, 3's, 6's, 9's, 4's, 8's, 7's to 100
By 1's from 100–200
One-to-one correspondence
Even and odd numbers
Tally marks
Word numbers to 100

2. ORDINAL AND CARDINAL NUMBERS
(Recognition and Use)

First, second, third, etc. to 10
The number that comes between
The number that comes after
The number that comes before a given number
The number that comes before and after a given number

3. CORRESPONDENCE OF QUANTITIES
(Distinguish Between)

Big—little
Large—small
Tall—short
Less than—greater than
Long—short
Equal—not equal

4. PLACE VALUE
(Digit Value)

Ones
Tens
Hundreds

5. ADDITION

Addition facts 1–18
Two double- and triple-digit numbers
Three single- and double-digit numbers
Horizontal and vertical addition
Carrying in the ones' place
Word problems

6. CALENDAR
(Memorize and Use)

Months of the year
Days of the week

7. TIME
(Read and Write)

Hour
Half hour
Quarter hour

8. SUBTRACTION

Subtraction facts 1–18
Two double- and triple-digit numbers
without borrowing
Horizontal and vertical subtraction
Word problems

9. MONEY

(Recognition, Value, and Use)

Penny, nickel, dime, quarter, and
   dollar
Adding

10. MEASUREMENT

(Practice and Use)

Inches
Centimeters

11. FRACTIONS

(Meaning and Recognition)

1/2, 1/3, 1/4, 1/5, 1/6, 1/8

12. SETS

(Count and Use)

Groups

13. SHAPES

(Recognition and
Characteristics)

Circle	Oval	Cylinder
Square	Diamond	Cube
Triangle	Octagon	Cone
Rectangle	Sphere	

14. GRAPHS

(Read and Draw)

Bar Graph

15. UNITS OF MEASURE

(Identify)

Dozen
Ounce, cup, pint, quart, and gallon
   (liquid)
Pound

16. SEQUENCE

(Create and Identify)

Numbers
Events

17. ESTIMATION

(Practice)

Rounding numbers using the number
   line
Height
Length
Quantity

Manipulatives

(Italic numbers indicate optional use of a manipulative.)

Manipulative Name	Description	Used In Lesson
Alarm clock or timer		*53, 54*
Bags	(self closing)	*79*
Balls	(2 small)	*75*
Bar graph		113
Bread	lb. loaf	132, 137
Butter	lb.	132, 137
Calendar	(picture)	*14*, 15, 17, 23, 24, *28*, 30, *39*, *41*, *45*, 71, 72, 86, 101, *127*, 129, *130*, 143, 144, 154, 155
Cardboard	(8" x 10")	*62*
Clock model	(large)	16, 17, 18, 19, 20, 21, 27, 28, 29, 42, 43, 44, 45, 56, 74, 75, 76, 86, 89, 90, *91*, 118, 119, 120, 144, 145, 154, 155, 156
Clock model	(small)	19, 20, 28, 30, 43, 45, 54, 55, 68, 69, 75, 76, 87, 118, 119, 120, 133, 145, 155, 156
Construction paper		*19*, *39*, *41*, *43*, 44, *67*, *78*, *83*, *93*, *105*,*106*, *121*
Counting chips		*5*, 72, 73, *75*, *76*, 78, 102, *103*, *110*, 115, 117, *120*, *131*, *138*, *139*, *140*, 150, *158*
Crayons		2, *41*, 52, 68, 71, 105, 113
Egg carton		*75*, 104
Flannel board		4, *10*, 12, 13, 33, 35, 38, 39, 43, 49, 51, 53, 116, 157, 158
Flannel board materials		4, *10*, 53, 59, 157, 158

Manipulative Name	Description	Used In Lesson
Flash cards	addition facts 1–9	7, 9, 10, 11, 12
Flash cards	addition facts 1–18	13, 14, 15, 16, 17, 18, 19, 20, 21, 22, 23, 24, 25, 26, 27, 28, 29, 30, 31, 32, 33, 34, 35, 36, 37, 38, 39, 40, *65*, 73, 104, 118, 119, 122, 124, 127, 129, 132, 134, *136*, 137, 139, 142, 144, 147, 149, 152, 154, 157, 159
Flash cards	days of the week	*40*, *41*, *71*, *72* , 86, 104, 105, 130, 143, *155*
Flash cards	= and ≠ symbols	13, 14, 18, 29, 31, 41, *42*, *51*, *52*, 53, *67*, 79, *80*, 109, *133*, 134, *159*
Flash cards	< and > symbols	7, 8, *10*, 20, 21, 32, 43, 65, *77*, *88*, 114, 139, 160
Flash cards	liquid measure	97, 98, 99, 119
Flash cards	minus sign	53, *63*
Flash cards	months of the year	12, 13, *15*, 27, 61, *62*, 84, 85, 101, 127, 128, *141*, *152*, 153
Flash cards	ordinal numbers	*2*, *6*, *58*, 70, 92, 114, 156
Flash cards	shapes	82, 83, 84, 93, 94, 95, 104, 105, 106, 115, 116, 117, 126, 127, 146, 147, 158
Flash cards	solids	108, 109, 110, *111*, *121*, 132, 133, 153
Flash cards	subtraction 1–9	56, 57, 58, 59, 60, 61, 62, 63, 64, 65, 66, 67, 68, 69, 70, 71, 72, 73, 74, 75
Flash cards	subtraction 1–18	76, 77, 78, 79, 80, 116, 117, 118, 121, 123, 126, 128, 131, 133, 136, 138, 141, 143, 146, 148, 151, 153, 156, 158
Flash cards	subtraction 10–18	81, 82, 83, 84, 85, 86, 87, 88, 89, 90, 91, 92, 93, 94, 95, 96, 97, 98, 99, 100, 101, 102, 103, 104, 105, 106, 107, 108, 109, 110, 111, 112, 113, 114, 115, 150
Flash cards	tally marks	*12*, *18*, 22, 24, 25, *66*
Flash cards	whole numbers	*3*, 6, 8, *12*, 13, 25, 26, 28, *32*, 53, 72, 77, *82*

Manipulative Name	Description	Used In Lesson
Flash cards	word numbers	*12*, 13, 18, 24, 25, *32*, 47, 48, *53*, 60, *63*, *68*, 82, 84, 85, 86, 100, 110, *111*, 122, 135, *136*, 141, 142, *146*, *147*
Flour	5 lb. bag	132, 137
Fraction materials		35, 38, 39, 43, 49, *50*, 51, *52*, *53*, *54* , *55*, *64*, *65*, *66*, *67*, *78*, *79*, *80*, 81, 116, 148, *149*, *159*
Graph paper		*148*
Growth chart		47, *93*
Jelly beans	(Glass jar of)	*101*
Happy face stamp		*46*, 47, 48, 49, 51, 52, 53, 54
Liquid measure containers		97, 98, 99, 119, 120, 142, 143
Meter stick		*130*
Newspaper	Word numbers *grocery ads*	*112*, *134* , *142*
Number line		1, 6, 7, 8, 9, 10, 11, 12, 13, 14, 15, 16, 18, *19*, *36*, *42*, 55, 56, 57, 58, 59, 60, 61, 62, 63, *71*, 76, 99, *106*, 112, 119, 125, 138, 148
Number chart		1, 2, 3, 4, 5, 6, 7, 8, 9, 10, 11, 12, 13, 14, 15, 16, 17, 18, 19, 20, 21, 22, 23, 24, 25, 26, 27, 28, 29, 30, 31, 32, 33, 36, 37, 38, 39, 40, 41, 42, 44, 45, 48, 49, 52, 53, 54, 55, 56, 58, 59, 60, 61, 62, 63, 64, 65, 66, 67, 68, 69, 70, 71, 72, 73, 74, *75*, 77, 78, 79, 80, 82, 88, 89, 90, 91, 92, 93, 94, 95, 96, 98, 99, 101, 105, 106, 107, 108, 112, 113, 114, 115, 118, 120, 123, 124, 125, 126, 127, 128, 129, 131, 136, 137, 138, 139, 141, 142, 143, 144, 151, 152, 153, 154, 159
Number chart	100–199	83, 84, 85, 86, 95, 96, 87, 88, 93, 94, 95, 96, 97, 98, 99, 102, 103, 105, 107, 109, 110, 111, 116, 121, 122, 123, 133, 134, 135, 137, 145, 146, 153
Paper plate	1 per student	*43*
Paste or glue		*19*, *66*, *67*, *75*, *142*
Place value game cards		*131*

Manipulative Name	Description	Used In Lesson
Place value materials		5, *6*, 7, 9, *10*, *11*, 13, *36*, *37*, *48*, *49* , *59*, *60*, *61*, 81, 82, *83*, *84*, *85*, *86*, *96*, *100*, *107*, 123, 124, *128*, 131, 132, *157*
Plastic rings	from 6-pack of pop	128
Play money		4, 15, *23*, 26, *27*, 28, 29, 32, 33, 34, 35, *36*, 37, *38*, *41*, *43*, *45*, 46, *47*, 48, 49, *51*, 52, 53, 54, *56*, *57*, 58, 59, *60*, 63, 64, 73, 87, 88, 89, *98*, *99*, 103, 104, 114, *118*, *119*, 122, 123, 124, 126, 127, 129, 130, 136, 137, 138, *139*, *140*, 151, 152, 153, 154
Poster board		*19*, *66*, *77*, *78*, *79*, *90*
Real money		*29*, *33*, *34*, *48*, *51*, *64*, *89*
Rock		132, 137
Ruler	(centimeter)	91, 92, 93, 94, 95, 105, 106, 107, 113, 114, *119*, 126, 130, 140, 141, 158, 159
Ruler	(12")	20, 31, 32, 33, 34, 35, 45, 46, 47, 57, 69, 70, 81, *102*, 124, 144, 145, 149, 150, 157, 159, 160
Scales		132, 135, *136*
Solid models		*108*, *109*, 110, 111, 112, 121, 122, 142, 143, 152, 153
Spinner		*58*
Straws		*57*, *72*, *82*
Sales receipt		*56*
String or yarn		*19*
Typing paper		57, *105*, *142*
World Book Encyclopedia	Vol. 3	*61*
Yardstick		20, 102, 139, *160*
3" x 5" cards		*35*, *50*, *69*, *80*

Where To Use
Mathematics Worksheets

*In this handbook you will find eighty worksheets to be used as **Duplication Masters.***

This chart shows where worksheets may be used. You will need to **duplicate** any worksheet used more than once.

No.	Master Worksheet Name	Lessons Where Worksheets Are Used
1	Writing numbers 0–9	1
2	Number order, Dot-to-dot	2
3	Ordinal numbers, counting by tens, number order	4
4	Place Value	6, 30, 31
5	Number chart	1, 8, 18, 30, 31, 36, 82, 99, 138, 139, 144
6	Number line	9, 58, 59
7	Addition on the number line	11
8	Addition facts 1–18	13, 24
9	Addition facts 1–18	18, 24, 35
10	General review	19
11	Addition facts 1–18	22, 24, 35
12	Calendar	24, 40
13	Fill in the blank number chart	26
14	Addition facts	28, 35
15	Adding money	29
16	Addition facts 10–18	32, 35
17	Addition facts for 10–18	34, 35
18	Word number addition facts	36
19	Dot-to-dot counting by 6's	37
20	Addition drill sheet	41
21	Pennies and dimes	43
22	Adding three single-digit numbers	45
23	Addition drill sheet.	46
24	Harvest color page with addition facts practice	48
25	Addition drill sheet	51
26	Thanksgiving dot-to-dot by ones	52
27	Subtraction with visual representation	54
28	Addition drill sheet	56
29	Inches	58
30	Addition drill sheet	61
31	Christmas math maze	62
32	Subtraction by number line	64, 76
33	Addition drill sheet	66
34	Counting by fives, sixes, sevens, and eights	68
35	Addition drill sheet	71
36	Christmas addition	72

Where To Use Mathematics Worksheets, continued:

No.	Master Worksheet Name	Lesson Where Worksheets Are Used
37	Visual representation of subtraction word problems	74
38	Addition drill sheet	76
39	Subtraction 10–18 with number line.	78, 105
40	Addition and subtraction drill sheet	81
41	Subtraction with number line 0–19	82, 105
42	Number chart 100–199	84, 85
43	Addition and subtraction drill sheet	86
44	Shapes color sheet	88
45	Addition and subtraction drill sheet	91
46	Subtraction 10–18 with number line	92, 105
47	Word problems (add and subtract)	94
48	Addition and subtraction drill sheet	96
49	Subtraction 10–18 with number line	98, 105
50	Addition and subtraction drill sheet	101
51	Corresponding subtraction facts for addition fact	102
52	Color sheet with < and >	104
53	Subtraction 10–18 with number line	105
54	Addition and subtraction drill sheet	106
55	Addition and subtraction without the number line	108
56	Addition and subtraction drill sheet	111
57	Patriotic color sheet	114
58	Addition and subtraction drill sheet	116
59	Number sequence	118
60	Addition and subtraction drill sheet	121
61	Cube pattern	121
62	Addition of money	124
63	Addition and subtraction drill sheet	126
64	Addition with answers in ones' column double-digit	128
65	Addition and subtraction drill sheet	131
66	Word problems from pictures	132
67	Addition with carrying and double-digit subtraction	134
68	Addition and subtraction drill sheet	136
69	Addition of money	138
70	Addition and subtraction drill sheet	141
71	Measuring a boat in centimeters	142
72	Dot to Dot over 100	144
73	Fill in the blank number chart 100–199	145
74	Addition and subtraction drill sheet	146
75	81 addition facts	148
76	Addition and subtraction drill sheet	151
77	81 subtraction facts	154
78	Addition and subtraction drill sheet	156
79	Estimation	158
80	Double-digit addition	159

APPEARANCE OF CONCEPTS
MATHEMATICS 1

1. COUNTING 1–200	Appears in Lesson
By 1's	1, 2, 3, 4, 5, 48, 49, 79, 80, 117
By 10's	4, 5, 50, 81, 118
By 5's	6, 7, 51, 82, 118
By 2's	8, 9, 10, 11, 12, 52, 53, 54, 88, 89, 117
By 3's	13, 14, 15, 16, 17, 55, 56, 58, 90, 91, 124, 125
By 6's	18, 19, 20, 21, 22, 59, 60, 61, 92, 93, 126, 127, 128, 129, 138, 139
By 9's	23, 24, 25, 26, 27, 62, 63, 64, 95, 96, 130, 131, 132, 149, 150, 159
By 4's	28, 29, 30, 31, 32, 65, 66, 67, 105, 106, 136, 137
By 8's	33, 34, 35, 36, 37, 68, 69, 70, 107, 108, 140, 141, 147, 148, 158
By 7's	38, 39, 40, 41, 42, 71, 72, 73, 74, 112, 113, 114, 115, 142, 143, 144, 151, 152, 153, 154, 160
Counting by 1's from 100–200	83, 84, 85, 87, 97, 98, 99, 109, 110, 111, 121, 122, 123, 133, 134, 135, 145, 146, 156, 157
One-to-one correspondence	3, 4, 10, 11, 12, 14, 74, 76, 125, 157
Even numbers	65, 66, 77, 96, 97, 117, 130, 141, 142, 152, 154
Odd numbers	94, 95, 97, 107, 108, 120, 130, 141, 143, 153, 154
Tally marks	10, 11, 12, 14, 17, 18, 22, 23. 24, 25, 66, 98
Word numbers	
one to ten	11, 12, 13, 24, 25, 33, 43
eleven to twenty	35, 47, 48, 53
eleven to 100	60, 62, 63
all	68, 80, 82
over 100	84, 85, 86, 87, 100, 101, 110, 111, 112, 122, 123, 134, 135, 136, 141, 142, 146, 147, 158, 159
2. ORDINAL AND CARDINAL NUMBERS	
First, second, third, etc. to last	2, 6, 15, 58, 70, 71, 92, 114, 133, 155, 156
Between	
by ones	4, 5, 7
by twos	9
by fives	11
by tens	13
by ones over 100	83, 84, 85
After	
by ones	15, 16
by twos	18, 19
by fives	21, 22
by tens	24, 25
by ones over 100	93, 94, 95

Before	
by ones	28, 30, 31
by twos	32, 33, 34, 36, 37
by ones over 100	96, 97, 98
Before and After	
by ones	39, 41, 42
by tens	44, 46, 59
by ones over 100	105, 106, 107

3. CORRESPONDENCE OF QUANTITIES

Big and little	4, 50
Large and Small	8
Tall and short	14
Less/greater than	6, 7, 8, 9, 10, 20, 21, 23, 32, 33, 43, 44, 53, 54, 65, 66, 76, 77, 150, 151, 160
(over 100)	88, 90, 102, 103, 114, 116, 139, 140
Long and Short	20
Equal and not equal	13, 14, 18, 29, 30, 31, 41, 42, 51, 52, 67, 68, 79, 80, 98, 99, 109, 110, 133, 134, 146, 147, 159

4. PLACE VALUE

Ones and Tens	5, 6, 7, 8, 9, 10, 11, 13, 14, 15, 17, 25, 26, 27, 37, 38, 46, 48, 49, 59, 60, 61, 71, 72, 73
Hundreds	81, 82, 83, 84, 85, 86, 87, 88, 96, 97, 107, 108, 109, 119, 120, 121, 131, 132, 133, 143, 144, 145, 155, 156, 157

5. ADDITION

1–9 w/number line	7, 8, 9, 10, 11, 12
1–18 w/number line	13, 14, 15, 16, 17, 19, 20, 21, 22, 23, 24, 25, 26, 27, 28, 31, 35
1–18 w/out number line	30, 32, 39, 40, 41, 42, 43, 44, 46, 48, 54, 58, 60, 65, 67, 80, 109, 125
Horizontal and	
vertical addition	18, 37, 38, 39, 40, 62, 68, 77
Two numbers	
double digit	36, 37, 38, 39, 40, 41, 42, 43, 46, 47, 48, 49, 50, 51, 55, 60, 61, 63, 64, 69, 70, 75, 79, 99, 109, 111, 116, 118, 122, 123, 124, 127, 128, 129, 130, 141, 143, 145, 146, 148, 149, 150, 152, 153, 154, 155, 156, 157
Two numbers	
triple digit	100, 102, 104, 105, 106, 110, 111. 112, 113, 116, 121, 138, 140, 144, 146
Three numbers	
single digit	45, 46, 47, 49, 50, 54, 55, 57, 58, 60, 61, 63, 64, 66, 69, 70, 72, 74, 75, 99, 111, 112, 113, 116, 118, 121
Three numbers	
double digit	92, 93, 99, 111
Adding with	
carrying in 1's	131, 132, 133, 134, 135, 136, 137, 138, 139, 140, 141, 143, 144, 145, 146, 148, 149, 150, 152, 153, 154, 155, 156, 157
Word problems	
visualized	15, 16, 17, 18
with lines for fact	19, 22, 23
with lines for fact	
and label given	24, 25, 30, 36, 38, 41, 44

Word problems (continued)	
with lines for fact	
and label	45, 46, 47, 48, 50, 51, 53, 56, 57, 59, 61, 62
with nothing	64, 65, 68, 69, 78, 79, 86, 89, 91, 110, 111, 117, 126, 127, 129, 130, 134, 136, 138, 139, 142, 147, 155, 156, 159

6. CALENDAR

Months	12, 14, 15, 23, 24, 25, 26, 27, 61, 62, 85, 101, 103, 126,127, 128, 141, 142, 152, 153
Days of the week	17, 30, 40, 41, 71, 72, 86, 104, 105, 129, 130, 143, 144, 154, 155
"Thirty Days Hath	
September"	23, 24, 25, 26, 27, 28, 29, 30, 44, 45, 55, 56, 61, 62, 77, 78, 85, 101, 103, 126, 127, 128, 141, 142, 152, 153

7. TIME

Hour	16, 17, 18, 19, 20, 21, 54, 68, 69
Half hour	27, 28, 29, 30, 43, 54, 74, 75, 76
Quarter hour	42, 43, 44, 45, 55, 86, 87, 120
All time	56, 89, 90, 91, 100, 101,102, 103, 118, 119, 132, 133, 144, 145, 154, 155, 156

8. SUBTRACTION

Visual representation	52, 53, 54
1–9 w/number line	55, 56, 57, 58, 59, 60, 62, 64, 65, 66, 67, 68, 69, 70, 72, 74, 75, 79
w/out number line	106, 107, 109, 110, 112, 113, 115, 118, 119, 121, 122, 125, 131
Horizontal to vertical	61, 63
10–18 w/number line	76, 77, 78, 79, 80, 81, 90, 92, 93, 94, 97, 99, 102
10–18 w/out number line	106, 107, 109, 110, 112, 113, 115, 116, 118, 119, 121, 122, 124, 125, 128, 130, 131, 132, 134, 139, 140, 141, 143, 144, 145, 146, 147, 149, 150, 151, 152, 154, 155, 156, 157, 160
Two numbers	
double digit	134, 135, 136, 138, 139, 140, 141, 143, 145, 147, 149, 150
Two numbers triple digit	151, 152, 154, 155, 156, 157
Word Problems (visualized)	71, 73, 75
with lines for	
fact and label	82, 84, 85, 89, 91, 94, 99, 102, 103, 108
with nothing	110, 111, 114, 117, 120, 123, 126, 132, 135, 140, 141, 142, 144, 146, 149, 159

9. MONEY

Penny	26, 27, 29, 32, 36, 37, 43, 46, 47, 56, 57, 58, 98
Nickel	33, 34, 35, 36, 37, 48, 49, 59, 60, 100
Dime	28, 29, 32, 43, 46, 47, 56, 57, 58, 99
Quarter	51, 52, 53, 63, 101
All coins	51, 64, 85, 87, 88, 103, 104, 140, 151, 152, 153, 154
Dollar	89, 103, 104
Adding	122, 123, 124, 126, 137, 138, 139

10. MEASUREMENT

Inches	31, 32, 33, 34, 35, 45, 46, 47, 57, 69, 70, 81, 144, 145, 149, 150, 159, 160
Centimeters	91, 92, 93, 94, 95, 105, 106, 107, 113, 114, 126, 130, 140, 141

11. **FRACTIONS**	
Whole	34
Half	38, 39, 43, 44, 53, 55, 66, 78, 157, 158
One fourth	49, 50, 51, 53, 54, 64, 65, 66, 79
One third	80
All fractions	35, 52, 67, 81,116, 131, 132, 148, 149, 159

12. **SETS**	
Groups	3, 4, 39, 74, 76, 125, 157

13. **SHAPES**	
Circle, square, triangle, rectangle	82, 83, 84, 104, 105, 106, 115, 116, 117, 126, 127, 128, 146, 147, 158
Oval, diamond, octagon	93, 94, 95, 104, 105, 106, 115, 116, 117, 126, 127, 128, 146, 147, 158
Sphere, cylinder, cube, cone	108, 109, 110, 111, 112, 121, 122, 132, 133, 142, 143, 152, 153

14. **GRAPHS**	
Bar graph	87, 88, 89, 90, 91, 101, 102, 103, 113, 114, 115, 136, 137, 147, 148, 158, 160

15. **UNITS OF MEASURE**	
Dozen	104, 105, 117, 128, 150
Ounce, cup, pint, quart, gallon	97, 98, 99, 119, 120, 142, 143
Pound	132, 133, 134, 135, 137

16. **SEQUENCE**	
Numbers	98, 99, 100, 101, 102, 116, 117, 118, 125, 126, 127, 138, 139, 140, 149, 150, 159, 160
Events	95, 96, 97, 98, 107, 108, 119, 120, 129, 130, 151, 152, 153
17. **ESTIMATION**	
	99, 100, 101, 102, 112, 113, 114, 124, 125, 126, 137, 138, 139, 148, 149, 158, 159

Development

Grades 1

GENERAL PATTERN:

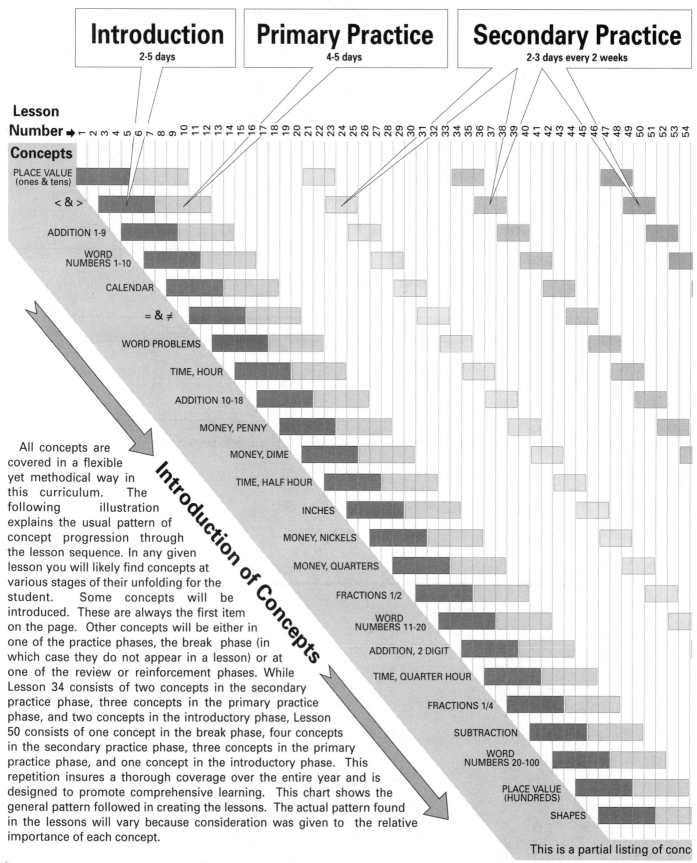

Introduction	Primary Practice	Secondary Practice
2-5 days	4-5 days	2-3 days every 2 weeks

Lesson Number → 1 2 3 4 5 6 7 8 9 10 11 12 13 14 15 16 17 18 19 20 21 22 23 24 25 26 27 28 29 30 31 32 33 34 35 36 37 38 39 40 41 42 43 44 45 46 47 48 49 50 51 52 53 54

Concepts

PLACE VALUE (ones & tens)

< & >

ADDITION 1-9

WORD NUMBERS 1-10

CALENDAR

= & ≠

WORD PROBLEMS

TIME, HOUR

ADDITION 10-18

MONEY, PENNY

MONEY, DIME

TIME, HALF HOUR

INCHES

MONEY, NICKELS

MONEY, QUARTERS

FRACTIONS 1/2

WORD NUMBERS 11-20

ADDITION, 2 DIGIT

TIME, QUARTER HOUR

FRACTIONS 1/4

SUBTRACTION

WORD NUMBERS 20-100

PLACE VALUE (HUNDREDS)

SHAPES

Introduction of Concepts

All concepts are covered in a flexible yet methodical way in this curriculum. The following illustration explains the usual pattern of concept progression through the lesson sequence. In any given lesson you will likely find concepts at various stages of their unfolding for the student. Some concepts will be introduced. These are always the first item on the page. Other concepts will be either in one of the practice phases, the break phase (in which case they do not appear in a lesson) or at one of the review or reinforcement phases. While Lesson 34 consists of two concepts in the secondary practice phase, three concepts in the primary practice phase, and two concepts in the introductory phase, Lesson 50 consists of one concept in the break phase, four concepts in the secondary practice phase, three concepts in the primary practice phase, and one concept in the introductory phase. This repetition insures a thorough coverage over the entire year and is designed to promote comprehensive learning. This chart shows the general pattern followed in creating the lessons. The actual pattern found in the lessons will vary because consideration was given to the relative importance of each concept.

This is a partial listing of conc

# of Concepts

& 2

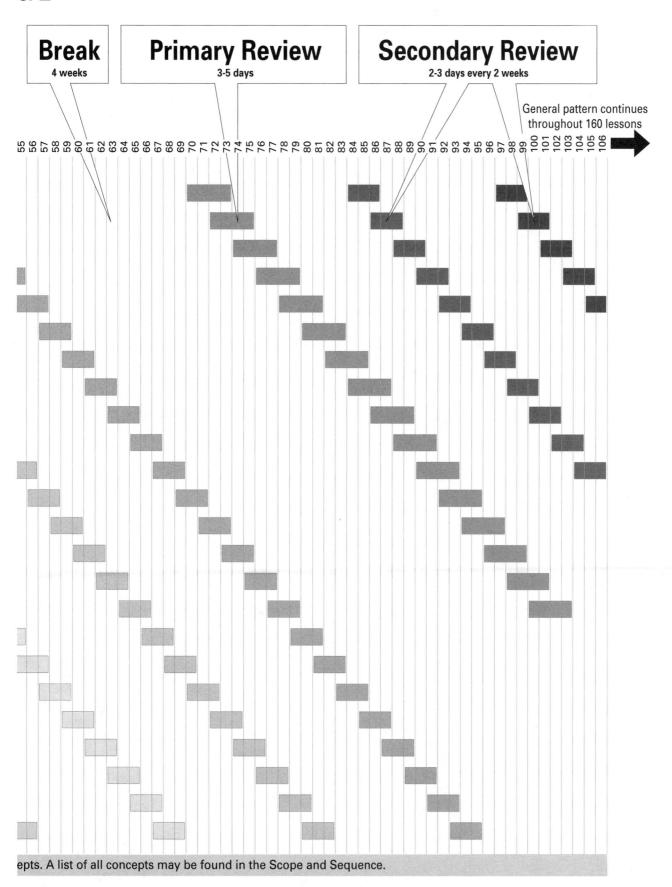

L e s s o n s

NUMBERS

Concepts:
>   Counting by ones and number line
>   *Definition:*   A number line is a graphic representation of how far a number is from zero.

Objectives:
1. The student shall be able to count by ones and twos up to 100 out loud from memory.

2. The student shall be able to correctly form all the numerals from zero through nine with a pencil.

Teaching Tips:
1. When doing activity 4, have each student stand up when the name of each number family (10, 20, 30, 40) is called while counting out loud. For example, when counting by ones to 100 the student would stand on ten, twenty, thirty, forty, fifty, etc.

2. If a student asks about the arrows at the ends of the number line in activity 3, give the illustration of standing on a railroad track. If you look in either direction the tracks seem to go on forever. In the same way, the number line seems to have no end.

Materials, Supplies, & Equipment:
1. Number line segments in families [or draw on chalkboard]

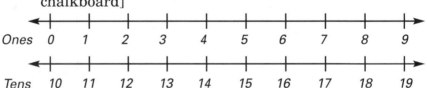

| Ones | 0 | 1 | 2 | 3 | 4 | 5 | 6 | 7 | 8 | 9 |

| Tens | 10 | 11 | 12 | 13 | 14 | 15 | 16 | 17 | 18 | 19 |

2. Number chart arranged in families either horizontally or vertically.

Vertical

0	10	20	30	40	50	60	70	80	90
1	11	21	31	41	51	61	71	81	91
2	12	22	32	42	52	62	72	82	92
3	13	23	33	43	53	63	73	83	93
4	14	24	34	44	54	64	74	84	94
5	15	25	35	45	55	65	75	85	95
6	16	26	36	46	56	66	76	86	96
7	17	27	37	47	57	67	77	87	97
8	18	28	38	48	58	68	78	88	98
9	19	29	39	49	59	69	79	89	99

Horizontal

0	1	2	3	4	5	6	7	8	9
10	11	12	13	14	15	16	17	18	19
20	21	22	23	24	25	26	27	28	29
30	31	32	33	34	35	36	37	38	39
40	41	42	43	44	45	46	47	48	49
50	51	52	53	54	55	56	57	58	59
60	61	62	63	64	65	66	67	68	69
70	71	72	73	74	75	76	77	78	79
80	81	82	83	84	85	86	87	88	89
90	91	92	93	94	95	96	97	98	99

Note: For a complete listing of materials and where they are used in the curriculum, see page 40 in the introduction.

Activities:

1. Work the student(s) through the printed guide a number at a time, reiterating the place to begin the strokes and the complete forming of the number in *Student Activity One*. If you want the numerals formed differently, you will need to provide a guide and follow it.

2. Now that the student(s) have been instructed, have them practice writing numerals without guides in *Student Activity Two*. You may wish to set a time limit on this activity to see how well each student can form their numbers. However, there is no need to create artificial pressure on the student(s) by telling them there is a time limit. Simply tell them when it's time to stop. For additional practice of writing numbers use *Worksheet 1*.

3. Explain the number line using the definition under **Concepts**. Draw a number line on the chalkboard and demonstrate the relation of the number line to counting. Erase some of the numbers and have a student tell you the missing numbers. When you feel the student(s) have grasped the relation of the number line to counting, let them do *Student Activity Three*.

4. Count out loud with the student(s) by ones to 100 using a number chart. Discuss with the student(s) how counting by ones means to count over one each time on the number chart or to add one to each previous number.

5. To begin *Student Activity Four*, have the student(s) place their pencil point on the star at number one. Guide them from number to number, referring to the number chart. You may want to give them a copy of *Worksheet 5* so that they have their own number chart at their desk and put it into a folder in their desk for future reference.

Worksheets:

1. *Worksheet 1* – Writing numbers 0–9

2. *Worksheet 5* – Number chart

*There is a place for everything and
everything should be in its place.*

NUMBER ORDER – ORDINAL NUMBERS

Concepts:

Cardinal and ordinal numbers and their relationship to counting and counting by ones

Definitions: Cardinal numbers are the counting numbers. Ordinal numbers are the numbers that show order like first, second, third, and fourth.

Objectives:

1. The student shall be able to identify ordinal numbers from memory by marking the item at the teacher's instruction (cover first through tenth).

2. The student shall be able to correctly arrange numbers in sequence by re-writing the numbers.

Teaching Tips:

1. When doing activity 2, have the student(s) tell you what grade they are in. Then ask them if "first" is an ordinal or cardinal number. Have them name the other grades using ordinal numbers. Discuss other examples of ordinal and cardinal numbers distinguishing which is which. Examples might include how old they are, how many brothers and sisters they have, if they are the "first" born in their family, and at what desk they sit.

2. If the student(s) find the presence of four or five different activities in one lesson a little overwhelming at the beginning, start guiding the student(s) through each activity each day. By the end of two weeks, they should be able to work more independently as they adjust to the format. Mastery of a new concept is not necessary the first time it is presented to be successful. Complete understanding of a new concept will come as the concept is approached from different views using different methods at different intervals.

Materials, Supplies, & Equipment:

1. Number chart

2. Crayons

3. *Flash cards for cardinal and ordinal numbers*

Activities:

1. Count out loud with the student(s) by ones to 100 using a number chart. Discuss with the student(s) the idea that when they are counting they are using cardinal numbers. They are also called natural numbers. Don't spend more than seven minutes on this or you won't have the time you need for the rest of the lesson.

2. Discuss with the student(s) that ordinal numbers (in the title for this lesson) are numbers that show order or position. Select groups of ten objects, count them out loud, and point out first through tenth. For example, lay ten crayons on your desk. Count them out loud and identify first through tenth (*flash cards for cardinal and ordinal numbers* would be a help). Write the cardinal number for the days of creation as you identify them by ordinal number in **Student Activity One**.

3. Look at the numbers on the sailboats that show order in **Student Activity Two**. Direct the student(s) in counting them out loud using ordinal numbers. Next have them draw an "X" on the first sailboat and draw a circle around the fifth sailboat in **Student Activity Three**.

4. In **Student Activity Four** count the balls with the student(s) and have them put an "X" on the third ball and circle the eighth ball.

5. Count the fish in **Student Activity Five** with the student(s) and have them put an "X" on the second fish.

6. Write the numbers 0–10 on the chalk board leaving several blanks. Ask the student(s) to fill in the missing numbers. Then begin **Student Activity Six**.

7. Write four numbers out of order on the chalk board. Let a student put them in correct order. Do this for several sets of numbers. Have student(s) rearrange the scrambled list of numbers into correct order in **Student Activity Seven**.

Worksheets:

1. *Worksheet 2 –* Ordinal numbers

"Let everything be done decently and in order."

SETS

Concepts:

One-to-one correspondence, sets, number line, and counting by ones

Definition: A set is any group of objects or numbers.

Objectives:

1. The student shall be able to count out loud by ones to 100.

2. The student shall be able to draw a set of a given number of objects.

3. The student shall be able to count a set of objects and write the numeral which represents them.

Teaching Tips:

1. When you are counting out loud in activity 1, have the student(s) do a different motion for each number within a family. For example, clap their hands on ones. Have them pat their head on tens. On twenties they might bend their knees.

2. In activity 2 the student(s) may use their finger to trace on their desk as you write on the board.

Materials, Supplies, & Equipment:

1. Number chart

2. *Flash cards 0–100*

Activities:

1. Count out loud by ones to 100 using a number chart. (*Flash cards*)

2. According to the style you have selected, practice writing the numerals 0–9 on the chalkboard. Encourage the student(s) to be neat as they do **Student Activity One**.

3. Draw sets of fives and tens on the board or represent sets of fives and tens with objects. Point out the sets and count them with the student(s). Direct the student(s) to do **Student Activity Two**.

4. Read the directions with the student(s) and have them count to themselves by ones as they write the missing numbers in the blanks in **Student Activity Three**.

5. In **Student Activity Four**, have the student(s) write the missing numbers in the blanks under the number line.

6. Count the nickels in the first box of **Student Activity Five** out loud with your student(s). Place the number in the box at the lower right corner. Instruct the student(s) to continue the activity on their own.

7. As the student(s) count to themselves by ones, they should write the missing numbers in the blanks in **Student Activity Six**.

Men do less than they ought, unless they do all that they can.

BIG AND LITTLE

Concepts:
Big and little, the number that comes between by ones, sets, one-to-one correspondence, and counting by ones and tens

Objectives:
1. The student shall be able to count out loud by ones and tens to 100.

2. The student shall be able to identify the bigger or littler object by drawing a circle around it.

3. The student shall be able to draw a set of a given number of objects.

4. The student shall be able to count a set of objects and write the numeral which represents them.

Teaching Tips:
1. To aid in the understanding of **Student Activity One** and **Two**, the teacher may need to instruct the student(s) to put their finger on the bigger or littler rectangle before they circle it with their pencil.

2. When doing activity 5, the student's crayons may be used to illustrate different sets by color, number, size, etc.

3. Give the student(s) a blank sheet of paper. Have them draw a set of one triangle, then a set of two triangles, then a set of three triangles, continuing until they have a set for each of the numbers from one through nine as practice for **Student Activity Four**.

4. The student(s) may use pages in one of their textbooks to practice finding what number comes between two numbers that you give them in preparing them for **Student Activity Five**.

Materials, Supplies, & Equipment:
1. Number chart

2. Flannel board and numbers

3. Flannel board materials

4. Money (real or play)

Activities:

1. Count out loud by tens to 100 using the number chart. Discuss with the student(s) that counting by tens means to count over ten places on the number chart, to count every tenth number, or to add ten to each number.

2. Using the number chart, review counting out loud by ones to 100.

3. Demonstrate big and little with several different objects. An example of this would be a big apple and a little apple. Hold them up and ask the student(s) which is the big apple and which is the little apple. Try not to use objects that are long and short because this can be confusing. Have the student(s) choose which is big and which is little in *Student Activity One* and *Two*.

4. Practice re-arranging numbers on the chalk board or a flannel board to prepare the student(s) for doing *Student Activity Three*.

5. Illustrate sets using common objects. Example: Put 5 objects on the flannel board. Let the student(s) count them. This is a set — any group of objects. Have them draw the sets in *Student Activity Four*.

6. Direct the student(s) in practicing what comes between two numbers using the number chart. Proceed with **Student Activity Five**.

7. Have the student(s) count several sets of money (play or real) and write the number on scrap paper. Then have the student(s) do *Student Activity Six* after you go over the directions with them.

Worksheets:

1. *Worksheet 3* – Ordinal numbers, counting by tens, and number order.

Is Bigger Better?
A nickel is bigger than a dime, but a dime is worth more.
Don't let size be your only measure for judging worth.

PLACE VALUE – TENS AND ONES

Concepts:

Place value for tens' and ones' place, counting by tens, the number that comes between by ones, and counting by ones

Objectives:

1. The student shall be able to count by tens to 100 out loud.

2. The student shall be able to correctly write the digit in the tens' place and ones' place.

3. The student shall be able to correctly write the missing numbers when counting by tens.

4. The student shall be able to correctly write the missing number between two given numbers.

Teaching Tips:

1. When you explain place value in activity 3, tell the student that when the tenth block is added to the ones, the group of ten ones must be replaced by one stack of ten in the tens' place and zero blocks in the ones' place.

2. If a student is having trouble with place value, use *counting sticks*, *blocks*, *colored stickers*, or other manipulatives to demonstrate the concept.

Materials, Supplies, & Equipment:

1. Number chart

2. Place value materials – many are available for purchase. To make them yourself, look at the student book to see how they should look. Cut ten 1" or 2" cardboard squares to represent the ones' place. Color them blue. For the tens' place cut ten stacks of ten squares. Color them pink. Glue a magnet on the back of each piece to allow you to display place value concepts on any magnetic surface.

3. *Counting sticks*, *blocks*, and *colored stickers*

Activities:

1. Count out loud by tens to 100 using the number chart.

2. Count out loud by ones to 100 using the number chart.

3. Before **Student Activity One**, discuss the number of places a single-digit numeral (such as 4) takes. Using the numbers chart, ask what the largest number is that takes only one place (9). Discuss how many ones in this number (9). Discuss the next number (10). How many places does it take? What is in the tens' place? What is in the ones' place? Read over the instructions with the student(s). Do other examples using place value materials for the student(s). The student(s) should tell you how many groups of ten in the number and write them; then, how many ones and write them.

4. **Student Activity Two** and **Three** need the teacher to guide the student(s) through each exercise. Have them count the groups of ten and write the number. Then, count the ones and write the number.

5. Guide the student(s) in counting by tens by giving examples on the board or using the number chart. They need to count by tens to themselves with the aid of the number chart as they do **Student Activity Four**.

6. With the aid of the number chart, have the student(s) write the number as they count to themselves in **Student Activity Five**.

Great minds have purposes, others have wishes.

LESS AND GREATER

Concepts:
Less and greater, ordinal numbers, place value, and counting by fives

Objectives:
1. The student shall be able to count out loud by fives to 100.

2. The student shall be able to identify the number that is less or greater by drawing a circle around it.

3. The student shall be able to identify ordinal numbers from memory by marking the item first through tenth at the teacher's instruction.

4. The student shall be able to correctly write the digit in the tens' place and the ones' place and the number that they represent.

Teaching Tips:
1. When doing activity 1, have the student(s) count by fives to 100 by filling in missing numbers from the sequence written on the board.

2. Before the student(s) start **Student Activity One**, tell the student(s) to point to the number which is less (5 or 6, 7 or 4, 2 or 9).

3. Have the student(s) point to each greater number in **Student Activity Two** before beginning the exercise.

4. The student(s) could create groups of ten and ones with their crayons as you dictate the number to them in activity 5. Be sure to keep the tens' digit small. For more place value practice be sure to see *Worksheet 4*.

Materials, Supplies, & Equipment:
1. Number chart

2. Number line 0–10

3. *Flash cards for cardinal and ordinal numbers*

4. Flash cards for whole numbers

5. *Place value materials*

Activities:

1. Count out loud by fives to 100 using a number chart. Discuss with the student(s) that counting by fives means to count over five places on the number chart, to count every fifth number, or to add five to each number.

2. Before **Student Activity One**, the student needs to orally identify two numerals on the number line. State which is less and which is greater or more. Repeat the activity several times. Have the student(s) circle which is less and which is greater in **Student Activity One** and **Two**.

3. Practice ordinal numbers by having the student(s) point to the first, fourth, and seventh teddy bear in **Student Activity Three** (*Flash cards for cardinal and ordinal numbers* may be a help). Go through the instructions with the student(s) making sure that they understand what they are to do.

4. Choose six consecutive whole number flash cards. Arrange the cards out of order. Have the student(s) put them in correct order. Repeat this four or five times with different sets of six numbers. The student(s) should now be ready to do **Student Activity Four**.

5. In the first set in **Student Activity Five**, have the student(s) count the tens and write the number. Then have them count the ones and write the number. This is the number 36. Write it down (*place value materials* may be a help). The student(s) will need the teacher's guidance through each of these sets.

6. As the student(s) count to themselves by fives, they should write the missing numbers in the blanks in **Student Activity Six** with the aid of the number chart.

Worksheets:

1. *Worksheet 4* – Place value.

True greatness is found in serving others.

ADDITION 1–9

Concepts:
> Addition facts 1–9, < and >, the number that comes between by ones, place value, and counting by fives

Objectives:
1. The student shall be able to count out loud by fives to 100.

2. The student shall be able to write the answers to the addition facts 1–9 using the number line.

3. The student shall be able to read the less than and greater than symbols.

4. The student shall be able to determine the number that comes between two given numbers by ones.

5. The student shall be able to write the number represented by a given number of groups of tens and ones.

Teaching Tips:
1. Before doing **Student Activity Two**, give two students a number and one student a symbol. Have the student(s) arrange them in order and read them. You may do the same thing by having a student correctly arrange jumbled cards.

2. If you wish to drill the addition facts by families in activity 2, you may want to set up your own schedule. If the schedule does not match the addition problems given in the student lesson, allow the student(s) to use the number line as long as necessary to arrive at the correct answer.

Materials, Supplies, & Equipment:
1. Number chart

2. Flash cards for 1–9 addition facts and < and >

3. Number line

4. Place value materials

Activities:

1. Count out loud by fives to 100 using a number chart.

2. Discuss with the student(s) the fact that any number added to zero is equal to the same number. Then discuss the fact that the number that comes after a given number is equal to the given number plus 1 (e.g. the number that comes after 5 is equal to 5 + 1). Using flash cards, drill the addition facts in which the answer is 1–9. For the first three weeks this drill needs to be done for five minutes with the answers showing. The student(s) need to repeat the complete addition fact and its opposite, not just the answer. They should say, "Four plus two equals six" and "two plus four equals six." Concentrate on the following 12 facts and their opposites: 2 + 2, 2 + 3, 2 + 4, 2 + 5, 2 + 6, 2 + 7, 3 + 3, 3 + 4, 3 + 5, 3 + 6, 4 + 4, and 4 + 5.

3. Use the number line to introduce addition facts. Draw lines on the number line to show the process of addition. For example, above the number line draw a line from zero to three and then from three to five. This shows that three plus two equals five. Do several problems like those in *Student Activity One* orally with the student(s). Write the addition fact. The student(s) need to understand that addition is "putting together." Carefully check each student's progress on *Student Activity One*.

4. Remind the student(s) to refer to the number line to help distinguish between the less than and the greater than symbols. The arrow at the end of the number line where the numbers are increasing is the greater than arrow and the arrow at the end where the numbers are decreasing is the less than arrow. Go over several examples before having the student(s) read *Student Activity Two*.

5. Review counting by ones with the student(s) as a refresher. To do the problems in *Student Activity Three* they need to count by ones to themselves. The number chart may be a help to the student(s).

6. Review counting by tens with the student(s) to aid in *Student Activity Four*. Using the place value materials, have the student(s) count the groups of ten, then continue to count by ones to arrive at the number. Example: first set — 10, 20, 30, 40, 41, 42, 43, 44, 45, 46, 47, 48. Write the number 48. Do the first three activities in *Student Activity Four* with the student(s). They may work the remaining sets by themselves.

There must be absolutes, else nothing can be known and no one can be trusted.

LARGE AND SMALL

Concepts:
Large and small, place value, addition 1–9, < and >, and counting by twos

Objectives:
1. The student shall be able to count out loud by twos to 100.

2. The student shall be able to circle the larger or smaller of two given objects.

3. The student shall be able to state how many tens and how many ones are in a given number.

4. The student shall be able to write the addition fact demonstrated on the number line.

5. Given two numbers, the student shall be able to write the correct symbol to identify whether the first number is less than or greater than the second number.

Teaching Tips:
1. Activity 1 can be demonstrated by having the student(s) take a number chart and circle all the twos. This could be done as an activity sheet later in the day on *Worksheet 5*. *Worksheet 5* will be used again on later assignments. Be sure to save your master copy.

2. The review in activity 6 may be done by using flash cards, counting objects, or writing on the chalk board.

Materials, Supplies, & Equipment:
1. Number chart

2. Flash cards for whole numbers

3. Number line

4. Flash cards for < and >

Activities:

1. Count out loud by twos to 100 using a number chart. Discuss with the student(s) that counting by twos means to count every other number, to count every second number, or to add two to each number.

2. Drill addition facts 1–9 with flash cards for five minutes with answers showing.

3. Start **Student Activity One** and **Two** by choosing objects of different size in the room. Compare pencils, books, crayons, chairs, etc. in relationship to large and small. Now have the student(s) work through these activities.

4. Hold up different flash cards of any number from 0–99 and have the student(s) tell you how many tens and how many ones are in the number. Do as many of these as you feel necessary, then begin **Student Activity Three**.

5. In preparation for **Student Activity Four**, use a number line on the chalk board to demonstrate several addition facts. Example: 3 + 2 = 5

   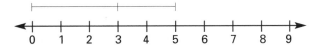

   Have the student(s) find the first number of the addition fact by counting from zero to three. Write three above the line. The second number is found by counting from three to five. Write two above the second line. Five is the answer. Have the student(s) tell you the addition fact, 3 + 2 = 5. Be sure the student(s) follow each step as they do **Student Activity Four**.

6. Review with the student(s) which is the less than and which is the greater than symbol. Remind the student(s) that the arrows' names correspond to the arrows on the number line. Tell the student(s) to point to the number that is less in **Student Activity Five**. Then remind them that the arrow points towards the number that is less. After writing in the symbol have the student(s) then read the expression to themselves.

Worksheets:

1. *Worksheet 5* – Number Chart. (Be sure to save your master copy.)

ADDITION ON THE NUMBER LINE

Concepts:
Addition on the number line, between by twos, < and >, place value, and counting by twos

Objectives:
1. The student shall be able to count out loud by twos to 100.

2. The student shall be able to write the solution to an addition fact using the number line.

3. The student shall be able to write the number that comes between two given numbers by counting by twos.

4. The student shall be able to write the correct symbol (< or >) between two given numbers.

5. The student shall be able to write the value of the digit in the tens' place.

Teaching Tips:
1. Use *Worksheet 6* to provide the practice needed before doing **Student Activity One**.

2. If you use the number chart to help the student(s) choose the correct number between two given numbers by twos in **Student Activity Two** remind them that counting by twos is the same as counting over two on the number chart or adding two to each number.

Materials, Supplies, & Equipment:
1. Number chart

2. Flash cards for addition facts 1–9

3. Number line

4. Place value materials

Activities:

1. Count out loud by twos to 100 using the number chart.

2. For five minutes, drill the addition facts 1–9 using flash cards with the answers showing.

3. In presenting addition, point out to the student(s) that zero means "nothing." When you add zero to a number you are putting nothing with it. To add zero on the number line means that you add nothing. Zero added to any number is the same number. In preparation for **Student Activity One**, the student(s) need to be reminded to begin at zero on the number line with a vertical mark. They then draw a straight line to the first number with a vertical mark at the end. Next they count over on the marks to equal the second number. The second straight line is drawn to this mark with a vertical mark at the end. Where the second straight line ends is the answer to the addition fact. After the student(s) practice several of these problems have them attempt the activity while you work closely with them.

4. Review counting by twos to help the student(s) as they complete **Student Activity Two**. The number chart may be helpful to the student(s).

5. In **Student Activity Three**, remind the student(s) that they read the less than and greater than symbols by referring to the arrows on the number line. Also remind them that the arrow always points to the smaller number. Go over the directions with the student(s) emphasizing that they read each set.

6. Using place value materials for groups of ten and then counting them by tens will increase the student's understanding as they start **Student Activity Four**. Display 5 groups of ten and have the student(s) count them by tens. Example: 10, 20, 30, 40, 50. Therefore, the value of 5 groups of ten is 50.

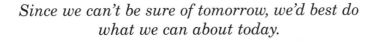

Worksheets:

1. *Worksheet 6* – Number line

Since we can't be sure of tomorrow, we'd best do what we can about today.

TALLY MARKS

Concepts:
One-to-one correspondence with tally marks, < and >, place value, addition 1–9, and counting by twos

Objectives:
1. The student shall be able to count out loud by twos to 100.

2. The student shall be able to make a tally mark for each given object.

3. The student shall be able to write the correct symbol (< or >) between two given numbers.

4. The student shall be able to write the value of the number in the tens' place and the ones' place.

5. The student shall be able to write the addition fact represented on the number line.

Teaching Tips:
1. Tell the student(s) to lay down their pencil when they finish each activity on **Test 1** to indicate that they are ready to proceed.

2. Before starting **Student Activity One** have five *objects* for the *flannel board*. Make a set of one. Have a student go to the board and make one tally mark for the set of one. Do the same for sets of two, three, four, and five.

3. Let the student(s) choose which *flash card* for less than and greater than goes between two numbers written on the board when introducing **Student Activity Three**.

Materials, Supplies, & Equipment:
1. Number chart

2. Flash cards for addition facts 1–9 and < *and* >

3. Number line

4. *Flannel board and objects*

5. *Place value materials*

Activities:

1. Administer **Test 1**. Proceed through the test as a regular lesson to avoid any unnecessary anxiety by the student(s). Go over the directions for each activity with the student(s) as they are ready to begin that activity.

2. Count out loud by twos to 100 using a number chart.

3. Drill the addition facts 1–9 with flash cards for five minutes with the answers showing.

4. In **Student Activity One**, explain that the student(s) make a mark for each object in the group. Have the student(s) point to the elephant and trace the tally mark with their pencil. In the second box, have the student(s) point to the first camel and trace the first tally mark with their pencil. Point to the second camel and trace the second tally mark with their pencil. Repeat this exercise with remaining boxes.

5. In **Student Activity Two**, have the student(s) put a tally mark in the box for one piano. The student(s) now point to the first french horn and make a tally mark in the box. Point to the second french horn and make a second tally mark in the box. Allow the student(s) to complete the page independently.

6. Remind the student(s) that the arrow points towards the number that is less as they do **Student Activity Three**.

7. Before starting **Student Activity Four**, be sure that the student(s) can correctly identify and give the value for the tens' place and the ones' place (*place value materials* may be helpful). The student(s) must answer the question, "How many tens are there and how many ones ?" The student(s) need to remember that 1 ten is the same as 10, 2 tens 20, 3 tens 30 etc. Check their progress as they do **Student Activity Four**.

8. On the chalk board demonstrate several addition facts (1–9) on the number line. Read the directions to the student(s) in **Student Activity Five**. Have them count on the number line to find the first number in the addition fact. Write the number. Then count to find the second and write that number. Write the answer to the addition fact. Do the same for the remaining problems.

WORD NUMBERS

Concepts:
Word numbers, place value, the number that comes between by fives, tally marks, addition 1–9, and counting by twos

Objectives:
1. The student shall be able to count out loud by twos to 100.

2. The student shall be able to draw a line to match the numeral with its corresponding word number.

3. The student shall be able to write the value of the number in the tens' place and the ones' place.

4. The student shall be able to write the number that comes between two given numbers when counting by fives.

5. The student shall be able to make a tally mark for each given object.

6. The student shall be able to write the addition fact represented on the number line.

Teaching Tips:
1. If the student(s) have difficulty with activity 4, put 4 stacks of ten on the board or use the *place value materials*. Have the student(s) count the stacks by counting by tens. Repeat with several other sets of stacks.

2. Use the number chart to help the student(s) understand how to write the number that comes between when counting by fives in activity 5.

Materials, Supplies, & Equipment:
1. Number chart

2. Flash cards for addition facts 1–9.

3. *Place value materials*

4. Number line

Activities:

1. Count out loud by twos to 100, using the number chart.

2. Drill addition facts 1–9 with flash cards for five minutes with the answers showing.

3. Write the words one, two, three, four, and five on the chalk board. Have the student(s) say the words, spell them orally, and then write them as you point to each one. To start **Student Activity One** have the student(s) point to the number "one." Count the block. Find the word "one." Draw a line from the one block to the word "one." Repeat for the number "two." Allow the student(s) to work the remainder of the activity independently.

4. Put on the board "1 ten," "2 tens," "3 tens," up to "9 tens," out of order. Have the student(s) tell you the value of 1 ten (10), the value of 8 tens (80), etc. Follow the same procedure for "1 one," "2 ones," "3 ones," etc. On **Student Activity Two** discuss the fact that 36 is the same as 3 tens or 30 and 6 ones or 6. Do the first column together with the student(s), then allow the student(s) to complete the remainder of the activity independently.

5. In **Student Activity Three**, have the student(s) count by fives and write the missing number.

6. Go over the directions for **Student Activity Four** with the student(s). Review how to make tally marks for one through five. Remind the student(s) they must make a tally mark for each object as they do the activity.

7. Demonstrate several addition facts 1–9 on the number line. In starting **Student Activity Five**, to find the first addition fact, have the student(s) write the number where the first straight line ends. Now the student(s) must count the marks to where the second straight line ends. This is the second number of this addition fact. The point on the number line where the second straight line ends is the answer to the addition fact. Let them finish the remaining problems independently.

Worksheets:

1. *Worksheet 7* – Addition on the number line

75

CALENDAR – MONTHS OF THE YEAR

Concepts:
> Months of the year, tally marks, word numbers, addition 1–9, and counting by twos

Objectives:
1. The student shall be able to say the months of the year in order.

2. The student shall be able to make tally marks for each given object.

3. The student shall be able to draw a line to match the word number with the counted objects.

4. The student shall be able to find the answer to an addition fact by use of the number line.

Teaching Tips:
1. To vary the drill in activity 2, have the student(s) stand up out of their chair the first ten facts, clap their hands softly the second ten, run in place the third ten, sing the fourth ten, and whisper the fifth ten.

2. Put up a permanent display of the months of the year on a bulletin board to aid activity 3.

3. Point out to the student(s) that the equivalent for ten in tally marks is the same as five plus five in activity 4. 5 + 5 = 10.

4. If the student(s) have difficulty with activity 5, use flash cards of the *word numbers 1–5* and *whole numbers 1–5*. Let the student(s) match the number to its word number on the flannel board.

Materials, Supplies, & Equipment:
1. Number chart

2. Flash cards for addition facts 1–9, months of the year, *whole numbers 1–5*, *word numbers 1–5*, and *tally marks*

3. Flannel board

4. Number line

Activities:

1. Count out loud by twos to 100 using the number chart.

2. Drill the addition facts 1–9 with flash cards for five minutes with the answers showing.

3. Have the student(s) recite the months of the year as you point to them on the chalk board, displayed by flash cards or on the flannel board. On **Student Activity One** have the student(s) point to each month of the year as you say it out loud together. Read the directions with the student(s). Have them point to the correct answer and circle it.

4. Put the numbers 1–5 on the chalk board and have the student(s) make the correct tally marks to represent each number (*flash cards for tally marks* may be a helpful reference). Let the student(s) tell you how they think you would make the tally marks for 6 objects, 7 objects, 8 objects, up to 10 objects. Leave the tally marks on display as the student(s) do **Student Activity Two**.

5. Write the word numbers to five on the chalk board. Have the student(s) read them and spell them out loud as you point to them. Count the first set of apples in **Student Activity Three**. Tell the student(s) to point to the word number and then draw the line from the set to the word number. Follow the same procedure for the rest of the activity.

6. Using a number line, let the student(s) find the answer to several addition facts 1–9. Start at zero and go to the first number in the addition fact.   Count the number of marks needed for the second number. The mark you end on is the answer to the addition fact. Guide the student(s) through the first activity in **Student Activity Four**. Allow them to finish the rest of the activity independently, helping only those who need it.

Never waste time, for that is what life is made of.

EQUAL AND NOT EQUAL

Concepts:

1. Equal and not equal, word numbers, the number that comes between by tens, place value, addition facts 10–18, and counting by threes

   Definitions: Equal means two objects are the same. Not equal means two objects are not the same.

Objectives:

1. The student shall be able to count by threes to 99.

2. The student shall be able to write the equal and not equal symbols correctly between two given objects.

3. The student shall be able to draw a line to match the word numbers (six–ten) with the correct numerals.

4. The student shall be able to write the number that comes between two given numbers when counting by tens.

5. The student shall be able to find the answer to addition facts 10–18 using the number line.

Teaching Tips:

1. When discussing = and ≠, compare ages. Is the student(s) age equal to a friend's age or a brother's age?

2. Point out to the student that the pages of his math book have both the word number and the numeral on them.

3. Use the number chart to show what comes between when counting by tens in ***Student Activity Three***.

Materials, Supplies, & Equipment:

1. Number chart

2. Flash cards for addition facts 1–18, months of the year, = and ≠, numerals 6–10, and word numbers six–ten

3. Flannel board

4. Place value materials

5. Number line 0–19

Activities:

1. Count out loud by threes to 99 using the number chart. Discuss with the student(s) that counting by three means to count over to every third number or to add three to each number.

2. Drill the addition facts 1–18 with flash cards for five minutes with the answers showing.

3. Review the months of the year by having the student(s) read them from the chalk board or flash cards as you point to them.

4. Write the = and ≠ symbols on the blackboard or make flash cards of them. Discuss the definition of equal and not equal with the student(s). Tell the student(s) that the slash mark means not or no. Refer to the no parking signs or no smoking signs as similar uses of the slash mark to mean not or no. Work through **Student Activity One** with the student(s) step by step.

5. Put flash cards of the word numbers and the numerals for 6–10 on the flannel board. Arrange them out of order and have the student(s) choose the matching pairs. Read the directions for **Student Activity Two** to the student(s) as they follow along. Have them point to the numeral 6 and then have them draw a line from the word number to the numeral and finish the activity by themselves.

6. Count by tens to 100 as preparation for **Student Activity Three**. The student(s) should count to themselves as they do each of the activities.

7. Put 3 tens and 5 ones on the chalk board using place value materials. Have the student(s) count the groups of ten and ones. Then have them tell you what the number is. Repeat this procedure with several other numbers. When starting **Student Activity Four**, check each student's work carefully.

8. Using a number line, find the answer to addition facts 10–18 in **Student Activity Five**. Addition facts 10–18 are those single-digit facts with an answer from 10–18. *Worksheet 8* will provide additional work in this area.

Worksheets:

1. *Worksheet 8* – Addition facts 1–18

TALL AND SHORT

Concepts:

Tall and short, tally marks, = and ≠, place value, addition 1–18, months of the year, and counting by threes

Objectives:

1. The student shall be able to circle the given object that is shorter or taller.

2. The student shall be able to make the correct tally marks for a set of objects.

3. The student shall be able to put the correct symbol (= or ≠) between two sets.

4. The student shall be able to write the number represented by a given number of groups of ten and ones.

5. The student shall be able to find the answers to addition facts 1–18 using the number line.

Teaching Tips:

1. Have a large *picture calendar* for the student(s) to look at when discussing the months of the year in activity 3. Many businesses make them available to the public.

2. Have the student(s) use tally marks to keep score in a game at recess.

Materials, Supplies, & Equipment:

1. Number chart

2. Flash cards for addition facts 1–18 and = and ≠

3. *Picture calendar*

4. Number line 0–19

Activities:

1. Count out loud by threes to 99 using the number chart.

2. Drill the addition facts 1–18 with flash cards for five minutes with the answers showing.

3. Review the months of the year and discuss which month has Thanksgiving in it, which has Christmas, and which is the month your school started.

4. Put two stacks of books on your desk. Have the student(s) point to the tall stack. Have the student(s) draw a tall building and a short one. As you start **Student Activity One**, the student(s) should point to the taller object and then circle it. In **Student Activity Two** have the student(s) point to the shorter object and then circle it.

5. Before starting **Student Activity Three**, make the tally marks for 1–10 on the chalk board. When the student(s) start the activity, they must make a mark for each object.

6. Display the equal and not equal flash card symbols. Explain that equal means two things that are the same and not equal means two things that are not the same. Read the directions for **Student Activity Four**. Work through each exercise with the student(s) being sure that they make the decision as to what is the correct answer before they start to make the symbol.

7. In **Student Activity Five** count the groups of ten by tens with the student(s) in the first activity. They can then finish the rest of the activity independently.

8. Using a number line 0–19, find the answers to several addition facts. Start at zero and count over the number of marks equal to the first number in the addition fact. Continue counting over the number of marks to equal the second number in the addition fact. Where you stop is the answer to the addition fact. Instruct the student(s) to do **Student Activity Six** independently. If the student(s) have the addition fact memorized, they may write the answer without using the number line.

Willful waste brings woeful want.

WORD PROBLEMS

Concepts:

Word problems, place value, the number that comes after by ones, addition 1–18, months of the year, ordinal numbers, and counting by threes

Objectives:

1. The student shall be able to visualize a word problem by making the appropriate number of "X's" for each given set of a word problem.

2. The student shall be able to determine the value of the digit in the tens' place.

3. The student shall be able to write the number that comes after a given number.

4. The student shall be able to find the answer to an addition fact 1–18 using the number line.

Teaching Tips:

1. Read the student(s) the poem: "Thirty Days Hath September" (Lesson 23, page 99, activity three). Show the student(s) how the poem tells you how many days in each month. The poem will be memorized at a later date.

Materials, Supplies, & Equipment:

1. Number chart

2. Flash cards for addition facts 1–18 and *months of the year*

3. Calendar display

4. Play money

5. Number line 0–19

Activities:

1. Count out loud by threes to 99 using the number chart.

2. Drill the addition facts 1–18 with flash cards for five minutes with the answers showing.

3. Using a calendar display (*flash cards or other calendar visual* may be used), have the student(s) read the months of the year together. See if anyone can recite the 12 months from memory. Ask which is the second month, the eighth month, and the third month.

4. Word problems will be taught for the next 2 weeks. The student(s) will not be expected to do a word problem on their own until after this time. To begin **Student Activity One**, read the word problem to the student(s) as they follow along. Emphasize that the word, "altogether," means to put together or add. Instruct the student(s) to make an "X" for each ball John has in the first set. Make an "X" for each ball Sally gave John in the second set. Count the "X's" in the two sets to see how many balls John has "altogether." Discuss with them the addition fact that supports the answer. Follow the same procedure for the next two word problems.

5. Have the student(s) count groups of ten using dimes (play money). **Student Activity Two** should be worked independently.

6. Using the number chart, have the student(s) tell you what number comes after a given number. They will need the aid of the number chart as they work through **Student Activity Three**.

7. Lead the student(s) through one addition fact on the chalk board using the number line 0–19. **Student Activity Four** should be worked independently. Check to see if individual help is needed.

Liberty means responsibility.

TIME – HOUR

Concepts:
Time (hour), after by ones, word problems, addition 1–18, and counting by threes

Objectives:
1. The student shall be able to write the correct time displayed on the face of a clock for the hour.

2. The student shall be able to do word problems with addition facts 1–9.

3. The student shall be able to find the answer to addition facts 1–18 using the number line.

Teaching Tips:
1. The student(s) may check their own answer to the word problem in **Student Activity Three** by working it on the number line.

2. When doing **Student Activity Four**, suggest that the student(s) do the addition facts 1–18 by going directly to the number on the number line for the first addition fact as opposed to starting at zero and counting over to the first number fact.

Materials, Supplies, & Equipment:
1. Number chart

2. Flash cards for addition facts 1–18

3. Clock model

4. Number line

Activities:

1. Count out loud by threes to 99 using the number chart.

2. Drill the addition facts 1–18 with flash cards for five minutes with the answers showing.

3. Discuss with the student(s) that the short hand is the hour hand and points to the hour in the day (24 hours in a day). The long hand points to the minutes in an hour and is called the minute hand (60 minutes in an hour). The long hand is on 12 when the short hand tells the hour. Demonstrate 1 o'clock, 3 o'clock, 7 o'clock, etc. using a clock model. When starting **Student Activity One**, have the student(s) check to see if the long hand is on 12. Have the student(s) look at the hour hand to see where the short hand is located.

4. The student(s) may refer to the pages in one of their textbooks or a library book to see what number comes after a given number. They should be able to do **Student Activity Two** independently.

5. In **Student Activity Three** read the word problem with the student(s). Emphasize that the word "altogether" means to put together or add. Have the student(s) make an "X" for each cookie and count them. Then, have the student(s) write the number of cookies eaten "altogether." Discuss the addition fact that supports the answer.

6. Carefully review the steps for finding the answer to an addition fact on the number line. It is important for the student(s) to have complete understanding of this procedure at this time. As they complete **Student Activity Four**, be sure to set aside time to give individual help if there is difficulty.

Whether you are rich or poor depends on what you are,
not what you have.

CALENDAR – DAYS OF THE WEEK

Concepts:

1. Days of the week, place value, hour, tally marks, addition 1–18, word problems, and counting by threes

Objectives:

1. The student shall be able to name the days of the week in the correct order.

2. The student shall be able to write the correct number of tens and ones in a given number and the value of each of the digits.

3. The student shall be able to write the correct time, displayed on the face of a clock, in two ways for the hour.

4. The student shall be able to draw a line to match a number to the correct number of tally marks.

5. The student shall be able to find the answers for addition facts 1–18 by using the number line.

Teaching Tips:

1. In connection with activity 3, help the student(s) determine what the date and day of the week is using a current calendar.

2. When doing activity 5, have the student(s) look at a *digital watch* as an example of another way to write time.

Materials, Supplies, & Equipment:

1. Number chart

2. Flash cards for addition facts 1–18

3. Calendar

4. Clock model *and digital watch*

Activities:

1. Count out loud by threes to 99 using the number chart.

2. Drill addition facts 1–18 with flash cards with the answers showing.

3. Use a calendar to discuss the days of the week. Include 7 days in a week, about four weeks in a month, and each week begins with Sunday. Ask what days of the week the student(s) go to school. In **Student Activity One**, read the days of the week with the student(s). Read the directions as they follow along.

4. Review counting by tens before starting **Student Activity Two**. Be sure that the student(s) understand the tens' place and the ones' place. Put several two-digit numbers on the chalk board. Ask the student(s) how many tens in the number, the value of that many tens, how many ones, and the value of that many ones. The student(s) should be able to do **Student Activity Two** on their own.

5. Inform the student that "o'clock" and ":00" are synonymous. Put the hands on the clock model at 8 o'clock. Show two ways of writing time (8 o'clock, 8:00). Do several other times, have the student(s) tell what time it is, then write it both ways. Complete **Student Activity Three**.

6. As the student(s) start **Student Activity Four**, have them count the tally marks and draw a line to the number it represents.

7. The student(s) will do **Student Activity Five** independently.

8. Read the word problem in **Student Activity Six** as the student(s) follow along. Ask what the word "altogether" means. Have the student(s) make an "X" for each basket, then count them. Write the number of baskets the boys made "altogether." Discuss the addition fact that supports the answer.

Lost time is never found again.

VERTICAL ADDITION

Concepts:

Vertical addition, the number that comes after by twos, hour, = and ≠, word problems, and counting by sixes

Objectives:

1. The student shall be able to count by sixes to 96.

2. The student shall be able to write the correct answer for a vertical addition problem.

3. The student shall be able to write a number that comes after a given number when counting by twos.

4. The student shall be able to circle the correct time displayed on the face of the clock for the hour.

5. The student shall be able to write the = and ≠ symbol correctly between two given sets.

Teaching Tips:

1. Have the student(s) circle the numbers when counting by sixes on *Worksheet 5* after finishing activity 1.

2. Discuss with the student(s) what time they get up, when they eat supper, and what time they go to bed in connection with activity 5.

Materials, Supplies, & Equipment:

1. Number chart

2. Flash cards for addition facts 1–18, = and ≠, word numbers, and *tally marks*

3. Number line

4. Clock model

Activities:

1. Count out loud with the student(s) by sixes to 96 using the number chart. Discuss with the student(s) that counting by sixes means to count every sixth number by counting over six or adding six to each number.

2. Drill the addition facts 1–18 with flash cards with the answers showing.

3. Explain the two ways (horizontal and vertical) of writing addition facts. Show how the number line may still be used to work vertical addition facts. If the student(s) have the answer to an addition fact memorized, encourage them to just write the answer on their paper when doing **Student Activity One**.

4. Review counting by twos. Have the student(s) use *Worksheet 5* as an aid while doing **Student Activity Two**.

5. Remind the student(s) of the two ways to write time. Using the clock model, show several times on the hour and have the student(s) tell what time it is and how to write it two ways. Have them do **Student Activity Three** independently.

6. Using the = and ≠ flash cards, review the names of the symbols and their meaning. Quickly go over the word numbers and tally marks 1–9 (you may use *tally mark flash cards*). In working with the sets in **Student Activity Four**, be sure the student(s) make a conscious effort to determine the correct symbol before they begin to write.

7. Read the word problem in **Student Activity Five** as the student(s) follow along. Have the student(s) make an "X" for each cow. Then count them and write the answer. Discuss the addition fact that supports the answer.

Worksheets:

1. *Worksheet 9* – Addition facts 1–18

2. *Worksheet 5* – Number Chart

ADDITION – OPPOSITES

Concepts:

Addition of opposites, after by twos, hour, word problems, addition 1–18, and counting by sixes

Objectives:

1. The student shall be able to identify opposite pairs in addition as having the same answer by writing the correct answer for each.

2. The student shall be able to write the number that comes after a given number when counting by twos.

3. The student shall be able to draw a line to match a given time to the clock face that displays the same time.

4. The student shall be able to write the correct answer for a vertical addition problem.

Teaching Tips:

1. You might take activity 3 one step further in talking about the importance of the order of numbers if the student(s) are ready. Discuss with the student(s) what happens when you write numbers with the digits in different order. Does the value of the number change? Yes it does. In place value, you cannot change the order of the digits without changing the value of the number.

2. In activity 5, show the student(s) how a *number line* can be used to make a clock. Lay a length of heavy string or yarn on a number line 0–12 and make a mark for each number. Put the *string* in a circle to form the clock face and use *paste* to put it on *heavy construction paper* or *poster board*. Write the numbers 1 to 12 on it. Make a big dot in the center. You may use this for an art project.

Materials, Supplies, & Equipment:

1. Number chart

2. Flash cards for addition facts 1–18

3. Clock model and small clock models for student(s)

4. *Number line*

5. *Heavy string or yarn, construction paper or poster board, and paste*

Activities:

1. Count out loud by sixes to 96 using the number chart.

2. Drill the addition facts 1–18 with flash cards with the answers showing.

3. Choose several opposite pairs of addition facts (flash cards) such as "3 + 4" and "4 + 3." Ask the student(s) how they are alike (same numbers and same answer). How are they different? (order) Explain to them that when you add two numbers, the order can be changed without changing the answer. Therefore if they know the answer to "9 + 7," they also know the answer to "7 + 9." The student(s) should then be able to complete *Student Activity One* independently.

4. Count by twos to 100. Then allow the student(s) to do *Student Activity Two* independently with the aid of the number chart.

5. Give each student a small clock model. Call out 4 or 5 hour times and have them put the hands in the correct position. Demonstrate the correct placement of the hour and minute hands on the clock model for the student(s) to compare with their efforts on the small clock models. When doing *Student Activity Three*, have the student(s) pick out the correct time for each clock. Then draw the line from the given time to the matching clock face.

6. In *Student Activity Four*, have a student read the word problem out loud. Notice there is no set with the problem. Ask why the problem is addition. Discuss what the addition fact would be. Use the number line to find the answer if needed. Write the answer.

7. The student(s) should be able to do *Student Activity Five* independently.

Worksheets:

1. *Worksheet 10* – General review

The reward of a thing well done is to have done it.

LONG AND SHORT

Concepts:
  Long and short, hour, < and >, addition 1–18, and counting by sixes

Objectives:
  1. The student shall be able to correctly circle the longer or shorter object when comparing two given objects.

  2. The student shall be able to draw the hour hand on the face of the clock for a given time.

  3. The student shall be able to correctly place the < or > symbols between two given numbers.

  4. The student shall be able to find the answer to addition facts 1–18 using the number line.

Teaching Tips:
  1. Along with **_Student Activity Three_**, call attention to the clock in the room throughout the day. Have the student(s) tell the time on the hour. Emphasize the positions of the long hand and the short hand.

  2. In **_Student Activity Four_**, another way of determining which symbol (< or >) to use is to mention that the open side of the symbol is always next to the larger number.

Materials, Supplies, & Equipment:
  1. Number chart

  2. Flash cards for addition facts 1–18

  3. Inch ruler and yardstick

  4. Clock model and small clock models for student(s)

Activities:

1. Administer **Test 2**. As the student(s) begin each test activity, go over the directions carefully.

2. Count out loud by sixes to 96 using the number chart.

3. Drill the addition facts 1–18 with flash cards with the answers showing.

4. Have the student(s) put two pencils on their desk. Have them pick up the longer one in their right hand. Have them pick up the shorter one in the left hand. Compare an inch ruler and a yardstick. Have the student(s) tell which is the longer and which is the shorter. When doing **Student Activity One** and **Two**, have the student(s) point to the correct object before they circle it.

5. Each student will need a small clock model. Have them put the long hand (minute hand) on twelve. As you call out or write on the chalk board several hour times, have them put the short hand (hour hand) pointing to the correct number. Have the student(s) point to where the short hand (hour hand) is to be drawn for each activity in **Student Activity Three**. Draw the hour hand, making sure it is shorter than the long hand.

6. Remind each student that "<" means less than, and ">" means greater than. The point of the arrow always goes towards the smaller number. When doing **Student Activity Four**, have the student(s) point to the smaller number, draw the arrow, and then read the set.

7. The student(s) should be able to do **Student Activity Five** independently. If they have the answer memorized, they should be encouraged to just write it without referring to the number line.

The only way to have a friend is to be one.

NUMBER ORDER – AFTER BY 5'S

Concepts:
The number that comes after by fives, hour, < and >, addition 1–18, and counting by sixes

Objectives:
1. The student shall be able to write a number that comes after a given number when counting by fives.

2. The student shall be able to write the correct time displayed on the face of a clock for the hour in two ways.

3. The student shall be able to write the < and > symbols correctly between two given numbers.

4. The student shall be able to write the correct answer to the addition facts 1–18 using the number line.

Teaching Tips:
1. You may reinforce "after" in activity 3 by asking the student(s) what time it is 5 minutes after 3:00, 6:00, 7:00, etc. Show them how to write it. This is good introductory work for telling time other than on the hour.

2. Another way of reading the < or > symbols in activity 5 is to read "less than" if the pointed end comes first and read "greater than" if the open end comes first.

Materials, Supplies, & Equipment:
1. Number chart

2. Flash cards for addition facts 1–18

3. Clock model

4. Flash cards for < and >

Activities:

1. Count out loud by sixes to 96 using the number chart.

2. Drill the addition facts 1–18 with flash cards with the answers showing.

3. Count out loud by fives up to 100 in preparation for ***Student Activity One***. Point to several multiples of five on the number chart and have the student(s) tell what the next number is when counting by fives. The student(s) should count by fives to themselves as they work through ***Student Activity One***.

4. Using the clock model, set the hands for several different times on the hour and have the student(s) tell what time it is. When starting ***Student Activity Two***, have each student point to the short hand of the clock on their lesson page before writing down the number indicated.

5. Use the < and > flash cards to practice naming the symbols. Have the student(s) tell you how to name the symbols (the greater than arrow is at the end of the number line where the numbers are getting greater and the less than arrow is at the end where the numbers are getting less). Read each set after completing ***Student Activity Three***.

6. Allow the student(s) to work on ***Student Activity Four*** independently as you check to observe any difficulty the student(s) may be having. Do not allow the student(s) to count on their fingers to find the answer.

Great works are performed, not by strength, but by perseverance.

WORD PROBLEMS

Concepts:
Word problems, after by fives, tally marks, addition 1–18, and counting by sixes

Objectives:
1. The student shall be able to write the correct answer to a word problem by writing the addition fact.

2. The student shall be able to write the correct number that comes after a given number when counting by fives.

3. The student shall be able to write the missing numbers when counting by sixes.

4. The student shall be able to draw a line to match the correct number to the corresponding tally marks.

5. The student shall be able to write the correct answer to the addition facts 1–18 using the number line.

Teaching Tips:
1. When working with word problems in **Student Activity One**, explain to the student(s) that as two numbers are put together, the result will always be the same or a larger number.

2. When the student(s) do **Student Activity Three**, notice the progression of the sum of the digits in the first seven multiples of six 6, 3, 9, 6, 3, 9, 6. For example 12 would be 1 + 2 = 3, eighteen would be 1 + 8 = 9.

3. *Worksheet 11* has further practice in addition if needed.

Materials, Supplies, & Equipment:
1. Number chart

2. Flash cards for addition facts 1–18

3. Flash cards for tally marks

Activities:

1. Count out loud by sixes to 96 using the number chart.

2. Drill the addition facts 1–9 with flash cards without the answers showing from now on. Continue to drill addition facts 10–18 with the answers showing. Total drill time should be 5 minutes. If you feel the student(s) are not ready to drill the addition facts 1–9 without the answers showing, adjust the schedule to meet individual needs.

3. To begin **Student Activity One**, read the word problem to the student(s) as they follow along. Have the student(s) make an "X" for each bunny Jane has in the first set and an "X" for each bunny Ann has in the second set, then count the X's and write the number of bunnies that the girls have "altogether." Write the addition fact that supports that answer. Read the second word problem aloud. Have the student(s) tell what two numbers are to be put together. Write the addition fact needed to find the answer. Follow the same procedure with the third word problem.

4. Before starting **Student Activity Two**, count out loud by fives to 100. As you point to multiples of five on the number chart, have the student(s) tell what is the next number when counting by fives. They must follow this same procedure as they begin **Student Activity Two**.

5. The student(s) may need the aid of the number chart to complete **Student Activity Three**.

6. Review how to make the tally marks from 1–9. Mix up flash cards of the tally marks to drill them on the number that corresponds to each set of tally marks. Have the student(s) point to the number that matches the corresponding correct set of tally marks and draw a line to it for **Student Activity Four**.

7. Allow the student(s) to do **Student Activity Five** independently.

Worksheets:

1. *Worksheet 11* – Addition facts 1–18

Encouragement to do wrong is not an act of friendship.

WORD PROBLEMS

Concepts:

Word problems, < and >, tally marks, addition 1–18, months of the year, "Thirty Days Hath September," and counting by nines

Objectives:

1. The student shall be able to count out loud by nines to 99 using the number chart.

2. The student shall be able to say the months of the year in the correct order from memory.

3. The student shall be able to write the addition fact to support the answer in a word problem.

4. The student shall be able to write the correct < or > symbol between two given numbers.

5. The student shall be able to circle the number that represents the corresponding tally marks.

Teaching Tips:

1. The question "Why does February only have 28 days?" may come up in activity 3. If you would like to go into a little history, the answer may be a good springboard to some discussion on how various cultures use different calendars. The Julian calendar had July named for Julius Caesar and August for the emperor Augustus. Tradition says Augustus took a day from February (which had 29) and added it to August so that his month, August, had as many days as Julius Caesar's July had.

2. The first word problem in *Student Activity One* may be demonstrated by the students using *play money*.

Materials, Supplies, & Equipment:

1. Number chart

2. Flash cards for addition facts 1–18 and < *and* >

3. Calendar

4. *Play money*

Activities:

1. Count out loud by nines to 99 using the number chart. Discuss with the student(s) that counting by nines means to count every ninth number by counting over nine places on the number chart or by adding nine to each number.

2. Drill the addition facts 1–9 with flash cards without the answers showing. Drill addition facts 10–18 with the answers showing.

3. Go over the months of the year in order with the student(s) using a calendar. Discuss how many days are in each month. Recite:

   > *Thirty days hath September,*
   > *April, June, and November.*
   > *All the rest have thirty-one*
   > *Except February alone*
   > *Which has twenty-eight*
   > *Until leap year gives it twenty-nine.*

   with the student(s). Have them repeat the first two lines several times. Then go through the verse again.

4. Have the student(s) read the first word problem in **Student Activity One** out loud. Pick out the key word, "altogether." Ask what two numbers should be put together. Have the student(s) write the correct addition fact on the blanks. Follow this procedure with the next two word problems.

5. Quickly go over the names of the < and > symbols (you may use *flash cards*). As the student(s) do **Student Activity Two,** check to see if help is needed. Ask them if they remember the ways you have shown to distinguish the symbols.

6. Put the tally marks for 1–10 on the chalk board out of order. Have the student(s) tell the number to match each set. Read the directions with the student(s) as they start **Student Activity Three**.

7. No help should be required with **Student Activity Four** except to check to see if the student(s) are making the same error consistently.

   > *You will never "find" time for anything.*
   > *If you want time, you must make it.*

NUMBER ORDER – AFTER BY 10'S

Concepts:
The number that comes after by 10's, word numbers, tally marks, word problems, addition 1–18, months of the year, "Thirty Days Hath September," and counting by nines

Objectives:
1. The student shall be able to say the months of the year in the correct order from memory.

2. The student shall be able to write the number that comes after a given number when counting by 10's.

3. The student shall be able to draw a line to match a number, a word number, and tally marks correctly.

4. The student shall be able to write the addition fact to support the answer in a word problem.

Teaching Tips:
1. Drilling the student(s) on the addition facts 10–18 without the answers showing will continue for one week. At that time they should have the answers memorized. In two weeks they will be given the facts in the student lessons without a number line. If a student is having difficulty, extra drill may be needed using flash cards or addition *Worksheets 8, 9,* and *11*.

2. Suggest to the student(s) that they use tally marks to keep score in a game involving team competition.

Materials, Supplies, & Equipment:
1. Number chart

2. Flash cards for addition facts 1–18

3. Calendar

4. Flash cards for word numbers

5. Flash cards for tally marks

Activities:

1. Count out loud by nines to 99 using the number chart.

2. Drill the addition facts 1–9 with flash cards without the answers showing. Drill addition facts 10–18 with the answers showing.

3. Go over the months of the year in order with the student(s). See if the student(s) can name them without looking at the calendar or the bulletin board. Read "Thirty Days Hath September" to the student(s). Have them repeat the first two lines several times. Further work with the calendar may be found on *Worksheet 12*.

4. Count by tens to 100. The student(s) should be able to do this without the number chart. Discuss what number comes after a given number when counting by tens. Guide the student(s) through several sets in ***Student Activity One*** and then allow them to finish on their own.

5. Drill word numbers and tally marks using flash cards. After reading the directions with the student(s), they may proceed with ***Student Activity Two***.

6. In ***Student Activity Three***, have the student(s) read the first word problem out loud. Pick out the key word, "altogether." Ask what two numbers are to be put together and have the student(s) write the addition fact on the blanks. Notice that the label for the answer has been added. Discuss its necessity with the student(s). Follow this procedure with the next two word problems.

7. Encourage the student(s) to answer as many of the addition facts as possible without looking at the number line when doing ***Student Activity Four***. They may use the number line to check their answers.

Worksheets:

1. *Worksheet 12* – Calendar

Those things which we wish to be able to do with ease must first be practiced with diligence.

PLACE VALUE

Concepts:
Place value, word numbers, tally marks, after by tens, word problems, addition 1–18, months of the year, "Thirty Days Hath September," and counting by nines

Objectives:
1. The student shall be able to say the months of the year in the correct order from memory.

2. The student shall be able to write the correct number of tens and ones in a two-digit number and then write the value of each digit.

3. The student shall be able to write the numerals for word numbers and tally marks.

4. The student shall be able to write the number after a given number when counting by tens.

5. The student shall be able to write the addition fact to support the answer in a word problem.

Teaching Tips:
1. Requiring the student(s) to do the last step in **Student Activity One** (27 = 20 + 7) is the beginning of instruction in expanded notation. It is important for the student(s) to have a clear understanding of this principle.

2. You may begin to check each student individually in regard to his proficiency with the addition facts 1–18 in activity 2. If a student is proficient, he may be allowed to skip every other day of drill.

Materials, Supplies, & Equipment:
1. Number chart

2. Flash cards for addition facts 1–18, whole numbers 0–99, word numbers, and tally marks

Activities:

1. Count out loud by nines to 99 using the number chart.

2. Drill the addition facts 1–9 with flash cards without the answers showing. Drill addition facts 10–18 with the answers showing.

3. Have the student(s) go over the months of the year without looking at a calendar or flash cards. Read the poem "Thirty Days Hath September." Have the student(s) recite the first two lines. Go over the third and fourth lines, "All the rest have thirty-one except February alone," several times.

4. Using whole number flash cards 0–99, ask the student(s) to tell how many tens and how many ones are in several numbers. Ask them to tell the value of the digit in the tens' place and the ones' place. They should be able to complete **Student Activity One** with no help.

5. Review the word numbers and tally marks with flash cards. Read the directions to **Student Activity Two** and allow them to complete the activity independently.

6. Quickly count by tens to 100. Choose several multiples of ten and ask the student(s) what comes after when counting by tens. They should be able to complete **Student Activity Three** by themselves.

7. Read the first word problem of **Student Activity Four** to the student(s) as they follow along. Ask what the key word is (altogether) and what it tells you to do. What two numbers are to be put together? Have the student(s) write the addition fact necessary to support the answer. Allow the student(s) to do the next two word problems on their own giving help only if needed.

8. **Student Activity Five** can be done with no help.

Putting off an easy thing makes it hard,
and putting off a hard thing makes it impossible.

MONEY – PENNY

Concepts:
Penny, place value, addition 1–18, months of the year, "Thirty Days Hath September," and counting by nines

Objectives:
1. The student shall be able to recognize the penny both front and back and count using pennies.

2. The student shall be able to write the correct number of tens and ones in a two-digit number and the value of each digit.

Teaching Tips:
1. In reference to activity 1, the student(s) may be given added practice by taking *Worksheet 13* and writing the numbers used for counting by nines first. Have them notice their placement on the chart.

2. Give the student(s) play pennies when doing activity 4. Allow them to make different sets with the pennies. Then count the sets. Two students could work as partners in this project.

Materials, Supplies, & Equipment:
1. Number chart

2. Flash cards for addition facts 1–18

3. Play money

4. Flash cards for whole numbers 0–99

Activities:

1. Count out loud by nines to 99 using the number chart.

2. Drill the addition facts 1–9 with flash cards without the answers showing. Drill addition facts 10–18 with the answers showing.

3. Display whole number flash cards for 1–12. Have a student name a month of the year as they point to each of the cards starting with one. Discuss today's date. What is the difference between today's date and the same date last year? Recite "Thirty Days Hath September," repeating the third and fourth lines several times. Then say the first through fourth lines together from memory.

4. Use play money for the student(s) to see the front and back of a penny. Ask, "What color is the penny?" "Whose picture is on the front of the penny?" (Abraham Lincoln) "What building is on the back of a penny?" (The Lincoln Memorial) Explain that you can write a penny's name in three ways – penny, 1 cents, or 1¢. The ¢ symbol is the short way to write cents. Read the directions for **Student Activity One** to the student(s). Be sure they point to each penny as they count. Notice any time you count money, you need to use a label to show that you are talking about money. For example, in writing, money must be labeled with the dollar sign or cent sign. When reading money, $4.95, would be read, "four dollars and ninety-five cents."

5. Ask the student(s) to tell how many tens and how many ones are in several numbers using whole number flash cards 0–99. Then ask what the value of the digit in the tens' place and the ones' place is. As the student(s) do **Student Activity Two**, be sure they understand that the value of the digit in the tens' place and the ones' place also goes into the last two blanks.

6. **Student Activity Three** can be done independently. Encourage the student(s) to use the number line only if they are having difficulty.

Worksheets:

1. *Worksheet 13 – Fill in the blank number chart*

Beware of little expenses, a small leak can sink a large ship.

TIME – HALF HOUR

Concepts:

Half hour, addition 1–18, pennies, place value, months of the year, "Thirty Days Hath September," and counting by nines

Objectives:

1. The student shall be able to say the months of the year in the correct order from memory.

2. The student shall be able to write the correct time displayed on the face of a clock on the half hour.

3. The student shall be able to write the correct answers to addition facts as they relate to pennies.

4. The student shall be able to write the correct number of tens and ones in a two-digit number and the value of each digit.

Teaching Tips:

1. When doing activity 4, you may tell the student(s) that telling time on the half hour can be expressed in three different ways. 3:30 may also be expressed as half past three or 30 minutes "after" 3.

2. In activity 5 give the student(s) *play pennies*. Have them make up two sets with the pennies. Then determine the addition fact they would use to find out how many pennies they would have altogether. Several students may take turns arranging the sets and finding the addition fact.

Materials, Supplies, & Equipment:

1. Number chart

2. Flash cards for addition facts 1–18 and months of the year

3. Clock model

4. *Play money*

Activities:

1. Count out loud by nines to 99 using the number chart.

2. Drill the addition facts 1–9 with flash cards without the answers showing. Drill addition facts 10–18 with the answers showing.

3. Use the flash cards to drill the student(s) on the months of the year in order. Recite the first four lines of "Thirty Days Hath September" with the student(s). Go over the last two lines several times. Then recite the whole poem.

4. When starting **Student Activity One**, talk about cutting the clock into two half-hours as in the picture of the first clock. Explain how the minutes can be found by counting by fives. Each half hour is 30 minutes. When the time is on the hour, the long hand is on the 12 (second picture). When 30 minutes have passed on the clock, the long hand is then on the 6 (third picture). Point out that the short hand is half way between the 3 and the 4. Show on a clock model the distance the two hands move with the passage of 30 minutes. To help the student(s) begin finding the time on the remaining clocks, ask the following questions: "Where is the long hand?" "How many minutes is that?" Write it. "Where is the short hand?" "What hour is that?" Write it.

5. As student(s) do **Student Activity Two**, point out that a label (in this case cents, ¢, or pennies) is always used when you add money.

6. Point to different numbers on the number chart and ask how many tens and how many ones are in the number. Ask what is the value of the digit in the tens' place and the ones' place. They should be able to complete **Student Activity Three** on their own.

Tomorrow is never guaranteed to anyone.

MONEY – DIME

Concepts:
Dimes, half hour, the number that comes before by ones, addition 1–18, date, "Thirty Days Hath September," and counting by fours

Objectives:
1. The student shall be able to count out loud by fours to 100 using the number chart.

2. The student shall be able to state the date for a given day.

3. The student shall be able to recognize a dime both front and back and write the value of a given number of dimes.

4. The student shall be able to write the time displayed on the face of a clock for the half hour correctly.

5. The student shall be able to write the number that comes before a given number.

Teaching Tips:
1. A student who has mastered the addition facts may be directed to drill another student who needs added practice. One student may even drill himself if he has extra time at some point during the day.

2. Show the student(s) several different types of calendars as you discuss today's date in activity 3. Examples: *a pretty picture calendar, a desk calendar, a pocket calendar, an appointment calendar*, etc.

Materials, Supplies, & Equipment:
1. Number chart

2. Flash cards for addition facts 1–18 and the whole numbers 1–99

3. *Different types of calendars*

4. Dime and play money

5. Clock model and small clock models for student(s)

Activities:

1. Count out loud by fours to 100 using the number chart. Discuss with the student(s) that counting by fours means to count over four on the number chart or to add four to each number.

2. Drill the addition facts 1–9 with flash cards without the answers showing. Drill addition facts 10–18 with the answers showing.

3. Write today's date on the board. Discuss what the date was the day "before" today and the day "after" today. How are they different? What is different about the same date a month ago? Repeat the last two lines of "Thirty Days Hath September" several times. Recite the complete poem out loud with them.

4. Show the student(s) a real dime. Discuss its color, the picture on the front (of Franklin D. Roosevelt), what's on the back (the torch and sprigs of laurel and oak), its monetary value, and three ways of referring to it. When counting dimes, count by tens. One dime equals ten cents. Have a student count several sets of dimes and tell how much they are worth. In **Student Activity One**, read the directions with the student(s) and work the first two problems together. Have the student(s) finish the activity on their own.

5. Remind the student(s) that an half hour is 30 minutes. When the clock is at the half hour, the long hand is on the 6. The short hand will be half way between two numbers because it is half past the hour. The hour is indicated by the number the short hand just passed. Give the student(s) a small clock model. Write several times on the chalk board and have them put the hands in the correct position, placing the long (minute) hand first and then the short (hour) hand. Then have them hold up the clock so it can be checked. Have them do **Student Activity Two** by determining where the long hand is and then where the short hand is.

6. Review the meaning of "before." Hold several whole number flash cards up and have the student(s) tell what number comes before. Have a number chart handy for them to use if needed. After reading the directions for **Student Activity Three**, encourage the student(s) to use the number chart if necessary.

7. **Student Activity Four** should be done independently. Remind the student(s) to use the number line only if necessary. They may use it to check their answers.

Worksheets:

1. *Worksheet 14* – Addition facts

MONEY – PENNIES AND DIMES

Concepts:
Pennies and dimes, = and ≠, half hour, "Thirty Days Hath September," and counting by fours

Objectives:
1. The student shall be able to correctly recite the poem "Thirty Days Hath September" from memory.

2. The student shall be able to write the value of a given number of dimes and pennies.

3. The student shall be able to write = or ≠ between an addition fact and a whole number correctly.

4. The student shall be able to draw a line to match a given written time to the time displayed on the face of a clock.

5. The student shall be able to correctly determine the value of a given number of dimes.

Teaching Tips:
1. When doing activity 4, discuss with the student(s) how the value of a dime is more than the value of a penny even though the size of it is smaller. Size does not determine value. This can also be paralleled to the size of a student does not determine his value.

2. If you have not already done so, now would be a good time to let the student(s) use real pennies and dimes to do activity 4. Have them look at both sides of the coins.

Materials, Supplies, & Equipment:
1. Number chart

2. Flash cards for addition facts 1–18

3. Play money

4. Flash cards for = and ≠

5. Clock model

6. *Real pennies and dimes*

Activities:

1. Count out loud by fours to 100 using the number chart.

2. Drill the addition facts 1–9 with flash cards without the answers showing. Drill addition facts 10–18 with the answers showing.

3. Recite the poem "Thirty Days Hath September" several times with the student(s).

4. Give each student play money dimes and pennies. Tell them to put 3 dimes and 4 pennies on their desks. Ask "how many pennies equal a dime?" To find the value of 3 dimes, you count the dimes by tens. 3 dimes and 4 pennies equal 10, 20, 30, 31, 32, 33, 34 cents. Practice this with several sets. In **Student Activity One**, do the first problem with the student(s) and only give help where it is needed on the remaining ones.

5. Write "2 + 6 __ 8", "3 + 8 __ 12", "4 + 3 __ 8", and "6 + 6 __ 12" on the chalk board. Have the student(s) add 2 + 6 (8) and then compare 8 and 8. Since they are the same, ask the student(s) if they are equal or not equal. Write the = symbol between the two sets. Follow the same procedure for the other three sets. The student(s) should be allowed to work **Student Activity Two** by themselves.

6. Using the clock model, show the student(s) several different half hour times for them to read. Caution them to check whether the long hand is on the 12 or on the 6. Do one with the long hand on the 12. Read the directions for **Student Activity Three** with the student(s). Allow the student(s) to complete the activity independently.

7. Display a set of dimes. Have the student(s) count them by tens to find the value. Do this several times. On the number chart, point to the multiples of 10 and ask how many dimes it will take to equal that number of cents. In **Student Activity Four**, help the student(s) do the first column. Let the student(s) complete the second column independently.

Worksheets:

1. *Worksheet 15 – Adding money*

Life's great accomplishments are measured by what one does with the little tasks.

CALENDAR – DAYS OF THE WEEK

Concepts:

Days of the week, half hour, before by ones, = and ≠, word problems, "Thirty Days Hath September," and counting by fours

Objectives:

1. The student shall be able to write the day of the week a given date falls on from a calendar.

2. The student shall be able to draw the hour hand on the face of a clock for the half hour.

3. The student shall be able to write the number that comes before a given number.

4. The student shall be able to write = or ≠ between two given sets correctly.

Teaching Tips:

1. Give the student(s) a copy of *Worksheet 5* to aid them in completing ***Student Activity Three***.

2. If the question, "What is it called when two sets have a ≠ sign between them in activity 6?" comes up, it is called an inequality because they are not equal.

Materials, Supplies, & Equipment:

1. Number chart

2. Flash cards for addition facts 1–18

3. Calendar

4. Small clock models

Activities:

1. Administer **Test 3**. Go over the directions for each activity out loud with the student(s) as they are ready to begin the activity.

2. Count out loud by fours to 100 using the number chart.

3. Drill the addition facts 1–9 with flash cards without the answer showing. Drill addition facts 10–18 with the answers showing.

4. Recite "Thirty Days Hath September" and the days of the week in order. Using the calendar, discuss with the student(s) what day of the week certain dates fall on. Look at the month given in **Student Activity One**. Read the instructions out loud and guide the student(s) through the activity.

5. Give each student a small clock model. As you call out a time on the half hour, have them first put the long hand on the six. Then have them place the short hand. Remind them that the short hand goes half way between the two numbers because it is half past the hour. Do a couple of examples on the hour to remind them that the long hand goes on the 12 when reading a clock on the hour. Read the directions for **Student Activity Two**. Do the first clock as a group and let them do the remainder by themselves.

6. Direct the student(s) as they practice picking out the number that comes before a given number on the number chart. Instruct the student(s) to use the number chart as they continue **Student Activity Three**.

7. Write several sets on the chalk board similar to **Student Activity Four**. Have the student(s) tell which symbol (= or ≠) to put between the given sets to make a true statement. Then pick out which are equations. After reading the directions, allow the student(s) to complete the activity independently.

8. Have the student(s) read the word problem to themselves in **Student Activity Five**. Point out the key word "altogether." Ask, "What two numbers are to be put together?" Have them write the addition fact on the blanks. Discuss the label.

INCHES

Concepts:

Inches, before by ones, = and ≠, addition 1–18, and counting by fours

Objectives:

1. The student shall be able to correctly measure an object by using a ruler marked in inches.

2. The student shall be able to write the number that comes before a given number.

3. The student shall be able to correctly place an = or ≠ symbol between two given sets.

Teaching Tips:

1. Have the student(s) circle all of the multiples of 4 on *Worksheet 5* to get an overview of counting by fours.

2. When doing activity 3, the student(s) may measure the length of the leaf, toothbrush, pencil, and spoon with their own ruler to see the consistency of length for the unit of measurement, the inch.

Materials, Supplies, & Equipment:

1. Number chart

2. Flash cards for addition facts 1–18

3. Inch ruler

4. Flash cards for = and ≠ symbols

Activities:

1. Count out loud by fours to 100 using the number chart.

2. Drill the addition facts 1–9 with flash cards without the answer showing. Drill addition facts 10–18 with the answers showing.

3. Have the student(s) take out their own ruler that has only inches on it. Compare their ruler to the ruler in *Student Activity One*. When measuring with a ruler, always put one end of the object at zero. Where the other end stops is the length of the object expressed in inches. Have the student trace from the tip of the leaf down to the ruler to see that the leaf is 2 inches long. Then have them trace an upward line with their finger from the end of the toothbrush, pencil, and spoon to the ruler to give them the number to write in the blanks in *Student Activity One*.

4. Have the student(s) look at page 18 in any reading book. Look at the page that comes "before" it. Do this with several other pages. Allow them to use their reading book as an aid in doing *Student Activity Two*.

5. The student(s) should be able to do *Student Activity Three* independently. If you feel it is necessary, show them the = and ≠ flash card symbols and discuss them.

6. Encourage the student(s) to not use the number line unless absolutely necessary while working *Student Activity Four*. In five more lessons the number line will no longer be put on the student activity sheet for doing addition problems.

Seldom lend and never borrow, that will save a lot of sorrow.

NUMBER ORDER – BEFORE BY 2'S

Concepts:
> The number that comes before by 2's, dimes and pennies, inches, < and >, and counting by fours

Objectives:
1. The student shall be able to write the number that comes before a given number when counting by 2's.

2. The student shall be able to write the value of a given number of dimes and pennies.

3. The student shall be able to measure the length of a given object in inches.

4. The student shall be able to write the missing numbers when counting by fours.

5. The student shall be able to write < or > symbols between two given sets correctly.

Teaching Tips:
1. If added practice is still needed in addition facts after completing activity 2, use *Worksheet 16*.

2. If time permits, the student(s) would benefit from measuring some real objects in the room with their inch ruler during activity 5. Choose objects that are very nearly multiples of whole inches.

Materials, Supplies, & Equipment:
1. Number chart

2. Flash cards for addition facts 1–18, < and >, *whole numbers*

3. Play money

4. Inch ruler

Activities:

1. Count out loud by fours to 100 using the number chart.

2. Drill the addition facts 1–9 with flash cards without the answer showing. Drill addition facts 10–18 with the answers showing.

3. Quickly count by 2's to 100 out loud. Using the number chart, point to a number. Have the student(s) tell what number comes before that number when counting by twos. Be sure you choose an even number. Do this several times. Instruct the student(s) to use the number chart as they work through **Student Activity One**.

4, Give each student play money (dimes and pennies). Let them set up a group of dimes and a group of pennies. Count the dimes by tens and the pennies by ones to see the value of the money. Two students may work together, one setting up the sets and the other counting them and vice versa. Read the directions to **Student Activity Two**. Do the first problem together, then allow the student(s) to work independently giving help where it is needed.

5. Each student needs to take out his ruler, marked with inches, for **Student Activity Three**. Have them line up the zero on the ruler at the beginning of the candy cane. Tell them the vertical line at the beginning of the candy cane is the point of reference for zero on the ruler and that the length of the candy cane is where it ends on the ruler. Write that number on the blank. Follow the same procedure for each of the objects.

6. Allow the student(s) to use a number chart when doing **Student Activity Four** if necessary. (*Flash cards – multiples of four may also be used.*)

7. Discuss the names of the < and > symbols (*flash cards*). Always put the point of the arrow toward the smaller number while doing **Student Activity Five**.

Worksheets:

1. *Worksheet 16* – Addition facts 10–18

MONEY – NICKELS

Concepts:

Nickels, inches, before by twos, < and >, and counting by eights

Objectives:

1. The student shall be able to count out loud by eights to 96 using the number chart.

2. The student shall be able to write the correct value for a given number of nickels.

3. The student shall be able to correctly measure the length of a given object with an inch ruler.

4. The student shall be able to write the number that comes before a given number when counting by twos.

5. The student shall be able to write the < and > symbols correctly between two given sets.

Teaching Tips:

1. You might play a game while drilling addition facts in activity 2. Divide the class into two teams lined up single file. Show a fact to the first person in each line. The one that answers first scores a point for his team and both players move to the back of the line. If he misses the answer, the other team may try. Have each student think of the answer each time even if he isn't at the front of the line. Keep score by using tally marks. You may have one student play this by playing against the clock to see how many answers he can get right within a set period of time, like two minutes or five minutes.

2. In activity 3, allow the student(s) to handle a *real nickel* and feel the imprint on the front and back.

Materials, Supplies, & Equipment:

1. Number chart

2. Flash cards for addition facts 10–18

3. Play money

4. Flannel board

5. Inch ruler

6. *Real nickel*

Activities:

1. Count out loud by eights to 96 using the number chart. Discuss with the student(s) that counting by eights means to count over every eighth number on the number chart or to add eight to each number.

2. Drill the addition facts 1–9 with flash cards without the answer showing. Drill addition facts 10–18 with the answers showing.

3. Use play money for the student(s) to see the front and back of the nickel. Discuss the color of the nickel, whose picture is on the front of the nickel (Thomas Jefferson), what is on the back of a nickel (Monticello, Thomas Jefferson's home), and what is the value of a nickel. Point out the three ways to write a nickel's name on **Student Activity One**. Quickly review counting by fives. Put several different sets of nickels on the flannel board or chalk board and have the student(s) count them by fives to learn their value. In **Student Activity One**, let a student read the directions. Do the first problem together. They should be able to complete the activity on their own.

4. Before starting **Student Activity Two**, talk with the student(s) about the inch ruler, "What is it used for?" "How long is an inch?" "What do you measure with an inch ruler?" You wouldn't use it to measure the distance from home to the grocery store, but you would use it to find out how long your pencil is. Put the zero on the ruler at the front of the object where the vertical line is in **Student Activity Two**. Trace on the ruler with your finger to the point where the object ends. This is the length of the object. Allow the student(s) to complete the remainder of the activity with as little help as possible.

5. Quickly count by 2's to 100. Have the student(s) take out any reading book and turn to page 22. Next have them look back 2 pages "before" page 22. Ask what page it is. Help the student(s) visualize this as 2 before 22. Do this with several other pages. They will need a number chart handy to complete **Student Activity Three**.

6. The student(s) should be able to do **Student Activity Four** independently once you read the directions out loud with them.

NAMING FRACTIONS

Concepts:
Naming fractions, nickels, before by twos, inches, and counting by eights

Definition: Fractions are a part of a whole.

Objectives:
1. The student shall be able to correctly write a unit fraction from a picture.

2. The student shall be able to write the correct value of a given number of nickels by counting by fives.

3. The student shall be able to write the correct number that comes before a given number by counting by twos.

4. The student shall be able to correctly measure the length of a given object with an inch ruler and write the answer.

Teaching Tips:
1. When making the transition to **Student Activity Two,** discuss with the student(s) how money uses fractions. There is the half dollar and the quarter which is one fourth of a dollar. One fourth is a quarter. A quarter pound of hamburger is one fourth of a pound.

2. In activity 4, let each student take a real nickel and lay a piece of paper on top of it. With the side of the lead of his pencil, have him scribble back and forth over the nickel to get the imprint on his paper. Do both the front and the back of the nickel.

Materials, Supplies, & Equipment:
1. Number line

2. Flash cards for addition facts 10 –18

3. Nickels or play money

4. Inch ruler

Activities:

1. Count out loud by eights to 96 using the number chart.

2. Drill the addition facts 1–9 with flash cards without the answer showing. Drill addition facts 10–18 with the answers showing.

3. Fractions are a part of a whole. Fractions are named in respect to what part of the whole you are talking about. **Student Activity One** deals with unit (numerator being one) fractions. Ask the student(s) how many parts the rectangle is divided into? How many parts are shaded? Explain that this fraction is named one half (one half hour, one half gallon of milk, etc.). Have the student(s) practice writing a one over a two with a horizontal line in between on a sheet of paper. Follow the same procedure for the next three pictures. Work step by step with them as they complete **Student Activity One**. In following lessons each unit fraction will be dealt with in a more thorough fashion. This lesson serves as the introduction to naming fractions.

4. Give the student(s) a real nickel to examine. Discuss how many pennies are equal to one nickel. How many nickels are equal to one dime. Find the value of a set of nickels by counting by fives. Read the directions for **Student Activity Two** and give help where needed.

5. Quickly count by twos to 100. Practice finding the number that comes before by twos on the number chart. The student(s) may need to see a number chart as they do **Student Activity Three**.

6. Using their inch ruler, have each student measure the length of the knife and the lollipop in **Student Activity Four**. Start with the zero on the ruler at the left end of each object.

Worksheets:

1. *Worksheet 17* – Addition facts for 10–18

It is better to go to bed without supper than to rise in debt.

WORD NUMBERS 11–20

Concepts:

Word numbers for 11–20, nickels, fractions, inches, addition 1–18, and counting by eights

Objectives:

1. The student shall be able to correctly draw a line to match a word number and the corresponding numeral.

2. The student shall be able to write the correct value of a given number of nickels by counting by fives.

3. The student shall be able to correctly write a unit fraction that is pictured.

4. Using an inch ruler, the student shall be able to draw a line a given length.

Teaching Tips:

1. Make *twenty 3" X 5" cards*. After completing activity 3, write the numbers 11–20 on half of the cards. Write the word numbers on the other cards. Student(s) may make these cards. Put the cards all together and have each student draw one card. Student(s) then find their partner (example 12 – twelve). One student could take all the cards and match them correctly.

2. Begin to collect objects that could be used in a play store for the student(s). A play cash register, empty food boxes, paper sacks, empty pop cans, empty vegetable cans, a salt box, etc. will provide much entertainment for a rainy day.

Materials, Supplies, & Equipment:

1. Flash cards for addition facts 1–18

2. Play money

3. Flannel board

4. Fraction materials

5. Inch rulers

6. *Twenty 3" X 5" cards*

Activities:

1. Count out loud by eights to 96 using the number chart.

2. Drill the addition facts 1–9 with flash cards without the answer showing. Drill addition facts 10–18 with the answers showing.

3. Write, in list form, the word numbers from 11–20 on the chalk board. Have the student(s) read them together. Call out a number and have a student tell if it is the first, second, third, etc. listed on the board. Read the directions for **Student Activity One** with the student(s). Give help only where needed as they work this activity.

4. To introduce this next activity, give each student a set of play money nickels. Tell them to make a set of six nickels with play money. Have them count the nickels by fives and tell what the value is. Do this with several other sets. They should be able to complete **Student Activity Two** by themselves.

5. Discuss the naming of unit fractions by doing several examples with fraction materials for the flannel board. Put a whole divided into six parts on the board. Take all away but one part. Ask what part of the whole is left (one sixth). Do this also for a whole divided into 2, 3, 4, and 5 parts. In **Student Activity Three**, do the first line together. Allow them to do the second line by themselves if you feel they can do it successfully.

6. In **Student Activity Four**, have each student put their inch ruler on the paper with the zero at the dot. Draw a line from the dot to the number 2 on the ruler. This may be difficult for the student(s). Do not expect perfection. They will become better as they have more practice. Now they need positive encouragement. Put the zero on the ruler at the second dot. Draw a line to the number 4 on the ruler.

7. This is the last day the number line will appear as an aid in addition facts. Check to see which student(s) are still relying on it as they do **Student Activity Five**. Provide additional practice in drill for these student(s). *Worksheets 9, 11, 14, 16, and 17* can be used for this purpose. Parents need to know if the student(s) are still having difficulty in this area.

Worksheets:

1. *Worksheets 9, 11, 14, 16, and 17* – Addition 1–18

ADDITION – DOUBLE DIGIT

Concepts:
Double-digit addition, before by twos, nickels and pennies, word problems, and counting by eights

Objectives:
1. The student shall be able to correctly add two double-digit numbers without the use of a number line.

2. The student shall be able to write the correct number that comes before a given number when counting by 2's.

3. The student shall be able to write the correct value of a set of nickels and pennies.

4. The student shall be able to correctly identify the numbers to be added for a word problem and write the addition fact that gives the correct answer.

Teaching Tips:
1. At the end of activity 3, instruct each student to draw, on a sheet of paper, two items you would buy in a grocery store. Write a price less than 50 cents for each item. (The number in the ones' place should also be less than 5.) Each student then writes a word problem using the two items. If time permits, work some of the word problems together with the student(s).

2. Use the *number line* by moving back two marks to show what comes before when counting by twos in activity 4.

Materials, Supplies, & Equipment:
1. Flash cards for addition facts 1–18

2. *Place value materials*

3. Number chart

4. *Number line*

5. *Play money*

Activities:

1. Count out loud by eights to 96 using the number chart.

2. Drill the addition facts 1–9 with flash cards without the answers showing. Drill the addition facts for 10–18 with the answers showing. In five more lessons, the drill for addition facts 1–9 will be changed to timed drill sheets four times a week. Continue to use the flash card drill for the addition facts 1–9 to supplement the drill sheets, if you feel it is necessary for the student(s) success.

3. Discuss the ones' place and the tens' place in a two-digit number (you may want to use *place value materials*). When adding two numbers that are two digits each, have the student(s) add the ones' column first and write the answer under the ones' column. Then have them add the tens' column and write the answer under the tens' column. The student(s) will not be introduced to addition with carrying until the last six weeks of the year after the basic skill of addition has been mastered. In **Student Activity One,** go over the three examples given at the top of the page with the student(s). Check the progress of the student(s) carefully as they do this activity. There will no longer be a number line with the addition problems.

4. Count by twos to 100. Point to several even numbers on the number chart and have the student(s) tell what number comes before when counting by twos. Allow the student(s) to look at a number chart (you may also use *Worksheet 5*) as they do **Student Activity Two**.

5. (*Play money – nickels and pennies*) Read the directions carefully with the student(s) for **Student Activity Three**. Do the first problem together. Then let the student(s) continue independently.

6. Have a student read the word problem in **Student Activity Four** out loud. Ask how many flowers Chris has altogether? Write the correct addition fact that answers the question.

Worksheets:

1. *Worksheet 18* – Word number addition facts

2. *Worksheet 5* – Number chart

ADDITION – HORIZONTAL AND VERTICAL

Concepts:
Adding double-digit horizontal numbers vertically, place value, nickels, before by twos, and counting by eights

Objectives:
1. The student shall be able to write the correct answer for double-digit horizontal addition problems rewritten vertically.

2. The student shall be able to write the number represented by a given number of groups of tens and ones.

3. The student shall be able to write the correct value of a given set of nickels and pennies.

4. The student shall be able to write the correct number that comes before a given number when counting by twos.

Teaching Tips:

1. When doing counting in activity 1, have a student or row of students start counting when you clap your hands. Then each time you clap (every 5 or 6 numbers) a different student or row of students starts counting, picking up where the others left off. A single student can do this activity by standing up the first time you clap and sitting down the next time and continuing in this pattern.

2. Allow the student(s) to go to the chalk board and work two-digit addition problems during activity 3. Watch carefully for those who do not know their addition facts or understand the addition process.

Materials, Supplies, & Equipment:
1. Number chart

2. Flash cards for addition facts 1–18

3. *Place value materials*

4. Play money

Activities:

1. Count out loud by eights to 96 using the number chart.

2. Drill the addition facts 1–9 with flash cards without the answer showing. Drill addition facts 10–18 with the answers showing.

3. Tell the student(s) to look at the horizontal addition problem at the top of **Student Activity One**. Discuss with them how to write this problem vertically. Write the first double-digit number by itself. Underneath it, write the second double-digit number being careful to place the tens and ones in their corresponding color coded columns. Write the answer by first adding the ones' column and then adding the tens' column (you may want to use *place value materials*). Work the first two problems together and then let them do the last four on their own. Emphasize the importance of aligning the numbers in the proper place value column.

4. Have the student(s) follow along as you read the directions for **Student Activity Two**. Do the first problem together and then allow them to finish without further help.

5. Give each student nickels and pennies in play money. Write several sets of nickels and pennies on the chalk board (Example: 4 nickels, 6 pennies). Ask the student(s) to form each set one at a time at their seat and tell what the value of the set is by counting the nickels by fives and the pennies by ones. Have a student read the directions for **Student Activity Three** and work the problems independently.

6. Quickly count out loud by twos with the student(s). After reading the directions for **Student Activity Four**, encourage them to only use the number chart if necessary to complete the activity successfully.

Worksheets:

1. *Worksheet 19* – Dot-to-dot counting by 6's.

What we obtain too cheap, we esteem too lightly;
it is dearness only that gives everything its value.

FRACTIONS – ONE-HALF

Concepts:

Fractions (one half), place value, vertical addition, word problems, and counting by sevens

Objectives:

1. The student shall be able to count by sevens to 98.

2. The student shall be able to correctly draw a line to divide a whole into two equal halves.

3. The student shall be able to correctly write what number is represented by the value of the digit in the tens' place added to the value of the digit in the ones' place.

4. The student shall be able to write the correct answer for a double-digit horizontal addition problem rewritten vertically.

5. The student shall be able to correctly identify the numbers to be added for a word problem and write the addition fact that gives the correct answer.

Teaching Tips:

1. When doing activity 3 have the student(s) name some everyday objects that speak of one half (example: one half dollar, one half gallon of milk, one half pound of ground beef, etc.).

2. For activity 4 when thinking of 8 tens and 4 ones, show the student(s) the correlation of tens to dimes and ones to pennies (*play money* may be helpful).

Materials, Supplies, & Equipment:

1. Number chart

2. Flash cards for addition facts 1–18

3. Flannel board

4. Fraction materials

5. *Play money*

Activities:

1. Count out loud by sevens to 98 using the number chart. Discuss with the student(s) that counting by sevens means to count every seventh number by counting over seven on the number chart or adding seven to each number.

2. Drill the addition facts 1–9 with flash cards without the answer showing. Drill addition facts 10–18 with the answers showing.

3. Using flannel board fraction materials, demonstrate to the student(s) several halves that equal a whole when put together. Draw several geometric shapes on the chalk board and call the student(s) to come up and draw a line that will divide the shape into two equal halves. Have a student read the directions for **Student Activity One** as the rest of them follow along. Then complete the activity.

4. Put "80 + 4" on the chalk board. Ask the student(s): "How many tens does it take to equal 80?" "How many ones to equal 4?" "What is the number that equals 80 + 4?" Do this with several other combinations. Begin **Student Activity Two** by doing the first activity together.

5. Write several horizontal double-digit addition problems on the chalk board. Discuss with the student(s) how to write these problems vertically. When adding the numbers, remind the student(s) to always add the ones' column first and then write the number. Then add the tens' column and write the number. After going over the directions for **Student Activity Three** do the first activity together. Give guidance where needed for the remaining activities.

6. Read the word problem together with the student(s) in **Student Activity Four**. Allow them to write the addition fact independently.

To neglect one's physical, social, mental, or spiritual development is to neglect the whole man.

NUMBER ORDER – BEFORE AND AFTER

Concepts:
> The number that comes before and after by ones, fractions (one half), sets, vertical addition, and counting by sevens

Objectives:
1. The student shall be able to write the number that comes before and after a given number.

2. The student shall be able to draw a line to divide a given object into two equal parts and color half of the object.

3. The student shall be able to circle a given number in a set of objects.

4. The student shall be able to write the correct answer for a double-digit horizontal addition problem rewritten vertically.

Teaching Tips:
1. Discuss with the student(s) different aspects of "after" and "before" other than numbers when doing activity 3. What day comes after Monday? What month is before July? What year comes after 1992? (*Calendar*)

2. To give added practice in recognizing one half of an object in activity 4, you might divide several everyday objects in half (e.g. cut an *apple* in half, divide a *set of crayons* in half, divide the desk in half, or divide ten pennies [*play money*] in half).

3. A different activity you might use for activity 5 would be to give each student 10 *construction paper shapes*. Have them then make different sets at their desk as you call the shapes out to them.

Materials, Supplies, & Equipment:
1. Number chart
2. Flash cards for addition facts 1–18
3. Flannel board
4. Fraction materials
5. *Calendar*
6. *Everyday items to divide in half*
7. *Construction paper shapes* (10 per student)

Activities:

1. Count out loud by sevens to 98 using the number chart.

2. Drill the addition facts 1–9 with flash cards without the answer showing. Drill addition facts 10–18 with the answers showing.

3. Use the number chart to practice before and after a given number. Point out to the student(s) that the answers, if correct, should be three consecutive counting numbers. After reading the directions to **Student Activity One** with the student(s), allow them to finish the activity on their own.

4. On the flannel board, show the student(s) a whole. Now show the object cut into two equal halves. Show them how to write one half in words and using numbers (1/2). The 2 tells them how many parts the whole is divided into. When beginning **Student Activity Two** have the student(s) draw a line to divide the object in half and then color one half of it.

5. In **Student Activity Three,** the student(s) will need to be reminded that a set is a group of objects. Have the student(s) take out a clean sheet of paper. Ask them to make ten circles on their paper and circle eight of the circles. Do this with several other sets. After the student(s) read the directions to **Student Activity Three,** they can finish the activity alone.

6. The student(s) should be able to complete **Student Activity Four** and **Five** independently. Remind the student(s) to properly align the numbers in the correct place value column.

He who has no taste for order,
will often be wrong in his judgment,
and will seldom be considerate or conscientious in his actions.

CALENDAR – DAYS OF THE WEEK

Concepts:
> Days of the week, vertical addition, and counting by sevens

Objectives:
1. The student shall be able to fill in a calendar given a partially filled in calendar and be able to correctly identify in writing the month of the calendar, the correct date for a given occurrence of a day of the week, the number of days in a week, and the number of occurrences of a given day of the week within a given month.

2. The student shall be able to write the correct answer for a double-digit addition problem rewritten vertically.

3. The student shall be able to write the correct addition facts for 1–18 without a number line.

Teaching Tips:
1. Use the test as a learning experience for the student(s). Give individual help to those who were not successful by going over the test with them after it has been graded. Do not allow a student to miss the same area time after time. Some re-teaching may have to be done.

2. Student(s) may be given *Worksheet 12* to fill in the month and dates. Blank out the other activities on the worksheet when you copy the calendar. Let them draw a picture of their choosing at the top of the page to represent the current month and circle the date on their calendar. Point out any special days in that particular calendar month.

Materials, Supplies, & Equipment:
1. Number chart

2. Flash cards for addition facts 1–18

3. *Flash cards for days of the week*

Activities:

1. Administer **Test 4**. On activity 1 remind the student(s) to check to see where the long hand is in deciding what time it is. Be sure they understand the directions for each activity. While there is no specific time limit on these tests, it should be completed and still allow time for completion of the lesson for the day.

2. Count out loud by sevens to 98 using the number chart.

3. Drill the addition facts 1–9 with flash cards without the answer showing. Drill addition facts 10–18 with the answers showing.

4. Recite the days of the week (you may want to use *flash cards*) in order with the student(s). All of **Student Activity One** must be teacher directed. Go over the directions with them. Have a different student read each question as they answer individually to themselves.

5. **Student Activity Two** and **Three** may be completed by the student(s) independently. Be sure that the student(s) align the numbers correctly in their appropriate place value columns.

Lost money may be regained, but lost time can never be recovered. So be careful how you handle other people's time.

SHOW YOUR SKILLS

Concepts:
= and ≠, before and after by ones, days of the week, word problems, addition, and counting by sevens

Objectives:
1. The student shall be able to write the = or ≠ symbol correctly between two given sets.

2. The student shall be able to write the correct number that comes before and after a given number.

3. The student shall be able to correctly identify the numbers to be added for a word problem and write the addition fact that gives the correct answer.

4. The student shall be able to write the correct answer to single- and double-digit addition problems.

Teaching Tips:

1. To aid the student in understanding the concept of before and after in activity 4, use the days of the week and months of the year. Give several examples such as: "What comes before Wednesday?" and "What comes after May?" Before today refers to the past and after today refers to the future.

2. For a different approach to word problems in activity 6, give each student nine objects (*crayons, play money, construction paper shapes*). Tell them to divide them into two sets. Next, have them make up a word problem about the sets. Have them share the word problems with you.

Materials, Supplies, & Equipment:

1. Number chart

2. Flash cards for = and ≠

3. *Flash cards for days of the week*

4. *Calendar or calendar bulletin board.*

5. *Crayons, play money, construction paper shapes*

Activities:

1. Count out loud by sevens to 98 using the number chart.

2. Use *Drill #1, Worksheet 20* to drill the addition facts 1–9. Drill the addition facts 10–18 with flash cards without the answers showing. If you feel further drill practice of flash cards without the answers showing is necessary at the present, continue on a daily basis until lesson 117. Starting with that lesson, a set pattern of flash card drill is once again incorporated into the instructions. Don't cut the worksheet apart. You will save time by giving the whole worksheet to the student(s) at once. Have them keep it neat in a special folder for quick access when drill time comes. When the drill is over, remind them to return the drill sheet to the folder and the folder to a special place in their desk. After all four drills have been completed, make sure they are removed from the folder. At the beginning, the drills will be 2 minutes long. As the student(s) become accustomed to them, the time can be shortened.

3. Put different number sets on the board with a blank between them. (Example: three __ 3, 4 + 2 __7, 3 nickels __ 15¢) Hold the = and ≠ flash cards in your hands. Read a set and have the student(s) raise the same hand that has the correct flash card symbol in it. Their right hand will match your left hand. They should be able to complete **Student Activity One** by themselves.

4. Point to several numbers on the number chart and have the student(s) tell the number that comes before each of the numbers and the number that comes after each of the numbers. Allow the student(s) to use a number chart to complete **Student Activity Two**.

5. Recite the days of the week in order (you may use *flash cards, calendar, or bulletin board*). Talk about today's date. After the student(s) read the directions for **Student Activity Three**, have them do the rest of the activity.

6. Have a student read the first word problem in **Student Activity Four**. Allow the student(s) to write the correct addition fact necessary to solve the problem and then discuss what they have written. Do the same for the second word problem.

7. **Student Activity Five** can be done independently by each student.

Worksheets:

1. *Worksheet 20* – Addition drill sheet

TIME – QUARTER HOUR

Concepts:
Time (quarter hour), = and ≠, before and after by ones, addition, and counting by sevens

Objectives:
1. The student shall be able to correctly write the time displayed on the face of a clock for the quarter hour.

2. The student shall be able to write the = or ≠ symbol correctly between two given sets.

3, The student shall be able to write the number that comes before and after a given number.

4. The student shall be able to add single- and double-digit numbers without carrying.

Teaching Tips:
1. Use the *number line* in teaching the student how to tell time by the quarter hour in activity 3. Draw a number line and number it to 12. Then, on top of the number line, number by 5's to correspond to the 1–12 underneath the number line. Tell each student the hour numbers are each five minutes apart for the minute hand (long hand). For example, if the minute hand points to the three, that would represent fifteen minutes. Show the student(s) how to do 30 minutes and 45 minutes using the number line and the clock face.

Materials, Supplies, & Equipment:
1. Number chart

2. Clock model

3. *Flash cards for = and ≠*

4. *Number line*

Activities:

1. Count out loud by sevens to 98 using the number chart.

2. Use *Drill #2, Worksheet 20* to drill the addition facts 1–9. Drill the addition facts 10–18 with flash cards without the answers showing.

3. Review telling time on the hour and half hour. Show the student(s) how to count the minute numbers (in a clockwise direction) by fives using the numbers 1–12 on the clock model. Set the clock for 4:00. Have them read it. Move the minute hand and the hour hand so that the clock represents 4:15. Have them read the short (hour) hand first. The short (hour) hand is read as the number the hand is just past, not what it is nearest to. Tell them that the clock hands always move in the same direction (clockwise) on the face of the clock. To read the long (minute) hand start at 1 and count by fives until you reach the number the hand is pointing to. Do several more examples including 45 minutes past the hour. Have the student(s) look at the top of **Student Activity One** as you explain each clock. Follow the same procedure as above as you guide the student(s) to complete the activity.

4. A quick review of the = and ≠ symbols (you may want to use *flash cards*) should be sufficient for the student(s) to complete **Student Activity Two** on their own.

5. With the aid of the number chart, point to several numbers and have the student(s) tell what number comes before and after. Allow a student to read the directions to **Student Activity Three** and then continue without further help on their own.

6. Direct the student(s) to do **Student Activity Four** by themselves.

Worksheets:

1. *Worksheet 20* – Addition drill sheet

Great haste makes great waste.

MONEY – PENNIES AND DIMES

Concepts:
> Pennies and dimes, fractions (one half), quarter hour, < and >, and addition

Objectives:
1. The student shall be able to circle the number of dimes and pennies to equal a given amount of money.

2. The student shall be able to color one half of an object.

3. The student shall be able to write the correct time displayed on the face of a clock for the quarter hour.

4. The student shall be able to write < and > between two sets correctly.

5. The student shall be able to add single- and double-digit numbers without carrying.

Teaching Tips:

1. After **Student Activity One** give each student *play money* (dimes and pennies). Have an object such as a chalk board eraser with a price attached to it. Have the student(s) count the money they would need to purchase the object.

2. For an addition to activity 4 give each student a *paper plate, construction paper, and a brad*. Have the student(s) write the numbers on the face of the clock around the edge of the paper plate, make a long and a short hand from construction paper, and attach the hands to the center of the plate with the brad.

Materials, Supplies, & Equipment:

1. Flannel board

2. Fraction materials

3. Clock model and small clock models for the student(s)

4. *Flash cards for < and >*

5. *Paper plate, construction paper, and brad*

6. *Play money*

Activities:

1. Use *Drill #3, Worksheet 20* to drill the addition facts 1–9. Drill the addition facts 10–18 with flash cards without the answers showing.

2. Review counting dimes by tens and counting pennies by ones. Write "35¢" on the chalkboard. Ask how many dimes (3) and pennies (5) are needed to make 35¢. Do several other examples. In **Student Activity One,** work through the first two activities with the student(s). Let them try the other two on their own.

3. Display on the flannel board several wholes that have been divided into 2, 4, 6, and 8 parts. Show how a whole may be cut in half even though it has been divided into more than 2 parts. Take a circle that has been divided into 8 parts. Show how it can be divided in half in four different ways by using each of the diameters of the circle as a dividing line. Guide the student(s) in identifying one half of each shape in **Student Activity Two**.

4. Give each student a small clock model. Call out several times, both the hour and the half hour and have the student(s) set their clocks. Set the hands on the large clock model so they can check their work. Review the placement of the hands for the quarter hours (15 minutes after the hour and 45 minutes after the hour). This time, call out several quarter hour times letting the student(s) place the hands correctly. Check their work. Allow them to work **Student Activity Three** independently.

5. After quickly reviewing < and > symbols (you may want to use *flash cards*), allow the student(s) to complete **Student Activity Four** and **Five** by themselves.

Worksheets:

1. *Worksheet 21* – Pennies and dimes

2. *Worksheet 20* – Addition drill sheet

A person who believes that money will do everything will be suspected of doing everything for money.

NUMBER ORDER – BEFORE AND AFTER BY 10

Concepts:
> The number that comes before and after by tens, quarter hour, < and >, fraction (one half), word problems, and "Thirty Days Hath September"

Objectives:
1. The student shall be able to write the number that comes before and after a given number when counting by tens.

2. The student shall be able to draw a line to match a given written time to the time displayed on the face of a clock.

3. The student shall be able to write < and > between two given sets correctly.

4. The student shall be able to correctly match one half of a shape with the other half by drawing a line to the corresponding half.

Teaching Tips:
1. In connection with activity 4, hand out a slip of paper to each student with a time (hour, half hour, or quarter hour) written on it. Make sure the time will fall between the time you hand them out and the end of school. Have the student(s) quietly stand to their feet when the clock says their time and announce, "It is now ___:___."

2. Tell the students that when the short hand goes past "6" in activity 4, it tells us how many minutes *before* the next hour. Therefore 8:45 can also be read as 15 minutes before 9 o'clock.

Materials, Supplies, & Equipment:
1. Number chart

2. Clock model

3. Construction paper shapes cut in half

Activities:

1. Use *Drill #4, Worksheet 20* to drill the addition facts 1–9. Drill the addition facts 10–18 with flash cards without the answers showing. Since there are only four drills a week, you may omit drilling on whichever day of the week you choose. Just be sure that you do four drills every week. Do not skip more than one day a week. If a student has successfully completed all of the four drills in the allotted time, you might allow him the option of doing only the last drill the next week.

2. Recite the poem "Thirty Days Hath September" with the student(s) several times as a refresher.

3. Point to several multiples of 10 on the number chart. Discuss with the student(s) what before and after means when counting by tens. Allow the student(s) to use the number chart as they work **Student Activity One**.

4. Write three different times on the chalk board (e.g. 4:30, 8:15, 2:45). Set the clock model at one of the three times and have the student(s) tell you if the first, second, or third time is correct. Do this several times. To begin **Student Activity Two,** read the directions with them.

5. The student(s) should be able to complete **Student Activity Three** independently.

6. Cut several shapes out of construction paper. Cut each shape into two equal parts. Give a different part to each student. Have one student stand holding up his part and the student who has the mate then stands. You may try two students standing and the two mates stand. For one student, take all the mixed up parts and have them match the parts. Read the directions with the student(s) as they begin **Student Activity Four**.

7. After reading the word problems out loud, have the student(s) complete **Student Activity Five** on their own.

Worksheets:

1. *Worksheet 20* – Addition drill sheet

In delay there is no plenty.

ADDITION – THREE NUMBERS

Concepts:
Addition of three single-digit numbers, quarter hour, inches, word problems, and "Thirty Days Hath September"

Objectives:
1. The student shall be able to recite the poem "Thirty Days Hath September" from memory.

2. The student shall be able to write the sum of three single-digit numbers correctly.

3. The student shall be able to draw the short (hour) hand on the clock for the quarter hour.

4. The student shall be able to correctly measure the length of a given object with an inch ruler.

5. The student shall be able to correctly identify the numbers to be added for a word problem, write the correct addition fact that answers the word problem, and label the correct answer.

Teaching Tips:

1. When doing activity 2, show the student(s) how they can add from the bottom up as well as from the top down following the same procedures.

2. Let the student(s) use *play money dimes* to demonstrate the sets necessary for writing the correct addition fact to solve the word problem in **Student Activity Four**.

Materials, Supplies, & Equipment:
1. *Calendar*

2. Clock model and small clock models for student(s)

3. Inch ruler

4. Number chart

5. *Play money*

Activities:

1. Recite "Thirty Days Hath September" with the student(s). Talk about how many days are in the present month according to the poem (or use a *calendar*). Let a student volunteer to say it by himself.

2. Write several addition problems of three single-digit numbers on the chalkboard. The first two numbers must come from addition facts 1–9. Follow the procedure given at the beginning of **Student Activity One** to solve the problems. Then have the student(s) follow along as you go through the steps given in **Student Activity One**. Notice in the last row, the student(s) are to write the sum of the first two numbers by the bracket and then add the number by the bracket to the last number. Guide them as they complete the activity.

3. Hand out the small clock models to each student. Write several times on the chalk board including hour, half hour and quarter hour. Have the student(s) set their clocks at the given time. Instruct them to place the long (minute) hand first and then place the short (hour) hand. The placement of the hour hand is determined by where the minute hand is located. Then let them hold their clocks up so you can check them. Be sure the student(s) understand they are to draw the **short** hand on the clock when they begin **Student Activity Two**.

4. Draw several straight lines on the chalkboard of various whole number lengths (example: 2", 4", 1"). Have one student at a time come to the chalk board and measure the length of the line with their inch ruler. Be sure to point out that the beginning of the line must be at zero on the ruler. Allow the student(s) to do **Student Activity Three** independently.

5. Tell each student to read the word problem to himself in **Student Activity Four**. After writing the addition fact, the student(s) may need some guidance in labeling their answer. Help them to understand that they must identify the unit of measure they are adding. In this case the unit is dimes.

Worksheets:

1. *Worksheet 22* – Adding three single-digit numbers

SHOW YOUR SKILLS

Concepts:

Money, inches, before and after by tens, addition, and word problems

Objectives:

1. The student shall be able to write the number of dimes and pennies in a given amount of money.

2. The student shall be able to correctly measure the length of a line with an inch ruler.

Teaching Tips:

1. A great motivator for activity 1 is to put a happy face (*stamp*) in the upper right hand corner of each individual drill sheet each time the student completes the drill in the allotted time and has no errors. This should be done daily. You can then see at a glance when a student has completed all four of the drills satisfactorily.

2. When doing activity 3 include a hands-on measurement project of some objects you might have in the room. Make sure that their lengths are very near a whole inch length. If you cannot find objects very near a whole inch in length, do not do the activity because the student(s) may become confused.

Materials, Supplies, & Equipment:

1. Play money

2. Inch ruler

3. *Happy face stamp*

4. *Objects to measure*

Activities:

1. *Worksheet 23* has the drill sheet for the next four days. Do *Drill #1* to drill the addition facts 1–9. Reduce the two minute time limit but make sure that the majority of the students can still finish the drill in the allotted time. The object is to develop speed and accuracy, not frustrate the student(s). Drill the addition facts 10–18 with flash cards without the answers showing. If you feel further drill practice of the addition facts 1–9 with flash cards without the answers showing is necessary at the present, continue on a daily basis until lesson 117. Starting with that lesson, a set pattern of flash card drill is once again incorporated into the instructions.

2. Have the student(s) tell how many dimes and pennies are in several given amounts of money using play money. When starting ***Student Activity One***, remind the student(s) to ask themselves "How many dimes and how many pennies are there?"

3. The student(s) should be able to complete ***Student Activity Two*** on their own once they are reminded to put the zero on the inch ruler at the beginning of the line.

4. Give each student 4 dimes using play money. Tell them to take one dime away and see how many dimes they have left. 4 dimes equal 40¢. Take one away and you have 3 dimes which equals 30¢. Taking one dime away is the same as taking 10¢ away. When you take 10¢ away from 40¢, you have 30¢. The number that comes before 40 when counting by tens is 30. If you have 4 dimes and you add one dime, 40¢ becomes 50¢. Adding one dime is the same as adding 10¢. When you add 10¢ to 40¢, you have 50¢. The number that comes after 40 when counting by tens is 50. Follow the same pattern with other multiples of ten. The student(s) should use the number chart when doing ***Student Activity Three*** only when necessary.

5. Write several addition problems of three single-digit numbers (make sure the first two are from the addition facts 1–9) on the chalk board. Following the procedure given in Lesson 45, allow the student(s) to solve each problem. In ***Student Activity Four***, complete the first row together with the student(s), allowing them to do the remaining rows independently.

6. Have each of the student(s) read the word problem in ***Student Activity Five*** to himself. Give individual help where needed.

Worksheets:

1. *Worksheet 23*–Addition drill sheet

WORD NUMBERS – ELEVEN TO TWENTY

Concepts:
Word numbers eleven to twenty and multiples of ten, inches, pennies and dimes, word problems, and addition

Objectives:
1. The student shall be able to correctly match the word number by drawing a line to its corresponding numeral.

2. The student shall be able to accurately draw a line of a given length using an inch ruler.

3. The student shall be able to draw the correct number of pennies and dimes needed to equal a given amount.

4. The student shall be able to write the correct addition fact necessary to solve a word problem and correctly label the answer without help.

Teaching Tips:
1. In activity 2, write each of the word numbers and their corresponding numbers on separate slips of paper. Pass out one paper to each student. Call out a number and have the two student(s) with the corresponding number and word number stand. They may then be first in line at lunch. Call out the remaining numbers and let them line up to establish the order of your lunch line for the day. You may pass all the slips to one student and as you call out the numbers, have them match the word number and the numbers against the clock. Be sure to call out numbers as fast as the student is ready.

2. In connection with activity 3, the student(s) will enjoy being measured on a *growth chart*. Set a time later in the year (maybe after spring break) when they can be measured again.

Materials, Supplies, & Equipment:
1. Flash cards for word numbers 11–20 plus multiples of 10

2. Inch ruler

3. *Play money*

4. *Growth chart*

Activities:

1. Use *Drill #2, Worksheet 23* to drill the addition facts 1–9. Drill the addition facts 10–18 with flash cards without the answers showing.

2. Use flash cards having the word number on one side and the number on the other as an introduction to ***Student Activity One.*** The word numbers should be 11–20 plus the multiples of 10 to 100. As a reinforcement, read down the columns of word numbers in the activity together with the student(s) before they attempt to complete ***Student Activity One*** on their own.

3. Have the student(s) put a point on a clean sheet of paper. Using that point as a starting point and zero on the ruler, ask them to draw a line 3 inches long using their inch ruler. Start at several other points drawing different inch lengths. Follow the same procedure when the student(s) do ***Student Activity Two.***

4. Have the student(s) take out a clean sheet of paper. Write "35¢" on the chalk board and ask the student(s) how many dimes and pennies are in 35¢ or use *play money*. Next have them draw a picture of 3 dimes and 5 pennies by drawing three circles and writing 10¢ in them and 5 circles with 1¢ written in them. Use some other examples. When the student(s) begin ***Student Activity Three***, have them follow the same procedure.

5. Allow the student(s) to complete ***Student Activity Four*** and ***Five*** independently.

Worksheets:

1. *Worksheet 23* – Addition drill sheet

The love of money is the root of all evil.

MONEY – NICKELS

Concepts:
  Nickels, word problems, word numbers, place value, addition, and counting by ones

Objectives:
  1. The student shall be able to find the correct value of a given number of nickels by counting by fives.

  2. The student shall be able to write the correct number for a given word number.

  3. The student shall be able to write the correct number of tens and ones in a given number.

Teaching Tips:
  1. Have one dollar's worth of nickels (play money) in a special box on teacher's desk or special study area. Allow the student(s) to take turns counting by 5's with the nickels during the day in connection with activity 3.

  2. Suggest that the student(s) look for places that word numbers are used in every day life such as on dollar bills (1, 5, 10, etc.), advertising, and newspapers in connection with activity 4.

Materials, Supplies, & Equipment:
  1. Number chart

  2. Real nickel

  3. Play money

  4. Flash cards for word numbers

  5. *Place value materials*

Activities:

1. Count out loud by ones to 100 using the number chart.

2. Use *Drill #3, Worksheet 23* to drill the addition facts 1–9. Drill the addition facts 10–18 with flash cards without the answers showing.

3. Show the student(s) the front and back of a real nickel. Again discuss with the student(s) the man on the front (Thomas Jefferson), the building on the back (Monticello), the color of the nickel, and the value of a nickel. Using play money, display several different sets of nickels for the student(s). Have the student(s) find the total value of the nickels by counting them by fives. Guide the student(s) through the first activity in **Student Activity One.** Then allow them to finish on their own, giving help only where needed.

4. The student(s) should be able to read the word problem and write the addition fact without help in **Student Activity Two.** Check to make sure that they label the answer correctly.

5. Using the word number flash cards, have the student(s) read the word numbers. After going over the directions for **Student Activity Three**, let the student(s) do the activity by themselves.

6. Point to several different numbers on the number chart. Ask how many tens and ones are in the number or use *place value materials*. The student(s) should be able to complete **Student Activity Four** independently.

7. **Student Activity Five** can be completed independently by the student(s).

Worksheets:

1. *Worksheet 24* – Harvest color page with addition facts practice

2. *Worksheet 23* – Addition drill sheet

FRACTIONS – ONE FOURTH

Concepts:
Fractions (one fourth), place value, nickels, addition, and counting by ones

Objectives:
1. The student shall be able to correctly color one fourth of a given shape.

2. The student shall be able to write the correct value of a given number of tens.

3. The student shall be able to match a given number of nickels with their correct value by drawing a line.

4. The student shall be able to write the correct missing numbers on a number chart.

Teaching Tips:
1. In activity 5, check to see if the student(s) recognize the different coins by making up different sets of coins (example: 3 pennies, 2 dimes, and 5 nickels). Ask the student(s) to tell the number of pennies, the number of nickels, and the number of dimes in the set.

Materials, Supplies, & Equipment:
1. Number chart

2. Flannel board

3. Fraction materials

4. *Place value materials*

5. Play money

Activities:

1. Count out loud by ones to 100 using the number chart.

2. Use *Drill #4, Worksheet 23* to drill the addition facts 1–9. Drill the addition facts 10–18 with flash cards without the answers showing.

3. Using flannel board fraction materials, demonstrate several times to the student(s) that four fourths equal a whole when put together. Draw several geometric shapes on the chalk board and divide them into four parts. Discuss with the student(s) that each part is called one fourth because the whole has been divided into four equal parts. The fraction one fourth (1/4) tells you that you are using one of the four parts into which the whole has been divided. Have the student(s) come to the board and color 1/4 of each of the shapes. After discussing the directions for **Student Activity One**, guide the student(s) as they do each activity.

4. Orally review with the student(s) the value of 6 tens, 2 tens, etc. Equate it with 6 dimes, 2 dimes, etc. or use *place value materials*. They should then be able to complete **Student Activity Two** independently.

5. Using play money nickels, display several sets of nickels one at a time for the student(s). Have them determine the value of each set by counting the nickels by fives. Read the directions to the student(s) as they follow along for **Student Activity Three**. They should then complete the activity on their own.

6. Quickly review adding three single-digit numbers and two double-digit numbers. Then allow student(s) to do **Student Activity Four** without further help.

7. Have the student(s) fill in the missing numbers on **Student Activity Five**.

Worksheets:

1. *Worksheet 23* – Addition drill sheet

Few rich men own their property. Their property owns them.

SHOW YOUR SKILLS

Concepts:

 Big and little, fractions (one fourth), addition, word problems, and counting by tens

Objectives:

1. The student shall be able to correctly draw a big and little object.

2. The student shall be able to correctly divide an object into four equal parts and shade one fourth of the object.

3. The student shall be able to write correctly the missing numbers when counting by tens.

Teaching Tips:

1. After the student(s) complete ***Student Activity One,*** try using *3" x 5" cards* and drawing a big *A* on one and a little *a* on another. Do the same for other letters of the alphabet until you have a card for each student. Hand one card to each student. Ask the student with the big *A* to please stand and come up to write an addition problem (single digit) on the chalkboard. The student with the little *a* may then come up and write the answer. Continue until all students have been to the chalk board. If time is short, you may divide the activity into two or three days. With individual students you may alternate; one time writing the problem and the student writing the answer, then switching and have the student write the problem and answer it.

2. When doing activity 4, have the student(s) think of examples in every day life where one fourth is expressed as quarter (example: quarter pounder, quarter past the hour, quarter (25¢), a quart is a quarter of a gallon, quarter mile, etc.).

Materials, Supplies, & Equipment:

1. *Fraction materials*

2. *3" x 5" cards*

Activities:

1. Administer **Test 5**. Remind the student(s) to look at the placement of the long hand on each of the clocks in the first activity. In the second activity tell the student(s) to first identify the money and then to find the value of each set of money.

2. Count out loud by tens to 100 without the use of the number chart.

3. Choose different objects in the room that compare big and little. Before doing **Student Activity One,** let a student read the directions.

4. Show the student(s) how to draw lines on the chalk board to divide an object into four equal parts or use *fraction materials*. Be open to several different ways an object can be divided as long as all parts are equal in size. Explain the different ways you can express one fourth (one fourth, 1/4, quarter). Go over the directions for **Student Activity Two** carefully with the student(s). Guide them as they divide each object.

5. The student(s) should be able to complete **Student Activity Three** independently of the number chart.

6. As the student(s) complete **Student Activity Four** and **Five**, they should require no assistance, but check to be sure they are aligning the answer in the proper place value column.

True liberty is achieved only by exercising proper self government.

MONEY – QUARTER

Concepts:
Money (quarter), = and ≠, fractions (one fourth), addition, word problems, and counting by fives

Objectives:
1. The student shall be able to write the correct value of a given number of quarters.

2. The student shall be able to write the correct symbol (= or ≠) between a given number of coins and a given amount of money.

3. The student shall be able to determine if a whole has been divided into four equal parts and demonstrate it by coloring one quarter of each of the objects that have been divided into quarters.

Teaching Tips:
1. When all four drills on the addition drill worksheets are completed in activity 2, let the student(s) and family know their progress and/or deficiencies. This will allow you to elicit any additional help that may be needed by the student(s) and provide encouragement to all involved.

2. In activity 3, have the student(s) take out a clean sheet of paper and create an imprint (called a "rubbing") by shading over a real *quarter* with the side of their pencil point. Have them do several rubbings of both the front and the back.

Materials, Supplies, & Equipment:
1. Quarter

2. *Play money*

3. *Flash cards for = and ≠*

4. Fraction materials

5. Flannel board

Activities:

1. Count out loud by fives up to 100.

2. Use *Drill #1, Worksheet 25* to drill the addition facts 1–9. Drill the addition facts 10–18 with flash cards without the answers showing. If you feel further drill practice of the addition facts 1–9 with flash cards without the answers showing is necessary at the present, continue on a daily basis until lesson 117. Starting with that lesson, a set pattern of flash card drill is once again incorporated into the instructions.

3. Show the student(s) a real quarter. Allow them to hold it and feel the imprint as well as talk about the texture of the edge. Discuss the size, the man on the front (George Washington), the picture on the back (eagle), color, and value of the quarter. Practice counting four quarters by 25 or use *play money*. Talk about four quarters being the same as one dollar. One quarter is one fourth or a quarter of a dollar. Do **Student Activity One** together with the student(s).

4. Write several examples similar to those used in **Student Activity Two** on the chalk board or use *play money*. If necessary you might suggest the student(s) use tally marks for each coin when finding the value. Then count the tally marks by ones, fives, or tens. Or they could draw circles and put 1¢, 5¢, or 10¢ in the circles. Talk about the = and ≠ symbols (you may want to use *flash cards*). Check the progress of each student as they work on **Student Activity Two**.

5. Discuss with the student(s) by means of fraction materials on the flannel board the difference between 1/2, 1/3, and 1/4. The 2, 3, and 4 tell how many parts the whole has been divided into. Put different examples on the flannel board and let the student(s) tell you if the whole is divided into halves, thirds, or fourths. When giving the directions for **Student Activity Three**, have them discuss which shapes are divided into fourths before they begin to color.

6. **Student Activity Four** should be done independently by the student(s). Remind the student(s) to add the ones' column first then the tens' column. Some student(s) will actually add the tens' column first. While this will give them the correct answer now, it is obviously laying a foundation for future failure when addition with carrying is introduced.

7. The student(s) should need no assistance when doing **Student Activity Five**.

Worksheets:

1. *Worksheet 25* – Addition drill sheet

SUBTRACTION

Concepts:
Subtraction of one digit numbers, quarters, fractions, = and ≠, and counting by twos

Objectives:
1. The student shall be able to write the answer to subtraction problems using a visual representation of the subtraction problems.

2. The student shall be able to find the value of 1, 2, and 3 quarters by counting by 25.

3. The student shall be able to determine what fractional part of a whole is colored and write the fraction.

4. The student shall be able to correctly write = or ≠ between two sets of numbers to create a true statement.

Teaching Tips:
1. When the student(s) are doing the drill sheets in activity 2, suggest that they start on the bottom row and work up for variety.

2. When doing activity 3, have five children come to the front of the room. Put a five on the chalk board. Send two students back to their seat. Put minus two on the chalk board. Ask how many students are left. Have them complete the subtraction fact by writing the equal symbol and the answer.

Materials, Supplies, & Equipment:
1. Number chart

2. Crayons

3. Play money

4. *Flash cards for = and ≠*

5. *Fraction materials*

Activities:

1. Count out loud by twos to 100 using the number chart.

2. Use *Drill #2, Worksheet 25* to drill the addition facts 1–9. Drill the addition facts 10–18 with flash cards without the answers showing.

3. To introduce subtraction, teach the student(s) that the answer is always going to be the same or less. Subtraction is taking away. Have the student(s) put three crayons on their desk. Write "3" on the chalk board. Show them the symbol (–) used to tell you to subtract. Now tell them to take away one crayon. Write a "1" after the minus sign followed by the = sign. Ask them to count the crayons to see how many they have left (2) and write "2" on the chalk board. "3 – 1 = 2" is a subtraction problem. Show how this can be written both horizontally and vertically. Do several other examples using crayons following the same procedure. In *Student Activity One* have the student(s) actually count the blocks that are left to arrive at their answer. They will need your guidance throughout this activity.

4. Using the play money quarters, have the student(s) count by 25 to determine how many cents there are in 1, 2, 3, and 4 quarters. Draw sets of 1, 2, 3, and 4 circles on the chalk board and put 25¢ in each circle. Draw a line under each circle as in *Student Activity Two*. As they count three circles by 25 write "25," "50," "75" on the lines. Three quarters then equal 75¢ Do this for 1, 2, and 4 circles. Guide the student(s) to follow the same procedure in *Student Activity Two*.

5. In *Student Activity Three* discuss each individual shape separately (you may want to use *fraction materials*). How many parts is the whole divided into? How many of those parts are colored? Have the student(s) write the fractional part of the whole that is colored.

6. The student(s) should be able to complete *Student Activity Four* independently (or you may want to use *flash cards*).

Worksheets:

1. *Worksheet 26* – Thanksgiving dot-to-dot by ones

2. *Worksheet 25* – Addition drill sheet

157

NUMBER ORDER – < AND >

Concepts:

< and >, word numbers, fractions, word problems, subtraction, quarters, and counting by twos

Objectives:

1. The student shall be able to write the correct sign (< or >) between word numbers and numerals.

2. The student shall be able to draw lines to divide a whole into four equal parts or two equal parts and color one fourth or one half of the whole as indicated.

3. Using visual representation, the student shall be able to write the correct answer to subtraction problems.

4. The student shall be able to circle the correct value for a given number of quarters.

Teaching Tips:

1. To reinforce activity 1, set an *alarm clock* or *timer* periodically. When it rings have the student(s) you have designated count by twos.

2. If any student is still having difficulty doing activity 2, encourage them to practice the addition facts each night for ten minutes.

Materials, Supplies, & Equipment:

1. Number chart

2. *Flash cards for word numbers*

3. Flannel board

4. *Fraction materials*

5. 9 objects, numerals, minus sign, and equal sign for the flannel board

6. Play money

7. *Alarm clock or timer*

Activities:

1. Count out loud by twos to 100 using the number chart. Use your own judgment as to when the student(s) should be able to do this without the chart.

2. Use *Drill #3, Worksheet 25* to drill the addition facts 1–9. Drill the addition facts 10–18 with flash cards without the answers showing.

3. Go over the word numbers 0–10 and multiples of 10 up to 100 (you may want to use *flash cards*). The student(s) should be able to then do **Student Activity One** independently.

4. Draw different shapes on the chalk board and allow the student(s) to divide them into two and four equal parts (or use *fraction materials*). Have them color 1/4 or 1/2 of the object. Help them to understand that to color 1/2 they must first divide it into two equal parts and to color 1/4 they must first divide the shape into four equal parts. Give individual help as the student(s) complete **Student Activity Two**.

5. Allow the student(s) to complete **Student Activity Three** on their own.

6. Put six objects on the flannel board. Have the student(s) count them. Put a "6" on the chalk board. Take two objects away and put "minus 2" on the chalk board. Have the student(s) count how many you have left (4). Put "= 4" on the chalk board. They should then read the subtraction fact. Follow this procedure with several other sets of objects. Remind them that subtraction means to take away. When doing **Student Activity Four**, have the student(s) count how many stars there are at the beginning and write the number. Have them count to see how many were taken away and write that number. Now count to see how many are left and write that number. The student(s) should then read the subtraction fact. Do the first two subtraction facts together and then let them proceed on their own if possible.

7. Count four quarters by 25 to find their value using play money. A student can read the directions to **Student Activity Five** and complete it without help.

Worksheets:

1. *Worksheet 25* – Addition drill sheet

TIME – HOUR AND HALF HOUR

Concepts:

Hour, half hour, fractions (one fourth), subtraction, < and >, addition, and counting by twos

Objectives:

1. The student shall be able to write in digital form the time shown on a clock face for the hour and half hour.

2. The student shall be able to correctly color 1/4 of only those shapes divided into four equal parts.

3. Using a visual representation, the student shall be able to write the correct answer to subtraction problems.

Teaching Tips:

1. When doing activity 3, discuss the length of a minute. Help the student(s) understand the difference in length of time between one minute and one hour. Set an *alarm* and have the student(s) sit perfectly still until it goes off at the end of one minute. Then set the alarm for one hour and proceed with the class as usual until the alarm sounds. Help the student(s) appreciate how much has happened in that hour.

2. When doing activity 5, you may want to do some examples of taking nothing away so the student(s) will get the idea that subtracting zero leaves the number the same in the same way as adding zero also leaves it the same.

Materials, Supplies, & Equipment:

1. Number chart

2. Small clock models for the student(s)

3. *Fraction materials*

4. Play money

5. *Alarm clock* or *watch*

Activities:

1. Count out loud by twos to 100 using the number chart if necessary.

2. Use *Drill #4, Worksheet 25* to drill the addition facts 1–9. Drill the addition facts 10–18 with flash cards without the answers showing.

3. Give each student a small clock model. Write several times on the hour and half hour on the chalk board. Have the student(s) place the hands to say the correct time. Then have them hold the clocks up so that you can see them. Remind them to put the long (minute) hand in place first and then the short (hour) hand. Allow the student(s) to complete **Student Activity One** with as little help as possible.

4. Draw several shapes on the chalk board. Divide the shapes into 2, 3, or 4 parts (or you may want to use *fraction materials*). Ask the student(s) to tell which shapes show 1/2, 1/3, and 1/4 of a whole. When doing **Student Activity Two**, be sure the student(s) have a clear understanding of the directions.

5. Give each student seven pennies, nickels, or dimes (play money). Tell them to form a set of five. On a clean sheet of paper have them write "5." Ask them to take two away. Have them write "– 2" on their paper. Tell them to count the ones that are left (3). Write "= 3" on their paper. Now read the subtraction fact together. Do this with several other sets of seven or less. The student(s) will need your guidance for each problem in **Student Activity Three**. They must count how many items they start with, how many are taken away, and how many are left.

6. The student(s) should be able to complete **Student Activity Four** and **Five** independently.

Worksheets:

1. *Worksheet 27* – Subtraction with visual representation

2. *Worksheet 25* – Addition drill sheet

SUBTRACTION – NUMBER LINE

Concepts:
> Subtraction using the number line, quarter hour, fractions (one half), addition, "Thirty Days Hath September," and counting by threes

Objectives:
1. The student shall be able to recite all of the poem "Thirty Days Hath September" from memory.

2. The student shall be able to write the answer to a subtraction fact by using the number line.

3. The student shall be able to write, in digital form, the correct time displayed on the clock face for the quarter hour.

4. The student shall be able to determine if a shape is divided into two equal parts and then demonstrate it by coloring one half of it.

Teaching Tips:
1. Have the student(s) use crayons at their desks to demonstrate the subtraction facts that you have done on the number line in activity 3.

2. When doing activity 5 discuss with the student(s) how the fraction 1/2 is used in everyday life. (Example: 1/2 gallon of milk, 1/2 dollar, 1/2 gallon of ice cream, 1/2 yard of ribbon, etc.

Materials, Supplies, & Equipment:
1. Number chart

2. Number line

3. Small clock models for the student(s)

4. *Fraction materials*

Activities:

1. Quickly count out loud by threes to 99 with the number chart. For variety, alternate with the student(s) in counting each number.

2. Recite the poem "Thirty Days Hath September" several times with the student(s).

3. Draw a number line on the chalk board to introduce subtraction facts. Next, write a subtraction fact (9–5 = 4) on the chalk board. Above the number line draw a straight line starting at zero to 9 with vertical bars at each end. This represents how many you have at the beginning. Since you are taking away 5, you want to start counting back five marks from 9 toward zero. Draw a second straight line under the first one from 9 to 4 (5 marks back) with vertical bars at each end. The point where you end up is the answer (4). Do this with several subtraction facts using the number line. When starting **Student Activity One**, have the student(s) state how many there are at the beginning, how many were taken away, and how many are then left. The point where the second line ends moving toward zero is how many are left. Do each subtraction problem together.

4. Give each student a small clock model. Call out several times and have them set their clocks to the times given. Remind them to set the long (minute) hand first and the short (hour) hand next. As soon as they have each time set, have them hold up the clocks for you to see. After this practice, they should be able to complete **Student Activity Two** independently.

5. Put several shapes on the chalk board. Divide the shapes into 2, 3, or 4 equal parts (or use *fraction materials*). Ask the student(s) to tell which shapes show 1/2, 1/3, and 1/4 of a whole. When doing **Student Activity Three,** be sure the student(s) understand the directions.

6. The student(s) should require no assistance to complete **Student Activity Four.**

Never boast of what you will do tomorrow.
No one can be sure of what may happen in a day.

MONEY – PENNIES AND DIMES

Concepts:

Pennies and dimes, time, subtraction, word problems, "Thirty Days Hath September," and counting by threes

Objectives:

1. The student shall be able to correctly write how many dimes and how many pennies are in a given sum of money.

2. The student shall be able to write the correct time displayed on a clock face for the hour, half hour, and quarter hour in digital form.

3. The student shall be able to correctly write the subtraction fact demonstrated on the number line.

Teaching Tips:

1. When doing activity 5, show the student(s) several household items with prices on them or use a *sales receipt*. Be sure to choose articles that cost less than a dollar.

2. When doing activity 7, you might want to again do a real life demonstration (using students, crayons, *play money*) to go along with the subtraction facts that you write on the chalk board. This will make the idea of "taking away" more realistic to the student.

Materials, Supplies, & Equipment:

1. Number chart

2. Flash cards for subtraction facts 1–9

3. *Play money*

4. Clock model

5. Number line

6. *Sales receipt*

Activities:

1. Quickly count out loud by threes to 99 with the number chart.

2. Recite "Thirty Days Hath September" twice.

3. Use *Drill #1, Worksheet 28* to drill the addition facts 1–9. Drill the addition facts 10–18 with flash cards without the answers showing. If you feel further drill practice of the addition facts 1–9 with flash cards without the answers showing is necessary at the present, continue on a daily basis until lesson 117. Starting with that lesson, a set pattern of flash card drill is once again incorporated into the instructions.

4. Drill the subtraction facts 1–9 (minuend being 1–9), for no longer than five minutes with flash cards with the answers showing. The student(s) need to repeat the complete subtraction fact not just the answer. The student(s) should say, "Twelve minus (or take away) four equals eight."

5. Write several different sums of money on the chalk board and have the student(s) tell how many dimes and how many pennies are in each sum (or use *play money*). After going over the directions with the student(s) for **Student Activity One**, they should be able to complete the activity on their own.

6. Ask the student(s) which hand (hour or minute) they should read first when they are telling time. Show them several different times on the large clock model including the hour, half hour, and quarter hour. Have them write the answer on a clean sheet of paper and check their answer after you write it on the chalkboard. The student(s) should be able to complete **Student Activity Two** independently.

7. Using a number line on the chalk board, demonstrate several subtraction facts similar to those in **Student Activity Three**. Have the student(s) write the subtraction fact on the paper used in activity 6. Much practice may be needed for the student(s) to think "take away" instead of adding. When doing **Student Activity Three**, work the first three subtraction facts together and then allow them to continue without help if possible.

8. **Student Activity Four** should be done by the student(s) independently.

Worksheets:

1. *Worksheet 28* – Addition drill sheet

INCHES

Concepts:

Inches, dimes and pennies, word problems, subtraction, and addition

Objectives:

1. The student shall be able to measure a line of a given length with an inch ruler.

2. The student shall be able to draw the number of dimes and pennies needed to equal a given sum of money.

3. The student shall be able to write the subtraction fact demonstrated on the number line.

Teaching Tips:

1. When doing activity 3, you might have one student draw a line 5 inches long and then have another student measure it to see if it was drawn correctly. Then switch and let the second student draw the line and the first one measure it.

2. In activity 6 you may still want to visualize the subtraction fact you demonstrated on the number line at the chalk board. Pass out nine *straws* to each student. After they have arrived at the subtraction fact, have them make a set for the first number in the subtraction fact. Then take away the second number and check to see if they have the correct number left.

Materials, Supplies, & Equipment:

1. Flash cards for subtraction facts 1–9

2. 8 1/2" x 11" piece of paper for each student

3. Inch ruler

4. *Play money*

5. Number line

6. *9 straws per student*

Activities:

1. Use *Drill #2, Worksheet 28* to drill the addition facts 1–9. Drill the addition facts 10–18 with flash cards without the answers showing.

2. Drill the subtraction facts 1–9 with flash cards with the answers showing for no longer than five minutes.

3. Give each student an 8 1/2" x 11" piece of paper. Using their inch ruler, have the student(s) measure the length (longest side) of the paper. Suggest several other objects they could measure that would be near inch increments. Be sure the student(s) put the zero on the ruler at the beginning of the line in **Student Activity One**.

4. Write "21¢" on the chalk board and ask the student(s) how many dimes and pennies in 21 cents (or use *play money*). Using the clean sheet of paper from activity 3, have them draw a picture of 2 dimes and 1 penny by drawing two circles with "10¢" in them and 1 circle with "1¢" in it. Do several other examples. As the student(s) begin **Student Activity Two**, have them follow the same procedure.

5. In **Student Activity Three,** tell the student(s) that they should automatically write the addition fact in solving a word problem from this point on. Read the word problem to them. Ask them how many pieces of candy Alice had to start with. Tell them to write "6" on their paper as you write it on the chalk board. Ask what change was made (Karen gave her 8 more pieces of candy). Tell them to write "+ 8" as you write it on the chalk board. Ask what the answer is. Have them write "= 14" on their paper as you write it on the chalk board. Let the student(s) determine the correct label. Use this same procedure in the following lessons dealing with word problems.

6. On the chalk board, put a subtraction fact on the number line similar to those in **Student Activity Four**. Have the student(s) find the first number in the subtraction fact by seeing where the top line ends. Then write that number. Counting backwards (taking away) from that point to the beginning of the second line gives the second number. Write it down with the minus symbol in front of it. Where the second line begins is the answer to the subtraction fact. Write it down with the equal symbol in front of it. Do several more examples. Follow the same procedure as you guide the student(s) through **Student Activity Four**.

7. The student(s) should need no help in completing **Student Activity Five**.

Worksheets:

1. *Worksheet 28* – Addition drill sheet

NUMBER ORDER – ORDINAL NUMBERS

Concepts:
> Ordinal numbers, pennies and dimes, subtraction, addition, and counting by threes

Objectives:
1. The student shall be able to write the ordinal number corresponding to a given object in a given position.

2. The student shall be able to circle the number of dimes and pennies needed to equal a given sum of money.

3. The student shall be able to correctly represent a subtraction fact on the number line by drawing a line from zero to the first number of the subtraction fact on the number line, then from that number draw a line towards zero representing the number taken away to arrive at the correct answer.

Teaching Tips:

1. Try replacing or supplementing the drill sheet in activity 2 with a spinner game. A *spinner* can be made out of a circular piece of cardboard using numbers 0–9 and a brad to hold the cardboard arrow in place. Write a number on the board for the student(s) to add to the number that the spinner stops on. They are then given 5 seconds to write the answer down on a piece of paper. After five spins, change the number on the board and do five more spins.

2. When doing activity 6, give each student a page of blank number lines (*Worksheet 6*) and have the student(s) do each of the subtraction facts at their seat as another student is doing them on the chalk board.

Materials, Supplies, & Equipment:
1. Number chart

2. Flash cards for subtraction facts 1–9 and *ordinal numbers*

3. Play money

4. Number line

5. *Spinner*

Activities:

1. Count out loud by threes to 99 with the student(s) using the number chart.

2. Use *Drill #3, Worksheet 28* to drill the addition facts 1–9. Drill the addition facts 10–18 with flash cards without the answers showing.

3. Drill the subtraction facts 1–9 for no longer than five minutes with flash cards with the answers showing.

4. Line up five different objects so that the student(s) can see them. Ask the student(s) to give ordinal number responses as to where each of the objects are located (you may want to use *ordinal number flash cards*). After going over the directions for **Student Activity One**, they should be able to complete the activity on their own.

5. Give each student dimes and pennies in play money. Write a sum of money on the chalk board and have them make the set of the coins they would need to equal that sum. After doing several of these examples, discuss the directions for **Student Activity Two** with them. The student(s) should be able to complete the activity independently.

6. Display a number line and several subtraction facts on the chalk board. Have a student come to the chalk board and draw the subtraction fact, "6–2 = 4", on the number line. Have them start at zero and draw a line above the number line to 6 with vertical bars at each end. At 6, count 2 marks backwards to 4, drawing a line under the first line from 6 to 4 with vertical bars at each end. By taking 2 away from 6 you arrive at the answer (4). Follow this procedure for several more examples. The student(s) may need some guidance to finish **Student Activity Three**.

7. The student(s) should complete **Student Activity Four** independently.

Worksheets:

1. *Worksheet 29* – Inches

2. *Worksheet 28* – Addition drill sheet

PLACE VALUE

Concepts:
Place value, nickels, before and after by tens, subtraction, word problems, and counting by sixes

Objectives:
1. The student shall be able to write the value of a given number of tens.

2. The student shall be able to write the value of a given set of nickels by counting by fives.

3. The student shall be able to write the number that comes before and after a given number when counting by tens.

4. The student shall be able to write the answer to a subtraction fact by using the number line.

Teaching Tips:
1. To aid in doing activity 7, have each student make a number line from 0–9 and secure it to the top of his desk with contact paper or scotch tape. Or you might want to use the number line from *Worksheet 6*.

2. If any student(s) are still having difficulty doing the word problems in **Student Activity Five**, give them some *flannel board objects* to use and let them make a visual representation of what is happening in the word problem.

Materials, Supplies, & Equipment:
1. Number chart

2. Flash cards for subtraction facts 1–9

3. Play money

4. *Place value materials*

5. Number line

6. *Flannel board objects*

Activities:

1. Count out loud by sixes to 96 using the number chart.

2. Use *Drill #4, Worksheet 28* to drill the addition facts 1–9. Drill the addition facts 10–18 with flash cards without the answers showing.

3. Drill the subtraction facts 1–9 with flash cards with the answers showing.

4. Quickly review with the student(s) the value of 4 tens, 7 tens, etc. by using play money dimes (or *place value materials*). They should then be able to complete **Student Activity One** independently.

5. Give each student up to nine play money nickels. Ask them to pick out a set of 4 nickels and then count them by fives to find out how many cents they equal. Repeat this with several other sets. The student(s) should be able, then, to complete **Student Activity Two** on their own.

6. Remind the student(s) to count to themselves by tens as they do **Student Activity Three** by themselves.

7. Again, carefully go over the steps for using the number line to find the answer to a subtraction fact with the student(s) in **Student Activity Four**. Example: "8–5 = ___." Starting at zero go over to 8 on the number line. At 8 start counting backwards 5 marks. The point where you end up (3) is the answer to the subtraction fact. Remind the student(s) that subtraction means to "take away".

8. The student(s) should be able to complete **Student Activity Five** without any help.

Worksheets:

1. *Worksheet 28* – Addition drill sheet

No one can take your place in the family.
God has made each of us distinct.

WORD NUMBERS – ELEVEN TO ONE HUNDRED

Concepts:
> Word numbers, place value, nickels, subtraction, addition, and counting by sixes

Objectives:
1. The student shall be able to write the numerals for word numbers 1–20 and multiples of ten.

2. The student shall be able to write the number of tens and ones found in a given number.

3. The student shall be able to draw the number of nickels needed to represent a given sum of money.

4. The student shall be able to write the answer to a subtraction fact by using the number line.

Teaching Tips:
1. The students may enjoy doing some counting backwards. Use the number chart and count from ten to one. Sing "One Little, Two Little, Three Little Indians" to go along with the counting. Then do the backwards counting again using the number line.

Materials, Supplies, & Equipment:
1. Number chart

2. Flash cards for subtraction facts 1–9 and word numbers

3. *Place value materials*

4. *Play money*

5. Number line

Activities:

1. Administer **Test 6**. As the student(s) begin each section discuss the directions.

2. Count out loud by sixes to 96 using the number chart.

3. Drill subtraction facts 1–9 with flash cards with the answers showing.

4. Review all of the word numbers using flash cards. Have the student(s) match the word numbers with the numerals or recite the numerals orally as you hold up the cards. The student(s) should be able to complete **Student Activity One** independently.

5. Point to several numbers on the number chart and ask the student(s) to tell you how many tens and ones are in the numbers (*place value materials* may be helpful). **Student Activity Two** should require no help from the teacher.

6. On a clean sheet of paper have the student(s) use circles to draw the number of nickels (you may also use *play money*) needed for given sums of money (20¢, 35¢, etc.). Tell them to put "5¢" inside of each circle and count the nickels by fives. The student(s) should be able to complete **Student Activity Three** on their own.

7. On the chalk board, solve several subtraction facts using the number line. Check each student for individual difficulties as they work **Student Activity Four**.

8. The student(s) should be able to complete **Student Activity Five** by themselves.

The time that we take to serve other people
creates a wealth beyond calculation.

SUBTRACTION – VERTICAL

Concepts:

Subtraction (horizontal to vertical), word problems, place value, addition, months of the year, "Thirty Days Hath September," and counting by sixes

Objectives:

1. The student shall be able to correctly complete an addition drill sheet within one minute.

2. The student shall be able to arrange the months of the year on flash cards in the correct order.

3. The student shall be able to write the correct answer to a vertical subtraction problem using the number line.

4. The student shall be able to write the numbers that represent the values of the digit in the tens' and ones' place as a horizontal addition problem.

Teaching Tips:

1. For variety in activity 2, suggest that the student(s) do the next four drill sheets by starting at the bottom and working up. Or suggest they start at the end of the row and work backwards. This would be especially good for those who finish with time left over. Don't complicate the procedure with these variations if the student(s) have trouble finishing within the time limit for the drills.

2. Student(s) might enjoy some research on the origin of the names for the months of the year when doing activity 4. July was named for Julius Caesar and August for the Roman emperor Augustus. Make some material available to them on the origins of the other months (see "Calendar, History of"; *World Book Encyclopedia, Volume 3*). Either read through it with them or let them read it aloud.

Materials, Supplies, & Equipment:

1. Number chart

2. Flash cards for subtraction facts 1–9 and months of the year

3. Number line

4. *Place value materials*

5. *World Book Encyclopedia, Volume 3*

Activities:

1. Count out loud by sixes to 96 using the number chart.

2. Use *Drill #1, Worksheet 30* to drill the addition facts 1–9. If you have not already shortened the student(s) drill to one minute, do so now. Most student(s) should be able to complete the drill in one minute. Drill the addition facts 10–18 with flash cards without the answers showing. If you feel further drill practice of the addition facts 1–9 with flash cards without the answers showing is necessary at the present, continue on a daily basis until lesson 117. Starting with that lesson, a set pattern of flash card drill is once again incorporated into the instructions.

3. Drill the subtraction facts 1–9 with flash cards with the answers showing.

4. Review the months of the year using flash cards. Mix the months up and have a student put them in the correct order. Or put one on the chalk board rail. Pick up a second one and ask if it comes before or after the first one. Pick up a third one and ask where it fits in. Continue until all 12 are in the correct order. Recite "Thirty Days Hath September."

5. Write a horizontal subtraction fact on the chalk board. Discuss that both numerals are one digit and therefore are in the ones' place. When the numerals are then written vertically, they are written straight up and down. The ones always go under the ones' place. Work the first four problems in **Student Activity One** together using the number line and then let the student(s) do the remainder on their own.

6. The student(s) should be able to complete **Student Activity Two** independently.

7. Point to several numbers on the number chart and ask what the value of the digit in the tens' place is and what the value of the digit in the ones' place is (or use *place value material*). After discussing the directions of **Student Activity Three**, the student(s) should be able to finish by themselves.

8. The student(s) should need no help on **Student Activity Four**. Remind them to add the first two digits together and add the sum to the third number in three digit addition. Have them write the sum to the right of the first two digits if necessary.

Worksheets:

1. *Worksheet 30* – Addition drill sheet

WORD NUMBERS – TWENTY TO ONE HUNDRED

Concepts:
Word numbers from twenty to one hundred, addition, subtraction, word problems, months of the year, "Thirty Days Hath September," and counting by nines

Objectives:
1. The student shall be able to recite the months of the year from memory.
2. The student shall be able to match the word number with the corresponding numeral by drawing a line.
3. The student shall be able to rewrite horizontal addition facts vertically and then write the correct answers.
4. The student shall be able to write the correct answer to subtraction facts for numbers up through 9.

Teaching Tips:
1. For activity 2, obtain *three 8" x 10" pieces of heavy cardboard*. Divide two of the pieces each into 40 1" x 2" rectangles (10 rows of 4 each). On one piece write in the rectangles 40 addition facts from 1–18 without the answers. On the second piece write the answers to the addition facts in the corresponding rectangles and on the back glue an *8" x 10" colorful picture*. Cut the cardboard into the 40 rectangles (1" x 2"). Place the piece with addition facts down with the facts showing. Mix up answer pieces and give them to a student to match to the addition facts. Have them place the pieces with the answer showing and the picture side down. When completed put the third piece of cardboard on top of the other two. Carefully turn the three pieces over and remove the top one. If the answers are correct the picture will be put together correctly. This could also be set up for subtraction facts.

Materials, Supplies, & Equipment:
1. Number chart
2. Flash cards for subtraction facts 1–9 and *months of the year*
3. Number line
4. *3 pieces of 8" x 10" cardboard, 8" x 10" colorful picture.*

Activities:

1. Count out loud by nines to 99 using the number chart.

2. Use *Drill #2, Worksheet 30* to drill the addition facts 1–9. Drill the addition facts 10–18 with flash cards without the answers showing.

3. Drill the subtraction facts 1–9 with flash cards with the answers showing.

4. Review the months of the year (you may want to use *flash cards*) by telling something special about each month. See if the student(s) are able to repeat all the months in the correct order. Recite "Thirty Days Hath September."

5. Discuss with the student(s) the word numbers from 20–100. Point out that the hyphen is used when two words are brought together. Go over the spelling of thirty, forty, fifty, and so forth. Point to different numbers on the number chart and have the student(s) pronounce them and then write them on a clean sheet of paper. Be sure to point out the tens' family, twenties' family, etc. When doing **Student Activity One**, read the word numbers together and then let the student(s) choose the numeral to which they should draw the line.

6. Work several two digit addition problems starting in the horizontal position. Discuss putting all the ones in ones' column and all the tens in the tens' column when changing it to a vertical problem. All horizontal problems should be changed to vertical problems for ease in finding the solution. Check for any wrong patterns being followed by the student(s) as they complete **Student Activity Two**.

7. Quickly go over the steps for finding the answer to a vertical subtraction problem using the number line. As the student(s) are doing **Student Activity Three**, help individuals who may still be having difficulty.

8. The student(s) should have no difficulty completing **Student Activity Four** independently.

Worksheets:

1. *Worksheet 31* – Christmas math maze

2. *Worksheet 30* – Addition drill sheet

SHOW YOUR SKILLS

Concepts:

Subtraction, word numbers, quarters, addition, and counting by nines

Objectives:

1. The student shall be able to write a horizontal subtraction fact in a vertical position and write the answer using the number line.

2. The student shall be able to write the number that corresponds to a given word number.

3. The student shall be able to draw the number of quarters needed to equal a given sum of money.

Teaching Tips:

1. Using the *word number flash cards* for 1–10 and multiples of 10, illustrate how the families of twenty, thirty, etc. are formed before doing activity 5. Put twenty and one together with a hyphen (use a *minus sign flash card*) for 21, forty and six together with a hyphen for 46. Any number from 1 to 99 can be formed in this way.

2. When doing activity 6, discuss with the student(s) the different ways you can use pennies, dimes, and nickels to equal a quarter. Give them play money and see how many sets they can form that equal a quarter or 25¢.

Materials, Supplies, & Equipment:

1. Number chart

2. Flash cards for subtraction facts 1–9, *word numbers*, and *minus sign*

3. Number line

4. Play money

Activities:

1. Count out loud by nines to 99 using the number chart.

2. Use *Drill #3, Worksheet 30* to drill the addition facts 1–9. Drill the addition facts 10–18 with flash cards without the answers showing.

3. Drill the subtraction facts 1–9 using flash cards with the answers showing.

4. Write several horizontal subtraction facts on the chalk board. Write them in vertical form and use the number line to determine the answer. The student(s) should then be allowed to do **Student Activity One** on their own with you giving individual help where it is needed.

5. Write on the chalk board the list of the word numbers for 1–10 and all multiples of 10 up to 90. Using the number chart point to various numbers and have the student(s) write on a clean sheet of paper the word numbers that name the same number. Remember the hyphen if there are two words. When starting **Student Activity Two** be sure the student(s) can read each of the word numbers.

6. Count one, two, three and four quarters by 25 using play money. Have the student(s) tell you how many quarters it would take to have 50¢, 25¢, and 75¢. Draw on the chalk board or have them draw circles on a sheet of paper to represent quarters until they have enough to equal 50¢, 25¢, 75¢. Put "25¢" inside of each circle. You may still have to lead them through **Student Activity Three** step by step.

7. The student(s) should do **Student Activity Four** independently.

Worksheets:

1. *Worksheet 30* – Addition drill sheet

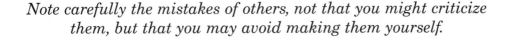

Note carefully the mistakes of others, not that you might criticize them, but that you may avoid making them yourself.

FRACTIONS – ONE FOURTH

Concepts:
Fractions (one fourth), money, word problems, addition, subtraction, and counting by nines

Objectives:
1. The student shall be able to draw the correct lines to divide an object into four equal parts and shade 1/4 of it.

2. The student shall be able to correctly identify a picture of a penny, nickel, dime, and quarter by writing their value in cents.

3. The student shall be able to write the correct answer to a subtraction fact by using the number line.

Teaching Tips:
1. For variety in activity 3, have the student(s) say the corresponding addition fact with each subtraction fact. Example: 9–4 = 5 and 5 + 4 = 9.

2. When doing activity 5, allow the student(s) to handle real *pennies, dimes,* and *nickels*, and see if they can identify them with their eyes closed. Tell them to think about the size, thickness, impression, and weight of the money as they feel it.

Materials, Supplies, & Equipment:
1. Number chart

2. Flash cards for subtraction facts 1–9

3. *Fraction materials*

4. Play money

5. *Real penny, dime, and nickel*

Activities:

1. Count out loud by nines to 99 using the number chart.

2. Use *Drill #4, Worksheet 30* to drill the addition facts 1–9. Drill the addition facts 10–18 with flash cards without the answers showing.

3. Drill the subtraction facts 1–9 with flash cards with the answers showing.

4. On the chalk board draw different shapes that can be divided into four equal parts (or use *fraction materials*). Have a student come to the chalk board and draw lines to divide one shape into four equal parts. Ask the student(s) to show a different way to divide the same shape into four equal parts. Then have them shade 1/4 of the shape with the chalk. Follow the same steps for each of the other shapes on the chalk board. Let a student read the directions for **Student Activity One** before they complete it on their own.

5. Using play money, hold up a penny, nickel, dime, and quarter both front and back in a mixed up order for the student(s) to identify and tell the value of each. After explaining the directions on **Student Activity Two**, the student(s) should be able to complete the activity independently.

6. The student(s) should be able to do **Student Activity Three**, **Four**, and **Five** without any assistance. Remind the student(s) to write the addition fact and label their answer since answer blanks are no longer printed for word problems in **Student Activity Three**. Be sure to check the student(s) answers in this new procedure.

Worksheets:

1. *Worksheet 32* – Subtraction by number line

2. *Worksheet 30* – Addition drill sheet

Good government begins with self government.

EVEN NUMBERS

Concepts:
Even numbers, fraction (one fourth), word problems, subtraction, < and >, addition, and counting by fours
Definition: Even numbers are the numbers used when counting by twos

Objectives:
1. The student shall be able to color the squares for all the even numbers on the number chart.

2. The student shall be able to circle the shape that has 1/4 of it colored.

3. The student shall be able to write the answer to a subtraction problem by using the number line.

4. The student shall be able to correctly write < or > between two sets to produce a true statement.

Teaching Tips:
1. If the student(s) ask about the odd numbers (those not divisible by two) in connection with activity 3, briefly discuss it with them. The concept of odd numbers will be taught at a later date.

2. When doing activity 6, hold up two *addition flash cards* without the answers showing. Have a student recite the answers. Repeat the two answers and have the student state which answer is greater. With the next set of cards follow the same procedure and have the student state which answer is least. Continue with several more sets switching back and forth between which is the greater and which is the least.

Materials, Supplies, & Equipment:
1. Number chart

2. Flash cards for subtraction facts 1–9, < and >, and *addition facts 1–18*

3. *Fraction materials*

Activities:

1. Count out loud by fours to 100 using the number chart.

2. Drill subtraction facts 1–9 with flash cards with the answers showing.

3. Discuss the meaning of even numbers. You should point out that an even number will always end in 2, 4, 6, 8, or 0. Point to several numbers on the number chart and have the student(s) tell you if the numbers are even or not. Go over the directions for **Student Activity One** with the student(s). Once you have them started, they should be able to complete the activity on their own.

4. Draw a large square on the chalk board and have the student(s) draw a square on a clean sheet of paper. Tell them to divide the square into four equal parts. As you divide the one on the chalk board (or use *fraction materials*), have them check their work. Follow the same procedure for a rectangle and a circle. Allow for different ways of dividing each shape. Divide one of the shapes into 3 equal parts and ask the student(s) if they can shade 1/4. (No, because there are not four equal parts). Discuss the directions with the student(s) for **Student Activity Two.** Remind them to be sure the shape is divided into four equal parts before they circle it and allow them to work independently.

5. **Student Activity Three** and **Four** should be completed without help. Since this is only the second time that the student(s) have been required to write the addition fact from word problems and label the answer without answer blanks being provided, remind them of what is expected.

6. Show the flash cards for < and > for the student(s) to identify. Discuss how to place the symbols correctly between two given sets. When they begin **Student Activity Five**, do the first row together orally to be sure they replace the addition fact with the answer before they determine what symbol to use. Discourage them from guessing which is correct.

There is no substitute for hard work.

FRACTIONS – ONE HALF AND ONE FOURTH

Concepts:

Fractions (one half and one fourth), addition, subtraction, even numbers, < and >, and counting by fours

Objectives:

1. The student shall be able to circle the pictures which represent one half and one fourth.

2. The student shall be able to write the answer to a subtraction problem using the number line.

3. The student shall be able to write the even numbers from 40–86 in sequence.

4. The student shall be able to write the < and > symbols between numerals and tally marks to create a true statement.

Teaching Tips:

1. If student(s) are still having difficulty with activity 2, cut a piece of *poster board* into fourths. Glue *library pockets* on them in rows (or seal some plain envelopes and cut them in half to create a pocket). On the pockets, write the addition facts that give the student(s) the most trouble. Mark the last pocket in the last row of each board the answer pocket. Write the answer for each addition fact on a separate 3" x 5" card so that the answer shows when the card is placed in the pocket. Have the student(s) put the cards in the correct pocket. Collect the ones that are correct and place them in the answer pocket. The ones that are missed need to be kept separate and practiced. The next day give the student(s) the same board and have them place only the answers to the problems they missed the day before. Continue until all of the answers can be placed correctly. Do the same for the other three pieces of poster board. The pockets could also be used for subtraction or multiplication facts.

Materials, Supplies, & Equipment:

1. Number chart

2. Flash cards for subtraction facts 1–9 and *tally marks*

3. Fraction materials

4. *Poster board, library pockets (or envelopes), and glue*

Activities:

1. Count out loud by fours to 100 using the number chart.

2. Use *Drill #1, Worksheet 33* to drill the addition facts 1–9. Drill the addition facts 10–18 with flash cards without the answers showing. In five more lessons, the drill for addition facts 10–18 will be changed to timed drill sheets four times a week. If you feel further drill practice of the addition facts 1–9 with flash cards without the answers showing is necessary at the present, continue on a daily basis until lesson 117. Starting with that lesson, a set pattern of flash card drill is once again incorporated into the instructions.

3. Drill subtraction facts 1–9 with flash cards with the answers showing.

4. Use fraction materials to show several sets with 1/2 and 1/4 of the whole missing. Have the student(s) determine which sets have 1/2 missing, which have 1/4 missing, and which have neither missing. The student(s) will need your help in working through **Student Activity One**.

5. The student(s) should be able to complete **Student Activity Two** and **Three** independently.

6. Ask the student(s) to tell you what even numbers are and what digits even numbers always end with (2, 4, 6, 8, 0). Have them give you examples of even numbers. They should be able to do **Student Activity Four** on their own.

7. Quickly review the tally marks from 1–10 (*flash cards* could be helpful). The student(s) should then be able to complete **Student Activity Five** with no help.

Worksheets:

1. *Worksheet 33* – Addition drill sheet

A diligent man will be honored by great men.

EQUAL AND NOT EQUAL

Concepts:
> = and ≠, fractions, subtraction, addition, and counting by fours

Objectives:
1. The student shall be able to form a true statement by writing equal or not equal between a fractional part and a whole that has been divided and shaded.

2. With the aid of the number line, the student shall be able to write the correct answer to a subtraction fact.

Teaching Tips:
1. After doing **Student Activity Three**, you might let the student(s) create their own addition flower. Give each student *four 1/4 sheets* of *construction paper*, each a different color. Out of one sheet, have them cut the centerpiece for the flower, cut eight smaller petals out of the second sheet, and cut the eight larger petals out of the third sheet. *Glue* them together and put them on the fourth sheet. Have the student(s) choose what number they want to put in the center and write "2–9" on the smaller petals. They are now ready to write in the answers on the larger petals.

Materials, Supplies, & Equipment:
1. Number chart

2. Flash cards for subtraction facts 1–9 and = *and* ≠

3. *Fraction materials*

4. *Construction paper and glue*

Activities:

1. Count out loud by fours to 100 using the number chart.

2. Use *Drill #2, Worksheet 33* to drill the addition facts 1–9. Drill the addition facts 10–18 with flash cards without the answers showing.

3. Drill subtraction facts 1–9 using flash cards with the answers showing.

4. Draw several different shapes on the chalk board and color a unit fraction (1/2, 1/3, 1/4, or 1/5) on each (or use *fraction materials*). Have the student(s) tell what fraction is colored for each shape. Then put a unit faction beside each shape, some being correct and some being incorrect. Let the student(s) tell you if you should put an = or ≠ symbol (flash cards) between each to make a true equation or inequality. On **Student Activity One** follow the same procedure for the first three items given. Then allow the student(s) to complete the remaining activities on their own.

5. The student(s) should be able to do **Student Activity Two** independently.

6. Ask the student(s) to point to the number 8 in the center of the first flower in **Student Activity Three**. Explain to them that they are to add 8 to each number in the petals around the center and write the answer on the large outer petal. (Example: "8 + 7 = 15" the answer 15 is written in for you). Do the first flower together with them, a petal at a time. The student(s) should be able to complete the remaining flower with little help.

Worksheets:

1. *Worksheet 33* – Addition drill sheet

Even if others do not treat us fairly,
we are always responsible to treat others fairly.

TIME – HOUR

Concepts:
Hour, = and ≠, word numbers, word problems, addition, subtraction, and counting by eights

Objectives:
1. The student shall be able to draw the hour hand on a clock face for a given time.

2. The student shall be able to create a true statement by writing = or ≠ correctly between given word numbers and numerals.

3. The student shall be able to write the correct addition fact and label the answer to a word problem without help.

Teaching Tips:
1. After doing activity 2, have the students take out a clean sheet of paper and 8 crayons. Ask them to see how many different sets they can make that add up to 8 (Example: 1 + 7, 2 + 6, etc.). Have them write each addition fact on their paper as they form it with the crayons.

2. When doing activity 4, discuss with the student(s) how long a second is. Have them see how many times they can blink their eye, tap their foot, say their name, count by fives, or stand up and sit down in 10 seconds, 15 seconds, or 20 seconds.

Materials, Supplies, & Equipment:
1. Number chart

2. Flash cards for subtraction facts 1–9 and *word numbers*

3. Small clock models for the student(s)

4. Crayons

Activities:

1. Count out loud by eights to 96 using the number chart.

2. Use *Drill #3, Worksheet 33* to drill the addition facts 1–9. Drill the addition facts 10–18 with flash cards without the answers showing.

3. Drill subtraction facts 1–9 with flash cards with the answers showing.

4. Give the small clock models to the student(s). Call out several hour times and have the student(s) set the hands to the correct time. Remind them to set the minute (long) hand on twelve first and then determine where to place the hour (short) hand. They should hold up their clock for you to see as soon as they are finished. After going over the directions with them, the student(s) should be able to finish ***Student Activity One*** on their own.

5. Review the word numbers 1–10 and multiples of ten (you may want to use *flash cards*). Have a student read the directions to ***Student Activity Two***. The student(s) should be able to complete the activity by themselves.

6. In ***Student Activity Three,*** notice that the word "altogether" has been omitted from the word problems. The next several word problems will ask for addition but not with the word "altogether." Discuss with the student(s) what makes the problem addition. What is the key word (joined)? Have the student(s) put 4 crayons on their desk. Next have 3 more join the ones on the desk. How many are on the desk? Ask a student to read the word problem out loud in ***Student Activity Three*** before they write the addition fact and label the answer.

7. ***Student Activity Four*** and ***Five*** should be completed independently by the student(s).

Worksheets:

1. *Worksheet 34* – Counting by fives, sixes, sevens, & eights

2. *Worksheet 33* – Addition drill sheet

INCHES

Concepts:
Inches, hour, word problems, addition, subtraction, and counting by eights

Objectives:
1. The student shall be able to draw a line of a given length using an inch ruler.

2. The student shall be able to draw the hands on the clock face at the correct position for a given hour.

Teaching Tips:
1. Replace or supplement the addition drill sheet in activity 2 with a memory game for those who have the facts memorized. Student(s) who are still struggling may have to wait for the game until they have extra time or at recess on a rainy day. On *3" x 5" cards* that have been cut in half, write 10 addition facts without the answers showing. On *colored (blue) 3" x 5" cards* that have been cut in half write the answers to these facts. Mix the cards up and place them face down on a flat surface in rows. Have a student turn over one white card and one blue card. If the addition fact and the answer match the student may keep the cards. If they do not match they return the cards to their place, face down, and the next student has a turn. The game ends when all cards have been matched and the winner is the one with the most cards. Since there are 90 different addition facts, you may want to make up several sets of 10 cards each. Some of the student(s) might enjoy the challenge of more than 10 facts used at a time.

Materials, Supplies, & Equipment:
1. Number chart

2. Flash cards for subtraction facts 1–9

3. Inch ruler

4. Small clock models for the student(s)

5. *3" x 5" cards – white and blue*

Activities:

1. Count out loud by eights to 96 using the number chart.

2. Use *Drill #4, Worksheet 33* to drill the addition facts 1–9. Drill the addition facts 10–18 with flash cards without the answers showing.

3. Drill subtraction facts 1–9 using flash cards with the answers showing.

4. On a clean sheet of paper, have each student draw several lines of a given length with his inch ruler. Show the student(s) how to hold the ruler so that it does not move when they draw the lines. Tell them to begin with a point, putting the zero on the ruler at that point. Suggest that they put a point at the end of their first line and use that as the beginning of the second line, forming what looks like a broken line. In **Student Activity One** the student(s) must use the given points to begin their lines.

5. Give each student a small clock model. As you tell them several times on the hour, have them set the hands of the clock correctly. They need to set the minute (long) hand first and then set the hour (short) hand. When they are finished, have them hold their clock up so you can check the accuracy of their work. They should be able to complete **Student Activity Two** independently.

6. Have the student(s) read the word problem in **Student Activity Three** out loud together. Discuss with them what you would do to find the answer (put them together or add). What is the key word? (and) What would the label be? (students) Ask them to write the addition fact and label on their paper.

7. **Student Activity Four** and **Five** should require no help from the teacher.

Worksheets:

1. *Worksheet 33* – Addition drill sheet

Anything worth doing is worth doing well.

NUMBER ORDER – ORDINAL NUMBERS

Concepts:
Ordinal numbers, inches, subtraction, addition, and counting by eights

Objectives:
1. The student shall be able to correctly place a set of letters numbered ordinally on blanks corresponding to the appropriate ordinal numbers.

2. Using an inch ruler, the student shall be able to measure the length of individual line segments and write their total length.

Teaching Tips:
1. For the student who has already mastered the ordinal numbers first through tenth in activity 4, you might want to teach the ordinal numbers eleventh through twentieth in accordance with the student(s) ability. Have them draw twenty objects. They can then tell you which is the fifteenth object, which is the eighteenth object, and so on.

2. Since this is a test day, you might want to have the student(s) do the first page of Lesson 70 before you give the test. The student(s) can then complete the second page after they have completed the test since the student(s) will be able to work independently. This prevents you from waiting for student(s) who need longer to finish the test before you can begin on the daily lesson. Do this only if the student(s) are capable of handling daily work before and after the test without confusion.

Materials, Supplies, & Equipment:
1. Number chart

2. Flash cards for subtraction facts 1–9 and ordinal numbers

3. Inch ruler

Activities:

1. Administer *Test 7*, making sure that the instructions are clear. Most student(s) should be able to complete the test with little teacher assistance.

2. Count out loud by eights to 96 using the number chart.

3. Drill subtraction facts 1–9 with flash cards with the answers showing.

4. Line the ordinal number flash cards up on the chalk board rail in mixed up order. Have the student(s) take turns coming to the chalk board and putting them into correct order. Ask the student(s) to read the directions to *Student Activity One* out loud together. Have them read the first ordinal number listed (fourth), point to the fourth blank, and write the letter V on it. Do the same for the next three ordinal numbers. Some student(s) may still need some help completing this activity.

5. The student(s) will need your guidance as they work through the first sequence of lines of *Student Activity Two*. Have the student(s) take out their inch ruler and put the zero at the first point (1). Tell them to measure the distance from point 1 to point 2 and write this length by the line. Next measure from point 2 to point 3 and write this length down. Continue this step by step until they have measured from point 5 to point 6. Now, after adding the various lengths, have the student(s) write the total length of the path, in inches, in the answer blank. Allow the student(s) who are capable to do the second path on their own, but give help if it is needed.

6. The student(s) should complete *Student Activity Three* and *Four* independently.

It is better to be faithful than famous.

WORD PROBLEMS – SUBTRACTION

Concepts:
> Subtraction word problems, days of the week, ordinal numbers, place value, and counting by sevens

Objectives:
1. The student shall be able to correctly write the answer to a subtraction word problem using visual representation of the subtraction problem.

2. The student shall be able to recite the days of the week in the correct order from memory.

3. The student shall be able to correctly write the name of the day of the week corresponding to the ordinal number of that day of the week.

4. The student shall be able to write the correct value of a given number of tens and ones and their sum.

Teaching Tips:
1. Have the student(s) take the word problems in **Student Activity One** and find the answers on the *number line*. It is important for them to understand that no matter how they work the problem, they are always going to get the same answer if they do it correctly.

2. Along with activity 3, start checking the student(s) to see if the subtraction facts for 1–9 have been mastered. The **Teaching Tip** for Lesson 66 would be a good aid for more practice if it is needed.

Materials, Supplies, & Equipment:
1. Number chart

2. Flash cards for subtraction facts 1–9 and *days of the week*

3. Calendar

4. Crayons

5. *Number line*

Activities:

1. Count out loud by sevens to 98 using the number chart.

2. Drill addition facts 1–18 using *Drill #1, Worksheet 35*.

3. Drill subtraction facts 1–9 with flash cards with the answers showing. This will be the last week that the answers will be shown in the subtraction drill for 1–9.

4. Have the student(s) put 4 crayons on their desk. Ask them to take one of them away and put it on their lap. Tell them to count the crayons that they have left. Have them state the subtraction fact they have just demonstrated (4–1 = 3). Ask them what the label for their answer would be (crayons). Now have them look at **Student Activity One**. Have a student read the first word problem out loud. Let them write the subtraction fact necessary to support the correct answer. Discuss what the label should be. Follow the same procedure for the remaining two word problems.

5. See if the student(s) can say the days of the week in order (*flash cards* might be helpful). Discuss what day today is and how you would write the date for today. Using a calendar, discuss what the date is for the first Monday, second Tuesday, etc. for this month. Give help on an individual basis in **Student Activity Two** as needed.

6. After the student(s) have read the directions for **Student Activity Three**, they should require little help to complete it.

Worksheets:

1. *Worksheet 35* – Addition drill sheet

Real courage is overcoming fear, not the absence of fear.

ADDITION AND SUBTRACTION

Concepts:

Subtraction (reverse of addition), place value, addition, subtraction, days of the week, and counting by sevens

Objectives:

1. The student shall be able to write the two corresponding subtraction facts that go with each addition fact.

2. The student shall be able to write the correct value of the digit in the tens' and the ones' place for a given number.

Teaching Tips:

1. When doing **Student Activity Two** you may use *straws* and have the student(s) do a visual representation of the numbers. Example: If the number is 38, have them put a rubber band around ten straws three times and then count out eight single straws. Have them also do an addition fact such as 8 + 6 = 14. Count out 8 straws and 6 straws. Then they would take ten of the straws and put a rubber band around them and have 4 straws left. One group of ten and 4 is equal to 14. They may also use the straws to demonstrate adding three single-digit numbers as in **Student Activity Three**. Example: 5 + 4 + 8 = 17 Count out 5 straws, add 4 more, and then add 8 more to the pile. Put a rubber band around one group of ten and they would have 7 straws left to represent 17.

Materials, Supplies, & Equipment:

1. Number chart

2. Flash cards for subtraction facts 1–9, *days of the week*, and whole numbers

3. Calendar

4. Counting chips

5. *Straws*

Activities:

1. Count out loud by sevens to 98 using the number chart.

2. Drill addition facts 1–18 using *Drill #2, Worksheet 35*.

3. Drill subtraction facts 1–9 with flash cards with the answers showing.

4. Recite out loud the days of the week in order with the student(s) (you may want to use *flash cards*). Using a calendar, have them tell you which day of the week the 24th, 16th, 8th, 4th, and 26th falls on.

5. Give each of the student(s) nine counting chips to demonstrate addition and subtraction facts. Start by putting 3 chips in one set and 2 chips in another. Have a student tell you the addition fact they have represented and write it on the chalk board. Now have them start with a set of 5 chips and take 2 away. Ask how many chips they have left and what subtraction fact is demonstrated. Write the subtraction fact on the chalk board underneath the addition fact. Next start with 5 chips and take 3 away. Again, ask how many chips they have left and what subtraction fact is demonstrated. Write this subtraction fact on the board underneath the first one. Discuss with the student(s) the three facts that can be written with the three numbers. Do several examples like this. Go over the first three equations in **Student Activity One** orally. Let the student(s) tell you what the two subtraction facts are for each addition fact. Have the student(s) attempt the remaining activities on their own.

6. Using the whole number flash cards, have the student(s) tell you the value of the digit in the tens' place and the ones' place for several numbers. The student(s) should be able to complete **Student Activity Two**, **Three**, and **Four** independently.

Worksheets:

1. *Worksheet 36* – Christmas addition

2. *Worksheet 35* – Addition drill sheet

PLACE VALUE

Concepts:
Place value, word problems, and counting by sevens

Objectives:
1. The student shall be able to write the correct value of a given number of tens.

2. Using a visual representation, the student shall be able to write the correct answer to subtraction word problems.

3. The student shall be able to write the two corresponding subtraction facts that go with each addition fact.

Teaching Tips:
1. When doing activity 5, give each student counting chips. Have them start with a set of 2 chips corresponding to the problem you write on the chalk board. Have them add 6 chips for the first answer, take away 3 chips for the second answer, add 2 chips for the third answer, and take away 1 chip for the last answer.

Materials, Supplies, & Equipment:
1. Number chart

2. Flash cards for subtraction facts 1–9 and addition 1–18

3. Play money

4. Counting chips

Activities:

1. Count out loud by sevens to 98 using the number chart.

2. Drill addition facts 1–18 using *Drill #3, Worksheet 35.*

3. Drill subtraction facts 1–9 with flash cards with the answers showing.

4. Give the student(s) play money dimes to practice counting by tens to determine the value of the digit in the tens' place. They should be able to do **Student Activity One** by themselves.

5. Write "2 + 6 = __ −3 = __ + 2 = __−1 = __" on the chalk board. Ask the student(s) to tell you what 2 + 6 equals and write "8" in the first blank. Then subtract 3 from 8. Have them tell you the answer and write "5" in the second blank. Now add 2 to 5 and have them tell you the answer. Write "7" in the third blank. Write the answer "6" for 7−1 in the last blank. Follow the same step by step procedure for each problem in **Student Activity Two**.

6. Write a simple subtraction word problem on the chalk board. Have the student(s) use counting chips at their desks to demonstrate what the problem is telling them. Discuss what the key word is that tells them if they are to add or subtract (left). Write the subtraction fact on the chalk board as the student(s) tell it to you. Discuss what the label for the answer would be. Follow the same procedure for **Student Activity Three,** guiding the student(s) through each step.

7. Put the numbers 2, 6, and 8 on the chalk board. Ask the student(s) to tell you what addition fact can be written with these three numbers. Then ask them what two subtraction facts can be written with the three numbers. Do this with several other sets of numbers. Discuss the directions for **Student Activity Four** with the student(s) and let them complete it with as little help as possible.

Worksheets:

1. *Worksheet 35* – Addition drill sheet

TIME – HALF HOUR

Concepts:
Half hour, sets, addition, subtraction, and counting by sevens

Objectives:
1. The student shall be able to write the correct time in digital form shown on the clock face for the half hour.

2. The student shall be able to write the correct number of objects in a given set.

3. The student shall be able to correctly identify the numbers used in counting by sevens by coloring the square on which they appear.

Teaching Tips:
1. In addition to activity 1, you may want to put a sequence of numbers on the chalk board that are used in counting by 7. Example: 49, 56, 63, 70. Ask the student(s) to tell you what the next three numbers would be.   Another would be 7, 14, 21, 28. Use the number chart if needed.

Materials, Supplies, & Equipment:
1. Number chart

2. Flash cards for subtraction facts 1–9

3. Clock model

Activities:

1. Count out loud by sevens to 98 using the number chart.

2. Drill addition facts 1–18 using *Drill #4, Worksheet 35.*

3. Drill subtraction facts 1–9 with flash cards with the answers showing. Tomorrow will be the last day for the answers to be showing when drilling the subtraction facts. Be sure that you know which student(s) still need additional help.

4. Write several sets of three numbers necessary to form an addition fact on the chalk board. Example: 1, 6, 7 (1 + 6 = 7 and 6 + 1 = 7). On a sheet of paper, have the student(s) write two addition facts and two subtraction facts using the three numbers (7–6 = 1 and 7–1 = 6). Write the addition and subtraction facts of each set of numbers on the chalk board after the student(s) have had sufficient time to complete them. Discuss those problems that were difficult for the student(s).

5. Using the clock model, set the clock for several half hour times and ask the student(s) to write the correct time in digital form on a piece of paper. Go over the answers one at a time so that any mistakes that the student(s) make can be corrected before continuing. The student(s) should be able to complete **Student Activity One** independently.

6. Read the directions together with the student(s) for **Student Activity Two**. They should then be able to do the activity on their own.

7. Explain to the student(s) that as they color the squares needed to count by sevens (you may want them to refer to the *number chart*) in **Student Activity Three**, they will be coloring a path for the mouse to take in order to find the cheese.

8. The student(s) should need no help in doing **Student Activity Four** and **Five**.

Worksheets:

1. *Worksheet 37* – Visual representation of subtraction word problems

2. *Worksheet 35* – Addition drill sheet

SHOW YOUR SKILLS

Concepts:
Half hour, word problems, addition, and subtraction

Objectives:
1. The student shall be able to correctly draw the hour hand on the clock face for a given half hour.

2. Using a visual representation, the student shall be able to write the correct answer to subtraction word problems.

Teaching Tips:
1. In addition to activity 1, play a game using subtraction with the student(s). Cut an *egg carton* in half so that you have two rows of three each in each half and remove the lids. Place the two halves side by side so that you now have three rows of four each. With a felt tip marker write a numeral (0–11) on the inside bottom of each cup. *Glue the bottom of the egg cartons to the bottom of a box (6" x 8")*. Have a student(s) take *two small balls (Ping-pong balls* are a possibility) and stand a set distance from the box. Toss the balls into the box. If the balls fall inside 5 and 3, the student subtracts the numbers and the answer is the score he receives (2 points). The teacher keeps score for each student. The student with the lowest total wins. This could also be used with addition and then the student with the highest total wins.

Materials, Supplies, & Equipment:
1. Flash cards for subtraction facts 1–9

2. Clock model and small clock models for student(s)

3. Counting chips

4. *Number chart*

5. *Egg carton, glue, 6" x 8" box, and 2 small balls*

Activities:

1. Drill subtraction facts 1–9 with flash cards with the answers showing. Today is the last day for the answers to be showing when drilling subtraction facts 1–9.

2. Write the numbers 1, 3, and 4 on the chalk board. On a sheet of paper, have the student(s) write two addition and two subtraction facts using these three numbers. Discuss any difficulties they might have. Do several more examples like 2, 3, and 5; 3, 4, and 7; 4, 5, and 9, etc. It is important for the student(s) to realize there is a relationship between addition and subtraction.

3. Give each student a small clock model. Write several half hour times on the chalk board. Have them set the clocks at the correct time by setting the minute (long) hand first and then setting the hour (short) hand. Set the large clock model for each time so that they can check to see if they have done each correctly. Have them raise their hand if they did it correctly. Notice the ones that do not raise their hand so that you can give them individual help while they are working on **Student Activity One**.

4. Discuss what makes a subtraction word problem with the student(s). Ask what the key word (left) is. Talk about the fact that something has to be taken away or given away. See if they can tell you a simple subtraction word problem that you could then write on the chalk board. If they can't, make one up for them. Visualize the problem using counting chips. Have the student(s) tell you the subtraction fact that supports the answer. Read the word problems in **Student Activity Two**. Allow the student(s) to write the subtraction fact, label the answer on their own, and then discuss the results with them.

5. The student(s) should be able to complete **Student Activity Three** and **Four** independently. Encourage the student(s) to not use the number line unless it is absolutely necessary.

Contentment is a most profitable habit but it must be cultivated.

SUBTRACTION 10–18

Concepts:
> Subtraction with minuend 10–18, < and >, half hour, and sets

Objectives:
1. The student shall be able to write the correct answer to a subtraction problem 10–18 using the number line.

2. The student shall be able to correctly circle the greater of two given numbers.

3. The student shall be able to correctly draw the hands on the face of a clock for a given half hour.

4. The student shall be able to correctly count the objects in a given set and write the number.

Teaching Tips:
1. You will want to take some time today to check the student(s) to see how proficient they are in the subtraction facts 1–9. Students who are still having difficulty should be given extra drill. *Worksheet 32* gives additional practice in subtraction.

2. When doing activity 3, the student(s) may want to visualize some of the subtraction facts. Give each student 18 *counting chips* and have them put the chips into a set to represent the subtraction fact. Take away the given number of chips and see if what they have left is the same as the answer received on the number line.

Materials, Supplies, & Equipment:
1. Flash cards for subtraction facts 1–18

2. Number line

3. Clock model and small clock models for student(s)

4. *Counting chips*

Activities:

1. Drill addition facts 1–18 using *Drill #1, Worksheet 38*.

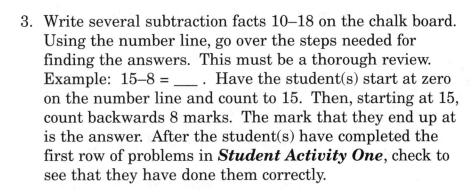

2. Drill subtraction facts 1–9 with flash cards with the answers **not** showing. Drill subtraction facts 10–18 with flash cards with the answers showing.

3. Write several subtraction facts 10–18 on the chalk board. Using the number line, go over the steps needed for finding the answers. This must be a thorough review. Example: 15–8 = ___ . Have the student(s) start at zero on the number line and count to 15. Then, starting at 15, count backwards 8 marks. The mark that they end up at is the answer. After the student(s) have completed the first row of problems in **Student Activity One**, check to see that they have done them correctly.

4. Discuss with the student(s) the word "greater" in the directions for **Student Activity Two**. Greater means greater than or larger. Once they have a clear understanding of the meaning, they should be able to complete the activity by themselves.

5. Give each child a small clock model. Write several half hour times on the chalk board. As you point to a time, have them set their clocks. Remind them to always set the minute (long) hand first. Set the large clock model for them to check their time by. As they begin **Student Activity Three**, ask them which hand should they draw first. Where should they draw it? Then, where do they draw the hour hand?

6. After going over the directions with the student(s) for **Student Activity Four**, they should be able to complete the activity by themselves.

Worksheets:

1. *Worksheet 38* – Addition drill sheet

No man is a fool who gives that which he cannot keep to gain that which he cannot lose.

ADDITION – HORIZONTAL TO VERTICAL

Concepts:

Addition (horizontal to vertical), < and >, subtraction, even numbers, and "Thirty Days Hath September"

Objectives:

1. The student shall be able to rewrite a horizontal addition problem vertically and write the correct answer.

2. The student shall be able to circle the least of two given numbers.

3. The student shall be able to write the answer to a subtraction problem 10–18 using the number line.

4. When given an even number, the student shall be able to write the next three even numbers in sequence.

Teaching Tips:

1. Here is a practice aid to use with activities 1 and 2. Cut a large apple out of a 1/4 sheet of *poster board*. Write "+4" in the middle of the apple. Around the edge of the apple, cut 16 "v" shaped notches evenly spaced. Write a number by each notch using the numbers 0–15 in non-sequential order. Determine what the answer would be if you added the number by the notch and "+ 4." Write this number on the back side by the same notch. Do this for all other notches. In the middle of the back write "– 4." Depending on which side you choose to use, this is a self check game for an individual student for addition or subtraction. Make several different apples with different numbers in the middle. If you use "+ 6" use numbers 0–13, (the number you are adding (+ 6) and the largest number you use around the notches (13) must equal 19 when added together), for "+ 8" use 0–11, for "+ 2" use 0–17, etc.

Materials, Supplies, & Equipment:

1. Flash cards for subtraction facts 1–18, < *and* >, and whole numbers

2. Number chart

3. *Addition subtraction game – poster board*

Activities:

1. Drill addition facts 1–18 using *Drill #2, Worksheet 38.*

2. Drill subtraction facts 1–9 with flash cards with the answers **not** showing. Drill subtraction facts 10–18 with flash cards with the answers showing.

3. Recite "Thirty Days Hath September."

4. Put a 3-number single digit horizontal addition problem and a 2-number double-digit horizontal addition problem on the chalk board. ("3 + 5 + 4 = ___ "and "25 + 34 = ___") When the student(s) write the addition problems vertically, show them how all the ones go in a straight line and all the tens go in a straight line. Remind them that this makes it easier to add the numbers correctly. As they begin **Student Activity One**, check each student to see if they are having any difficulty lining up the tens and the ones.

5. Read the directions for **Student Activity Two** to the student(s). Discuss with them how the meaning of the word "least" is the same as "less than" *(you might show the < and > flash cards).* When they have a clear understanding of that meaning, they should be able to complete the activity by themselves. If necessary, have them mentally or actually place the < or > sign between the numbers to identify the smaller number.

6. Allow the student(s) to complete **Student Activity Three** independently, giving individual help where needed.

7. Discuss with the student(s) the meaning of even numbers (the numbers used when counting by twos). After telling the student(s) an even number, have them tell you the next three to follow. This is their first formal work dealing with sequences. **Student Activity Four** should be completed together being sure each student knows the number that goes in the first blank of each series. The number chart may be a help to some student(s) when doing this activity.

Worksheets:

1. *Worksheet 38* – Addition drill sheet

WORD PROBLEMS – ADDITION

Concepts:
> Addition word problems, fractions (one half), subtraction, and "Thirty Days Hath September"

Objectives:
1. The student shall be able to correctly determine if a word problem is an addition or subtraction problem, write the appropriate fact, and correctly label the answer.

2. The student shall be able to correctly write the next three numbers when counting by eights.

3. The student shall be able to correctly identify the shape that has one of two equal parts shaded by marking it with an "X."

4. The student shall be able to write the correct answer to a subtraction problem 10–18 using the number line.

Teaching Tips:
1. For more practice in activity 6, make some dominoes with a unit fraction on one end and a shape with a factional part colored on the other end. Use 2" x 4" rectangles cut out of *poster board*. Make enough (20) for two to play the game of fraction dominoes.

2. When doing activity 6, cut out of *construction paper* some shapes that have been divided into two unequal parts. Cut the shapes on the dividing line and demonstrate that the parts are unequal by comparison. Emphasize that one part equals one half only if the two parts are equal.

Materials, Supplies, & Equipment:
1. Flash cards for subtraction facts 1–18

2. Counting chips

3. Number chart

4. *Fraction materials*

5. *Poster board and construction paper*

Activities:

1. Drill addition facts 1–18 using *Drill #3, Worksheet 38*.

2. Drill subtraction facts 1–9 with flash cards with the answers ***not*** showing. Drill subtraction facts 10–18 with flash cards with the answers showing.

3. Recite "Thirty Days Hath September."

4. Give the student(s) an addition word problem orally or on the chalk board without using the word "altogether." Instead, use "more" or "joined." Ask them for the key word and if that word tells them to add or subtract. Do a visualization of the problem with counting chips for each student to aid in determining what process to use. Discuss what they started out with and what change took place. Lead the student(s) through the same discussion as they do ***Student Activity One***.

5. The student(s) should be able to do ***Student Activity Two*** with little help. Allow them to use the number chart if necessary.

6. The emphasis in ***Student Activity Three*** is to identify those shapes that have been divided into two **equal** parts (you may want to use *fraction materials* to introduce this activity). Draw a square, triangle, and rectangle on the chalk board. Divide each of them into two unequal parts. Ask if any student can correct one and divide it into two equal parts. Emphasize that one half (½) means two equal parts not just two parts. Together discuss each shape in ***Student Activity Three*** before you allow the student(s) to pick up their pencil. Have them read the directions to themselves and then proceed.

7. While the student(s) are doing ***Student Activity Four,*** check their work to detect anyone who still needs individual help in using the number line to arrive at the answer for a subtraction problem. Encourage the student(s) who have some of the facts memorized to write the answers without using the number line.

Worksheets:

1. *Worksheet 39* – Subtraction 10–18 with number line

2. *Worksheet 38* – Addition drill sheet

EQUAL AND NOT EQUAL

Concepts:
= and ≠, fractions (one fourth), subtraction, addition, word problems, and counting by ones

Objectives:
1. The student shall be able to write the correct symbol (= or ≠) between two given sets.

2. The student shall be able to correctly identify the shape that has been divided into four equal parts by marking it with an "X."

3. By using the number line, the student shall be able to write the correct answer to a subtraction problem.

4. The student shall be able to correctly determine if a word problem is an addition or subtraction problem, write the correct fact, and correctly label the answer.

Teaching Tips:

1. When doing activity 5, use one sheet each of *blue, red, orange, green,* and *yellow poster board.* Cut six inch circles for each student out of each of the colors. Cut the red into halves, the orange into thirds, the green into fourths, and the yellow into sixths. Give them a large *self closing plastic bag* in which to keep their fraction materials for use later as you see the need. CAUTION the student(s) about keeping the plastic bag away from their faces. Have the student(s) tell you, by counting, how many halves it takes to make a whole, how many thirds, how many fourths, and how many sixths. Then let them put different combinations together to make a whole (for example: 1/2 + 1/4 +1/4).

Materials, Supplies, & Equipment:
1. Number chart

2. Flash cards for subtraction facts 1–18 and = and ≠

3. *Fraction materials*

4. *Poster board (blue, red, orange, green, yellow)* and *self closing plastic bags*

Activities:

1. Count out loud by ones to 100 using the number chart only where necessary.

2. Drill addition facts 1–18 using *Drill #4, Worksheet 38.*

3. Drill subtraction facts 1–9 with flash cards with the answers **not** showing. Drill subtraction facts 10–18 with flash cards with the answers showing.

4. Using flash cards for the symbols, discuss the difference between = and ≠. Put different subtraction facts on the chalk board, some with correct answers and some with incorrect answers. Have the student(s) tell you if the = or ≠ symbol should go between them. To keep them from guessing, have them defend their answer by telling the difference between the first set of numbers as compared to the numbers in the second set. They should be able to complete **Student Activity One** on their own.

5. In **Student Activity Two,** the student(s) learn to identify those shapes that have been divided into four equal parts (you may wish to review with *fraction materials*). After drawing squares, circles, and rectangles on the chalk board; divide some into four equal parts and some into four parts that are not equal. Discuss what makes the four parts equal and what keeps them from being equal. Emphasize that the part is only one fourth (1/4) if all four parts are equal. After the discussion, the student(s) should be able to complete **Student Activity Two** independently.

6. **Student Activity Three** and **Four** should be completed by the student(s) with little help. Use the time to help those who may still be struggling.

7. To begin **Student Activity Five,** first ask the student(s) what the problem tells them. Discuss whether the key word tells them to add or subtract. Have them write the fact they think would give them the correct answer. Be sure they label their answer.

Worksheets:

1. *Worksheet 38* – Addition drill sheet

FRACTIONS – ONE THIRD

Concepts:
    Fractions (one third), = and ≠, word numbers, subtraction, addition, and counting by ones

Objectives:

1. The student shall be able to correctly identify the shape that has been divided into three equal parts by marking it with an "X."

2. The student shall be able to write = or ≠ correctly between two given sets.

3. The student shall be able to write the correct answer to a subtraction problem using the number line.

4. The student shall be able to correctly write a letter above a corresponding number that matches the answer to an addition fact.

Teaching Tips:

1. To save time put the work for ***Student Activity Four*** on the chalk board during test time.

2. Since there is no addition drill today, here is a game you may like to use. Give each student five *3" x 5" cards* cut in half. Have them number each card from 0 to 9. Call out a number (8) and have them see what addition fact they can make that has that answer. As you call on the student(s), write the different facts on the chalk board as they write them on the back of their card. Do this with several other numbers. You might also want to use the game with subtraction facts. Save the cards to use later.

Materials, Supplies, & Equipment:

1. Number chart

2. Flash cards for subtraction facts 1–18 and = *and* ≠

3. *Fraction materials*

4. *3" x 5" cards*

Activities:

1. Administer **Test 8**.

2. Count out loud by ones to 100.

3. Drill subtraction facts 1–9 with flash cards with the answers **not** showing. Drill subtraction facts 10–18 with flash cards with the answers showing.

4. Draw several shapes on the chalk board (or use *fraction materials*). Divide some into three equal parts and some into three parts that are not equal. Have the student(s) tell you which shapes are divided into three equal parts and therefore could have one third shaded. Remind them that they can shade one third only if all three parts are equal. They should be able to complete **Student Activity One** on their own.

5. After going over the directions with the student(s) in **Student Activity Two**, they should be able to complete the activity independently (*flash cards* may be used to help before the activity).

6. **Student Activity Three** should be done independently. Remind the student(s) that some of the facts should be able to be answered without using the number line.

7. Tell the student(s) that they are going to decode a secret message. To decode the message, they must solve the addition fact and put the letter associated with the fact on the blank that has that sum beneath it. Put five blank lines (3" long) on the chalk board to put the practice message on. Put the number "8" under the first blank, "9" under the second, "10" under the third, etc. until you put "12" under the last blank. Write the following five addition problems on the chalk board with a line above each: "6+4," "7+5," "3+5," "9+2," "8+1." Above "6+4" put an "I," above "7+5" put an "H," above "3+5" put an "F," above "9+2" put an "T," and above "8+1" put an "A." Have the student(s) tell you what "6+4" equals. Find the blank that has a 10 under it and put the "I" on it. Do the same for the other four addition problems. What does this spell? (Faith) Ask the student(s) to look at **Student Activity Four**. Ask them what "6+3" equals and have them write the answer. What letter will they put on the blank above the number 9? (P) What does "7+7" equal? What letter will go above the number 14? (L) Allow them to complete the activity on their own if they are able.

PLACE VALUE –
ONE HUNDREDS

Concepts:
Place value (one hundreds), fractions, inches, subtraction, and counting by tens

Objectives:
1. The student shall be able to write the correct number of hundreds, tens, and ones that make up a given set of place value blocks and write that number.

2. The student shall be able to identify what fractional part of a shape has been shaded by circling the correct fraction.

3. Using an inch ruler, the student shall be able to measure the length of the three sides of a triangle and determine its total perimeter by writing the sum of the lengths.

4. The student shall be able to write the two corresponding subtraction facts that go with each given addition fact.

Teaching Tips:
1. In **Student Activity Four,** have the student(s) write the length of the longest side on the longest line and the shortest side on the shortest line after they measure each side. The side that remains is then the third side.

Materials, Supplies, & Equipment:
1. Flash cards for subtraction facts 10–18

2. Place value materials

3. Fraction materials

4. Inch ruler

Activities:

1. Count out loud by tens up to 100.

2. Drill the addition facts 1–18 using *Drill #1, Worksheet 40.*

3. Drill subtraction 10–18 with flash cards with the answers showing.

4. Have the student(s) look at **Student Activity One**. Read the top part together. Go over the meaning of the number, 135, with the student(s). Do several other three digit numbers with the student(s) using the place value materials. Allow them to tell you what number you have represented. When they are ready to begin **Student Activity Two**, do one place value problem together counting the hundreds, tens, and ones separately and then putting them together to make the number represented. The student(s) should then be able to complete the remaining problems by themselves. If they are not able to do so, work some more with them.

5. Using fraction materials, have the student(s) tell you what part of the whole has been shaded. Do this several times. Be sure to not use any fractions except unit fractions (those with one for the numerator). After going over the directions together, the student(s) should be able to finish **Student Activity Three** independently.

6. Ask the student(s) to take out their inch rulers. Looking at **Student Activity Four**, have them read the first question. Then tell them to point to the longest side. Measure that side and write the length on the blank. Read the second question. Have them point to the shortest side and measure it, writing the length on the blank. After reading the next question, ask them to point to the side they have not measured. Measure it and write the length on the blank. Discuss with the student(s) what the last question means. Have them write their answer on the blank.

7. Write three addition facts 1–9 on the chalk board. Beneath the addition facts, write the corresponding subtraction facts as the student(s) tell them to you. They should be able to complete **Student Activity Five** with little help.

8. **Student Activity Six** should be completed by the student(s) on their own.

Worksheets:

1. *Worksheet 40* – Addition and subtraction drill sheet

SHAPES

Concepts:

Shapes (circle, square, rectangle, and triangle), word numbers, place value (one hundreds), word problems, and counting by fives.

Objectives:

1. The student shall be able to identify a circle, rectangle, square, and triangle by coloring each a given color.

2. The student shall be able to write the numeral for the word numbers up to one hundred.

3. The student shall be able to write the correct number of hundreds, tens, and ones that make up a given set of place value blocks and write that number.

4. The student shall be able to write the correct subtraction fact and label the answer to subtraction word problems.

Teaching Tips:

1. When doing activity 1, you may want to have the student(s) use the number chart on *Worksheet 5* and color all the squares used in counting by fives. You may also want to use the multiples of five from the *whole number flash cards* to do the counting in activity 1.

2. Instead of place value materials for activity 7, you may want to use *straws*. Make up bundles of ten straws with a rubber band around them. Then take ten of these bundles and use a large rubber band to make a bundle of one hundred. Allow the student(s) to select the bundles they would need to represent the number you call out.

Materials, Supplies, & Equipment:

1. Number chart

2. Flash cards for subtraction facts 10–18, shapes, word numbers, and *whole numbers*

3. Place value materials

4. *Straws*

Activities:

1. Count out loud by fives to 100 using the number chart only where necessary.

2. Drill subtraction facts 1–9 using *Drill #2, Worksheet 40*. Remind the student(s) that this is a subtraction drill. Check the progress of the student(s) who may not have the subtraction facts memorized yet.

3. Drill subtraction 10–18 with flash cards with the answers showing. The student(s) will need to do *Worksheet 41* for practice in subtraction for this week.

4. Write four addition facts 1–9 on the chalk board. On a sheet of paper, have the student(s) write the subtraction facts that use the same three numbers used in the addition fact. Then, write the student(s) subtraction facts on the chalk board so the student(s) can check their work. Discuss any questions they might have.

5. Using shape flash cards, discuss the characteristics of the circle (round), square (4 sides same size), triangle (three sides), and rectangle (4 sides with opposite sides the same size). Go over the four shapes as the student(s) point to them in **Student Activity One**. Instruct the student(s) to follow the directions as they do the activity.

6. Using the flash cards for word numbers, review 1–20 and multiples of 10. Call out several numbers and allow a student to choose the words he would need from the flash cards to represent each number. Remind them to use the hyphen where it is appropriate. The student(s) should be able to do **Student Activity Two** without further help.

7. Give each of the student(s) place value materials. Call out a number in the hundreds and have them visually demonstrate the number with the place value materials. For 374 they would need 3 groups of one hundreds, 7 groups of tens and 4 ones. After doing this with several numbers, the student(s) should be able to complete **Student Activity Three** on their own.

8. Read the word problems in **Student Activity Four** together. Have the student(s) decide if they add or subtract and why. Remind them to label their answers since it is no longer a part of the word problem text.

Worksheets:

1. *Worksheet 41* – Subtraction with number line 0–19

2. *Worksheet 40* – Addition and subtraction drill sheet

COUNTING – TWO HUNDRED

Concepts:
Counting to 200, the number (over one hundred) that comes between by ones, place value (one hundreds), and shapes

Objectives:
1. The student shall be able to count out loud to 200 correctly using a number chart.

2. The student shall be able to write the number that comes between two given numbers greater than one hundred.

3. The student shall be able to correctly write the digit in the hundreds', tens', and ones' place in a given number.

4. The student shall be able to write the two corresponding subtraction facts that go with each given addition fact.

5. The student shall be able to correctly draw a line to match an object to its corresponding shape.

Teaching Tips:
1. When doing the drill sheets in activity 2, stress that accuracy is more important than speed. At the same time do not allow them to count to arrive at their answers since recall of the math facts is the objective. Neatness should also be encouraged. Do not allow them to become sloppy for the benefit of speed.

2. When doing activity 7, give each student a sheet of *construction paper* and let them cut out one of each of the shapes. Encourage them to make the shapes large. Then have them print the name on the shape.

Materials, Supplies, & Equipment:
1. Number chart 100–199

2. Flash cards for subtraction facts 10 –18 and shapes

3. *Place value materials*

4. *Construction paper*

Activities:

1. Count out loud with the student(s) from 100 to 200 using the number chart. Write "200" on the chalk board to point to after going through the number chart for 100–199. Help the student(s) count correctly by telling them that the number, 147, is read, "one hundred forty-seven." Be sure to instruct the student(s) that they must not put the word "and" between the word "hundred" and the word "forty-seven." "And" is used to denote the decimal point and should not be used unless the number has a decimal point in it. Students are more familiar with the numbers under one hundred, but will need the reinforcement of counting by ones to two hundred. With enough drill on this, they will not be confused when counting any number in the hundreds families.

2. Drill the addition facts 1 -18 using *Drill #3, Worksheet 40.*

3. Drill the subtraction facts 10–18 with flash cards with the answers showing.

4. Using the 100–199 number chart, choose two numbers and have the student(s) tell you what number comes between. Do this with several sets of numbers. The student(s) may need the help of the number chart to complete **Student Activity One** successfully.

5. Write several three digit numbers on the chalk board. Ask the student(s) what digit is in the tens' place, the hundreds' place, and the ones' place changing the order each time (*place value materials* might be helpful here). In **Student Activity Two,** do the first sentence together to be sure that the student(s) understand the directions. Allow them to finish it on their own.

6. Have the student(s) tell you three addition facts 1–9 to write on the board (e.g. 9 + 1 = 10). Write the two corresponding subtraction facts for each addition fact as the student(s) tell them to you (e.g. 10–1 = 9, 10–9 = 1). Allow the student(s) to do **Student Activity Three** with as little help as possible.

7. Go over the four shapes using the flash cards. Read the directions for **Student Activity Four** and allow the student(s) to finish the activity on their own.

Worksheets:

1. *Worksheet 40* – Addition and subtraction drill sheet

WORD NUMBERS – 100–199

Concepts:

Word numbers (100–199), place value (one hundreds), word problems, shapes, between by ones (numbers over 100), and counting to 200

Objectives:

1. By drawing a line, the student shall be able to correctly match the word number with the corresponding numeral.

2. The student shall be able to write the correct number of hundreds, tens, and ones in a given number.

3. The student shall be able to correctly circle the object which has a shape that does not match the shape of the first object given.

4. The student shall be able to correctly write the number that comes between two given numbers over one hundred.

Teaching Tips:

1. To provide some enrichment work in activity 8, ask the student(s) questions such as, "What is the difference between a triangle and a square?", "What is the difference between a square and a rectangle?", "What shape does not have straight sides?", "How many corners does a square, rectangle, or triangle have?".

Materials, Supplies, & Equipment:

1. Number chart 100–199

2. Flash cards for subtraction facts 10–18, word numbers, shapes, and months of the year

3. *Place value materials*

Activities:

1. Count out loud from 100–200 using the number chart.

2. Drill subtraction facts 1–9 using *Drill #4, Worksheet 40.* Remind the student(s) that today they will be subtracting.

3. Drill subtraction facts 10–18 with flash cards with the answers showing.

4. Have the student(s) tell you an addition fact and two subtraction facts using the same three numbers. Example: 2 + 4 = 6, 6–2 = 4, 6–4 = 2. Do this with several other sets of facts.

5. Using the word number flash cards, let the student(s) choose different cards to make up several numbers over one hundred. Have a student read the number and write it on the chalk board. In **Student Activity One,** read the word numbers together. Then have the student(s) point to the correct number and draw a line to it.

6. On the number chart 100–199, point to several numbers and ask the student(s) to tell you how many hundreds, tens, and ones are in the numbers (*place value materials* may be useful here). The student(s) should be able to complete **Student Activity Two** with little help.

7. Read the word problem in **Student Activity Three** together and let the student(s) work it independently. After they are done, go over the problem with them.

8. Ask the student(s) to look around the room and see if they can find any shapes that look like a circle, rectangle, square, and triangle (provide flash cards for reference). Give them some aid if necessary. In **Student Activity Four,** have the student(s) point to the objects that are the same and then circle the one that is different.

9. Discuss with the student(s) the number that comes between two given numbers on the number chart 100–199. They may need to use the number chart or *Worksheet 42* to complete **Student Activity Five.**

Worksheets:

1. *Worksheet 42* – Number chart 100–199

2. *Worksheet 40* – Addition and subtraction drill sheet

MONEY

Concepts:

Money, between by ones (numbers over 100), place value (one hundreds), word numbers (over 100), word problems, counting to 200, months of the year, and "Thirty Days Hath September"

Objectives:

1. The student shall be able to determine the cost of two given objects and write the value in cents.

2. The student shall be able to write the number that comes between two given numbers over 100.

3. The student shall be able to write the value of a given number of hundreds.

4. The student shall be able to write the numeral corresponding to the given word number.

Teaching Tips:

1. When doing activity 3, tell how many days are in each month as they are lined up on the chalk board rail applying the information learned in "Thirty Days Hath September."

2. When doing activity 4, tell the student(s) a little about the making of coins. All U.S. coins are made in Denver, Philadelphia, San Francisco, and West Point by the Bureau of the Mint. Circular disks the size of the coin are punched out of sheets of metal. A coining press imprints each side of the disk using coin stamping dies.

Materials, Supplies, & Equipment:

1. Number chart 100–199

2. Flash cards for subtraction facts 10–18, months of the year, and word numbers

3. *Place value materials*

Activities:

1. Count out loud from 100–200 using the number chart.

2. Drill subtraction facts 10–18 with flash cards with the answers showing.

3. Place one of the months of the year flash cards on the chalk board rail. Hold a second one up and ask the student(s) if it comes before or after the other month. Place it on the correct side of the other card. Do the same for all the remaining months until they are arranged in order. Recite "Thirty Days Hath September."

4. In **Student Activity One**, ask the price of an apple and have them write it on the blank. Do the same with the cherries. Now have the student(s) add the two numbers together to find the total cost. Do the same thing with the second group of fruit. Let them do the third group of fruit by themselves and then check to see if their total cost is correct. If it is, allow them to continue adding the rest of the groups on their own.

5. Using the number chart 100–199, point to several numbers and ask the student(s) to tell you what number comes between them. Allow the student(s) to use *Worksheet 42* or a number chart 100–199 as an aid in completing **Student Activity Two**.

6. Tell the student(s) that 4 hundreds means to add 100 together 4 times (100 + 100 + 100 + 100) (you may want to demonstrate this with *place value materials*). When you add 4 hundreds, count 100, 200, 300, 400. 4 hundreds equal 400. Ask the student(s) what 6 hundreds would equal. If they need to count 6 of them by hundreds, do so. Question them about several other given numbers of hundreds. They should then be able to complete **Student Activity Three** independently.

7. Display several word numbers (you may want to use flash cards) for the student(s) including one hundred. Have them tell you the number and then write it on their own sheet of paper. Write the number on the chalk board so that the student(s) can check to see that they wrote the number correctly. The student(s) should be able to complete **Student Activity Four** with no assistance.

8. When the student(s) begin **Student Activity Five**, remind them that they need to write the subtraction fact and label their answer.

Worksheets:

1. *Worksheet 42* – Number chart 100–199

CALENDAR–DAYS OF THE WEEK

Concepts:
> Days of the week, word problems, quarter hour, place value (one hundreds), and word numbers (over 100)

Objectives:
1. The student shall be able to correctly write the numbers on a calendar when given partial dates, the correct day for a given date, the correct date for a given occurrence of a day of the week, and the correct day for a given number of days before and after a given date.

2. The student shall be able to write, in digital form, the correct time displayed on the face of a clock for the quarter hour.

3. The student shall be able to write the value of each digit in the hundreds', tens', and ones' place and the numeral it represents.

4. By drawing a line, the student shall be able to match the word numbers over 100 with the corresponding numeral.

Teaching Tips:
1. For the student(s) who are still having difficulty with **Student Activity Six,** take the word number and break it into an addition problem. Example: one hundred sixty-three is made up of 100 + 60 + 3. When added together they equal 163.

Materials, Supplies, & Equipment:
1. Flash cards for subtraction facts 10–18, days of the week, word numbers

2. Calendar

3. Clock model

4. *Place value materials*

5. Number chart 100–199

Activities:

1. Drill addition facts 1–18 using *Drill #1, Worksheet 43.*

2. Drill the subtraction facts 10–18 with flash cards with the answers showing.

3. Recite the days of the week in order using flash cards or a calendar. See if the student(s) can say them by themselves. In **Student Activity One,** check carefully that the student(s) write the correct numbers in the boxes. When starting **Student Activity Two**, have the student(s) read the question together, point to the correct answer, and write it down. Do this for each of the questions in the activity.

4. The student(s) should be able to complete **Student Activity Three** with minimal help. Read the problem together and have the student(s) identify the key word (joined) and what it indicates (addition). Remind them to label their answer.

5. Display several different times on the clock model for 15 minutes after and 45 minutes after the hour. Have the student(s) write the correct time on a sheet of paper. Write the answer on the chalk board to enable the student(s) to check their answer. Allow them to complete **Student Activity Four** independently.

6. Write "2 hundreds," "5 tens," and "6 ones" on the chalk board (or use *place value materials*). Have the student(s) tell you the value of each and what number it represents (200, 50, and 6 = 256). Do this for several other groups of hundreds, tens, and ones. As the student(s) work on **Student Activity Five,** check to see they are not making any repetitious mistakes.

7. Point to a number on the number chart 100–199. Ask the student(s) to choose the word number flash cards needed to represent that number. Have the student(s) read the word number together. Do this for several other numbers. Choose a student to read the directions for **Student Activity Six** and allow them to complete it on their own.

Worksheets:

1. *Worksheet 43* – Addition and subtraction drill sheet

BAR GRAPH

Concepts:

Bar graph, place value (one hundreds), quarter hour, word numbers (over 100), money, and counting to 200.

Objectives:

1. The student shall be able to write the correct number of objects represented on a bar graph.

2. The student shall be able to write the correct value of the hundreds', tens', and ones' digit in a given number.

3. The student shall be able to correctly draw the hands on the face of a clock for a given quarter hour.

4. The student shall be able to write the correct number corresponding to a given word number.

5. The student shall be able to write the correct value of a given set of coins in cents.

Teaching Tips:

1. When doing activity 1, have the student(s) stand. As they begin to count, have them march in place. When you clap your hands, have them stop marching as they continue to count. Next time you clap your hands, have them start to march again as they continue to count. Switch back and forth until you have reached 200.

Materials, Supplies, & Equipment:

1. Flash cards for subtraction facts 10–18

2. Number chart 100–199

3. Small clock models for the student(s)

4. Play money

Activities:

1. Count out loud from 100–200 using the number chart. This is important to do though you may be inclined to pass over it if students can already count from 1–99 easily. This drill will help them avoid confusion students have when counting numbers over one hundred.

2. Drill subtraction facts 1–9 using *Drill #2, Worksheet 43.*

3. Drill the subtraction facts 10–18 with flash cards with the answers showing.

4. Tell the student(s) that a bar graph is used to help us count things. Have the student(s) look at the bar graph in **Student Activity One**. Ask them why it is called a bar graph. Help them see that the bars picture the number of objects. Tell them that this bar graph is going to help them count how many triangles, squares, and circles they have. If there are 5 blocks above the triangle, then they have 5 triangles. If there are 8 blocks then they have 8 objects, etc. Read the first question to them. Ask them to count the blue blocks and write the number on the blank. Then read the second question. If there are 2 blue blocks, how many triangles do they have? Repeat this procedure for each of the following questions.

5. Point to at least six different numbers one at a time on the number chart 100–199. Have the student(s) tell you the value of each digit in the number. Write it on the chalk board in the manner done in **Student Activity Two.** The student(s) should be able to complete the activity on their own.

6. Using the small clock models, have the student(s) set their clocks for several different quarter hour times. Check their work. When starting **Student Activity Three,** remind the student(s) to draw the minute (long) hand first and then the hour (short) hand.

7. **Student Activity Four** should be completed by the student(s) with no assistance.

8. After reviewing the different coins using play money, allow the student(s) to complete **Student Activity Five** independently.

Worksheets:

1. *Worksheet 43* – Addition and subtraction drill sheet

NUMBER ORDER – < AND > OVER 100

Concepts:
> < and > (over 100), bar graphs, place value (one hundreds), money, and counting by twos

Objectives:
1. The student shall be able to write < and > correctly between two given numbers over 100.

2. The student shall be able to correctly color on a bar graph the number of given objects to be represented.

3. The student shall be able to write the correct number when given the value of the digit in the hundreds', tens', and ones' place.

4. The student shall be able to write the correct value of a given number of pennies, dimes, nickels, and quarters in cents.

Teaching Tips:
1. When doing **Student Activity One**, have them read the set to themselves once they have placed the symbol correctly between the two numbers. This reinforces the meaning of the symbols as well as aiding proper placement.

2. If the student(s) have difficulty in comprehending activity 6, write the three addends similar to the problems in **Student Activity Three** vertically on the chalk board and have the student(s) add them. This could also be done as a check on their answer.

Materials, Supplies, & Equipment:
1. Number chart 0 – 99 and 100 – 199

2. Flash cards for subtraction facts 10 – 18 and < *and* >

3. Play money

Activities:

1. Count out loud by twos to 100 using the number chart.

2. Drill addition facts 1 - 18 using *Drill #3, Worksheet 43*.

3. Drill the subtraction facts 10 - 18 with flash cards with the answers showing.

4. Using the number chart 100 - 199 point to two numbers and have the student(s) determine which is the largest. Then write the two numbers on the chalk board and have them tell you which symbol (< or >) they should place between the numbers (or use *flash cards*). Follow this procedure several times with other numbers over 100. When the student(s) do **Student Activity One,** encourage them to decide which number is largest before they choose which symbol to use.

5. When starting **Student Activity Two,** tell the student(s) a bar graph is used to help us count things. Have a student read and answer the first question. Read the next statement and let them color three blue blocks above the triangle in the bar graph. Show the student(s) a sample bar graph like the one in this activity and show them how to color it. Continue with the second question and statement in the same manner. Allow the student(s) to complete the last question and statement on their own.

6. Write several problems on the chalk board similar to those in **Student Activity Three** (e.g. 700 + 70 + 2, 500 + 50 + 1, etc.). Have the student(s) tell you what number is represented by asking what digit will go in the hundreds', tens', and ones' place. Have the student(s) do the first two answers together and finish the remaining ones by themselves.

7. Using play money, display several sets of dimes and pennies, nickels and pennies, pennies, dimes, nickels, and quarters. Allow the student(s) to tell you the value of each set by counting by the appropriate number. They should be able to complete **Student Activity Four** independently.

Worksheets:

1. *Worksheet 44* – Shapes color sheet

2. *Worksheet 43* – Addition and subtraction drill sheet

MONEY – DOLLAR

Concepts:
Dollar, word problems, bar graph, time, and counting by twos

Objectives:
1. The student shall be able to write the correct value of a given number of one dollar bills in dollars and cents.

2. The student shall be able to correctly write the fact and label the answer to an addition or a subtraction word problem.

3. The student shall be able to correctly color a block for each given object to be represented on a bar graph.

4. The student shall be able to correctly write the time shown on a clock face for the hour, half hour, and quarter hour in digital form.

Teaching Tips:
1. When doing activity 4, tell them a little about how paper money is made. All United States paper money is made by the Bureau of Engraving and Printing. Special paper and ink are used to help the money last a long time. Thirty two one dollar bills are printed on a large sheet and then cut into individual dollar bills. Pass a *real one dollar bill* around to the student(s) so that they can feel its strength and texture compared to a sheet of regular notebook paper.

Materials, Supplies, & Equipment:
1. Number chart

2. Flash cards for subtraction facts 10–18

3. Play money

4. Clock model

5. *Real one dollar bill*

Activities:

1. Count out loud by twos to 100 using the number chart.

2. Drill subtraction facts 1–9 using *Drill #4, Worksheet 43.*

3. Drill the subtraction facts 10–18 with flash cards with the answers showing.

4. Give each student a play money dollar bill. Discuss the color, picture on the front (George Washington), and the word "ONE" on the back with the student(s). Tell them that one dollar can be written as cents (100¢) or it can be written as a dollar and cents ($1.00). The decimal point is used to separate the dollar from the cents. The number on the left of the point means dollar and the numbers on the right of the point mean cents. $1.00 means you have one dollar and no cents. In **Student Activity One** have the student(s) count the dollar bills and write the value. Encourage the student(s) to be conscious of prices on sales receipts which are printed with the dollar sign and the decimal point separating the dollars and cents. The half dollar will be introduced in second grade.

5. When starting **Student Activity Two,** have the student(s) read the word problem, pick out the key word, determine if they should add or subtract, write the fact, and label their answer.

6. Discuss with the student(s) that the bar graph is used to count things. In **Student Activity Three,** guide the student(s) to count the airplanes, ships, and cars and color the blocks to represent the objects.

7. Using a large clock model, set the clock for one hour, one half hour, and two quarter hour times. Have the student(s) write the times on a sheet of paper. Give them the correct times so they can check their answers. The student(s) should be able to complete **Student Activity Four** on their own.

8. The student(s) should be able to complete **Student Activity Five** without any help.

Worksheets:

1. *Worksheet 43* – Addition and subtraction drill sheet

SHOW YOUR SKILLS

Concepts:
Time, subtraction, graphs, < and >, and counting by threes

Objectives:
1. The student shall be able to correctly draw the hour hand on the clock face for the hour, half hour, and quarter hour.

2. The student shall be able to correctly draw the number of shapes represented on a bar graph.

3. The student shall be able to write < or > correctly between two given numbers over 100.

Teaching Tips:
1. When doing activity 3, you might have a different student answer each subtraction flash card and then give the addition fact that corresponds to it. Example: 16–7 = 9, 9 + 7 = 16. Or you might alternate giving addition and subtraction facts to a student and have them, in turn, give you the other one.

2. Prepare a bar graph on *poster board* ahead of time and then display it in front of the student(s) when doing activity 6, or draw it on the chalk board ahead of time.

Materials, Supplies, & Equipment:
1. Number chart

2. Flash cards for subtraction facts 10–18

3. Clock model

4. *Poster board*

Activities:

1. Administer **Test 9**. Read the directions carefully with the student(s) for each activity.

2. Count out loud by threes to 99 using the number chart.

3. Drill subtraction facts 10–18 with flash cards with the answers showing.

4. When starting **Student Activity One**, use a clock model to remind the students to first look at the minute (long) hand to determine where the hour (short) hand should be drawn and then draw the hour hand.

5. The student(s) should be able to complete **Student Activity Two** independently.

6. Draw a simple bar graph on the chalk board and let the student(s) tell you how many objects each bar represents. The student(s) will need you to guide them through each step of **Student Activity Three**.

7. The student(s) should require no assistance in completing **Student Activity Four**.

Life's great accomplishments are measured
by what one does in the little tasks.

CENTIMETERS

Concepts:
Centimeters, time, bar graph, word problems, and counting by threes

Objectives:
1. The student shall be able to correctly measure the length of an object by using a centimeter ruler.

2. The student shall be able to correctly draw the hands on the face of a clock for hour, half hour, and quarter hour.

3. The student shall be able to correctly write the number of objects represented on a bar graph.

Teaching Tips:
1. After the student(s) have completed ***Student Activity One***, have them take out their centimeter ruler and measure each of the objects in the activity. It is important for the student(s) to realize that all centimeter rulers will measure the same.

2. Suggest to the student(s) that they look in the newspaper to see if they can find any bar graphs as a practical application of ***Student Activity Three***. Make a bulletin board display of those that are brought in. Talk about how they are alike and different from the ones that the student(s) have done in class.

Materials, Supplies, & Equipment:
1. Number chart

2. Flash cards for subtraction facts 10–18

3. Centimeter ruler

4. *Clock model*

Activities:

1. Count out loud by threes to 99 using the number chart.

2. Drill addition facts 1–18 using *Drill #1, Worksheet 45*.

3. Drill the subtraction facts 10–18 with flash cards with the answers showing. This will be the last week that the drill will be done with the answers showing. You need to begin checking the student(s) individually using flash cards to be sure that they have mastered the subtraction facts. They will then be drilled for four weeks without the answers showing before the number line will be taken from the activity.

4. Discuss with the student(s) that there are two different rulers that can be used to measure lengths – the inch ruler and the centimeter ruler. Tell them the centimeter ruler is a metric measure while the inch ruler is an English measure. Have them take out their own ruler that has centimeters on it. Tell them to compare their ruler to the ruler in **Student Activity One**. Explain that you use a centimeter ruler in the same way that you use an inch ruler. Ask the student(s) to tell you the length of each object in the activity and then have them write it on the blank.

5. When doing **Student Activity Two**, remind the student(s) to draw the minute hand before they draw the hour hand (you may want to use the *clock model* to demonstrate the importance of this).

6. Have the student(s) look at the bar graph in **Student Activity Three**. Discuss with them how this bar graph is different than the one in the last lesson (bars are horizontal, numbers across bottom, objects are vertical). Talk together about how many objects are represented on the graph before they read the questions. Then allow them to complete the questions on their own.

7. Have the student(s) read the first word problem in **Student Activity Four** to themselves, pick out the key word, and determine if they should add or subtract (realizing the subtraction symbol is displayed). Tell them to then write the correct fact and label their answer. Follow the same procedure for the second word problem.

Worksheets:

1. *Worksheet 45* – Addition and subtraction drill sheet

ADDITION – THREE DOUBLE DIGIT NUMBERS

Concepts:
> Addition of three double-digit numbers, ordinal numbers, centimeters, subtraction, and counting by sixes

Objectives:
1. The student shall be able to correctly add three double-digit numbers by writing the answer for the ones' column and then writing the answer for the tens' column.

2. The student shall be able to correctly place a set of letters numbered ordinally on blanks corresponding to the appropriate ordinal numbers.

3. Using a centimeter ruler, the student shall be able to correctly measure the length of a given object.

Teaching Tips:
1. When doing activity 6, talk with the student(s) about the metric system. Discuss the ways that the metric system is used in the United States – 2 liter bottles, medicine measured in grams, some highway signs give distance in both miles and kilometers, millimeter wrenches, speedometers show both miles and kilometers, etc. The U.S. military services use metric units. In fact, the metric system is used extensively throughout most of the world. The modern metric system is known as the International System of Units. The name International System of Units with the international abbreviation SI was given to the system by the General Conference on Weights and Measures in 1960. However, the use of the metric system in the United States is very limited.

Materials, Supplies, & Equipment:
1. Number chart

2. Flash cards for subtraction facts 10–18 and ordinal numbers

3. Centimeter ruler

Activities:

1. Count out loud by sixes to 96 using the number chart.

2. Drill subtraction facts 1–9 using *Drill #2, Worksheet 45*.

3. Drill the subtraction facts 10–18 with flash cards with the answers showing.

4. Write several sets of three double-digit numbers on the chalk board to be added together. Remind the student(s) to always add the ones' column first and then to add the tens' column. This is essential when they begin carrying. Do not allow them to develop any wrong habits at this time. They should be able to complete **Student Activity One** on their own, but spot check to see that they are starting with the ones' column.

5. Review ordinal numbers by using the flash cards. Ask the student(s) to read the directions to **Student Activity Two** out loud together. Tell them to point to the fourth blank and then write the letter "W" on that blank. Do the same for the next two ordinal numbers. Some student(s) should be able to complete the blanks on their own while others may still need help.

6. Have the student(s) look at their centimeter ruler. Discuss with them what different objects they might measure with a centimeter ruler. Ask if they would measure the length of a football field with it or the length of their shoe. After reading the directions together, allow them to complete **Student Activity Three** by themselves.

7. Encourage the student(s) to complete **Student Activity Four** by looking at the number line only when necessary.

Worksheets:

1. *Worksheet 46* – Subtraction 10–18 with number line

2. *Worksheet 45* – Addition and subtraction drill sheet

SHAPES

Concepts:
Shapes (oval, diamond, and octagon), the number over 100 that comes after by ones, centimeters, addition, subtraction, and counting by sixes

Objectives:
1. The student shall be able to correctly identify an oval, diamond, and octagon by coloring each a given color.

2. The student shall be able to correctly write the number that comes after a given number over 100.

3. Using a centimeter ruler, the student shall be able to correctly measure the length of a given object.

Teaching Tips:
1. In activity 4, you may want to have the student(s) cut their own shapes out of *construction paper*. Tell the student(s) to write the name of the shape on one side. On the other side have them list all of the objects that they can see in the room for that shape.

2. In activity 6, put a vertical line marked in centimeters beside the *growth chart* and compare the student(s) heights in inches and centimeters. Discuss with them that even though the centimeter measurement is a larger number, the actual height is the same. See if they can tell you which is larger – a centimeter or an inch. This may be a difficult concept for them to understand so cover it briefly. It will be taught thoroughly in the next grade.

Materials, Supplies, & Equipment:
1. Number chart 0–99 and 100–199

2. Flash cards for subtraction facts 10–18 and shapes (oval, diamond, and octagon)

3. Centimeter ruler

4. *Construction paper*

5. *Growth chart*

Activities:

1. Count out loud by sixes to 96 using the number chart.

2. Drill addition facts 1–18 using *Drill #3, Worksheet 45.*

3. Drill the subtraction facts 10–18 with flash cards with the answers showing.

4. Display the three new shapes on flash cards. Discuss with the student(s) where they might see an oval (egg), a diamond (baseball diamond), and an octagon (stop sign). As you say the name of the shape, have the student(s) point to that shape in ***Student Activity One***. Then allow them to read the directions to themselves and color the shapes.

5, Point to several numbers on the number chart 100–199 and have the student(s) tell you the number that comes after the given number. With the aid of the number chart they should be able to complete ***Student Activity Two*** independently.

6. Have the student(s) look at their centimeter ruler. You may want to collect their inch rulers to prevent them from getting the two confused. To measure the length of the carrot in ***Student Activity Three,*** tell the student(s) to find the zero on the ruler and put it on the dotted line at the end of the carrot. Then read the point at which the other end of the carrot stops. They should be able to measure the lollipop and arrow by themselves.

7. The student(s) should be able to do ***Student Activity Four*** and ***Five*** on their own.

Worksheets:

1. *Worksheet 45* – Addition and subtraction drill sheet

Appearances are often deceiving.

ODD NUMBERS

Concepts:

Odd numbers, shapes, word problems, centimeters, after by ones (numbers over 100), and subtraction

Definition: An odd number is a whole number that is not even.

Objectives:

1. The student shall be able to correctly write the missing odd numbers from 1 to 55.

2. The student shall be able to correctly draw a line to match an object with its corresponding shape.

3. The student shall be able to correctly measure the length of a given line using a centimeter ruler.

4. The student shall be able to correctly write the number that comes after a given number over 100.

Teaching Tips:

1. In activity 4, suggest that the student(s) collect pictures of the three new shapes they are learning. Tell them to look in magazines, newspapers, advertisements, etc. Make a bulletin board display of their collection.

2. If student(s) are having difficulty with **Student Activity Five**, you may tell them to cover up the digit in the hundreds' place and decide what the answer would be. The answer is then the same with a one in front of it in the hundreds' place.

Materials, Supplies, & Equipment:

1. Flash cards for subtraction facts 10–18 and shapes (oval, diamond, and octagon)

2. Number chart 0–99 and 100–199

3. Centimeter ruler

Activities:

1. Drill subtraction facts 1–9 using *Drill #4, Worksheet 45*.

2. Drill the subtraction facts 10–18 with flash cards with the answers showing. The drill will be done only one more day with the answers showing. Provide further practice (using flash cards, make own drill sheets or, if not used before, *Worksheets 39, 41, 46, 49*, and *53*) for those who still have not mastered the subtraction facts.

3. Discuss the meaning of odd numbers (all whole numbers that are not even) with the student(s). Odd numbers begin with 1 and add 2 each time to get the next number (3). All odd numbers end in 1, 3, 5, 7, or 9. All counting numbers are either even or odd numbers. Using the number chart, count the odd numbers beginning at one. Show the student(s) how they can use the number chart (if they need it) to help them do **Student Activity One**.

4. Using flash cards, review the three new shapes. Discuss the different characteristics of each: oval – sides are curved, diamond – 4 sides the same length, octagon – 8 sides the same length. Discuss how a diamond is different than a square (square has equal angles) and how an oval is different than a circle (oval is not everywhere the same distance from the center). The student(s) should have no difficulty finishing **Student Activity Two** by themselves.

5. Remind the student(s) to write the subtraction fact and label their answer as they complete **Student Activity Three** independently.

6. Draw several lines on the chalk board. Have the student(s) come to the chalk board and measure the lines with their centimeter ruler. Remind them to put the zero on their ruler at the beginning of the line. As the student(s) do **Student Activity Four**, check to see that they are placing the zero at the beginning of the line.

7. Using the number chart for 100–199, point out several numbers. Have the student(s) name the number that comes after the given number. The student(s) should be able to complete **Student Activity Five** on their own.

8. The student(s) should be able to complete **Student Activity Six** without any help.

Worksheets:

1. *Worksheet 47* – Word problems (add and subtract)

2. *Worksheet 45* – Addition and subtraction drill sheet

SEQUENCE OF EVENTS

Concepts:
Sequences of events, after by ones (numbers over 100), centimeters, shapes (oval, diamond, and octagon), odd numbers, and counting by nines

Objectives:
1. The student shall be able to identify the event that comes first and last in a sequence of pictures by circling the correct number for the picture.

2. The student shall be able to correctly write the number that comes after a given number over 100.

3. The student shall be able to correctly draw a line of a given length using a centimeter ruler.

4. The student shall be able to correctly circle an object that is the same shape as the given shape.

5. The student shall be able to correctly color the squares that contain odd numbers.

Teaching Tips:
1. When doing activity 5, tell the student(s) about some early methods used in measurement. To know how large to make a jacket of skins, a mother would use her hands to see how many lengths of her hand it would take to go around the chest and down the back. Then she would measure the same number of hands on the flat skins. The height of horses is still measured in this way today. Other units of measure that were used were the length of the forearm, length of the foot, or the thickness of the finger. The unit of measure of a foot is still used today.

Materials, Supplies, & Equipment:
1. Number chart 0–99 and 100–199

2. Flash cards for subtraction facts 10–18 and shapes (oval, diamond, and octagon)

3. Centimeter ruler

Activities:

1. Count out loud by nines to 99 using the number chart.

2. Drill the subtraction facts 10–18 with flash cards with the answers showing. This is the last day for the answers to be showing on the subtraction drill. There will be four weeks of drill without the answers showing and then the drill sheets given on the worksheets will be used.

3. To aid in the teaching of the sequence of events, ask the student(s) which is the correct sequence. Do they get dressed and then get out of bed or do they get out of bed and then get dressed? Do they put their shirt on and then their coat or do they put their coat on and then their shirt? Do they drink their milk and then pour it or do they pour their milk and then drink it? Have the student(s) look at **Student Activity One**. Ask them to point to the picture that comes first and circle its number. Then have them point to the picture that comes last and circle its number. Now let them tell you the sequence that the three pictures should be in.

4. Using a number chart 100–199, the student(s) should be able to complete **Student Activity Two** on their own.

5. When the student(s) begin to draw the line in **Student Activity Three**, remind them to place the zero on their centimeter ruler at the dot. Show them how they need to hold their ruler (fingers of their free hand spread along the length of the ruler) so that it will not move while they are drawing the lines.

6. Review the oval, diamond, and octagon with the flash cards. After the student(s) circle the object in **Student Activity Four**, discuss with them why the other objects could not be circled.

7. See if the student(s) can tell you what an odd number is. Let them give you examples of an odd number. Ask what digits odd numbers always end with. Read the directions for **Student Activity Five** and help them get started with 1, 3, 5, etc. Have the number chart available for them to use if needed.

In labor there is profit, but idle talk tends to make one poor.

PLACE VALUE – ONE HUNDREDS

Concepts:

Place value (one hundreds), before by ones (number over 100), sequence of events, even numbers, and counting by nines

Objectives:

1. The student shall be able to write the correct value of the digit in the hundreds' place, tens' place, and ones' place for a given number.

2. The student shall be able to write the correct number when given the value of the digit in the hundreds', tens', and ones' place.

3. The student shall be able to correctly write the number that comes before a given number over 100.

4. The student shall be able to correctly identify the event that comes first and last in a sequence of pictures by circling the correct number for the picture.

5. The student shall be able to correctly write the missing even numbers from 130–176.

Teaching Tips:

1. When doing activity 7, the student(s) would find the history of even and odd numbers interesting. In early history when people first began to think about numbers, they discovered that some numbers could be divided into two equal parts and some numbers could not be divided into two equal parts. The numbers that could be divided into two equal parts were called "even" because they had the same or even number in each part. The numbers that could not be divided into two equal parts were called "odd" numbers because they had a different or "odd" number in each part.

Materials, Supplies, & Equipment:

1. Number chart 0–99 and 100–199

2. Flash cards for subtraction facts 10–18

3. *Place value materials*

Activities:

1. Count out loud by nines to 99 using the number chart.

2. Drill addition facts 1–18 using *Drill #1, Worksheet 48.*

3. Drill the subtraction facts 10–18 with flash cards *without* the answers showing.

4. Write several three digit numbers on the chalk board. Discuss with the student(s) what digit is in the hundreds', tens', and ones' place and the value of each digit (you may find *place value materials* valuable here). Write the values on the board in expanded notation (example: 295 = 200 + 90 + 5). Now write several expanded notations (400 + 60 + 5) on the chalk board and have the student(s) tell you what number they represent. The student(s) should be able to complete **Student Activity One** on their own.

5. Using the number chart 100–199, point to several numbers and ask the student(s) to tell you the number that comes before. Discuss with them that "before" means "take away" and "after" means "to add to." As the student(s) complete **Student Activity Two,** check their work for clear understanding of the concept.

6. Give the student(s) several sequences of events to put in correct order. Example: Getting ready for school and taking a test or taking a test and getting ready for school, the batter hitting the ball and the pitcher pitching the ball or the pitcher pitching the ball and the batter hitting the ball, the family eating dinner and washing the dinner dishes or washing the dinner dishes and the family eating dinner, etc. Have the student(s) discuss what is happening in the first three pictures of **Student Activity Three**. Let the student(s) read the questions and answer them. Allow them to answer the questions for the next three pictures by themselves. Then discuss the correct sequence for the three pictures.

7. Make the number chart 100–199 available to those student(s) who need it as they do **Student Activity Four** independently.

Worksheets:

1. *Worksheet 48* – Addition and subtraction drill sheet

MEASUREMENT – LIQUID

Concepts:

Ounce, cup, pint, quart, gallon, place value (one hundreds), before by ones (numbers over 100), even and odd numbers, sequence of events, subtraction, and counting to 200

Objectives:

1. The student shall be able to point to the ounce, cup, pint, quart, and gallon as they are called out by the teacher.

2. The student shall be able to correctly write the value of each digit in a three digit number as a sum.

3. The student shall be able to correctly write the number that comes before a given number over 100.

4. The student shall be able to correctly circle the word "even" or "odd" corresponding to a given number.

5. The student shall be able to correctly identify the event that comes first and last in a sequence of pictures by circling the correct number for the picture.

Teaching Tips:

1. In activity 5, it is not necessary for you to use the phrase "expanded notation" with the student(s). They will be introduced to the phrase and its meaning at a later grade but they can understand the concept as it is used in expressing the value of each digit in a given number.

2. When doing activity 8, allow the student(s) to make up a sequence of three events to share. Discuss what event happened first, last, and the correct order of the events.

Materials, Supplies, & Equipment:

1. Number chart 100–199

2. Flash cards for subtraction facts 10–18 and liquid measure

3. Liquid measure containers (one ounce container, one cup measuring cup, glass pint jar, glass quart jar, and one gallon milk jug)

Activities:

1. Count out loud from 100–200 using the number chart.

2. Drill subtraction facts 1–9 using *Drill #2, Worksheet 48*.

3. Drill the subtraction facts 10–18 with flash cards *without* the answers showing.

4. Display an ounce (medicine) container, a one cup glass measuring cup, pint and quart glass jars, and a gallon milk jug for the student(s) to examine. Explain that they are used to measure a given amount of liquid. Ask which of the five they are most familiar with, which is the largest, and which is the smallest. Using flash cards for each unit of measure, have the student(s) tell you which container goes with which name. Spend several minutes with the student(s) learning to name each container correctly. As you call out the name of the different containers, have the student(s) point to the correct container in *Student Activity One*.

5. Write several three digit numbers on the chalk board. Have the student(s) tell you the value of each digit as you write it on the chalk board in expanded notation form (600 + 30 + 2). The student(s) should be able to complete *Student Activity Two* by themselves.

6. With the help of the number chart 100–199, the student(s) should be able to complete *Student Activity Three* independently.

7. After going over the meaning of even and odd numbers, the student(s) should be able to complete *Student Activity Four* on their own.

8. Discuss each of the pictures in *Student Activity Five* concerning the order in which they should occur. Allow the student(s) to answer the questions by themselves.

9. The student(s) should be able to complete *Student Activity Six* with no help.

Worksheets:

1. *Worksheet 48* – Addition and subtraction drill sheets

NUMBER SEQUENCE

Concepts:

Number sequence, liquid measure, = and ≠, tally marks, pennies, sequence of events, before by ones (numbers over 100), and counting to 200

Definition: A number sequence is a list of numbers following a set pattern.

Objectives:

1. The student shall be able to correctly circle every third number in a sequence of numbers from two to twenty-eight and write the circled numbers in correct sequence.

2. The student shall be able to correctly draw a line to match the unit of measure for liquids to its name.

3. The student shall be able to write the correct symbol (= or ≠) between a number and tally marks.

4. The student shall be able to correctly circle the pennies that appear in a set of coins.

5. The student shall be able to correctly identify the event that comes first and last in a sequence of pictures by circling the correct number for the picture.

6. The student shall be able to correctly write the number that comes before a given number over 100.

Teaching Tips:

1. When doing activity 5, take the five flash cards for liquid measure and mix them up so that they are not according to size. Set one of them on the chalk board rail. Show them the second one and ask them to tell you where to place it so that they will be arranged from smallest to largest. Continue until all cards are placed on the rail and they are in order smallest to largest.

Materials, Supplies, & Equipment:

1. Number chart 0–99 and 100–199

2. Flash cards for subtraction facts 10–18 and liquid measure

3. Liquid measure containers

4. *Play money*

Activities:

1. Count out loud from 100–200 using the number chart.
2. Drill addition facts 1–18 using *Drill #3, Worksheet 48*.

3. Drill the subtraction facts 10–18 with flash cards **without** the answers showing. The student(s) need to do *Worksheet 49* for practice in subtraction.

4. Discuss with the student(s) how counting by threes, fours, fives, etc. gives them a number sequence (numbers listed in a set pattern). Show them how they can create their own number sequence by starting at a number other than zero. Example: Beginning with the number three, point to every fourth number by counting over four each time on the number chart and write it on the chalk board. Do several other number sequences in the same manner. Read the directions for **Student Activity One**. Work together in circling the first two numbers by counting over three each time. Then let the student(s) continue circling the remaining numbers. Have the student(s) point to the first circled number (2) and write it below in the first blank, the second number (5) in the second blank, etc.

5. Display the ounce, cup, pint, quart, and gallon containers. Ask the student(s) to guess at the number of cups in a pint, pints in a quart, and quarts in a gallon from observation of their comparative size. Do not tell them the correct answer at this time. Tell them that they will see an actual demonstration of quantities in the next lesson. Practice the names of each container using the flash cards. Have a student read the directions for **Student Activity Two**. Read each of the names and have the student(s) draw a line to the corresponding container.

6. The student(s) should be able to complete **Student Activity Three**, **Four**, and **Six** independently.

7. Discuss what is happening in the three pictures in **Student Activity Five**. Allow the student(s) to circle the picture number in answer to the questions by themselves.

Worksheets:

1. *Worksheet 49* – Subtraction 10–18 with number line

2. *Worksheet 48* – Addition and subtraction drill sheet

ESTIMATION

Concepts:
Estimation, number sequence, word problems, liquid measure, dimes, = and ≠, addition, subtraction, and counting to 200

Definition: An estimation is an approximate answer.

Objectives:
1. The student shall be able to correctly write the number (0 or 10) indicating which is closer to a given number.

2. The student shall be able to correctly write the next three numbers in a number sequence when starting with a number other than one and using every third number.

3. The student shall be able to correctly write the names of the units of measure for liquids.

4. The student shall be able to correctly circle the dimes that appear in a set of coins.

5. The student shall be able to write the correct symbol (= or ≠) between an addition fact and a number.

Teaching Tips:
1. Before doing **Student Activity Five**, have the student(s) put a mixture of coins (*play money*) on their desk and select the dimes from the set. Ask the student(s) to count the dimes and write their value in cents on a piece of paper. Check that they make the cent sign (¢) correctly.

Materials, Supplies, & Equipment:
1. Number chart 0–99 and 100–199

2. Flash cards for subtraction facts 10–18 and liquid measure

3. Number line

4. Liquid measure containers

5. *Play money*

Activities:

1. Count out loud from 100–200 using the number chart.

2. Drill subtraction facts 1–9 using *Drill #4, Worksheet 48*.

3. Drill the subtraction facts 10–18 with flash cards **without** the answers showing.

4. Point to several numbers between 0 and 10 on the number line. Ask the student(s) to tell you if the number is closer to 0 or to 10. Do not use 5, it will be taught later. If the student(s) ask about 5, tell them that because it is in the middle you cannot tell if it is closer to 0 or 10. Do all of **Student Activity One** together.

5. Tell the student(s) they are going to create a number sequence beginning with the number 4. Write the number "4" on the chalk board. On the number chart have the student(s) count over to the third number from 4 and you write "7" on the chalk board. Count over three more and write "10" on the chalk board. Now put three blanks after the 10 and ask if they can tell you how to find the next three numbers. Fill in the blanks as they give the correct responses. Try another sequence beginning at 12 and counting over three. Work with the student(s) in creating the first sequence in **Student Activity Two** and allow them to complete the second one by themselves if possible. The student(s) may use *Worksheet 5* as an aid.

6. The student(s) should require no help on **Student Activity Three**.

7. Discuss with the student(s) the units of measure used for liquids by pointing to each container and having them name it. Fill a large (at least a gallon) container with water. Ask the student(s) to estimate or guess how many ounces in a cup. Then pour enough ounces of water into the cup to fill it. It is not the intent of this lesson for them to memorize 8 oz. = 1 cup but to become familiar with the fact that there is a relationship between the two units of measure. Do the same for cups and pints, pints and quarts, and quarts and gallons. Display the liquid measure flash cards on the chalk board rail to aid the student(s) in completing **Student Activity Four**.

8. The student(s) should be able to complete **Student Activity Five**, **Six**, **Seven**, and **Eight** independently.

Worksheets:

1. *Worksheet 48* – Addition and subtraction drill sheet

2. *Worksheet 5* – Number chart

ADDITION – TWO TRIPLE DIGIT NUMBERS

Concepts:
>   Adding two triple-digit numbers, word numbers (over 100), time, nickels, estimation, and number sequence

Objectives:
1. The student shall be able to write the correct answer to a triple-digit addition problem.

2. The student shall be able to write the correct number that corresponds to the equivalent word number.

3. The student shall be able to write the correct time displayed on the face of a clock for the hour, half hour, and quarter hour.

4. The student shall be able to correctly circle the nickels that appear in a set of coins.

5. The student shall be able to correctly circle an object that is an approximate given height.

6. The student shall be able to correctly circle every fourth number in a sequence of numbers and then write the circled numbers in correct sequence.

Teaching Tips:
1. If the triple-digit numbers in ***Student Activity One*** are difficult for some of the student(s) to understand, tell them to cover the tens and hundreds while they add the ones, then cover the ones and hundreds while they add the tens, and finally cover the ones and tens while they add the hundreds.

Materials, Supplies, & Equipment:
1. Flash cards for subtraction facts 10–18 and word numbers

2. *Place value materials*

Activities:

1. Administer *Test 10.*

2. Drill the subtraction facts 10–18 with flash cards *without* the answers showing.

3. Write several addition problems consisting of two triple-digit numbers on the chalk board. Discuss with the student(s) the place value of each of the three digits (you may want to use *place value materials*). Remind them that when they add, they must always add the ones' column first, then the tens' column, and then the hundreds' column. The student(s) should be able to complete *Student Activity One* independently with you checking to see that they add the ones' column first.

4. Write a triple-digit number under 200 on the chalk board. Have the student(s) choose the word number flash cards they would need to represent that number. Do not forget the hyphen (you may want to use the minus sign). After the student(s) have done several numbers, they should be able to complete *Student Activity Two* by themselves.

5. The student(s) should be able to complete *Student Activity Three* and *Four* on their own.

6. Discuss with the student(s) the meaning of the word "estimation" (an approximate answer). When they look at *Student Activity Five*, tell them to visualize how tall each of the objects would be in real life. Show them how tall ten inches is on a ruler. Then have them point to the one that they think would be about 10 inches tall and circle it.

7. In *Student Activity Six*, have the student(s) count to the fourth number after three and circle it (7). Then have them to count to the fourth number after 7, circle it (11). Using the same procedure, continue to help those who need it until they are finished writing the circled numbers as a sequence below.

A wise man judges himself more harshly than he judges others.

BAR GRAPH

Concepts:

Bar graph, word numbers (over 100), number sequence, estimation, time, quarters, months of the year, and "Thirty Days Hath September"

Objectives:

1. The student shall be able to write the correct number of objects represented on a bar graph.

2. The student shall be able to write the correct numeral corresponding to the given word number.

3. The student shall be able to correctly write the next three numbers that come after a given sequence of numbers.

4. The student shall be able to circle the correct number that estimates how many objects are present.

5. The student shall be able to write the correct time shown on the face of a clock for the quarter hour.

6. The student shall be able to correctly circle the quarters that appear in a given set of coins.

Teaching Tips:

1. When doing activity 7, take a pint or quart glass jar and put jelly beans in it. Have the student(s) look at the jar and estimate how many jelly beans are in the jar keeping their answer to themselves. On a sheet of paper have the student(s) write their name and estimation of the number of beans in the jar. Collect the sheets of paper and reward the student with the best estimation by giving him the jelly beans.

Materials, Supplies, & Equipment:

1. Flash cards for subtraction facts 10–18 and months of the year

2. Calendar

3. Number charts 0–99

4. *Glass jar of jelly beans*

Activities:

1. Drill addition facts 1–18 using *Drill #1, Worksheet 50.*

2. Drill the subtraction facts 10–18 with flash cards without the answers showing. This will be the last week that the number line will appear with the subtraction facts. Check for student(s) who are still having difficulty. Make provision for further practice for them.

3. Using flash cards with the student(s), recite the months of the year in the correct order. See how many of the student(s) are able to recite them by themselves. Using a calendar, discuss with the student(s) what day of the week it is and what the date is. Ask what the date will be one week from today, how many days until a week from Monday, and how many Fridays in the month. Recite "Thirty Days Hath September."

4. Remind the student(s) that the bar graph tells them how many various items there are. Look at the bar graph in **Student Activity One**. Read the questions together but allow the student(s) to write the answers individually on their paper.

5. The student(s) should be able to do **Student Activity Two** independently.

6. Write several sets of three odd numbers in sequence on the chalk board. Have the student(s) give the next three numbers in the sequence. They may use the number chart 0–99, if necessary. In **Student Activity Three** do the first sequence together but allow them to finish on their own.

7. Ask the student(s) several questions involving estimation. Example: "About" how many crayons are in your desk? "About" how many books are in your desk? "About" how many pages are in your reading book? Be sure to point out that an estimation is not exact but "about" or close to being exact. When the student(s) do **Student Activity Four**, discuss with them why the two answers that are not correct would not be a good estimation.

8. The student(s) should be able to complete **Student Activity Five** and **Six** without any help.

Worksheets:

1. *Worksheet 50* – Addition and subtraction drill sheet

WORD PROBLEMS – SUBTRACTION

Concepts:
Word problems, number sequence, estimation, greater than, time, bar graph, addition, and subtraction

Objectives:
1. The student shall be able to circle every sixth number in a sequence of numbers and write the circled numbers on the blanks.

2. The student shall be able to write the two corresponding subtraction facts for each given addition fact.

3. The student shall be able to circle the object that is an approximate given length.

4. The student shall be able to circle the numbers that are greater than 150 in a set of given numbers.

5. The student shall be able to write the correct time shown on the face of the clock for the hour, half hour, and quarter hour.

6. The student shall be able to color a block for each given object to be represented on a bar graph.

Teaching Tips:
1. Before doing **Student Activity Four,** see "about" how long the student(s) think 3 inches, 8 inches, 14 inches, etc. is by holding their hands apart the given length. Measure with the *inch ruler* so they can see how close their estimation is.

2. You may save part of this lesson to go with the next lesson if necessary.

Materials, Supplies, & Equipment:
1. Flash cards for subtraction facts 10–18

2. Counting chips

3. Yardstick

4. Number chart 100–199

5. *Inch ruler*

Activities:

1. Drill subtraction facts 1–9 using *Drill #2, Worksheet 50*.

2. Drill the subtraction facts 10–18 with flash cards without the answers showing.

3. Have the student(s) read the first word problem in *Student Activity One* together. Give each student 8 counting chips to divide into a set of 5 and a set of 3. Tell the student(s) to match the two sets in a one to one correspondence. How many more are there in the set of 5 than in the set of 3 (2)? Point out that the key phrase is "how many more . . . than" and indicates that you are to compare or find the difference which means to subtract. Read the second word problem to the student(s) and ask them if they add or subtract and why (the problem asks how many more . . . than). Tell them to read the third word problem and finish it on their own. The label is the object that comes after the words "how many more." Check that the subtraction fact and its label are correct.

4. In *Student Activity Two* have the student(s) count to the sixth number after three, circle it (9), count to the sixth number after 9, circle it (15), and write the circled numbers in sequence. Using the same procedure, continue to help those who need it until they are finished.

5. Write "2 + 5 = 7" on the chalk board. Ask the student(s) to tell you the two corresponding subtraction facts that go with the addition fact. Follow the same procedure with "6 + 8 = 14." The student(s) should be able to complete *Student Activity Three* on their own.

6. Look at *Student Activity Four* as you discuss the meaning of estimation with the student(s). Have them tell you "about" how long they would think the length of each of the objects would be in real life. Using a yardstick show them how long 30 inches is. Have them point to the object that is "about" 30 inches long in real life and circle the object.

7. Allow the student(s) to complete *Student Activity Five*, *Six*, *Seven*, *Eight*, and *Nine* independently. The number chart 100–199 may be a help to some student(s) in *Student Activity Five*.

Worksheets:

1. *Worksheet 51* – Corresponding subtraction facts for addition fact

2. *Worksheet 50* – Addition and subtraction drill sheet

MONEY

Concepts:

Money, less than, word problems, bar graph, time, months of the year, and "Thirty Days Hath September"

Objectives:

1. The student shall be able to draw a line from a given coin to its value.

2. The student shall be able to circle the numbers that are less than 150 in a set of given numbers.

3. The student shall be able to write the number of given objects represented on a bar graph.

4. The student shall be able to write the two corresponding subtraction facts for each given addition fact.

5. The student shall be able to write the time shown on the face of a clock for the hour, half hour, and quarter hour.

Teaching Tips:

1. In activity 4, have the student(s) try to describe the different coins both front and back without seeing them.

2. If a student is having difficulty in gaining understanding in **Student Activity Three**, it may be necessary to use *counting chips* to visually demonstrate what the word problem is describing. Have the student(s) put 4 chips and 7 chips into one to one correspondence and see how many more seven has than four has.

Materials, Supplies, & Equipment:

1. Flash cards for subtraction facts 10–18

2. Play money

3. Number chart 100–199

4. *Counting chips*

Activities:

1. Drill addition facts 1–18 using *Drill #3, Worksheet 50*.

2. Drill the subtraction facts 10–18 with flash cards without the answers showing.

3. Recite with the student(s) the months of the year and "Thirty Days Hath September." Reward those who have mastered the months of the year and the poem.

4. Using play money have the student(s) identify each piece of money (front and back) they have studied and tell its value. They should be able to complete **Student Activity One** by themselves.

5. With the help of a number chart 100–199, the student(s) should be able to complete **Student Activity Two** without assistance.

6. Have the student(s) read the word problem in **Student Activity Three**. Ask them to give you the key phrase (how many more . . . than) in the problem and if they should add or subtract. Notice that the answer blanks provide the minus sign. Allow them to write the subtraction fact and label the answer on their own.

7. The student(s) should be able to complete **Student Activity Four** with you helping only those who need individual assistance.

8. Write "5," "6," and "11" on the chalk board. Ask the student(s) to tell you an addition fact using the three numbers. Now have them tell you two subtraction facts using the three numbers and write the facts below the addition fact. Remind them that each addition fact has two corresponding subtraction facts. The student(s) should be able to complete **Student Activity Five** with little help.

9. **Student Activity Six** should be completed independently by the student(s).

Worksheets:

1. *Worksheet 50* – Addition and subtraction drill sheet

DOZEN

Concepts:
Dozen, money, shapes, addition, and days of the week
Definition: A dozen is a set of twelve.

Objectives:
1. The student shall be able to color the correct number of objects needed to represent a dozen.

2. The student shall be able to write the correct value of a given set of coins.

3. The student shall be able to write the two corresponding subtraction facts for each given addition fact.

4. The student shall be able to draw a line to match a given shape to its name.

5. The student shall be able to write the correct answer to a three digit addition problem.

Teaching Tips:
1. When doing activity 7, discuss how a diamond and square are like and different, how a circle and oval are alike and different, and how a square and rectangle are alike and different.

Materials, Supplies, & Equipment:
1. Flash cards for subtraction facts 10–18, days of the week, addition, and shapes

2. Egg carton

3. Play money

Activities:

1. Drill subtraction facts 1–9 using *Drill #4, Worksheet 50*.

2. Drill the subtraction facts 10–18 with flash cards without the answers showing. The next lesson will be the last one with the number line showing with the subtraction problems. Flash cards should be used for two more weeks. After that, drill may be done with drill sheets on the worksheets, with flash cards, or both.

3. Recite with the student(s) the days of the week in the correct order using flash cards. Discuss with them how many days until and since the 25th, 16th, and 2nd. Equate this with "before" and "after."

4. Discuss with the student(s) the meaning of the word "dozen." Ask them what they can purchase by the dozen in the grocery store. Have them count the number of pockets in an egg carton. The student(s) should be able to do **Student Activity One** by themselves.

5. Give each student several pennies, dimes, nickels, and quarters in play money. Ask them to make up a set of 5 dimes and 3 pennies. Have them tell you the value of the money by counting the dimes by tens and the pennies by ones. Do the same with 4 nickels and 6 pennies, 2 quarters and 7 pennies. Allow the student(s) to complete **Student Activity Two** independently.

6. Hold up three addition fact flash cards. Have the student(s) copy the facts on a sheet of paper and write the two corresponding subtraction facts for each addition fact. Let the student(s) check their work by you writing the subtraction facts on the chalk board or by saying them for the student(s). **Student Activity Three** should be completed by the student(s) on their own.

7. Using the flash cards for the seven shapes, have each student name all seven as quickly as possible. The student(s) will need little help in completing **Student Activity Four**.

8. The student(s) should not require any assistance in doing **Student Activity Five**.

Worksheets:

1. *Worksheet 52* – Color sheet with < and >

2. *Worksheet 50* – Addition and subtraction drill sheet

NUMBER ORDER – BEFORE AND AFTER OVER 100

Concepts:

The number over 100 that comes before and after by ones, shapes, addition, centimeters, days of the week, dozen, and counting by fours

Objectives:

1. The student shall be able to write the correct number that comes before and after a given number over 100.

2. The student shall be able to write the correct name of a given shape.

3. The student shall be able to correctly write the answer to a three digit addition problem.

4. The student shall be able to write the correct measurement of the length of a given object.

5. The student shall be able to write the days of the week in the correct order.

6. The student shall be able to correctly draw a given object a dozen times.

Teaching Tips:

1. For activity 4, cut the seven shapes in different colors and sizes from *construction paper*. Give the student(s) a *white sheet of paper* and enough shapes for them to create their own picture. This activity could be combined with art class at another time during the day.

Materials, Supplies, & Equipment:

1. Number chart 0–99 and 100–199

2. Flash cards for subtraction facts 10–18, shapes, and days of the week

3. Centimeter ruler

4. Crayons

5. *Construction paper and white paper*

Activities:

1. Count out loud by fours to 100 using the number chart.

2. Drill the subtraction facts 10–18 with flash cards without the answers showing. The number line will no longer appear with the subtraction problems in the following lessons. *Worksheet 53* should be done as a part of this lesson. *Worksheets 39, 41, 46,* and *49* should be used for those student(s) who need further practice.

3. Discuss the terms before and after as they relate to addition and subtraction. Point to several numbers on the number chart 100–199 and have the student(s) tell you the number that comes before and the number that comes after each. The student(s) may need the aid of the number chart as they begin ***Student Activity One***.

4. Using the shape flash cards with the name showing, have the student(s) say the name and then describe what each of the shapes look like. They should be able to do ***Student Activity Two*** by themselves.

5. Remind the student(s) to begin with the ones column when they add the problems in ***Student Activity Three***.

6. Have the student(s) take their centimeter ruler and begin to measure the objects in ***Student Activity Four***. Remind them to put the zero on their ruler at the vertical dotted line as their beginning point for each object.

7. Recite the days of the week in order. Place the flash cards for the days of the week on the chalk board rail out of order. Have the student(s) choose the card that is the first day of the week and place it first, then the second, then third, etc. thus arranging them in the correct order. The student(s) should be able to complete ***Student Activity Five*** independently.

8. Ask the student(s) how many it takes to make a dozen objects. Have them count a dozen crayons. They should be able to complete ***Student Activity Six*** on their own.

Worksheets:

1. *Worksheet 53* – Subtraction 10–18 with number line

2. *Worksheets 39, 41, 46,* and *49* – Subtraction 10–18 with number line

SUBTRACTION – WITHOUT NUMBER LINE

Concepts:

Subtraction without the number line, shapes, centimeters, addition, before and after over 100, and counting by fours

Objectives:

1. The student shall be able to write the correct answer to a subtraction problem without the aid of the number line.

2. The student shall be able to correctly trace the outline of a given shape.

3. The student shall be able to write the correct length of a line measured with a centimeter ruler.

4. The student shall be able to write the correct number that comes before and after a given number over 100.

Teaching Tips:

1. Have the student(s) who still do not have their subtraction facts memorized continue to use the *number line*. They could make a number line to tape (or use contact paper) on the top of their desk if they have not done so already. Their centimeter ruler is also a good substitute for the number line. A real effort should be made by the student(s) to not rely on the number line much longer.

2. If a student finds **Student Activity Two** difficult, a ruler may be used to draw the lines for the shapes except for the circle and oval.

Materials, Supplies, & Equipment:

1. Number chart

2. Flash cards for subtraction facts 10–18 and shapes

3. Centimeter ruler

4. *Number line*

5. *Construction paper*

Activities:

1. Count out loud by fours to 100 using the number chart.

2. Drill addition facts 1–18 using *Drill #1, Worksheet 54.*

3. Drill the subtraction facts 10–18 with flash cards without the answers showing.

4. There is no number line given for use with the subtraction problems in this lesson. Be sure that the student(s) who have not mastered the subtraction facts are following your suggestions for further practice. The student(s) should do **Student Activity One** with no help.

5. Show each of the shape flash cards with the name showing to the student(s). Have them pronounce the name and then describe the shape. Turn the shape over to see if their description is correct. Put three dots on the chalk board and tell the student(s) to put three dots on their paper. As you draw each line of the triangle by connecting the three dots, have the student(s) make the same line on their paper. Do the same for the other six shapes in **Student Activity Two**. The student(s) should then complete **Student Activity Two** by tracing the outline of the given shapes.

6. As the student(s) begin **Student Activity Three**, remind them to place the zero on their centimeter ruler at the beginning of the line.

7. **Student Activity Four** and **Five** should be completed by the student(s) independently.

Worksheets:

1. *Worksheet 54* – Addition and subtraction drill sheet

Difficulties strengthen the mind as labor does the body.

ODD NUMBERS

Concepts:
   Odd numbers, sequence of events, before and after by ones (numbers over 100), place value (one hundreds), centimeters, subtraction, and counting by eights

Objectives:
1. The student shall be able to draw lines that connect consecutive odd numbers to form a picture.

2. The student shall be able to number a series of pictures in correct sequential order.

3. The student shall be able to write the correct number that comes before and after a given number over 100.

4. The student shall be able to write the correct value of each digit in a three digit number.

5. The student shall be able to draw a line of a given length using a centimeter ruler.

6. The student shall be able to write the correct answer to a subtraction problem without the use of the number line.

Teaching Tips:
1. For enrichment take the numbers given in **Student Activity Four** and equate them to dollars for hundreds' place, dimes for tens' place and pennies for ones' place. Ask how many dimes in 156¢ (5), how many dollars (1), and how many pennies (6). Follow the same procedure for the remaining numbers.

Materials, Supplies, & Equipment:
1. Number chart 0–99 and 100–199

2. Flash cards for subtraction facts 10–18

3. *Place value materials*

4. Centimeter ruler

Activities:

1. Count out loud by eights to 96 using the number chart.

2. Drill subtraction facts 1–9 using *Drill #2, Worksheet 54.*

3. Drill the subtraction facts 10–18 with flash cards without the answers showing.

4. Discuss with the student(s) the meaning of odd numbers. Say several numbers and have them tell you if they are odd numbers. Have the student(s) find the "1" on the dot-to-dot in **Student Activity One**. Tell them to connect the consecutive odd numbers to complete the picture.

5. Give the student(s) several events and ask them to tell you in what order they happen. Example: baking a cake and eating a cake, coloring the picture and drawing the picture, etc. Discuss the three pictures in **Student Activity Two**. When the student(s) have determined what happened first, have them put a "1" under the picture. Place a "2" under the picture that happened second, and a "3" under the picture that happened last.

6. The student(s) should be able to complete **Student Activity Three** by themselves. Do have a number chart 100–199 available for them to refer to if necessary.

7. Write several three digit numbers on the chalk board (or use *place value materials*). Point to a number and ask the student(s) to tell you what digit is in the tens', ones', and hundreds' place and its value. On the next number give them the digit and have them tell you if it is in the ones', tens', or hundreds' place and its value. Use both methods of questioning for the remaining three digit numbers. The student(s) should be able to complete **Student Activity Four** on their own.

8. Have the student(s) take their centimeter ruler and look at **Student Activity Five**. Placing the zero on their ruler at the point, let them draw the lines the given lengths.

9. **Student Activity Six** should be completed by the student(s) independently.

Worksheets:

1. *Worksheet 54* – Addition and subtraction drill sheet

SOLIDS

Concepts:
    Solids (cube, sphere, cylinder, and cone), word problems, place value (one hundreds), sequence of events, odd numbers, and counting by eights

Objectives:
1. The student shall be able to correctly identify a cube, sphere, cylinder, and cone by coloring each object with the correct color.

2. The student shall be able to write the correct number when given the value of the digit in the hundreds', tens', and ones' place as a sum.

3. The student shall be able to number a series of pictures in correct sequential order.

4. The student shall be able to correctly write the missing odd numbers when counting from 101 to 135.

Teaching Tips:
1. Show the student(s) *models of the four solids* discussed in activity 4. If you do not have wooden or plastic models, you could use a ball for the sphere; a can of vegetables for the cylinder; a block or box for the cube; and a pointed hat, paper drinking cup, or an ice cream cone for the cone. Let the student(s) handle the solids.

2. For enrichment take the sums in **Student Activity Three** and equate the 600 to 600¢, the 50 to 50¢, and the 4 to 4¢. Ask the student(s) how many dollars in 600¢, how many dimes in 50¢, and how many pennies in 4¢. As 600 + 50 + 4 = 654 so does 600¢ + 50¢ + 4¢ = $6.54.

Materials, Supplies, & Equipment:
1. Number chart

2. Flash cards for subtraction facts 10–18 and solids

3. *Solid models*

Activities:

1. Count out loud by eights to 96 using the number chart.

2. Drill addition facts 1–18 using *Drill #3, Worksheet 54.*

3. Drill the subtraction facts 10–18 with flash cards without the answers showing. *Worksheet 55* should be done with this lesson or the next lesson for practice in addition and subtraction.

4. Using the flash cards for solids, have the student(s) read the name of each solid and look at the picture. Then looking at the pictures, see how many of the solids they can name. Tell the student(s) to look at the pictures of the solids in **Student Activity One**. As you say the name of each, have them point to the solid on their paper. Read each sentence to the student(s) as they are ready to color each solid.

5. The student(s) should be able to do **Student Activity Two** by themselves.

6. Write the sum of the value of the digits in the hundreds', tens', and ones' place for several three digit numbers on the chalk board as is done in **Student Activity Three**. Beside each sum, make three short blanks to represent the hundreds', tens', and ones' place. Ask the student(s) to tell you what digit will go in the hundreds', tens', and ones' place for each sum. Have the student(s) read the number out loud. Do not let them use the word "and."

7. As the student(s) look at **Student Activity Four**, discuss with them the position of the sun during the day. Ask them which picture they should place a "1" under, a "2" under, and a "3" under.

8. The student(s) should be able to complete **Student Activity Five** on their own. When they have finished, ask them what kind of numbers they have written (odd).

Worksheets:

1. *Worksheet 55* – Addition and subtraction without the number line

2. *Worksheet 54* – Addition and subtraction drill sheet

SHOW YOUR SKILLS

Concepts:

Place value (one hundreds), solids, = or ≠, addition, subtraction, and counting to 200

Objectives:

1. The student shall be able to write the digit that is in the hundreds', tens', and ones' place for a given number.

2. The student shall be able to draw a line to match a given solid with its name.

3. The student shall be able to correctly write = or ≠ between a subtraction fact and a whole number.

Teaching Tips:

1. Have the student(s) look in the newspapers or magazines for pictures of the solids in activity 5. Let each student describe one picture and tell how the solid is used.

2. Also for activity 5, you might teach the student(s) how to draw a cube on their paper. Do not be too concerned over the accuracy of the student(s) drawings, but encourage them to do a careful job of following directions. First draw a square on the chalk board and have them copy it. Then make the three solid slanted lines out from the corners of the square. Next, draw the vertical and horizontal lines to connect the endpoints of the slanted lines. Now place a dot where the three dotted lines will meet. Then, use the dot as a guide to draw the remaining three dotted lines which represent the lines that would be hidden from the viewer.

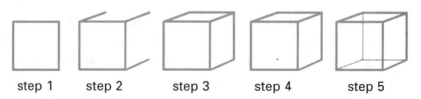

step 1   step 2   step 3   step 4   step 5

Materials, Supplies, & Equipment:

1. Number chart 100–199

2. Flash cards for subtraction facts 10–18, solids, and = and ≠

3. *Solid models*

Activities:

1. Count out loud to 200 using the number chart 100–199.

2. Drill subtraction facts 1–9 using *Drill #4, Worksheet 54.*

3. Drill the subtraction facts 10–18 with flash cards without the answers showing.

4. Write a three digit number on the chalk board. Ask the student(s) what digit is in the ten's, hundreds', and ones' place. Using several more three digit numbers, repeat the questions changing the order of the hundreds', tens', and ones' place each time. The student(s) should be able to complete **Student Activity One** by themselves after they read the first statement together.

5. Using the flash cards (or you may want to use your *models*), show the student(s) the solids, and have them name each of them. Discuss the characteristics of each solid by asking the student(s) to describe them. The student(s) should complete **Student Activity Two** on their own.

6. Using flash cards, quickly review the = and ≠ symbols and their meaning. **Student Activity Three** should be completed by the student(s) independently.

7. The student(s) should complete **Student Activity Four** and **Five** by themselves.

Worksheets:

1. *Worksheet 54* – Addition and subtraction drill sheet

The best training for being in authority is to be under authority.

WORD NUMBERS 100–199

Concepts:
> Word numbers 100–199, = and ≠, solids, word problems, addition, subtraction, and counting to 200

Objectives:
1. The student shall be able to write the symbols = or ≠ correctly between a word number and a whole number to form a true statement.

2. The student shall be able to write the correct name by the model of a cube, sphere, cylinder, and cone.

Teaching Tips:
1. In **Student Activity Two**, teach the student(s) how to draw a cylinder. Begin by drawing an oval on the chalk board. Have the student(s) then draw an oval on their paper. Next draw the two vertical lines down from the ends of the oval. Now they can draw the oval at the bottom with the top half of it being a dotted line. The dotted line is used to show that the edge is at the back of the solid and there are three dimensions (length, width, and height).

2. If the student(s) have difficulty solving a subtraction word problem with no visual helps, let them use *counting chips* to demonstrate what is happening in the word problems in **Student Activity Three** and **Six**. Have them pretend that the chips are dog biscuits and dips of ice cream.

Materials, Supplies, & Equipment:
1. Number chart 100–199

2. Flash cards for subtraction facts 10–18, word numbers, and solids

3. Solid models

4. *Counting chips*

Activities:

1. Administer *Test 11*.

2. Count out loud from 100 to 200 using the number chart 100–199. Put "200" on the chalk board before beginning the exercise. Point to it as the student(s) finish counting.

3. Drill the subtraction facts 10–18 with flash cards without the answers showing.

4. Using the flash cards, go over several word numbers for 100–200. On the chalk board write a few more three digit numbers greater than 200 and have the student(s) read them. Be sure the student(s) read them correctly with no "and." The student(s) may need your help to complete each set in *Student Activity One*. Have the student(s) read the word number, write the corresponding numeral, and then compare the two numerals.

5. Discuss with the student(s) the names of each of the solids using either the flash cards or models and display all of them in a row. Point to a solid and have them name it. Then name a solid and have the student(s) tell you if it is the first, second, third, etc. one. To do *Student Activity Two*, read the word "cube," have them point to the solid and write its name on the blank. Do the same for each of the other solids.

6. Notice the blanks for the subtraction fact have been omitted in *Student Activity Three*. Let the student(s) decide if they should add or subtract. They should be able to support their choice by telling the key word and if they are joining together or taking away. Have them write the subtraction fact and label their answer.

7. The student(s) should be able to complete *Student Activity Four*, *Five*, and *Six* independently.

The adversities of life can make us bitter or better,
the choice is ours to make.

ADDITION

Concepts:
    Addition, word numbers (over 100), solids, word problems, and counting to 200

Objectives:
1. The student shall be able to write the number that corresponds to a given word number.

2. The student shall be able to draw a line to correctly match a solid with pictures that have a corresponding shape.

3. The student shall be able to determine if a word problem is addition or subtraction, write the correct fact, and label the answer.

Teaching Tips:
1. Along with activity 2, do an oral drill with the student(s) using three single-digit numbers. Example: 4 + 5 + 6 = __, 2 + 6 + 7 = __, etc. Use addition facts 1–9 for the first two numbers and any single-digit number for the last one. Since the sum of the first two numbers is nine or less, the sum of the three numbers will be 18 or less. Say the numbers out loud about 2 seconds apart and have the student(s) raise their hand as soon as they have the answer. Each time you start say the numbers just a little bit faster. The more often you drill, the faster you will be able to say the numbers and have the student(s) still able to keep up with you.

Materials, Supplies, & Equipment:
1. Number chart 100–199

2. Flash cards for subtraction facts 10–18, *word number*, and *solids*

3. Solid models

Activities:

1. Count out loud from 100 to 200 using the number chart 100–199.

2. Drill addition facts 1–18 using *Drill #1, Worksheet 56.*

3. Drill the subtraction facts 10–18 with flash cards without the answers showing. This is the last week for drilling subtraction facts 10–18 on a daily basis. After this week the drill work will be done with drills sheets on the worksheets and by flash cards. You need to use flash cards to check each student individually to see who still needs further drill. Make provisions for further drill by using flash cards and having student drill student, teacher drill student, parent drill student, or sister or brother drill student, etc.

4. ***Student Activity One*** should be completed by the student(s) on their own.

5. Put several three digit numbers on the chalk board (or you may use w*ord number flash cards*) and have the student(s) read the numbers. Then say several three digit numbers out loud to the student(s) and have them write the numbers on a sheet of paper. Have the student(s) check their answers as you write the numbers on the chalk board. The student(s) should be able to complete ***Student Activity Two*** by themselves.

6. Display the solid models for the student(s) (or use *flash cards*). Name several objects (orange, carrot, vegetable can, facial tissue box, etc.) and have the student(s) tell you which solid has the same shape as the object. Look about the room for any objects that are the same shape as one of the solids. When doing ***Student Activity Three*** explain to the student(s) that they will draw two lines to each of the shapes in the middle column – one from the right hand column and one from the left hand column.

7. As the student(s) begin ***Student Activity Four***, caution them to first determine if the word problem is addition or subtraction, write the fact, and label the answer.

Worksheets:

1. *Worksheet 56* – Addition and subtraction drill sheet

ESTIMATION

Concepts:

Estimation, solids, word numbers (over 100), addition, subtraction, and counting by sevens

Objectives:

1. The student shall be able to correctly write the number (10 or 20) indicating which is closer to a given number.

2. The student shall be able to draw a line to match a solid with its name.

3. The student shall be able to write the number that corresponds to a given word number.

Teaching Tips:

1. Teach the student(s) how to draw a cone during activity 5. First draw an oval that is about one inch left-to-right and one half inch up and down with the top half of the oval being a dotted line (or erase the top half). Put a point about two to three inches above the center of the oval. Then draw lines from this point to the left and right ends of the oval. Guide the student(s) through this by doing each step on the chalk board as they draw on paper at their desk.

2. In addition to activity 6, have the student(s) look in the *newspaper* for several places where word numbers have been used and cut them out. Using a clean sheet of paper, guide the student(s) in making their own worksheet by pasting the word numbers on the paper and then writing the corresponding numeral.

Materials, Supplies, & Equipment:

1. Number chart

2. Flash cards for subtraction facts 10–18

3. Number line

4. Solid models

5. *Newspaper*

Activities:

1. Count out loud by sevens to 98 using the number chart.

2. Drill subtraction facts 1–9 using *Drill #2, Worksheet 56.*

3. Drill the subtraction facts 10–18 with flash cards without the answers showing.

4. Using the number line, point to several numbers between 10 and 20. Ask the student(s) to tell you if the number is closer to 10 or to 20. Read the first question in **Student Activity One** with the student(s). Let the student(s) who have a grasp of the concept of estimation answer the remaining questions on their own. Give help where help is needed.

5. Have the student(s) look at the solid models from different positions. Ask the student(s) if any of them look the same from all positions. (sphere) Do any of them look the same from at least two positions? (cylinder, cube, and cone– the cone as you rotate it on it circular base) Do any of them never look the same from any two positions? (no) Have the student(s) go over the names of the solids as you point to them. The student(s) should be able to complete **Student Activity Two** by themselves.

6. Call out to the student(s) several three digit numbers with the 0 in the tens' place or with the 0 in the ones' place. Have the student(s) write the numbers that you call out on their paper. Then write the numbers on the chalk board to enable the student(s) to check their answers. Write several more three digit numbers on the chalk board and have the student(s) read the numbers to you. They should be able to complete **Student Activity Three** with no further help.

7. **Student Activity Four** and **Five** should be completed by the student(s) independently.

Worksheets:

1. *Worksheet 56*–Addition and subtraction drill sheet

BAR GRAPH

Concepts:
Bar graph, estimation, centimeters, addition, subtraction, and counting by sevens

Objectives:
1. The student shall be able to write the correct number of objects represented on a bar graph.

2. The student shall be able to circle the number that is closer to the length of a given line measured by a centimeter ruler.

Teaching Tips:
1. While doing activity 5, lead the student(s) in a discussion of how tall they are and how much they have grown in the last three months. Have the student(s) describe each student's height and growth in terms of "about" four feet or three feet (whatever is applicable) to give them practice with estimation. Some answers may be far from accurate but reinforce the idea that an estimation is not exact but an educated guess. Remind them to think about what they are saying. Encourage them to show what they are saying by holding their hand above the floor to represent the measurement of one student's height. They might talk about how much taller or shorter one student is than a brother or sister or friend. You may also discuss approximately how long ago they measured their height.

Materials, Supplies, & Equipment:
1. Number chart

2. Flash cards for subtraction facts 10–18

3. Bar graph

4. Centimeter ruler

5. Crayons

Activities:

1. Count out loud by sevens to 98 using the number chart.

2. Drill addition facts 1–18 using *Drill #3, Worksheet 56*.

3. Drill the subtraction facts 10–18 with flash cards without the answers showing.

4. Discuss with the student(s) the purpose of a bar graph (to tell how many). Display a bar graph (draw it on the chalk board or make one on poster board ahead of class) with each box of the bar to represent 10 objects as in ***Student Activity One***. Have the student(s) tell you how many objects are represented on each bar by counting the boxes that make up the bar by tens. Read each question with the student(s) in ***Student Activity One*** but allow them to determine their answer by themselves.

5. Have the student(s) take out their centimeter ruler and several used crayons. Discuss the meaning of estimation (an approximate answer or an educated guess). Tell them they are going to determine "about" how long their crayons are. Have them put the end of the crayon at the zero on their ruler. Ask them, "The other end of the crayon is between what two numbers?" Have them write the two numbers on paper. Then ask them which of the two numbers the end of the crayon is closer to. Circle that number. As you follow the same procedure for several more crayons, check the work of the student(s). Guide the student(s) through ***Student Activity Two*** in the same way that they measured their crayons.

6. ***Student Activity Three*** and ***Four*** should be completed by the student(s) on their own.

Worksheets:

1. *Worksheet 56* – Addition and subtraction drill sheet

Kind words are always welcome.

NUMBER ORDER – ORDINAL NUMBERS

Concepts:
Ordinal numbers, < and >, word problems, bar graph, centimeters, estimation, and counting by sevens

Objectives:

1. The student shall be able to correctly place a set of letters numbered ordinally on blanks corresponding to the appropriate ordinal numbers.

2. The student shall be able to write the correct symbol (< and >) between two given numbers over one hundred.

3. The student shall be able to read a word problem, determine if it is addition or subtraction, write the correct fact, and label the answer.

4. The student shall be able to color a block for each given object to be represented on a bar graph.

5. The student shall be able to circle the number that is closer to the length of a given object measured by a centimeter ruler.

Teaching Tips:

1. When the student(s) are coloring the bars for the graph in **Student Activity Four**, have them find the top box to be colored and do it first. Then color the boxes below it. This will prevent them from forgetting how high on the bar they are to color.

Materials, Supplies, & Equipment:

1. Number chart

2. Flash cards for subtraction 10–18, ordinal numbers, and < and >

3. Play money

4. Centimeter ruler

Activities:

1. Count out loud by sevens to 98 using the number chart.

2. Drill subtraction facts 1–9 using *Drill #4, Worksheet 56.*

3. Drill the subtraction facts 10–18 with flash cards without the answers showing. The next lesson will be the last time that drill will be done with flash cards for subtraction on a daily basis.

4. Place the flash cards for ordinal numbers in a mixed up order on the chalk board. Allow the student(s) to arrange them in the correct order one card at a time. To start ***Student Activity One***, ask the student(s) to read the first word (fourth) then point to the fourth blank and write the letter A on that blank. Do the same for the next two ordinal numbers. The student(s) should then be able to finish the blanks by themselves. Encourage them to check each ordinal number once they are finished in case they figured out the answer and wrote some of the letters in the blanks without counting.

5. Use the < and > flash cards to refresh the student(s) minds for reading and writing the symbols correctly. Have the student(s) read each set once they have completed ***Student Activity Two*** on their own.

6. Allow the student(s) to do ***Student Activity Three*** independently. Once they are finished, discuss the word problem, what the key words are, whether they added or subtracted, and what they used for the label.

7. Using play money, discuss the names of the coins used on the bar graph in ***Student Activity Four***. Allow the student(s) to complete the graph with you giving help to those who need it.

8. Discuss how all objects are not exactly a given number of centimeters in length. An object may be more than 6 centimeters long but less than 7 centimeters long. When this is true they need to decide if the length of the object is closer to 6 or to 7. If it is closer to 6, then they say it is "about" 6 centimeters long. This is estimating how long an object is. Using their centimeter ruler, have the student(s) measure the first object in ***Student Activity Five***. Tell them to circle the number (7 or 8) to which the end of the object is closer. Do the same steps for the next three objects.

Worksheets:

1. *Worksheet 57* – Patriotic color sheet

2. *Worksheet 56* – Addition and subtraction drill sheet

SHAPES

Concepts:
Shapes, bar graph, subtraction, and counting by sevens

Objectives:
1. The student shall be able to identify a circle, rectangle, square, triangle, diamond, oval, and octagon by coloring each a given color.

2. The student shall be able to write the two corresponding subtraction facts for each given addition fact.

3. The student shall be able to write the correct number of objects represented on a bar graph.

Teaching Tips:
1. After activity 3 or during art class, have the student(s) take out a clean sheet of paper. Tell them they are going to create a picture using shapes. You will draw the picture on the board as they draw on their paper. Put a circle for the sun in the upper right hand area with rays of light coming out from it. To make a house, use the triangle to form the roof, a rectangle for the walls, squares for the windows, a rectangle for the door, and a circle for the door knob. Make a picket fence out of a rectangle with a triangle on top of it for the fence posts and long narrow rectangles for the cross sections. Flowers (stems and leaves–rectangles, bloom–circle encircled by small diamonds) could be drawn around an oval pond. Draw triangular mountains in the background. Ask the student(s) how to use the octagon (stop sign, flower pot, dormer window, etc.).

Materials, Supplies, & Equipment:
1. Number chart

2. Flash cards for subtraction facts 10–18 and shapes

3. Counting chips

Activities:

1. Count out loud by sevens to 98 using the number chart.

2. Drill subtraction facts 10–18 with flash cards without the answers showing. This should be the last day to drill subtraction using flash cards on a daily basis. The subtraction drill will be done from now on with the drill sheets on the worksheets or with flash cards. If you feel the student(s) are not ready to leave the flash cards at this time, continue with them for a few more days. Set your own goal for the termination of the flash cards on a daily basis.

3. Review with the student(s) the names of the seven shapes using flash cards. Then show them the name of a shape and have the student(s) describe it. Discuss with the student(s) the difference between the shapes and the solids (two and three dimensional – three dimensional has thickness). The student(s) should complete **Student Activity One** with little help.

4. Write several addition facts on the board in a horizontal position. Ask the student(s) to tell you the two corresponding subtraction facts that use the same three numbers. Visualize the three facts using counting chips as done in Lesson 72 if you feel it is necessary for understanding by the student(s). Do the first set of facts in **Student Activity Two** together. Allow the student(s) to finish the remaining facts by themselves giving help where needed.

5. The student(s) should be able to complete **Student Activity Three** on their own. Use the time to correct any recurring mistake a student might be making.

6. The student(s) should complete **Student Activity Four** independently.

Most decisions made in haste cause us to repent in leisure.

NUMBER SEQUENCE

Concepts:
    Number sequence, fractions, < and >, shapes, addition, and subtraction

Objectives:
1. The student shall be able to place an "X" on the number that is incorrect in a sequence of numbers.

2. The student shall be able to write the correct fraction that shows what part of a shape has been shaded.

3. The student shall be able to write the correct symbol (< or >) between two numbers over 100.

4. The student shall be able to draw a line to match a shape to its correct name.

Teaching Tips:
1. For enrichment when doing activity 5, write several pairs of three digit numbers over 200 on the board (435 ___ 444). Have the student(s) tell you if you would place a < or > symbol between the numbers. If they are of the same hundreds' family, the student(s) can cover the hundreds' place and consider the 35___44. If 35 < 44, then 435 < 444. If the student(s) are capable, you may want to try one of different hundreds' families (378___162). If the hundreds' families are different, they need only to compare the hundreds' digit (3___1).

Materials, Supplies, & Equipment:
1. Flash cards for subtraction facts 1–18 and shapes

2. Fraction materials

3. Flannel board

4. Number chart 100–199

Activities:

1. Drill addition facts 1–18 using *Drill #1, Worksheet 58*.

2. Drill the subtraction facts 1–18 using flash cards without the answers showing.

3. Write the numbers used in counting by twos up to 30 on the chalk board. Change three of the numbers to be incorrect. Example: 2, 4, 6, 8, 11, 12, 14, etc. Have the student(s) tell you the numbers that are incorrect in the sequence. Do the same for counting by threes up to 45. Guide the student(s) through the first row of **Student Activity One** by counting by twos. Allow them to complete the remaining rows on their own.

4. Using fraction materials, discuss what is necessary for a shape to have 1/2, 1/3, 1/4, 1/5, or 1/6 shaded (the shape cut into 2, 3, 4, 5, or 6 equal parts and one part shaded). Place several shapes on the flannel board that are divided into 2, 3, 4, 5, or 6 parts. Remove one part. Ask the student(s) to tell you what fractional part has been removed. The student(s) should be able to complete **Student Activity Two** by themselves.

5. Choose two numbers from the number chart 100–199 and have the student(s) tell you if they would place an < or > symbol between them. Do the same for several other sets of numbers. The student(s) should complete **Student Activity Three** independently.

6. Using the shape flash cards, display the name and have the student(s) describe how it looks. **Student Activity Four** should be completed by the student(s) with little assistance. Point out to the student(s) that some lines will be drawn from the shapes on the left to the names in the center and some lines will also be drawn from the shapes on the right to the names in the middle.

7. The student(s) should complete **Student Activity Five**, **Six**, and **Seven** on their own.

Worksheets:

1. *Worksheet 58* – Addition and subtraction drill sheet

DOZEN

Concepts:
Dozen, shapes, number sequence, word problems, even numbers, and counting by ones and twos

Objectives:
1. The student shall be able to count a dozen eggs by putting an "X" on 12 eggs.

2. The student shall be able to write the correct name for a given shape.

3. The student shall be able to place an "X" on the number that is incorrect in a sequence of numbers.

4. The student shall be able to determine if a word problem is addition or subtraction, write the correct fact, and label the answer.

5. The student shall be able to write the missing even numbers from 154 to 200.

Teaching Tips:
1. When doing activity 4, suggest to the student(s) that they accompany one of their parents to the grocery store and have them make a list of all the products they can find packaged by the dozen. Compile a single list to read to the student(s). Encourage the student(s) to do this at the convenience of their parents and not as a must for tonight's work.

Materials, Supplies, & Equipment:
1. Flash cards for addition facts 1–18 and shapes

2. Counting chips

Activities:

1. Count out loud by ones and twos to 100 from memory.

2. Drill subtraction facts 1–18 using *Drill #2, Worksheet 58.*

3. Drill the addition facts 1–18 using the flash cards without the answers showing.

4. Ask the student(s) how many objects are needed to have a dozen. Have them count a dozen counting chips. Allow the student(s) to read the question in ***Student Activity One*** and write the answer in the blank. After reading the directions they should be able to mark the "X"s on one dozen eggs by themselves.

5. Using shape flash cards, have the student(s) tell the names of each of the shapes. Arrange the cards on the chalk board rail, with the names showing, for the student(s) to refer to while doing ***Student Activity Two***.

6. Write the odd numbers from 1 to 30 on the chalk board having changed any four of the numbers to the next even number. Have the student(s) identify the sequence used (odd numbers) and tell you the numbers that do not follow the sequence. Then have them tell what numbers are needed to make the sequence correct. Read the directions for ***Student Activity Three*** and have the student(s) identify the sequence (odd numbers). They should then be able to complete the activity by themselves.

7. Allow the student(s) to complete ***Student Activity Four*** independently after reminding them to find the key word, write the correct fact, and label their answer. When the student(s) have completed a word problem, review it with them a step at a time.

8. After discussing the sequence of even numbers used in ***Student Activity Five***, the student(s) should be able to write the missing numbers without any help.

Worksheets:

1. *Worksheet 58* – Addition and subtraction drill sheet

TIME

Concepts:
Time, number sequence, addition, subtraction, and counting by fives and tens

Objectives:
1. The student shall be able to write the correct time displayed on the face of the clock by the hour, half hour, and quarter hour.

2. The student shall be able to correctly write the next three numbers that come in a given sequence of numbers.

3. The student shall be able to write the two corresponding subtraction facts for each given addition fact.

4. The student shall be able to write the answer to a subtraction problem without the aid of the number line.

Teaching Tips:
1. When doing activity 1, count by fives and tens using nickels and dimes *play money*. Allow the student(s) to individually count the nickels and dimes. Then allow them to count how many dimes and nickels are needed in counting to one hundred.

2. Allow those student(s) who have not mastered their subtraction facts to use their centimeter ruler as a number line for **Student Activity Five**.

Materials, Supplies, & Equipment:
1. Flash cards for subtraction facts 1–18 and addition facts 1–18

2. Clock model

3. Small clock model for student(s)

4. Number chart

5. *Play money*

Activities:

1. Count out loud by fives and tens to 100 from memory.

2. Drill addition facts 1–18 using *Drill #3, Worksheet 58.*

3. Drill the subtraction facts 1–18 using flash cards without the answers showing.

4. At this point the student(s) should be able to read the time on the face of a clock for the hour and half hour by themselves. Have the student(s) practice setting the hands on the clock face for several quarter hour times using the small clock models. Watch for those student(s) who are having difficulty. Arrange for individual help using the small clock model for those who have not mastered the quarter hour. The student(s) should complete **Student Activity One** independently.

5. Write the following sequences on the board with three blanks after each "8, 10, 12;" "17, 19, 21;" "12, 15, 18." Ask the student(s) to identify each sequence [even numbers (or counting by twos), odd numbers, and counting by threes] and name the next three numbers for each. Point out how they can find the sequence by counting from the first number to the second number on the number chart. (Example: From 12 to 15 is 3 spaces and from 15 to 18 is three spaces–counting by threes.) Have the student(s) look at **Student Activity Two**. After they tell you the sequence for each line of numbers, they should be able to finish on their own.

6. Using the addition flash cards, have the student(s) state the opposite addition fact and the two corresponding subtraction facts for each addition fact (5 + 4 = 9, 4 + 5 = 9, 9–4 = 5, 9–5 = 4). The student(s) should be able to complete **Student Activity Three** without any help.

7. The student(s) should be able to complete **Student Activity Four** and **Five** by themselves.

Worksheets:

1. *Worksheet 59* – Number sequence

2. *Worksheet 58* – Addition and subtraction drill sheet

SEQUENCE OF EVENTS

Concepts:
> Sequence of events, place value (one hundreds), liquid measure, time, and subtraction

Objectives:
1. The student shall be able to number a series of pictures in correct sequential order.

2. The student shall be able to write the value of a given number of tens and hundreds.

3. The student shall be able to draw a line to match a liquid measure container with its correct name.

4. The student shall be able to correctly draw the short (hour) hand on the face of the clock for a given hour, half hour, and quarter hour.

5. The student shall be able to write the correct answer to a subtraction problem without the use of the number line.

Teaching Tips:
1. Before starting **Student Activity Five**, discuss with the student(s) the names of the answer to an addition problem (sum) and the answer to a subtraction problem (difference). Put a subtraction problem on the chalk board. Discuss with them the relationship between the top number in subtraction and the sum of the other number and the answer. They should discover that the sum of the bottom two numbers will always equal the top number if the problem has the correct answer. Suggest that they could check their answer in subtraction by adding the bottom two numbers and checking to see if it equals the top number.

Materials, Supplies, & Equipment:
1. Flash cards for addition facts 1–18 and liquid measure

2. *Play money*

3. Liquid measure containers

4. Clock model and small clock models for student(s)

5. Number line

6. *Centimeter ruler*

Activities:

1. Drill subtraction facts 1–18 using *Drill #4, Worksheet 58*.

2. Drill the addition facts 1–18 using flash cards without the answers showing.

3. Discuss with the student(s) the correct order of several sequences of events (planting a seed, going shopping, growth of an animal, etc.). Talk with the student(s) about each of the pictures in ***Student Activity One***. Let them think about the order for about 30 seconds by choosing which comes first and which comes last. Number the picture that comes first "1," the one that comes second "2," and the one that comes last "3."

4. Write several sets of tens and hundreds on the chalk board (or use dimes and dollar bills in *play money*) and have the student(s) tell the value of each. Equate the dimes and dollar bills with the tens' and hundreds' place. The value of 4 dimes is 4 tens which equals 40 cents. The student(s) should require no assistance in completing ***Student Activity Two***.

5. Display the liquid measure containers for the student(s) to identify. Using the flash cards, show the names of the containers and have the student(s) describe them. ***Student Activity Three*** should be completed by the student(s) on their own.

6. Do several practice times for 15 minutes and 45 minutes after the hour on the clock model. Give the student(s) a small clock model to set the hands at a given time. Quickly review an hour and half hour time. The student(s) should be able to complete ***Student Activity Four*** by themselves.

7. The student(s) should do ***Student Activity Five*** independently. Have a number line (or use *centimeter ruler*) for those student(s) who need it.

Worksheets:

1. *Worksheet 58* – Addition and subtraction drill sheet

ODD NUMBERS

Concepts:
>Odd numbers, sequence of events, time, liquid measure, place value (one hundreds), and word problems

Objectives:
1. The student shall be able to correctly circle the odd numbers in a given set of numbers.

2. The student shall be able to number a series of pictures in correct sequential order.

3. The student shall be able to correctly draw both hands on the face of the clock for a given quarter hour.

4. The student shall be able to write the correct name for the containers used in liquid measure.

5. The student shall be able to write the correct value of a given number of hundreds, tens, and ones as a sum and the numeral it represents.

Teaching Tips:
1. When doing **Student Activity Six**, have the student(s) demonstrate one to one correspondence with *counting chips* for the numbers in the two word problems. This will help to cement the idea of "how many more . . . than" being the difference of the two numbers.

Materials, Supplies, & Equipment:
1. Number chart

2. Clock model and small clock models for student(s)

3. Liquid measure containers

4. *Counting chips*

Activities:

1. Administer *Test 12.*

2. Do an oral drill with the student(s) using three single-digit numbers for 4 minutes. Use the addition facts 1–9 for the first two numbers and any single-digit number for the last one. Say the numbers out loud, 2 seconds apart, and have the student(s) raise their hand as soon as they have the answer. Increase speed with each new problem.

3. Point to several sets of two numbers (one odd and one even) on the number chart and have the student(s) tell you which of the two numbers is an odd number. Discuss with them the possible digits (1, 3, 5, 7, 9) that an odd number must have as its last digit. Read the directions for *Student Activity One* together. Have the student(s) point to the number in the first set that is odd (19) and circle it. Allow them to finish the activity on their own.

4. Make up several sequences of events that are out of order (days of the week, baking a cake, etc.). Have the student(s) put them in correct sequence. Let them do *Student Activity Two* independently, giving help where it is needed.

5. Give each student a small clock model. Write several quarter hour times on the chalk board (use both 15 and 45 minutes after the hour). Tell the student(s) to set the hands on their clock and check their work with your clock. Ask them which hand to place first [long (minute) hand]. Remind them that the minute hand tells them where to place the short (hour) hand. Let them do *Student Activity Three* independently.

6. Review the names of the liquid measure containers by pointing to each container and having the student(s) say the name. Call out a name and have the student(s) tell you if it is the first, second, third, etc., container. Have them complete *Student Activity Four* by themselves.

7. The student(s) should be able to complete *Student Activity Five* with no help.

8. Discuss "how many more . . . than" as the key words in the subtraction problems in *Student Activity Six*. When finding "how many more one number is than another," you are finding the difference, which means you are subtracting. To find the difference between 9 and 5, subtract 5 from 9. Have the student(s) point to the words "how many more ... than" in the first word problem. Tell them to write the subtraction fact and label the answer. Do the same for the second word problem.

SOLIDS

Concepts:
Solids, place value (one hundreds), addition, subtraction, and counting to 200

Objectives:
1. The student shall be able to draw a line to match a solid to its name.

2. The student shall be able to write the correct value of each digit in a given three digit number as a sum.

3. The student shall be able to write the correct number when given the value of the digit in the hundreds', tens', and ones' place.

4. The student shall be able to write the correct answer to a subtraction problem without a number line.

Teaching Tips:
1. When doing activity 4, have the student(s) look around the room to name some objects that are the same shape as the solids. Tell them to think of objects they see outside or at the store and name the solid that is similar to it. Discuss what makes the object and the solid similar (they have the same shape).

2. Have the student(s) make a cube out of *construction paper*. A pattern is given on *Worksheet 61*. You may want to have these patterns already cut out for the student(s). Have one cube already put together to show the student(s) and instruct them in folding their pattern on the dotted lines and then gluing it together.

Materials, Supplies, & Equipment:
1. Number chart 100–199

2. Flash cards for subtraction facts 1–18 and *solids*

3. Solid models

4. *Construction paper*

Activities:

1. Count out loud from 100 to 200 using the number chart.

2. Drill addition facts 1–18 using *Drill #1, Worksheet 60.*

3. Drill the subtraction facts 1–18 using flash cards without the answers showing.

4. Using the solid models (or use *flash cards*), have the student(s) identify each of the solids by name and describe what the solid looks like. When doing **Student Activity One**, have the student(s) repeat the word "cylinder" after you, point to the shape, and then draw a line from the word to the shape. Follow the same procedure for each of the names of the solids.

5. Write several three digit numbers on the chalk board. As you point to each digit have the student(s) tell you its value and write it on the chalk board as a sum. Then write "500 + 30 + 6 = __," "200 + 70 + 2 = __," and "800 + 10 + 0 = __" and have the student(s) tell you the number the expanded notation represents. Allow the student(s) to complete **Student Activity Two** by themselves.

6. Introduce **Student Activity Three** by having the student(s) count the spaces between the first given number and the second number. From this they should be able to tell you the sequence of numbers being used. Have them fill in the missing numbers.

7. The student(s) should complete **Student Activity Four** and **Five** independently.

Worksheets:

1. *Worksheet 60* – Addition and subtraction drill sheet

2. *Worksheet 61* – Cube pattern

Ignorance is a voluntary misfortune.

MONEY

Concepts:
> Money, solids, word numbers (over 100), addition, subtraction, and counting to 200

Objectives:
1. The student shall be able to write the correct value of a given number of coins and their sum.

2. The student shall be able to write the correct name for the given solids.

3. The student shall be able to write the correct numeral that corresponds to a given word number over 100.

Teaching Tips:
1. When doing activity 4, give each student a variety of play money coins. Ask them to select the coins necessary to equal several given amounts of money (e.g. 34¢). When they have finished, write the different combinations they have found on the chalk board (3 dimes and 4 pennies; 2 dimes, 2 nickels, and 4 pennies; 1 quarter, 1 nickel, and 4 pennies etc.). This concept may be difficult for some student(s) but encourage them to start with any coins and count until they get to 30¢ and add the 4 pennies. If they use 6 nickels, you may then ask them if they can replace any of the nickels with a larger coin (1 dime for 2 nickels). They could use 34 pennies and replace 5 pennies for a nickel or 10 pennies for a dime.

Materials, Supplies, & Equipment:
1. Number chart 100–199

2. Flash cards for addition facts 1–18 and word numbers

3. Play money

4. Solid models

Activities:

1. Count out loud from 100 to 200 using the number chart.

2. Drill subtraction facts 1–18 using *Drill #2, Worksheet 60.*

3. Drill the addition facts 1–18 using flash cards without the answers showing.

4. Using play money, display several sets of coins (3 quarters, 1 dime, and 1 nickel; 4 dimes, 5 nickels, and 3 pennies; 3 dimes, 6 nickels, and 7 pennies). Have the student(s) tell you the value of 3 quarters, then 1 dime, and then 1 nickel as you write them on the chalk board similar to the answers in **Student Activity One**. Point out to the student(s) the importance of writing the pennies and one nickel in the ones' column when you are finding the sum. Follow the same procedure for the next two sets. When the student(s) start **Student Activity One**, guide them through each step as you did on the chalk board for all sets of coins.

5. Have a student close his eyes. Hand him a solid model. Ask him to tell the name of it and describe it as he feels its shape. Do the same for the other three solids. In **Student Activity Two** have the student(s) point to the name of the first solid (cube) and write it on the line. Follow the same procedure for the next three shapes.

6. Using the word number flash cards, form word numbers on the chalk board rail (or you may want to write them on the chalk board). Have the student(s) write the number on a sheet of paper while you write it on the chalk board. Ask if any student has a question as to why his number was not correct. Point out the placement of a zero in a number such as one hundred three. Do several more examples before having the student(s) complete **Student Activity Three**.

7. The student(s) should be able to complete **Student Activity Four** and **Five** independently.

Worksheets:

1. *Worksheet 60* – Addition and subtraction drill sheet

SHOW YOUR SKILLS

Concepts:
Counting to 200, word numbers (over 100), word problems, money, and addition

Objectives:
1. The student shall be able to write the missing numbers in counting from 177 to 200.

2. The student shall be able to write the correct numeral that corresponds to a given word number.

3. The student shall be able to write the correct value of a given number of coins and their sum.

4. The student shall be able to write the correct sum of two double-digit numbers when the tens' column has a double-digit answer.

Teaching Tips:
1. When doing activity 1, you may want to count from 400 to 500 instead of 100 to 200. Use the *number chart 0–99* and have the student(s) say four hundred in front of each number. It is important for the student(s) to understand that once they can count to 200, they could count to nine hundred ninety-nine if they so desired.

Materials, Supplies, & Equipment:
1. Number chart 100–199 and *0–99*

2. Flash cards for subtraction facts 1–18

3. Play money

4. Place value materials

Activities:

1. Count out loud to 200 using the number chart 100–199.

2. Drill addition facts 1–18 using *Drill #3*, *Worksheet 60*.

3. Drill the subtraction facts 1–18 using flash cards without the answers showing.

4. The student(s) should complete **Student Activity One** on their own.

5. Call out several word numbers over 100 and have the student(s) write the numeral on a sheet of paper. Include word numbers that have zeros in the corresponding numerals. Write the correct numerals on the chalk board to enable the student(s) to check their papers. The student(s) should be able to complete **Student Activity Two** by themselves.

6. Ask a student to read the word problem in **Student Activity Three**. Have the student(s) point to the key word(s) and discuss if they are to add or subtract. Ask them to write the correct subtraction fact. Discuss the label (is it goldfish or guppies?). The label is the larger set which comes after the word "more" in the question.

7. Give the student(s) play money. Ask them to choose two dimes, two nickels, and two pennies. On a sheet of paper have them write the value of each set of coins in a column to add. Emphasize putting the pennies and one nickel in the ones' column. Write the values and the answer on the chalk board to enable the student(s) to check their answer. Do several different sets of coins in this manner requiring no carrying. Allow the student(s) to complete **Student Activity Four** with as little help as possible.

8. Notice that the addition in **Student Activity Five** has a double-digit answer in the tens' column. Write "84 + 52" on the chalk board as a vertical addition problem. Ask the student(s) to add the ones' column, write the number, add the tens' column, and write the number. Using place value materials show that 13 tens equal 10 tens (100) and 3 tens (30) or 130 (100 + 30). 130 + 6 = 136. Discuss the answer (three digits, the "1" is in the hundreds' place, "3" is in the tens' place, and the "6" is in the ones' place). Do several more examples making the sum in the ones' column 9 or less and in the tens' column between 10 and 18 before allowing the student(s) to complete **Student Activity Five**.

Worksheets:

1. *Worksheet 60* – Addition and subtraction drill sheet

ESTIMATION

Concepts:

Estimation, money, addition, subtraction, and counting by threes

Objectives:

1. The student shall be able to circle the animal that corresponds in size most closely to the size indicated in the instructions.

2. The student shall be able to write the correct value of a given number of coins and their sum.

3. The student shall be able to write the correct sum of two double-digit numbers when the tens' column has a double-digit answer.

Teaching Tips:

1. When doing activity 4, tell the student(s) a given height and have them name some objects that they think are about that high. Be ready to accept almost any answer. Since an estimation is not exact, the student(s) may have difficulty coming very close. The primary benefit of the exercise will be derived by allowing them to express their best guesses and to think in the area of estimation.

2. For enrichment, encourage the faster student(s) to check their work in *Student Activity Two* by counting the coins as was illustrated in activity 5.

Materials, Supplies, & Equipment:

1. Number chart

2. Flash cards for addition facts 1–18

3. Inch ruler

4. Play money

5. Place value materials

Activities:

1. Count out loud by threes to 99 using the number chart.

2. Drill subtraction facts 1–18 using *Drill #4, Worksheet 60*.

3. Drill the addition facts 1–18 using flash cards without the answers showing.

4. With the student(s), estimate how tall an object is (a chair, table, desk, ant, dog, cat, horse, etc.). Talk about how estimation deals with "about" how tall an object is and that it is not an exact measurement. Have the student(s) use their hands to show "about" how tall they think 8 inches is. Then compare their estimate with 8 inches on an inch ruler. As the student(s) look at the animals in **Student Activity One**, have them pick out the largest one and the smallest one. Ask them to point to the one they think would be "about" 8 inches tall and circle it. Do the next series of pictures the same way.

5. Using play money, display 5 dimes, 4 nickels, and 3 pennies. Have the student(s) tell you the value of the 5 dimes and write it on the chalk board. Do the same with the 4 nickels and 3 pennies. Point out the importance of lining the pennies up in the ones' column. Add the values together. Check your answer by counting the coins (10, 20, 30, 40, 50, 55, 60, 65, 70, 71, 72, 73). Follow the same procedure for several more sets. Then let the student(s) proceed with **Student Activity Two**, on their own if possible.

6. Write several double-digit numbers (e.g. 73 + 91) on the chalk board to be added. Make the sum in the ones' column 9 or less and in the tens' column between 10 and 18. Using place value materials, show how 16 tens equal 10 tens (100) and 6 tens (60) or 160 (100 + 60). 160 + 4 = 164. Have the student(s) work the first problem in **Student Activity Three** together. Allow those student(s) who understand to continue on their own as you guide the remaining student(s) where needed.

7. The student(s) should be able to complete **Student Activity Four** by themselves.

Worksheets:

1. *Worksheet 62* – Addition of money

2. *Worksheet 60* – Addition and subtraction drill sheet

NUMBER SEQUENCE

Concepts:

Number sequence, estimation, sets, addition, subtraction, and counting by threes

Objectives:

1. The student shall be able to correctly write the next three numbers after a given sequence of numbers.

2. The student shall be able to write the correct number (10 or 20) to which a given number is closer on the number line.

3. The student shall be able to count a given set of objects and write the number in the box.

4. The student shall be able to correctly write a letter above a corresponding number that matches the answer to an addition fact.

Teaching Tips:

1. When doing activity 3, ask the student(s) to be aware of places that they can see number sequences such as on the speedometer in a car, a thermometer, scales, numbered checks, etc. Ask them to be ready to discuss number sequences in every day life during their next lesson.

Materials, Supplies, & Equipment:

1. Number chart

2. Number line

Activities:

1. Count out loud by threes to 99 using the number chart where necessary.

2. Do an oral drill with the student(s) using three single-digit numbers for about 4 minutes. Use the addition facts 1–9 for the first two numbers and any single-digit number for the last one. Say the numbers out loud about 2 seconds apart and have the student(s) raise their hand as soon as they have the answer. Increase your speed just a little each time you give them a new problem.

3. Write "16," "19," and "22" on the chalk board. Have the student(s) tell you how many places you must count on the number chart to go from 16 to 19 (3). Ask how many places you must count to go from 19 to 22 (3). Then ask them to tell what number would be next in the sequence if they counted 3 places from 22 (25). Write "25" after 22 and continue with the next two numbers. Follow the same procedure with "14, 17, 20" and "21, 24, 27." Complete the first sequence in **Student Activity One** with the student(s). They should be able to finish the next two on their own.

4. Point to several numbers between 10 and 20 on the number line (except 15 which will be dealt with when the student(s) study the rounding off of numbers). Ask the student(s) to decided if each number is closer to 10 or 20. This exercise is only a preparation for rounding numbers. For now, if there are questions, tell them that 15 is the same distance from 10 and 20. The student(s) should be able to complete **Student Activity Two** with little help.

5. The student(s) should be able to complete **Student Activity Three** by themselves.

6. To decode the message in **Student Activity Four**, the student(s) must solve the addition fact and put the letter associated with the fact on the blank that has that sum beneath it. Have the student(s) look at the first addition fact (7 + 4) and write the sum beside it. Ask what letter they will put on the blank above the number 11 (I). What does 6 + 8 equal? Write the sum beside it. What letter will they put on the blank above the number 14 (O)? Allow them to complete the activity on their own if they are able.

7. **Student Activity Five** should be completed by the student(s) independently.

SHAPES

Concepts:
Shapes, number sequence, word problems, money, estimation, centimeters, months of the year, "Thirty Days Hath September," and counting by sixes

Objectives:
1. The student shall be able to draw a line to match a given shape to its name.

2. The student shall be able to circle every fourth number in a sequence of numbers and write the circled numbers on the blanks.

3. The student shall be able to determine if a given word problem is addition or subtraction, write the correct fact, and label the answer.

4. The student shall be able to write the correct value of a given number of coins and their sum.

5. The student shall be able to circle the number that is closer to the length of a given line measured by a centimeter ruler.

Teaching Tips:
1. When doing activity 9, have the student(s) measure a pencil to the nearest whole centimeter. Remind them to put the zero on their ruler at the end of the pencil. Have them write, on a sheet of paper, the two numbers between which the end of the pencil falls. Circle the number to which the end of the pencil is closer. Let the student(s) measure a crayon in the same way.

Materials, Supplies, & Equipment:
1. Number chart

2. Flash cards for subtraction facts 1–18 and shapes

3. Play money

4. Centimeter ruler

Activities:

1. Count out loud by sixes to 96 using the number chart when necessary.

2. Drill addition facts 1–18 using *Drill #1, Worksheet 63.*

3. Drill the subtraction facts 1–18 using flash cards without the answers showing.

4. Quickly recite the months of the year and "Thirty Days Hath September."

5. Using the shape flash cards with the name showing, have the student(s) say each name and describe what the shape looks like. Then have them name each shape as you quickly show the pictures on the flash cards. They should be able to complete **Student Activity One** independently.

6. Point to the number 5 on the number chart. Have the student(s) tell you the fourth number after 5 (count the next 4 numbers) and write "9" on the chalk board. Follow the same procedure for several more numbers. Help the student(s) to see they have created their own number sequence. Read the directions for **Student Activity Two** with the student(s). After you guide them to find the first number they circle, allow them to complete the activity by themselves.

7. Read each of the word problems in **Student Activity Three** together with the student(s). Let them determine if they add or subtract, write the fact, and label their answer. Once they have finished, discuss the reason they chose to add or subtract and why the label is what it is.

8. Give the student(s) play money. Ask them to choose the necessary coins to equal 62¢, 38¢, 57¢, and 29¢. Discuss the different possible combinations. They should be able to complete **Student Activity Four** with little help.

9. Have the student(s) take out their centimeter ruler. Ask them what number (0) on their ruler they are to put at the dotted vertical line when measuring the first line in **Student Activity Five**. As they measure the length of the first line, ask them if the line is exactly a given number of centimeters long. Then ask them what are the two numbers (8 & 9) between which the length falls. The length is closer to which number (8)? Tell them that the line is "about" 8 centimeters long. This is an estimation of the length of the line. Allow the student(s) to measure the second line and circle the answer on their own.

Worksheets:

1. *Worksheet 63* – Addition and subtraction drill sheet

CALENDAR – MONTHS OF THE YEAR

Concepts:
Months of the year, "Thirty Days Hath September," number sequence, word problems, shapes, addition, and counting by sixes

Objectives:
1. The student shall be able to write the months of the year in the correct order.

2. The student shall be able to write the next three numbers that come in a given sequence of numbers.

3. In a word problem, the student shall be able to write the correct value of a given number of dimes as cents.

4. The student shall be able to write the correct name of a given shape.

5. The student shall be able to write the correct sum of two double-digit numbers when the tens' column has a double-digit answer.

Teaching Tips:
1. Look up the birthdays of the student(s). When doing activity 4, give each student the opportunity to tell when his birthday is. Help them along if they cannot recall the date. Using a current *calendar*, let the student(s) find what day of the week their birthday will be on this year. Share with the student(s) when your birthday is. See who has the first and the last birthday in the year. Are any birthdays on major holidays?

Materials, Supplies, & Equipment:
1. Number chart

2. Flash cards for addition facts 1–18, months of the year, and shapes

3. Play money

4. *Calendar*

Activities:

1. Count out loud by sixes to 96 using the number chart if necessary.

2. Drill subtraction facts 1–18 using *Drill #2, Worksheet 63*.

3. Drill the addition facts 1–18 using the flash cards without the answers showing.

4. Have the student(s) recite "Thirty Days Hath September" and the months of the year using the flash cards. Then have them recite the months without the flash cards. Line the flash cards for the months on the chalk board rail and have the student(s) tell you the third month after January, the second month after June, the fifth month after March, etc. After the student(s) read the directions to **Student Activity One** together, they should be able to finish on their own. Recite "Thirty Days Hath September" with the student(s) again.

5. Write three consecutive numbers counting backwards (e.g. 6, 5, 4) on the chalk board followed by three blanks. Ask the student(s) what would be the next numbers if they were counting backwards. You may want to use the number chart. Do several other sets such as "17, 16, 15" and "25, 24, 23." You will need to guide the student(s) in doing each number sequence in **Student Activity Two**.

6. Have each student read the word problem in **Student Activity Three**. Give the student(s) the opportunity to answer the question on their own. Discuss the answer to guide the thinking of the student(s) who could not comprehend the concept. Play money may be helpful.

7. The student(s) should be able to complete **Student Activity Four** by themselves. If you find there are student(s) who still need help, display the shapes flash cards with only the names showing.

8. **Student Activity Five** should be completed by the student(s) with little help from you.

Worksheets:

1. *Worksheet 63* – Addition and subtraction drill sheet

DOZEN

Concepts:
> Dozen, shapes, addition, subtraction, months of the year, "Thirty Days Hath September," and counting by sixes

Objectives:
1. The student shall be able to recite the months of the year in correct order and "Thirty Days Hath September" from memory.

2. The student shall be able to write the number of objects in a dozen and color a dozen objects in a given set.

3. The student shall be able to draw a line to match an object to its corresponding shape.

4. The student shall be able to write the correct sum of two double-digit numbers when the tens' column has a double-digit answer.

Teaching Tips:
1. Continue to check the student(s) to see if they can recite "Thirty Days Hath September" from memory. You can also use the knuckles on your hand and the spaces between to tell how many days in each month. Each knuckle is a 31 day month. Each space is a 30 day month with the exception of February. The first knuckle is January, space February, second knuckle March, second space April, third knuckle May, third space June, fourth knuckle July, (starting over again) first knuckle is August, first space September, etc.

Materials, Supplies, & Equipment:
1. Number chart

2. Flash cards for subtraction facts 1–18 and months of the year

3. Plastic rings from two 6 packs of soda pop

4. *Place value materials*

Activities:

1. Count out loud by sixes to 96 using the number chart only if necessary.

2. Drill addition facts 1–18 using *Drill #3, Worksheet 63.*

3. Drill the subtraction facts 1–18 using flash cards without the answers showing.

4. Line up the months of the year flash cards on the chalk rail. Point to a month and have a student name it and tell you something special about that month (it's cold or hot, birthday, holiday, vacation, spring, fall, begins with a "J," has 30 days, etc.). Recite the months of the year in order and "Thirty Days Hath September" from memory.

5. Show the student(s) two plastic rings used to hold two 6 packs of soda pop cans together. Have the student(s) count the holes. Tell them there are a dozen holes to hold a dozen cans of soda pop. (You may want to bring two 6 packs, instead of just the rings.) Discuss dividing the dozen in half (one 6 pack, each) and how many are in each half. Read the question in **Student Activity One** to the student(s) and have them write the answer. Have them read the directions and finish coloring on their own.

6. Have the student(s) look at the shapes in **Student Activity Two** and name each of them. The student(s) should be able to draw the lines by themselves.

7. Write "65 + 73" vertically on the chalk board. Have the student(s) add the ones' column. Write the answer under the ones' column. Tell them to add the tens' column. Write the answer under the tens' and hundreds' columns. Ask them to tell you what column the "1" (in the number 13) is in. 6 tens added to 7 tens equals 13 tens which equals 10 tens + 3 tens which equals 100 + 30 (you may want to use *place value materials* to illustrate this). Putting the ones' column with this, they have 100 + 30 + 8 = 138. Do several more problems before the student(s) complete **Student Activity Three.** Check the student(s) work for any reoccurring errors.

8. The student(s) should be able to complete **Student Activity Four** on their own.

Worksheets:

1. *Worksheet 64* – Addition with answer in tens' column double digit

2. *Worksheet 63* – Addition and subtraction drill sheet

CALENDAR – DAYS OF THE WEEK

Concepts:
Days of the week, word problems, sequence of events, addition, and counting by sixes

Objectives:
1. The student shall be able to correctly write the numbers on a calendar when given partial dates, the correct day for a given date, the correct day for a given number of days before and after a given date, and the correct date for a given occurrence of a day of the week.

2. The student shall be able to write the number of cents in a given set of coins in a word problem.

3. The student shall be able to number a series of pictures in correct sequential order.

4. The student shall be able to write the correct sum of two double-digit numbers when the tens' column has a double-digit answer.

Teaching Tips:

1. Allow the student(s) to make up a sequence of events when you are doing activity 6. You decide the order and let them tell you if you are right or wrong. Do some of the orders incorrectly and see if they can correct you and tell you why. This is a good thinking exercise for the student(s).

Materials, Supplies, & Equipment:

1. Number chart

2. Flash cards for addition facts 1–18

3. Calendar

4. Play money

Activities:

1. Count out loud by sixes to 96 using the number chart only when necessary.

2. Drill subtraction facts 1–18 using *Drill #4, Worksheet 63*.

3. Drill the addition facts 1–18 using flash cards without the answers showing.

4. Using a calendar for the present month, have the student(s) practice locating the day for a given date (22nd), the date for a given occurrence of a day of the week (third Tuesday), and the day for a given number of days before and after a given date (3 days after or before the 16th). Spend about 5 minutes doing several examples. Allow the student(s) to fill in the missing numbers in **Student Activity One**. Read each question with the student(s) as they finish **Student Activity Two**.

5. Have the student(s) read the word problem in **Student Activity Three**. Display 9 nickels (play money) for them to count (or have them draw 9 nickels on their paper). When the student(s) write their answer, have them use the "¢" sign or write the word "cents" as the label.

6. Discuss with the student(s) several sequences of events (eat lunch and then eat breakfast or eat breakfast and then eat lunch, brush your teeth and then put toothpaste on your toothbrush or put toothpaste on your toothbrush and then brush your teeth, etc.). Discuss the three pictures in **Student Activity Four**. Allow the student(s) to number the picture that comes first "1," the picture that comes second "2," and the picture that comes last "3" by themselves.

7. The student(s) should be able to complete **Student Activity Five** independently. Check to see that they are adding the one's column first.

Worksheets:

1. *Worksheet 63* – Addition and subtraction drill sheet

CENTIMETERS

Concepts:
Centimeters, odd and even numbers, subtraction, sequence of events, word problems, addition, days of the week, and counting by nines

Objectives:
1. The student shall be able to measure a line of a given length using a centimeter ruler.

2. The student shall be able to correctly circle the word "even" or "odd" corresponding to a given number.

3. The student shall be able to number a series of pictures in correct sequential order.

4. The student shall be able to write the correct sum of two double-digit numbers when the tens' column has a double-digit answer.

Teaching Tips:
1. When doing activity 5, show the student(s) a *meter stick*. Let them see how many centimeters in a meter. This could be compared with how many cents in a dollar or how many years in a century. Discuss some objects that they would rather measure with a meter stick than with a centimeter ruler.

Materials, Supplies, & Equipment:
1. Flash cards for days of the week

2. *Calendar*

3. Centimeter ruler

4. Play money

5. *Meter stick*

Activities:

1. Administer **Test 13**.

2. Count out loud by nines to 99 from memory.

3. Do an oral drill with the student(s) using three single-digit numbers for about 4 minutes. Use the addition facts 1–9 for the first two numbers and any single-digit number for the last one. Say the numbers out loud about 2 seconds apart and have the student(s) raise their hand as soon as they have the answer. Increase your speed just a little each time you give them a new problem.

4. Have the student(s) recite the days of the week using flash cards and then without flash cards. Discuss what day of the week today is and what day one week from today will be (you may want to use a *calendar*). Discuss what day yesterday was and what day tomorrow will be.

5. Ask the student(s) to take their centimeter ruler and look at **Student Activity One**. Ask them to tell you the first thing they must do when they are measuring a line (put the zero on the ruler at the beginning of the line). Allow them to measure the three lines and write their answers by themselves.

6. After discussing the words "odd" and "even" with the student(s), have them tell you with which digits an odd and even number ends. After circling the first word together, allow the student(s) to complete **Student Activity Two** on their own.

7. **Student Activity Three** should be completed by the student(s) independently.

8. Discuss the three pictures in **Student Activity Four**. Allow the student(s) to number the picture that comes first "1," the picture that comes second "2," and the picture that comes last "3." Then discuss the reason for the correct picture order.

9. Have each student read the word problem in **Student Activity Five** to himself. Ask them to write the fact they need to solve the word problem. Write how many dimes Rose had and label the answer (dimes). Using play money, if necessary, let the student(s) then determine how many cents Rose had. Have them rewrite the answer and label it cents(¢).

10. The student(s) should be able to complete **Student Activity Six** without any help.

ADDITION – CARRYING

Concepts:
> Addition (carrying), fractions, place value (one hundreds), subtraction, and counting by nines

Objectives:
1. The student shall be able to write the correct sum for an addition problem when the ones' column has a double-digit answer.

2. The student shall be able to write the correct fraction that shows what part of a shape has been shaded.

3. The student shall be able to write the correct value of the hundreds', tens', and ones' digit in a given number and their sum.

Teaching Tips:
1. Here is a place value game to go with activity 6. From a sheet of typing paper make a *game card* for each student. Under the heading HUNDREDS write 100, 200, 300, . . . 900 in a column. Under the second heading TENS write 10, 20, 30, . . . 90 in a column. Under the third heading ONES write 1, 2, 3, . . . 9 in a column. Write a three digit number on the chalk board. Using *counting chips*, have the student(s) put a chip over the value of each digit in the number (e.g. 483–put a chip over 400, 80, and 3). Continue to write numbers on the chalk board until all of the numbers in one column are covered. Choose your numbers so that all numbers are used for each digit. The student(s) should all arrive at this point at the same time. If they do not, it indicates a student missed placing a chip on the correct number. Those student(s) may need additional help if the number of misses is very high.

Materials, Supplies, & Equipment:
1. Flash cards for subtraction facts 1–18

2. Place value materials

3. Number chart

4. *Counting chips* and *game cards*

Activities:

1. Count out loud by nines to 99 from memory.

2. Drill addition facts 1–18 using *Drill #1, Worksheet 65*.

3. Drill the subtraction facts 1–18 using flash cards without the answers showing.

4. Write "7 + 5 = 12" vertically on the chalk board. Discuss the place value (use place value materials) for the number 12 (1 ten + 2 ones) with the student(s). Write "37 + 5" vertically on the chalk board. Have the student(s) add the ones' column (12). Write the 2 ones in the ones'

$$\begin{array}{r} \boxed{1} \\ 37 \\ +5 \\ \hline 42 \end{array}$$

column and add the 1 ten to the 3 in the tens' column. Show them how this can be done by putting the 1 above the three in the tens' column. Use the small square above the 3 in the tens' column in which to put the 1. Now have the student(s) add the tens' column and you write the answer (4) in the tens' column. Have the student(s) verify their answer by counting over 5 from 37 on the number chart. Work several more examples on the chalk board following this same procedure. As the student(s) begin working the problems in **Student Activity One**, check their work for reoccurring errors that should be corrected now before they become a habit.

5. The student(s) should be able to complete writing the fractions in **Student Activity Two** independently.

6. Write several 3 digit numbers on the chalk board. Ask what digit is in the hundreds', tens', and ones' place. Then have them tell the value of the digit in the hundreds', tens', and ones' place. After doing the first sentence in **Student Activity Three** together, the student(s) should be able to complete the remaining sentences on their own.

7. The student(s) should be able to complete **Student Activity Four** independently.

Worksheets:

1. *Worksheet 65* – Addition and subtraction drill sheet

315

POUND

Concepts:
Pound, time, place value (one hundreds), solids, fractions, word problems, subtraction, addition (carrying), and counting by nines

Definition: A pound is a unit of measure for weight.

Objectives:
1. The student shall be able to write the weight in pounds of a given object.

2. The student shall be able to write the correct time on the face of the clock for the hour, half hour, and quarter hour.

3. The student shall be able to write the correct value of the hundreds', tens', and ones' digit in a given number.

4. The student shall be able to draw a line to match a solid with its name.

5. The student shall be able to draw the necessary lines to divide a given object into the necessary number of equal segments to shade a given fractional part.

Teaching Tips:
1. When doing activity 4, allow each of the student(s) to weigh themselves. Have them each tell you what they think their approximate weight is. You may even allow them to tell you what they think your approximate weight is. Make it a fun time for them.

Materials, Supplies, & Equipment:
1. Flash cards for addition facts 1–18 and solids

2. 5 pound bag of flour

3. Pound loaf of bread

4. Pound of butter

5. Rock

6. Scale for weighing pounds

7. Place value materials

Activities:

1. Count out loud by nines to 99 from memory.

2. Drill subtraction facts 1–18 using *Drill #2, Worksheet 65*.

3. Drill the addition facts 1–18 using flash cards.

4. Introduce the student(s) to the pound (unit of measure for weight) by displaying a 5 pound bag of flour, a 1 pound loaf of bread, a pound of butter, and a rock weighing near a whole pound(s). If a scale is available, weigh each object and have the student(s) write the weight on the blank in **Student Activity One**. If a scale is not available tell the student(s) the weight to write in the blank. Let each student lift each of the objects to give them an idea of how heavy 1 pound and 5 pounds are. Compare the weight of the pound of butter and the loaf of bread. Explain that size does not determine weight.

5. The student(s) should be able to complete **Student Activity Two** and **Three** independently.

6. Using the flash cards for solids, review each of the names of the solids. Have the student(s) look at **Student Activity Four** and name each solid before they pick up their pencils. Then ask them to read the names of the solids together before drawing the lines by themselves.

7. Look at **Student Activity Five** with the student(s). Discuss how many parts an object must be divided into if they are to shade 1/2, 1/3, 1/4, and 1/5. Let the student(s) divide the objects into the appropriate number of parts by drawing lines and then complete the shading without any assistance.

8. **Student Activity Six** and **Seven** should be completed by the student(s) on their own.

9. Write "68 + 6" vertically on the chalk board as an addition problem. Discuss the place value for the number 68 in the same manner as was done in Lesson 131. Work several more examples on the chalk board following this same procedure. The student(s) should complete **Student Activity Eight** independently receiving individual help where needed.

$$\begin{array}{r} \boxed{1} \\ 68 \\ +6 \\ \hline 74 \end{array}$$

Worksheets:

1. *Worksheet 66* – Word problems from pictures

2. *Worksheet 65* – Addition and subtraction drill sheet

NUMBER ORDER – ORDINAL NUMBERS

Concepts:
> Ordinal numbers, solids, time, place value (one hundreds), = and ≠, addition (carrying), pound, and counting to 200

Objectives:
1. The student shall be able to write the name of a given solid in respect to its ordinal position.

2. The student shall be able to draw both hands on the face of the clock for the hour, half hour, and quarter hour.

3. The student shall be able to write the correct symbol (= or ≠) between a digit and the value of that digit in a given three-digit number.

4. The student shall be able to write the correct sum of an addition problem when the ones' column has a double-digit answer.

Teaching Tips:
1. When doing activity 6, tell the student(s) about the sundial, the first known instrument used in telling time. As the sun moved across the sky it would cast a shadow on the dial. The length and angle of the shadow told the time of the day. The shadow was shortest and had the smallest angle at noon. Ask if any student has seen a sundial. They are frequently found on the grounds of historical buildings.

Materials, Supplies, & Equipment:
1. Number chart 100–199

2. Flash cards for subtraction facts 1–18, solids, and = *and* ≠

3. Small clock models for student(s)

Activities:

1. Count out loud to 200 using the number chart 100–199.

2. Drill addition facts 1–18 using *Drill #3, Worksheet 65*.

3. Drill the subtraction facts 1–18 using flash cards without the answers showing.

4. Discuss the pound unit of measure for weight with the student(s). Ask what items are sold by the pound that are not food. Ask them to look at the grocery store or in their kitchen to see how many different kinds of food they can find that are sold by the pound or 5 pounds. Ounces will not be taught in the first grade.

5. Have the student(s) give the names of each solid by lining the flash cards up on the chalk rail and asking the student(s) to name the second, fourth, third, and first solid. The student(s) should be able to complete **Student Activity One** on their own.

6. Give each student a small clock model. Write three quarter hour and one each of hour and half hour times in digital form on the chalk board. Have the student(s) place the minute (long) hand in position and then the hour (short) hand. Let the student(s) hold up their clocks as they finish each time to enable you to check their work. When you finish, let the student(s) complete **Student Activity Two** independently.

7. Write "In 593 the 9 is _____ 9 tens." Also put "= or ≠" (or you may want to us the *flash cards*) on the chalk board. Ask the student(s) what place value the 9 is in for the number 593. Then, pointing to the symbols, ask them if 9 is = or ≠ to 9 tens. Place an = sign in the blank. On the chalk board write several other examples similar to this one with some of them = and some of them ≠. You will need to guide the student(s) as they do each sentence in **Student Activity Three**.

8. The student(s) should be able to complete **Student Activity Four** by themselves. Check to see if there is an individual who may still need direction in following the correct steps given in Lesson 131.

Worksheets:

1. *Worksheet 65* – Addition and subtraction drill sheet

SUBTRACTION – DOUBLE DIGIT

Concepts:
Subtraction, word numbers (over 100), = and ≠, addition (carrying), word problems, pounds, and counting to 200

Objectives:
1. The student shall be able to write the correct difference of two double-digit numbers.

2. The student shall be able to write the correct symbol (= or ≠) between a word number and a numeral.

3. The student shall be able to write the correct sum for an addition problem when the ones' column has a double-digit answer.

Teaching Tips:
1. When doing activity 6, allow the student(s) to go to the chalk board and work an addition problem involving carrying. Watch for individual difficulties. Once a problem is completed, give the student(s) an opportunity to explain why they worked the problem as they did. Remind them that accuracy is to be the goal not speed. You may also want to have the student(s) work some subtraction problems on the chalk board as in activity 4.

2. For activity 8, show the student(s) the grocery ads from a *newspaper* to see what they can find that is sold by the pound. Make a bulletin board display of the different kinds of food that can be bought by the pound.

Materials, Supplies, & Equipment:
1. Number chart 100–199

2. Flash cards for addition facts 1–18 and = and ≠

3. *Newspaper, grocery advertisements*

Activities:

1. Count out loud to 200 using the number chart 100–199.

2. Drill subtraction facts 1–18 using *Drill #4, Worksheet 65*.

3. Drill the addition facts 1–18 using flash cards without the answers showing.

4. Put several double-digit subtraction problems (without borrowing) on the chalk board. Instruct the student(s) to subtract the ones' column first and then the tens' column. If the two columns are confusing to some student(s) have them cover up the tens' column when they add the ones' column and cover up the ones' column when adding the tens' column. Have the student(s) work the first three problems in **Student Activity One** together and then continue on their own.

5. Review the = and ≠ symbols using flash cards. Allow the student(s) to tell you a statement using the = or ≠ symbol (they may use word numbers, tally marks, money, etc.). When beginning **Student Activity Two**, have the student(s) read the word numbers together. They should be able to place the symbols correctly by themselves.

6. Review addition with carrying using a double-digit and single-digit number on the chalk board. Do not put the little box over the tens' column. The next lesson will be the last time it will appear in the student lessons. The student(s) should be able to complete **Student Activity Three** independently.

7. **Student Activity Four** should be completed by the student(s) without any assistance.

8. Discuss with the student(s) the different items they found in the grocery store or their kitchen that are sold by the pound. Ask them what unit of measure the pound is (weight). They should be able to do **Student Activity Five** on their own.

Worksheets:

1. *Worksheet 67* – Addition with carrying and double-digit subtraction

2. *Worksheet 65* – Addition and subtraction drill sheet

SHOW YOUR SKILLS

Concepts:
> Word numbers (over 100), word problems, pound, addition (carrying), subtraction, and counting to 200

Objectives:
1. The student shall be able to write the two corresponding subtraction facts for each given addition fact.

2. The student shall be able to write the word number for a given numeral.

3. The student shall be able to write the correct sum for an addition problem when the ones' column has a double-digit answer.

4. The student shall be able to write the correct difference of two double-digit numbers.

Teaching Tips:
1. When doing activity 5, the student(s) would enjoy hearing about the first scales that were used in Egypt about 3000 B.C. These scales were called balances. They consisted of a horizontal bar with a pan hanging from each end. The bar is supported on a thin edge of metal. In one pan they put what is to be weighed and in the other they put weights of a known quantity until the two pans balance. This type of scale is often seen used to represent justice because it symbolizes a balance of equality.

Materials, Supplies, & Equipment:
1. Number chart 100–199

2. Flash cards for word numbers

3. Scale for weighing pounds

Activities:

1. Count out loud to 200 using the number chart 100–199.

2. Do an oral drill with the student(s) using three single-digit numbers for about 4 minutes. Use the addition facts 1–9 for the first two numbers and any single-digit number for the last one. Say the numbers out loud about 2 seconds apart and have the student(s) raise their hand as soon as they have the answer. Increase speed with each new problem.

3. The student(s) should be able to complete **Student Activity One** independently.

4. Display the word numbers for 1–10 and multiples of 10 using flash cards. Say several numbers over 100 for the student(s) and have them write the word numbers on a sheet of paper. Encourage them to refer to the flash cards if they have difficulty with the spelling. The student(s) should be able to complete **Student Activity Two** by themselves.

5. Discuss how a scale is used to measure weight by the pound. Show them a scale that is used to find a persons weight if you have not done so already. Talk about the scale at the meat counter that weighs meat and the scales on the interstate highways that weigh large trucks. The student(s) should be able to complete **Student Activity Three** on their own. Remind them that they are comparing pounds and that the "three weeks" is not used to find the answer.

6. Write "64 + 9" vertically on the chalk board. Have the student(s) copy the problem on a sheet of paper and work it without any help. Have them raise their hand when they have the answer. Check to see if it is correct. Continue with other examples if necessary. The student(s) should be able to complete **Student Activity Four** and **Five** without further help.

The only thing necessary for evil to triumph
is for good men to do nothing.

BAR GRAPH

Concepts:
>   Bar graph, word numbers (over 100), word problems, addition, subtraction, and counting by fours

Objectives:
1. The student shall be able to correctly write the number of objects represented on a bar graph.

2. The student shall be able to write the correct numeral corresponding to a given word number.

3. The student shall be able to write the two corresponding subtraction facts for each given addition fact.

4. The student shall be able to write the correct sum for an addition problem when the ones' column has a double-digit answer.

5. The student shall be able to write the correct difference of two double-digit numbers.

Teaching Tips:
1. Instead of activity 3, use the *addition facts flash cards* and have the student(s) give the two corresponding subtraction facts for each addition fact. Allow each student to do a separate fact. Then have the student(s) give the opposite addition fact as well as the corresponding subtraction facts. Take note of any student who would profit from additional practice with the flash cards and schedule a time for individual drill practice.

Materials, Supplies, & Equipment:
1. Number chart

2. Flash cards for subtraction facts 1–18, *word numbers,* and *addition facts 1–18*

3. Play money

Activities:

1. Count out loud by fours to 100 using the number chart where necessary.

2. Drill addition facts 1–18 using *Drill #1, Worksheet 68*.

3. Drill the subtraction facts 1–18 using flash cards without the answers showing.

4. Ask the student(s) to name each of the objects on the bar graph in **Student Activity One**. Read the first question together with the student(s). Allow them to answer it and complete the remaining questions by themselves.

5. Say several word numbers over 100 (or you may want to create them with *flash cards*) and have the students write the number on a sheet of paper. Include word numbers that have a zero in the ones' or tens' place. Write the numbers (e.g. 120, 204, etc.) on the chalk board to enable the student(s) to check their answers. Go over any questions that the student(s) might have. **Student Activity Two** should be complete by the student(s) on their own.

6. Have the student(s) read the word problem in **Student Activity Three** to themselves. Using play money have the student(s) count 7 dimes to see how many cents they have. When they write their answer, have them label it either "¢" or "cents."

7. The student(s) should be able to complete **Student Activity Four**, **Five**, and **Six** independently. In **Student Activity Five**, note that the small box is not above the tens' column. Insist that the student(s) continue to write the "1" above the tens' column for each of the problems.

Worksheets:

1. *Worksheet 68* – Addition and subtraction drill sheet

Even a fool may be thought wise when he keeps quiet.

ESTIMATION

Concepts:
Estimation, pound, bar graph, money, addition, and counting by fours

Objectives:
1. The student shall be able to circle the object that is an approximate given weight.

2. The student shall be able to color a block for each given object to be represented on a bar graph.

3. The student shall be able to write the two corresponding subtraction facts for each given addition fact.

4. The student shall be able to write the correct value of a given number of coins and their sum.

5. The student shall be able to write the correct sum for an addition problem when the ones' column has a double-digit answer.

Teaching Tips:
1. For activity 7, allow the student(s) to make their own combinations of coins using play money. Limit them to 4 pennies, 6 nickels, and 6 dimes to be sure their combinations will not require carrying. Have the student(s) write the value of each denomination of coins and add them together.

Materials, Supplies, & Equipment:
1. Number chart 0–99 and 100–199

2. Flash cards for addition facts 1–18

3. Weight objects (bag flour, butter, rock, etc.)

4. Play money

Activities:

1. Count out loud by fours to 100 using the number chart where necessary.

2. Drill subtraction facts 1–18 using *Drill #2, Worksheet 68.*

3. Drill the addition facts 1–18 using flash cards without the answers showing.

4. Show the student(s) objects that weigh "about" 1 pound, 5 pounds, and a larger weight. Discuss the comparison of the weight of each object. Look at the three objects given in **Student Activity One**. Discuss which is the heaviest and lightest. Ask "about" how much each of the objects would weigh. Read the directions with the student(s) and allow them to choose which object they should circle.

5. Have the student(s) look at the bar graph in **Student Activity Two** and note the numbers are given in multiples of ten. Discuss the names of each of the fruit given. Read the first sentence. Remind them to color the block at 60 first and then color the remaining blocks to the picture of the banana. Allow them to complete the last three sentences on their own.

6. The student(s) should be able to do **Student Activity Three** independently.

7. Using play money, display several combinations of quarters, dimes, nickels, and pennies similar to **Student Activity Four**. Have the student(s) tell the value of each denomination of coins as you write it on the chalk board in columns to enable them to add the values together. The selection of coins must be such as to require no carrying when doing the addition. It may be necessary to give help to some student(s) to complete **Student Activity Four** successfully.

8. **Student Activity Five** should be completed by the student(s) without any assistance.

Worksheets:

1. *Worksheet 68* – Addition and subtraction drill sheet

NUMBER SEQUENCE

Concepts:
Number sequence, money, subtraction, estimation, addition, word problem, and counting by sixes

Objectives:
1. The student shall be able to correctly write the next three numbers that come in a given sequence of numbers.

2. The student shall be able to write the correct value of a given number of coins and their sum.

3. The student shall be able to write the correct difference of two double-digit numbers.

4. The student shall be able to correctly write the number (20 or 30) indicating which is closer to a given number.

5. The student shall be able to write the correct sum for an addition problem when the ones' column has a double-digit answer.

Teaching Tips:
1. For enrichment in activity 7, number a number line from 120–130 and point to several numbers for the student(s) to tell you if they are closer to 120 or 130. Ask them what number is half way between 120 and 130. Then change the numbers to 420–430 and follow the same procedure.

Materials, Supplies, & Equipment:
1. Flash cards for subtraction facts 1–18

2. Number chart

3. Play money

4. *Counting chips*

5. Number line

Activities:

1. Count out loud by sixes to 96 from memory.

2. Drill addition facts 1–18 using *Drill #3, Worksheet 68.*

3. Drill the subtraction facts 1–18 using flash cards without the answers showing.

4. Write "16 14 12 __ __ __" on the chalk board. Point out that the sequence is going backwards by twos. With the help of a number chart, have the student(s) tell the next three numbers in the sequence to be written in the blanks by counting back two numbers each time. Write "19 17 15 __ __ __" and "30 28 26 __ __ __" on the chalk board, discuss the sequence, and determine what should be written in the blanks. Allow the student(s) to use the number chart (*Worksheet 5* may be helpful) to complete **Student Activity One** where needed.

5. Write "2 quarters, 3 dimes, and 8 pennies" in a vertical column on the chalk board. Give each student play money (or use *counting chips*) if they need it to find the value of each denomination of coins. Write the value of each denomination of coins as the student(s) tell you and let a student find the sum. Point out the importance of placing the value of the pennies or one nickel in the ones' column. Follow the same procedure with 3 quarters, 4 nickels, 4 pennies; and 1 quarter, 5 dimes, and 4 nickels. They should be able to do **Student Activity Two** on their own.

6. The student(s) should be able to complete **Student Activity Three** independently.

7. Using a number line from 20–30, point to several numbers and ask the student(s) if the number is closer to 20 or 30. Point out that 25 is half way between the two numbers. Any numbers less than 25 is closer to 20 and any number greater than 25 is closer to 30. They should be able to do **Student Activity Four** by themselves.

8. **Student Activity Five** should be completed by the student(s) without assistance.

9. Have the student(s) read **Student Activity Six** and tell you how they are to find the answer. Have them draw nickels on their paper and count them or use play money. Remind them to label the answer correctly.

Worksheets:

1. *Worksheet 69* – Addition of money

2. *Worksheet 68* – Addition and subtraction drill sheet

3. *Worksheet 5* – Number chart

NUMBER ORDER – < AND >

Concepts:
< and >, money, number sequence, estimation, word problems, addition, subtraction, and counting by sixes

Objectives:
1. The student shall be able to write the correct symbol (< or >) between a given number of coins and a given number of cents.

2. The student shall be able to circle every fifth number in a sequence of numbers and write the circled numbers in the blanks provided.

3. The student shall be able to circle the object that is an approximate given height.

4. The student shall be able to write the correct sum for an addition problem when the ones' column has a double-digit answer.

5. The student shall be able to write the correct difference of two double-digit numbers.

Teaching Tips:
1. When doing activity 5, give each student *Worksheet 5* and allow the student(s) to create their own number sequence. Begin with them choosing with what number they want to start (circle it) and by what number they want to count. Have them circle the numbers to 30 and write the circled numbers in sequence.

Materials, Supplies, & Equipment:
1. Flash cards for addition facts 1–18 and < and >

2. *Play money*

3. *Counting chips*

4. Number chart

5. Yard stick

Activities:

1. Count out loud by sixes to 96 from memory.

2. Drill subtraction facts 1–18 using *Drill #4, Worksheet 68.*

3. Drill the addition facts 1–18 using flash cards without the answers showing.

4. Review the names of the symbols < and > using flash cards. Write "2 quarters (¢) __ 60¢, 5 dimes (¢) __ 48¢, 8 nickels (¢) __ 35¢, and 14 pennies (¢) __ 15¢" on the chalk board. Have the student(s) determine the value of 2 quarters (*play money* or *counting chips* may be a help) and write it in the parentheses for each problem. Then ask the student(s) if 50¢ is < or > 60¢ and write the symbol in the blank. Follow the same procedure with the other examples. Work the first set of problems in *Student Activity One* together and then allow the student(s) to complete the last one on their own.

5. Using the number chart, ask the student(s) to count to the fifth number after three (8) and write "3" and "8" in a sequence. Count to the fifth number after 8 (13) and write "13" after the 8. Continue in the same manner until they reach 30. Point out to the student(s) that they have just created their own number sequence counting by fives but beginning with a number other than zero. The student(s) should be able to complete *Student Activity Two* by themselves.

6. Look at the three pictures in *Student Activity Three*. Have the student(s) show, with their hands being held apart, how tall they think each of the objects in the pictures is in real life. With a yard stick show them how tall 30 inches is. Then have them circle the picture that they think is about 30 inches tall.

7. Have the student(s) read the word problem in *Student Activity Four* to themselves. Let them find the answer on their own, giving guidance only where necessary. Remind them that they are comparing quarters and cents and that the "five pounds" is not used to find the answer.

8. The student(s) should complete *Student Activity Five* and *Six* without any assistance.

Worksheets:

1. *Worksheet 68* – Addition and subtraction drill facts

CENTIMETERS

Concepts:
Centimeters, number sequence, < and >, money, addition, subtraction, word problems, and counting by eights

Objectives:
1. The student shall be able to correctly measure a given line with a centimeter ruler.

2. The student shall be able to correctly circle every third number in a sequence of numbers and then write the circled numbers in correct sequence.

3. The student shall be able to write the correct symbol (< or >) between a given number of coins and a given number of cents.

4. The student shall be able to write the correct sum for an addition problem when the ones' column has a double-digit answer.

5. The student shall be able to write the correct difference of two double-digit numbers.

Teaching Tips:
1. When doing **Student Activity Six**, ask the student(s) to make up a word problem of their own. Give them a mental picture from which to draw. Tell them to think of 3 dogs and 2 cats, 5 cookies, and 1 cupcake or 28 chairs and 13 people. Have the student(s) tell the word problem, if they add or subtract, what the answer is, and what the label is.

Materials, Supplies, & Equipment:
1. Centimeter ruler

2. *Play money*

3. *Counting chips*

Activities:

1. Administer **Test 14.**

2. Count out loud by eights to 96 from memory.

3. Do an oral drill with the student(s) for 4 minutes using three single-digit numbers. Use the addition facts 1–9 for the first two numbers and any single-digit number for the last one. Say the numbers out loud about 2 seconds apart and have the student(s) raise their hand as soon as they have the answer. Increase speed with each problem.

4. Using their centimeter ruler, have the student(s) measure the lines given in **Student Activity One**. Instruct them to put the zero on their ruler at the beginning of the line and write the number of centimeters on the blanks.

5. In **Student Activity Two,** have the student(s) count to the third number after one, circle it (4), count to the third number after 4, circle it (7), and write the circled numbers in sequence on the blanks. Using the same procedure, continue to help those who need it until they are finished.

6. Using flash cards, discuss the symbols < and >. Write:

    1   quarter   (¢) __   30¢
    3   dimes   (¢) __   25¢
    7   nickels   (¢) __   40¢
    11   pennies   (¢) __   10¢

    on the chalk board. Have the student(s) determine the value of 1 quarter (you may want to use *play money* or *counting chips*) and write it in the parenthesis. Then ask the student(s) if 25¢ is < or > 30¢ and write the symbol in the blank. Follow the same procedure with the other examples. Work the first set of problems in **Student Activity Three** together and then allow the student(s) to complete the rest on their own.

7. The student(s) should be able to complete **Student Activity Four** and **Five** by themselves.

8. Have the student(s) read the word problem in **Student Activity Six** to themselves. Ask them to tell you if there is a key word (left), if they are to add or subtract, and what the label is. Point out to the student(s) that once they find the answer to be 1 dime and the question asks how many "cents," they now need to change the 1 dime into ten cents.

EVEN AND ODD NUMBERS

Concepts:

Even and odd numbers, centimeter, word numbers, addition, subtraction, word problems, months of the year, "Thirty Days Hath September," and counting by eights

Objectives:

1. The student shall be able to correctly circle the word "even" or "odd" corresponding to a given number.

2. The student shall be able to draw a line a given length using a centimeter ruler.

3. The student shall be able to write the correct numeral that corresponds to a given word number.

4. The student shall be able to write the correct sum for two double-digit numbers when the ones' column has a double-digit answer.

Teaching Tips:

1. Allow a student to choose a word number from the flash cards during activity 7. Have the other student(s) write down the number on a sheet of paper. Then let the student write the correct number on the chalk board by which the other student(s) may check their answer. If the student is capable, allow him to answer any questions about the word number.

Materials, Supplies, & Equipment:

1. Flash cards for subtraction facts 1–18, *months of the year*, and word numbers

2. Number chart

3. Centimeter ruler

Lesson 141

Activities:

1. Count out loud by eights to 96 from memory.

2. Drill addition facts 1–18 using *Drill #1, Worksheet 70.*

3. Drill the subtraction facts 1–18 using flash cards without the answers showing.

4. Recite with the student(s) the months of the year in correct order (you may want to use *flash cards*). Discuss the present month and what is special about it. Recite "Thirty Days Hath September" together.

5. Discuss with the student(s) the concept that all whole numbers are either even or odd. Using the number chart, point to several numbers and have them tell you if the numbers are even or odd and why (if the last digit of the number is 0, 2, 4, 6, or 8 the number is even and if the last digit of the number is 1, 3, 5, 7, or 9 the number is odd). They should be able to complete **Student Activity One** by themselves.

6. Put a dot on the chalk board. Have a student take his centimeter ruler to the chalk board and draw a line 12 centimeters long. If the student has difficulty holding the ruler steady, show him how to use his fingers on his non-writing hand to steady the ruler. Have the student(s) draw several lines of given lengths on the chalk board. They should be able to complete **Student Activity Two** on their own beginning each line at the dot.

7. Using flash cards, show several word numbers and have the student(s) write the numerals on a sheet of paper. Then, you write the numerals on the chalk board to enable the student(s) to check their work. Use some numbers with the zero in the tens' or the ones' place. The student(s) should be able to complete **Student Activity Three** with no further help.

8. Write "16 + 68," "57 + 26," and "43 + 29" on the chalk board as vertical addition problems. Work through each problem step by step with the student(s). Note that the tens' column is a three-digit addition problem. Be sure that they always add the ones' column first and then the tens' column. The student(s) should be able to complete **Student Activity Four** and **Five** independently.

9. After the student(s) read the word problem in **Student Activity Six** and determine if they add or subtract, encourage them to write the fact vertically before they solve the problem.

Worksheets:

1. *Worksheet 70* – Addition and subtraction drill sheet

335

MEASUREMENT – LIQUID

Concepts:
Liquid measure, even numbers, word numbers, solids, word problems, months of the year, "Thirty Days Hath September," and counting by sevens

Objectives:
1. The student shall be able to draw a line to match the liquid measure container to its name.

2. The student shall be able to circle the even numbers in a given set of numbers.

3. The student shall be able to write the word number that corresponds to a given numeral.

4. The student shall be able to mark an "X" on the solid that is different from the first solid given.

Teaching Tips:
1. In ***Student Activity One*** have the student(s) cut out ads from the *newspaper* that advertise items sold by liquid measure. Give them a sheet of *white paper* on which to *paste* their ads. Then ask them to write the name of the liquid measure used beside each ad.

Materials, Supplies, & Equipment:
1. Number chart

2. Flash cards for addition facts 1–18 and word numbers

3. Liquid measure containers

4. Solid models

5. *Newspaper*

6. *White paper* and *paste*

Activities:

1. Count out loud by sevens to 98 using the number chart only where necessary.

2. Drill subtraction facts 1–18 using *Drill #2, Worksheet 70*.

3. Drill the addition facts 1–18 using flash cards without the answers showing.

4. Recite the months of the year with the student(s) without the flash cards or the use of a calendar. Have them tell the number of days in each month using "Thirty Days Hath September" as reference after reciting the poem with the student(s) from memory.

5. Display the containers used when measuring liquids. Have the student(s) name each container as you point to it. Look at **Student Activity One**. As you read the first name "quart," have the student(s) point to the quart container on their paper and draw a line from the word to the container. Read the rest of the words and allow time for the student(s) to draw a line to the correct container.

6. Point to several numbers on the number chart and have the student(s) tell if they are even or odd numbers. The student(s) should be able to complete **Student Activity Two** by themselves.

7. Display the word number flash cards. Write several two and three-digit numbers on the chalk board and have the student(s) write the corresponding word number on a sheet of paper. Point out the word numbers using the flash cards so the student(s) can check their answers. Allow the student(s) to refer to the flash cards as they complete **Student Activity Three**.

8. Review the names of the solids using models. Have the student(s) look at **Student Activity Four** and read the directions together. Ask them to name the first solid and point to the picture that is not a cone. Have the student(s) mark it with an "X." Discuss why the pyramid is not a cone (the base is a square and not a circle). Follow the same procedure with the other three solids.

9. After the student(s) have determined to add in the first word problem in **Student Activity Five**, discuss the label with them. It may be necessary to remind them to write the second problem vertically before they attempt to find the answer.

Worksheets:

1. *Worksheet 71* – Measuring a boat in centimeters

2. *Worksheet 70* – Addition and subtraction drill sheet

PLACE VALUE – ONE HUNDREDS

Concepts:
Place value (one hundreds), liquid measure, odd numbers, solids, addition, subtraction, days of the week, and counting by sevens

Objectives:
1. The student shall be able to write the correct value of each digit in the hundreds', tens', and ones' place and the numeral it represents.

2. The student shall be able to correctly write the names of the units of measure for liquids.

3. The student shall be able to correctly circle the odd numbers in a given set of numbers.

4. The student shall be able to write the correct names of the given solids.

5. The student shall be able to write the correct sum for two double-digit numbers when the ones' column has a double-digit answer.

Teaching Tips:
1. When doing activity 6, have the student(s) look in the grocery store to see how many items they can find that are packaged by liquid measure.

Materials, Supplies, & Equipment:
1. Number chart

2. Flash cards for subtraction facts 1–18 and days of the week

3. Calendar

4. Liquid measure containers

5. Solid models

Activities:

1. Count out loud by sevens to 98 using the number chart only when necessary.

2. Drill addition facts 1–18 using *Drill #3, Worksheet 70.*

3. Drill subtraction facts 1–18 with flash cards without the answers showing.

4. Recite the days of the week in order with the student(s), using flash cards if necessary. Discuss what day today is and what the date is. Using a calendar, look at this date for the next month to see on what day of the week it will be. Recite the days of the week again without any aids.

5. Write several three-digit numbers on the chalk board (e.g. 631). Have the student(s) name the digits in the ones', tens', and hundreds' place. Then have them tell the value of each digit in each number and write it on the chalk board in expanded notation (e.g. 600 + 30 + 1). The student(s) should be able to complete **Student Activity One** by themselves.

6. Review the names of the containers used to measure liquids using the models. Discuss the items they are familiar with that use liquid measure. In **Student Activity Two**, have them point to the ounce container and write its name, then have them point to the cup and write its name, continue in the same way for the other three names.

7. The student(s) should be able to complete **Student Activity Three** on their own.

8. Using the solid models, have the student(s) name each of the solids. Ask one child to describe one of the solids and see if another student can determine what solid he is describing. In **Student Activity Four** have them point to the cone and write its name, then point to the cube and write its name, continuing with the next two solids in the same manner.

9. Write several two double-digit vertical addition problems. The ones' column should require carrying but the tens' column must not total more than 8. Work through each step needed (add the ones' column first, carry the 1 to the tens' column, and add the tens' column) for finding the sum. They should be able to complete **Student Activity Five** and **Six** by themselves as you check their work.

Worksheets:

1. *Worksheet 70* – Addition and subtraction drill sheet

339

TIME

Concepts:
Time, place value (one hundreds), word problems, inches, addition, subtraction, days of the weeks, and counting by sevens

Objectives:
1. The student shall be able to write the correct time shown on the face of a clock for the hour, half hour, and the quarter hour.

2. The student shall be able to write the correct value of the hundreds', tens', and ones' digit in a given number.

3. The student shall be able to measure the length of a given line using the inch ruler.

4. The student shall be able to write the correct sum for two double-digit numbers when the ones' column has a double-digit answer.

Teaching Tips:
1. When doing activity 1, give each student a copy of *Worksheet 5* and have them color the boxes that are used in counting by sevens. If a student is still having difficulty in counting by sevens, have him count over seven numbers each time to determine the next number in the sequence. Then have them write the numbers that are colored in a sequence at the bottom of the worksheet.

Materials, Supplies, & Equipment:
1. Number chart

2. Flash cards for addition facts 1–18

3. Calendar

4. Clock model

5. Inch ruler

Activities:

1. Count out loud by sevens to 98 using the number chart only when necessary.

2. Drill subtraction facts 1–18 using *Drill #4, Worksheet 70*.

3. Drill the addition facts 1–18 using flash cards without the answers showing.

4. Recite the days of the week from memory. Using a calendar for the present month, have the student(s) tell on which day of the week the 1st is, the last day of the month, the date of the first Thursday, the third Tuesday, how many Wednesdays in the month, and other similar things related to the calendar.

5. Setting the clock model for several times (15 minutes after and 45 minutes after the hour), have the student(s) tell you what time it is. The student(s) should then be able to complete **Student Activity One** on their own.

6. Write several three-digit numbers on the chalk board. Ask the student(s) to tell you the value of the digit in the hundreds' place, the tens' place, and the ones' place. Write them as a sum. The student(s) should complete **Student Activity Two** and **Three** by themselves.

7. Give the student(s) their inch ruler. Discuss with them the two different units of measure for length they have used – inches and centimeters. They will be measuring inches instead of centimeters for two lessons. Look at **Student Activity Four**. Allow the student(s) to measure the lines on their own, with you checking to see that they put the zero on the ruler at the beginning of the line.

8. **Student Activity Five** and **Six** should be completed by the student(s) independently.

Worksheets:

1. *Worksheet 72* – Dot to dot over 100

2. *Worksheet 70* – Addition and subtraction drill sheet

SHOW YOUR SKILLS

Concepts:
Place value (one hundreds), time, inches, addition, subtraction, and counting to 200

Objectives:
1. The student shall be able to write the correct digit that is in the hundreds' place, tens' place, and ones' place for a given number.

2. The student shall be able to correctly draw both hands on the face of the clock for the hour, half hour, and the quarter hour.

3. The student shall be able to draw a line a given length with an inch ruler.

4. A student shall be able to write the correct sum for two double-digit numbers when the ones' column has a double-digit answer.

Teaching Tips:
1. Instead of doing activity 1, you may want to have the student(s) fill in the missing numbers on the number chart given for *Worksheet 73*. This activity will give the student(s) practice in counting from 100 to 200 but will also provide practice in writing these large numbers.

Materials, Supplies, & Equipment:
1. Number chart 100–199

2. Clock model

3. Small clock models for student(s)

4. Inch ruler

Activities:

1. Count out loud from 100 to 200 using the number chart if necessary.

2. Do an oral drill of three single-digit numbers. Use the addition facts 1–18 for the first two numbers and any single-digit number as the third number to be subtracted. (e.g. 5 + 9–8 = __).

3. Write several three-digit numbers on the chalk board. Have the student(s) tell what digit is in the ones', tens', and hundreds' place changing the order with each number. Complete the first three sentences in **Student Activity One** together with the student(s) if necessary. Allow them to do the last three on their own.

4. Give the student(s) the small clock models. Write four times on the chalk board one at a time. Ask them which hand they are to set first and why (minute hand – because the minute hand tells where to place the hour hand). As the student(s) set their clocks for the given time, check their work with your clock. Allow the student(s) to complete **Student Activity Two** by themselves.

5. Tell the student(s) to take out a sheet of paper and their inch ruler. Ask them to put several points on their paper and draw a line a given length from each point. Observe any difficulty a student may be encountering. The student(s) should be able to complete **Student Activity Three** without any further help.

6. Write "43 + 28," "85 + 62," and "74 + 52" on the chalk board as three vertical addition problems. Allow the student(s) to copy the problems on a sheet of paper and work them at their seat. Then work the problems on the chalk board allowing the student(s) to tell you what to write. Have the student(s) check the work they did on their paper with what was written on the chalk board. **Student Activity Four** and **Five** should be completed by the student(s) independently.

Worksheets:

1. *Worksheet 73* – Fill in the blank number chart 100–199

EQUAL AND NOT EQUAL

Concepts:
= and ≠, word numbers, shapes, word problems, addition, subtraction, and counting to 200

Objectives:

1. The student shall be able to write the correct symbol (= or ≠) between a word number and a numeral.

2. The student shall be able to draw the given shapes by following the outline of the examples provided.

3. The student shall be able to write the correct sum for two double-digit numbers when the ones' column has a double-digit answer.

Teaching Tips:

1. Play a drill game with the student(s) in place of activity 3. Divide the student(s) into two teams. Using 30 subtraction flash cards, show one subtraction fact letting anyone from either team answer. The first to answer receives a point for his team (use tally marks to keep score on the chalk board). That person must then drop out of competition until everyone on their team has answered one fact. Then they may all rejoin the competition with the same rule. The team with the highest score at the end of the 30 cards will be the winner.

Materials, Supplies, & Equipment:

1. Number chart 100–199

2. Flash cards for subtraction facts 1–18, *word numbers*, and shapes

Activities:

1. Count out loud from 100 to 200 using the number chart if necessary.

2. Drill addition facts 1–18 using *Drill #1, Worksheet 74.*

3. Drill the subtraction facts 1–18 using flash cards without the answers showing.

4. Write several word numbers on the chalk board (or you may want to use *flash cards*). Ask the student(s) to read the numbers out loud. Then have them tell you what digits are needed to write each word number as a numeral. Beside half of the word numbers, write the corresponding numeral and by the other half, write numerals that do not correspond but are close. Ask the student(s) to tell you which symbol (= or ≠) should be placed between each set. Have the student(s) write the corresponding numeral for each word number in **Student Activity One** to help them decide which symbol (= or ≠) is the correct symbol for each set.

5. Using flash cards, review with the student(s) the names of the seven shapes given in **Student Activity Two**. Have the student(s) trace the white outline of the square with their pencils. After you are sure that they understand what to do, allow them to complete the activity for the other shapes.

6. Have the student(s) read the word problem in **Student Activity Three,** choose the key word(s), and decide if they are to add or subtract. Guide them in labeling their answer "nickels" and then changing the answer to cents.

7. The student(s) should be able to complete **Student Activity Four** and **Five** independently.

Worksheets:

1. *Worksheet 74* – Addition and subtraction drill sheet

A job well done is its own reward.

BAR GRAPH

Concepts:
    Bar graph, = and ≠, shapes, word problems, word
    numbers (over 100), subtraction, and counting by eights

Objectives:
1. The student shall be able to correctly write the number of objects represented on a bar graph.

2. The student shall be able to write the correct symbol (= or ≠) between a shape and a given name of a shape.

3. The student shall be able to write the correct numeral that corresponds to a given word number.

Teaching Tips:
1. When doing activity 1, have the student(s) use *Worksheet 5* to circle the numbers that are used in counting by fours. Then have them write the numbers that are circled in a sequence at the bottom of the worksheet. Now have them color the numbers used in counting by eights and write them in a sequence on the back of the worksheet.

2. In **Student Activity Four**, list 10 triple-digit numbers on the chalk board. Have the student(s) write them on a clean sheet of paper down the left side. Next have them write the word numbers that correspond to the numerals. Place the *word number flash cards* on the rail of the chalk board for reference.

Materials, Supplies, & Equipment:
1. Flash cards for addition facts 1–18, shapes, and *word numbers*

Activities:

1. Count out loud by eights to 96 from memory.

2. Drill subtraction facts 1–18 using *Drill #2, Worksheet 74.*

3. Drill the addition facts 1–18 using flash cards without the answers showing.

4. Have the student(s) look at the bar graph on **Student Activity One**. Ask them the value of an individual box on the bar graph. Count the boxes by tens. After reading the first question together with the student(s), allow them to complete the remaining questions on their own.

5. Using the flash cards, hold up a shape and have the student(s) say the name of the shape. Let them tell you if the shape and the name are the same or not the same (= or ≠). Continue with each shape making some names the same (=) and some not the same (≠). After discussing the directions for **Student Activity Two**, the student(s) should continue by themselves.

6. When the student(s) complete **Student Activity Three**, remind them to change their answer from quarters to cents.

7. The student(s) should be able to complete **Student Activity Four** and **Five** independently.

Worksheets:

1. *Worksheet 74* – Addition and subtraction drill sheet

*If you want to do mighty deeds
you must first learn to handle little responsibilities.*

ESTIMATION

Concepts:
Estimation, bar graph, fractions, addition, and counting by eights

Objectives:
1. The student shall be able to write the correct number (20 or 30) indicating which is closer to a given number.

2. The student shall be able to color a block for each given object to be represented on a bar graph.

3. The student shall be able to determine what fractional part of a whole is shaded and write the fraction.

4. The student shall be able to write the correct sum for two double-digit numbers when the ones' and tens' column have a double-digit answer.

Teaching Tips:
1. For enrichment when doing activity 5, have the student(s) create their own bar graph. Give each student a sheet of *large squared graph paper* with a box 5 units by 8 units drawn on it. Allow them to choose three items for their graph. Tell them to use the graph in **Student Activity Two** as a guide for placing the items they have chosen on their graph. Help them number the boxes on the left hand side. Let each student determine how many of each item they want to represent on their graph. Have them write it down and then color the boxes to represent the quantity they have for each item.

Materials, Supplies, & Equipment:
1. Flash cards for subtraction facts 1–18

2. Number line

3. Fraction materials

4. *Large squared graph paper*

Activities:

1. Count out loud by eights to 96 from memory.

2. Drill addition facts 1–18 using *Drill #3, Worksheet 74.*

3. Drill the subtraction facts 1–18 using flash cards without the answers showing.

4. Using a number line for 20 to 30, point to a number (23) and have the student(s) tell you if the number is closer to 20 or 30. Discuss with them that 23 is then "about" 20 (an approximate answer). Tell them that they are rounding off the number 23 to the nearest ten. Follow the same thought process with several other numbers. The student(s) should be able to complete **Student Activity One** by themselves.

5. Have the student(s) look at the bar graph in **Student Activity Two** and follow along as you read the first sentence. Ask them to point to the star on the graph and count each box above it by tens until they reach the box for 60. Color that box first and then each box below it. Allow those who are capable to color the last two bars on their own giving help where needed.

6. Using fraction materials, display wholes divided into 2, 3, 4, 5, 6, and 8 parts. As you take one part away from each set, have the student(s) tell you what part you have removed and have them write the fraction on a blank sheet of paper. Next let them complete **Student Activity Three** and **Four** independently.

Worksheets:

1. *Worksheet 75 – 81 addition facts*

2. *Worksheet 74 – Addition and subtraction drill sheet*

The worst kind of failure is never trying.

NUMBER SEQUENCE

Concepts:

Number sequence, inches, estimation, word problems, fractions, addition, subtraction, and counting by nines

Objectives:

1. The student shall be able to place an "X" on the number that is incorrect in a sequence of numbers.

2. The student shall be able to circle the number that is closer to the length of a given line measured with an inch ruler.

3. The student shall be able to draw the necessary lines to divide a given object into the number of equal segments needed to shade a given fractional part.

4. The student shall be able to write the correct sum for two double-digit numbers when the ones' and the tens' column have a double-digit answer.

Teaching Tips:

1. On a clean sheet of paper, have the student(s) draw the shapes you put on the chalk board in activity 7. Ask them to divide the shapes into the given number of parts and shade one part as a student is doing the same on the chalk board. Discuss the different ways a shape may be divided into a given number of parts. Ask if it makes a difference which one of the given parts is shaded.

Materials, Supplies, & Equipment:

1. Flash cards for addition facts 1–18

2. Inch ruler

3. *Fraction materials*

Activities:

1. Count out loud by nines to 99 from memory.

2. Drill subtraction facts 1–18 using *Drill #4, Worksheet 74.*

3. Drill the addition facts 1–18 using flash cards without the answers showing.

4. On the chalk board, write the following number sequence: "3, 6, 9, 11, 15, 18, 22, 24, 27, 30, 32, 36, 39, 42, 46, 48, 51, 54, 57, 61." Have the student(s) tell you the numbers that are not in sequence by counting by threes and put an "X" on them. Then ask the student(s) to tell you the correct numbers needed to replace the "X"s. Discuss with the student(s) the sequence used in **Student Activity One**. Help the student(s) find the first number that is not in sequence and then allow them to continue on their own.

5. Give each student an inch ruler. For the remaining lessons dealing with measurement of length, the student(s) will be using the inch ruler. Remind the student(s) to place the zero on the inch ruler at the beginning of the first line in **Student Activity Two**. Have each student determine if the length of the line is closer to 2 or 3 inches and circle the number. Discuss the number they circled and why they chose it. Instruct the student(s) to measure the last three lines by themselves.

6. After the student(s) have read the word problem in **Student Activity Three** and written the correct subtraction fact, remind them to write the fact vertically before they find the answer and to label the answer.

7. Draw five shapes on the chalk board that can be easily divided into 2, 3, 4, 5, or 6 parts. Ask a student to come to the chalk board and divide one shape into 2 parts. Then have him shade 1/2 of the shape. Do the same for each of the other shapes using 3, 4, 5, and 6 respectively (*fraction materials* may be a help). Allow the student(s) to complete **Student Activity Four** independently.

8. The student(s) should complete **Student Activity Five** and **Six** without any assistance.

Worksheets:

1. *Worksheet 74* – Addition and subtraction drill sheet

351

DOZEN

Concepts:
Dozen, number sequence, inches, < and >, addition, subtraction, and counting by nines

Objectives:
1. The student shall be able to write the number of objects in a dozen and circle a dozen objects in a given set.

2. The student shall be able to place an "X" on the number that is incorrect in a sequence of numbers.

3. The student shall be able to draw a line of a given length using an inch ruler.

4. The student shall be able to correctly write < or > between a subtraction fact and a whole number.

5. The student shall be able to write the correct sum for two double-digit numbers when the tens' column has a double-digit answer.

Teaching Tips:
1. Once the student(s) have finished **Student Activity Two**, have them write the correct number above each number on which they have put an "X."

2. If a student has difficulty with **Student Activity Four**, tell him to write the answer to the subtraction fact above the subtraction fact and then make the comparison of the two numbers.

Materials, Supplies, & Equipment:
1. Counting chips

2. Inch ruler

3. Flash cards for subtraction facts 10 –18

Activities:

1. Administer *Test 15*.

2. Count out loud by nines to 99 from memory.

3. Do an oral drill of three single-digit numbers. Use the addition facts 1–18 for the first two numbers and any single-digit number as the third number to be subtracted. (e.g. 7 + 4–3 = __).

4. Discuss with the student(s) how many cookies are in a dozen. Give each student 30 counting chips and ask them to count out two sets of one dozen each. Have them put the two sets together and count the chips to see how many are in 2 dozen. Tell the student(s) to read the question in *Student Activity One*, write the answer, and circle one dozen in each group.

5. Write the following number sequence on the chalk board: "4, 8, 11, 16, 20, 24, 29, 32, 36, 39, 44, 48, 53, 56, 60, 64, 69, 72, 76, 81." Have the student(s) tell you the numbers that are in sequence by counting by fours and put an "X" on the numbers that do not belong. Then ask the student(s) to tell you the correct numbers to replace the "X"s. Discuss the sequence used in *Student Activity Two*. Find the first number that is not in sequence with them and then allow them to continue on their own.

6. Have the student(s) take out a sheet of paper and their inch ruler. Ask them to put three dots on their paper in a vertical line about an inch apart. Tell them to place the zero on their ruler at the first dot on the paper and draw a line 4 inches long. Remind them to hold their ruler steady by using the fingers on their free hand spread along the ruler (a visual demonstration would help). Give the student(s) two more lengths to draw. Help those student(s) who do not put the zero at the dot. The student(s) should be able to complete *Student Activity Three* with little help.

7. Hold up a flash card for subtraction facts 10–18 (e.g. 15–9). Have the student(s) give the answer (6). Then say a number that is close to the answer (e.g. 8). Ask the student(s) to tell you if the answer (6) is < or > than the number (8) you gave. Show several flash cards and follow the same procedure. Encourage the student(s) not to guess what the symbol should be in *Student Activity Four*. They need to first think of the answer to the subtraction fact and then make the comparison.

8. The student(s) should be able to complete *Student Activity Five* and *Six* independently.

MONEY

Concepts:

Money, sequence of events, < and >, subtraction, and counting by sevens

Objectives:

1. The student shall be able to circle a given amount of money, in cents, from a group of coins.

2. The student shall be able to number a series of pictures in correct sequential order.

3. The student shall be able to write the correct symbol (< or >) between a subtraction fact and a whole number.

4. The student shall be able to write the difference of two triple-digit numbers without borrowing.

5. The student shall be able to write the missing numbers from 0 to 49.

Teaching Tips:

1. When doing activity 6, write several sets of two numbers on the chalk board that are > 200 and < 999. Allow the student(s) to tell you which symbol (< or >) should be placed between the two numbers. Remind them that when the hundreds' digits are the same they should compare only the tens' and ones' place and when the hundreds' digits are different they compare only the hundreds' digits.

Materials, Supplies, & Equipment:

1. Number chart

2. Flash cards for subtraction facts 1–18

3. Play money

Activities:

1. Count out loud by sevens to 98 using the number chart only where necessary.

2. Drill addition facts 1–18 using *Drill #1, Worksheet 76*.

3. Drill the subtraction facts 1–18 using flash cards without the answers showing.

4. Give the student(s) play money and have them select the coins needed to equal 72¢, 87¢, 36¢, and 54¢. Guide them in selecting the larger coins first. For 72¢ encourage them to select the 70¢ (7 dimes, 2 quarters and 2 dimes, or 2 quarters, 2 nickels, and 1 dime) first and then the 2¢. Discuss the many different combinations they may use. Read the directions for **Student Activity One** with the student(s) and allow them to continue on their own.

5. Have the student(s) look at the three pictures in **Student Activity Two**. Point out that the beginning event is the child climbing up a slide as the title indicates. Have them number that picture "1" and then choose on their own in what order the other two pictures happen and write the number by the appropriate picture.

6. When beginning **Student Activity Three**, encourage the student(s) to solve for the answer to the subtraction fact and then compare the two numbers. Discourage guessing.

7. Write several sets of two triple-digit numbers on the chalk board to be used as subtraction problems that do not involve borrowing. For the first two problems, work with the student(s) by starting the subtraction with the ones' column, then the tens' column, and last the hundreds' column. Have the student(s) copy the third problem onto a sheet of paper and work it by themselves. Have one of the student(s) give his answer and then discuss how he arrived at that answer. Continue with several more problems in this manner before the student(s) do **Student Activity Four** by themselves.

8. The student(s) should be able to complete **Student Activity Five** independently.

Worksheets:

1. *Worksheet 76* – Addition and subtraction drill sheet

355

SOLIDS

Concepts:
Solids, money, sequence of events, even numbers, addition, subtraction, months of the year, "Thirty Days Hath September," and counting by sevens

Objectives:
1. The student shall be able to draw a line to match a given solid to its name.

2. The student shall be able to circle a given amount of money in cents from a group of coins.

3. The student shall be able to number a series of pictures in correct sequential order.

4. The student shall be able to write seven even numbers.

5. The student shall be able to write the difference of two triple-digit numbers without borrowing.

Teaching Tips:
1. When doing activity 4, place the *months of the year flash cards* on the chalk board rail and allow the student(s) to read them backwards. Encourage them to think about the month that comes "before" as they read each one. Then have them read the months in the correct order encouraging them to think about the month that comes "after" as they read each one.

Materials, Supplies, & Equipment:
1. Number chart

2. Flash cards for addition facts 1–18 and *months of the year*

3. Solid models

4. Play money

Activities:

1. Count out loud by sevens to 98 using the number chart where necessary.

2. Drill subtraction facts 1–18 using *Drill #2, Worksheet 76.*

3. Drill the addition facts 1–18 using flash cards without the answers showing.

4. Recite the months of the year in order and "Thirty Days Hath September" from memory.

5. Using the solid models, have the student(s) tell the name of each solid. Allow them to describe what each solid looks like. With the solids in a row, call out a solid and have them tell you if it is the first, second, third, or fourth solid. The student(s) should be able to complete ***Student Activity One*** by themselves.

6. Give each student play money. Write several amounts of money, less than a dollar, on the chalk board. Have the student(s) select the coins necessary to equal the given amounts. Discuss the different combinations that are possible. The student(s) should be able to complete ***Student Activity Two*** by themselves.

7. Give the student(s) several sequences of events (e.g. butter the bread and then toast it or toast it and then butter the toast). Allow the student(s) to select the correct order. They should then be able to complete ***Student Activity Three*** on their own.

8. Read the directions for ***Student Activity Four*** with the student(s). Allow them to pick out any even numbers they choose and write them on the blanks.

9. The student(s) should be able to complete ***Student Activity Five*** and ***Six*** without any assistance.

Worksheets:

1. *Worksheet 76* – Addition and subtraction drill sheet

SHOW YOUR SKILLS

Concepts:

Money, solids, sequence of events, odd numbers, addition, months of the year, "Thirty Days Hath September," and counting by sevens

Objectives:

1. The student shall be able to circle a given amount of money, in cents, from a group of coins.

2. The student shall be able to write the correct name by the model of a cube, sphere, cylinder, and cone.

3. The student shall be able to number a series of pictures in correct sequential order.

4. The student shall be able to write seven odd numbers.

5. The student shall be able to write the missing numbers from 50 to 99.

Teaching Tips:

1. Before doing **Student Activity One**, play store with the student(s). Ask one student to be the store keeper. Allow them to come to the store, purchase an item, and count out the correct amount of money they need. Then let them decide if they have enough money left to make a second purchase.

Materials, Supplies, & Equipment:

1. Number charts 0–99 and *100–199*

2. Flash cards for subtraction facts 1–18, months of the year, and solids

3. Play money

4. Solid models

Activities:

1. Count out loud by sevens to 98 using the number chart where necessary.

2. Drill addition facts 1–18 using *Drill #3, Worksheet 76.*

3. Drill the subtraction facts 1–18 using flash cards without the answers showing.

4. Mix up the months of the year flash cards and have a student arrange them in the correct order on the chalk board rail. Give each student an opportunity to recite the months of the year from memory. Have the student(s) recite "Thirty Days Hath September" together.

5. Give each student play money. Ask them to select the coins necessary to have 26¢, 41¢, 66¢, and 93¢. Discuss the different combinations that are possible for each amount. The student(s) should be able to complete **Student Activity One** independently.

6. Using the solid models, ask the student(s) to identify each solid by writing its name on a piece of paper as you point to the solid. Displaying the solid flash cards with the names showing will help the student(s) in using correct spelling. The student(s) should complete **Student Activity Two** on their own.

7. After discussing what is happening in the three pictures in **Student Activity Three**, allow the student(s) to number the pictures in the correct sequential order without any assistance.

8. Ask the student(s) to give you examples of odd numbers under 100 and over 100 (you may want to use the *number charts*). Have one student say an odd number and another student tell if he is correct or not and why (last digit in the number). Allow the student(s) to complete **Student Activity Four** by themselves using any odd numbers they choose.

9. The student(s) should be able to complete **Student Activity Five** and **Six** independently.

Worksheets:

1. *Worksheet 76* – Addition and subtraction drill sheet

TIME

Concepts:
Time, money, even and odd numbers, addition, subtraction, days of the week, and counting by seven

Objectives:
1. The student shall be able to write the correct time on the face of the clock by the hour, half hour, and quarter hour.

2. The student shall be able to circle a given amount of money, in cents, from a group of coins.

3. The student shall be able to color the even and odd numbered marbles a given color.

4. The student shall be able to write the correct sum for two double-digit numbers when the ones' and the tens' column have a double-digit answer.

5. The student shall be able to write the difference of two triple-digit numbers without borrowing.

Teaching Tips:
1. For enrichment when doing activity 6, give the student(s) dollar bills with their play money. Ask the student(s) to count out $3.47, $1.04, $2.67, and $4.80. For $1.04 they could use 4 quarters and 4 pennies. Next have a student operate an imaginary store while another student goes to the store and purchases two items. Have the store keeper add up the cost of the items. The shopper should pay for the items and allow the storekeeper to make change.

Materials, Supplies, & Equipment:
1. Number chart

2. Flash cards for addition facts 1–18

3. Calendar

4. Clock model

5. Play money

Activities:

1. Count out loud by sevens to 98 using the number chart where necessary.

2. Drill subtraction facts 1–18 using *Drill #4, Worksheet 76.*

3. Drill the addition facts 1–18 using flash cards without the answers showing.

4. Recite the days of the week in the correct order with the student(s). Using a calendar for the present month, discuss with the student(s) how many days in the month, how many Mondays there are, what the date of the third Wednesday is, and on what day the 18th is.

5. Using the large clock model, practice with the student(s) telling the time for the quarter hour (using both 15 minutes and 45 minutes after the hour). They should be able to complete **Student Activity One** by themselves.

6. Using play money, allow the student(s) to select the coins needed for a given amount of money under a dollar. The student(s) should complete **Student Activity Two** on their own.

7. Read the directions for **Student Activity Three** together with the student(s). Tell them to look at the first marble and decide if it has an even or an odd number on it and color it the corresponding color. Encourage them to continue by looking at each marble and deciding if it is even or odd and coloring it the corresponding color.

8. The student(s) should be able to complete **Student Activity Four** and **Five** independently.

Worksheets:

1. *Worksheet 77 – 81 subtraction facts*

2. *Worksheet 76 – Addition and subtraction drill sheet*

Make the best of today for it is all you have.

NUMBER ORDER – ORDINAL NUMBERS

Concepts:

Ordinal numbers, time, place value (one hundreds), addition, subtraction, word problems, and days of the week

Objectives:

1. The student shall be able to draw a line to match a written ordinal number to the corresponding abbreviated form of the ordinal number.

2. The student shall be able to correctly draw the short (hour) hand on the face of the clock for a given hour, half hour, and quarter hour.

3. The student shall be able to write the value of each digit in the hundreds', tens', and ones' place and the numeral it represents.

4. The student shall be able to write the correct sum for two double-digit numbers when the ones' and the tens' column have a double-digit answer.

5. The student shall be able to write the difference of two triple-digit numbers without borrowing.

Teaching Tips:

1. Before completing activities 2 and 3, place the *days of the week flash cards* on the chalk board rail and have the student(s) tell you which is the fourth day, second day, etc. Then mix the flash cards up and have a student choose the one that is the first day and place it on the chalk rail, the second day, the third day, etc.

Materials, Supplies, & Equipment:

1. Calendar

2. Small clock models for student(s)

3. Clock model

4. *Flash cards for days of the week*

Activities:

1. Do an oral drill of three single-digit numbers. Use the addition facts 1–18 for the first two numbers and any single-digit number as the third number to be subtracted. (e.g. 8 + 5–6 = __).

2. Recite the days of the week in the correct order. Using a calendar for the present month, discuss what today's date is, what day of the week it is, what the date is three days after today, what day of the week is three days after today, what was the date three days before today, and what day of the week was three days before today.

3. Point out to the student(s) the abbreviated form of the ordinal numbers in **Student Activity One**. Read each column together with the student(s). Allow the student(s) to then draw the lines to match the ordinal numbers on their own.

4. Give the student(s) small clock models. Review with them the placement of the hour hand when setting the clock for the hour, half hour and quarter hour. Ask them to tell you which hand they need to place in position first when setting the clock for a given time (the long minute hand). Write several times on the chalk board in digital form and ask the student(s) to place the hands in the correct position for each given time. Have the student(s) check their clocks with your clock. The student(s) should be able to complete **Student Activity Two** by themselves.

5. Write several three-digit numbers on the chalk board. Have the student(s) tell you the value of each digit for each number, changing the digit you start with each time (e.g. 10's, 1's, and 100's; 100's, 1's, and 10's; 1's, 10's, and 100's). Write "600 + 40 + 2; 300 + 70 + 9; and 100 + 50 + 8" on the chalk board and have the student(s) tell what number they represent. The student(s) should complete **Student Activity Three** without any further assistance.

6. The student(s) should be able to complete **Student Activity Four**, **Five**, and **Six** independently.

He who would have friends must show himself friendly.

PLACE VALUE –
ONE HUNDREDS

Concepts:

Place value (one hundreds), time, ordinal numbers, addition, subtraction, word problems, and counting to 200

Objectives:

1. The student shall be able to write the correct value of the digit in the hundreds', tens', and ones' place for a given number.

2. The student shall be able to write the correct number when given the value of the digit in the hundreds', tens', and ones' place.

3. The student shall be able to correctly draw both hands on the face of the clock for a given hour, half hour, and quarter hour.

4. The student shall be able to correctly place a set of letters numbered ordinally on blanks corresponding to the appropriate ordinal numbers.

5. The student shall be able to write the correct sum for two double-digit numbers when the ones' and the tens' column have a double-digit answer.

6. The student shall be able to write the difference of two triple-digit numbers without borrowing.

Teaching Tips:

1. Show the student(s) how to make their own coded message as in **Student Activity Three**. On the chalk board write "I like to swim." On a sheet of paper have them draw eleven blanks like this: _ _ _ _ _ _ _ (first row) _ _ _ _ (second row). Underneath the blanks, in three columns, have them write "second, sixth, ninth, first, tenth, third, eighth, eleventh, fourth, seventh, and fifth" with a blank beside each word similar to **Student Activity Three**. On the blank beside the word "first" put an "I," beside the word "second" put an "l," beside the word "third" put an "i," continuing until all blanks are filled. The message is now ready to decode.

Materials, Supplies, & Equipment:

1. Flash cards for subtraction facts 1–18 and ordinal numbers

2. Small clock models for student(s)

3. Clock model

Activities:

1. Count out loud from 100 to 200 without the number chart.

2. Drill addition facts 1–18 using *Drill #1, Worksheet 78*.

3. Drill the subtraction facts 1–18 using flash cards without the answers showing.

4. The student(s) should be able to complete **Student Activity One** on their own.

5. Give the student(s) small clock models. Write several quarter hour times in digital form on the chalk board. Have the student(s) tell you what hand they will place in position first when setting their clock (long minute hand). Have the student(s) check their clocks with your clock. The student(s) should be able to complete **Student Activity Two** by themselves.

6. Review the ordinal numbers using flash cards if necessary. Ask the student(s) to read the directions to **Student Activity Three** out loud together. Tell them to point to the second blank and then write the letter "U" on that blank. Do the same for the next two ordinal numbers. Some student(s) should be able to complete the blanks on their own while others may still need help.

7. The student(s) should complete **Student Activity Four**, **Five**, and **Six** independently.

Worksheets:

1. *Worksheet 78* – Addition and subtraction drill sheet

*Wisdom is better than precious jewels and
more valuable than anything that can be bought.*

FRACTIONS – ONE HALF

Concepts:
Fractions (one half), place value (one hundreds), sets, addition, subtraction, and counting to 200

Objectives:
1. The student shall be able to circle the number of objects that represent one half of a set.

2. The student shall be able to write the digit that is in the hundreds', tens', and ones' place for a given number.

3. The student shall be able to write the numeral that represents the number of objects counted in a set.

4. The student shall be able to write the correct sum for two double-digit numbers when the ones' and tens' column have a double-digit answer.

5. The student shall be able to write the difference of two triple-digit numbers without borrowing.

Teaching Tips:
1. When doing activity 7, give each student *place value materials*. For reinforcement of carrying in addition, write "37 + 8" on the chalk board as a vertical addition problem. From the place value materials, have the student(s) select 3 tens and 7 ones and then have them select 8 ones. Ask them how many ones they will have when adding the 7 ones and 8 ones together (15). Tell them to take 10 of the ones and replace them with 1 ten and see how many ones they have left (5). Now ask them how many tens they have altogether and how many ones (4 tens and 5 ones) and what number that represents (45). Next work the problem on the chalk board by carrying the 1 to the tens' column and compare with the place value answer. Complete several more problems following the same procedure.

Materials, Supplies, & Equipment:
1. Flash cards for addition facts 1 -18

2. Flannel board

3. Flannel board materials

4. Inch ruler

5. *Place value materials*

Activities:

1. Count out loud from 100 to 200 without the number chart.

2. Drill subtraction facts 1–18 using *Drill #2, Worksheet 78.*

3. Drill the addition facts 1–18 using flash cards without the answer showing.

4. Display several sets of an even number of objects on the flannel board so that a straight line can be used to divide each set in half. Explain to the student(s) that they are going to be taking one half of each set away. This means they are going to be dividing the sets in half or into two equal parts. Using an inch ruler (or any other straight edge) as the dividing line, show them how they can divide the first set so that they have the same number of objects on each side of the line. If the set can be divided more than one way (e.g. 2 rows of 2), show them all the possibilities. Let them tell you how to divide the remaining sets. The student(s) will need your help as they complete each set in *Student Activity One.*

5. Write several three-digit numbers on the chalk board. Ask the student(s) to tell you what number is in the tens', hundreds', and ones' place and the value of each digit. The student(s) should be able to complete *Student Activity Two* by themselves.

6. *Student Activity Three* should be completed by the student(s) independently.

7. Write several sets of two double-digit numbers (the sum of both the ones' and the tens' columns should be greater than 9) on the chalk board. Ask the student(s) to copy the problems on a sheet of paper and find their sum. Then work each of the problems on the chalk board and have them check each of their answers. Encourage the student(s) that have an incorrect answer to find out what they did wrong. Carefully check the student(s) work as they complete *Student Activity Four.*

8. The student(s) should complete *Student Activity Five* on their own.

Worksheets:

1. *Worksheet 78* – Addition and subtraction drill sheet

ESTIMATION

Concepts:
   Estimation, fractions (one half), word numbers (over 100), bar graphs, shapes, and counting by eights

Objectives:
1. The student shall be able to correctly write the number (0 or 10) indicating which is closer to a given number without the number line.

2. The student shall be able to circle the number of objects that represent one half of a set.

3. The student shall be able to write the numeral that corresponds to a given word number.

4. The student shall be able to write the correct number of objects represented on a bar graph.

5. The student shall be able to draw a line to match one half of a shape with the other half.

Teaching Tips:
1. When doing activity 5, give each student *counting chips*. Tell them to count out 10 chips and line them up into two equal rows. Have them then divide the ten chips into two equal sets and count how many are in each set. Ask them how many counting chips they have when they take one half of 10. Then ask them what 5 plus 5 equals. Using several other sets with an even number of objects, have the student(s) discover how many one half of a number is.

Materials, Supplies, & Equipment:
1. Flash cards for subtraction facts 1–18 and shapes

2. Centimeter ruler

3. Flannel board

4. Flannel board materials

5. *Counting chips*

Activities:

1. Count out loud by eights to 96 from memory.

2. Drill addition facts 1–18 using *Drill #3, Worksheet 78.*

3. Drill the subtraction facts 1–18 using flash cards without the answers showing.

4. Without the use of the number line, ask the student(s) if the following numbers (3, 7, 4, 9, 6, 2, and 8) are closer to 0 or 10. Remind them that if the number is less than 5 the number is closer to 0 and if the number is greater than 5 the number is closer to 10. Allow the student(s) to complete **Student Activity One** by themselves using their centimeter ruler as a number line if necessary.

5. On the flannel board, display several sets of an even number of objects so that a straight line can be used to divide each set in half. Explain to the student(s) that they are going to be dividing the sets into two equal parts or taking away one half of the set. Have the student(s) come to the flannel board and tell you where the line should be drawn so that the set is divided into two equal parts. Have them count the number of objects on each side of the line to be sure that there is an equal number. Allow the student(s) to complete **Student Activity Two** on their own helping only where necessary.

6. **Student Activity Three** and **Four** should be completed by the student(s) independently.

7. Using the shape flash cards, cover up one half of each shape and have the student(s) draw on a sheet of paper what they think the other half should look like. When starting **Student Activity Five**, have the student(s) tell you the name of the first half shape in the top row and point to the other half in the bottom row. Then draw a line to connect the two halves. Follow this procedure for each of the half shapes in the first row.

Worksheets:

1. *Worksheet 79* – Estimation

2. *Worksheet 78* – Addition and subtraction drill sheet

NUMBER SEQUENCE

Concepts:

Number sequence, estimation, inches, fractions, = and ≠, word numbers (over 100), word problems, and counting by nines

Objectives:

1. The student shall be able to correctly write the next three numbers that come in a given sequence of numbers.

2. The student shall be able to correctly write the number (0 or 10) indicating which is closer to a given number without the number line.

3. The student shall be able to write the correct length of a line measured with an inch ruler.

4. The student shall be able to write the correct symbol (= or ≠) between a unit fraction and a whole that has been divided and shaded.

5. The student shall be able to write the numeral that corresponds to a given word number.

Teaching Tips:

1. For enrichment when doing activity 4, write "436 439 442 ___ ___ ___" on the chalk board. Guide the student(s) in determining how many numbers they must count to go from 436 to 439, and then from 439 to 442. Ask them to tell you the number that will go in the next three blanks. Write several more sequences on the chalk board using numbers over 200 and allow them to determine the next three numbers.

Materials, Supplies, & Equipment:

1. Flash cards for addition facts 1–18 and = *and* ≠

2. Number chart

3. Centimeter ruler

4. Inch ruler

5. *Fraction materials*

Activities:

1. Count out loud by nines to 99 from memory.

2. Drill subtraction facts 1–18 using *Drill #4, Worksheet 78.*

3. Drill the addition facts 1–18 using flash cards without the answers showing.

4. Have the student(s) look at the first number sequence in **Student Activity One**. Ask them how many numbers they must count to go from 12 to 15 (3) and from 15 to 18 (3). Counting over 3 more places gives them the number to go in the first blank. Let them fill in the remaining blanks on their own using a number chart if necessary.

5. Without the use of the number line, ask the student(s) if the following numbers (13, 17, 14, 11, 19, 16, 12, and 18) are closer to 10 or 20. Remind them if the number is less than 15 the number is closer to 10 and if the number is greater than 15 the number is closer to 20. Allow them to complete **Student Activity Two** on their own using their centimeter ruler as a number line if necessary.

6. After reminding the student(s) to put the zero on their inch ruler at the beginning of the line, the student(s) should be able to complete **Student Activity Three** independently.

7. Review the = and ≠ symbols (you may want to use *flash cards*). Draw several different shapes on the chalk board and shade a unit fraction (1/2, 1/3, 1/4, 1/5, 1/6, or 1/8) on each (or use *fraction materials*). Have the student(s) tell what fractional part is shaded for each shape. Then have the student(s) look at the first shape in **Student Activity Four** and determine what fractional part is shaded. If the shaded part is the same as the given fraction put the = symbol. If the shaded part is not the same put the ≠ symbol. Guide the student(s) as they consider each shape but allow them to determine which symbol (= or ≠) to use by themselves.

8. The student(s) should complete **Student Activity Five** and **Six** without any assistance.

Worksheets:

1. Worksheet 80 – Double-digit addition

2. *Worksheet 78* – Addition and subtraction drill sheet

NUMBER ORDER – < AND >

Concepts:
    < and >, number sequence, inches, bar graph, subtraction, and counting by sevens

Objectives:
1. The student shall be able to write the correct symbol (< or >) between a subtraction fact and a numeral.

2. The student shall be able to correctly circle every third number in a sequence of numbers and then write the circled numbers in correct sequential order.

3. The student shall be able to draw a line of a given length using an inch ruler.

4. The student shall be able to color a block for each given object to be represented on a bar graph.

Teaching Tips:
1. When doing activity 6, show the student(s) a *yardstick*. Let them see how many inches in a yard. Discuss some objects that they would rather measure with a yardstick than with an inch ruler. Since a yardstick measures distance, ask if there are some distances they would not want to measure with a yardstick and what unit they would use to measure those distances (e.g. by the mile).

Materials, Supplies, & Equipment:
1. Flash cards for < and >

2. Inch ruler

3. *Yardstick*

Activities:

1. Administer ***Test 16***. Notice that it is 4 pages long. There are no new concepts covered in this test and all the concepts were reviewed in the last few weeks. Because of the length of the test and the lesson together, you may want to delay the test until the next school day, do the test in place of Lesson 160, or do half of the test at one sitting and the other half at another sitting in one day or two days. Of course, you may also do both the test and lesson today as in previous test days. Administer the test in the way you feel is best suited to your student(s).

2. Count out loud by sevens to 98 from memory.

3. Do an oral drill of three single-digit numbers. Use the addition facts 1–18 for the first two numbers and any single-digit number as the third number to be subtracted. (e.g., 7 + 8 – 9 = __).

4. Using the flash cards, discuss the reading and writing of the < and > symbols. Write "13 – 7 __ 8," "15 – 9 __ 4," and "11 – 7 __ 5" on the chalk board. Have a student read the first problem on the chalk board and tell the answer for the subtraction fact. Then have him compare the answer (6) and the other number (8) and point to the correct symbol (< or >) to be placed between the two sets. After you have written the symbol in the blank, have the student read the statement. Follow the same procedure for the remaining two problems. The student(s) should complete ***Student Activity One*** on their own.

5. Have the student(s) read the directions for ***Student Activity Two*** to themselves. Guide them in circling the first number three numbers over from 5 and then let them continue by themselves. Remind them to write all of the circled numbers on the blanks below, starting with 5.

6. Tell the student(s) to get their inch ruler. After reading the directions for ***Student Activity Three***, have them draw the lines without help, checking to be sure they put the zero on their ruler at each point on their paper.

7. Allow the student(s) to complete ***Student Activity Four*** on their own only helping where necessary.

8. ***Student Activity Five*** should be completed by the student(s) independently.

Answer Key

NUMBERS

(1) Trace the numbers.

0 1 2 3 4 5 6 7 8 9

(2) Write numbers 0–9.

Teacher check according to your style.

(3) Write in the missing numbers on the number line.

0 1 2 3 4 5 6 7 8 9

0 1 2 3 4 5 6 7 8 9

0 1 2 3 4 5 6 7 8 9

1 (one)

---

(4) Connect the dots.

Draw dot to dot.

2 (two)

NUMBER ORDER – ORDINAL NUMBERS

(1)

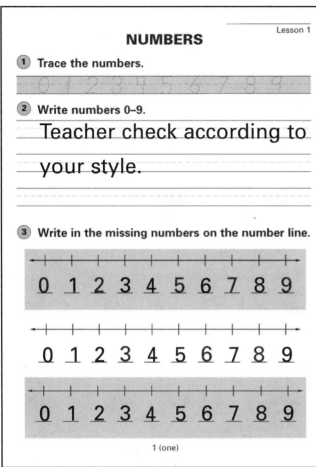

God used numbers to put the world in order.

Day 1
Day 2
Day 3
Day 4
Day 5
Day 6
Day 7

GOD RESTED

(2) Look at the numbers on the sailboats. These numbers show order. Count the sailboats.

(3) Put an X on the first (1) sailboat. Circle the fifth (5) sailboat.

3 (three)

---

(4) Count the balls. Put an X on the third (3) ball. Circle the eighth (8) ball.

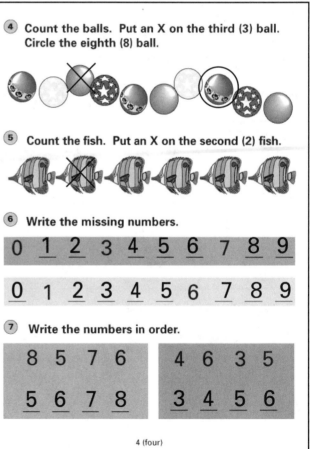

(5) Count the fish. Put an X on the second (2) fish.

(6) Write the missing numbers.

0 1 2 3 4 5 6 7 8 9

0 1 2 3 4 5 6 7 8 9

(7) Write the numbers in order.

8 5 7 6	4 6 3 5
5 6 7 8	3 4 5 6

4 (four)

SETS

1 Write the numbers 0–9.

Teacher check according to your style.

2 Draw a set of 5 X's.   Draw a set of 10 circles.

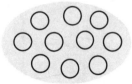

3 Write the missing numbers by 1's.

1	_2_	_3_	4	_5_	6	7
8	_9_	10	_11_	12	13	_14_
15	_16_	_17_	18	_19_	20	21

4 Write the missing numbers on the number line.

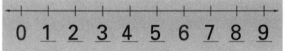

0 _1_ 2 _3_ 4 _5_ 6 7 _8_ 9

5 (five)

---

5 Count the objects in each set. Write the number in the box.

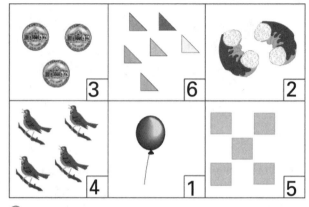

3   6   2

4   1   5

6 Write the missing numbers by 1's.

22	23	_24_	_25_	_26_	27	_28_
29	_30_	31	_32_	_33_	34	_35_
36	_37_	38	_39_	_40_	41	_42_
43	_44_	45	_46_	_47_	48	_49_

6 (six)

BIG AND LITTLE

1 Circle the bigger object.

2 Circle the littler object.

3 Write the numbers in order.

8 6 9 7   16 17 15 14

_6_ _7_ _8_ _9_   _14_ _15_ _16_ _17_

7 (seven)

---

4 Draw a set of 3 sticks. Draw a set of 9 balls.

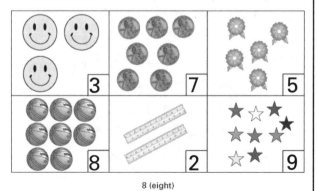

5 Write the number that comes between.

6 _7_ 8   9 _10_ 11   5 _6_ 7

13 _14_ 15   24 _25_ 26   38 _39_ 40

6 Count the objects in each set. Write the number in the box.

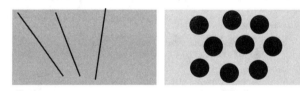

3   7   5

8   2   9

8 (eight)

378

PLACE VALUE – TENS AND ONES

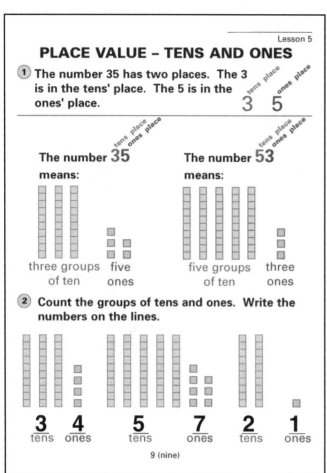

(1) The number 35 has two places. The 3 is in the tens' place. The 5 is in the ones' place.

3 5

The number **35** means:

three groups of ten — five ones

The number **53** means:

five groups of ten — three ones

(2) Count the groups of tens and ones. Write the numbers on the lines.

3 tens **4** ones **5** tens **7** ones **2** tens **1** ones

9 (nine)

(3) Count the groups of tens and ones. Write the numbers on the lines.

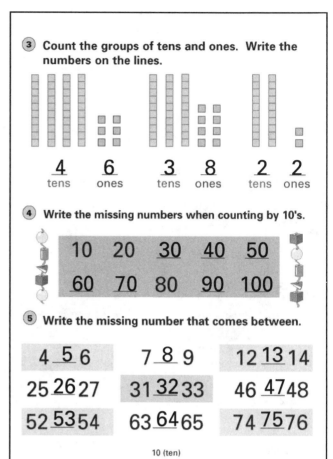

4 tens **6** ones **3** tens **8** ones **2** tens **2** ones

(4) Write the missing numbers when counting by 10's.

10 20 **30** **40** **50**
60 **70** 80 **90** 100

(5) Write the missing number that comes between.

4 **5** 6   7 **8** 9   12 **13** 14
25 **26** 27   31 **32** 33   46 **47** 48
52 **53** 54   63 **64** 65   74 **75** 76

10 (ten)

LESS AND GREATER

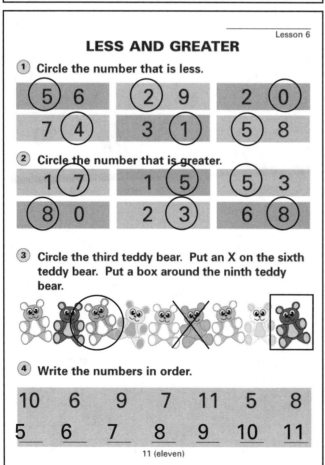

(1) Circle the number that is less.

⑤ 6   ② 9   2 ⓪
7 ④   3 ①   ⑤ 8

(2) Circle the number that is greater.

1 ⑦   1 ⑤   ⑤ 3
⑧ 0   2 ③   6 ⑧

(3) Circle the third teddy bear. Put an X on the sixth teddy bear. Put a box around the ninth teddy bear.

(4) Write the numbers in order.

10 6 9 7 11 5 8

5 6 7 8 9 10 11

11 (eleven)

(5) Count the tens. Count the ones. Write the number.

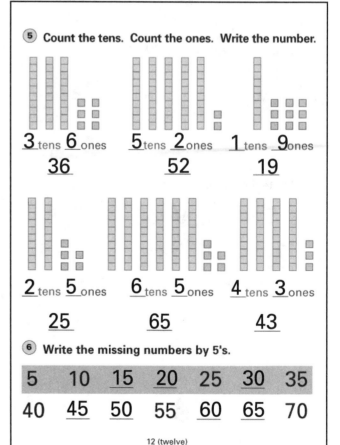

3 tens **6** ones   **5** tens **2** ones   **1** tens **9** ones
36   **52**   **19**

2 tens **5** ones   **6** tens **5** ones   **4** tens **3** ones
25   **65**   **43**

(6) Write the missing numbers by 5's.

5 10 **15** 20 25 **30** 35
40 **45** **50** 55 **60** **65** 70

12 (twelve)

379

ADDITION 1-9

① Write the answer to these addition facts using the number line.

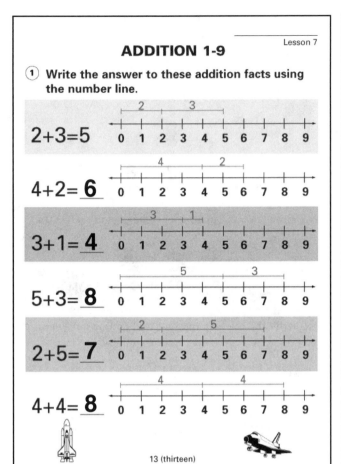

$2+3=5$

$4+2=\underline{6}$

$3+1=\underline{4}$

$5+3=\underline{8}$

$2+5=\underline{7}$

$4+4=\underline{8}$

13 (thirteen)

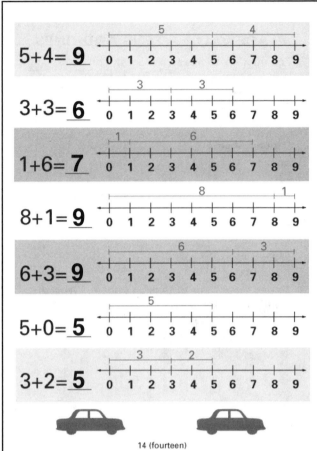

$5+4=\underline{9}$

$3+3=\underline{6}$

$1+6=\underline{7}$

$8+1=\underline{9}$

$6+3=\underline{9}$

$5+0=\underline{5}$

$3+2=\underline{5}$

14 (fourteen)

② Read out loud.
< means less than
> means greater than

$3 < 7$ $6 > 1$ $2 < 6$

$2 < 4$ $9 > 4$ $1 < 8$

$5 < 8$ $7 > 3$ $9 > 5$

③ Write the missing numbers, counting by 1's.

6 **7** 8   8 **9** 10   4 **5** 6

12**13**14   18**19**20   26**27**28

④ Count the groups of ten by 10's. Count the ones. Write the number.

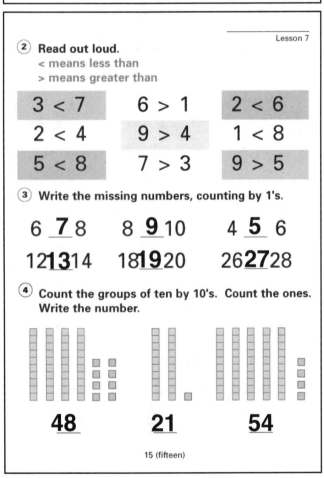

48   **21**   **54**

15 (fifteen)

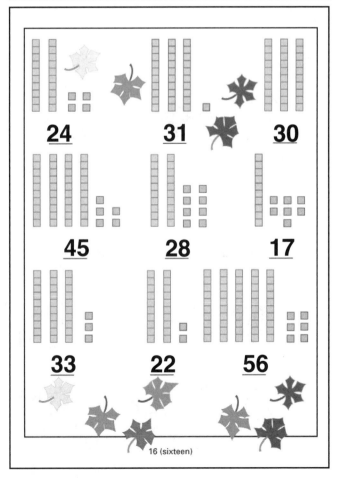

24   **31**   **30**

45   **28**   **17**

33   **22**   **56**

16 (sixteen)

380

LARGE AND SMALL

(1) Circle the larger object.

(2) Circle the smaller object.

(3) Write the number of tens and ones.

$72 = \underline{7}$ tens + $\underline{2}$ ones $28 = \underline{2}$ tens + $\underline{8}$ ones

$57 = \underline{5}$ tens + $\underline{7}$ ones $46 = \underline{4}$ tens + $\underline{6}$ ones

$35 = \underline{3}$ tens + $\underline{5}$ ones $64 = \underline{6}$ tens + $\underline{4}$ ones

17 (seventeen)

$12 = \underline{1}$ ten + $\underline{2}$ ones $23 = \underline{2}$ tens + $\underline{3}$ ones

$38 = \underline{3}$ tens + $\underline{8}$ ones $81 = \underline{8}$ tens + $\underline{1}$ one

(4) Write the addition fact shown on the number line.

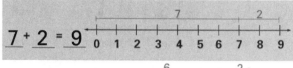

$\underline{7} + \underline{2} = \underline{9}$

$\underline{6} + \underline{2} = \underline{8}$

$\underline{3} + \underline{6} = \underline{9}$

(5) Write < or > between each set of numbers.

1 $\underline{<}$ 7	6 $\underline{>}$ 2	3 $\underline{<}$ 4
4 $\underline{>}$ 1	2 $\underline{<}$ 9	5 $\underline{<}$ 8
3 $\underline{<}$ 6	8 $\underline{>}$ 7	4 $\underline{<}$ 9

18 (eighteen)

ADDITION ON THE NUMBER LINE

(1) Draw the addition fact on the number line.

$2+7=9$

$2+0=2$

$1+8=9$

$4+5=9$

$3+4=7$

$5+1=6$

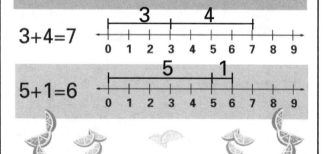

19 (nineteen)

---

(2) When counting by 2's write the number that comes between.

2 $\underline{4}$ 6   42 $\underline{44}$ 46   76 $\underline{78}$ 80

66 $\underline{68}$ 70   34 $\underline{36}$ 38   82 $\underline{84}$ 86

28 $\underline{30}$ 32   10 $\underline{12}$ 14   54 $\underline{56}$ 58

(3) Write < or > between each set of numbers. Read each set.

16 $\underline{<}$ 19	23 $\underline{>}$ 4	35 $\underline{<}$ 38
19 $\underline{<}$ 37	21 $\underline{>}$ 12	41 $\underline{>}$ 34
28 $\underline{<}$ 32	32 $\underline{>}$ 23	42 $\underline{<}$ 45

(4) Write the number for the groups of ten.

2 tens = $\underline{20}$ 8 tens = $\underline{80}$ 9 tens = $\underline{90}$

4 tens = $\underline{40}$ 5 tens = $\underline{50}$ 7 tens = $\underline{70}$

6 tens = $\underline{60}$ 3 tens = $\underline{30}$ 1 ten = $\underline{10}$

20 (twenty)

TEST 1

(1) Put an X on the third tepee. Circle the seventh one. Put a box around the fifth tepee. 3 pts.

(2) Draw a set of 4 circles.   Draw a set of 6 X's. 2 pts.

(3) Count the objects in each set. Write the number in the box. 3 pts. total for this exercise.

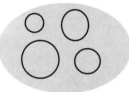

8   2   5

21 (twenty-one)

---

(4) Count the groups of ten. Count the ones. Write the number. 6 pts. total for this exercise.

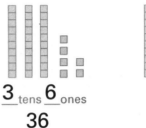 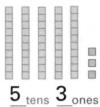

3 tens 6 ones   5 tens 3 ones

36   53

(5) Write the answer to the addition facts shown on the number line. 3 pts. total for this exercise.

3+5= 8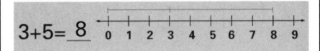

2+3= 5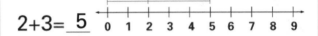

5+1= 6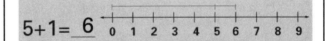

22 (twenty-two)   17 pts. Total

TALLY MARKS

(1) Count the objects. Trace over the tally marks with your pencil.

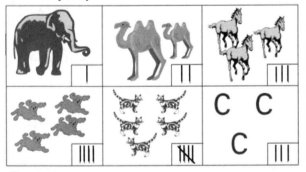

(2) Make a tally mark for each object.

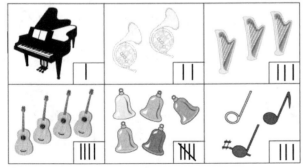

23 (twenty-three)

---

(3) Write < or > between each set of numbers. Read each set.

8 < 15   25 < 32   34 < 79

29 < 30   16 > 12   49 > 36

(4) Write the numbers in the blanks.

53 = 5 tens + 3 ones = 50 + 3

36 = 3 tens + 6 ones = 30 + 6

27 = 2 tens + 7 ones = 20 + 7

(5) Write the addition facts shown on the number line.

3 + 2 = 5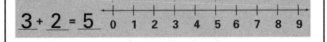

4 + 1 = 5

1 + 5 = 6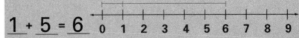

24 (twenty-four)

382

WORD NUMBERS

① Count the objects. Draw a line to match the number of objects with the word number.

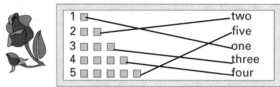

1		two
2		five
3		one
4		three
5		four

② Write the value of the tens. Write the value of the ones.

$36 = \underline{30} + \underline{6}$ $96 = \underline{90} + \underline{6}$

$45 = \underline{40} + \underline{5}$ $23 = \underline{20} + \underline{3}$

$89 = \underline{80} + \underline{9}$ $11 = \underline{10} + \underline{1}$

$57 = \underline{50} + \underline{7}$ $78 = \underline{70} + \underline{8}$

③ When counting by 5's write the number that comes between.

| 5 <u>10</u> 15 | 50 <u>55</u> 60 | 45 <u>50</u> 55 |
| 35 <u>40</u> 45 | 20 <u>25</u> 30 | 10 <u>15</u> 20 |

25 (twenty-five)

---

④ Make a tally mark for each object.

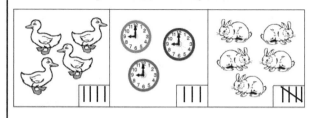

⑤ Write the addition facts shown on the number lines.

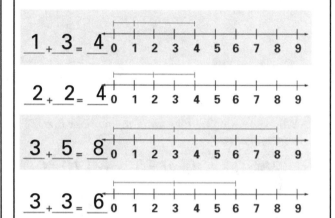

$\underline{1} + \underline{3} = \underline{4}$

$\underline{2} + \underline{2} = \underline{4}$

$\underline{3} + \underline{5} = \underline{8}$

$\underline{3} + \underline{3} = \underline{6}$

26 (twenty-six)

CALENDAR – MONTHS OF THE YEAR

January February March April May June July August September October November December

① Circle the first month of the year.

| May | (January) | November |

Circle the last month of the year.

| February | August | (December) |

② Make a tally mark for each object.

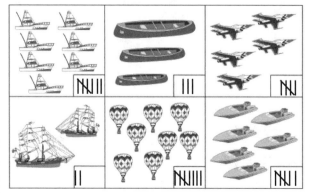

27 (twenty-seven)

---

③ Count the objects. Draw a line to match the word number with the number of objects.

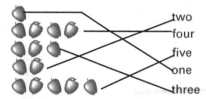

two
four
five
one
three

④ Write the answer to each addition fact by using the number line.

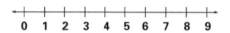

$1 + 6 = \underline{7}$ $3 + 3 = \underline{6}$

$2 + 3 = \underline{5}$ $8 + 1 = \underline{9}$

$3 + 1 = \underline{4}$ $4 + 2 = \underline{6}$

$6 + 3 = \underline{9}$ $5 + 3 = \underline{8}$

$4 + 4 = \underline{8}$ $6 + 0 = \underline{6}$

28 (twenty-eight)

383

EQUAL AND NOT EQUAL

① Write = or ≠ between each set.

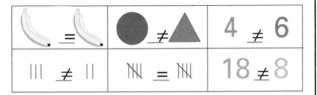

🍌 = 🍌	● ≠ ▲	4 ≠ 6
||| ≠ ||	||||| = |||||	18 ≠ 8

② Draw a line to match the word number with the number.

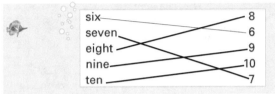

six —— 8
seven —— 6
eight —— 9
nine —— 10
ten —— 7

③ When counting by tens write the number that comes between.

10 _20_ 30   30 _40_ 50   60 _70_ 80

40 _50_ 60   20 _30_ 40   70 _80_ 90

50 _60_ 70   ⭐ ⭐   80 _90_ 100

29 (twenty-nine)

---

④ Count the tens. Count the ones. Write the number.

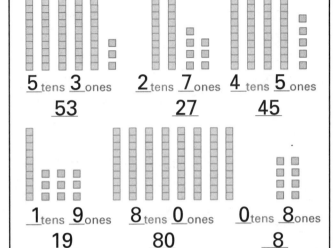

5 tens **3** ones
_53_

2 tens **7** ones
_27_

4 tens **5** ones
_45_

1 tens **9** ones
_19_

8 tens **0** ones
_80_

0 tens **8** ones
_8_

⑤ Write the answer to the addition facts using the number line.

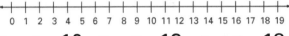

0 1 2 3 4 5 6 7 8 9 10 11 12 13 14 15 16 17 18 19

2 + 8 = _10_   5 + 8 = _13_   9 + 9 = _18_
4 + 7 = _11_   9 + 6 = _15_   7 + 3 = _10_

30 (thirty)

TALL AND SHORT

① Circle the taller object.

② Circle the shorter object.

③ Make a tally mark for each object.

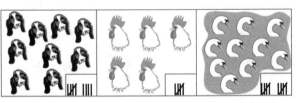

31 (thirty-one)

---

④ Write = or ≠ between each set.

||| _=_ 3   two _≠_ 4 ||||| _≠_ four

nine _=_ ||||||| |||| _≠_ 5   six _=_ 6

⑤ Count the groups of ten by 10's. Count the ones. Write the number.

_24_   _51_   _46_

⑥ Write the answer to the addition facts using the number line.

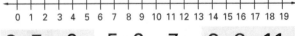

0 1 2 3 4 5 6 7 8 9 10 11 12 13 14 15 16 17 18 19

2+7 = _9_   5+2 = _7_   3+8 = _11_
8+3 = _11_   4+6 = _10_   6+6 = _12_

32 (thirty-two)

WORD PROBLEMS

Lesson 15

1. John has 5 balls. Sally gave him 4 more balls. How many balls does John have altogether?

John's balls   Sally's balls

X X X   +   X X
X X   X X

5+4=9

Joe has 3 pears. Dick has 5 pears. How many pears did the boys have altogether?

Joe's pears   Dick's pears

X X X   +   X X X
            X X

3+5=8

Amy had 5 hair ribbons. Mother gave her 1 more. How many hair ribbons does Amy have altogether?

Amy's ribbons   Amy's ribbons

X X X   +   X
X X

5+1=6

33 (thirty-three)

---

2. Write the number for the groups of ten.

4 tens = 40   3 tens = 30   7 tens = 70

5 tens = 50   8 tens = 80   2 tens = 20

1 ten = 10   6 tens = 60   9 tens = 90

3. Write the number that comes after.

| 5 | 6 | | 34 | 35 | | 27 | 28 |

| 78 | 79 | | 19 | 20 | | 65 | 66 |

4. Write the answer to the addition facts using the number line.

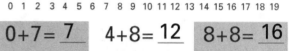

0 1 2 3 4 5 6 7 8 9 10 11 12 13 14 15 16 17 18 19

0+7= 7   4+8= 12   8+8= 16

1+2= 3   7+7= 14   9+6= 15

3+5= 8   5+9= 14   7+4= 11

34 (thirty-four)

TIME – HOUR

Lesson 16

1. Write the correct time. 1 hour = 60 minutes

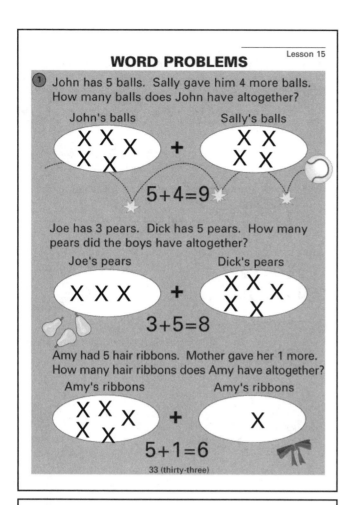

5 o'clock   10 o'clock   8 o'clock   2 o'clock

1 o'clock   3 o'clock   7 o'clock   11 o'clock

4 o'clock   6 o'clock   9 o'clock   12 o'clock

2. Write the number that comes after.

8 9   37 38   23 24

75 76   12 13   69 70

35 (thirty-five)

---

3. Susie ate 4 cookies. Mary ate 2 cookies. How many cookies did the girls eat altogether?

Susie's cookies   Mary's cookies

X X
X X   +   X   X

4+2= 6

4. Write the answer to the addition facts using the number line.

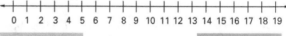

0 1 2 3 4 5 6 7 8 9 10 11 12 13 14 15 16 17 18 19

8+2=10   7+3=10   9+2=11

5+5=10   8+1= 9   7+1= 8

6+5=11   6+4=10   9+3=12

7+2= 9   9+0= 9   6+7=13

5+4= 9   8+3=11   7+7=14

36 (thirty-six)

CALENDAR – DAYS OF THE WEEK

① Circle the second day of the week.
Put an X on the fourth day of the week.
Put a box around the seventh day of the week.

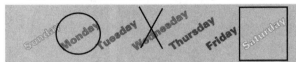

Sunday (Monday) Tuesday ✗Wednesday Thursday Friday [Saturday]

② Write the numbers in the blanks.

76 = **7** tens + **6** ones = **70** + **6**

28 = **2** tens + **8** ones = **20** + **8**

41 = **4** tens + **1** ones = **40** + **1**

③ Write the correct time in two ways.

9 : **00**
9 o'clock

4 : **00**
4 o'clock

7 : **00**
7 o'clock

6 : **00**
6 o'clock

37 (thirty-seven)

---

④ Draw a line to match the number to the tally marks.

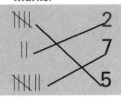 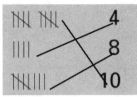

⑤ Write the answer to the addition facts using the number line.

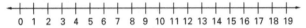
0 1 2 3 4 5 6 7 8 9 10 11 12 13 14 15 16 17 18 19

4+7 = **11**   3+6 = **9**   8+9 = **17**

6+2 = **8**   5+4 = **9**   3+4 = **7**

⑥ Seth made 3 baskets. His brother Joseph made 1 . How many baskets did they make altogether?

Seth's baskets   Joseph's baskets

 + = **4**

3 + 1 = **4**

38 (thirty-eight)

VERTICAL ADDITION

① Write the answers.

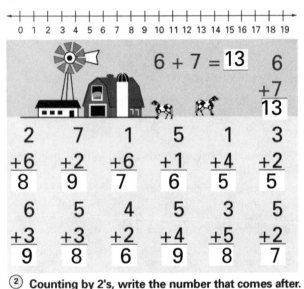

0 1 2 3 4 5 6 7 8 9 10 11 12 13 14 15 16 17 18 19

6 + 7 = **13**

6
+7
13

2	7	1	5	1	3
+6	+2	+6	+1	+4	+2
8	**9**	**7**	**6**	**5**	**5**

6	5	4	5	3	5
+3	+3	+2	+4	+5	+2
9	**8**	**6**	**9**	**8**	**7**

② Counting by 2's, write the number that comes after.

8 **10**   14 **16**   26 **28**

30 **32**   42 **44**   54 **56**

68 **70**   70 **72**   86 **88**

39 (thirty-nine)

---

③ Circle the correct time.

  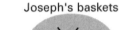

5:00
(1:00)

(11 o'clock)
6 o'clock

9 o'clock
(3 o'clock)

(12:00)
8:00

④ Write = or ≠ between each set.

six **=** 6 |||| **≠** 5   one **≠** 2

11 **≠** 3   nine **=** 𝍷𝍷𝍷𝍷   7 **=** 𝍷𝍷𝍷

eight **=** 𝍷𝍷𝍷   four **=** 4   five **≠** 𝍷𝍷𝍷

⑤ Bill counted four cows by the fence. Jonathan counted three more by the barn. How many cows were there altogether?

 + = **7**

4 + 3 = **7**

40 (forty)

ADDITION – OPPOSITES

1 Add.

3	6	5	4	2	3
+6	+3	+4	+5	+3	+2
9	9	9	9	5	5

7	3	1	2	5	9
+3	+7	+2	+1	+9	+5
10	10	3	3	14	14

8	7	2	5	6	9
+7	+8	+5	+2	+9	+6
15	15	7	7	15	15

2 Counting by 2's, write the number that comes after.

94	**96**	32	**34**	58	**60**
70	**72**	46	**48**	4	**6**
12	**14**			28	**30**

41 (forty-one)

---

3 Draw a line to match the time to the clock.

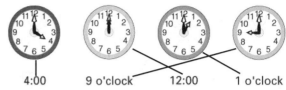

4:00   9 o'clock   12:00   1 o'clock

4 Paul has 7 marbles in his pocket. James gave him 2 more marbles. How many marbles do Paul and James have altogether?   **7** + **2** = **9**

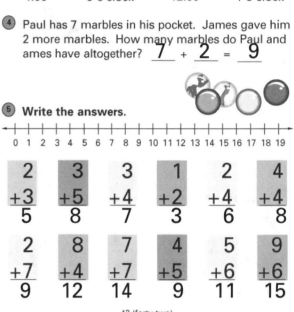

5 Write the answers.

0 1 2 3 4 5 6 7 8 9 10 11 12 13 14 15 16 17 18 19

2	3	3	1	2	4
+3	+5	+4	+2	+4	+4
5	8	7	3	6	8

2	8	7	4	5	9
+7	+4	+7	+5	+6	+6
9	12	14	9	11	15

42 (forty-two)

TEST 2

1 Count the groups of tens by 10's. Count the ones. Write the number. 3 pts. total for this exercise.

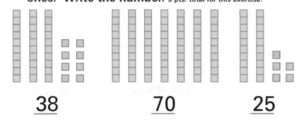

38   **70**   **25**

2 Write the numbers in the blanks. 10 pts.

18 = **1** tens + **8** ones = **10** + **8**

42 = **4** tens + **2** ones = **40** + **2**

69 = **6** tens + **9** ones = **60** + **9**

3 Make a tally mark for each object. 3 pts.

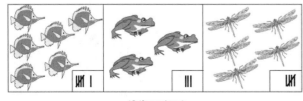

ⅧⅠ	Ⅲ	Ⅷ

43 (forty-three)

---

4 Draw a line to match the word number and number.
8 pts. total for this exercise.

4 — three
7 — four
3 — seven
10 — ten

SIX

8 — five
5 — eight
9 — two
2 — nine

5 Write < or > between each set of numbers. 3 pts.

5 **<** 8   16 **<** 24   35 **>** 28

6 Write = or ≠ between each set. 3 pts. total for this exercise.

3+5 **≠** 7   4+2 **=** 6   7+1 **≠** 9

7 Counting by 2's, write the number that comes between.
3 pts. total for this exercise.

16 **18** 20   34 **36** 38   50 **52** 54

8 Counting by 5's, write the number that comes between.
3 pts. total for this exercise.

15 **20** 25   40 **45** 50   75 **80** 85

44 (forty-four)   36 pts. Total

387

LONG AND SHORT

① Circle the longer object.

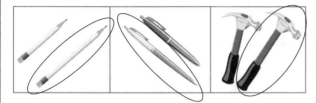

② Circle the shorter object.

③ Draw the short hand for each clock.

2:00   7 o'clock   10:00   6:00

45 (forty-five)

---

④ Write < or > between each set. Read the set.

16 _>_ 7   38 _<_ 42   57 _>_ 50

86 _>_ 79   24 _<_ 27   60 _<_ 65

⑤ Write the answers.

5	3	4	2	5	2
+2	+3	+1	+2	+4	+3
7	6	5	4	9	5

3	3	1	2	6	7
+5	+4	+2	+6	+8	+4
8	7	3	8	14	11

8	7	6	9	3	9
+3	+5	+5	+7	+9	+2
11	12	11	16	12	11

46 (forty-six)

NUMBER ORDER – AFTER BY 5'S

① Counting by 5's, write the number that comes after.

5 _10_   20 _25_   35 _40_   50 _55_

65 _70_   80 _85_   95 _100_   15 _20_

② Write the correct time.

_7_ o'clock   _2_ o'clock   _9_ o'clock   _4_ o'clock

_11_:00   _6_:00   _3_:00   _10_:00

_1_ o'clock   _5_ o'clock   _8_ o'clock   _12_ o'clock

47 (forty-seven)

---

③ Write < or > between each set. Read the set.

7 _>_ 2   18 _<_ 20   26 _>_ 25

32 _<_ 33   45 _<_ 46   51 _>_ 50

④ Write the answers.

0	1	6	3	4	5
+8	+8	+2	+8	+9	+7
8	9	8	11	13	12

3	6	5	2	9	7
+2	+9	+0	+5	+1	+2
5	15	5	7	10	9

6	8	7	9	8	3
+3	+1	+8	+6	+5	+7
9	9	15	15	13	10

48 (forty-eight)

388

WORD PROBLEMS

1 Jane has 3 bunnies. Ann has 6 bunnies. How many bunnies do they have altogether?

Jane's 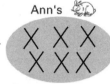 Ann's

$\underline{3} + \underline{6} = \underline{9}$

Joan has 5 pencils. Jill has 2 pencils. How many do they have altogether?

$\underline{5} + \underline{2} = \underline{7}$

Mike has 4 cars. Peter gave Mike 1 more. How many cars does Mike have altogether?

$\underline{4} + \underline{1} = \underline{5}$

2 Counting by 5's, write the number that comes after.

| 25 __30__ | 90 __95__ | 55 __60__ | 60 __65__ |
| 10 __15__ | 85 __90__ | 20 __25__ | 45 __50__ |

49 (forty-nine)

---

3 Counting by 6's, write the missing numbers.

6   12   __18__   __24__   30   __36__   42
48   __54__   __60__   66   __72__   78   __84__

4 Draw a line to match the number and the tally marks.

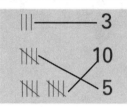   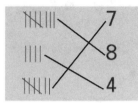

5 Write the answers.

0 1 2 3 4 5 6 7 8 9 10 11 12 13 14 15 16 17 18 19

4	2	0	4	2	5
+4	+8	+9	+6	+1	+8
8	10	9	10	3	13

7	1			9	8
+6	+6			+9	+6
13	7			18	14

50 (fifty)

WORD PROBLEMS

1 Joe found 3 pennies on the floor. Ruth found 3 pennies on her desk. How many pennies did they find altogether?

$\underline{3} + \underline{3} = \underline{6}$

Sherry did 2 pages of math. Kay did 6 pages of math. How many pages of math did the girls do altogether?

$\underline{2} + \underline{6} = \underline{8}$

Johnny had 3 cowboy hats. Jay gave Johnny 2 more cowboy hats. How many cowboy hats did Johnny have altogether?

$\underline{3} + \underline{2} = \underline{5}$

2 Write < or > between each set. Read the set.

| 55 _<_ 57 | 23 _>_ 21 | 66 _>_ 64 |
| 18 _>_ 16 | 72 _<_ 74 | 99 _>_ 97 |

51 (fifty-one)

---

3 Circle the correct number to match the tally marks.

1 (4) 9   (6) 5 4   (10) 7 5   0 (3) 8

2 9 (7)   7 3 (5)   (2) 3 4   7 (8) 9

4 Write the answers.

0 1 2 3 4 5 6 7 8 9 10 11 12 13 14 15 16 17 18 19

2	9	0	4	4	3
+7	+5	+4	+9	+4	+5
9	14	4	13	8	8

7	6	3	7	8	8
+7	+8	+3	+2	+8	+0
14	14	6	9	16	8

1	9			5	6
+0	+9			+6	+6
1	18			11	12

52 (fifty-two)

NUMBER ORDER – AFTER BY 10'S

① Counting by 10's, write the number that comes after.

10 **20** 40 **50** 70 **80** 20 **30**

30 **40** **60** **70** 50 **60** **90** **100**

② Draw a line to match.

one — ||

two — |||

three — |

four — ||||

five — ||||

six — ||||

seven — ||||

eight — 10

nine — ||||

ten — 9

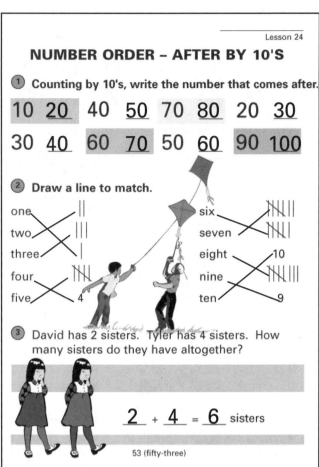

③ David has 2 sisters. Tyler has 4 sisters. How many sisters do they have altogether?

2 + **4** = **6** sisters

53 (fifty-three)

Wendy picked 4 oranges. Eva gave Wendy 3 more oranges. How many oranges did Wendy have altogether?

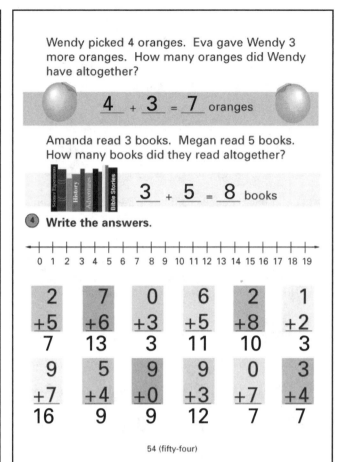

4 + **3** = **7** oranges

Amanda read 3 books. Megan read 5 books. How many books did they read altogether?

3 + **5** = **8** books

④ Write the answers.

0 1 2 3 4 5 6 7 8 9 10 11 12 13 14 15 16 17 18 19

2	7	0	6	2	1
+5	+6	+3	+5	+8	+2
7	13	3	11	10	3

9	5	9	9	0	3
+7	+4	+0	+3	+7	+4
16	9	9	12	7	7

54 (fifty-four)

PLACE VALUE

① Write the numbers in the blanks.

27 = **2** tens + **7** ones = **20** + **7**

51 = **5** tens + **1** one = **50** + **1**

43 = **4** tens + **3** ones = **40** + **3**

68 = **6** tens + **8** ones = **60** + **8**

② Write the number for each.

two **2**

seven **7**

three **3**

five **5**

nine **9**

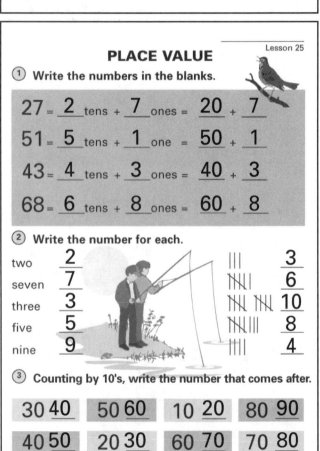

||| **3**

|||| **6**

|||| |||| **10**

|||| ||| **8**

|||| **4**

③ Counting by 10's, write the number that comes after.

30 **40**   50 **60**   10 **20**   80 **90**

40 **50**   20 **30**   60 **70**   70 **80**

55 (fifty-five)

---

④ Janice has 4 people in her family. Jerry has 4 people in his family. How many people are in the two families altogether?

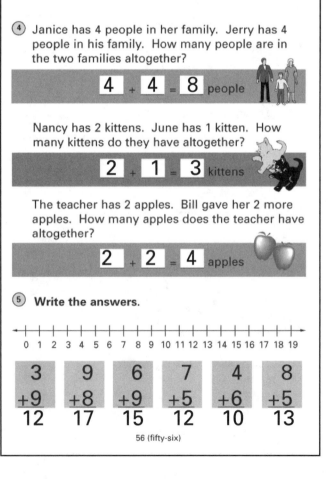

4 + **4** = **8** people

Nancy has 2 kittens. June has 1 kitten. How many kittens do they have altogether?

2 + **1** = **3** kittens

The teacher has 2 apples. Bill gave her 2 more apples. How many apples does the teacher have altogether?

2 + **2** = **4** apples

⑤ Write the answers.

0 1 2 3 4 5 6 7 8 9 10 11 12 13 14 15 16 17 18 19

3	9	6	7	4	8
+9	+8	+9	+5	+6	+5
12	17	15	12	10	13

56 (fifty-six)

390

MONEY – PENNY

Penny

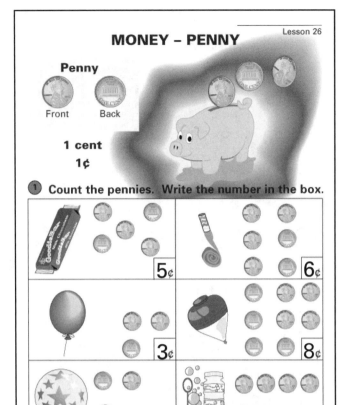

Front   Back

1 cent

1¢

① Count the pennies. Write the number in the box.

5¢	6¢
3¢	8¢
4¢	7¢

57 (fifty-seven)

---

② Write the numbers in the blanks.

$12 = \underline{1}$ ten $+ \underline{2}$ ones $= \underline{10} + \underline{2}$

$76 = \underline{7}$ tens $+ \underline{6}$ ones $= \underline{70} + \underline{6}$

$35 = \underline{3}$ tens $+ \underline{5}$ ones $= \underline{30} + \underline{5}$

$89 = \underline{8}$ tens $+ \underline{9}$ ones $= \underline{80} + \underline{9}$

$42 = \underline{4}$ tens $+ \underline{2}$ ones $= \underline{40} + \underline{2}$

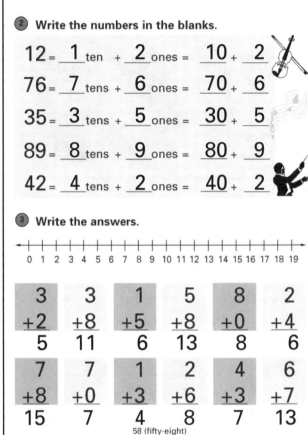

③ Write the answers.

```
+--+--+--+--+--+--+--+--+--+--+--+--+--+--+--+--+--+--+--+--+
0  1  2  3  4  5  6  7  8  9 10 11 12 13 14 15 16 17 18 19
```

3	3	1	5	8	2
+2	+8	+5	+8	+0	+4
5	11	6	13	8	6

7	7	1	2	4	6
+8	+0	+3	+6	+3	+7
15	7	4	8	7	13

58 (fifty-eight)

TIME – HALF HOUR

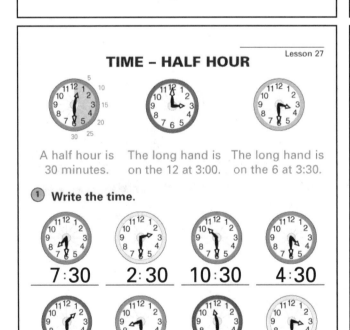

A half hour is 30 minutes.

The long hand is on the 12 at 3:00.

The long hand is on the 6 at 3:30.

① Write the time.

7:30	2:30	10:30	4:30
1:30	8:30	11:30	3:30
6:30	12:30	9:30	5:30

59 (fifty-nine)

---

② Write the answers.

```
+--+--+--+--+--+--+--+--+--+--+--+--+--+--+--+--+--+--+--+--+
0  1  2  3  4  5  6  7  8  9 10 11 12 13 14 15 16 17 18 19
```

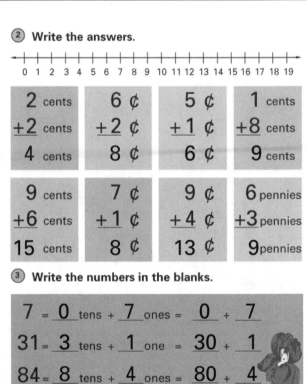

2 cents	6 ¢	5 ¢	1 cents
+2 cents	+2 ¢	+1 ¢	+8 cents
4 cents	8 ¢	6 ¢	9 cents

9 cents	7 ¢	9 ¢	6 pennies
+6 cents	+1 ¢	+4 ¢	+3 pennies
15 cents	8 ¢	13 ¢	9 pennies

③ Write the numbers in the blanks.

$7 = \underline{0}$ tens $+ \underline{7}$ ones $= \underline{0} + \underline{7}$

$31 = \underline{3}$ tens $+ \underline{1}$ one $= \underline{30} + \underline{1}$

$84 = \underline{8}$ tens $+ \underline{4}$ ones $= \underline{80} + \underline{4}$

$50 = \underline{5}$ tens $+ \underline{0}$ ones $= \underline{50} + \underline{0}$

60 (sixty)

391

MONEY – DIME

Dime

Front   Back

10 cents

10¢

① Count the dimes by 10's. Write the number.

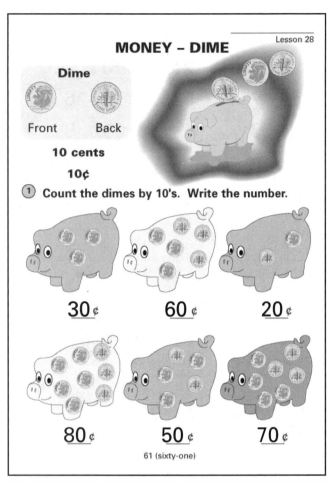

30¢   60¢   20¢

80¢   50¢   70¢

61 (sixty-one)

---

② Write the correct time.

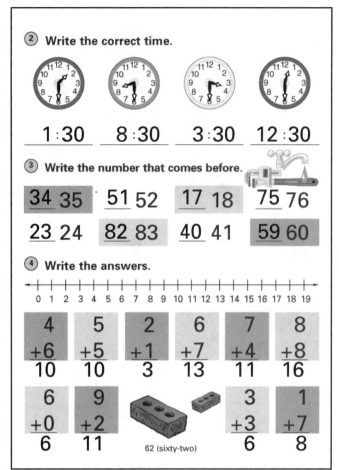

1:30   8:30   3:30   12:30

③ Write the number that comes before.

34 35   51 52   17 18   75 76

23 24   82 83   40 41   59 60

④ Write the answers.

0 1 2 3 4 5 6 7 8 9 10 11 12 13 14 15 16 17 18 19

4	5	2	6	7	8
+6	+5	+1	+7	+4	+8
10	10	3	13	11	16

6	9			3	1
+0	+2			+3	+7
6	11			6	8

62 (sixty-two)

MONEY – PENNIES AND DIMES

① Count the dimes by 10's. Count the pennies.
Write the value of each set.

=

10 pennies   1 dime

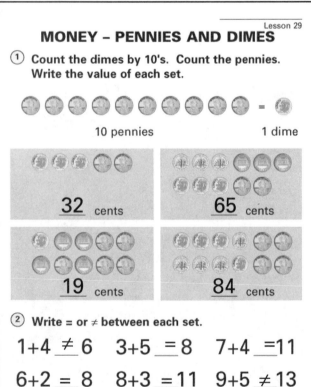

32 cents   65 cents

19 cents   84 cents

② Write = or ≠ between each set.

1+4 ≠ 6   3+5 = 8   7+4 =11

6+2 = 8   8+3 =11   9+5 ≠ 13

3+4 = 7   6+4 ≠ 9   8+6 ≠ 15

63 (sixty-three)

---

③ Draw a line to match the time with the clock.

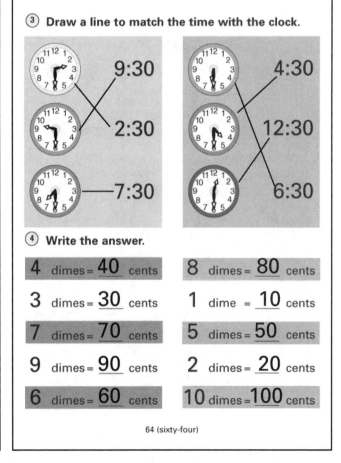

9:30

2:30

7:30

4:30

12:30

6:30

④ Write the answer.

4 dimes = 40 cents   8 dimes = 80 cents

3 dimes = 30 cents   1 dime = 10 cents

7 dimes = 70 cents   5 dimes = 50 cents

9 dimes = 90 cents   2 dimes = 20 cents

6 dimes = 60 cents   10 dimes =100 cents

64 (sixty-four)

392

TEST 3

(1) Write the correct time. 4 pts. total for this exercise.

<u>2</u> : 00   <u>10</u> : 00   <u>6</u> : 00   <u>8</u> : 00

(2) Counting by 5's, write the number that comes after.
8 pts. total for this exercise.

40 <u>45</u>   25 <u>30</u>   75 <u>80</u>   60 <u>65</u>

10 <u>15</u>   90 <u>95</u>   35 <u>40</u>   55 <u>60</u>

(3) Lisa baked 5 cakes. Rose gave Lisa 1 cake she baked. How many cakes did Lisa have altogether?
2 pts. total for this exercise.

<u>5</u> + <u>1</u> = <u>6</u> cakes

Bob sang 2 songs. Dan sang 2 songs. How many songs did they sing altogether?

<u>2</u> + <u>2</u> = <u>4</u> songs

65 (sixty-five)

---

(4) Draw a line to match each set. 10 pts.

six — 1
eight — 6
one — 8
three — 10
ten — 3

(5) Write the answers. 16 pts. total for this exercise.

0 1 2 3 4 5 6 7 8 9 10 11 12 13 14 15 16 17 18 19

1	7	2	3	4	9
+3	+0	+4	+5	+1	+9
4	7	6	8	5	18

6	4	5	6	9	0
+2	+7	+9	+8	+4	+1
8	11	14	14	13	1

8	7			4	4
+6	+2			+4	+2
14	9			8	6

66 (sixty-six)   40 pts. Total

CALENDAR – DAYS OF THE WEEK

(1) Circle the correct answer.

October

Sunday	Monday	Tuesday	Wednesday	Thursday	Friday	Saturday
			1	2	3	4
5	6	7	8	9	10	11
12	13	14	15	16	17	18
19	20	21	22	23	24	25
26	27	28	29	30	31	

What is the month on the calendar?
(October)   May   August

What day of the week is October 1?
Monday   Tuesday   (Wednesday)

What day of the week is October 10?
Thursday   (Friday)   Saturday

What day of the week is October 27?
(Monday)   Tuesday   Wednesday

What day of the week is October 25?
Thursday   Friday   (Saturday)

67 (sixty-seven)

---

(2) Draw the short hand for each clock.

2:30   8:30   4:30   10:30

(3) Write the number that comes before.

<u>15</u> 16   <u>47</u> 48   <u>24</u> 25   <u>98</u> 99

<u>31</u> 32   <u>79</u> 80   <u>2</u> 3   <u>73</u> 74

(4) Write = or ≠ between each set.

5+4 <u>=</u> 9   7+1 <u>≠</u> 9   8+4 <u>≠</u> 11

2+8 <u>=</u> 10   6+3 <u>=</u> 9   9+5 <u>=</u> 14

3+4 <u>≠</u> 6   5+7 <u>≠</u> 13   6+2 <u>=</u> 8

(5) Todd picked 7 apples. Dick gave Todd 1 apple he picked. How many apples did Todd have altogether?

<u>7</u> + <u>1</u> = <u>8</u> apples

68 (sixty-eight)

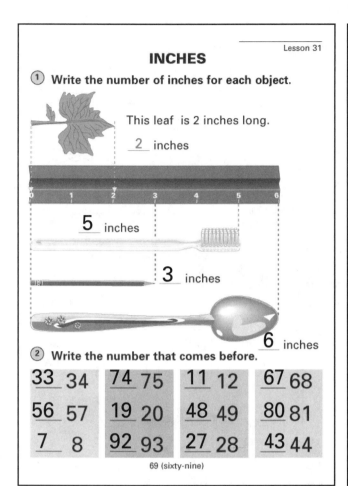

INCHES

① Write the number of inches for each object.

This leaf is 2 inches long.

__2__ inches

__5__ inches

__3__ inches

__6__ inches

② Write the number that comes before.

33 34	74 75	11 12	67 68
56 57	19 20	48 49	80 81
7 8	92 93	27 28	43 44

69 (sixty-nine)

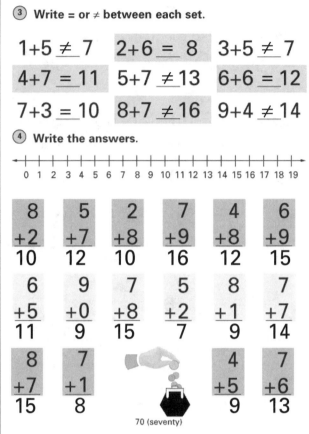

③ Write = or ≠ between each set.

$1+5 \neq 7$ $2+6 = 8$ $3+5 \neq 7$

$4+7 = 11$ $5+7 \neq 13$ $6+6 = 12$

$7+3 = 10$ $8+7 \neq 16$ $9+4 \neq 14$

④ Write the answers.

0 1 2 3 4 5 6 7 8 9 10 11 12 13 14 15 16 17 18 19

8	5	2	7	4	6
$+2$	$+7$	$+8$	$+9$	$+8$	$+9$
10	12	10	16	12	15

6	9	7	5	8	7
$+5$	$+0$	$+8$	$+2$	$+1$	$+7$
11	9	15	7	9	14

8	7			4	7
$+7$	$+1$			$+5$	$+6$
15	8			9	13

70 (seventy)

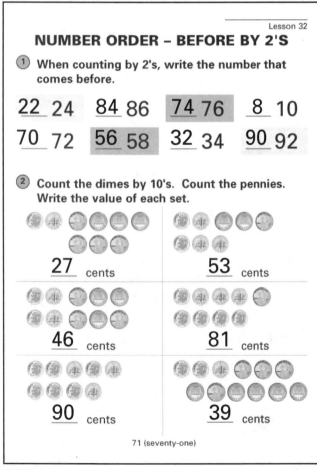

NUMBER ORDER – BEFORE BY 2'S

① When counting by 2's, write the number that comes before.

22 24   84 86   74 76   8 10

70 72   56 58   32 34   90 92

② Count the dimes by 10's. Count the pennies. Write the value of each set.

__27__ cents

__53__ cents

__46__ cents

__81__ cents

__90__ cents

__39__ cents

71 (seventy-one)

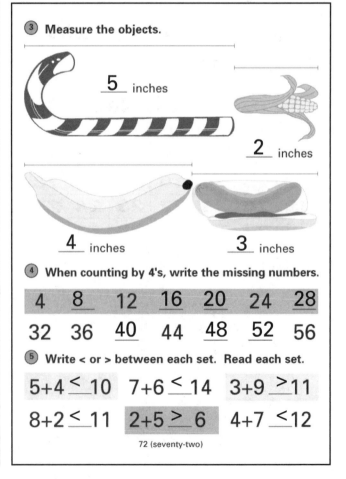

③ Measure the objects.

__5__ inches

__2__ inches

__4__ inches

__3__ inches

④ When counting by 4's, write the missing numbers.

4	8	12	16	20	24	28
32	36	40	44	48	52	56

⑤ Write < or > between each set. Read each set.

$5+4 < 10$ $7+6 < 14$ $3+9 > 11$

$8+2 < 11$ $2+5 > 6$ $4+7 < 12$

72 (seventy-two)

394

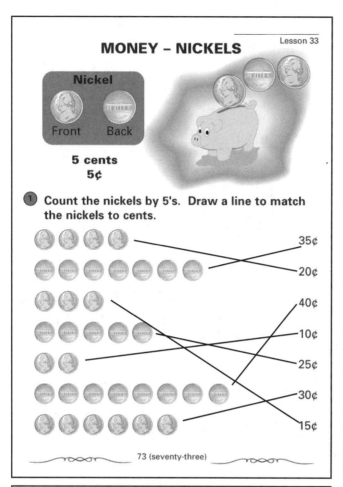

MONEY – NICKELS

Lesson 33

Nickel
Front   Back

5 cents
5¢

① Count the nickels by 5's. Draw a line to match the nickels to cents.

35¢
20¢
40¢
10¢
25¢
30¢
15¢

73 (seventy-three)

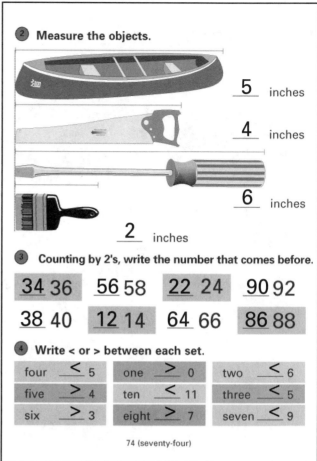

② Measure the objects.

5 inches

4 inches

6 inches

2 inches

③ Counting by 2's, write the number that comes before.

34 36   56 58   22 24   90 92

38 40   12 14   64 66   86 88

④ Write < or > between each set.

four	< 5	one	> 0	two	< 6
five	> 4	ten	< 11	three	< 5
six	> 3	eight	> 7	seven	< 9

74 (seventy-four)

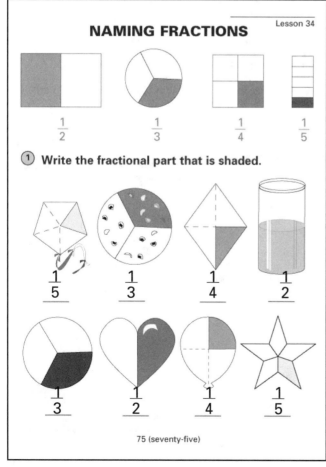

NAMING FRACTIONS

Lesson 34

$\frac{1}{2}$ $\frac{1}{3}$ $\frac{1}{4}$ $\frac{1}{5}$

① Write the fractional part that is shaded.

$\frac{1}{5}$ $\frac{1}{3}$ $\frac{1}{4}$ $\frac{1}{2}$

$\frac{1}{3}$ $\frac{1}{2}$ $\frac{1}{4}$ $\frac{1}{5}$

75 (seventy-five)

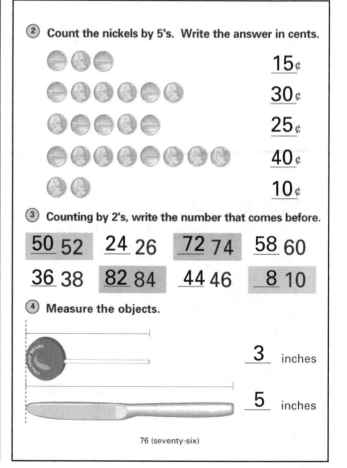

② Count the nickels by 5's. Write the answer in cents.

15¢
30¢
25¢
40¢
10¢

③ Counting by 2's, write the number that comes before.

50 52   24 26   72 74   58 60

36 38   82 84   44 46   8 10

④ Measure the objects.

3 inches

5 inches

76 (seventy-six)

395

WORD NUMBERS 11-20

① Draw a line to match the number and the word number.

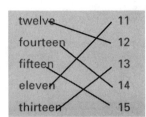

twelve	11
fourteen	12
fifteen	13
eleven	14
thirteen	15

eighteen	16
sixteen	17
seventeen	18
twenty	19
nineteen	20

② Count the nickels by 5's. Write the answer.

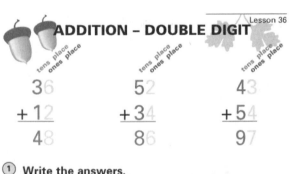

15 ¢   25 ¢   30 ¢

10 ¢   35 ¢   20 ¢

77 (seventy-seven)

③ Write the fractional part that is shaded.

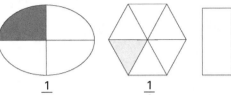

$\frac{1}{4}$ $\frac{1}{6}$ $\frac{1}{3}$

$\frac{1}{2}$ $\frac{1}{4}$ $\frac{1}{5}$

④ Draw a line with the ruler.

2 inches .
4 inches .
}Measure the student's lines.

⑤ Write the answers.

0 1 2 3 4 5 6 7 8 9 10 11 12 13 14 15 16 17 18 19

2	4	5	6	5	3
+8	+7	+5	+8	+9	+8
10	11	10	14	14	11

78 (seventy-eight)

ADDITION – DOUBLE DIGIT

tens place ones place
tens place ones place
tens place ones place

3 6   5 2   4 3
+ 1 2   + 3 4   + 5 4
4 8   8 6   9 7

① Write the answers.

22	46	72	34	61	82
+31	+41	+16	+51	+18	+17
53	87	88	85	79	99

72	45	53	32	77	60
+20	+30	+24	+24	+11	+35
92	75	77	56	88	95

23	45	60	52	14	16
+54	+23	+24	+44	+31	+50
77	78	84	96	45	66

79 (seventy-nine)

---

② Counting by 2's, write the number that comes before.

| 12 | 14 | 54 | 56 | 36 | 38 | 18 | 20 |
| 94 | 96 | 42 | 44 | 80 | 82 | 58 | 60 |

③ Count the nickels by 5's. Count the pennies. Write the cents.

28 ¢   39 ¢

23 ¢   26 ¢

④ Chris picked 8 flowers. Kim picked 3 more and gave them to Chris. How many did Chris have altogether?

8 + 3 = 11 flowers

80 (eighty)

396

ADDITION – HORIZONTAL AND VERTICAL

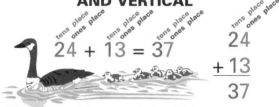

$$24 + 13 = 37$$

$$\begin{array}{r} 24 \\ +13 \\ \hline 37 \end{array}$$

1 Write the problems vertically. Write the answers.

$17 + 42 =$ $\begin{array}{r} 1\,7 \\ +4\,2 \\ \hline 5\,9 \end{array}$ $\quad$ $22 + 51 =$ $\begin{array}{r} 2\,2 \\ +5\,1 \\ \hline 7\,3 \end{array}$

$12 + 53 =$ $\begin{array}{r} 1\,2 \\ +5\,3 \\ \hline 6\,5 \end{array}$ $\quad$ $83 + 14 =$ $\begin{array}{r} 8\,3 \\ +1\,4 \\ \hline 9\,7 \end{array}$

$66 + 22 =$ $\begin{array}{r} 6\,6 \\ +2\,2 \\ \hline 8\,8 \end{array}$ $\quad$ $14 + 72 =$ $\begin{array}{r} 1\,4 \\ +7\,2 \\ \hline 8\,6 \end{array}$

81 (eighty-one)

---

2 Count the tens by 10's. Count the ones. Write the number.

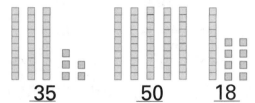

35 **50** **18**

3 Count the nickels by 5's. Count the pennies by 1's. Circle the correct answer.

(19¢) 34¢ 23¢   19¢ 43¢ (23¢)   (35¢) 7¢ 70¢

18¢ 41¢ (13¢)   (30¢) 55¢ 10¢

4 Counting by 2's, write the number that comes before.

82 84   **34** 36   **50** 52   **16** 18

38 40   **92** 94   **26** 28   **60** 62

82 (eighty-two)

FRACTIONS – ONE HALF

1 Draw a line to divide each object in half.

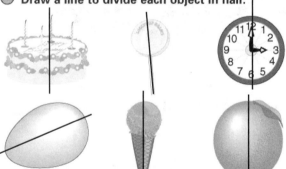

2 Write the numbers in the blanks.

$90 + 1 = \underline{91}$ $80 + 0 = \underline{80}$

$50 + 4 = \underline{54}$ $40 + 6 = \underline{46}$

$30 + 8 = \underline{38}$ $60 + 7 = \underline{67}$

$70 + 5 = \underline{75}$ $10 + 3 = \underline{13}$

$20 + 9 = \underline{29}$ $30 + 2 = \underline{32}$

83 (eighty-three)

---

3 Write the problems vertically. Write the answers.

$43 + 31 =$ $\begin{array}{r} 4\,3 \\ +3\,1 \\ \hline 7\,4 \end{array}$ $\quad$ $55 + 33 =$ $\begin{array}{r} 5\,5 \\ +3\,3 \\ \hline 8\,8 \end{array}$

$12 + 15 =$ $\begin{array}{r} 1\,2 \\ +1\,5 \\ \hline 2\,7 \end{array}$ $\quad$ $65 + 14 =$ $\begin{array}{r} 6\,5 \\ +1\,4 \\ \hline 7\,9 \end{array}$

$86 + 12 =$ $\begin{array}{r} 8\,6 \\ +1\,2 \\ \hline 9\,8 \end{array}$ $\quad$ $34 + 22 =$ $\begin{array}{r} 3\,4 \\ +2\,2 \\ \hline 5\,6 \end{array}$

$17 + 21 =$ $\begin{array}{r} 1\,7 \\ +2\,1 \\ \hline 3\,8 \end{array}$ $\quad$ $70 + 16 =$ $\begin{array}{r} 7\,0 \\ +1\,6 \\ \hline 8\,6 \end{array}$

4 Pat walked 2 blocks to the store. She then walked 7 blocks to her grandparents house. How many blocks did Pat walk altogether?

$$\underline{2} + \underline{7} = \underline{9} \text{ blocks}$$

84 (eighty-four)

397

NUMBER ORDER – BEFORE AND AFTER

Lesson 39

① Write the number that comes before and after.

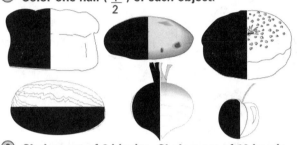

_7_	8	_9_	_15_	16	_17_	23	24	25
_34_	35	_36_	_46_	47	_48_	_50_	51	_52_
_68_	69	_70_	_71_	72	_73_	82	83	84

② Color one half ($\frac{1}{2}$) of each object.

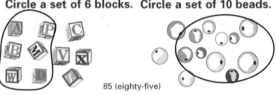

③ Circle a set of 6 blocks. Circle a set of 10 beads.

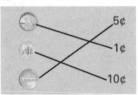 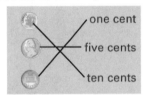

85 (eighty-five)

---

④ Write the problems vertically. Write the answers.

$$83 + 15 = \quad \begin{array}{r} 8\,3 \\ +\,1\,5 \\ \hline 9\,8 \end{array} \qquad 75 + 10 = \quad \begin{array}{r} 7\,5 \\ +\,1\,0 \\ \hline 8\,5 \end{array}$$

$$52 + 25 = \quad \begin{array}{r} 5\,2 \\ +\,2\,5 \\ \hline 7\,7 \end{array} \qquad 36 + 21 = \quad \begin{array}{r} 3\,6 \\ +\,2\,1 \\ \hline 5\,7 \end{array}$$

$$77 + 12 = \quad \begin{array}{r} 7\,7 \\ +\,1\,2 \\ \hline 8\,9 \end{array} \qquad 44 + 33 = \quad \begin{array}{r} 4\,4 \\ +\,3\,3 \\ \hline 7\,7 \end{array}$$

⑤ Write the answers.

2	7	0	6	2	1
+5	+6	+3	+5	+8	+2
7	13	3	11	10	3

9	5			0	3
+7	+4			+7	+4
16	9	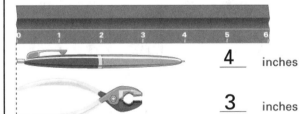		7	7

86 (eighty-six)

TEST 4
Lesson 40

① Write the correct time. 4 pts. total for this exercise.

2:30   7:30   11:30   4:00

② Draw a line to match the coin to cents. 6 pts.

5¢
1¢
10¢

one cent
five cents
ten cents

③ Write the number that comes before. 12 pts.

_31_	32	_59_	60	_27_	28	_73_	74
_15_	16	_54_	55	_7_	8	_46_	47
_80_	81	_38_	39	_92_	93	_65_	66

87 (eighty-seven)

---

④ Measure the objects using the ruler. 2 pts.

<u>4</u> inches

<u>3</u> inches

⑤ Write the answers. 16 pts. total for this exercise.

7	4	9	3	8	3
+9	+5	+6	+2	+9	+4
16	9	15	5	17	7

2	5	8	6	9	9
+9	+3	+6	+1	+2	+7
11	8	14	7	11	16

0	7			6	4
+8	+8			+7	+3
8	15			13	7

88 (eighty-eight)   40 pts. Total

398

CALENDAR – DAYS OF THE WEEK

1 Write the missing numbers.

November

Sunday	Monday	Tuesday	Wednesday	Thursday	Friday	Saturday
					1	**2**
3	4	5	6	**7**	8	9
10	**11**	12	**13**	14	15	**16**
17	18	19	20	21	**22**	23
24	25	**26**	27	28	29	**30**

The calendar is for what month? **November**

What is the date on the first Monday? **4**

What is the date on the last Sunday? **24**

What is the date on the fourth Friday? **22**

How many days are in a week? **7**

How many Tuesdays are in November? **4**

89 (eighty-nine)

---

2 Write the problems vertically. Write the answers.

$$19 + 30 = \begin{array}{r} 19 \\ + 30 \\ \hline 49 \end{array} \qquad 46 + 41 = \begin{array}{r} 46 \\ + 41 \\ \hline 87 \end{array}$$

$$31 + 52 = \begin{array}{r} 31 \\ + 52 \\ \hline 83 \end{array} \qquad 29 + 40 = \begin{array}{r} 29 \\ + 40 \\ \hline 69 \end{array}$$

3 Write the answers.

8	7	4	6	5	6
+3	+6	+7	+8	+9	+4
11	13	11	14	14	10

1	9	9	8	8	9
+9	+9	+4	+7	+5	+1
10	18	13	15	13	10

3	4			2	7
+9	+8			+8	+5
12	12			10	12

90 (ninety)

SHOW YOUR SKILLS

1 Write = or ≠ between each set.

five **≠** 4

3+3 **≠** 5

5+2 **=** 7

10¢ **=** dime

5¢ **=** nickel

eight **≠** 7

3+8 **≠** 10

6+3 **=** 9

20¢ **≠** 2 nickels

30¢ **=** 3 dimes

2 Write the number that comes before and after.

48 49 **50** **67** 68 **69** **14** 15 **16**

80 81 **82** **5** 6 **7** **31** 32 **33**

23 24 **25** **72** 73 **74** **56** 57 **58**

3 Circle the correct answer.

What is the first day of the week?

Saturday   Friday   (Sunday)

What is the last day of the week?

(Saturday)   Friday   Sunday

91 (ninety-one)

---

4 Brad caught 5 fish. David caught 6 fish. How many fish did they catch altogether?

5 + **6** = **11** fish

Wade has 3 library books to return to the library. Beth gave him 6 to return for her. How many library books did Wade return altogether?

3 + **6** = **9** books

5 Write the answers.

6	7	3	3	5	6
+5	+8	+8	+6	+5	+7
11	15	11	9	10	13

6	8	5	6	0	12
+9	+7	+8	+5	+9	+0
15	15	13	11	9	12

72	45	53	32	77	60
+20	+30	+24	+24	+11	+35
92	75	77	56	88	95

92 (ninety-two)

TIME – QUARTER HOUR

The long hand is on the 3 at 4:15.　　The long hand is on the 6 at 4:30.　　The long hand is on the 9 at 4:45.

① Write the correct time.

7 :15　　　　2 :45　　　　10 :45

6 :45　　　　12 :15　　　　9 :15

93 (ninety-three)

---

② Write = or ≠ between each set.

8+3 ≠ 12　　7+5 = 12　　3+9 = 12

4+2 ≠ 5　　6+7 ≠ 14　　2+3 = 3+2

6+4 = 10　　7+6 ≠ 14　　8+5 = 13

③ Write the number that comes before and after.

23 24 25　　　59 60 61　　　81 82 83

58 59 60　　　6　7 8　　　92 93 94

40 41 42　　　35 36 37　　　17 18 19

④ Write the answers.

6	7	5	3	3	5
+5	+8	+5	+7	+8	+8
11	15	10	10	11	13

27	42			73	80
+42	+51			+25	+12
69	93			98	92

94 (ninety-four)

MONEY – PENNIES AND DIMES

① Circle the dimes and pennies needed.

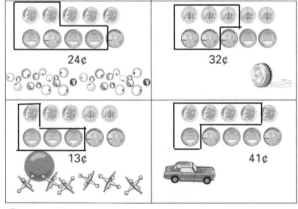

24¢　　　　32¢

13¢　　　　41¢

② Color one half (½) of each object.

95 (ninety-five)

---

③ Write the correct time.

1 :15　　3 :45　　6 :45　　8 :30

④ Write < or > between each set.

seven < 8	4 + 6 > 9	three < 30
ten > 8	7 + 5 > 10	eight < 9
four > 3	3 + 4 < 8	nine > 6

⑤ Write the answers.

6	3	5	4	7	8
+9	+8	+7	+6	+4	+5
15	11	12	10	11	13

66	61	12	43	80	33
+22	+18	+53	+31	+16	+12
88	79	65	74	96	45

96 (ninety-six)

400

NUMBER ORDER – BEFORE AND AFTER BY 10
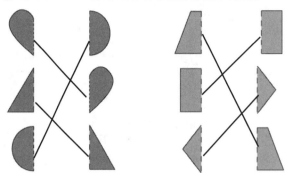

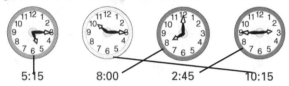

Lesson 44

1 When counting by 10's, write the number that comes before and after.

<u>10</u> 20 <u>30</u>	<u>40</u> 50 <u>60</u>	<u>70</u> 80 <u>90</u>
<u>30</u> 40 <u>50</u>	<u>60</u> 70 <u>80</u>	<u>50</u> 60 <u>70</u>
<u>0</u> 10 <u>20</u>	<u>80</u> 90 <u>100</u>	<u>20</u> 30 <u>40</u>

2 Draw a line to match the clock with the time.

5:15   8:00   2:45   10:15

3 Write < or > between each set.

5+6 <u>></u> 10	9+7 <u>></u> 15	8+3 <u><</u> 14
4+7 <u><</u> 14	6+8 <u>></u> 12	9+6 <u><</u> 16
2+9 <u>></u> 10	7+7 <u><</u> 15	3+9 <u>></u> 11

97 (ninety-seven)

---

4 Draw a line to match one half to the other.

5 Mother baked 4 loaves of bread on Monday. She baked 6 more on Wednesday. Altogether Mother baked how many loaves of bread?

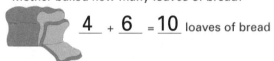

<u>4</u> + <u>6</u> = <u>10</u> loaves of bread

Barb painted 5 pictures in art class. Tye painted 9 pictures at home. How many pictures did they paint altogether?

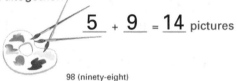

<u>5</u> + <u>9</u> = <u>14</u> pictures

98 (ninety-eight)

ADDITION – THREE NUMBERS

Lesson 45

1 Add the numbers.

3
2 add 3+2= 5
+1 ------→ +1
6   6

2
2 add 2+2= 4
+5 ------→ +5
            9

1
2 add 1+2= 3
+2 ------→ +2
            5

4
1 add 4+1= 5
+3 ------→ +3
            8

4 7	1 7	3 4	4 6	7 9	5 8
3	6	1	2	2	3
+1	+2	+2	+2	+1	+2
8	9	6	8	10	10

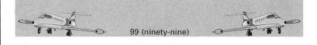

99 (ninety-nine)

---

2 Draw the short (hour) hand on the clock.

12:15   8:30   1:45   5:15

3 Measure each object with a ruler.

<u>5</u> inches

<u>3</u> inches

<u>4</u> inches

4 Chad had 8 dimes in his left pocket and 6 dimes in his right pocket. Chad had how many dimes altogether? Write the addition fact and label the answer.

<u>8</u> + <u>6</u> = <u>14</u> dimes

100 (one hundred)

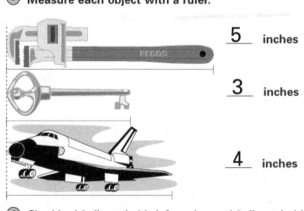

401

SHOW YOUR SKILLS

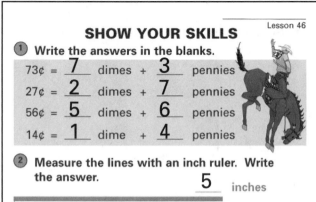

1. Write the answers in the blanks.

73¢ = __7__ dimes + __3__ pennies

27¢ = __2__ dimes + __7__ pennies

56¢ = __5__ dimes + __6__ pennies

14¢ = __1__ dime + __4__ pennies

2. Measure the lines with an inch ruler. Write the answer.

__5__ inches

__3__ inches

__6__ inches

__4__ inches

3. When counting by 10's, write the number that comes before and after.

__80__ 90 __100__   __20__ 30 __40__   __0__ 10 __20__

__10__ 20 __30__   __40__ 50 __60__   __30__ 40 __50__

101 (one hundred one)

---

4. Write the answers.

| 2 4 +1 = 7 | 2 5 +3 = 10 | 1 2 +7 = 10 | 2 7 +4 = 13 | 6 2 +3 = 11 | 7 2 +9 = 18 |

| 3 +8 = 11 | 5 +9 = 14 | 4 +7 = 11 | 7 +3 = 10 | 8 +2 = 10 | 6 +7 = 13 |

| 82 +17 = 99 | 14 +72 = 86 | 25 +50 = 75 | 72 +17 = 89 | 36 +43 = 79 | 20 +35 = 55 |

5. Chuck gave Shawn 2 donuts. Shawn already had 7 donuts. Shawn had how many donuts altogether? Write the addition fact and label the answer.

__2__ + __7__ = __9__ donuts

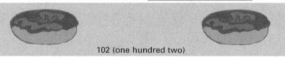

102 (one hundred two)

WORD NUMBERS – ELEVEN TO TWENTY

1. Draw a line to match the word number and number.

11	twelve
12	fourteen
13	eleven
14	fifteen
15	thirteen
16	eighteen
17	seventeen
18	sixteen
19	nineteen

20	forty
30	twenty
40	fifty
50	thirty
60	eighty
70	sixty
80	one hundred
90	seventy
100	ninety

2. Draw a line with the ruler.

2 inches

• Measure student's line

5 inches

• Measure student's line

3 inches

• Measure student's line

4 inches

• Measure student's line

103 (one hundred three)

---

3. Draw the pennies and dimes needed.

23¢ 10¢ 10¢ 1¢ 1¢ 1¢

41¢ 10¢ 10¢ 10¢ 10¢ 1¢

16¢ 10¢ 1¢ 1¢ 1¢ 1¢ 1¢ 1¢

34¢ 10¢ 10¢ 10¢ 1¢ 1¢ 1¢ 1¢

4. Ron read 10 pages on Tuesday and 8 pages on Wednesday. How many pages did Ron read altogether? Write the addition fact and label the answer.

__10__ + __8__ = __18__ pages

5. Write the answers.

| 5 3 +7 = 15 | 4 4 +9 = 17 | 2 6 +4 = 12 | 3 3 +8 = 14 | 1 5 +9 = 15 | 5 4 +7 = 16 |

| 36 +23 = 59 | 25 +41 = 66 | | | 76 +20 = 96 | 22 +44 = 66 |

104 (one hundred four)

402

MONEY – NICKELS
Lesson 48

1 Count the nickels by 5's. Circle the correct cents.

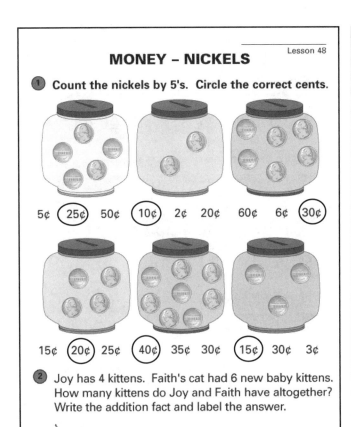

5¢　(25¢)　50¢　　(10¢)　2¢　20¢　　60¢　6¢　(30¢)

15¢　(20¢)　25¢　　(40¢)　35¢　30¢　　(15¢)　30¢　3¢

2 Joy has 4 kittens. Faith's cat had 6 new baby kittens. How many kittens do Joy and Faith have altogether? Write the addition fact and label the answer.

$\underline{4} + \underline{6} = \underline{10}$ kittens

105 (one hundred five)

---

3 Write the number in the blank.

thirteen	13	fifteen	15
nineteen	19	sixty	60
forty	40	twenty	20
eighty	80	eleven	11
twelve	12	seventy	70

4 Write the numbers in the blanks.

72 = __7__ tens + __2__ ones　　　50 = __5__ tens + __0__ ones

54 = __5__ tens + __4__ ones　　　17 = __1__ ten + __7__ ones

8 = __0__ tens + __8__ ones　　　43 = __4__ tens + __3__ ones

39 = __3__ tens + __9__ ones　　　26 = __2__ tens + __6__ ones

81 = __8__ tens + __1__ one　　　65 = __6__ tens + __5__ ones

5 Write the answers.

2	4	5	6	8	9
+9	+6	+8	+9	+8	+7
11	10	13	15	16	16

16	44			72	21
+53	+22			+12	+74
69	66			84	95

106 (one hundred six)

FRACTIONS – ONE FOURTH
Lesson 49

1 Color one fourth ($\frac{1}{4}$) of each shape.

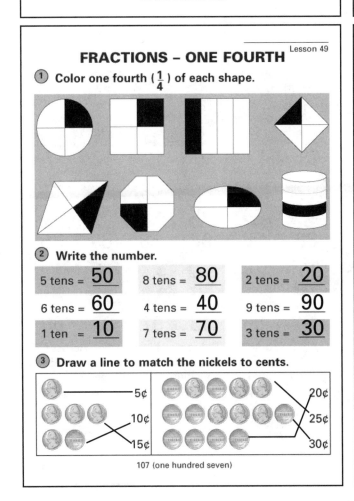

2 Write the number.

5 tens = 50	8 tens = 80	2 tens = 20
6 tens = 60	4 tens = 40	9 tens = 90
1 ten = 10	7 tens = 70	3 tens = 30

3 Draw a line to match the nickels to cents.

—5¢
10¢
15¢
20¢
25¢
30¢

107 (one hundred seven)

---

4 Write the answers.

2	6	4	1	5	2
4	1	3	8	1	6
+8	+9	+7	+7	+9	+9
14	16	14	16	15	17

82	14	25	56	53	30
+17	+72	+50	+32	+22	+35
99	86	75	88	75	65

32	45	74	61	24	20
+16	+51	+11	+38	+25	+73
48	96	85	99	49	93

5 Write the missing numbers.

50	51	52	53	54	55	56	57	58	59
60	61	62	63	64	65	66	67	68	69
70	71	72	73	74	75	76	77	78	79
80	81	82	83	84	85	86	87	88	89
90	91	92	93	94	95	96	97	98	99

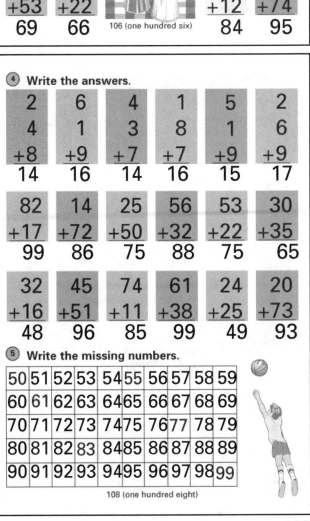

108 (one hundred eight)

TEST 5

① Write the correct time. 4 pts. total for this exercise.

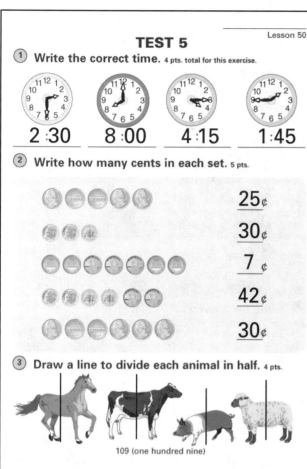

2:30   8:00   4:15   1:45

② Write how many cents in each set. 5 pts.

25¢

30¢

7¢

42¢

30¢

③ Draw a line to divide each animal in half. 4 pts.

109 (one hundred nine)

---

④ Write the number that comes before and after.
12 pts. total for this exercise.

22 23 24   55 56 57   7 8 9

29 30 31   86 87 88   40 41 42

⑤ Write the answers. 12 pts. total for this exercise.

3	6	5	8	7	7
3	3	3	1	1	0
+3	+2	+3	+5	+1	+2
9	11	11	14	9	9

16	44	72	21	54	10
+53	+22	+12	+74	+25	+33
69	66	84	95	79	43

⑥ Amy brought 4 dimes for lunch. Anita brought 6 dimes. Amy and Anita had how many dimes altogether? Write the addition fact and label the answer. 4 pts.

4 + 6 = 10 dimes

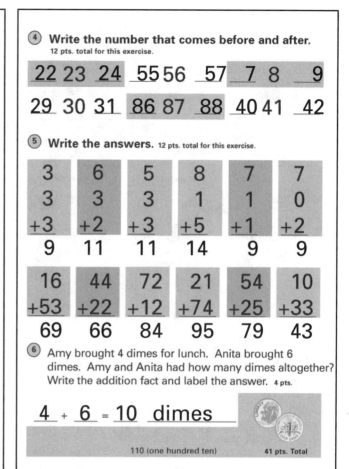

110 (one hundred ten)   41 pts. Total

SHOW YOUR SKILLS

① Draw the objects.

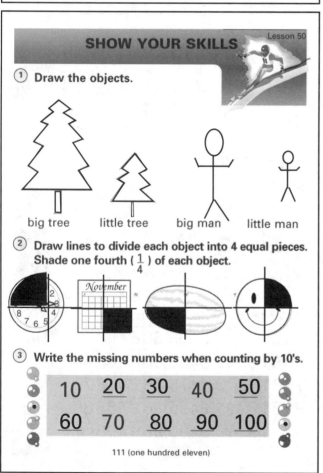

big tree   little tree   big man   little man

② Draw lines to divide each object into 4 equal pieces. Shade one fourth ($\frac{1}{4}$) of each object.

November

③ Write the missing numbers when counting by 10's.

10	20	30	40	50
60	70	80	90	100

111 (one hundred eleven)

---

④ Write the answers.

1	5	9	1	3	2
8	5	1	6	2	4
+4	+3	+0	+5	+5	+1
13	13	10	12	10	7

14	56	63	65	53	15
+72	+32	+35	+23	+16	+20
86	88	98	88	69	35

70	63	14	81	82	46
+22	+23	+34	+16	+15	+23
92	86	48	97	97	69

⑤ Sam could see 7 blue birds in his tree. Across the road he could see 9 black birds on the fence. Sam could see how many birds altogether? Write the addition fact and label the answer.

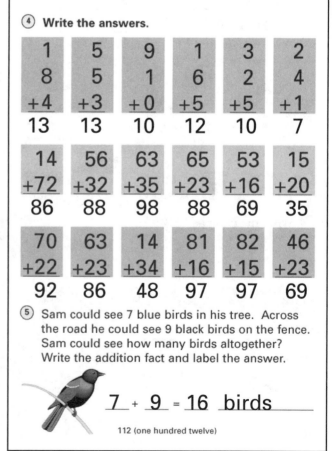

7 + 9 = 16 birds

112 (one hundred twelve)

MONEY – QUARTER

Front　　Back

25 cents
25¢

① Count the quarters by 25's.

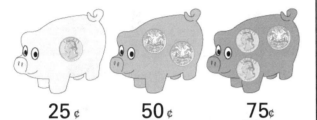

25¢　　**50**¢　　**75**¢

② Write = or ≠ between each set.

3 dimes   **=**   30¢   4 nickels   **=**   20¢

7 pennies **=**   7¢   1 quarter   **≠**   75¢

2 dimes and
3 pennies **≠**   32¢   5 dimes   **≠**   25¢

113 (one hundred thirteen)

---

③ Color $\frac{1}{4}$ of the objects divided into 4 parts.

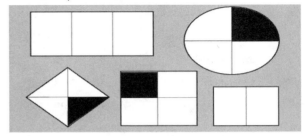

④ Write the answers.

81	63	72	25	41	22
+15	+35	+14	+32	+54	+12
96	98	86	57	95	34

37	33	63	60	22	44
+42	+44	+15	+29	+57	+10
79	77	78	89	79	54

⑤ Ron bought a drink with 7 nickels and a candy bar with 4 nickels. How many nickels did Ron need altogether? Write the addition fact and label the answer.

7 + **4** = **11 nickels**

114 (one hundred fourteen)

SUBTRACTION

① Write the answers.

7-3=4

$\begin{array}{r} 7 \\ -3 \\ \hline 4 \end{array}$

5-2=3

$\begin{array}{r} 5 \\ -2 \\ \hline 3 \end{array}$

7-1= 6

$\begin{array}{r} 7 \\ -1 \\ \hline 6 \end{array}$

6-2= 4

$\begin{array}{r} 6 \\ -2 \\ \hline 4 \end{array}$

115 (one hundred fifteen)

---

② Write the value.

   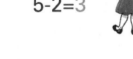

25 50 75   25 50   25

75 ¢   **50** ¢   **25** ¢

③ Write the fraction that shows what part is shaded.

$\frac{1}{3}$ $\frac{1}{2}$ $\frac{1}{4}$

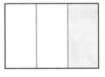 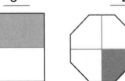 

$\frac{1}{2}$ $\frac{1}{4}$ $\frac{1}{3}$

④ Write = or ≠ between each set.

7+8 **=** 15   9+4 **≠** 14   5+4 **=** 9

7+5 **≠** 13   6+9 **≠** 17   8+5 **=** 13

116 (one hundred sixteen)

405

NUMBER ORDER – < AND >

(1) Write < or > in the blanks.

18 __>__ sixteen	four __<__ 8	16 __<__ twenty
6 __<__ fourteen	fifty __>__ 36	71 __>__ thirty
14 __>__ twelve	forty __>__ 26	6 __<__ eleven
67 __<__ eighty	thirty __>__ 21	23 __>__ nineteen

(2) Color $\frac{1}{4}$ Color $\frac{1}{2}$ Color $\frac{1}{2}$

Color $\frac{1}{2}$ Color $\frac{1}{4}$ Color $\frac{1}{4}$

(3) Lee had 5 baseball cards. Gene gave him 9 more cards. How many baseball cards does Lee now have? Label the answer.

__5__ + __9__ = __14__ baseball cards

117 (one hundred seventeen)

---

(4) Write the answers.

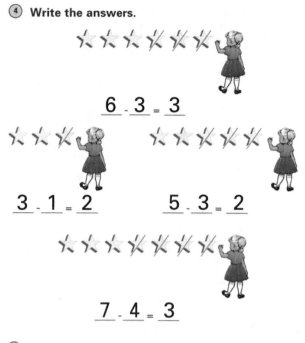

__6__ - __3__ = __3__

__3__ - __1__ = __2__   __5__ - __3__ = __2__

__7__ - __4__ = __3__

(5) Circle the correct answer.

10¢   25¢   (50¢) | 25¢   50¢   (75¢) | 5¢   10¢   (25¢)

118 (one hundred eighteen)

TIME – HOUR AND HALF HOUR

(1) Write the correct time.

2:00   8:00   9:30   5:30

3:00   11:30   10:00   6:00

4:30   1:30   12:30   7:00

(2) If divided into 4 parts, color $\frac{1}{4}$.

119 (one hundred nineteen)

---

(3) Write the answers.

__4__ - __1__ = __3__   __6__ - __5__ = __1__

__6__ - __1__ = __5__   __5__ - __4__ = __1__

Write < or > between each set.

6+5 __>__ 10	7+4 __<__ 12	8+9 __>__ 10
8+2 __<__ 17	9+9 __<__ 34	2+3 __>__ 0

(5) Write the answers.

1	3	6	1	0	2
5	7	3	8	7	6
+8	+2	+4	+9	+8	+9
14	12	13	18	15	17

120 (one hundred twenty)

SUBTRACTION – NUMBER LINE

1 Write the answer to these addition facts using the number line.

$2-1=1$

$3-2=$ _1_

$5-5=$ _0_

$7-0=$ _7_

$4-2=$ _2_

121 (one hundred twenty-one)

---

2 Write the correct time.

4:15   8:45   3:45   11:15

3 If divided into 2 parts, color $\frac{1}{2}$.

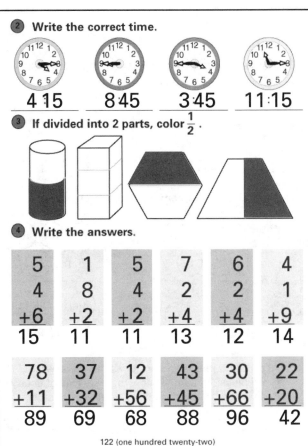

4 Write the answers.

5	1	5	7	6	4
4	8	4	2	2	1
+6	+2	+2	+4	+4	+9
15	11	11	13	12	14

78	37	12	43	30	22
+11	+32	+56	+45	+66	+20
89	69	68	88	96	42

122 (one hundred twenty-two)

MONEY – PENNIES AND DIMES

1 Write the number on the line.

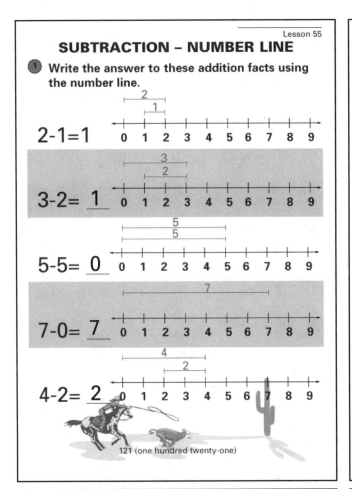

67¢	98¢	59¢
6 dimes	9 dimes	5 dimes
7 pennies	8 pennies	9 pennies
73¢	16¢	84¢
7 dimes	1 dime	8 dimes
3 pennies	6 pennies	4 pennies

2 Write the correct time.

3:00   9:30   7:15   10:45

1:30   4:45   2:00   11:15

123 (one hundred twenty-three)

---

3 Write the subtraction fact.

$9 - 3 = 6$

$8 - 8 = 0$

$9 - 7 = 2$

$2 - 0 = 2$

$4 - 3 = 1$

4 Doug picked 3 quarts of berries. Joyce picked 7 quarts of berries. They picked how many quarts of berries altogether? Write the addition fact and label the answer.

$3 + 7 = 10$ quarts

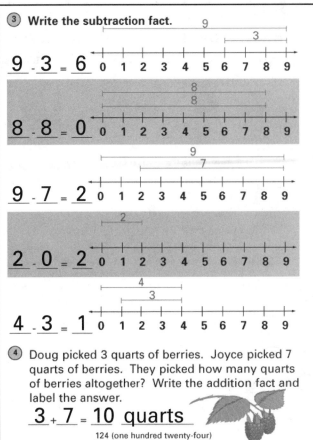

124 (one hundred twenty-four)

407

INCHES
Lesson 57

1 Measure the lines with an inch ruler. Write the answers.

__4__ inches

__5__ inches

__3__ inches

2 Draw dimes and pennies for each object.

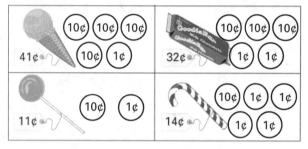

41¢ 10¢ 10¢ 10¢ 10¢ 1¢

32¢ 10¢ 10¢ 10¢ 1¢ 1¢

11¢ 10¢ 1¢

14¢ 10¢ 1¢ 1¢ 1¢ 1¢

3 Alice has 6 pieces of candy. Karen gave Alice 8 more pieces of candy. How many pieces of candy does Alice have altogether? Label the answer.

__6__ + __8__ = __14__ pieces of candy

125 (one hundred twenty-five)

---

4 Write the subtraction fact.

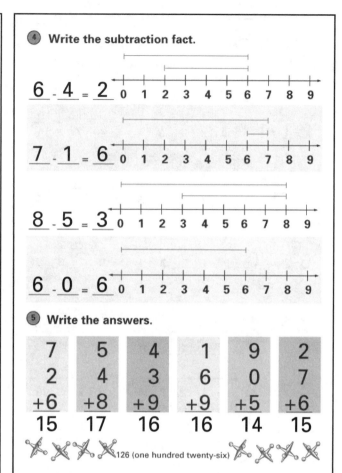

6 - 4 = 2

7 - 1 = 6

8 - 5 = 3

6 - 0 = 6

5 Write the answers.

7	5	4	1	9	2
2	4	3	6	0	7
+6	+8	+9	+9	+5	+6
15	17	16	16	14	15

126 (one hundred twenty-six)

NUMBER ORDER – ORDINAL NUMBERS
Lesson 58

1 Write first, second, third, fourth or fifth in the blanks.

The ship is the __third__ toy.
The teddy bear is the __second__ toy.
The airplane is the __first__ toy.
The doll is the __fourth__ toy.
The car is the __fifth__ toy.

2 Circle the number of dimes and pennies needed.

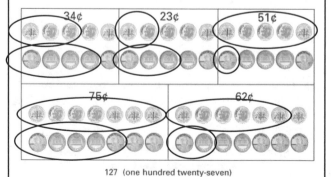

34¢   23¢   51¢
75¢   62¢

127 (one hundred twenty-seven)

---

3 Draw the subtraction fact on the number line.

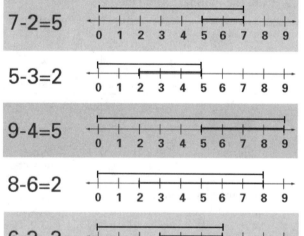

7-2=5

5-3=2

9-4=5

8-6=2

6-3=3

4 Write the answers.

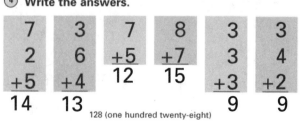

7	3	7	8	3	3
2	6	+5	+7	3	4
+5	+4	12	15	+3	+2
14	13			9	9

128 (one hundred twenty-eight)

408

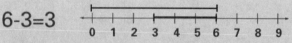

PLACE VALUE

1 Write the numbers.

5 tens = **50**	8 tens = **80**	9 tens = **90**
7 tens = **70**	3 tens = **30**	4 tens = **40**
1 ten = **10**	2 tens = **20**	6 tens = **60**

2 Write the value of each set.

  **35**¢

 **15**¢

 **25**¢

  40¢

3 Counting by 10's, write the number that comes before and after.

0 10 **20** 40 50 60 **30** 40 **50**

60 70 80 **20** **30** 40 80 90 100

129 (one hundred twenty-nine)

---

4 Write the answers using the number line.

```
+--+--+--+--+--+--+--+--+--+
0  1  2  3  4  5  6  7  8  9
```

2 - 2 = **0**   5 - 4 = **1**

6 - 2 = **4**   8 - 4 = **4**

7 - 3 = **4**   9 - 4 = **5**

9 - 1 = **8**   5 - 0 = **5**

4 - 1 = **3**   6 - 6 = **0**

5 Alice made her brother Joe's bed for 8 mornings. Then she made Jack's bed for 7 mornings. How many mornings did she make a bed for her brothers? Label the answer.

8 + **7** = **15 mornings**

Allen had 9 crayons in his desk. He found 7 more in his book bag. How many crayons did he have altogether? Label the answer.

9 + **7** = **16 crayons**

130 (one hundred thirty)

TEST 6

1 Write the correct time. 4 pts. total for this exercise.

2 : **30**   **8** : **00**   **4** : **45**   **1** : **15**

2 Shade $\frac{1}{2}$ of each object. 3 pts. total for this exercise.

3 Shade $\frac{1}{4}$ of each object. 3 pts. total for this exercise.

131 (one hundred thirty-one)

---

4 Counting by 10's, write the number that comes before and after. 18 pts. total for this exercise.

50 60 **70** **80** 90 100 **30** 40 **50**

40 50 **60** **10** 20 **30** **70** 80 **90**

0 10 **20** 60 70 **80** **20** 30 **40**

5 Write the answers. 12 pts. total for this exercise.

7	5	4	7	5	2
1	3	3	1	4	6
+3	+4	+2	+1	+7	+1
11	**12**	**9**	**9**	**16**	**9**

63	42	83	75	23	35
+13	+21	+16	+24	+ 6	+11
76	**63**	**99**	**99**	**29**	**46**

6 Mae had 5 pennies in her bank. Her mother gave her 8 more to put in her bank. Mae's bank now has how many pennies in it altogether? Label the answer. 4 pts.

5 + **8** = **13 pennies**

132 (one hundred thirty-two)   44 pts. Total

409

WORD NUMBERS – ELEVEN TO ONE HUNDRED

Lesson 60

① Write the number in the blank.

eighteen	18	twenty	20
forty	40	fifteen	15
eleven	11	seventy	70
ninety	90	eighty	80
sixteen	16	twelve	12

② Write the numbers in the blanks.

34 = **3** tens+ **4** ones   12 = **1** ten + **2** ones

27 = **2** tens+ **7** ones   75 = **7** tens+ **5** ones

9 = **0** tens+ **9** ones   98 = **9** tens+ **8** ones

56 = **5** tens+ **6** ones   41 = **4** tens+ **1** one

83 = **8** tens+ **3** ones   60 = **6** tens+ **0** ones

③ Draw the number of nickels needed.

5¢ 5¢ 5¢ 5¢ 5¢ 5¢ 5¢ 5¢ 5¢ 45¢

5¢ 5¢ 5¢ 15¢

5¢ 5¢ 5¢ 5¢ 5¢ 5¢ 30¢

133 (one hundred thirty-three)

④ Write the answers using the number line.

0 1 2 3 4 5 6 7 8 9

3 - 0 = **3**   4 - 4 = **0**   5 - 3 = **2**

7 - 2 = **5**   1 - 1 = **0**   6 - 1 = **5**

8 - 3 = **5**   6 - 5 = **1**   7 - 6 = **1**

⑤ Write the answers.

5	3	6	5	4	6
3	4	2	4	4	1
+6	+7	+9	+9	+8	+7
14	14	17	18	16	14

5	6	6	5	6	5
+9	+7	+8	+8	+9	+7
14	13	14	13	15	12

54	72			14	16
+45	+17			+13	+22
99	89			27	38

134 (one hundred thirty-four)

SUBTRACTION – VERTICAL

Lesson 61

① Write the answers using the number line.

0 1 2 3 4 5 6 7 8 9

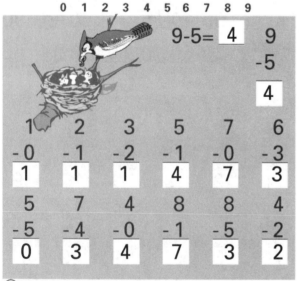

9-5= **4**

9
-5
4

1	2	3	5	7	6
-0	-1	-2	-1	-0	-3
1	1	1	4	7	3

5	7	4	8	8	4
-5	-4	-0	-1	-5	-2
0	3	4	7	3	2

② Anna picked 6 lemons from the tree. Eva picked 8 more. How many lemons did the girls pick altogether? Label the answer.

6 + **8** = **14 lemons**

135 (one hundred thirty-five)

③ Write the value of the tens and ones.

72 = **70** + **2**   16 = **10** + **6**

57 = **50** + **7**   43 = **40** + **3**

38 = **30** + **8**   61 = **60** + **1**

84 = **80** + **4**   25 = **20** + **5**

④ Write the answers.

6	1	2	5	7	3
2	2	3	2	1	5
+3	+7	+8	+9	+2	+9
11	10	13	16	10	17

6	4	6	6	7	3
2	3	3	2	1	5
+4	+5	+2	+6	+5	+7
12	12	11	14	13	15

42	82			41	45
+36	+ 6			+58	+24
78	88			99	69

136 (one hundred thirty-six)

410

WORD NUMBERS –
TWENTY TO ONE HUNDRED

1 Match the word number to the number.

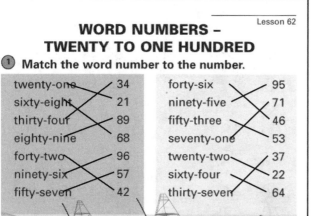

twenty-one	34	forty-six	95
sixty-eight	21	ninety-five	71
thirty-four	89	fifty-three	46
eighty-nine	68	seventy-one	53
forty-two	96	twenty-two	37
ninety-six	57	sixty-four	22
fifty-seven	42	thirty-seven	64

2 Write the problems vertically. Write the answers.

$16 + 23 =$
$$\begin{array}{r} 16 \\ +23 \\ \hline 39 \end{array}$$

$17 + 2 =$
$$\begin{array}{r} 17 \\ +2 \\ \hline 19 \end{array}$$

$43 + 36 =$
$$\begin{array}{r} 43 \\ +36 \\ \hline 79 \end{array}$$

$10 + 11 =$
$$\begin{array}{r} 10 \\ +11 \\ \hline 21 \end{array}$$

137 (one hundred thirty-seven)

---

3 Write the answers.

Number line: 0 1 2 3 4 5 6 7 8 9

$$\begin{array}{r} 9 \\ -0 \\ \hline 9 \end{array} \quad \begin{array}{r} 5 \\ -3 \\ \hline 2 \end{array} \quad \begin{array}{r} 6 \\ -5 \\ \hline 1 \end{array} \quad \begin{array}{r} 4 \\ -4 \\ \hline 0 \end{array} \quad \begin{array}{r} 7 \\ -2 \\ \hline 5 \end{array} \quad \begin{array}{r} 1 \\ -1 \\ \hline 0 \end{array}$$

$$\begin{array}{r} 9 \\ -4 \\ \hline 5 \end{array} \quad \begin{array}{r} 2 \\ -0 \\ \hline 2 \end{array} \quad \begin{array}{r} 2 \\ -1 \\ \hline 1 \end{array} \quad \begin{array}{r} 9 \\ -8 \\ \hline 1 \end{array} \quad \begin{array}{r} 8 \\ -7 \\ \hline 1 \end{array} \quad \begin{array}{r} 7 \\ -4 \\ \hline 3 \end{array}$$

$$\begin{array}{r} 6 \\ -1 \\ \hline 5 \end{array} \quad \begin{array}{r} 7 \\ -6 \\ \hline 1 \end{array} \quad \begin{array}{r} 3 \\ -0 \\ \hline 3 \end{array} \quad \begin{array}{r} 6 \\ -3 \\ \hline 3 \end{array} \quad \begin{array}{r} 4 \\ -3 \\ \hline 1 \end{array} \quad \begin{array}{r} 6 \\ -2 \\ \hline 4 \end{array}$$

4 Roy had 5 paper airplanes. Rod gave him 7 more. Roy now has how many paper airplanes altogether? Label the answer.

$\underline{5} + \underline{7} = \underline{12}$ airplanes

Lori skipped rope 9 times. Jan skipped rope only 4 times. How many times did they skip rope altogether? Label the answer.

$\underline{9} + \underline{4} = \underline{13}$ times

138 (one hundred thirty-eight)

SHOW YOUR SKILLS

1 Write the answers.

Number line: 0 1 2 3 4 5 6 7 8 9

$9-6 =$
$$\begin{array}{r} 9 \\ -6 \\ \hline 3 \end{array}$$

$8-3 =$
$$\begin{array}{r} 8 \\ -3 \\ \hline 5 \end{array}$$

$1-0 =$
$$\begin{array}{r} 1 \\ -0 \\ \hline 1 \end{array}$$

$4-1 =$
$$\begin{array}{r} 4 \\ -1 \\ \hline 3 \end{array}$$

$5-0 =$
$$\begin{array}{r} 5 \\ -0 \\ \hline 5 \end{array}$$

$8-2 =$
$$\begin{array}{r} 8 \\ -2 \\ \hline 6 \end{array}$$

$$\begin{array}{r} 8 \\ -8 \\ \hline 0 \end{array} \quad \begin{array}{r} 2 \\ -0 \\ \hline 2 \end{array} \quad \begin{array}{r} 4 \\ -3 \\ \hline 1 \end{array} \quad \begin{array}{r} 5 \\ -2 \\ \hline 3 \end{array} \quad \begin{array}{r} 9 \\ -9 \\ \hline 0 \end{array} \quad \begin{array}{r} 6 \\ -4 \\ \hline 2 \end{array}$$

$$\begin{array}{r} 7 \\ -1 \\ \hline 6 \end{array} \quad \begin{array}{r} 7 \\ -5 \\ \hline 2 \end{array} \quad \begin{array}{r} 8 \\ -0 \\ \hline 8 \end{array} \quad \begin{array}{r} 8 \\ -4 \\ \hline 4 \end{array} \quad \begin{array}{r} 3 \\ -3 \\ \hline 0 \end{array} \quad \begin{array}{r} 6 \\ -0 \\ \hline 6 \end{array}$$

139 (one hundred thirty-nine)

---

2 Write the number.

forty-one	41	twenty-nine	29
ninety-two	92	fifty-one	51
sixty-five	65	thirty-eight	38
thirty-six	36	ninety-three	93
eighty-four	84	seventy-two	72

3 Draw the number of quarters needed.

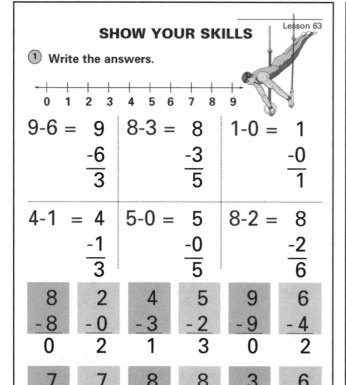

75¢ (25¢) (25¢) (25¢)

50¢ (25¢) (25¢)

4 Write the answers.

$$\begin{array}{r} 1 \\ 2 \\ +7 \\ \hline 10 \end{array} \quad \begin{array}{r} 5 \\ 3 \\ +6 \\ \hline 14 \end{array} \quad \begin{array}{r} 3 \\ 4 \\ +7 \\ \hline 14 \end{array} \quad \begin{array}{r} 7 \\ 2 \\ +8 \\ \hline 17 \end{array} \quad \begin{array}{r} 3 \\ 6 \\ +3 \\ \hline 12 \end{array} \quad \begin{array}{r} 2 \\ 5 \\ +9 \\ \hline 16 \end{array}$$

$$\begin{array}{r} 40 \\ +47 \\ \hline 87 \end{array} \quad \begin{array}{r} 19 \\ +20 \\ \hline 39 \end{array} \quad \begin{array}{r} 24 \\ +43 \\ \hline 67 \end{array} \quad \begin{array}{r} 55 \\ +20 \\ \hline 75 \end{array} \quad \begin{array}{r} 54 \\ +22 \\ \hline 76 \end{array} \quad \begin{array}{r} 63 \\ +14 \\ \hline 77 \end{array}$$

140 (one hundred forty)

411

FRACTIONS – ONE FOURTH

1 Divide each object into fourths. Shade $\frac{1}{4}$.

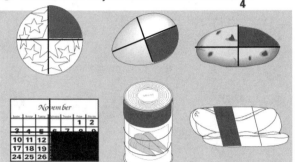

2 Write the value of each coin.

 __10__ ¢   __25__ ¢

__5__ ¢   __1__ ¢   __25__ ¢

__1__ ¢   __5__ ¢   __10__ ¢

3 Polly dusted 6 rows of library books. Sally dusted the next 8 rows. How many rows did they dust altogether?

$6 + 8 = 14$ rows

141 (one hundred forty-one)

---

4 Write the answers.

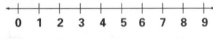

7	3	2	3	7	6
2	6	2	4	2	2
+9	+9	+5	+3	+8	+4
18	18	9	10	17	12

30	26	43	13	32	52
+40	+12	+14	+54	+55	+46
70	38	57	67	87	98

5 Write the answers.

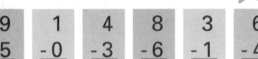

```
0 1 2 3 4 5 6 7 8 9
```

9	1	4	8	3	6
-5	-0	-3	-6	-1	-4
4	1	1	2	2	2

8	9			8	1
-7	-4			-1	-1
1	5			7	0

142 (one hundred forty-two)

EVEN NUMBERS

1 Color all the even numbers.

1	2	3	4	5	6	7	8	9	10	11	12
13	14	15	16	17	18	19	20	21	22	23	24
25	26	27	28	29	30	31	32	33	34	35	36
37	38	39	40	41	42	43	44	45	46	47	48

2 Circle the shapes that have $\frac{1}{4}$ colored.

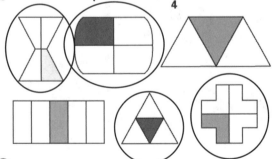

3 Ed colored 5 pictures in the coloring book. Rex colored 7 pictures. How many pictures in the book did they color altogether?

$5 + 7 = 12$ pictures

143 (one hundred forty-three)

---

4 Write the answers.

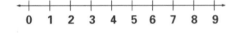

```
0 1 2 3 4 5 6 7 8 9
```

2	9	7	6	4	8
-1	-9	-6	-1	-1	-0
1	0	1	5	3	8

7	9	8	7	5	7
-1	-5	-6	-5	-1	-3
6	4	2	2	4	4

9	9	7	5	8	7
-8	-6	-0	-4	-7	-7
1	3	7	1	1	0

5 Write < or > between each set. Read the set.

$3+4$ __<__ 10 $7+5$ __<__ 16 $6+3$ __<__ 11

$9+4$ __<__ 15 $7+7$ __>__ 7 $2+6$ __>__ 7

$4+5$ __>__ 8 $6+5$ __<__ 14 $7+2$ __<__ 11

144 (one hundred forty-four)

412

FRACTIONS – ONE HALF AND ONE FOURTH

1 Circle the picture that matches the fraction problem.

Ann ate $\frac{1}{2}$ of a donut. Karen ate $\frac{1}{4}$ of a pizza.

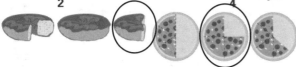

John ate $\frac{1}{2}$ of an apple pie. Susan ate $\frac{1}{4}$ of a watermelon slice.

2 Write the answers.

4	3	3	5	7	5
2	5	6	2	2	3
+3	+2	+4	+9	+4	+6
9	10	13	16	13	14

145 (one hundred forty-five)

---

3 Write the answers.

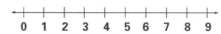

0 1 2 3 4 5 6 7 8 9

3	9	5	2	8	6
-1	-9	-4	-0	-3	-6
2	0	1	2	5	0

4	5	3	7	6	8
-2	-2	-3	-2	-4	-1
2	3	0	5	2	7

4 Write the even numbers from 40 - 86.

40	42	44	46	48	50	52	54	56	58	60	62
64	66	68	70	72	74	76	78	80	82	84	86

5 Write < or > between each set.

5 > |||| 7 < ||||||||| 3 > ||

6 > ||||| 2 < ||| 4 < |||||||

146 (one hundred forty-six)

EQUAL AND NOT EQUAL

1 Write = or ≠ between each set.

$\frac{1}{2}$ ≠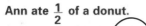

$\frac{1}{4}$ =

$\frac{1}{3}$ =

$\frac{1}{2}$ ≠

$\frac{1}{4}$ ≠

$\frac{1}{5}$ =

$\frac{1}{6}$ ≠

$\frac{1}{2}$ =

$\frac{1}{4}$ =

$\frac{1}{3}$ ≠

147 (one hundred forty-seven)

---

2 Subtract.

0 1 2 3 4 5 6 7 8 9

7	9	1	6	5	6
-6	-2	-1	-0	-5	-1
1	7	0	6	0	5

9	4	9	7	2	9
-4	-0	-1	-4	-2	-3
5	4	8	3	0	6

8	5	8	6	5	8
-4	-2	-2	-3	-1	-0
4	3	6	3	4	8

3 Add.

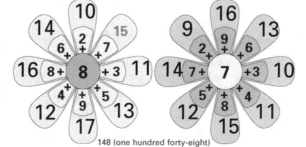

148 (one hundred forty-eight)

413

TIME – HOUR

1 Draw the short hand for each clock.

3:00   10:00   7:00   1:00

2 Write = or ≠ between each set.

fifteen	≠	50	thirty-six	≠	34
twenty-one	=	21	twelve	=	12
fourteen	≠	44	eighteen	=	18
nine	≠	6	seventy-one	=	71

3 There were 5 frogs on a lilly pad. 4 more joined them. How many frogs were on the lilly pad?

$$5 + 4 = 9 \text{ frogs}$$

Freddy Frog ate 9 bugs. Fran Frog ate 4 bugs. How many bugs did the two frogs eat?

$$9 + 4 = 13 \text{ bugs}$$

149 (one hundred forty-nine)

---

4 Write the problems vertically. Write the answers.

42 + 16 =	42	15 + 14 =	15
	+ 16		+ 14
	58		29
12 + 20 =	12	43 + 15 =	43
	+ 20		+ 15
	32		58

5 Subtract.

0 1 2 3 4 5 6 7 8 9

1	9	8	3	8	9
-0	-8	-5	-0	-1	-2
1	1	3	3	7	7

9	7	6	6	5	6
-3	-2	-2	-5	-5	-4
6	5	4	1	0	2

150 (one hundred fifty)

INCHES

1 Draw a line with the ruler.

4 inches

Teacher check.

3 inches

Teacher check.

6 inches

Teacher check.

5 inches

Teacher check.

2 Draw both hands on the clock.

4:00   11:00   8:00   2:00

3 There were 8 boys and 6 girls in a van going to the zoo. How many children were in the van?

$$8 + 6 = 14 \text{ children}$$

151 (one hundred fifty-one)

---

4 Add.

23	56	15	17	83	17
+32	+13	+43	+62	+12	+42
55	69	58	79	95	59

7	1	6	3	7	6
2	6	2	4	2	2
+0	+9	+5	+3	+8	+4
9	16	13	10	17	12

5 Subtract.

0 1 2 3 4 5 6 7 8 9

3	9	1	5	2	9
-2	-4	-0	-2	-1	-6
1	5	1	3	1	3

3	9			8	8
-3	-0			-3	-2
0	9			5	6

152 (one hundred fifty-two)

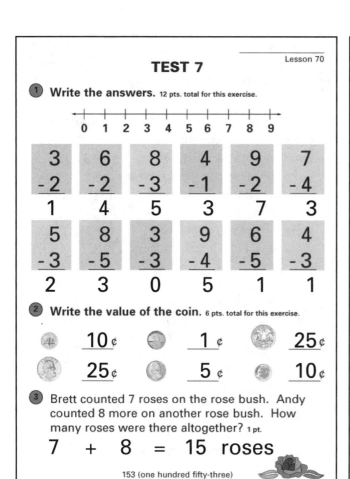

TEST 7

1 Write the answers. 12 pts. total for this exercise.

```
0 1 2 3 4 5 6 7 8 9
```

3	6	8	4	9	7
-2	-2	-3	-1	-2	-4
1	4	5	3	7	3

5	8	3	9	6	4
-3	-5	-3	-4	-5	-3
2	3	0	5	1	1

2 Write the value of the coin. 6 pts. total for this exercise.

10 ¢   1 ¢   25 ¢

25 ¢   5 ¢   10 ¢

3 Brett counted 7 roses on the rose bush. Andy counted 8 more on another rose bush. How many roses were there altogether? 1 pt.

7 + 8 = 15 roses

153 (one hundred fifty-three)

---

4 Draw a line with the ruler. 2 pts. total for this exercise.

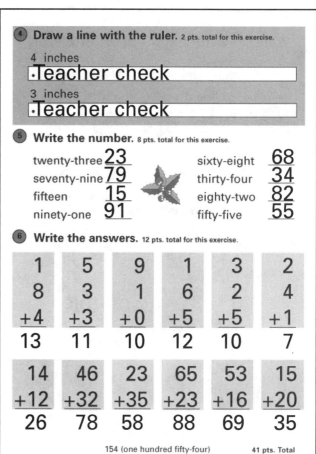

4 inches
·Teacher check

3 inches
·Teacher check

5 Write the number. 8 pts. total for this exercise.

twenty-three 23   sixty-eight 68
seventy-nine 79   thirty-four 34
fifteen 15   eighty-two 82
ninety-one 91   fifty-five 55

6 Write the answers. 12 pts. total for this exercise.

1	5	9	1	3	2
8	3	1	6	2	4
+4	+3	+0	+5	+5	+1
13	11	10	12	10	7

14	46	23	65	53	15
+12	+32	+35	+23	+16	+20
26	78	58	88	69	35

154 (one hundred fifty-four)   41 pts. Total

NUMBER ORDER – ORDINAL NUMBERS

1 Write the letters in the blanks.

I   L   O   V   E   Y   O   U

fourth __V__   second __L__   sixth __Y__
first __I__   eighth __U__   seventh __O__
fifth __E__   third __O__

2 How long is the path?

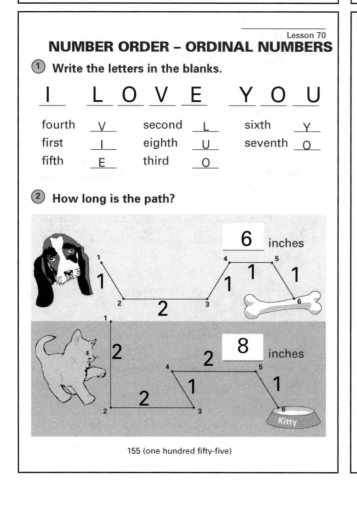

6 inches

1   1   1   1
2

8 inches

2   2
2   1   1

Kitty

155 (one hundred fifty-five)

---

3 Subtract.

```
0 1 2 3 4 5 6 7 8 9
```

5	8	2	6	2	5
-3	-4	-0	-1	-2	-1
2	4	2	5	0	4

9	6	7	9	4	6
-1	-3	-5	-5	-1	-6
8	3	2	4	3	0

4 Add.

4	1	4	5	7	3
2	2	3	2	2	5
+3	+6	+5	+9	+2	+9
9	9	12	16	11	17

49	15			26	68
+30	+62			+33	+31
79	77			59	99

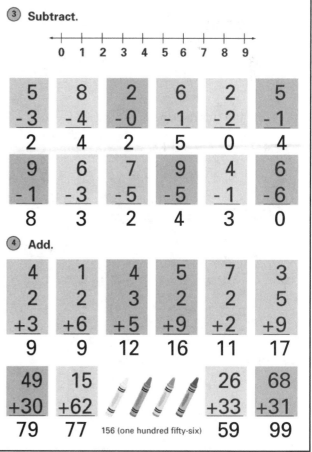

156 (one hundred fifty-six)

415

WORD PROBLEMS – SUBTRACTION

① Stan had 4 cookies in his lunch. He gave 1 of them to Glen. How many cookies did he have left?

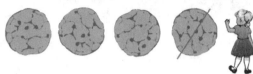

$$\underline{4} - \underline{1} = \underline{3} \quad \text{cookies}$$

Wade had 8 marbles in his pocket. He gave 3 of them to Luke. How many marbles did he have left?

$$\underline{8} - \underline{3} = \underline{5} \quad \text{marbles}$$

There were 7 birds on the fence. 2 of the birds flew away. How many birds were left on the fence?

$$\underline{7} - \underline{2} = \underline{5} \quad \text{birds}$$

157 (one hundred fifty-seven)

---

②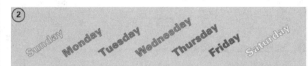

Sunday	Monday	Tuesday	Wednesday	Thursday	Friday	Saturday

Write the third day of the week. **Tuesday**
Write the first day of the week. **Sunday**
Write the sixth day of the week. **Friday**
Write the seventh day of the week. **Saturday**
Write the fifth day of the week. **Thursday**
Write the fourth day of the week. **Wednesday**
Write the last day of the week. **Saturday**
Write the middle day of the week. **Wednesday**

③ **Write the answers in the blanks.**

6 tens + 4 ones	=	60	+	4	=	64
5 tens + 3 ones	=	50	+	3	=	53
7 tens + 6 ones	=	70	+	6	=	76
3 tens + 8 ones	=	30	+	8	=	38
0 tens + 8 ones	=	0	+	8	=	8
0 tens + 0 ones	=	0	+	0	=	0
4 tens + 5 ones	=	40	+	5	=	45
8 tens + 2 ones	=	80	+	2	=	82

158 (one hundred fifty-eight)

ADDITION AND SUBTRACTION

6+2=8	3+4=7	5+4=9
8-2=6	7-4=3	9-5=4
8-6=2	7-3=4	9-4=5

① **Write the subtraction facts.**

2+1=3	3+5=8	3+2=5
3 - 1 = 2	8 - 5 = 3	5 - 2 = 3
3 - 2 = 1	8 - 3 = 5	5 - 3 = 2
2+4=6	3+6=9	7+1=8
6 - 4 = 2	9 - 6 = 3	8 - 1 = 7
6 - 2 = 4	9 - 3 = 6	8 - 7 = 1

② **Write the numbers in the blanks.**

$$84 = \underline{80} + \underline{4} \qquad 42 = \underline{40} + \underline{2}$$
$$36 = \underline{30} + \underline{6} \qquad 25 = \underline{20} + \underline{5}$$

159 (one hundred fifty-nine)

$$13 = \underline{10} + \underline{3} \qquad 8 = \underline{0} + \underline{8}$$
$$79 = \underline{70} + \underline{9} \qquad 65 = \underline{60} + \underline{5}$$
$$57 = \underline{50} + \underline{7} \qquad 91 = \underline{90} + \underline{1}$$

③ **Add.**

6	4	2	6	5	2
2	3	3	2	3	4
+9	+5	+5	+5	+7	+7
17	12	10	13	15	13

④ **Subtract.**

```
0  1  2  3  4  5  6  7  8  9
```

5	7	9	8	7	6
-4	-0	-6	-5	-7	-5
1	7	3	3	0	1

8	6	7	5	8	9
-1	-3	-4	-2	-0	-2
7	3	3	3	8	7

160 (one hundred sixty)

416

PLACE VALUE

1 Write the numbers.

6 tens = **60**	7 tens = **70**	1 ten = **10**
2 tens = **20**	3 tens = **30**	4 tens = **40**
5 tens = **50**	8 tens = **80**	9 tens = **90**

2 Write the answers in the blanks.

4+5= 9   -3= 6   -4= 2   +7= 9

2+5= 7   -2= 5   +3= 8   -4= 4

3+2= 5   +4= 9   -4= 5   -5= 0

1+4= 5   +3= 8   -7= 1   +6= 7

6+3= 9   -2= 7   -3= 4   +4= 8

2+4= 6   +3= 9   -5= 4   +2= 6

3+4= 7   -5= 2   +6= 8   -3= 5

161 (one hundred sixty-one)

---

3 Jason had 6 lollipops. He gave 2 of them to Ned. How many lollipops did he have left?

_6_ - _2_ = _4_ lollipops

There were 9 squirrels in Joan's backyard. 4 of them climbed over the fence. How many were left in Joan's backyard?

_9_ - _4_ = _5_ squirrels

4 Write the subtraction facts.

4+2=6	2+7=9	5+2=7
6 - 2 = 4	9 - 7 = 2	7 - 5 = 2
6 - 4 = 2	9 - 2 = 7	7 - 2 = 5

162 (one hundred sixty-two)

TIME – HALF HOUR

1 Write the correct time.

8:30   5:30   10:30   7:30

1:30   9:30   4:30   12:30

2 Count the objects in each set. Write the number.

10

8

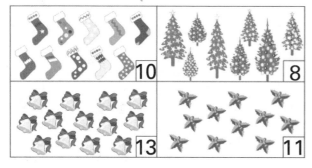

13

11

163 (one hundred sixty-three)

---

3 Color the squares used in counting by 7's.

7	14	21	28	6	4	52	57	60	64	62
2	3	5	35	42	49	56	59	50	68	61
13	8	22	24	26	43	63	70	77	84	90
23	25	27	12	32	36	40	55	67	91	98

4 Add.

7	6	4	2	1	4
2	3	4	3	5	1
+4	+7	+6	+8	+5	+9
13	16	14	13	11	14

5 Subtract.

0 1 2 3 4 5 6 7 8 9

2	1	4	6	7	8
-2	-0	-2	-1	-1	-2
0	1	2	5	6	6

7	6		8	3
-5	-4		-7	-3
2	2		1	0

164 (one hundred sixty-four)

417

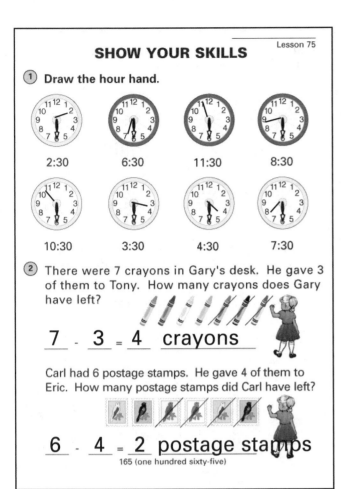

SHOW YOUR SKILLS
Lesson 75

1 Draw the hour hand.

2:30　　6:30　　11:30　　8:30

10:30　　3:30　　4:30　　7:30

2 There were 7 crayons in Gary's desk. He gave 3 of them to Tony. How many crayons does Gary have left?

_7_ - _3_ = _4_ crayons

Carl had 6 postage stamps. He gave 4 of them to Eric. How many postage stamps did Carl have left?

_6_ - _4_ = _2_ postage stamps

165 (one hundred sixty-five)

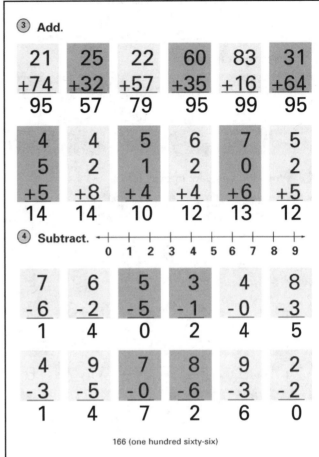

3 Add.

21	25	22	60	83	31
+74	+32	+57	+35	+16	+64
95	57	79	95	99	95

4	4	5	6	7	5
5	2	1	2	0	2
+5	+8	+4	+4	+6	+5
14	14	10	12	13	12

4 Subtract.

0 1 2 3 4 5 6 7 8 9

7	6	5	3	4	8
-6	-2	-5	-1	-0	-3
1	4	0	2	4	5

4	9	7	8	9	2
-3	-5	-0	-6	-3	-2
1	4	7	2	6	0

166 (one hundred sixty-six)

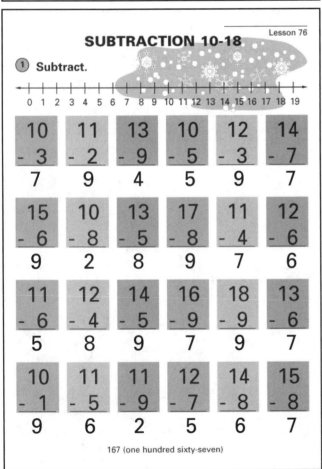

SUBTRACTION 10-18
Lesson 76

1 Subtract.

0 1 2 3 4 5 6 7 8 9 10 11 12 13 14 15 16 17 18 19

10	11	13	10	12	14
- 3	- 2	- 9	- 5	- 3	- 7
7	9	4	5	9	7

15	10	13	17	11	12
- 6	- 8	- 5	- 8	- 4	- 6
9	2	8	9	7	6

11	12	14	16	18	13
- 6	- 4	- 5	- 9	- 9	- 6
5	8	9	7	9	7

10	11	11	12	14	15
- 1	- 5	- 9	- 7	- 8	- 8
9	6	2	5	6	7

167 (one hundred sixty-seven)

2 Circle the greater number.

16 (38)　(72) 64　27 (53)　49 (71)　8 (80)

3 Draw both hands on the clocks.

1:30　　6:30　　11:30　　3:30

9:30　　2:30　　12:30　　5:30

4 Count each set. Write the number.

9　　12

168 (one hundred sixty-eight)

ADDITION – HORIZONTAL TO VERTICAL

1 Write the problems vertically. Add.

$5+2+3=$

```
  5
  2
+ 3
———
 10
```

$1+7+6=$

```
  1
  7
+ 6
———
 14
```

$8+0+7=$

```
  8
  0
+ 7
———
 15
```

$4+3+9=$

```
  4
  3
+ 9
———
 16
```

$43+51=$

```
 43
+51
———
 94
```

$24+32=$

```
 24
+32
———
 56
```

2 Circle the number that is least.

(28) 82 54 (17) 63 (29) 93 (39) 12 (9)

169 (one hundred sixty-nine)

---

3 Subtract.

```
0 1 2 3 4 5 6 7 8 9 10 11 12 13 14 15 16 17 18 19
```

14	13	11	12	10	16
- 9	- 4	- 3	- 8	- 9	- 8
5	9	8	4	1	8

15	12	10	15	13	14
- 6	- 5	- 6	- 7	- 8	- 6
9	7	4	8	5	8

11	10	11	17	15	10
- 8	- 4	- 5	- 9	- 9	- 2
3	6	6	8	6	8

4 Write the next 3 even numbers.

16 __18__ __20__ __22__   38 __40__ __42__ __44__

24 __26__ __28__ __30__   74 __76__ __78__ __80__

52 __54__ __56__ __58__   46 __48__ __50__ __52__

170 (one hundred seventy)

WORD PROBLEMS – ADDITION

1 There were 6 boys playing basketball. 2 more boys joined them. How many boys were now playing basketball?

$6 + 2 = 8$ boys

Susan had 5 baby ducks. Toni gave her 3 more baby ducks. Susan now has how many baby ducks?

$5 + 3 = 8$ ducks

8 children were going up the hill to ride their sleds. 3 more children followed them up. How many children went up the hill to go sledding?

$8 + 3 = 11$ children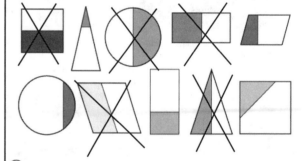

2 Write the next 3 numbers when counting by 8's.

8	16	24	32	40	48
48	56	64	72	80	88

171 (one hundred seventy-one)

---

3 Put an X on each shape that has one half ($\frac{1}{2}$) shaded.

4 Subtract.

```
0 1 2 3 4 5 6 7 8 9 10 11 12 13 14 15 16 17 18 19
```

10	12	14	15	13	12
- 4	- 6	- 7	- 8	- 6	- 9
6	6	7	7	7	3

14	10	17	18	16	11
- 5	- 6	- 8	- 9	- 7	- 8
9	4	9	9	9	3

172 (one hundred seventy-two)

419

EQUAL AND NOT EQUAL

1 Write = or ≠ between each set.

7-5 ≠ 12	6-3 ≠ 4	5-1 ≠ 6
7-7 ≠ 1	5-4 = 1	9-7 ≠ 3
4-3 = 1	7-2 ≠ 9	6-4 = 2
8-2 ≠ 10	9-4 = 5	8-5 = 3
9-2 = 7	3-3 = 0	2-1 ≠ 2

2 Put an X on each shape that has one fourth ($\frac{1}{4}$) shaded.

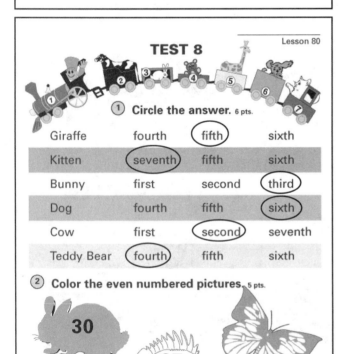

173 (one hundred seventy-three)

---

3 Subtract.

0 1 2 3 4 5 6 7 8 9 10 11 12 13 14 15 16 17 18 19

13 - 9	11 - 2	10 - 1	12 - 5	14 - 6	13 - 7
4	9	9	7	8	6

14 - 8	11 - 4	13 - 4	15 - 7	11 - 9	10 - 5
6	7	9	8	2	5

4 Add.

15 +72	85 +11	24 +33	17 +50	46 +12	58 +31
87	96	57	67	58	89

5 Nancy's cat had 7 kittens. Susie's cat had 3 kittens. How many kittens did the girls have altogether?

7 + 3 = 10 kittens

174 (one hundred seventy-four)

TEST 8

1 Circle the answer. 6 pts.

Giraffe	fourth	(fifth)	sixth
Kitten	(seventh)	fifth	sixth
Bunny	first	second	(third)
Dog	fourth	fifth	(sixth)
Cow	first	(second)	seventh
Teddy Bear	(fourth)	fifth	sixth

2 Color the even numbered pictures. 5 pts.

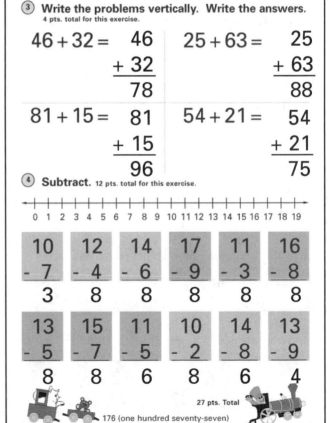

30
27
15
45
18

175 (one hundred seventy-five)

---

3 Write the problems vertically. Write the answers.
4 pts. total for this exercise.

46 + 32 =	46 +32 78	25 + 63 =	25 +63 88
81 + 15 =	81 +15 96	54 + 21 =	54 +21 75

4 Subtract. 12 pts. total for this exercise.

0 1 2 3 4 5 6 7 8 9 10 11 12 13 14 15 16 17 18 19

10 - 7	12 - 4	14 - 6	17 - 9	11 - 3	16 - 8
3	8	8	8	8	8

13 - 5	15 - 7	11 - 5	10 - 2	14 - 8	13 - 9
8	8	6	8	6	4

27 pts. Total

176 (one hundred seventy-seven)

FRACTIONS – ONE THIRD

1 Put an X on each shape that has one third ($\frac{1}{3}$) shaded.

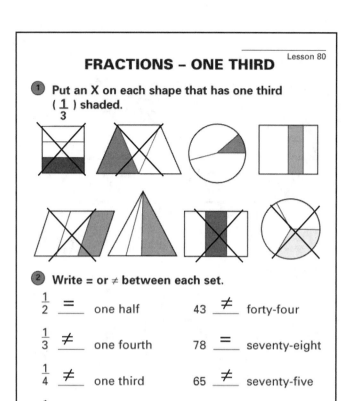

2 Write = or ≠ between each set.

$\frac{1}{2}$ **=** one half   43 **≠** forty-four

$\frac{1}{3}$ **≠** one fourth   78 **=** seventy-eight

$\frac{1}{4}$ **≠** one third   65 **≠** seventy-five

$\frac{1}{5}$ **=** one fifth   52 **≠** forty-two

$\frac{1}{6}$ **≠** one seventh   89 **≠** ninety-eight

177 (one hundred seventy-seven)

---

3 Subtract.

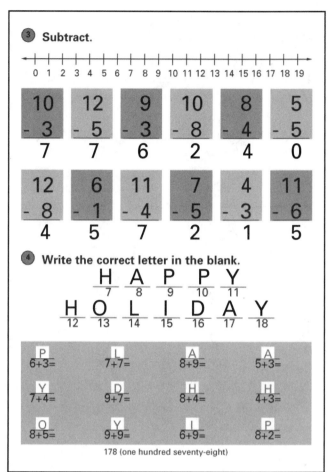

10 − 3 = 7	12 − 5 = 7	9 − 3 = 6	10 − 8 = 2	8 − 4 = 4	5 − 5 = 0
12 − 8 = 4	6 − 1 = 5	11 − 4 = 7	7 − 5 = 2	4 − 3 = 1	11 − 6 = 5

4 Write the correct letter in the blank.

H A P P Y
7 8 9 10 11

H O L I D A Y
12 13 14 15 16 17 18

P 6+3=   L 7+7=   A 8+9=   A 5+3=

Y 7+4=   D 9+7=   H 8+4=   H 4+3=

O 8+5=   Y 9+9=   I 6+9=   P 8+2=

178 (one hundred seventy-eight)

PLACE VALUE – ONE HUNDREDS

1 The number 135 has three places. The 1 is in the hundreds' place. The 3 is in the tens' place. The 5 is in the ones' place.

1 3 5

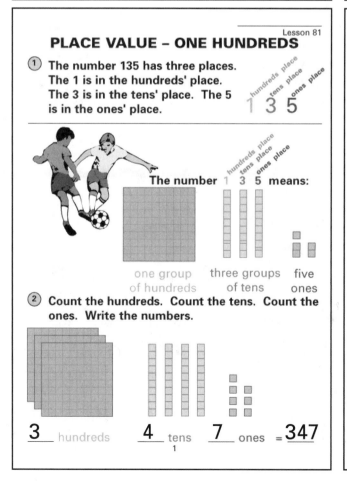

The number 1 3 5 means:

one group of hundreds   three groups of tens   five ones

2 Count the hundreds. Count the tens. Count the ones. Write the numbers.

3 hundreds   **4** tens   **7** ones **= 347**

1

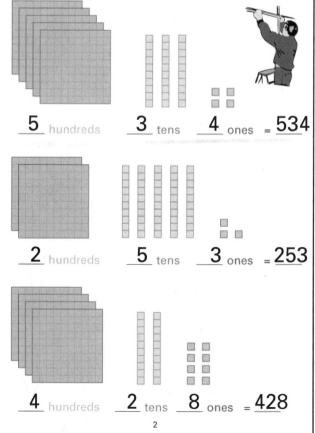

5 hundreds   **3** tens   **4** ones **= 534**

2 hundreds   **5** tens   **3** ones **= 253**

4 hundreds   **2** tens   **8** ones **= 428**

2

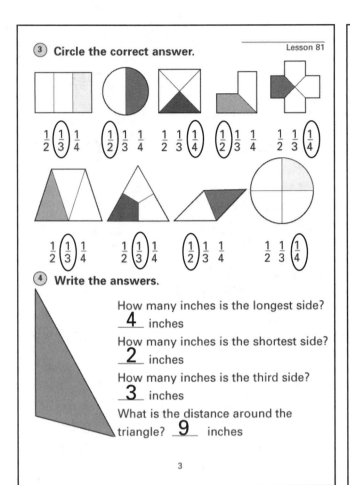

③ Circle the correct answer.   Lesson 81

$\frac{1}{2}$ $\boxed{\frac{1}{3}}$ $\frac{1}{4}$ $\boxed{\frac{1}{2}}$ $\frac{1}{3}$ $\frac{1}{4}$ $\frac{1}{2}$ $\frac{1}{3}$ $\boxed{\frac{1}{4}}$ $\boxed{\frac{1}{2}}$ $\frac{1}{3}$ $\frac{1}{4}$ $\frac{1}{2}$ $\frac{1}{3}$ $\boxed{\frac{1}{4}}$

$\frac{1}{2}$ $\boxed{\frac{1}{3}}$ $\frac{1}{4}$ $\frac{1}{2}$ $\boxed{\frac{1}{3}}$ $\frac{1}{4}$ $\boxed{\frac{1}{2}}$ $\frac{1}{3}$ $\frac{1}{4}$ $\frac{1}{2}$ $\frac{1}{3}$ $\boxed{\frac{1}{4}}$

④ Write the answers.

How many inches is the longest side?
__4__ inches

How many inches is the shortest side?
__2__ inches

How many inches is the third side?
__3__ inches

What is the distance around the
triangle? __9__ inches

3

---

⑤ Write the subtraction facts.

6+1=7	2+6=8	4+3=7
7 - 1 = 6	8 - 6 = 2	7 - 3 = 4
7 - 6 = 1	8 - 2 = 6	7 - 4 = 3
7+2=9	2+5=7	1+7=8
9 - 2 = 7	7 - 5 = 2	8 - 7 = 1
9 - 7 = 2	7 - 2 = 5	8 - 1 = 7

⑥ Subtract.

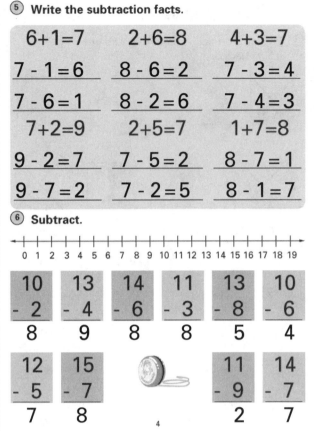

0 1 2 3 4 5 6 7 8 9 10 11 12 13 14 15 16 17 18 19

10	13	14	11	13	10
- 2	- 4	- 6	- 3	- 8	- 6
8	9	8	8	5	4

12	15		11	14
- 5	- 7		- 9	- 7
7	8		2	7

4

SHAPES   Lesson 82

○ circle   □ square   △ triangle   ▭ rectangle

① Color the circle red.
Color the triangle blue.
Color the square yellow.
Color the rectangle green.

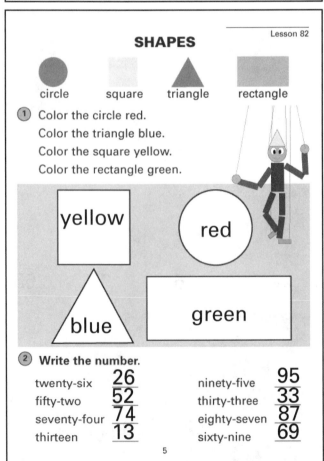

yellow   red

blue   green

② Write the number.

twenty-six	26	ninety-five	95
fifty-two	52	thirty-three	33
seventy-four	74	eighty-seven	87
thirteen	13	sixty-nine	69

5

---

③ Write the numbers.

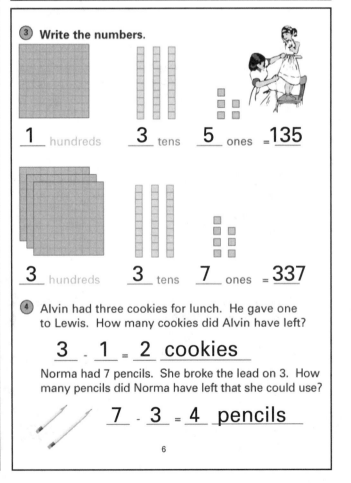

__1__ hundreds   __3__ tens   __5__ ones = 135

__3__ hundreds   __3__ tens   __7__ ones = 337

④ Alvin had three cookies for lunch. He gave one
to Lewis. How many cookies did Alvin have left?

__3__ - __1__ = __2__ cookies

Norma had 7 pencils. She broke the lead on 3. How
many pencils did Norma have left that she could use?

__7__ - __3__ = __4__ pencils

6

COUNTING – TWO HUNDRED

① **Write the number that comes between.**

165	**166**	167		134	**135**	136
127	**128**	129		142	**143**	144
150	**151**	152		176	**177**	178

② **Write the number.**

124 has a __4__ in the ones' place.

421 has a __1__ in the ones' place.

142 has a __4__ in the tens' place.

412 has a __1__ in the tens' place.

241 has a __2__ in the hundreds' place.

142 has a __1__ in the hundreds' place.

③ **Write the subtraction facts.**

$3 + 1 = 4$	$4 + 5 = 9$	$1 + 5 = 6$
$4 - 1 = 3$	$9 - 5 = 4$	$6 - 5 = 1$
$4 - 3 = 1$	$9 - 4 = 5$	$6 - 1 = 5$

7

---

④ **Draw a line to match the object with the shape.**

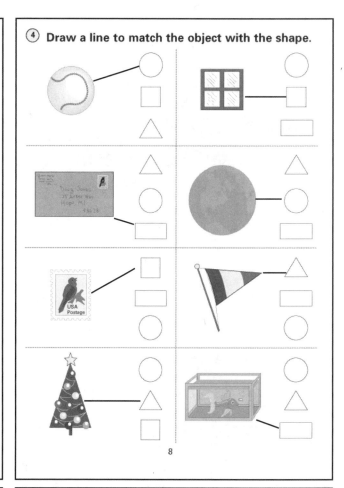

8

WORD NUMBERS – 100-199

① **Draw a line to match the word number to the number.**

one hundred sixty — 141

one hundred forty-one — 185

one hundred eighty-five — 160

one hundred twenty-two — 170

one hundred seventy — 122

one hundred fifty-six — 138

one hundred thirty-eight — 156

② **Write the number.**

129 = __1__ hundred __2__ tens __9__ ones

363 = __3__ hundreds __6__ tens __3__ ones

941 = __9__ hundreds __4__ tens __1__ one

502 = __5__ hundreds __0__ tens __2__ ones

655 = __6__ hundreds __5__ tens __5__ ones

③ Julia cut the pie into 8 pieces. Jared ate 2 pieces. Julia had how many pieces left?

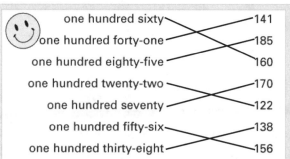

__8__ - __2__ = __6__ pieces of pie

9

---

④ **Circle the object that has a different shape.**

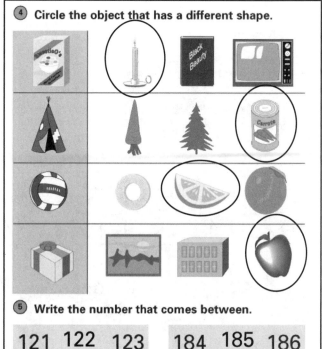

⑤ **Write the number that comes between.**

121	**122**	123		184	**185**	186
153	**154**	155		167	**168**	169
132	**133**	134		179	**180**	181

10

MONEY

① Write the numbers in the blanks.

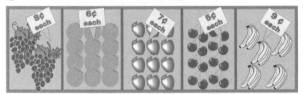

apple	7 ¢	orange	6 ¢	banana	9 ¢
cherry	+5 ¢	grape	+8 ¢	orange	+6 ¢
total	12 ¢	total	14 ¢	total	15 ¢

apple	7 ¢	cherry	5 ¢	grape	8 ¢
grape	+8 ¢	banana	+9 ¢	orange	+6 ¢
total	15 ¢	total	14 ¢	total	14 ¢

② Write the number that comes between.

126	**127**	128		158	**159**	160
135	**136**	137		172	**173**	174
104	**105**	106		143	**144**	145

11

---

③ Write the numbers.

1 hundred = **100**	3 hundreds = **300**
4 hundreds = **400**	7 hundreds = **700**
6 hundreds = **600**	5 hundreds = **500**
9 hundreds = **900**	8 hundreds = **800**
2 hundreds = **200**	

④ Write the numbers.

one hundred eighty-two	**182**
one hundred twenty-six	**126**
one hundred forty	**140**
one hundred sixty-seven	**167**
one hundred thirteen	**113**
one hundred five	**105**

⑤ Bert had 8 horses on his farm. His father sold 3 of them. Bert has how many horses left?

8 - **3** = **5** horses

12

CALENDAR – DAYS OF THE WEEK

① Write the missing numbers.

January

Sunday	Monday	Tuesday	Wednesday	Thursday	Friday	Saturday
			1	**2**	3	4
5	**6**	7	8	9	**10**	11
12	13	**14**	15	**16**	17	18
19	20	21	22	23	**24**	25
26	**27**	28	29	30	**31**	

② Write the answers.

What day is January 1? **Wednesday**

What day is the last day of January? **Friday**

What day is 2 days after January 15? **Friday**

What day is 1 day before January 20? **Sunday**

③ Jill saw 6 birds on the bird bath. 4 more birds joined them. How many birds were on the bird bath?

6 + 4 = 10 birds

13

---

④ Write the correct time.

4 :**15**   **7** :**45**   **1** :**45**   **11** :**15**

⑤ Write the hundreds, tens, and ones. Write the number.

1 hundred 8 tens 5 ones = **100** + **80** + **5** = **185**

3 hundreds 6 tens 3 ones = **300** + **60** + **3** = **363**

7 hundreds 3 tens 8 ones = **700** + **30** + **8** = **738**

5 hundreds 5 tens 4 ones = **500** + **50** + **4** = **554**

⑥ Draw a line to match the word number to the number.

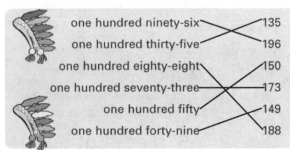

one hundred ninety-six	135
one hundred thirty-five	196
one hundred eighty-eight	150
one hundred seventy-three	173
one hundred fifty	149
one hundred forty-nine	188

14

424

BAR GRAPH

1 Write the answers.

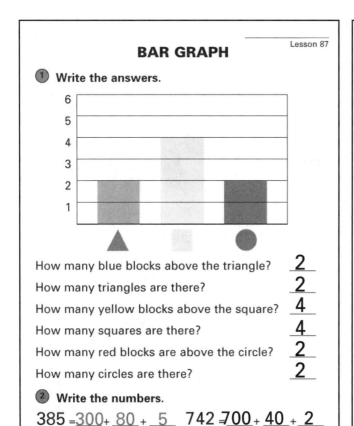

How many blue blocks above the triangle? __2__

How many triangles are there? __2__

How many yellow blocks above the square? __4__

How many squares are there? __4__

How many red blocks are above the circle? __2__

How many circles are there? __2__

2 Write the numbers.

385 = __300__ + __80__ + __5__   742 = __700__ + __40__ + __2__

521 __500__ + __20__ + __1__   690 = __600__ + __90__ + __0__

15

---

3 Draw the hands on the clocks.

6:15   3:45   2:45   9:15

4 Write the numbers.

one hundred fifteen __115__

one hundred fifty-nine __159__

one hundred seventy-seven __177__

one hundred twenty-eight __128__

one hundred ninety-two __192__

one hundred thirty-one __131__

one hundred forty-five __145__

5 Write the value of each set.

__43__¢   __75__¢

__34__¢   __70__¢

16

NUMBER ORDER –
< AND > OVER 100

1 Write < or > in the blanks.

137	__<__	140		154	__>__	151
163	__>__	136		195	__>__	159
183	__>__	181		168	__<__	175

2 Color the blocks for the bar graph.

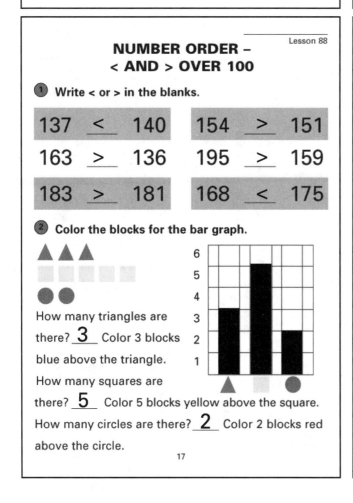

How many triangles are there? __3__ Color 3 blocks blue above the triangle.

How many squares are there? __5__ Color 5 blocks yellow above the square.

How many circles are there? __2__ Color 2 blocks red above the circle.

17

---

3 Write the numbers.

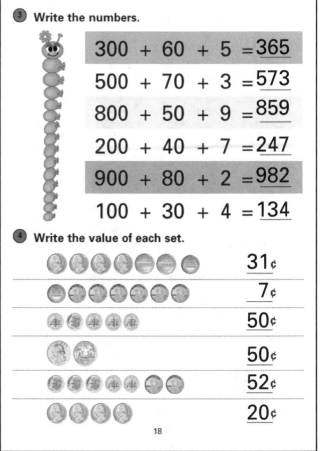

300 + 60 + 5 = __365__

500 + 70 + 3 = __573__

800 + 50 + 9 = __859__

200 + 40 + 7 = __247__

900 + 80 + 2 = __982__

100 + 30 + 4 = __134__

4 Write the value of each set.

__31__¢

__7__¢

__50__¢

__50__¢

__52__¢

__20__¢

18

425

MONEY – DOLLAR

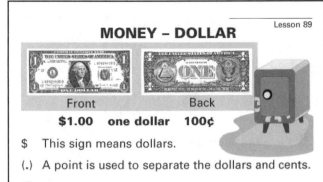

Front   Back

$1.00   one dollar   100¢

$ This sign means dollars.

(.)   A point is used to separate the dollars and cents.

① Count the dollars.

 $ **3** .00

 $ **2** .00

 $ **4** .00

② Henry had 8 balloons for his birthday. 5 of the balloons broke during his party. How many balloons did he have left when the party was over?

8 - 5 = 3 balloons

19

---

③ Color the blocks on the bar graph.

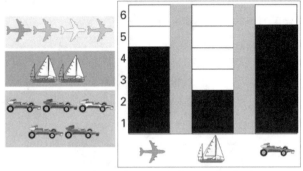

Color a block on the graph for each airplane.

Color a block on the graph for each ship.

Color a block on the graph for each car.

④ Write the correct time.

2:30   7:45   3:00   5:15

⑤ There were 8 boys and 8 girls at Jackie's party. How many children were at Jackie's party?

8 + 8 = 16 children

20

TEST 9

① Write the correct time. 8 pts. total for this exercise.

5:00   6:45   10:30   9:15

2:45   4:30   11:00   1:15

② Write the fractional part that is shaded. 8 pts.

 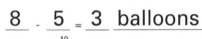

$\frac{1}{2}$ $\frac{1}{3}$ $\frac{1}{4}$ $\frac{1}{4}$

$\frac{1}{2}$ $\frac{1}{5}$ $\frac{1}{3}$ $\frac{1}{5}$

21

---

③ Write the numbers. 9 pts. total for this exercise.

483 has a **3** in the ones' place.

297 has a **9** in the tens' place.

165 has a **1** in the hundreds' place.

340 has a **4** in the tens' place.

628 has a **8** in the ones' place.

512 has a **1** in the tens' place.

734 has a **7** in the hundreds' place.

856 has a **6** in the ones' place.

971 has a **9** in the hundreds' place.

④ Draw a line to match a shape to its name. 4 pts.

circle

rectangle

triangle

square

⑤ Jay had 6 keys on his ring. Kay had 8 keys on her ring. How many keys do Jay and Kay have? 1 Pt.

6 + 8 = 14 keys

22   30 pts. Total

SHOW YOUR SKILLS

① **Draw the hour (short) hand on the clocks.**

10:30　　8:15　　4:45　　6:00

11:15　　7:00　　1:30　　3:45

② **Subtract.**

0 1 2 3 4 5 6 7 8 9 10 11 12 13 14 15 16 17 18 19

13	11	10	12	11	14
- 4	- 6	- 8	- 9	- 4	- 5
9	5	2	3	7	9

15	10	13	14	15	12
- 7	- 6	- 7	- 8	- 6	- 3
8	4	6	6	9	9

23

---

③

Draw the number of triangles shown on the graph.

Draw the number of squares shown on the graph.

Draw the number of circles shown on the graph.

Draw the number of rectangles shown on the graph.

④ **Write < or > between each set.**

138	<	142		141	>	114
175	<	184		108	<	111
156	>	123		160	<	197

24

CENTIMETERS

① **Write the numbers.**

_7_ centimeters

_5_ centimeters

_12_ centimeters

② **Draw both hands on the clocks.**

4:15　　8:30　　10:00　　12:45

2:00　　11:30　　9:15　　6:45

25

---

③ **Write the number.**

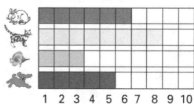

1 2 3 4 5 6 7 8 9 10

How many rabbits are on the graph?　_6_

How many dogs are on the graph?　_5_

How many fish are on the graph?　_3_

How many kittens are on the graph?　_8_

④ 8 cows were in the barnyard. 5 cows then went into the barn. How many cows were left in the yard?

 _8_ - _5_ = _3_ cows

Sue picked 7 flowers in the woods. Mae picked 5 flowers. How many flowers did they pick?

_7_ + _5_ = _12_ flowers

26

427

ADDITION – THREE
DOUBLE DIGIT NUMBERS

① Write the answers.

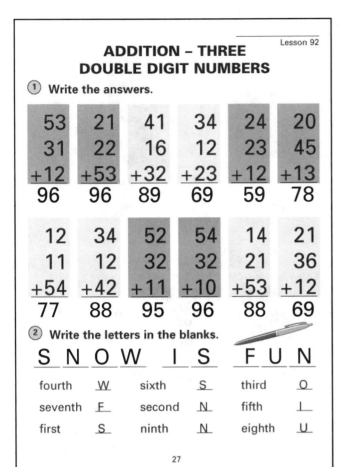

53	21	41	34	24	20
31	22	16	12	23	45
+12	+53	+32	+23	+12	+13
96	96	89	69	59	78

12	34	52	54	14	21
11	12	32	32	21	36
+54	+42	+11	+10	+53	+12
77	88	95	96	88	69

② Write the letters in the blanks.

S N O W   I S   F U N

fourth	W	sixth	S	third	O
seventh	F	second	N	fifth	I
first	S	ninth	N	eighth	U

27

③ Write the number.

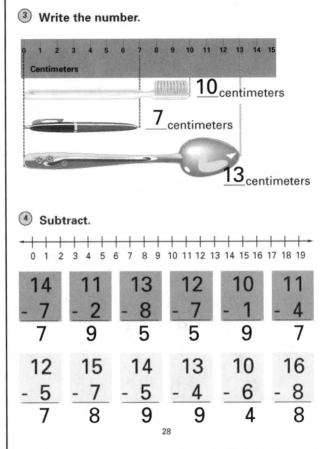

10 centimeters

7 centimeters

13 centimeters

④ Subtract.

0 1 2 3 4 5 6 7 8 9 10 11 12 13 14 15 16 17 18 19

14	11	13	12	10	11
- 7	- 2	- 8	- 7	- 1	- 4
7	9	5	5	9	7

12	15	14	13	10	16
- 5	- 7	- 5	- 4	- 6	- 8
7	8	9	9	4	8

28

SHAPES

①

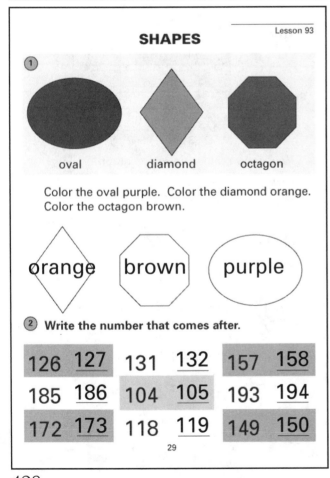

oval   diamond   octagon

Color the oval purple. Color the diamond orange.
Color the octagon brown.

orange   brown   purple

② Write the number that comes after.

126	127	131	132	157	158
185	186	104	105	193	194
172	173	118	119	149	150

29

③ Measure the objects.

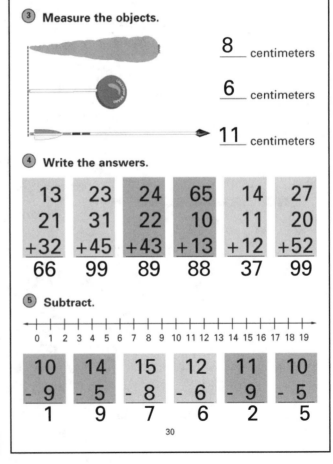

8 centimeters

6 centimeters

11 centimeters

④ Write the answers.

13	23	24	65	14	27
21	31	22	10	11	20
+32	+45	+43	+13	+12	+52
66	99	89	88	37	99

⑤ Subtract.

0 1 2 3 4 5 6 7 8 9 10 11 12 13 14 15 16 17 18 19

10	14	15	12	11	10
- 9	- 5	- 8	- 6	- 9	- 5
1	9	7	6	2	5

30

428

ODD NUMBERS

① Write the missing odd numbers.

1	3	_5_	_7_	9	_11_	_13_
15	_17_	_19_	21	_23_	_25_	_27_
_29_	_31_	_33_	_35_	37	_39_	_41_
43	_45_	_47_	49	_51_	_53_	_55_

② Draw a line to match the object to the shape.

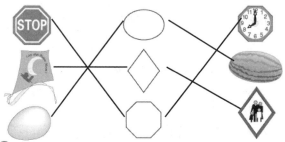

③ Jack had 12 baseball cards. He gave 4 of them to Joe. How many baseball cards did Jack have left?

_12_ - _4_ = _8_ baseball cards

31

---

④ Measure the lines with a centimeter ruler. Write the answers.

_9_ centimeters

_5_ centimeters

_12_ centimeters

⑤ Write the number that comes after.

186	_187_	125	_126_	134	_135_
101	_102_	197	_198_	153	_154_
178	_179_	112	_113_	140	_141_

⑥ Subtract.

0 1 2 3 4 5 6 7 8 9 10 11 12 13 14 15 16 17 18 19

11	15	13	12	14	11
- 5	- 7	- 4	- 8	- 7	- 2
6	8	9	4	7	9

32

SEQUENCE OF EVENTS

① John just got out of bed.

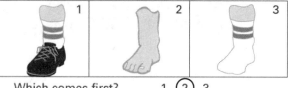

Which comes first? 1 ②3
Which comes last? ① 2 3

Making a snow man.

Which comes first? 1 ②3
Which comes last? ① 2 3

② Write the number that comes after.

| 108 | _109_ | 192 | _193_ | 150 | _151_ |
| 171 | _172_ | 117 | _118_ | 143 | _144_ |

33

---

③ Draw a line with the ruler.

4 centimeters

Teacher Check

11 centimeters

Teacher Check

④ Circle the object that is the same shape.

⑤ Color the squares blue that have odd numbers.

2	1	8	11	13	15	4	31	33	35	10
6	3	12	14	16	17	18	37	20	22	24
30	5	32	34	21	19	36	39	41	43	38
44	7	46	48	50	23	52	54	56	45	58
64	9	66	29	27	25	68	51	49	47	70

34

429

PLACE VALUE – ONE HUNDREDS

① Write the answers.

458 = 400 + 50 + 8

369 = 300 + 60 + 9

217 = 200 + 10 + 7

764 = 700 + 60 + 4

300 + 60 + 5 = 365

500 + 70 + 3 = 573

800 + 50 + 9 = 859

600 + 30 + 2 = 632

② Write the number that comes before.

180	181	105	106	126	127
194	195	132	133	153	154
171	172	109	110	147	148

35

---

③ Mother is making cookies.

Which picture comes first? ① 2 3

Which picture comes last? 1 ② 3

Jack planted a tree.

Which picture comes first? 1 2 ③

Which picture comes last? ① 2 3

④ Write the missing even numbers.

130	132	134	136	138	140
142	144	146	148	150	152
154	156	158	160	162	164
166	168	170	172	174	176

36

MEASUREMENT – LIQUID

①

ounce   cup   pint   quart   gallon

② Write the answers.

390 = 300 + 90 + 0

428 = 400 + 20 + 8

746 = 700 + 40 + 6

274 = 200 + 70 + 4

③ Write the number that comes before.

181	182	99	100	127	128
190	191	135	136	156	157
174	175	112	113	143	144

37

---

④ Circle the correct word.

183	even	⭕odd		127	even	⭕odd
25	even	⭕odd		64	⭕even	odd
76	⭕even	odd		30	⭕even	odd

⑤ Father is getting ready for work.

Which picture comes first? 1 ② 3

Which picture comes last? 1 2 ③

⑥ Subtract.

0 1 2 3 4 5 6 7 8 9 10 11 12 13 14 15 16 17 18 19

15	13	18	14	16	12
- 6	- 5	- 9	- 8	- 7	- 5
9	8	9	6	9	7

11	17	10	11	10	15
- 4	- 8	- 1	- 8	- 4	- 9
7	9	9	3	6	6

38

430

NUMBER SEQUENCE

1 Circle every third number after 2.

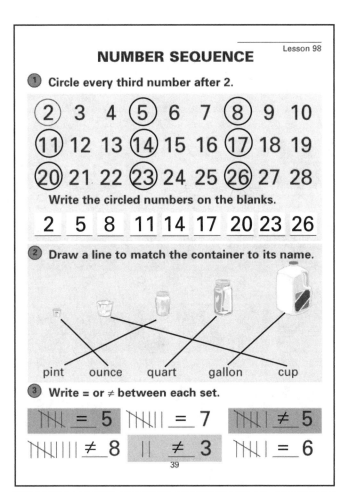

(2) 3 4 (5) 6 7 (8) 9 10
(11) 12 13 (14) 15 16 (17) 18 19
(20) 21 22 (23) 24 25 (26) 27 28

Write the circled numbers on the blanks.

2 5 8 11 14 17 20 23 26

2 Draw a line to match the container to its name.

pint   ounce   quart   gallon   cup

3 Write = or ≠ between each set.

卌 **=** 5   卌|| **=** 7   卌| **≠** 5

卌||||| **≠** 8 || **≠** 3   卌| **=** 6

39

---

4 Circle the pennies.

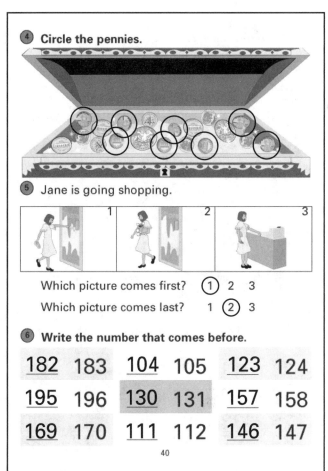

5 Jane is going shopping.

Which picture comes first?   (1) 2 3
Which picture comes last?   1 (2) 3

6 Write the number that comes before.

<u>182</u> 183   <u>104</u> 105   <u>123</u> 124
<u>195</u> 196   <u>130</u> 131   <u>157</u> 158
<u>169</u> 170   <u>111</u> 112   <u>146</u> 147

40

ESTIMATION

1 Write the answers.

0 1 2 3 4 5 6 7 8 9 **10** 11 12 13 14 15 16 17 18 19

Is 3 closer to 0 or 10?   **0**
Is 7 closer to 0 or 10?   **10**
Is 9 closer to 0 or 10 ?   **10**
Is 2 closer to 0 or 10 ?   **0**
Is 4 closer to 0 or 10?   **0**

2 Write the next 3 numbers.

5 8 11 **14 17 20**
7 10 13 **16 19 22**

3 There were 12 cookies on the plate. Sue and Jan ate 4 of them. How many cookies were left on the plate?

<u>12</u> - <u>4</u> = <u>8</u> cookies

41

---

4 Write the name.

ounce

quart

cup

pint

gallon

5 Circle the dimes.

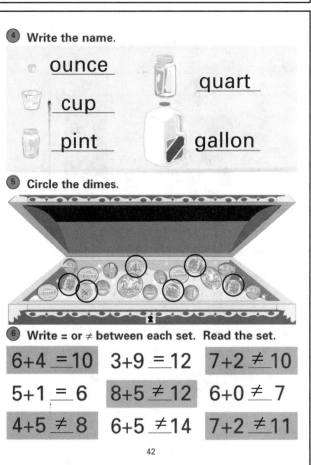

6 Write = or ≠ between each set. Read the set.

6+4 **=** 10   3+9 **=** 12   7+2 **≠** 10

5+1 **=** 6   8+5 **≠** 12   6+0 **≠** 7

4+5 **≠** 8   6+5 **≠** 14   7+2 **≠** 11

42

431

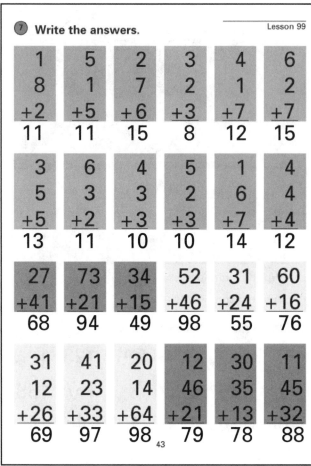

⑦ Write the answers.　　　　Lesson 99

1 8 +2 11	5 1 +5 11	2 7 +6 15	3 2 +3 8	4 1 +7 12	6 2 +7 15

3 5 +5 13	6 3 +2 11	4 3 +3 10	5 2 +3 10	1 6 +7 14	4 4 +4 12

27 +41 68	73 +21 94	34 +15 49	52 +46 98	31 +24 55	60 +16 76

31 12 +26 69	41 23 +33 97	20 14 +64 98	12 46 +21 79	30 35 +13 78	11 45 +32 88

43

⑧ Write the answers.

0 1 2 3 4 5 6 7 8 9 10 11 12 13 14 15 16 17 18 19

11 - 6 5	14 - 6 8	12 - 7 5	15 - 6 9	14 - 9 5	10 - 2 8

12 - 4 8	13 - 5 8	10 - 3 7	11 - 3 8	12 - 9 3	14 - 7 7

10 - 6 4	15 - 8 7	13 - 8 5	12 - 6 6	11 - 7 4	17 - 9 8

16 - 9 7	16 - 8 8	11 - 9 2	13 - 7 6	10 - 8 2	12 - 8 4

44

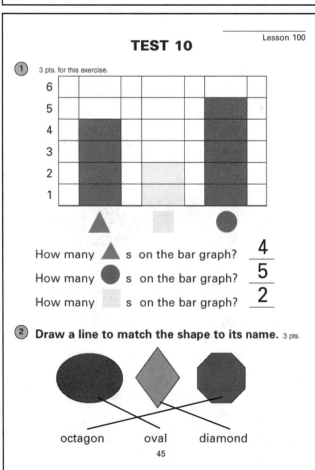

TEST 10　　　　Lesson 100

① 3 pts. for this exercise.

6
5
4
3
2
1
　　▲　　　■　　　●

How many ▲ s on the bar graph?　4

How many ● s on the bar graph?　5

How many ■ s on the bar graph?　2

② Draw a line to match the shape to its name. 3 pts.

octagon　　oval　　diamond

45

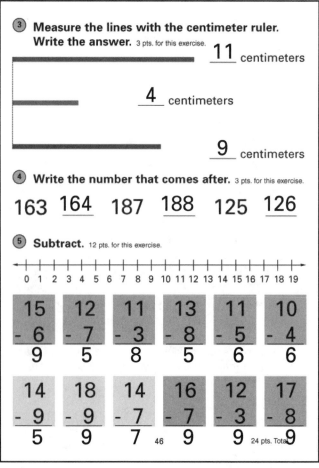

③ Measure the lines with the centimeter ruler. Write the answer. 3 pts. for this exercise.

_11_ centimeters

_4_ centimeters

_9_ centimeters

④ Write the number that comes after. 3 pts. for this exercise.

163 _164_　187 _188_　125 _126_

⑤ Subtract. 12 pts. for this exercise.

0 1 2 3 4 5 6 7 8 9 10 11 12 13 14 15 16 17 18 19

15 - 6 9	12 - 7 5	11 - 3 8	13 - 8 5	11 - 5 6	10 - 4 6

14 - 9 5	18 - 9 9	14 - 7 7	16 - 7 9	12 - 3 9	17 - 8 9

46　　24 pts. Total

432

ADDITION – TWO
TRIPLE DIGIT NUMBERS

① Write the answers.

153	261	427	523	214
+234	+405	+151	+246	+733
387	666	578	769	947

350	627	462	162	124
+413	+351	+123	+532	+124
763	978	585	694	248

② Write the numbers.

one hundred eighty-three   183

one hundred fifty-one   151

one hundred fourteen   114

③ Write the correct time.

3:30   1:15   8:00   5:45

47

---

④ Circle the nickels.

⑤ Circle the object that is about 10 inches tall.

⑥ Circle every fourth number after 3.

(3) 4 5 6 (7) 8 9 10 (11)
12 13 14 (15) 16 17 18 (19) 20
21 22 (23) 24 25 26 (27) 28 29

Write the circled numbers on the blanks.

3   7   11   15   19   23   27

48

BAR GRAPH

①

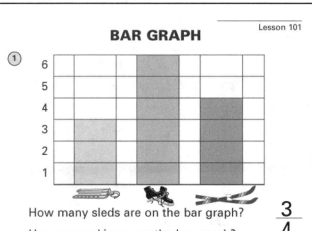

How many sleds are on the bar graph?   3

How many skis are on the bar graph?   4

How many ice skates are on the bar graph?   6

② Write the numbers.

one hundred thirty   130

one hundred forty-seven   147

one hundred eighteen   118

③ Write the next 3 numbers.

5	7	9	11	13	15
41	43	45	47	49	51

49

---

④ Circle "about" how many fish there are.

(15)
4
40

⑤ Write the correct time.

1:15   10:45   3:45   6:15

8:15   5:45   7:15   2:45

⑥ Circle the quarters.

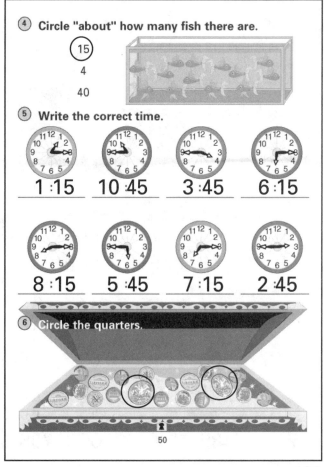

50

433

WORD PROBLEMS – SUBTRACTION

① John has 5 matchbox cars. Kyle has 3 matchbox cars. John has how many more cars than Kyle?

 $\underline{5} - \underline{3} = \underline{2}$ cars

Mary ate 8 marshmallows. Sally ate 5 marshmallows. Mary ate how many more marshmallows than Sally?

$\underline{8} - \underline{5} = \underline{3}$ marshmallows

There were 9 ducks and 6 swans on the pond. How many more ducks were there than swans?

 $\underline{9} - \underline{6} = \underline{3}$ ducks

② Circle every sixth number after 3. Write the circled numbers on the blanks.

③ 4 5 6 7 8 ⑨ 10 11
12 13 14 ⑮ 16 17 18 19 20
㉑ 22 23 24 25 26 ㉗ 28 29

| 3 | 9 | 15 | 21 | 27 |

51

③ Write the subtraction facts.

$6+2=8 \qquad 2+4=6 \qquad 1+5=6$
$8 - 2 = 6 \quad\; 6 - 4 = 2 \quad\; 6 - 5 = 1$
$8 - 6 = 2 \quad\; 6 - 2 = 4 \quad\; 6 - 1 = 5$

④ Circle the object that is about 30 inches long.

⑤ Circle the numbers greater than 150.

⓰⓰⓰ 168 127 146 ⑯172 115
130 ⑮151 ⑯180 108 ⑲197
⑯159 ⑰173 112 ⑯164 146

⑥ Write the correct time.

3:45   5:00   7:15   10:30

52

⑦ Color the blocks on the bar graph.   Lesson 102

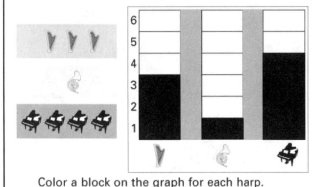

Color a block on the graph for each harp.

Color a block on the graph for each french horn.

Color a block on the graph for each piano.

⑧ Add.

112	214	142	536	234
+131	+251	+603	+233	+512
243	465	745	769	746

214	325		243	496
+584	+161		+722	+302
798	486	53	965	798

⑨ Subtract.

0 1 2 3 4 5 6 7 8 9 10 11 12 13 14 15 16 17 18 19

13	11	15	10	12	14
- 8	- 3	- 6	- 3	- 9	- 5
5	8	9	7	3	9

12	13	17	11	10	11
- 8	- 6	- 8	- 7	- 4	- 2
4	7	9	4	6	9

10	11	15	18	13	12
- 6	- 4	- 8	- 9	- 5	- 7
4	7	7	9	8	5

12	16	13	14	11	10
- 5	- 7	- 4	- 9	- 6	- 7
7	9	9	5	5	3

54

434

MONEY

1 Draw a line to match each coin to its value.

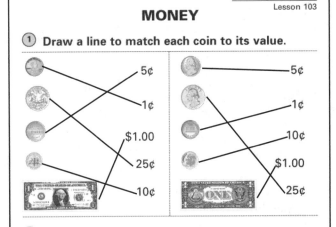

- 5¢
- 1¢
- $1.00
- 25¢
- 10¢

- 5¢
- 1¢
- 10¢
- $1.00
- 25¢

2 Circle the numbers less than 150.

(147) 165 (113) 174 160
(131) 181 (109) 152 198
(146) (128) 169 173 (116)

3 Susie has 7 people in her family. Jane has 4 people in her family. Susie has how many more people in her family than Jane?

$7 - 4 = 3$ people

55

4

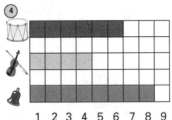

1 2 3 4 5 6 7 8 9

How many drums are on the bar graph? __6__

How many violins are on the bar graph? __4__

How many bells are on the bar graph? __8__

5 Write the subtraction facts.

$3+5=8$	$2+1=3$	$4+3=7$
$8 - 5 = 3$	$3 - 1 = 2$	$7 - 3 = 4$
$8 - 3 = 5$	$3 - 2 = 1$	$7 - 4 = 3$

6 Write the correct time.

11:30   4:15   6:00   1:45

56

DOZEN

1 Color a dozen objects in each set.

2 Write the value of each set of money.

 __34__¢

 __27__¢

 __76__¢

 $ __5.00__

3 Write the subtraction facts.

$5+7=12$	$3+8=11$	$6+9=15$
$12 - 7 = 5$	$11 - 8 = 3$	$15 - 9 = 6$
$12 - 5 = 7$	$11 - 3 = 8$	$15 - 6 = 9$

57

---

4 Draw a line to match the shape to its name.

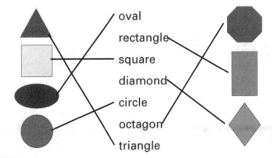

- oval
- rectangle
- square
- diamond
- circle
- octagon
- triangle

5 Add.

242	623	473	726	134
+115	+126	+221	+172	+424
357	749	694	898	558

124	331	416	521	832
+735	+535	+333	+242	+146
859	866	749	763	978

152	275		100	531
+830	+304		+568	+104
982	579	58	668	635

435

NUMBER ORDER – BEFORE AND AFTER OVER 100

① Write the number that comes before and after.

135 136 **137**   **171** 172 **173**

149 150 **151**   **126** 127 **128**

190 191 **192**   **148** 149 **150**

107 108 **109**   **182** 183 **184**

② Write the name of each shape.

square   rectangle   circle   triangle
oval   diamond   octagon

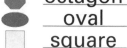

triangle
octagon
oval
square

rectangle
diamond
circle

③ Add.

325	123		732	508
+410	+345		+163	+341
735	468		895	849

59

---

④ Measure each object. Write the number.

__8__ centimeters

__11__ centimeters

__4__ centimeters

⑤ Write the days of the week in order.

Monday   Wednesday   Saturday   Friday
Tuesday   Sunday   Thursday

1. __Sunday__   2. __Monday__   3. __Tuesday__
4. __Wednesday__ 5. __Thursday__ 6. __Friday__
7. __Saturday__

⑥ Draw a dozen triangles.

△ △ △ △ △ △ △ △ △ △ △ △

60

SUBTRACTION – WITHOUT NUMBER LINE

① Subtract.

12	5	15	2	13	3
- 6	- 4	- 7	- 1	- 9	- 3
6	1	8	1	4	0

6	10	14	9	11	4
- 1	- 5	- 6	- 3	- 8	- 4
5	5	8	6	3	0

10	8	16	9	17	7
- 1	- 7	- 8	- 0	- 9	- 5
9	1	8	9	8	2

② Draw the outlines of the shapes.

square   triangle   rectangle   circle

octagon   oval   diamond

61

---

③ Measure the lines with a centimeter ruler. Write the answers.

__10__ centimeters

__6__ centimeters

__12__ centimeters

④ Add.

482	372	164	153	150
+515	+322	+832	+546	+229
997	694	996	699	379

758	405	623	643	321
+140	+461	+270	+210	+248
898	866	893	853	569

⑤ Write the number that comes before and after.

130 131 **132**   **178** 179 **180**

156 157 **158**   **119** 120 **121**

195 196 **197**   **141** 142 **143**

62

436

ODD NUMBERS

① Dot to dot using odd numbers.

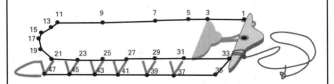

② Number the pictures in the correct order.
Joe is building a dog house.

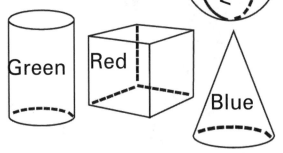

<u>1</u>   <u>3</u>   <u>2</u>

③ Write the number that comes before and after.

<u>138</u> 139 <u>140</u>   <u>170</u> 171 <u>172</u>

<u>152</u> 153 <u>154</u>   <u>114</u> 115 <u>116</u>

<u>191</u> 192 <u>193</u>   <u>145</u> 146 <u>147</u>

63

---

④ Write the answers.

156 = <u>100</u>+ <u>50</u>+ <u>6</u>

427 = <u>400</u>+ <u>20</u>+ <u>7</u>

389 = <u>300</u>+ <u>80</u>+ <u>9</u>

734 = <u>700</u>+ <u>30</u>+ <u>4</u>

265 = <u>200</u>+ <u>60</u>+ <u>5</u>

⑤ Draw a line with the centimeter ruler.

7 centimeters
· Teacher Check

11 centimeters
· Teacher Check

4 centimeters
· Teacher Check

⑥ Subtract.

12	5	15	2	13	3
- 6	- 4	- 7	- 1	- 9	- 3
6	1	8	1	4	0

64

SOLIDS

cube   sphere   cylinder   cone

① Color the sphere yellow.
Color the cylinder green.
Color the cube red.
Color the cone blue.

Yellow

Green Red

Blue

② Jonathan had 12 chicks. James had 7 chicks.
Jonathan had how many more chicks than
James had?

<u>12</u> - <u>7</u> = <u>5</u> chicks

65

---

③ Write the answers.

600 + 50 + 4 = <u>654</u>

700 + 30 + 8 = <u>738</u>

100 + 40 + 9 = <u>149</u>

500 + 70 + 1 = <u>571</u>

④ Number the pictures in the correct order.
It is morning.

noon	morning	evening
2	1	3

⑤ Write the missing numbers.

101	103	105	<u>107</u>	<u>109</u>	111
113	<u>115</u>	117	<u>119</u>	121	<u>123</u>
<u>125</u>	127	<u>129</u>	131	<u>133</u>	135

66

437

SHOW YOUR SKILLS

1 Write the numbers.

367 has a **7** in the ones' place.

637 has a **3** in the tens' place.

763 has a **7** in the hundreds' place.

736 has a **3** in the tens' place.

673 has a **6** in the hundreds' place.

376 has a **6** in the ones' place.

2 Draw a line to match the solid to its name.

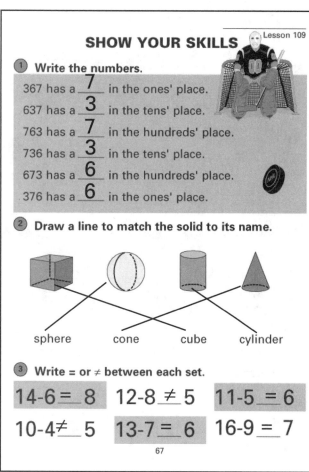

sphere   cone   cube   cylinder

3 Write = or ≠ between each set.

14-6 **=** 8   12-8 **≠** 5   11-5 **=** 6

10-4 **≠** 5   13-7 **=** 6   16-9 **=** 7

67

---

4 Add.

5	7	3	9	6	8
+8	+5	+7	+2	+4	+6
13	12	10	11	10	14

16	24	38	15	72	46
+23	+53	+60	+11	+26	+41
39	77	98	26	98	87

5 Subtract.

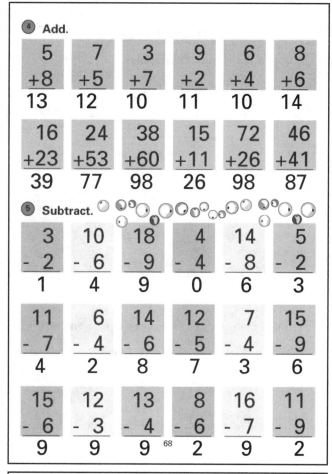

3	10	18	4	14	5
- 2	- 6	- 9	- 4	- 8	- 2
1	4	9	0	6	3

11	6	14	12	7	15
- 7	- 4	- 6	- 5	- 4	- 9
4	2	8	7	3	6

15	12	13	8	16	11
- 6	- 3	- 4	- 6	- 7	- 9
9	9	9	2	9	2

68

TEST 11

1 A baby is born. 2 pts. for this exercise.

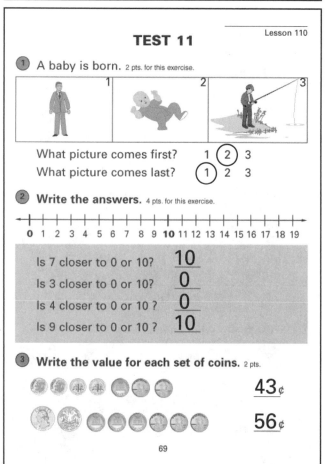

What picture comes first?   1 ②　3

What picture comes last?   ①　2　3

2 Write the answers. 4 pts. for this exercise.

0　1　2　3　4　5　6　7　8　9　**10**　11　12　13　14　15　16　17　18　19

Is 7 closer to 0 or 10? **10**

Is 3 closer to 0 or 10? **0**

Is 4 closer to 0 or 10? **0**

Is 9 closer to 0 or 10? **10**

3 Write the value for each set of coins. 2 pts.

43¢

56¢

69

---

4 Add. 11 pts.

5	6	5	3	4	6
4	2	1	2	3	3
+6	+3	+8	+9	+7	+4
15	11	14	14	14	13

124	321	243	517	163
+134	+362	+750	+241	+504
258	683	993	758	667

5 Subtract. 12 pts.

0　1　2　3　4　5　6　7　8　9　10　11　12　13　14　15　16　17　18　19

11	13	8	10	14	15
- 6	- 7	- 5	- 2	- 5	- 8
5	6	3	8	9	7

12	14	11	9	10	13
- 8	- 6	- 3	- 3	- 7	- 5
4	8	8	6	3	8

70   31 pts. Total

WORD NUMBERS 100-199

① Write = or ≠ between each set.

one hundred sixty-two	≠	126
one hundred eighty-five	=	185
one hundred thirty	≠	103
one hundred thirteen	=	113
one hundred fifty-eight	=	158
one hundred forty-three	≠	134

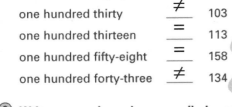

② Write cone, cube, sphere, or cylinder on the lines.

<u>cube</u> <u>sphere</u> <u>cylinder</u> <u>cone</u>

③ Paul gave his dog 13 dog biscuits. The dog ate 7 of them. How many dog biscuits were left?

13 - 7 = 6 dog biscuits

71

---

④ Add.

4	3	6	8	9	7
+7	+9	+8	+4	+6	+7
11	12	14	12	15	14

332	321	340	134	254
+ 54	+374	+217	+702	+720
386	695	557	836	974

⑤ Subtract.

10	8	14	11	10	12
- 8	- 5	- 7	- 5	- 2	- 6
2	3	7	6	8	6

13	12	15	6	11	9
- 9	- 3	- 7	- 4	- 3	- 6
4	9	8	2	8	3

⑥ Joan ate 3 scoops of ice cream. Bill ate 5 scoops. They ate how many scoops of ice cream altogether?

3 + 5 = 8 scoops

72

ADDITION

① Add.

3	3	5	7	32	14
6	5	2	1	13	61
+4	+5	+6	+7	+23	+23
13	13	13	15	68	98

13	21	84	17	61	65
+ 3	+31	+12	+22	+13	+31
16	52	96	39	74	96

211	328	253	243	147
+486	+170	+632	+554	+740
697	498	885	797	887

② Write the numbers.

one hundred twenty-three	<u>123</u>
one hundred forty-seven	<u>147</u>
one hundred ninety-five	<u>195</u>
one hundred eighteen	<u>118</u>

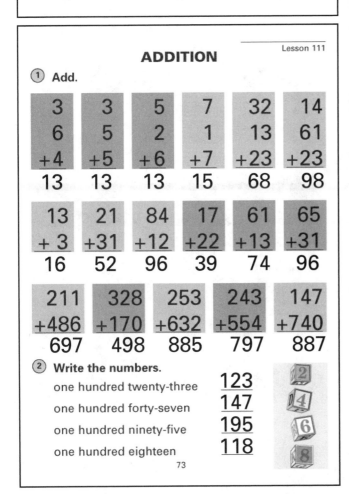

73

---

③ Draw a line to match the solid with the picture.

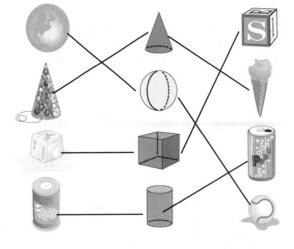

④ Mike gathered 5 eggs from one nest in the chicken house and 7 from another nest. Mike gathered how many eggs?

5 + 7 = 12 eggs

There were 13 cars and 6 trucks in the parking lot. How many more cars were there than trucks?

 13 - 6 = 7 cars

74

439

ESTIMATION

① Write the answers.

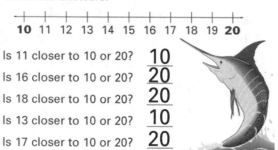

```
   10  11  12  13  14  15  16  17  18  19  20
```

Is 11 closer to 10 or 20? **10**

Is 16 closer to 10 or 20? **20**

Is 18 closer to 10 or 20? **20**

Is 13 closer to 10 or 20? **10**

Is 17 closer to 10 or 20? **20**

② Draw a line to match the solid to its name.

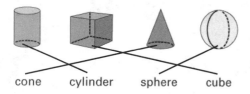

cone   cylinder   sphere   cube

③ Write the numbers.

one hundred fifty-one   **151**

one hundred eighty   **180**

one hundred thirty-two   **132**

75

---

④ Add.

4	6	3	6	5	2
3	3	2	1	4	2
+3	+4	+6	+8	+7	+9
10	13	11	15	16	13

213	345	415	362	173
+714	+134	+121	+325	+312
927	479	536	687	485

⑤ Subtract.

13	12	16	11	16	8
- 6	- 6	- 9	- 2	- 8	- 2
7	6	7	9	8	6

12	17	10	13	12	10
- 8	- 8	- 7	- 8	- 7	- 2
4	9	3	5	5	8

76

BAR GRAPH

①

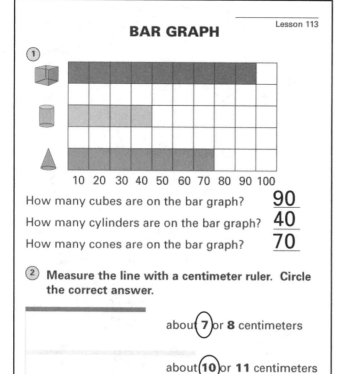

```
10  20  30  40  50  60  70  80  90  100
```

How many cubes are on the bar graph? **90**

How many cylinders are on the bar graph? **40**

How many cones are on the bar graph? **70**

② Measure the line with a centimeter ruler. Circle the correct answer.

about **(7)** or **8** centimeters

about **(10)** or **11** centimeters

about **7** or **(8)** centimeters

77

---

③ Add.

4	4	7	3	2	6
4	2	2	3	3	3
+3	+6	+5	+9	+7	+8
11	12	14	15	12	17

321	813	249	102	621
+504	+156	+150	+662	+147
825	969	399	764	768

④ Subtract.

13	10	11	9	8	7
- 5	- 3	- 6	- 9	- 5	- 5
8	7	5	0	3	2

8	10	7	12	9	14
- 1	- 9	- 6	- 9	- 7	- 9
7	1	1	3	2	5

78

NUMBER ORDER – ORDINAL NUMBERS

① Write the letters in the blanks.

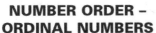

M	Y

V	A	L	E	N	T	I	N	E

fourth	A	tenth	N	fifth	L
eleventh	E	sixth	E	eighth	T
ninth	I	second	Y	third	V
seventh	N	first	M		

② Write < or > between each set.

156 > 124   173 > 147

108 < 111   135 < 162

189 < 190   140 > 129

③ Sherry found 7 seashells on the beach. Ruth found 16 seashells. Ruth found how many more seashells than Sherry?

16 - 7 = 9 seashells

79

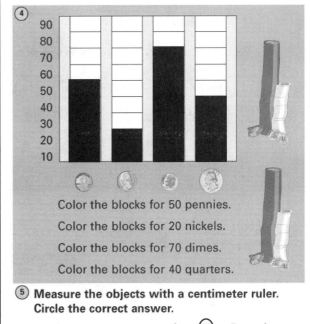

④

Color the blocks for 50 pennies.

Color the blocks for 20 nickels.

Color the blocks for 70 dimes.

Color the blocks for 40 quarters.

⑤ Measure the objects with a centimeter ruler. Circle the correct answer.

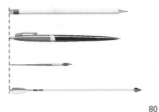

about ⑦ or 8 centimeters

about 6 or ⑦ centimeters

about 3 or ④ centimeters

about ⑧ or 9 centimeters

80

SHAPES

① Color the circle red.

Color the rectangle green.

Color the square yellow.

Color the triangle blue.

Color the octagon brown.

Color the diamond orange.

Color the oval purple.

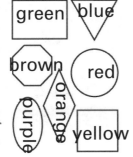

green   blue

brown   red

purple   orange   yellow

② Write the subtraction facts.

6+3=9	7+8=15	4+8=12
9 - 3 = 6	15 - 8 = 7	12 - 8 = 4
9 - 6 = 3	15 - 7 = 8	12 - 4 = 8
5+9=14	9+2=11	4+1=5
14 - 9 = 5	11 - 2 = 9	5 - 1 = 4
14 - 5 = 9	11 - 9 = 2	5 - 4 = 1

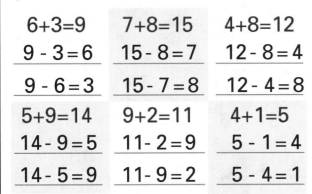 81

---

③

10 20 30 40 50 60 70 80 90 100

How many pints are on the bar graph? 90

How many gallons are on the bar graph? 70

How many cups are on the bar graph? 60

How many quarts are on the bar graph? 30

④ Subtract.

11	12	4	13	10	14
- 2	- 6	- 2	- 4	- 5	- 6
9	6	2	9	5	8

12	6	10	5	11	15
- 8	- 3	- 3	- 4	- 4	- 7
4	3	7	1	7	8

82

441

NUMBER SEQUENCE

① Put an X on the numbers that are not in sequence.

2　4　6　X̶　10　12　14　16　X̶X̶

20　22　X̶2̶3̶　26　28　X̶2̶9̶　32　34　36

38　X̶4̶　42　44　X̶4̶7̶　48　50　X̶5̶　54

② Write the fraction that shows what part is shaded.

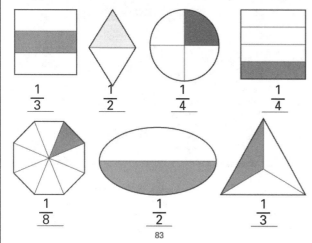

$\frac{1}{3}$ $\frac{1}{2}$ $\frac{1}{4}$ $\frac{1}{4}$

$\frac{1}{8}$ $\frac{1}{2}$ $\frac{1}{3}$

83

③ Write < or > between each set.

186 > 159   173 < 191

135 < 142   168 > 114

127 > 103   121 < 130

④ Draw a line to match the shape to its name.

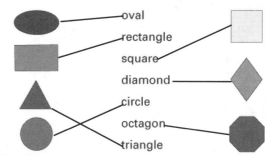

oval

rectangle

square

diamond

circle

octagon

triangle

⑤ Write the subtraction facts.

4+3=7	5+7=12	6+9=15
7 - 3 = 4	12 - 7 = 5	15 - 9 = 6
7 - 4 = 3	12 - 5 = 7	15 - 6 = 9

84

⑥ Add.

6	4	3	1	2	5
2	3	3	6	3	1
+4	+5	+9	+6	+8	+7
12	12	15	13	13	13

2	3	5	2	4	6
4	5	2	2	4	1
+8	+5	+4	+9	+7	+6
14	13	11	13	15	13

45	10	53	25	48	15
+21	+14	+46	+13	+10	+70
66	24	99	38	58	85

138	230	716	701	142
+421	+718	+223	+123	+856
559	948	939	824	998

85

⑦ Subtract.

12	11	16	10	14	13
- 3	- 3	- 7	- 2	- 9	- 5
9	8	9	8	5	8

14	10	15	12	11	17
- 7	- 6	- 9	- 7	- 5	- 8
7	4	6	5	6	9

15	11	13	12	10	16
- 8	- 6	- 8	- 5	- 7	- 9
7	5	5	7	3	7

12	14	10	13	11	13
- 4	- 8	- 8	- 6	- 8	- 9
8	6	2	7	3	4

10	17	15	11	10	18
- 4	- 9	- 6	- 9	- 1	- 9
6	8	9	2	9	9

86

442

DOZEN

1. How many eggs in a dozen? __12__

   Put an X on one dozen.

2. Write the name of each shape.

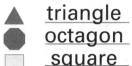 __triangle__
   __octagon__
   __square__
   __oval__

 __diamond__
   __circle__
   __rectangle__

3. Put an X on the numbers that are not in sequence.

   21 23 25 X̶8̶ 29 31 33 35 37

   39 X̶4̶0̶ 43 X̶4̶6̶ 47 49 X̶5̶2̶ 53 55

   57 59 X̶6̶0̶ 63 65 X̶6̶6̶ 69 71 73

87

---

4. Tyler has 16 grapes for lunch. He gave 8 of them to Bob. Tyler had how many grapes left?

   16 - 8 = 8   grapes

   Janice had 12 blue marbles and 5 red marbles. Janice has how many more blue marbles than red marbles?

   12 - 5 = 7   blue marbles

   The children saw 17 black bears and 21 polar bears at the zoo. How many bears did the children see at the zoo?

   17 + 21 = 38   bears

5. Write the missing numbers.

   154 __156__ __158__ 160 __162__ 164

   166 __168__ __170__ 172 __174__ __176__

   178 __180__ __182__ __184__ 186 __188__

   __190__ 192 __194__ __196__ __198__ 200

88

TIME

1. Write the correct time.

   10:00   6:45   5:15   12:30

   8:30   11:15   4:00   4:45

2. Write the next three numbers.

   12 14 16 __18__ __20__ __22__

   23 25 27 __29__ __31__ __33__

3. Write the subtraction facts.

   3+8=11   5+4=9   9+7=16

   11 - 8 = 3   9 - 5 = 4   16 - 7 = 9

   11 - 3 = 8   9 - 4 = 5   16 - 9 = 7

89

---

4. Add.

2	5	4	1	8	4
5	3	1	6	1	2
+4	+7	+6	+5	+3	+8
11	15	11	12	12	14

47	71	51	20	67	30
+51	+20	+17	+54	+30	+16
98	91	68	74	97	46

5. Subtract.

2	9	16	14	4	13
- 2	- 5	- 7	- 6	- 1	- 4
0	4	9	8	3	9

17	4	15	3	12	11
- 9	- 3	- 8	- 1	- 5	- 6
8	1	7	2	7	5

90

443

SEQUENCE OF EVENTS

① Number the pictures in the correct order.

___2___   ___1___   ___3___

② Write the numbers.

3 tens = __30__   7 hundreds = __700__

5 tens = __50__   2 hundreds = __200__

8 tens = __80__   9 hundreds = __900__

4 tens = __40__   6 hundreds = __600__

③ Draw a line to match the container to its name.

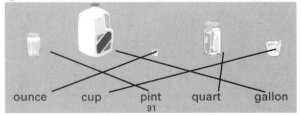

ounce   cup   pint   quart   gallon

91

---

④ Draw the short (hour) hand.

2:45   4:15   1:00   7:45

9:15   10:45   3:30   6:15

⑤ Subtract.

11	12	13	10	17	15
- 8	- 7	- 6	- 4	- 8	- 7
3	5	7	6	9	8

17	14	6	10	15	11
- 9	- 8	- 6	- 7	- 9	- 3
8	6	0	3	6	8

9	16	7	12	18	13
- 1	- 8	- 2	- 8	- 9	- 7
8	8	5	4	9	6

92

TEST 12

① Write the numbers. 18 pts. for this exercise.

654 = __600__ + __50__ + __4__   465 = __400__ + __60__ + __5__

138 = __100__ + __30__ + __8__   873 = __800__ + __70__ + __3__

589 = __500__ + __80__ + __9__   210 = __200__ + __10__ + __0__

② Draw a line to match the shape to its name. 7 pts.

octagon

square

rectangle

triangle

oval

circle

diamond

③ Write the answers. 3 pts.

+—+—+—+—+—+—+—+—+—+—+—+—+—+—+—+—+—+—+—+
0 1 2 3 4 5 6 7 8 9 **10** 11 12 13 14 15 16 17 18 19

Is 6 closer to 0 or 10? __10__

Is 8 closer to 0 or 10   __10__

Is 3 closer to 0 or 10 ? __0__

93

---

④ Add. 11 pts.

3	4	2	7	3	4
2	2	5	2	5	1
+7	+9	+4	+5	+6	+8
12	15	11	14	14	13

120	512	106	371	283
+324	+364	+731	+618	+111
444	876	837	989	394

⑤ Subtract. 12 pts.

16	13	11	12	10	14
- 7	- 6	- 5	- 9	- 3	- 8
9	7	6	3	7	6

12	15	13	11	12	11
- 6	- 9	- 8	- 8	- 3	- 7
6	6	5	3	9	4

51 pts. Total

94

ODD NUMBERS

Lesson 120

① Circle the odd number in each set.

16 (19)	(23) 28	74 (77)	52 (55)
30 (31)	(87) 88	(5) 6	(61) 64

② Number the pictures in the correct order.

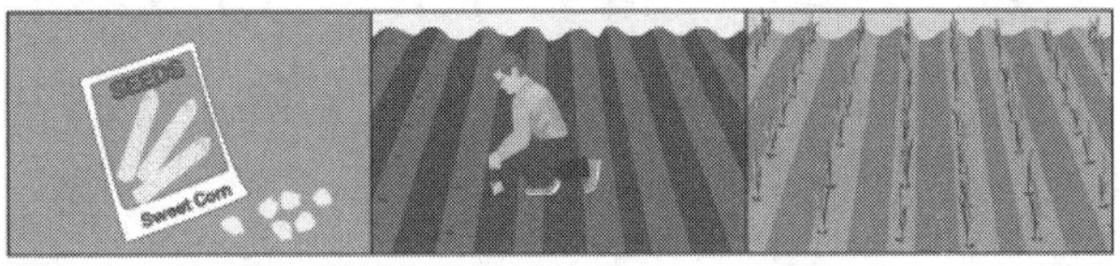

1   2   3

③ Draw both hands on the clock.

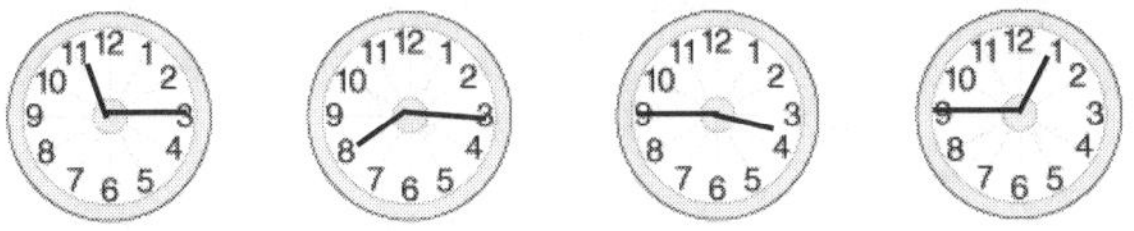

11:15   8:15   3:45   12:45

95

④ Write the name.

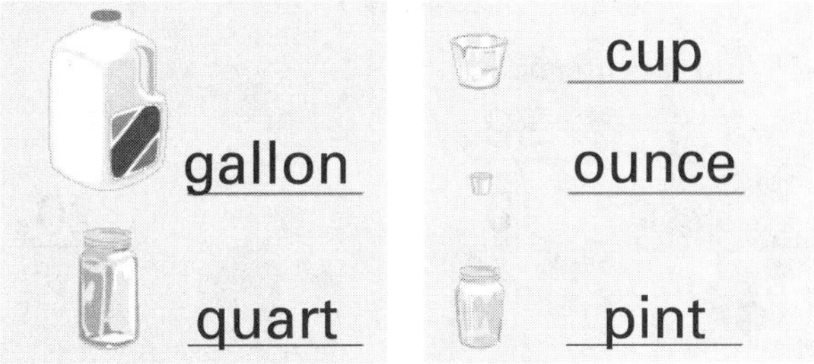

gallon   cup   ounce

quart   pint

⑤ Write the numbers.

4 hundreds 6 tens 5 one = 400 + 60 + 5 = 465

7 hundreds 3 tens 1 one = 700 + 30 + 1 = 731

1 hundred 2 tens 6 ones = 100 + 20 + 6 = 126

8 hundreds 0 tens 9 one = 800 + 0 + 9 = 809

⑥ Megan ran around the circle 12 times. Lisa ran around the circle 8 times. Megan ran around the circle how many more times than Lisa?

12 - 8 = 4 times

There were 11 hens and 3 roosters in the barnyard. There were how many more hens than roosters in the barnyard?

11 - 3 = 8 hens

96

SOLIDS

Lesson 121

① Draw a line to match the solid to its name.

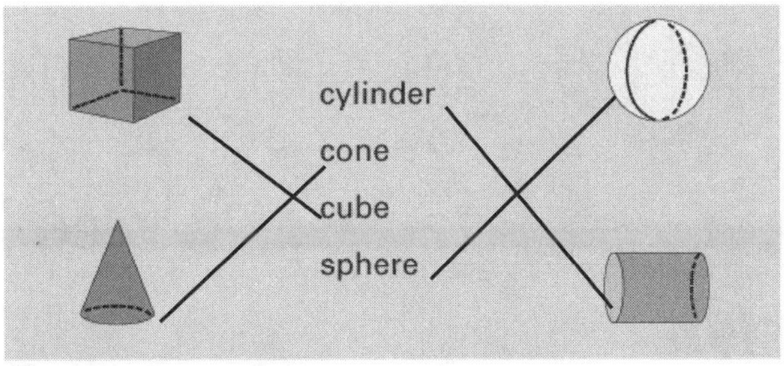
cylinder
cone
cube
sphere

② Write the numbers.

385 = 300 + 80 + 5   700 + 40 + 8 = 748

476 = 400 + 70 + 6   200 + 50 + 4 = 254

527 = 500 + 20 + 7   600 + 00 + 3 = 603

③ Write the numbers.

160 161 162 163 164 165

166 167 168 169 170 171

172 173 174 175 176 177

97

④ Add.

2 + 6 + 8 = 16	5 + 1 + 5 = 11	2 + 4 + 5 = 11	3 + 4 + 9 = 16	1 + 3 + 6 = 10	4 + 5 + 1 = 10

251 + 341 = 592	245 + 213 = 458	312 + 647 = 959	643 + 125 = 768	136 + 822 = 958

⑤ Subtract.

10 - 5 = 5	11 - 2 = 9	14 - 5 = 9	9 - 3 = 6	12 - 4 = 8	15 - 7 = 8
16 - 9 = 7	7 - 7 = 0	11 - 5 = 6	13 - 5 = 8	10 - 6 = 4	14 - 7 = 7

98

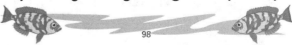

MONEY

① Add the money.

 = **30** ¢   = **50** ¢

= **10** ¢   = **20** ¢

= **1** ¢   = **5** ¢

Total **41** ¢   Total **75** ¢

= **40** ¢   = **20** ¢

= **15** ¢   = **20** ¢

= **4** ¢   = **3** ¢

Total **59** ¢   Total **43** ¢

② Write cube, cone, sphere, or cylinder on the lines.

cube   cylinder

sphere   cone

99

---

③ Write the numbers.

one hundred seventy-eight **178**

one hundred forty **140**

one hundred six **106**

④ Add.

16	42	43	61	52	26
+10	+52	+41	+14	+43	+43
26	94	84	75	95	69

74	21	53	50	38	40
+22	+67	+14	+24	+50	+12
96	88	67	74	88	52

⑤ Subtract.

13	11	15	8	12	6
- 4	- 2	- 6	- 3	- 5	- 4
9	9	9	5	7	2

7	10	12	13	11	16
- 5	- 4	- 8	- 8	- 6	- 8
2	6	4	5	5	8

100

SHOW YOUR SKILLS

① Write the missing numbers.

177	178	179	180	181	182
183	184	185	186	187	188
189	190	191	192	193	194
195	196	197	198	199	200

② Write the numbers.

one hundred thirty-one **131**

one hundred twenty **120**

one hundred nineteen **119**

one hundred two **102**

one hundred sixty-four **164**

③ Bill had 14 goldfish and 8 guppies in his fish tank. Bill has how many more goldfish than guppies?

14 - 8 = 6 goldfish

101

---

④ Add the money.

= **50** ¢   = **75** ¢

= **20** ¢   = **20** ¢

= **2** ¢   = **1** ¢

Total **72** ¢   Total **96** ¢

⑤ Add.

12	86	81	27	95	24
+91	+93	+25	+82	+92	+94
103	179	106	109	187	118

44	45	36	53	52	60
+63	+80	+92	+51	+73	+65
107	125	128	104	125	125

73	81	82	58	73	97
+73	+37	+65	+91	+44	+21
146	118	147	149	117	118

102

ESTIMATION

(1) Circle the animal that is about 8 inches tall.

Circle the animal that is about 2 inches long.

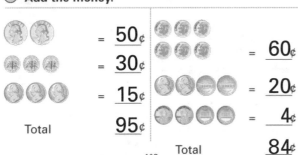

(2) Add the money.

(coins)	=	50¢
(coins)	=	30¢
(coins)	=	15¢
Total		95¢

(coins)	=	60¢
(coins)	=	20¢
(coins)	=	4¢
Total		84¢

103

---

(3) Add.

56	43	21	83	62	77
+72	+86	+95	+72	+81	+90
128	129	116	155	143	167

91	82	54	55	93	67
+48	+35	+83	+93	+63	+41
139	117	137	148	156	108

(4) Subtract.

12	16	10	15	11	13
- 7	- 9	- 5	- 7	- 4	- 5
5	7	5	8	7	8

13	11	14	12	10	17
- 6	- 8	- 5	- 3	- 3	- 8
7	3	9	9	7	9

14	10	18	12	11	13
- 8	- 9	- 9	- 9	- 5	- 7
6	1	9	3	6	6

104

NUMBER SEQUENCE

(1) Write the next three numbers.

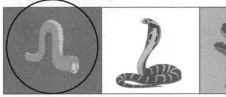

4	7	10	13	16	19
3	6	9	12	15	18
5	8	11	14	17	20

(2) Write the answers.

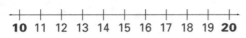

10 11 12 13 14 15 16 17 18 19 20

Is 16 closer to 10 or 20? 20
Is 12 closer to 10 or 20? 10
Is 18 closer to 10 or 20? 20
Is 14 closer to 10 or 20? 10

(3) Count each set. Write the number.

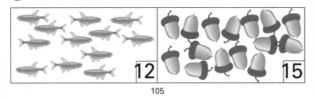

12   15

105

---

(4) Write the correct letter in the blank.

S P R I N G I S
5 6 7 8 9 10 11 12

C O M I N G
13 14 15 16 17 18

I	O	P	M	C
7+4=	6+8=	5+1=	8+7=	5+8=

N	S	S	I	R
7+2=	3+2=	7+5=	5+3=	4+3=

I	G	N	G	
7+9=	6+4=	8+9=	9+9=	

(5) Subtract.

15	12	13	11	16	10
- 8	- 4	- 9	- 7	- 7	- 2
7	8	4	4	9	8

9	11	8	10	7	10
- 5	- 9	- 4	- 6	- 5	- 1
4	2	4	4	2	9

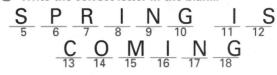

106

447

SHAPES

① **Draw a line to match the shape to its name.**

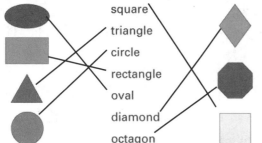

square
triangle
circle
rectangle
oval
diamond
octagon

② **Circle every fourth number after 7.**

⑦ 8 9 10 ⑪ 12 13 14 ⑮
16 17 18 ⑲ 20 21 22 ㉓ 24
25 26 ㉗ 28 29 30 ㉛ 32 33

Write the circled numbers on the blanks.

| 7 | 11 | 15 | 19 | 23 | 27 | 31 |

③ June had 30¢ in her left pocket and 20¢ in her right pocket. How many cents did June have?

30¢ + 20¢ = 50¢

107

There were 13 children swimming in a pool. There were 8 children sitting on the edge of the pool. How many more children were in the pool than on the edge?

13 - 8 = 5   children

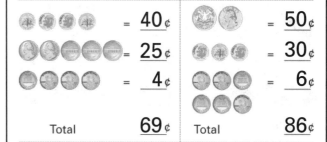

④ **Add the money.**

= 40¢   = 50¢

= 25¢   = 30¢

= 4¢   = 6¢

Total   69¢   Total   86¢

⑤ **Measure the line with a centimeter ruler. Circle the correct answer.**

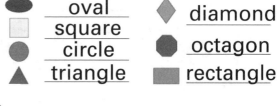

about ⑧ or **9** centimeters

about **9** or ⑩ centimeters

about ⑥ or **7** centimeters

108

CALENDAR – MONTHS OF THE YEAR

① **Write the months of the year in the correct order.**

June   October   December   March
May   January   November   July
February   September   August   April

1. January   2. February   3. March
4. April   5. May   6. June
7. July   8. August   9. September
10. October   11. November   12. December

② **Write the next three numbers.**

9	8	7	6	5	4
14	13	12	11	10	9
26	25	24	23	22	21

③ Nancy paid 8 dimes for some french fries. How many cents did she pay?

8 dimes = 80¢

109

---

④ **Write the name of each shape.**

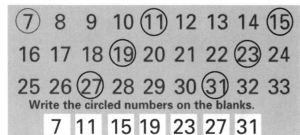

oval
square
circle
triangle

diamond
octagon
rectangle

⑤ **Add.**

41	62	94	75	40	22
+63	+93	+21	+54	+75	+87
104	155	115	129	115	109

82	81	52	96	73	87
+86	+26	+60	+32	+72	+51
168	107	112	128	145	138

78	94	71	35	93	69
+41	+84	+82	+73	+75	+70
119	178	153	108	168	139

110

448

DOZEN

① How many apples are in a dozen? __12__
Color a dozen apples.

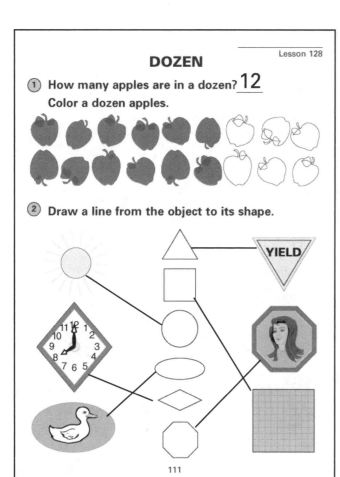

② Draw a line from the object to its shape.

YIELD

111

③ Add.

16	66	85	31	54	75
+91	+53	+41	+94	+50	+32
107	119	126	125	104	107

32	82	83	47	64	70
+86	+62	+94	+92	+63	+65
118	144	177	139	127	135

④ Subtract.

14	15	10	11	13	12
- 6	- 6	- 8	- 6	- 8	- 6
8	9	2	5	5	6

16	15	14	11	10	12
- 8	- 9	- 8	- 3	- 2	- 3
8	6	6	8	8	9

17	10	12	11	13	15
- 8	- 5	- 7	- 8	- 4	- 7
9	5	5	3	9	8

112

CALENDAR – DAYS OF THE WEEK

① Write the missing numbers.

March

Sunday	Monday	Tuesday	Wednesday	Thursday	Friday	Saturday
1	2	3	4	5	6	7
8	9	10	11	12	13	14
15	16	17	18	19	20	21
22	23	24	25	26	27	28
29	30	31				

② Write the answers.

What day is March 20th? __Friday__

What day is 4 days after March 13th? __Tuesday__

What day is 3 days before March 28th? __Wednesday__

What date is the third Monday? __16th__

③ Jerry paid 9 nickels for a candy bar. How many cents did he pay?

9 nickels = __45__ cents

113

---

④ Number the pictures in the correct order.

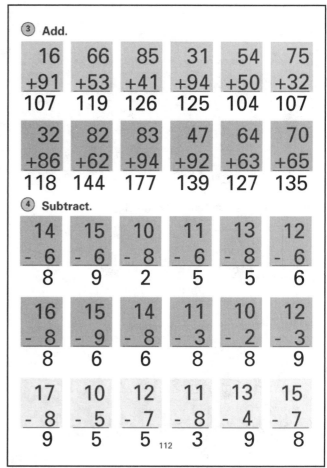

__3__   __1__   __2__

⑤ Add.

64	91	22	43	91	35
+61	+63	+81	+72	+97	+90
125	154	103	115	188	125

62	75	56	94	73	89
+94	+73	+50	+54	+45	+30
156	148	106	148	118	119

87	91	98	50	92	81
+91	+38	+71	+87	+17	+65
178	129	169	137	109	146

114

449

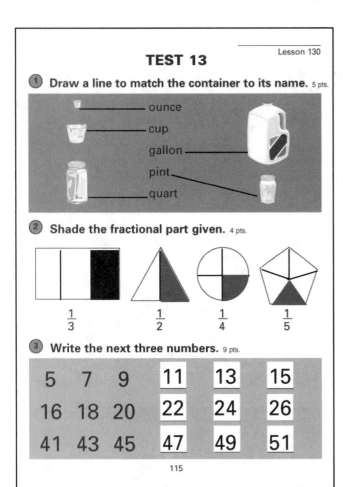

TEST 13 — Lesson 130

① Draw a line to match the container to its name. 5 pts.

- ounce
- cup
- gallon
- pint
- quart

② Shade the fractional part given. 4 pts.

$\frac{1}{3}$ $\frac{1}{2}$ $\frac{1}{4}$ $\frac{1}{5}$

③ Write the next three numbers. 9 pts.

5	7	9	11	13	15
16	18	20	22	24	26
41	43	45	47	49	51

115

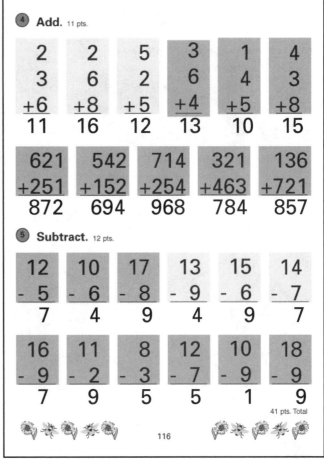

④ Add. 11 pts.

2	2	5	3	1	4
3	6	2	6	4	3
+6	+8	+5	+4	+5	+8
11	16	12	13	10	15

621	542	714	321	136
+251	+152	+254	+463	+721
872	694	968	784	857

⑤ Subtract. 12 pts.

12	10	17	13	15	14
- 5	- 6	- 8	- 9	- 6	- 7
7	4	9	4	9	7

16	11	8	12	10	18
- 9	- 2	- 3	- 7	- 9	- 9
7	9	5	5	1	9

41 pts. Total

116

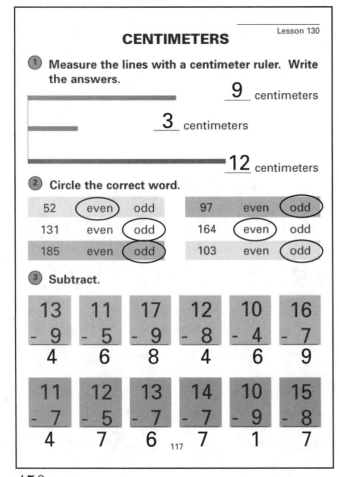

CENTIMETERS — Lesson 130

① Measure the lines with a centimeter ruler. Write the answers.

_9_ centimeters

_3_ centimeters

_12_ centimeters

② Circle the correct word.

52	(even) odd	97	even (odd)
131	even (odd)	164	(even) odd
185	even (odd)	103	even (odd)

③ Subtract.

13	11	17	12	10	16
- 9	- 5	- 9	- 8	- 4	- 7
4	6	8	4	6	9

11	12	13	14	10	15
- 7	- 5	- 7	- 7	- 9	- 8
4	7	6	7	1	7

117

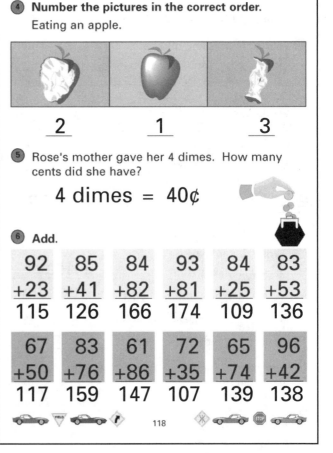

④ Number the pictures in the correct order.
Eating an apple.

2   1   3

⑤ Rose's mother gave her 4 dimes. How many cents did she have?

4 dimes = 40¢

⑥ Add.

92	85	84	93	84	83
+23	+41	+82	+81	+25	+53
115	126	166	174	109	136

67	83	61	72	65	96
+50	+76	+86	+35	+74	+42
117	159	147	107	139	138

118

450

ADDITION – CARRYING

1 Add.

① 32 +8	① 86 +5	① 58 +4	① 47 +8	① 25 +9	① 63 +8
40	91	62	55	34	71

① 72 +9	① 64 +9	① 55 +7	① 73 +7	① 34 +8	① 81 +9
81	73	62	80	42	90

① 35 +6	① 57 +6	① 44 +8	① 24 +6	① 46 +4	① 17 +5
41	63	52	30	50	22

2 Write the fraction that shows what part is shaded.

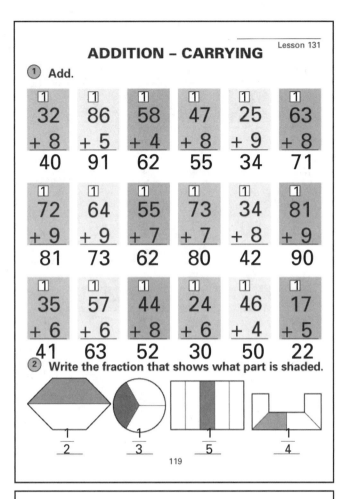

$\frac{1}{2}$ $\frac{1}{3}$ $\frac{1}{5}$ $\frac{1}{4}$

119

---

3 Write the hundreds, tens, and ones. Write the number.

4 hundreds 3 tens 6 ones = 400 + 30 + 6 = 436

7 hundreds 5 tens 1 one = 700 + 50 + 1 = 751

8 hundreds 2 tens 9 ones = 800 + 20 + 9 = 829

2 hundreds 8 tens 4 ones = 200 + 80 + 4 = 284

6 hundreds 7 tens 8 ones = 600 + 70 + 8 = 678

4 Subtract.

10 -7	13 -6	12 -4	18 -9	8 -5	11 -4
3	7	8	9	3	7

14 -9	11 -2	16 -7	10 -6	12 -9	9 -3
5	9	9	4	3	6

6 -2	11 -9	7 -3	14 -5	10 -3	5 -3
4	2	4	9	7	2

120

POUND

1 Write the weight of each object.

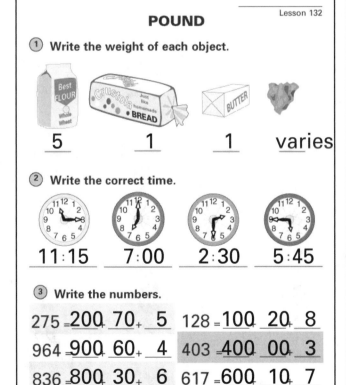

5   1   1   varies

2 Write the correct time.

11:15   7:00   2:30   5:45

3 Write the numbers.

275 = 200 + 70 + 5   128 = 100 + 20 + 8

964 = 900 + 60 + 4   403 = 400 + 00 + 3

836 = 800 + 30 + 6   617 = 600 + 10 + 7

590 = 500 + 90 + 0   359 = 300 + 50 + 9

121

---

4 Draw a line to match the solid to its name.

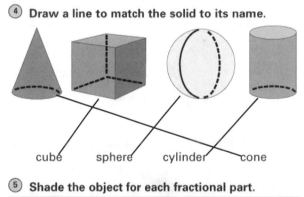

cube   sphere   cylinder   cone

5 Shade the object for each fractional part.

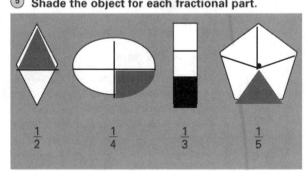

$\frac{1}{2}$ $\frac{1}{4}$ $\frac{1}{3}$ $\frac{1}{5}$

6 Todd is 15 years old. Dick is 8 years old. How many years older is Todd than Dick?

15 - 8 = 7 years

122

451

⑦ Subtract.

12 − 3 = 9	16 − 7 = 9	11 − 2 = 9	15 − 6 = 9	10 − 4 = 6	13 − 4 = 9
12 − 5 = 7	10 − 2 = 8	13 − 6 = 7	15 − 8 = 7	11 − 5 = 6	14 − 8 = 6
17 − 8 = 9	10 − 6 = 4	11 − 3 = 8	12 − 6 = 6	14 − 6 = 8	16 − 9 = 7
14 − 7 = 7	12 − 4 = 8	11 − 7 = 4	10 − 7 = 3	13 − 9 = 4	15 − 7 = 8
11 − 9 = 2	12 − 8 = 4	18 − 9 = 9	10 − 8 = 2	13 − 5 = 8	14 − 5 = 9

⑧ Add.

19 + 4 = 23	53 + 7 = 60	48 + 6 = 54	86 + 6 = 92	59 + 9 = 68	29 + 2 = 31
68 + 7 = 75	14 + 6 = 20	28 + 9 = 37	37 + 5 = 42	39 + 6 = 45	74 + 8 = 82
57 + 9 = 66	35 + 7 = 42	26 + 8 = 34	45 + 9 = 54	86 + 4 = 90	67 + 8 = 75
69 + 8 = 77	58 + 2 = 60	12 + 9 = 21	75 + 5 = 80	48 + 4 = 52	77 + 3 = 80

NUMBER ORDER – ORDINAL NUMBERS

①

cylinder   sphere   cone   cube

The **cone** is the third solid.
The **cylinder** is the first solid.
The **cube** is the fourth solid.
The **sphere** is the second solid.

② Draw both hands on the clock.

11:45   8:15   6:00   10:30

7:45   12:15   2:45   1:15

---

③ Write = or ≠ between each set.

In 783 the 8 is = to 8 tens.
In 256 the 6 is = to 6 ones.
In 429 the 4 is = to 4 hundreds.
In 375 the 5 is ≠ to 5 tens.
In 948 the 9 is = to 9 hundreds.
In 261 the 6 is ≠ to 6 ones.

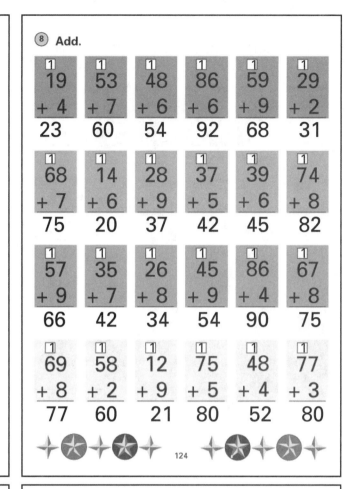

④ Add.

27 + 6 = 33	38 + 5 = 43	76 + 7 = 83	43 + 8 = 51	34 + 7 = 41	69 + 1 = 70
86 + 5 = 91	45 + 8 = 53	67 + 7 = 74	19 + 3 = 22	28 + 3 = 31	84 + 9 = 93
21 + 9 = 30	57 + 4 = 61	19 + 7 = 26	75 + 6 = 81	53 + 9 = 62	12 + 8 = 20

Lesson 134

SUBTRACTION – DOUBLE DIGIT

① Subtract.

58	97	39	56	85	69
-27	-52	-19	-16	-63	-51
31	45	20	40	22	18

49	84	76	91	73	28
-46	-23	-40	-81	-63	-21
3	61	36	10	10	7

74	96	58	35	95	27
-12	-71	-54	-24	-20	-17
62	25	4	11	75	10

② Write = or ≠ between each set.

one hundred fifty-four	≠	145
one hundred eighty-three	=	183
one hundred ten	=	110
one hundred twenty-nine	=	129
one hundred seven	≠	170

127

---

③ Add.

☐1	☐1	☐1	☐1	☐1	☐1
66	38	89	23	26	59
+ 6	+ 8	+ 2	+ 8	+ 7	+ 6
72	46	91	31	33	65

☐1	☐1	☐1	☐1	☐1	☐1
48	74	16	48	14	37
+ 5	+ 6	+ 7	+ 9	+ 9	+ 8
53	80	23	57	23	45

④ Subtract.

13	16	10	11	15	13
- 7	- 8	- 3	- 4	- 9	- 8
6	8	7	7	6	5

⑤ Henry weighs 34 pounds and Harry weighs 75 pounds. How many pounds do the boys weigh altogether?

75 + 34 =   75
          + 34
        109 pounds

128

Lesson 135

SHOW YOUR SKILLS

① Write the subtraction facts.

3+8=11	5+7=12	5+8=13
11 - 8 = 3	12 - 7 = 5	13 - 8 = 5
11 - 3 = 8	12 - 5 = 7	13 - 5 = 8

6+2=8	7+8=15	8+9=17
8 - 2 = 6	15 - 8 = 7	17 - 9 = 8
8 - 6 = 2	15 - 7 = 8	17 - 8 = 9

② Write the word numbers.

138	one hundred thirty–eight
152	one hundred fifty–two
194	one hundred ninety–four
165	one hundred sixty–five
170	one hundred seventy

129

---

③ Rover eats a 24 pound bag of dog food in three weeks. Blacky eats a 10 pound bag in three weeks. Rover eats how many more pounds of dog food than Blacky eats?

24 - 10 =   24
           - 10
          14 pounds

④ Add.

☐1	☐1	☐1	☐1	☐1	☐1
52	19	28	63	47	14
+ 8	+ 1	+ 6	+ 9	+ 7	+ 7
60	20	34	72	54	21

☐1	☐1	☐1	☐1	☐1	☐1
45	39	56	28	87	79
+ 8	+ 5	+ 9	+ 3	+ 3	+ 8
53	44	65	31	90	87

⑤ Subtract.

96	23	67	85	94	59
-82	-12	-50	-61	-12	-35
14	11	17	24	82	24

130

453

BAR GRAPH

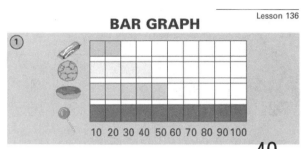

10 20 30 40 50 60 70 80 90 100

How many cookies are on the bar graph? __40__
How many lollipops are on the bar graph? __100__
How many donuts are on the bar graph? __50__
How many candies are on the bar graph? __20__

② Write the numbers.

one hundred sixty-nine __169__
one hundred fifty __150__
one hundred two __102__
one hundred fourteen __114__
one hundred seven __107__
one hundred twenty-one __121__

③ Susie had 7 dimes to buy an ice cream cone. How many cents did she have?

7 dimes = 70 cents (¢)

131

---

④ Write the subtraction facts.

7+6=13   5+9=14   8+4=12
13 - 6 = 7   14 - 9 = 5   12 - 4 = 8
13 - 7 = 6   14 - 5 = 9   12 - 8 = 4

⑤ Add.

37	65	59	28	75	42
+ 5	+ 5	+ 4	+ 7	+ 9	+ 9
42	70	63	35	84	51

⑥ Subtract.

81	73	94	87	97	58
-50	-23	-73	-25	-37	-47
31	50	21	62	60	11

95	86	65	86	74	72
-63	-41	-32	-34	-61	-41
32	45	33	52	13	31

132

ESTIMATION

① **Circle the object that weighs "about" 5 pounds.**

②

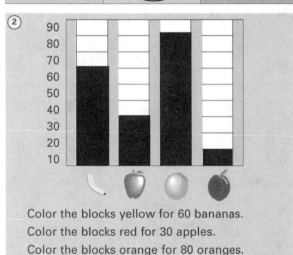

Color the blocks yellow for 60 bananas.
Color the blocks red for 30 apples.
Color the blocks orange for 80 oranges.
Color the blocks purple for 10 plums.

133

---

③ **Write the subtraction facts.**

4+6=10   8+6=14   5+4=9
10 - 6 = 4   14 - 6 = 8   9 - 4 = 5
10 - 4 = 6   14 - 8 = 6   9 - 5 = 4

④ **Add the money.**

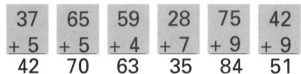 = __30__ ¢   = __50__ ¢
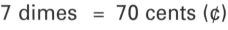 = __20__ ¢   = __40__ ¢
= __5__ ¢   = __5__ ¢

Total __55__ ¢   Total __95__ ¢

⑤ **Add.**

28	46	24	18	47	63
+ 4	+ 5	+ 8	+ 2	+ 6	+ 8
32	51	32	20	53	71

134

NUMBER SEQUENCE

Lesson 138

1 Write the next three numbers.

12	10	8	6	4	2
13	11	9	7	5	3
20	18	16	14	12	10

2 Add the money.

= 50¢   = 25¢

= 20¢   = 20¢

= 4¢   = 2¢

Total 74¢   Total 47¢

3 Subtract.

68	59	75	84	38	48
-30	-56	-24	-12	-18	-27
38	3	51	72	20	21

135

---

4 Write the answers.

20 21 22 23 24 25 26 27 28 29 30

Is 22 closer to 20 or 30? 20
Is 24 closer to 20 or 30? 20
Is 28 closer to 20 or 30? 30
Is 21 closer to 20 or 30? 20
Is 26 closer to 20 or 30? 30

5 Add.

69	45	23	16	51	38
+ 9	+ 7	+ 9	+ 8	+ 9	+ 5
78	52	32	24	60	43

471	560	412	543	136
+513	+315	+457	+220	+252
984	875	869	763	388

6 Jared had 7 nickels to spend on a drink. How many cents did he have?

7 nickels = 35¢ (cents)

136

NUMBER ORDER – < AND >

Lesson 139

1 Write the value of the coins. Write < or > in the blanks.

3 quarters (75¢) < 80¢   5 pennies (5 ¢) > 4¢
4 dimes (40¢) < 50¢   8 dimes (80¢) < 90¢
6 nickels (30¢) > 25¢   18 pennies (18¢) > 15¢

2 Circle every fifth number after 2. Write the circled numbers on the blanks.

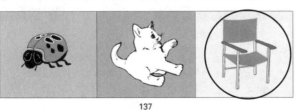

(2) 3 4 5 6 (7) 8 9 10
11 (12) 13 14 15 16 (17) 18 19
20 21 (22) 23 24 25 26 (27) 28

2   7   12   17   22   27

3 Circle the one that is "about" 30 inches tall.

137

---

4 A five pound bag of flour costs 3 quarters. How many cents does the bag of flour cost?

3 quarters = 75¢ (cents)

5 Add.

86	19	57	24	48	78
+ 5	+ 7	+ 6	+ 6	+ 7	+ 4
91	26	63	30	55	82

37	53	61	46	72	15
+ 9	+ 9	+ 9	+ 8	+ 9	+ 6
46	62	70	54	81	21

6 Subtract.

86	53	79	48	67	97
-12	-23	-65	-38	-61	-42
74	30	14	10	6	55

17	13	11	16	12	15
- 9	- 9	- 7	- 8	- 9	- 6
8	4	4	8	3	9

138

455

TEST 14

1 Draw a line to match the solid to its name. 4 pts.

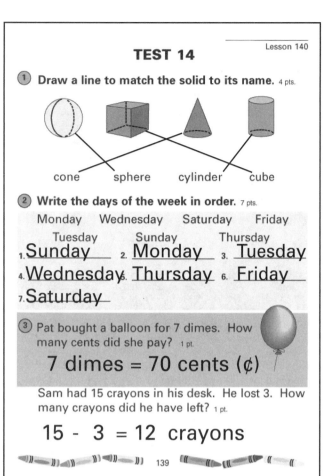

cone   sphere   cylinder   cube

2 Write the days of the week in order. 7 pts.

Monday   Wednesday   Saturday   Friday
Tuesday   Sunday   Thursday

1. Sunday   2. Monday   3. Tuesday
4. Wednesday 5. Thursday 6. Friday
7. Saturday

3 Pat bought a balloon for 7 dimes. How many cents did she pay? 1 pt.

7 dimes = 70 cents (¢)

Sam had 15 crayons in his desk. He lost 3. How many crayons did he have left? 1 pt.

15 - 3 = 12 crayons

139

---

4 Add. 11 pts.

① 46 + 5	① 54 + 6	① 16 + 7	① 39 + 7	① 68 + 4	① 27 + 8
51	60	23	46	72	35

322 +514	740 +226	182 +607	351 +332	352 +140
836	966	789	683	492

5 Subtract. 12 pts.

68 -38	49 -11	75 -52	57 -12	96 -26	85 -24
30	38	23	45	70	61

16 - 9	11 - 2	14 - 8	15 - 6	12 - 5	10 - 6
7	9	6	9	7	4

36 pts. Total

140

CENTIMETERS

1 Measure the lines with a centimeter ruler. Write the answers.

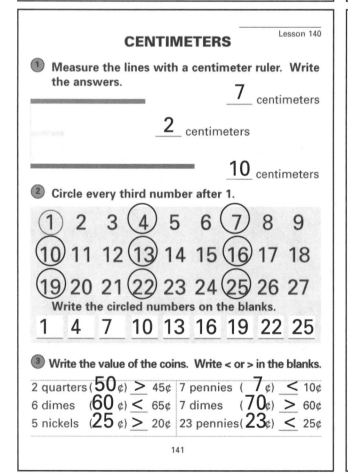

_7_ centimeters

_2_ centimeters

_10_ centimeters

2 Circle every third number after 1.

(1) 2 3 (4) 5 6 (7) 8 9
(10) 11 12 (13) 14 15 (16) 17 18
(19) 20 21 (22) 23 24 (25) 26 27

Write the circled numbers on the blanks.

1   4   7   10   13   16   19   22   25

3 Write the value of the coins. Write < or > in the blanks.

2 quarters	**50**¢	>	45¢	7 pennies	(**7**¢	<	10¢
6 dimes	**60**¢	<	65¢	7 dimes	(**70**¢	>	60¢
5 nickels	**25**¢	>	20¢	23 pennies	**23**¢	<	25¢

141

---

4 Add.

36 + 4	59 + 8	14 + 7	66 + 9	29 + 4	47 + 5
40	67	21	75	33	52

253 +612	361 +408	306 +123	224 +310	247 +232
865	769	429	534	479

5 Subtract.

59 -27	43 -13	76 -36	93 -22	78 -53	86 -65
32	30	40	71	25	21

10 - 7	13 - 5	16 - 9	11 - 4	14 - 6	12 - 6
3	8	7	7	8	6

6 Sam had 6 dimes. He spent 5 dimes on a can of soda pop. How many cents did he have left?

6 - 5 = 1 dime = 10 cents (¢)

142

456

EVEN AND ODD NUMBERS
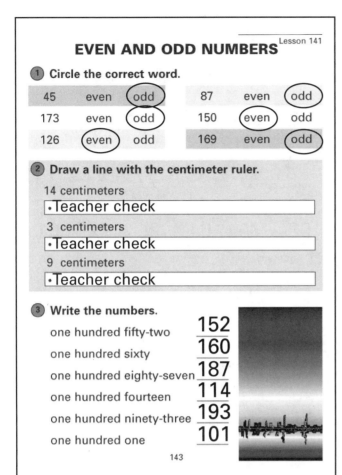

Lesson 141

1 Circle the correct word.

45	even	**(odd)**		87	even	**(odd)**
173	even	**(odd)**		150	**(even)**	odd
126	**(even)**	odd		169	even	**(odd)**

2 Draw a line with the centimeter ruler.

14 centimeters
· Teacher check

3 centimeters
· Teacher check

9 centimeters
· Teacher check

3 Write the numbers.

one hundred fifty-two __152__

one hundred sixty __160__

one hundred eighty-seven __187__

one hundred fourteen __114__

one hundred ninety-three __193__

one hundred one __101__

143

---

4 Add.

14	56	63	13	27	29
+69	+16	+28	+17	+47	+51
83	72	91	30	74	80

28	35	58	36	49	69
+17	+16	+29	+27	+16	+13
45	51	87	63	65	82

5 Subtract.

68	94	52	87	67	94
-42	-53	-31	-57	-14	-34
26	41	21	30	53	60

10	12	14	11	12	17
- 4	- 8	- 5	- 9	- 4	- 8
6	4	9	2	8	9

6 The room has 47 chairs. 25 people came into the room and sat down in the chairs. How many chairs were left empty?

47 - 25 =

$$\begin{array}{r} 47 \\ - 25 \\ \hline 22 \end{array}$$ chairs

144

MEASUREMENT – LIQUID
Lesson 142

1 Draw a line to match the container to its name.

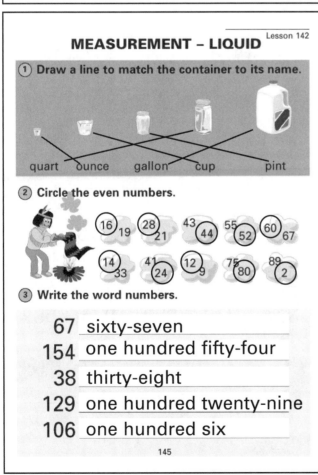

quart   ounce   gallon   cup   pint

2 Circle the even numbers.

(16) 19   (28) 21   43 (44)   55 (52) (60) 67

(14) 33   41 (24)   (12) 9   75 (80)   89 (2)

3 Write the word numbers.

67	sixty-seven
154	one hundred fifty-four
38	thirty-eight
129	one hundred twenty-nine
106	one hundred six

145

---

4 Put an X on the solid that is different.

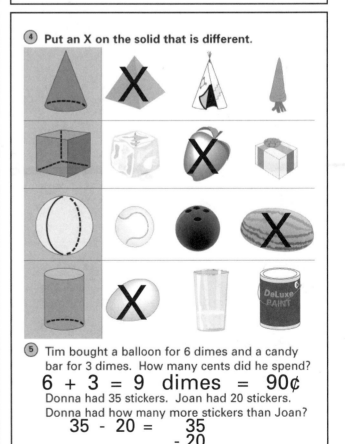

5 Tim bought a balloon for 6 dimes and a candy bar for 3 dimes. How many cents did he spend?

6 + 3 = 9 dimes = 90¢

Donna had 35 stickers. Joan had 20 stickers. Donna had how many more stickers than Joan?

35 - 20 =

$$\begin{array}{r} 35 \\ - 20 \\ \hline 15 \end{array}$$ stickers

146

457

PLACE VALUE – ONE HUNDREDS

① Write the hundreds, tens, and ones. Write the number.

5 hundreds 6 tens 3 ones = 500 + 60 + 3 = 563

8 hundreds 4 tens 7 ones = 800 + 40 + 7 = 847

2 hundreds 1 ten 9 ones = 200 + 10 + 9 = 219

6 hundreds 0 tens 4 ones = 600 + 00 + 4 = 604

② Write ounce, cup, pint, quart, gallon on the lines.

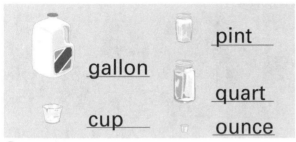

pint

gallon

quart

cup

ounce

③ Circle the odd number.

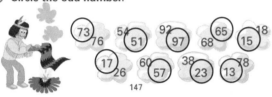

73 76 54 51 92 97 68 65 15 18
17 26 60 57 38 23 13 78

147

---

④ Write cone, cube, sphere, or cylinder on the lines.

 cylinder   cube

sphere   cone

⑤ Add.

65	47	29	77	54	12
+28	+23	+35	+19	+18	+49
93	70	64	96	72	61

⑥ Subtract.

12	13	13	18	14	11
- 5	- 7	- 4	- 9	- 8	- 2
7	6	9	9	6	9

89	96	78	25	67	91
-46	-80	-67	-21	-21	-11
43	16	11	4	46	80

148

TIME

① Write the correct time.

7:15   2:45   12:45   1:30

4:45   5:00   9:15   11:15

② Write the numbers.

194 = 100 + 90 + 4   629 = 600 + 20 + 9

376 = 300 + 70 + 6   852 = 800 + 50 + 2

248 = 200 + 40 + 8   461 = 400 + 60 + 1

③ Brad weighed 48 pounds. Steve weighed 35 pounds. Brad weighed how many more pounds than Steve?   48 - 35 = 48
- 35

149

13 pounds

---

④ Measure the lines with an inch ruler. Write the answers.

4 inches

2 inches

6 inches

⑤ Add.

32	85	27	19	68	78
+ 8	+ 9	+ 4	+ 2	+ 2	+ 3
40	94	31	21	70	81

135	714	232	826	261
+202	+162	+751	+150	+328
337	876	983	976	589

⑥ Subtract.

10	12	10	11	10	13
- 8	- 3	- 5	- 8	- 3	- 7
2	9	5	3	7	6

150

Panel 1 (top left):

SHOW YOUR SKILLS

1 **Write the number.**

259 has a **9** in the ones' place.

295 has a **2** in the hundreds' place.

925 has a **2** in the tens' place.

952 has a **5** in the tens' place.

592 has a **2** in the ones' place.

529 has a **5** in the hundreds' place.

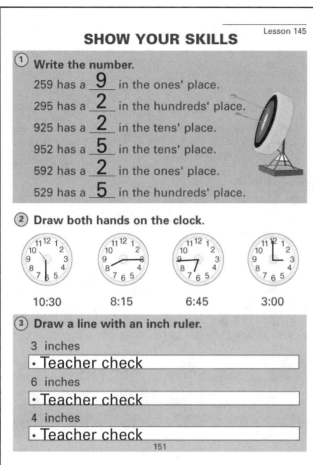

2 **Draw both hands on the clock.**

10:30   8:15   6:45   3:00

3 **Draw a line with an inch ruler.**

3 inches
• Teacher check

6 inches
• Teacher check

4 inches
• Teacher check

151

Panel 3 (top right):

4 **Add.**

14	38	25	44	19	57
+36	+45	+27	+19	+75	+14
50	83	52	63	94	71

27	52	75	33	44	81
+92	+86	+73	+73	+83	+75
119	138	148	106	127	156

5 **Subtract.**

10	14	16	11	12	15
- 2	- 9	- 9	- 6	- 4	- 8
8	5	7	5	8	7

13	14	10	17	12	11
- 7	- 6	- 9	- 8	- 7	- 3
6	8	1	9	5	8

83	6	46	78	54	97
-41	- 4	-20	-35	-51	-37
42	2	26	43	3	60

152

Panel 2 (bottom left):

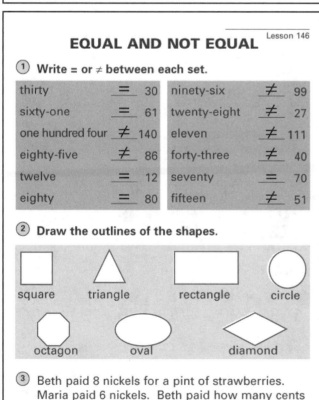

EQUAL AND NOT EQUAL

1 **Write = or ≠ between each set.**

thirty	= 30	ninety-six	≠ 99
sixty-one	= 61	twenty-eight	≠ 27
one hundred four	≠ 140	eleven	≠ 111
eighty-five	≠ 86	forty-three	≠ 40
twelve	= 12	seventy	= 70
eighty	= 80	fifteen	≠ 51

2 **Draw the outlines of the shapes.**

square   triangle   rectangle   circle

octagon   oval   diamond

3 Beth paid 8 nickels for a pint of strawberries. Maria paid 6 nickels. Beth paid how many cents more than Maria paid?

8 - 6 = 2 nickels = 10¢

153

Panel 4 (bottom right):

4 **Add.**

13	49	37	15	56	29
+18	+14	+55	+45	+28	+29
31	63	92	60	84	58

90	43	84	92	70	66
+73	+72	+65	+24	+38	+61
163	115	149	116	108	127

139	316	402	372	527
+710	+423	+267	+306	+431
849	739	669	678	958

5 **Subtract.**

14	12	13	10	11	15
- 7	- 8	- 8	- 5	- 4	- 9
7	4	5	5	7	6

11	12	13	14	16	10
- 2	- 6	- 9	- 8	- 8	- 7
9	6	4	6	8	3

154

BAR GRAPH

①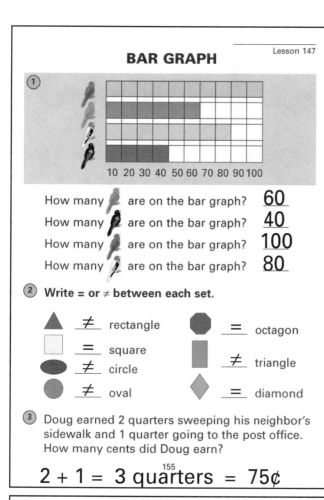

How many 🐦 are on the bar graph? **60**
How many 🐦 are on the bar graph? **40**
How many 🐦 are on the bar graph? **100**
How many 🐦 are on the bar graph? **80**

② Write = or ≠ between each set.

🔺 ≠ rectangle   ⬡ = octagon
⬜ = square   ▬ ≠ triangle
⬭ ≠ circle   ◆ = diamond
⬤ ≠ oval

③ Doug earned 2 quarters sweeping his neighbor's sidewalk and 1 quarter going to the post office. How many cents did Doug earn?

2 + 1 = 3 quarters = 75¢

155

④ **Write the numbers.**

one hundred thirty-six   136
one hundred seventy   170
one hundred five   105
one hundred twenty-nine   129
one hundred eleven   111
one hundred eighty-four   184

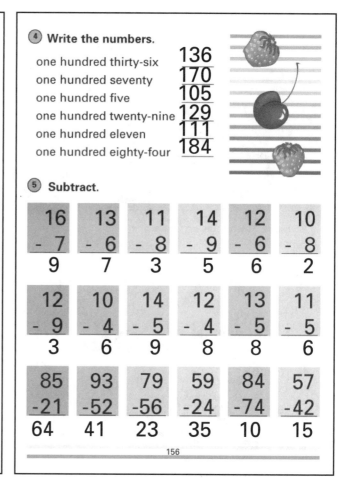

⑤ **Subtract.**

16	13	11	14	12	10
- 7	- 6	- 8	- 9	- 6	- 8
9	7	3	5	6	2

12	10	14	12	13	11
- 9	- 4	- 5	- 4	- 5	- 5
3	6	9	8	8	6

85	93	79	59	84	57
-21	-52	-56	-24	-74	-42
64	41	23	35	10	15

156

ESTIMATION

① **Write the answers.**

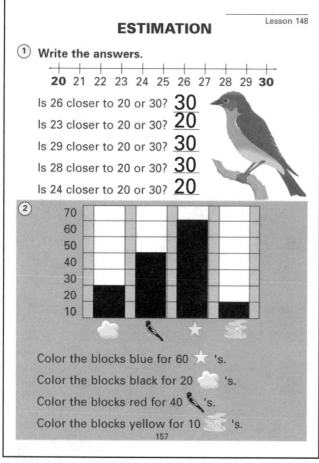

20 21 22 23 24 25 26 27 28 29 30

Is 26 closer to 20 or 30? **30**
Is 23 closer to 20 or 30? **20**
Is 29 closer to 20 or 30? **30**
Is 28 closer to 20 or 30? **30**
Is 24 closer to 20 or 30? **20**

②

Color the blocks blue for 60 ⭐'s.
Color the blocks black for 20 ☁'s.
Color the blocks red for 40 🐦's.
Color the blocks yellow for 10 ✂'s.

157

③ **Write the fractional part that is shaded.**

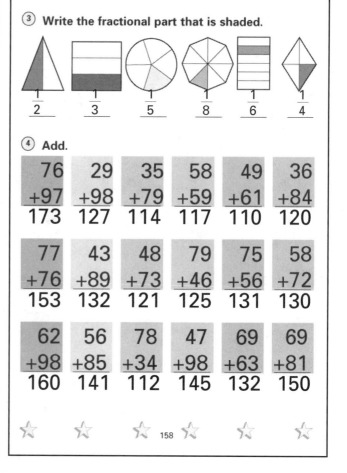

$\frac{1}{2}$ $\frac{1}{3}$ $\frac{1}{5}$ $\frac{1}{8}$ $\frac{1}{6}$ $\frac{1}{4}$

④ **Add.**

76	29	35	58	49	36
+97	+98	+79	+59	+61	+84
173	127	114	117	110	120

77	43	48	79	75	58
+76	+89	+73	+46	+56	+72
153	132	121	125	131	130

62	56	78	47	69	69
+98	+85	+34	+98	+63	+81
160	141	112	145	132	150

☆ ☆ ☆ 158 ☆ ☆ ☆

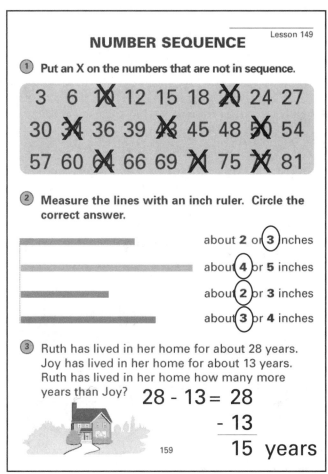

NUMBER SEQUENCE

① Put an X on the numbers that are not in sequence.

3 6 ~~10~~ 12 15 18 ~~20~~ 24 27
30 ~~34~~ 36 39 ~~43~~ 45 48 ~~51~~ 54
57 60 ~~64~~ 66 69 ~~72~~ 75 ~~78~~ 81

② Measure the lines with an inch ruler. Circle the correct answer.

about **2** or ③ inches

about ④ or **5** inches

about ② or **3** inches

about ③ or **4** inches

③ Ruth has lived in her home for about 28 years. Joy has lived in her home for about 13 years. Ruth has lived in her home how many more years than Joy?

$$28 - 13 = \begin{array}{r} 28 \\ -13 \\ \hline 15 \end{array} \text{ years}$$

159

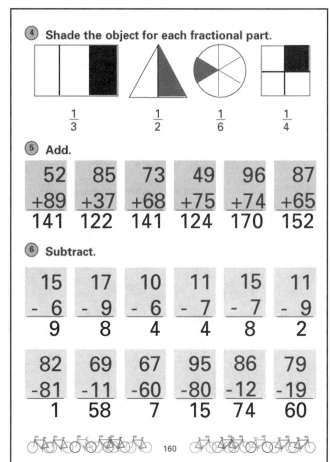

④ Shade the object for each fractional part.

$\frac{1}{3}$ $\frac{1}{2}$ $\frac{1}{6}$ $\frac{1}{4}$

⑤ Add.

52	85	73	49	96	87
+89	+37	+68	+75	+74	+65
141	122	141	124	170	152

⑥ Subtract.

15	17	10	11	15	11
- 6	- 9	- 6	- 7	- 7	- 9
9	8	4	4	8	2

82	69	67	95	86	79
-81	-11	-60	-80	-12	-19
1	58	7	15	74	60

160

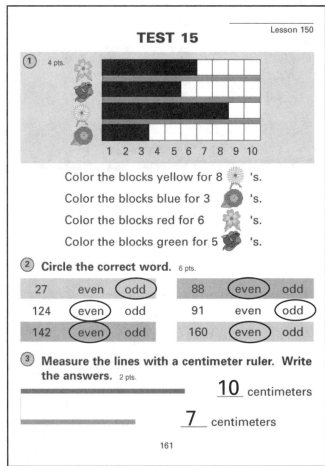

TEST 15

Lesson 150

① 4 pts.

1 2 3 4 5 6 7 8 9 10

Color the blocks yellow for 8 🌼 's.

Color the blocks blue for 3 🌺 's.

Color the blocks red for 6 🌸 's.

Color the blocks green for 5 🌷 's.

② Circle the correct word. 6 pts.

27	even	**odd**		88	**even**	odd
124	**even**	odd		91	even	**odd**
142	**even**	odd		160	**even**	odd

③ Measure the lines with a centimeter ruler. Write the answers. 2 pts.

_10_ centimeters

_7_ centimeters

161

---

④ Add. 12 pts.

14	28	49	46	18	36
+47	+55	+18	+26	+77	+84
61	83	67	72	95	120

42	75	71	96	53	87
+84	+90	+38	+22	+55	+91
126	165	109	118	108	178

⑤ Subtract. 18 pts.

14	12	10	11	13	17
- 9	- 5	- 9	- 9	- 9	- 8
5	7	1	2	4	9

15	16	10	18	12	11
- 7	- 9	- 1	- 9	- 7	- 4
8	7	9	9	5	7

45	76	78	68	69	89
-35	-74	-64	-58	-58	-65
10	2	14	10	11	24

162

42 pts. total

461

DOZEN

① How many cookies are in a dozen? __12__
Circle one dozen in each group.

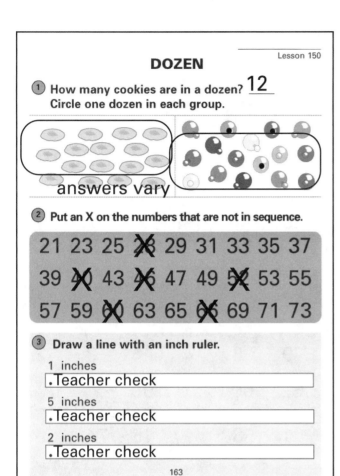

answers vary

② Put an X on the numbers that are not in sequence.

21 23 25 ✗ 29 31 33 35 37

39 ✗ 43 ✗ 47 49 ✗ 53 55

57 59 ✗ 63 65 ✗ 69 71 73

③ Draw a line with an inch ruler.

1 inches
.Teacher check

5 inches
.Teacher check

2 inches
.Teacher check

163

---

④ Write < or > between each set.

15-9 > 5   12-7 < 6   18-9 > 8

16-7 < 10   17-8 > 8   11-3 < 9

⑤ Add.

44	56	54	65	47	79
+27	+46	+28	+19	+48	+22
71	102	82	84	95	101

82	37	72	64	83	91
+27	+91	+45	+83	+46	+45
109	128	117	147	129	136

⑥ Subtract.

10	13	12	15	18	11
- 3	- 7	- 8	- 7	- 9	- 8
7	6	4	8	9	3

93	75	87	84	96	86
-12	-34	-50	-21	-56	-23
81	41	37	63	40	63

164

MONEY

① Circle 68¢ in coins.   answers vary

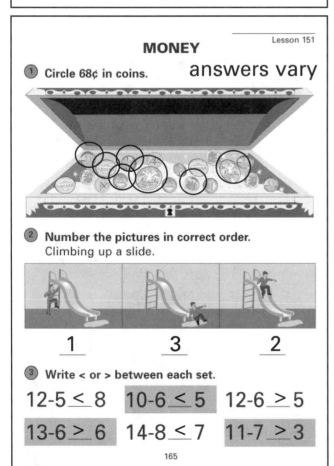

② Number the pictures in correct order.
Climbing up a slide.

1   3   2

③ Write < or > between each set.

12-5 < 8   10-6 < 5   12-6 > 5

13-6 > 6   14-8 < 7   11-7 > 3

165

---

④ Subtract.

764	837	972	683	458
- 150	- 614	- 522	- 473	- 138
614	223	450	210	320

982	746	597	658	939
- 741	- 522	- 183	- 123	- 609
241	224	414	535	330

17	15	14	11	16	14
- 8	- 6	- 7	- 4	- 7	- 9
9	9	7	7	9	5

⑤ Write the missing numbers.

0	1	2	3	4	5	6	7	8	9
10	11	12	13	14	15	16	17	18	19
20	21	22	23	24	25	26	27	28	29
30	31	32	33	34	35	36	37	38	39
40	41	42	43	44	45	46	47	48	49

166

SOLIDS

1 Draw a line to match the solid to its name.

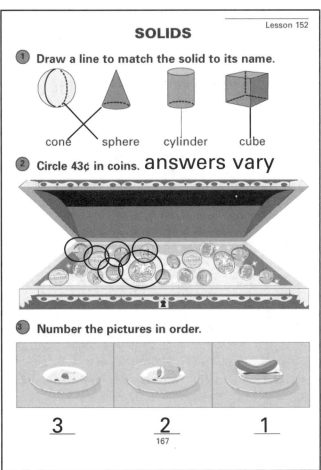

cone   sphere   cylinder   cube

2 Circle 43¢ in coins. answers vary

3 Number the pictures in order.

3   2   1

167

---

4 Write seven even numbers.

___ answers vary ___

5 Add.

21	68	89	29	59	48
+29	+15	+ 9	+31	+28	+49
50	83	98	60	87	97

23	65	92	73	95	84
+82	+50	+61	+65	+83	+41
105	115	153	138	178	125

6 Subtract.

11	14	12	16	10	13
- 7	- 8	- 7	- 9	- 6	- 8
4	6	5	7	4	5

297	548	975	768	759
- 136	- 326	- 274	- 431	- 250
161	222	701	337	509

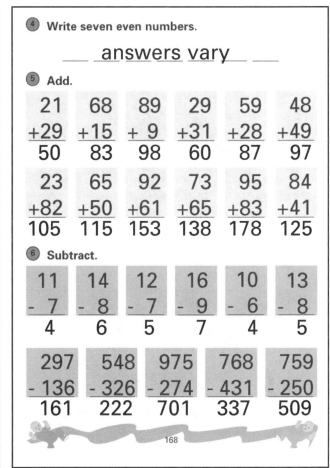

168

SHOW YOUR SKILLS

1 Circle 87¢ in coins. answers vary

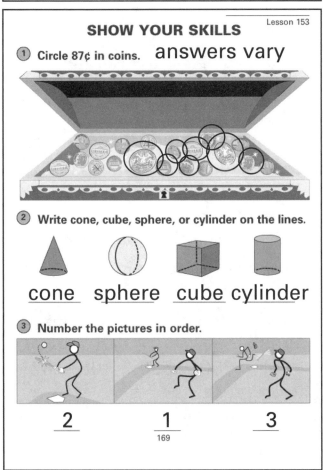

2 Write cone, cube, sphere, or cylinder on the lines.

cone   sphere   cube   cylinder

3 Number the pictures in order.

2   1   3

169

---

4 Write seven odd numbers.

___ answers vary ___

5 Add.

19	38	24	86	65	47
+67	+46	+47	+19	+28	+35
86	84	71	105	93	82

31	95	82	51	27	65
+72	+41	+83	+74	+90	+83
103	136	165	125	117	148

6 Write the missing numbers.

50	51	52	53	54	55	56	57	58	59
60	61	62	63	64	65	66	67	68	69
70	71	72	73	74	75	76	77	78	79
80	81	82	83	84	85	86	87	88	89
90	91	92	93	94	95	96	97	98	99

170

TIME

① Write the correct time.

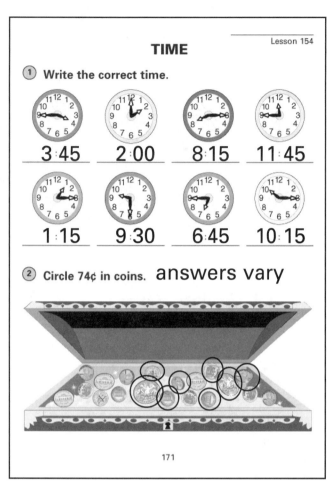

3:45　2:00　8:15　11:45

1:15　9:30　6:45　10:15

② Circle 74¢ in coins.　answers vary

171

---

③ Color the even numbers red. Color the odd numbers blue.

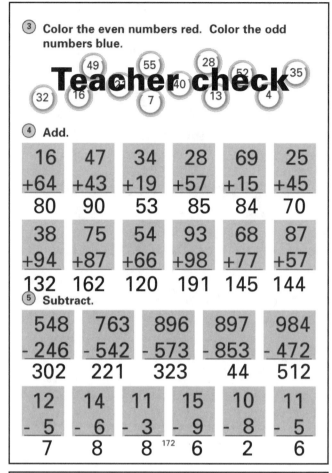

Teacher check

49　55　28　52　35
32　16　61　40　13　4
7

④ Add.

16	47	34	28	69	25
+64	+43	+19	+57	+15	+45
80	90	53	85	84	70

38	75	54	93	68	87
+94	+87	+66	+98	+77	+57
132	162	120	191	145	144

⑤ Subtract.

548	763	896	897	984
- 246	- 542	- 573	- 853	- 472
302	221	323	44	512

12	14	11	15	10	11
- 5	- 6	- 3	- 9	- 8	- 5
7	8	8	6	2	6

172

NUMBER ORDER - ORDINAL NUMBERS

① Draw a line to match the ordinal numbers.

4th　first
6th　fourth
9th　sixth
1st　seventh
7th　ninth

5th　second
2nd　third
10th　fifth
8th　eighth
3rd　tenth

② Draw the short (hour) hand.

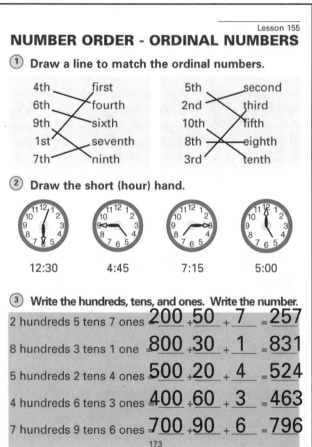

12:30　4:45　7:15　5:00

③ Write the hundreds, tens, and ones. Write the number.

2 hundreds 5 tens 7 ones	200 + 50 + 7 = 257
8 hundreds 3 tens 1 one	800 + 30 + 1 = 831
5 hundreds 2 tens 4 ones	500 + 20 + 4 = 524
4 hundreds 6 tens 3 ones	400 + 60 + 3 = 463
7 hundreds 9 tens 6 ones	700 + 90 + 6 = 796

173

---

④ Add.

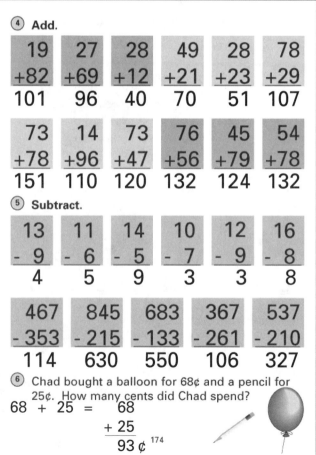

19	27	28	49	28	78
+82	+69	+12	+21	+23	+29
101	96	40	70	51	107

73	14	73	76	45	54
+78	+96	+47	+56	+79	+78
151	110	120	132	124	132

⑤ Subtract.

13	11	14	10	12	16
- 9	- 6	- 5	- 7	- 9	- 8
4	5	9	3	3	8

467	845	683	367	537
- 353	- 215	- 133	- 261	- 210
114	630	550	106	327

⑥ Chad bought a balloon for 68¢ and a pencil for 25¢. How many cents did Chad spend?

68 + 25 =　68
　　　　　+ 25
　　　　　93 ¢　174

464

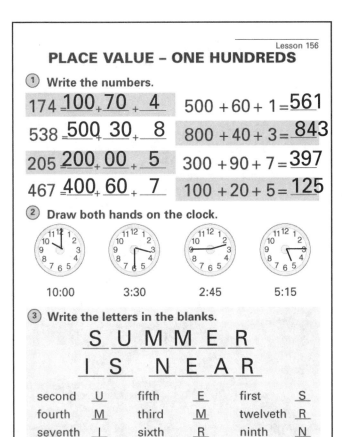

PLACE VALUE – ONE HUNDREDS

Lesson 156

① Write the numbers.

174 = <u>100</u> + <u>70</u> + <u>4</u>   500 + 60 + 1 = <u>561</u>

538 = <u>500</u> + <u>30</u> + <u>8</u>   800 + 40 + 3 = <u>843</u>

205 = <u>200</u> + <u>00</u> + <u>5</u>   300 + 90 + 7 = <u>397</u>

467 = <u>400</u> + <u>60</u> + <u>7</u>   100 + 20 + 5 = <u>125</u>

② Draw both hands on the clock.

10:00   3:30   2:45   5:15

③ Write the letters in the blanks.

S U M M E R

I S   N E A R

second <u>U</u>	fifth <u>E</u>	first <u>S</u>
fourth <u>M</u>	third <u>M</u>	twelveth <u>R</u>
seventh <u>I</u>	sixth <u>R</u>	ninth <u>N</u>
eleventh <u>A</u>	eighth <u>S</u>	tenth <u>E</u>

175

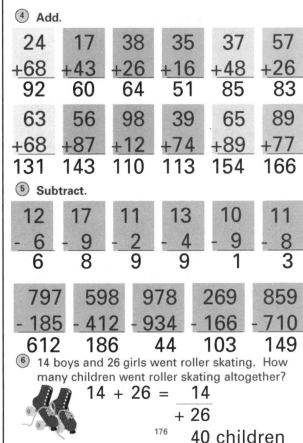

④ Add.

24	17	38	35	37	57
+68	+43	+26	+16	+48	+26
92	60	64	51	85	83

63	56	98	39	65	89
+68	+87	+12	+74	+89	+77
131	143	110	113	154	166

⑤ Subtract.

12	17	11	13	10	11
- 6	- 9	- 2	- 4	- 9	- 8
6	8	9	9	1	3

797	598	978	269	859
- 185	- 412	- 934	- 166	- 710
612	186	44	103	149

⑥ 14 boys and 26 girls went roller skating. How many children went roller skating altogether?

14 + 26 =
$$\begin{array}{r} 14 \\ + 26 \\ \hline \end{array}$$
176   **40 children**

FRACTIONS – ONE HALF

Lesson 157

① Circle $\frac{1}{2}$ of each set.   answers vary

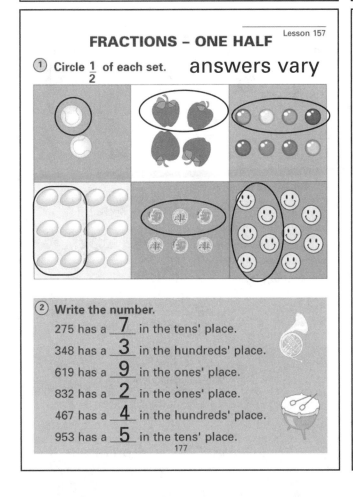

② Write the number.

275 has a <u>7</u> in the tens' place.

348 has a <u>3</u> in the hundreds' place.

619 has a <u>9</u> in the ones' place.

832 has a <u>2</u> in the ones' place.

467 has a <u>4</u> in the hundreds' place.

953 has a <u>5</u> in the tens' place.

177

③ Count the objects in each set. Write the number in the box.

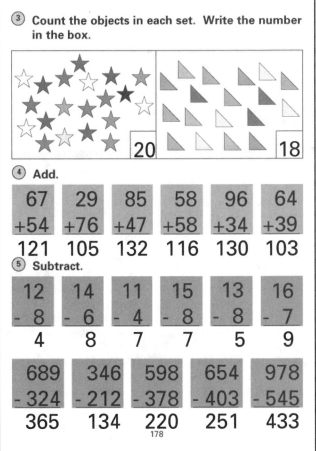

20   18

④ Add.

67	29	85	58	96	64
+54	+76	+47	+58	+34	+39
121	105	132	116	130	103

⑤ Subtract.

12	14	11	15	13	16
- 8	- 6	- 4	- 8	- 8	- 7
4	8	7	7	5	9

689	346	598	654	978
- 324	- 212	- 378	- 403	- 545
365	134	220	251	433

178

465

ESTIMATION

① Write the answers.

Is 1 closer to 0 or 10? 0
Is 6 closer to 0 or 10? 10
Is 3 closer to 0 or 10? 0
Is 8 closer to 0 or 10? 10
Is 7 closer to 0 or 10? 10
Is 2 closer to 0 or 10? 0
Is 9 closer to 0 or 10? 10

② Circle $\frac{1}{2}$ of each set.   answers vary

③ Write the numbers.

one hundred thirty-one 131
one hundred twenty 120
one hundred nineteen 119
one hundred two 102

179

---

④

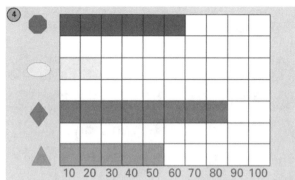

How many ovals are on the bar graph? 20
How many diamonds are on the bar graph? 80
How many octagons are on the bar graph? 60
How many triangles are on the bar graph? 50

⑤ Draw a line to match one half to the other half.

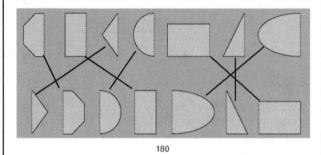

180

NUMBER SEQUENCE

① Write the next three numbers.

12	15	18	21	24	27
10	13	16	19	22	25
8	11	14	17	20	23

② Write the answers.

Is 12 closer to 10 or 20? 10
Is 16 closer to 10 or 20? 20
Is 18 closer to 10 or 20? 20
Is 14 closer to 10 or 20? 10
Is 13 closer to 10 or 20? 10
Is 17 closer to 10 or 20? 20

③ Measure the lines with an inch ruler. Write the answers.

_____ 4 inches

_____ 3 inches

_____ 5 inches

181

---

④ Write = or ≠ between each set.

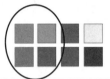 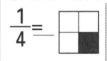

$\frac{1}{4} =$ $\frac{1}{3} \neq$ $\frac{1}{5} =$

 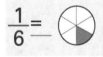

$\frac{1}{6} =$ $\frac{1}{2} \neq$ $\frac{1}{7} \neq$

⑤ Write the numbers.

one hundred fifty-one 151
one hundred nine 109
one hundred seventeen 117
one hundred thirty-eight 138
one hundred ten 110

⑥ Ron read 16 books in June and 23 books in July. How many books did he read in June and July?

16 + 23 =   16
              + 23
            39 books

Amy scored 98 points bowling. Joy scored 92 points. Amy scored how many more points than Joy?

98 - 92 =   98
              - 92
182   6 points

466

TEST 16

① Write the numbers. 12 pts.

265 = <u>200</u> <u>60</u> + <u>5</u>   600 + 20 + 7 = <u>627</u>

183 = <u>100</u> <u>80</u> + <u>3</u>   400 + 50 + 8 = <u>458</u>

549 = <u>500</u> <u>40</u> + <u>9</u>   900 + 30 + 1 = <u>931</u>

② Write the numbers. 3 pts.

367 has a <u>7</u> in the ones' place.

452 has a <u>4</u> in the hundreds' place.

819 has a <u>1</u> in the tens' place.

③ Write < or > between each set. 4 pts.

156 <u><</u> 165   142 <u><</u> 199

137 <u>></u> 131   183 <u><</u> 200

④ Write = or ≠ between each set. 6 pts.

6+4 <u>=</u> 10   7+9 <u>=</u> 16   8+6 <u>≠</u> 13

3+8 <u>≠</u> 12   5+2 <u>≠</u> 9   9+5 <u>=</u> 14

183

⑤ How many eggs are in a dozen? <u>12</u>   1 pt.

⑥ Circle every fourth number after 7. 7 pts.

⑦ 8 9 10 ⑪ 12 13 14 ⑮
16 17 18 ⑲ 20 21 22 ㉓ 24
25 26 ㉗ 28 29 30 ㉛ 32 33

Write the circled numbers on the blanks.

<u>7</u> <u>11</u> <u>15</u> <u>19</u> <u>23</u> <u>27</u> <u>31</u>

⑦ Write the correct time. 4 pts.

<u>7:00</u>   <u>2:45</u>   <u>10:30</u>   <u>5:15</u>

⑧ Write the value of each coin. 8 pts.

= <u>1</u>¢   = <u>5</u>¢

= <u>25</u>¢   = <u>25</u>¢

= <u>5</u>¢   = <u>1</u>¢

= <u>10</u>¢   = <u>10</u>¢

184

---

⑨ Draw a line to match the shape to its name. 7 pts.

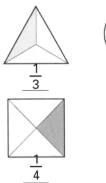

circle
octagon
square
oval
diamond
rectangle
triangle

⑩ Write the fractional part that is shaded. 6 pts.

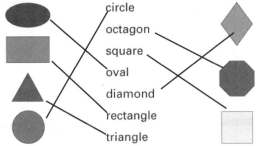

$\frac{1}{3}$ $\frac{1}{6}$ $\frac{1}{5}$

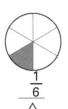 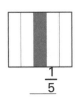 

$\frac{1}{4}$ $\frac{1}{2}$ $\frac{1}{8}$

185

⑪ Add. 12 pts.

25	39	43	14	19	58
+35	+53	+27	+69	+39	+23
60	92	70	83	58	81

37	68	53	42	97	92
+87	+92	+49	+78	+18	+89
124	160	102	120	115	181

⑫ Subtract. 12 pts.

17	15	11	13	16	12
- 8	- 9	- 7	- 6	- 8	- 7
9	6	4	7	8	5

63	98	75	38	79	52
-40	-34	-53	-26	-25	-42
23	64	22	12	54	10

82 pts. Total

186

467

NUMBER ORDER – < AND >

① Write < or > between each set.

18-9 $>$ 8   11-4 $>$ 6   14-8 $<$ 8

12-7 $\leq$ 6   13-5 $\leq$ 9   12-5 $\leq$ 9

16-8 $>$ 7   17-8 $>$ 7   10-4 $>$ 5

② Circle every third number after 5.

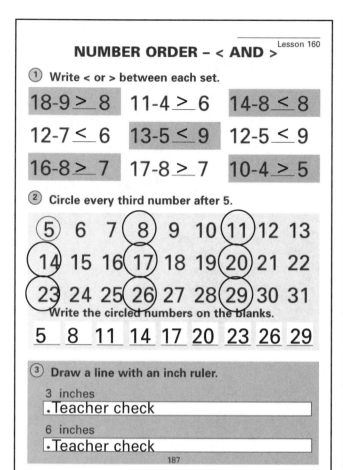

⑤ 6 7 ⑧ 9 10 ⑪ 12 13

⑭ 15 16 ⑰ 18 19 ⑳ 21 22

㉓ 24 25 ㉖ 27 28 ㉙ 30 31

Write the circled numbers on the blanks.

5 8 11 14 17 20 23 26 29

③ Draw a line with an inch ruler.

3 inches
.Teacher check

6 inches
.Teacher check

187

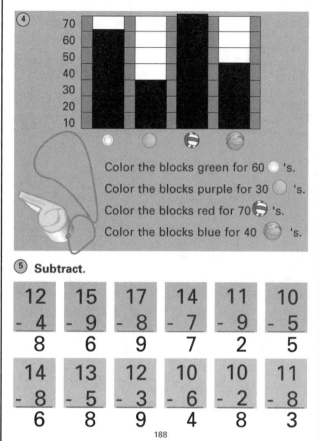

④

Color the blocks green for 60 ◯ 's.

Color the blocks purple for 30 ◯ 's.

Color the blocks red for 70 ◯ 's.

Color the blocks blue for 40 ◯ 's.

⑤ Subtract.

12	15	17	14	11	10
- 4	- 9	- 8	- 7	- 9	- 5
8	6	9	7	2	5

14	13	12	10	10	11
- 8	- 5	- 3	- 6	- 2	- 8
6	8	9	4	8	3

188

468

Worksheets

Reproducible Worksheets
for use with Horizons
Mathematics 1

① Trace the numbers.

0 1 2 3 4 5 6 7 8 9

② Practice writing your numbers.

Circle the first child to get a sailboat. Put an X on the sixth child. Color the pants of the ninth child blue. Then color the rest of the picture.

(1) **Circle the seventh lollipop.**
Put an X on the second lollipop.
Put a box around the fourth lollipop.

(2) **Write in the missing numbers by 10's.**

10 ___ ___ 40 ___ ___ 70

30 ___ 50 ___ ___ 80 ___

20 ___ ___ ___ 60 ___ ___

(3) **Write the numbers in order.**

10 8 7 9
___ ___ ___ ___

4 7 6 5
___ ___ ___ ___

Count the tens and ones. Write the number.

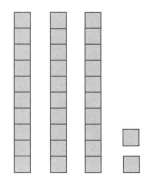
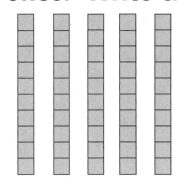
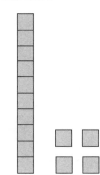

___tens ___ones   ___tens ___ones   ___tens ___ones

_____   _____   _____

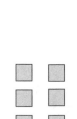
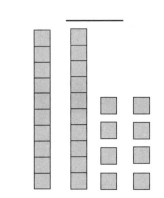
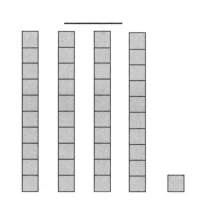

___tens ___ones   ___tens ___ones   ___tens ___ones

_____   _____   _____

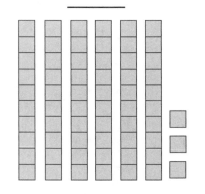
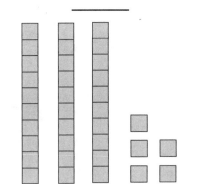
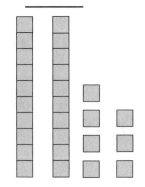

___tens ___ones   ___tens ___ones   ___tens ___ones

_____   _____   _____

474

0	1	2	3	4	5	6	7	8	9
10	11	12	13	14	15	16	17	18	19
20	21	22	23	24	25	26	27	28	29
30	31	32	33	34	35	36	37	38	39
40	41	42	43	44	45	46	47	48	49
50	51	52	53	54	55	56	57	58	59
60	61	62	63	64	65	66	67	68	69
70	71	72	73	74	75	76	77	78	79
80	81	82	83	84	85	86	87	88	89
90	91	92	93	94	95	96	97	98	99

(1)
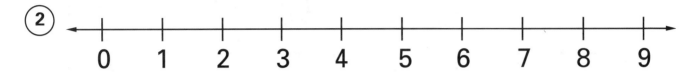

(2)
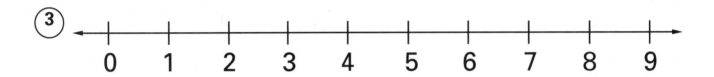

(3)
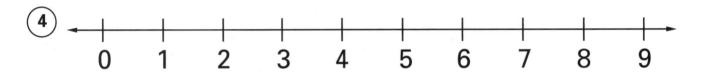

(4)
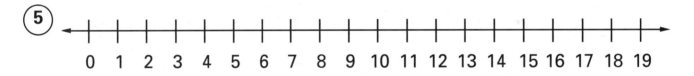

(5)
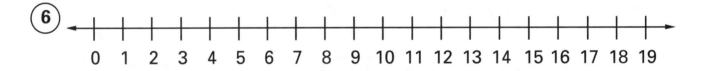

(6)
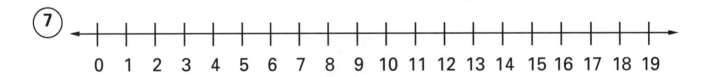

(7)
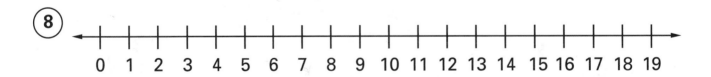

(8)
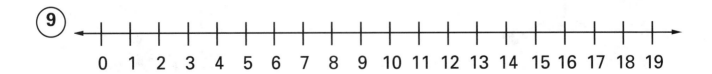

(9)

(1) ____ + ____ = ____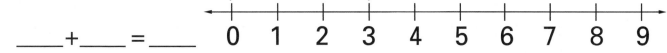

(2) ____ + ____ = ____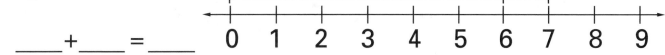

(3) ____ + ____ = ____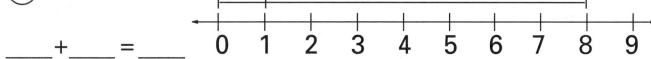

(4) ____ + ____ = ____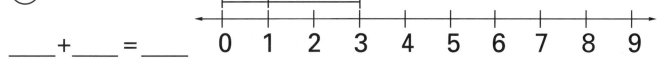

(5) ____ + ____ = ____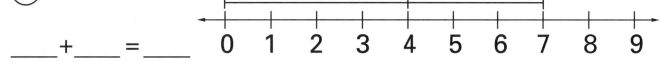

(6) ____ + ____ = ____

(7) ____ + ____ = ____

① **Write the answers.**

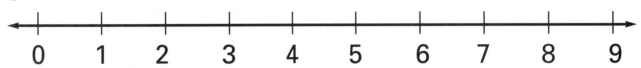

$2 + 1 = \underline{\hspace{1cm}}$ $3 + 4 = \underline{\hspace{1cm}}$ $5 + 3 = \underline{\hspace{1cm}}$

$6 + 2 = \underline{\hspace{1cm}}$ $5 + 1 = \underline{\hspace{1cm}}$ $3 + 6 = \underline{\hspace{1cm}}$

$4 + 5 = \underline{\hspace{1cm}}$ $1 + 4 = \underline{\hspace{1cm}}$ $7 + 2 = \underline{\hspace{1cm}}$

$2 + 4 = \underline{\hspace{1cm}}$ $2 + 6 = \underline{\hspace{1cm}}$ $4 + 1 = \underline{\hspace{1cm}}$

② **Write the answers.**

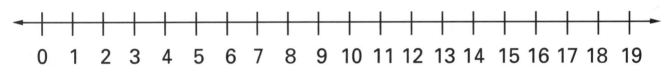

$3 + 9 = \underline{\hspace{1cm}}$ $5 + 6 = \underline{\hspace{1cm}}$ $9 + 8 = \underline{\hspace{1cm}}$

$8 + 5 = \underline{\hspace{1cm}}$ $9 + 3 = \underline{\hspace{1cm}}$ $6 + 8 = \underline{\hspace{1cm}}$

$8 + 2 = \underline{\hspace{1cm}}$ $8 + 7 = \underline{\hspace{1cm}}$ $9 + 1 = \underline{\hspace{1cm}}$

$3 + 7 = \underline{\hspace{1cm}}$ $4 + 9 = \underline{\hspace{1cm}}$ $7 + 6 = \underline{\hspace{1cm}}$

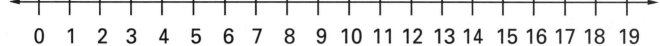

0 1 2 3 4 5 6 7 8 9 10 11 12 13 14 15 16 17 18 19

①
$$1 \atop +4$$
$$2 \atop +7$$
$$3 \atop +6$$
$$4 \atop +0$$
$$5 \atop +1$$
$$2 \atop +9$$

②
$$4 \atop +7$$
$$6 \atop +7$$
$$5 \atop +6$$
$$7 \atop +9$$
$$8 \atop +4$$
$$5 \atop +9$$

③
$$8 \atop +2$$
$$6 \atop +6$$
$$9 \atop +8$$
$$8 \atop +5$$
$$7 \atop +3$$
$$9 \atop +4$$

④
$$0 \atop +5$$
$$1 \atop +9$$
$$5 \atop +5$$
$$1 \atop +3$$
$$9 \atop +5$$
$$6 \atop +4$$

⑤
$$2 \atop +1$$
$$4 \atop +3$$
$$2 \atop +8$$
$$0 \atop +9$$
$$8 \atop +8$$
$$1 \atop +7$$

① Make a tally mark for each object.

② Write the number for each word number.

six ____   four ____   two ____

ten ____   seven ____   nine ____

③ Write < or > between each set.

24 ___ 38   91 ___ 89   60 ___ 54

69 ___ 96   12 ___ 70   74 ___ 49

④ When counting by 2's, write the number that comes between.

16 ___ 20   30 ___ 34   78 ___ 82

54 ___ 58   92 ___ 96   60 ___ 64

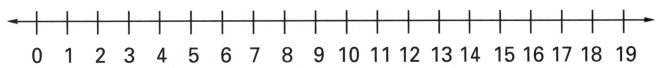

0 1 2 3 4 5 6 7 8 9 10 11 12 13 14 15 16 17 18 19

① $\begin{array}{r} 3 \\ +0 \\ \hline \end{array}$ $\begin{array}{r} 4 \\ +8 \\ \hline \end{array}$ $\begin{array}{r} 8 \\ +7 \\ \hline \end{array}$ $\begin{array}{r} 1 \\ +5 \\ \hline \end{array}$ $\begin{array}{r} 9 \\ +6 \\ \hline \end{array}$ $\begin{array}{r} 1 \\ +7 \\ \hline \end{array}$

② $\begin{array}{r} 7 \\ +7 \\ \hline \end{array}$ $\begin{array}{r} 3 \\ +6 \\ \hline \end{array}$ $\begin{array}{r} 5 \\ +9 \\ \hline \end{array}$ $\begin{array}{r} 3 \\ +1 \\ \hline \end{array}$ $\begin{array}{r} 8 \\ +3 \\ \hline \end{array}$ $\begin{array}{r} 0 \\ +2 \\ \hline \end{array}$

③ $\begin{array}{r} 2 \\ +4 \\ \hline \end{array}$ $\begin{array}{r} 9 \\ +9 \\ \hline \end{array}$ $\begin{array}{r} 0 \\ +6 \\ \hline \end{array}$ $\begin{array}{r} 8 \\ +9 \\ \hline \end{array}$ $\begin{array}{r} 4 \\ +3 \\ \hline \end{array}$ $\begin{array}{r} 8 \\ +1 \\ \hline \end{array}$

④ $\begin{array}{r} 6 \\ +1 \\ \hline \end{array}$ $\begin{array}{r} 7 \\ +0 \\ \hline \end{array}$ $\begin{array}{r} 4 \\ +1 \\ \hline \end{array}$ $\begin{array}{r} 8 \\ +4 \\ \hline \end{array}$ $\begin{array}{r} 7 \\ +3 \\ \hline \end{array}$ $\begin{array}{r} 4 \\ +7 \\ \hline \end{array}$

⑤ $\begin{array}{r} 4 \\ +5 \\ \hline \end{array}$ $\begin{array}{r} 8 \\ +8 \\ \hline \end{array}$ $\begin{array}{r} 9 \\ +2 \\ \hline \end{array}$ $\begin{array}{r} 5 \\ +3 \\ \hline \end{array}$ $\begin{array}{r} 1 \\ +1 \\ \hline \end{array}$ $\begin{array}{r} 6 \\ +0 \\ \hline \end{array}$

CALENDAR

We use a calendar to help us remember the days and months in a year. It helps us know the time of the year.

① **Write the name of today's month and year.**

② **Use a current calendar to write the numbers that stand for the days in the current month.**

③ **Circle today's date on the calendar on this page.**

④ **Put an X on the second Saturday of the month.**

month _____			year _____			
Sunday	**Monday**	**Tuesday**	**Wednesday**	**Thursday**	**Friday**	**Saturday**

Write the missing numbers on the number chart.

0									9
				14					
								38	
		52							
				75					
									99

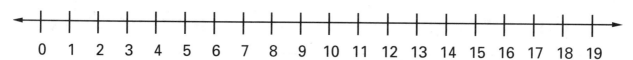

0 1 2 3 4 5 6 7 8 9 10 11 12 13 14 15 16 17 18 19

①
$$\begin{array}{r} 3 \\ +7 \\ \hline \end{array}$$
$$\begin{array}{r} 2 \\ +0 \\ \hline \end{array}$$
$$\begin{array}{r} 2 \\ +9 \\ \hline \end{array}$$
$$\begin{array}{r} 8 \\ +3 \\ \hline \end{array}$$
$$\begin{array}{r} 9 \\ +1 \\ \hline \end{array}$$
$$\begin{array}{r} 3 \\ +8 \\ \hline \end{array}$$

②
$$\begin{array}{r} 5 \\ +8 \\ \hline \end{array}$$
$$\begin{array}{r} 3 \\ +6 \\ \hline \end{array}$$

$$\begin{array}{r} 8 \\ +0 \\ \hline \end{array}$$
$$\begin{array}{r} 4 \\ +9 \\ \hline \end{array}$$

③
$$\begin{array}{r} 6 \\ +4 \\ \hline \end{array}$$
$$\begin{array}{r} 5 \\ +1 \\ \hline \end{array}$$

$$\begin{array}{r} 3 \\ +2 \\ \hline \end{array}$$
$$\begin{array}{r} 5 \\ +6 \\ \hline \end{array}$$

④
$$\begin{array}{r} 4 \\ +0 \\ \hline \end{array}$$
$$\begin{array}{r} 6 \\ +3 \\ \hline \end{array}$$
$$\begin{array}{r} 8 \\ +5 \\ \hline \end{array}$$
$$\begin{array}{r} 7 \\ +3 \\ \hline \end{array}$$
$$\begin{array}{r} 2 \\ +3 \\ \hline \end{array}$$
$$\begin{array}{r} 6 \\ +6 \\ \hline \end{array}$$

⑤
$$\begin{array}{r} 2 \\ +7 \\ \hline \end{array}$$
$$\begin{array}{r} 3 \\ +9 \\ \hline \end{array}$$
$$\begin{array}{r} 1 \\ +9 \\ \hline \end{array}$$
$$\begin{array}{r} 9 \\ +7 \\ \hline \end{array}$$
$$\begin{array}{r} 5 \\ +3 \\ \hline \end{array}$$
$$\begin{array}{r} 7 \\ +5 \\ \hline \end{array}$$

484

Write the answer

(1)

   2 pennies
+ 4 pennies
_____
    pennies

   3 dimes
+ 6 dimes
_____
    dimes

   4 pennies
+ 4 pennies
_____
    pennies

(2)

   2 dimes
+ 8 dimes
_____
    dimes

   3 cents
+ 8 cents
_____
    cents

   4 pennies
+ 8 pennies
_____
    pennies

(3)

   5 ¢
+ 3 ¢
_____
   ¢

   6 dimes
+ 4 dimes
_____
    dimes

   9 dimes
+ 7 dimes
_____
    dimes

   7 ¢
+ 8 ¢
_____
   ¢

(4)

   8 dimes
+ 6 dimes
_____
    dimes

   9 dimes
+ 2 dimes
_____
    dimes

   6 cents
+ 3 cents
_____
    cents

(5)

   1 penny
+ 1 penny
_____
    pennies

   6 dimes
+ 4 dimes
_____
    dimes

   3 ¢
+ 8 ¢
_____
   ¢

   5 ¢
+ 8 ¢
_____
   ¢

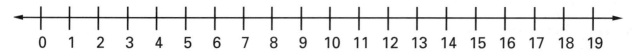

(1) 9   5   8   7   8   4
    + 7   + 5   + 4   + 3   + 2   +6
    ___   ___   ___   ___   ___   ___

(2) 6   9   7   2   8   5
    + 4   + 1   + 4   +8   + 5   + 7
    ___   ___   ___   ___   ___   ___

(3) 9   3   8   6   9   7
    + 8   + 7   + 8   + 7   + 4   + 7
    ___   ___   ___   ___   ___   ___

(4) 4   1   8   9   3   6
    + 7   + 9   + 7   + 2   + 8   + 5
    ___   ___   ___   ___   ___   ___

(5) 5   7   4   6   7   9
    + 8   + 9   + 9   + 8   + 6   + 5
    ___   ___   ___   ___   ___   ___

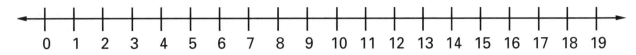

① 2   4   6   7   8   3
 + 9   + 8   + 6   + 5   + 3   +7
 ___   ___   ___   ___   ___   ___

② 9   1   5   3   4   6
 + 9   + 9   + 6   +9   + 6   + 7
 ___   ___   ___   ___   ___   ___

③ 5   6   5   6   4   8
 + 9   + 4   + 7   + 9   + 9   + 6
 ___   ___   ___   ___   ___   ___

④ 7   9   8   8   9   7
 + 8   + 1   + 9   + 4   + 3   + 6
 ___   ___   ___   ___   ___   ___

⑤ 9   9   7   8   7   9
 + 7   + 6   + 3   + 7   + 9   + 4
 ___   ___   ___   ___   ___   ___

Draw a line from the word addition facts to the word number answer.

(1) five   + six   =   sixteen

eight   + five   =   fourteen

nine   + seven =   eleven

six   + eight =   thirteen

nine   + eight =   twelve

seven   + five   =   seventeen

nine   + six   =   eighteen

nine   + nine   =   fifteen

(2) seven + four   =   fifteen

five   + nine   =   eleven

ten   + five   =   sixteen

eight   + eight =   fourteen

four   + eight =   thirteen

eight   + nine   =   twelve

six   + seven =   seventeen

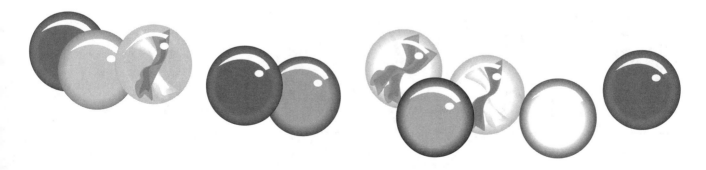

DOT-TO DOT
COUNTING BY SIXES

84
90
78
96
6
12
18
24
72
30
66
60
36
54
42
48

Drill #1

1	1	2	3
+ 0	+ 3	+ 4	+ 6

2	5	2	0
+ 1	+ 3	+ 3	+ 2

1	3	0	1
+ 4	+ 2	+ 4	+ 7

2	3	4	8
+ 5	+ 3	+ 2	+ 0

Drill #2

3	2	1	4
+ 5	+ 6	+ 8	+ 4

5	6	0	4
+ 4	+ 3	+ 6	+ 3

5	4	6	4
+ 2	+ 1	+ 2	+ 0

3	2	4	7
+ 4	+ 7	+ 5	+ 0

Drill #3

1	2	0	3
+ 5	+ 7	+ 7	+ 4

2	0	6	4
+ 2	+ 8	+ 1	+ 3

6	7	8	1
+ 2	+ 2	+ 1	+ 1

6	3	1	4
+ 3	+ 0	+ 2	+ 4

Drill #4

5	1	3	4
+ 0	+ 6	+ 1	+ 5

5	6	3	7
+ 2	+ 0	+ 6	+ 1

2	5	5	0
+ 4	+ 1	+ 4	+ 3

2	9	3	0
+ 3	+ 0	+ 5	+ 5

14¢ 46¢ 28¢ 99¢

56¢ 87¢ 8¢ 35¢ 12¢

Write the answers in the blanks.

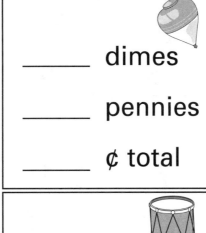		
_____ dime	_____ dimes	_____ dimes
_____ pennies	_____ pennies	_____ pennies
_____ ¢ total	_____ ¢ total	_____ ¢ total
_____ dimes	_____ dimes	_____ dimes
_____ pennies	_____ pennies	_____ pennies
_____ ¢ total	_____ ¢ total	_____ ¢ total
_____ dimes	_____ dime	_____ dimes
_____ pennies	_____ pennies	_____ pennies
_____ ¢ total	_____ ¢ total	_____ ¢ total

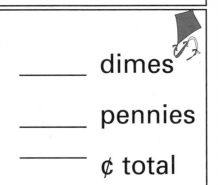
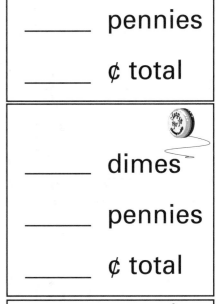

Add the numbers.

$$\left.\begin{array}{c}1\\2\end{array}\right]\ \text{add } 1+2=3 \qquad \left.\begin{array}{c}2\\4\end{array}\right]\ \text{add } 2+4=\underline{}$$

$$\begin{array}{c}+7\\\hline 10\end{array}\ \text{------}\!\!\blacktriangleright\ +7 \qquad +\ 5\ \text{------}\!\!\blacktriangleright\ +5$$

①
$$\begin{array}{c}6\\1\\+2\\\hline\end{array}7 \quad \begin{array}{c}8\\1\\+2\\\hline\end{array} \quad \begin{array}{c}5\\3\\+6\\\hline\end{array} \quad \begin{array}{c}2\\6\\+3\\\hline\end{array} \quad \begin{array}{c}6\\3\\+4\\\hline\end{array} \quad \begin{array}{c}7\\2\\+6\\\hline\end{array}$$

②
$$\begin{array}{c}1\\6\\+2\\\hline\end{array} \quad \begin{array}{c}4\\2\\+7\\\hline\end{array} \quad \begin{array}{c}7\\1\\+5\\\hline\end{array} \quad \begin{array}{c}3\\4\\+5\\\hline\end{array} \quad \begin{array}{c}5\\1\\+4\\\hline\end{array} \quad \begin{array}{c}3\\2\\+6\\\hline\end{array}$$

③
$$\begin{array}{c}3\\1\\+7\\\hline\end{array} \quad \begin{array}{c}5\\2\\+2\\\hline\end{array} \quad \begin{array}{c}8\\1\\+8\\\hline\end{array} \quad \begin{array}{c}4\\5\\+9\\\hline\end{array} \quad \begin{array}{c}6\\2\\+5\\\hline\end{array} \quad \begin{array}{c}5\\3\\+2\\\hline\end{array}$$

Drill #1

5	1	8	6
+ 1	+ 6	+ 0	+ 1

2	3	1	9
+ 7	+ 1	+ 2	+ 0

7	2	6	3
+ 1	+ 3	+ 0	+ 2

4	3	0	4
+ 0	+ 4	+ 2	+ 1

Drill #2

3	3	0	1
+ 2	+ 0	+ 8	+ 1

5	2	2	2
+ 4	+ 1	+ 6	+ 2

2	0	2	6
+ 5	+ 9	+ 3	+ 2

5	1	4	1
+ 3	+ 4	+ 3	+ 0

Drill #3

3	4	5	1
+ 3	+ 5	+ 3	+ 3

4	0	7	2
+ 2	+ 4	+ 2	+ 4

5	1	0	3
+ 2	+ 7	+ 6	+ 6

2	4	5	3
+ 0	+ 3	+ 4	+ 5

Drill #4

4	8	6	3
+ 2	+ 1	+ 3	+ 3

2	1	7	3
+ 6	+ 8	+ 0	+ 4

7	2	4	5
+ 2	+ 5	+ 4	+ 3

1	3	6	4
+ 5	+ 5	+ 2	+ 5

Write the answers to the addition facts. Then color the harvest picture.

7	4	4	8	8	6	10
+ 5	+ 8	+ 7	+ 3	+ 7	+ 9	+ 5

				2	1	6
12	13	23	32	4	3	2
+ 3	+ 6	+ 45	+ 67	+ 7	+ 5	+ 9

Drill #1

3	7	0	2
+ 3	+ 2	+ 4	+ 7

6	8	1	0
+ 2	+ 1	+ 5	+ 7

7	8	4	3
+ 1	+ 0	+ 3	+ 4

2	1	5	5
+ 4	+ 7	+ 2	+ 0

Drill #2

3	3	6	1
+ 3	+ 4	+ 0	+ 6

6	0	5	3
+ 1	+ 3	+ 3	+ 1

4	7	1	4
+ 4	+ 0	+ 2	+ 5

4	2	3	4
+ 1	+ 5	+ 2	+ 0

Drill #3

3	6	2	7
+ 2	+ 3	+ 3	+ 1

9	1	5	2
+ 0	+ 2	+ 1	+ 6

6	8	4	5
+ 1	+ 0	+ 2	+ 4

1	3	1	3
+ 0	+ 3	+ 4	+ 5

Drill #4

6	1	0	2
+ 3	+ 8	+ 9	+ 5

2	4	2	1
+ 2	+ 4	+ 1	+ 3

1	0	3	3
+ 1	+ 8	+ 0	+ 2

3	5	2	2
+ 5	+ 4	+ 0	+ 3

495

Connect the numbers and color the picture.

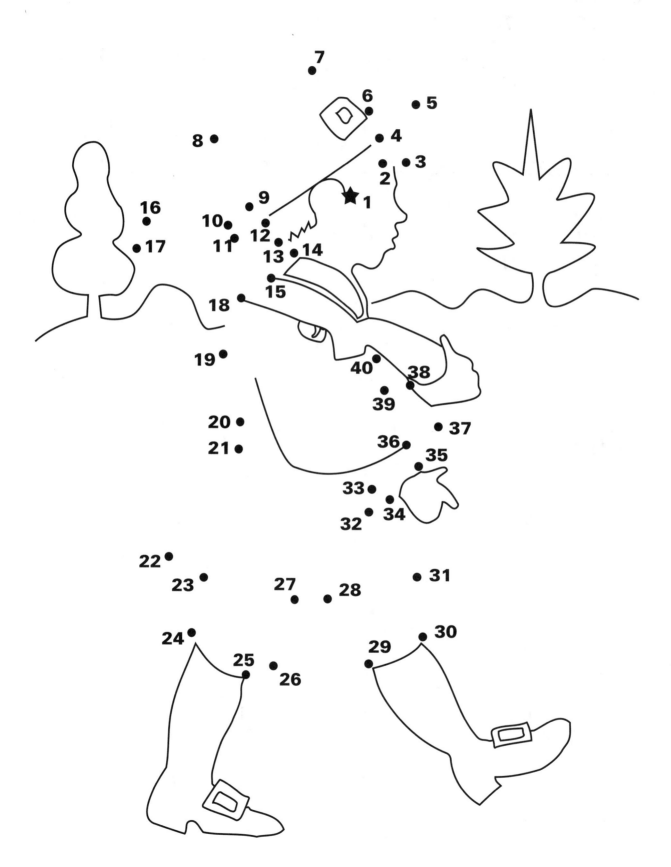

Write the answers in the blanks.

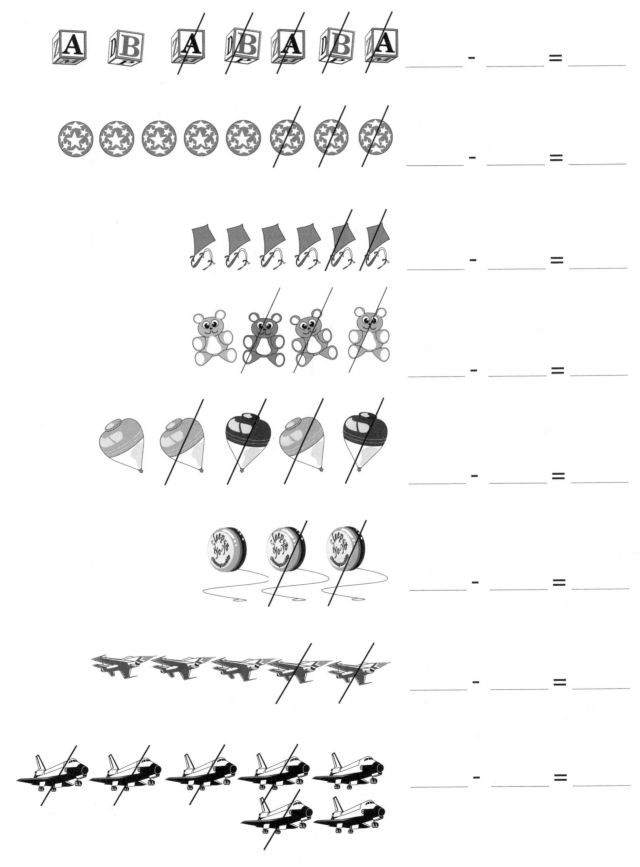

_____ - _____ = _____

_____ - _____ = _____

_____ - _____ = _____

_____ - _____ = _____

_____ - _____ = _____

_____ - _____ = _____

_____ - _____ = _____

_____ - _____ = _____

Drill #1

3	2	1	3
+ 6	+ 3	+ 7	+ 5

2	2	0	4
+ 4	+ 2	+ 4	+ 2

1	5	3	3
+ 3	+ 3	+ 0	+ 3

6	6	0	1
+ 1	+ 2	+ 9	+ 5

Drill #2

8	4	5	6
+ 0	+ 4	+ 1	+ 2

4	7	1	2
+ 3	+ 0	+ 8	+ 6

5	6	0	2
+ 4	+ 3	+ 6	+ 5

5	5	1	7
+ 0	+ 2	+ 3	+ 1

Drill #3

3	4	9	2
+ 4	+ 3	+ 0	+ 1

0	5	8	2
+ 7	+ 4	+ 1	+ 0

2	1	7	0
+ 7	+ 1	+ 2	+ 5

0	3	2	4
+ 4	+ 2	+ 5	+ 1

Drill #4

4	2	1	2
+ 5	+ 7	+ 5	+ 6

3	1	4	5
+ 1	+ 2	+ 4	+ 3

1	6	3	2
+ 6	+ 0	+ 3	+ 2

5	1	2	1
+ 2	+ 4	+ 4	+ 0

MEASURING WITH INCHES

Measure the house using an inch ruler.

1. The house is _____ inches wide.

2. The walls of the house are _____ inches high.

3. The door is _____ inches high.

4. The door is _____ inches wide.

5. The windows are _____ inches wide.

6. Each side of the roof is _____ inches.

7. The doorknob is _____ inches from the ground.

Drill #1

1	5	7	2
+ 8	+ 4	+ 1	+ 3

5	4	8	1
+ 2	+ 4	+ 0	+ 2

0	3	9	6
+ 1	+ 2	+ 0	+ 1

1	6	2	2
+ 4	+ 3	+ 0	+ 5

Drill #2

0	2	3	2
+ 9	+ 1	+ 0	+ 7

5	0	4	0
+ 4	+ 8	+ 5	+ 5

3	2	1	3
+ 2	+ 2	+ 1	+ 5

3	2	1	6
+ 6	+ 4	+ 3	+ 0

Drill #3

6	5	0	5
+ 2	+ 3	+ 6	+ 1

1	0	2	2
+ 7	+ 4	+ 6	+ 4

1	3	4	7
+ 5	+ 3	+ 2	+ 0

0	2	0	3
+ 3	+ 7	+ 7	+ 4

Drill #4

4	5	3	5
+ 3	+ 2	+ 3	+ 0

5	7	8	3
+ 3	+ 2	+ 1	+ 6

2	4	3	4
+ 5	+ 2	+ 5	+ 1

0	1	3	4
+ 2	+ 6	+ 1	+ 5

Help the wise man find his way to the manger. The correct answer to each subtraction problem tells the correct path to take.

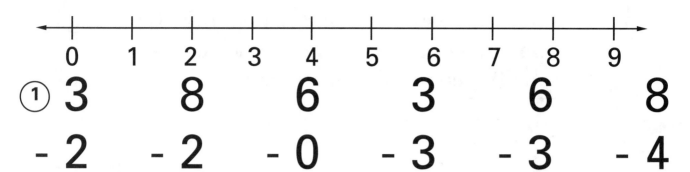

①
$$\begin{array}{r} 3 \\ -\ 2 \\ \hline \end{array}$$
$$\begin{array}{r} 8 \\ -\ 2 \\ \hline \end{array}$$
$$\begin{array}{r} 6 \\ -\ 0 \\ \hline \end{array}$$
$$\begin{array}{r} 3 \\ -\ 3 \\ \hline \end{array}$$
$$\begin{array}{r} 6 \\ -\ 3 \\ \hline \end{array}$$
$$\begin{array}{r} 8 \\ -\ 4 \\ \hline \end{array}$$

②
$$\begin{array}{r} 4 \\ -\ 4 \\ \hline \end{array}$$
$$\begin{array}{r} 7 \\ -\ 2 \\ \hline \end{array}$$
$$\begin{array}{r} 8 \\ -\ 8 \\ \hline \end{array}$$
$$\begin{array}{r} 6 \\ -\ 6 \\ \hline \end{array}$$
$$\begin{array}{r} 3 \\ -\ 0 \\ \hline \end{array}$$
$$\begin{array}{r} 5 \\ -\ 3 \\ \hline \end{array}$$

③
$$\begin{array}{r} 5 \\ -\ 5 \\ \hline \end{array}$$
$$\begin{array}{r} 9 \\ -\ 1 \\ \hline \end{array}$$
$$\begin{array}{r} 5 \\ -\ 0 \\ \hline \end{array}$$
$$\begin{array}{r} 9 \\ -\ 5 \\ \hline \end{array}$$
$$\begin{array}{r} 7 \\ -\ 5 \\ \hline \end{array}$$
$$\begin{array}{r} 4 \\ -\ 2 \\ \hline \end{array}$$

④
$$\begin{array}{r} 6 \\ -\ 5 \\ \hline \end{array}$$
$$\begin{array}{r} 2 \\ -\ 0 \\ \hline \end{array}$$
$$\begin{array}{r} 9 \\ -\ 7 \\ \hline \end{array}$$
$$\begin{array}{r} 7 \\ -\ 7 \\ \hline \end{array}$$
$$\begin{array}{r} 9 \\ -\ 6 \\ \hline \end{array}$$
$$\begin{array}{r} 8 \\ -\ 3 \\ \hline \end{array}$$

⑤
$$\begin{array}{r} 7 \\ -\ 4 \\ \hline \end{array}$$
$$\begin{array}{r} 9 \\ -\ 3 \\ \hline \end{array}$$
$$\begin{array}{r} 8 \\ -\ 6 \\ \hline \end{array}$$
$$\begin{array}{r} 7 \\ -\ 1 \\ \hline \end{array}$$
$$\begin{array}{r} 6 \\ -\ 2 \\ \hline \end{array}$$
$$\begin{array}{r} 9 \\ -\ 0 \\ \hline \end{array}$$

Drill #1

1	4	1	2
+ 4	+ 4	+ 0	+ 6

3	6	5	1
+ 1	+ 0	+ 2	+ 6

4	1	4	3
+ 1	+ 8	+ 3	+ 5

4	1	0	2
+ 0	+ 2	+ 8	+ 1

Drill #2

1	2	5	0
+ 3	+ 2	+ 4	+ 9

2	1	3	3
+ 4	+ 1	+ 6	+ 5

5	3	2	2
+ 1	+ 0	+ 3	+ 0

2	9	8	4
+ 5	+ 0	+ 1	+ 2

Drill #3

0	3	7	5
+ 5	+ 2	+ 2	+ 3

4	0	6	8
+ 5	+ 0	+ 1	+ 0

7	6	1	2
+ 1	+ 3	+ 2	+ 3

3	4	0	6
+ 4	+ 2	+ 4	+ 2

Drill #4

0	3	1	2
+ 7	+ 3	+ 7	+ 7

1	0	2	3
+ 5	+ 4	+ 5	+ 6

5	7	6	4
+ 3	+ 0	+ 3	+ 2

4	3	7	4
+ 5	+ 4	+ 2	+ 3

Write the numbers in the boxes when:

counting by fives:

```
      5
              20          35
 10
              35
 30                   60
```

counting by sevens:

```
      7          28
 7
                  42
 28
            56          77
```

counting by sixes:

```
      6
 6
         30
            48
 48          72
```

counting by eights:

```
 8
            40
         48
                  80
 40
```

Drill #1

1	3	7	9
+ 8	+ 8	+ 6	+ 7

3	2	7	2
+ 1	+ 8	+ 8	+ 4

6	8	0	4
+ 9	+ 8	+ 4	+ 2

0	5	8	6
+ 7	+ 5	+ 1	+ 5

Drill #2

2	6	9	1
+ 6	+ 3	+ 2	+ 3

5	6	9	3
+ 3	+ 7	+ 8	+ 3

9	7	4	2
+ 6	+ 2	+ 6	+ 7

1	6	5	9
+ 6	+ 0	+ 7	+ 1

Drill #3

5	3	7	1
+ 6	+ 6	+ 5	+ 7

4	7	4	8
+ 4	+ 0	+ 9	+ 3

7	9	3	4
+ 9	+ 3	+ 4	+ 3

9	3	4	6
+ 5	+ 9	+ 5	+ 6

Drill #4

5	4	9	5
+ 0	+ 8	+ 9	+ 2

8	1	6	2
+ 5	+ 5	+ 2	+ 9

8	4	2	1
+ 2	+ 7	+ 5	+ 0

3	5	5	8
+ 5	+ 4	+ 8	+ 7

Add and color the picture.

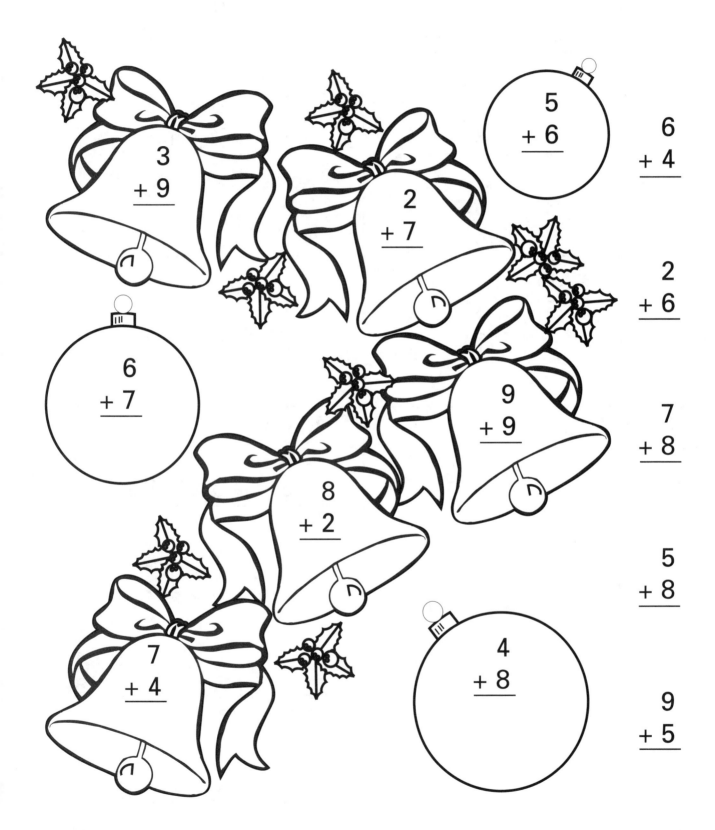

$$
\begin{array}{r} 3 \\ + 9 \\ \hline \end{array}
$$

$$
\begin{array}{r} 5 \\ + 6 \\ \hline \end{array}
$$

$$
\begin{array}{r} 6 \\ + 4 \\ \hline \end{array}
$$

$$
\begin{array}{r} 2 \\ + 7 \\ \hline \end{array}
$$

$$
\begin{array}{r} 2 \\ + 6 \\ \hline \end{array}
$$

$$
\begin{array}{r} 6 \\ + 7 \\ \hline \end{array}
$$

$$
\begin{array}{r} 9 \\ + 9 \\ \hline \end{array}
$$

$$
\begin{array}{r} 7 \\ + 8 \\ \hline \end{array}
$$

$$
\begin{array}{r} 8 \\ + 2 \\ \hline \end{array}
$$

$$
\begin{array}{r} 5 \\ + 8 \\ \hline \end{array}
$$

$$
\begin{array}{r} 7 \\ + 4 \\ \hline \end{array}
$$

$$
\begin{array}{r} 4 \\ + 8 \\ \hline \end{array}
$$

$$
\begin{array}{r} 9 \\ + 5 \\ \hline \end{array}
$$

Al has 5 tomatoes on a plant in his garden. He
picked 1 tomato from the plant. How many
tomatoes were left on the plant? Label the answer.

____ - ____ = ____ _____

There are 4 trumpet players in the band. 2 of them
are sick today. How many trumpet players are left
to play in the band today? Label the answer.

____ - ____ = ____ _____

Hal had 8 cupcakes. He gave 4 to his friends. How
many cupcakes did Hal have left? Label the answer.

____ - ____ = ____ _____

Drill #1

9	7	8	2
+ 4	+ 7	+ 9	+ 5

7	4	6	5
+ 1	+ 0	+ 4	+ 1

1	5	6	2
+ 6	+ 3	+ 7	+ 7

3	9	4	0
+ 3	+ 8	+ 3	+ 5

Drill #2

3	7	5	1
+ 6	+ 5	+ 6	+ 7

3	2	7	8
+ 7	+ 3	+ 3	+ 4

3	0	2	1
+ 0	+ 9	+ 1	+ 4

6	3	4	9
+ 1	+ 2	+ 1	+ 0

Drill #3

8	5	1	6
+ 0	+ 9	+ 2	+ 8

1	1	2	1
+ 1	+ 9	+ 2	+ 0

0	8	7	4
+ 8	+ 2	+ 4	+7

1	7	2	2
+ 8	+ 6	+ 8	+ 4

Drill #4

3	9	3	7
+ 8	+ 7	+ 1	+ 8

6	5	0	6
+ 9	+ 5	+ 4	+ 5

0	8	8	4
+ 7	+ 8	+ 1	+ 2

2	9	6	1
+ 6	+ 2	+ 3	+ 3

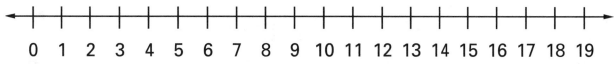

0 1 2 3 4 5 6 7 8 9 10 11 12 13 14 15 16 17 18 19

① 10   11   13   17   12   14
  - 1   - 2   - 5   - 9   - 4   - 5

② 11   15   10   16   14   10
  - 3   - 8   - 2   - 7   - 6   - 3

③ 16   13   10   11   10   12
  - 8   - 4   - 6   - 6   - 4   - 5

④ 10   14   11   13   12   10
  - 5   - 8   - 5   - 8   - 7   - 9

⑤ 11   15   10   17   14   11
  - 8   - 7   - 7   - 8   - 9   - 4

Drill #1

5	9	6	3
+ 3	+ 8	+ 7	+ 3

9	6	4	2
+ 6	+ 0	+ 6	+ 7

1	7	5	3
+ 6	+ 2	+ 7	+ 7

5	7	7	8
+ 6	+ 0	+ 5	+ 3

Drill #2

9	4	8	6
- 1	- 3	- 2	- 4

9	5	7	8
- 3	- 0	- 4	- 5

9	8	6	7
- 8	- 7	- 1	- 2

9	5	8	7
- 6	- 2	- 3	- 5

Drill #3

9	9	4	4
+ 5	+ 3	+ 5	+ 3

5	1	9	2
+ 0	+ 5	+ 9	+ 9

8	4	6	5
+ 5	+ 8	+ 2	+2

4	3	4	1
+ 4	+ 6	+ 9	+ 7

Drill #4

5	1	6	9
- 5	- 1	- 2	- 9

2	8	9	8
- 0	- 6	- 7	- 8

7	3	2	9
- 7	- 1	- 1	- 2

5	9	7	3
- 1	- 4	- 0	- 3

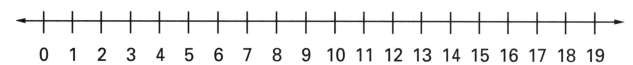

0　1　2　3　4　5　6　7　8　9　10　11　12　13　14　15　16　17　18　19

①
| 10 | 12 | 11 | 15 | 10 | 13 |
| - 1 | - 3 | - 5 | - 9 | - 3 | - 6 |

②
| 12 | 16 | 10 | 13 | 11 | 17 |
| - 7 | - 7 | - 9 | - 4 | - 8 | - 8 |

③
| 10 | 14 | 12 | 11 | 15 | 14 |
| - 5 | - 5 | - 9 | - 2 | - 6 | - 8 |

④
| 10 | 11 | 13 | 10 | 12 | 14 |
| - 7 | - 3 | - 7 | - 2 | - 4 | - 7 |

⑤
| 14 | 13 | 10 | 12 | 11 | 13 |
| - 9 | - 5 | - 6 | - 6 | - 6 | - 9 |

100	101	102	103	104	105	106	107	108	109
110	111	112	113	114	115	116	117	118	119
120	121	122	123	124	125	126	127	128	129
130	131	132	133	134	135	136	137	138	139
140	141	142	143	144	145	146	147	148	149
150	151	152	153	154	155	156	157	158	159
160	161	162	163	164	165	166	167	168	169
170	171	172	173	174	175	176	177	178	179
180	181	182	183	184	185	186	187	188	189
190	191	192	193	194	195	196	197	198	199

Drill #1

7	7	6	5
+ 1	+ 7	+ 4	+ 1

1	9	6	0
+ 3	+ 8	+ 9	+ 4

3	5	4	2
+ 3	+ 3	+ 2	+ 4

3	7	7	1
+ 7	+ 5	+ 3	+ 7

Drill #2

2	3	5	6
- 1	- 3	- 4	- 2

9	4	8	6
- 7	- 2	- 4	- 5

2	4	8	1
- 0	- 3	- 8	- 1

6	7	9	8
- 6	- 3	- 5	- 6

Drill #3

1	5	2	1
+ 1	+ 9	+ 2	+ 0

0	7	7	2
+ 8	+ 6	+ 4	+ 5

1	8	2	4
+ 8	+ 2	+ 8	+7

3	3	2	9
+ 0	+ 2	+ 1	+ 0

Drill #4

6	5	9	8
- 1	- 0	- 8	- 2

9	7	8	6
- 6	- 7	- 5	- 3

8	5	9	7
- 1	- 2	- 3	- 0

6	3	4	5
- 0	- 1	- 4	- 3

Color each area. The shapes below will tell you which color to use.

■ Yellow   ▲ Orange
▲ Blue   ▌ Red
● Purple   ▶ Green
▬ Black

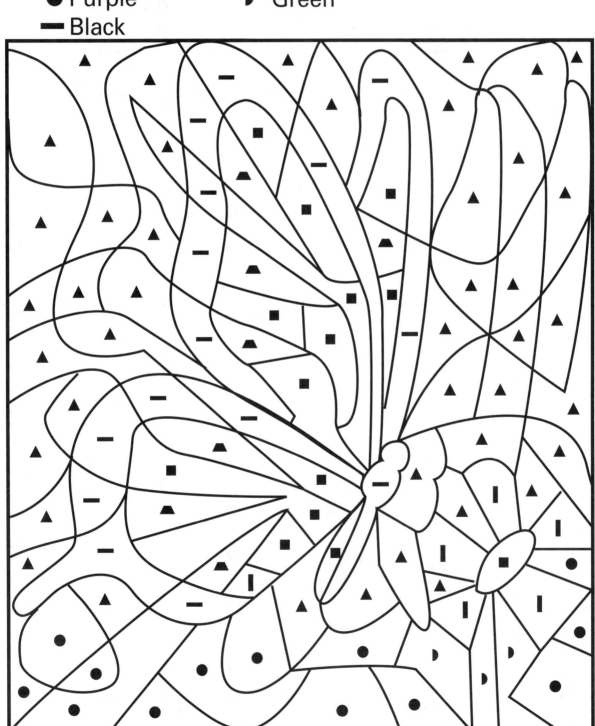

Drill #1

6	9	0	7
+ 9	+ 7	+ 4	+ 8

0	9	8	1
+ 7	+ 2	+ 1	+ 3

2	8	6	4
+ 6	+ 8	+ 3	+ 2

5	6	2	6
+ 3	+ 0	+ 7	+ 7

Drill #2

1	3	6	7
- 1	- 0	- 3	- 7

5	9	8	2
- 1	- 2	- 0	- 2

1	6	8	9
- 0	- 4	- 7	- 9

4	7	5	7
- 1	- 6	- 5	- 1

Drill #3

5	3	7	1
+ 6	+ 6	+ 5	+ 7

4	3	4	6
+ 4	+ 9	+ 9	+ 6

7	9	3	4
+ 9	+ 3	+ 4	+3

9	9	4	3
+ 6	+ 8	+ 6	+ 3

Drill #4

9	8	5	7
- 1	- 3	- 3	- 5

3	4	7	5
- 3	- 0	- 2	- 4

9	7	8	4
- 5	- 4	- 6	- 4

3	9	9	8
- 2	- 0	- 4	- 1

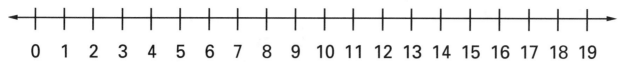

① 18   10   11   13   14   12
   - 9   - 1   - 3   - 4   - 8   - 9
   ___   ___   ___   ___   ___   ___

② 15   10   16   12   11   10
   - 8   - 5   - 9   - 4   - 5   - 2
   ___   ___   ___   ___   ___   ___

③ 12   17   16   10   15   13
   - 6   - 9   - 7   - 6   - 9   - 5
   ___   ___   ___   ___   ___   ___

④ 15   14   10   14   11   14
   - 6   - 6   - 4   - 7   - 2   - 5
   ___   ___   ___   ___   ___   ___

⑤ 10   13   16   11   13   12
   - 3   - 9   - 8   - 6   - 6   - 5
   ___   ___   ___   ___   ___   ___

(1) Donna has 25 stamps. Joan gave 30 more stamps to Donna. How many stamps does Donna have in all?

(2) Tim had 15 problems on his math paper on Monday. He had 12 problems on his math paper on Tuesday. How many problems did Tim have on Monday and Tuesday?

(3) Sarah's father had 13 baseball caps. He gave 4 of them to Joyce's father. How many caps did Sarah's father have left?

_____ - _____ = _____ _____

(4) Jerry had a stack of 16 blocks. 8 of the blocks fell off. How many blocks did Jerry have left in his stack?

_____ - _____ = _____ _____

Drill #1

8	4	2	1
+ 2	+ 7	+ 5	+ 0

3	4	5	5
+ 5	+ 0	+ 8	+ 1

9	7	8	2
+ 4	+ 2	+ 9	+ 7

7	9	6	0
+ 1	+ 8	+ 4	+ 4

Drill #2

2	4	6	3
- 1	- 4	- 2	- 1

7	9	8	5
- 5	- 6	- 3	- 4

9	3	7	8
- 4	- 3	- 2	- 5

9	2	6	8
- 9	- 0	- 3	- 2

Drill #3

3	5	7	2
+ 7	+ 3	+ 3	+ 4

3	0	2	1
+ 0	+ 9	+ 1	+ 4

6	3	4	8
+ 1	+ 2	+ 1	+0

1	7	6	5
+ 3	+ 7	+ 9	+ 4

Drill #4

1	8	4	5
- 0	- 8	- 3	- 2

6	4	2	7
- 5	- 0	- 2	- 1

4	6	8	9
- 2	- 1	- 4	- 5

7	7	8	9
- 4	- 0	- 6	- 3

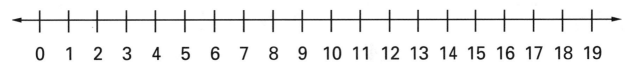

0 1 2 3 4 5 6 7 8 9 10 11 12 13 14 15 16 17 18 19

①
10	12	14	11	13	10
− 3	− 8	− 6	− 4	− 6	− 1

②
13	10	15	13	11	12
− 5	− 5	− 6	− 9	− 6	− 3

③
11	15	14	10	12	18
− 8	− 7	− 8	− 7	− 7	− 9

④
13	11	10	13	12	15
− 7	− 5	− 9	− 4	− 4	− 9

⑤
11	16	12	14	17	10
− 2	− 8	− 6	− 9	− 8	− 4

Drill #1

8	3	5	4
+ 2	+ 6	+ 6	+ 7

8	5	6	6
+ 0	+ 5	+ 8	+ 5

3	1	3	1
+ 8	+ 9	+ 1	+ 2

4	8	8	0
+ 2	+ 1	+ 8	+ 7

Drill #2

5	6	9	7
- 0	- 3	- 2	- 7

9	8	8	5
- 1	- 7	- 0	- 1

9	6	7	3
- 8	- 4	- 5	- 0

4	6	8	7
- 1	- 6	- 2	- 6

Drill #3

2	0	6	6
+ 7	+ 4	+ 0	+ 9

8	4	7	9
+ 3	+ 6	+ 0	+ 6

3	5	9	1
+ 3	+ 7	+ 8	+6

1	6	9	2
+ 3	+ 3	+ 2	+ 6

Drill #4

3	5	6	8
- 2	- 4	- 1	- 4

7	8	6	4
- 3	- 5	- 0	- 2

9	5	8	1
- 7	- 5	- 1	- 1

9	7	9	5
- 0	- 2	- 5	- 3

Write the subtraction facts.

① $3+7=10$ $4+5=9$ $8+3=11$

_____   _____   _____

_____   _____   _____

② $2+6=8$ $4+8=12$ $3+4=7$

_____   _____   _____

_____   _____   _____

③ $5+7=12$ $8+6=14$ $7+8=15$

_____   _____   _____

_____   _____   _____

④ $7+6=13$ $7+9=16$ $5+9=14$

_____   _____   _____

_____   _____   _____

Color the numbers > 150 brown.
Color the numbers < 150 yellow.
Color the nose and blocks.

```
  0  1  2  3  4  5  6  7  8  9  10 11 12 13 14 15 16 17 18 19
```

① 12   15   11   10   14   16
  - 3   - 7   - 5   - 4   - 8   - 9

② 10   15   13   11   17   12
  - 1   - 9   - 6   - 4   - 8   - 5

③ 11   18   12   10   13   15
  - 3   - 9   - 7   - 9   - 4   - 6

④ 10   13   15   11   16   14
  - 7   - 5   - 8   - 2   - 8   - 6

⑤ 11   14   16   12   10   13
  - 6   - 5   - 7   - 4   - 3   - 8

Drill #1

2	7	1	5
+ 9	+ 5	+ 5	+ 6

8	9	4	5
+ 7	+ 9	+ 8	+ 0

3	6	5	8
+ 4	+ 2	+ 4	+ 5

7	3	5	6
+ 9	+ 9	+ 2	+ 6

Drill #2

9	6	8	5
- 4	- 1	- 2	- 2

8	1	9	7
- 3	- 0	- 8	- 4

3	5	4	6
- 2	- 5	- 3	- 4

9	8	7	2
- 6	- 1	- 6	- 2

Drill #3

8	2	8	3
+ 2	+ 5	+ 4	+ 5

4	5	1	9
+ 7	+ 8	+ 0	+ 4

4	8	5	1
+ 0	+ 9	+ 1	+6

7	5	8	9
+ 0	+ 7	+ 3	+ 5

Drill #4

5	9	4	8
- 1	- 3	- 0	- 7

9	2	7	6
- 7	- 1	- 3	- 6

9	6	8	4
- 0	- 2	- 4	- 2

3	6	6	9
- 1	- 0	- 5	- 9

①
82	21	50	31	52
11	35	42	12	31
+ 34	+ 90	+ 86	+ 76	+ 24

②
| 249 | 643 | 154 | 384 | 743 |
| + 540 | + 125 | + 823 | + 405 | + 216 |

③
| 12 | 13 | 2 | 13 | 8 | 12 |
| - 5 | - 5 | - 2 | - 4 | - 4 | - 7 |

④
| 15 | 9 | 10 | 5 | 17 | 7 |
| - 6 | - 7 | - 7 | - 3 | - 8 | - 5 |

⑤
| 6 | 11 | 16 | 9 | 11 | 18 |
| - 1 | - 4 | - 8 | - 3 | - 7 | - 9 |

Drill #1

1	7	5	8
+ 6	+ 0	+ 7	+ 3

9	1	4	2
+ 5	+ 5	+ 5	+ 9

5	4	9	5
+ 0	+ 8	+ 9	+ 2

8	5	6	8
+ 5	+ 4	+ 2	+ 7

Drill #2

1	7	4	8
- 1	- 7	- 1	- 3

6	8	2	7
- 3	- 5	- 0	- 2

8	7	9	5
- 8	- 5	- 1	- 2

3	5	7	9
- 0	- 4	- 1	- 2

Drill #3

6	0	4	1
+ 1	+ 9	+ 1	+ 4

3	2	5	7
+ 6	+ 3	+ 6	+ 3

8	1	6	1
+ 0	+ 9	+ 8	+2

3	5	3	6
+ 8	+ 5	+ 1	+ 5

Drill #4

9	5	6	7
- 5	- 0	- 1	- 6

5	8	9	7
- 3	- 7	- 3	- 0

9	4	7	3
- 6	- 3	- 4	- 1

8	9	8	6
- 0	- 8	- 2	- 2

Color the first, third, fifth, seventh, ninth, eleventh, and thirteenth stripe red.

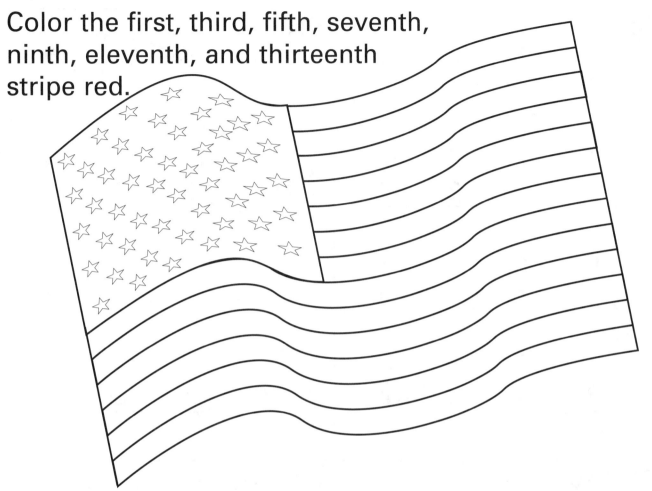

Color the second, fourth, sixth, eighth, tenth, and twelfth stripe white.

Color the box that the stars are in blue.

Color Washington's birth date green on the calendar.

Color Lincoln's birth date red on the calendar.

Feb. 22

Feb. 12

February

Sunday	Monday	Tuesday	Wednesday	Thursday	Friday	Saturday
			1	2	3	4
5	6	7	8	9	10	11
12	13	14	15	16	17	18
19	20	21	22	23	24	25
26	27	28				

527

Drill #1

3	7	4	1
+ 3	+ 5	+ 2	+ 7

1	7	2	2
+ 1	+ 6	+ 2	+ 4

0	5	7	1
+ 8	+ 7	+ 4	+ 0

1	2	2	8
+ 8	+ 3	+ 8	+ 4

Drill #2

10	4	14	12
- 3	- 2	- 5	- 3

13	16	9	15
- 8	- 8	- 5	- 6

12	8	10	11
- 7	- 3	- 7	- 8

17	11	14	6
- 9	- 4	- 8	- 1

Drill #3

2	7	8	3
+ 6	+ 3	+ 8	+ 7

8	9	4	9
+ 5	+ 5	+ 5	+ 8

6	6	4	9
+ 4	+ 2	+ 7	+2

5	7	6	7
+ 5	+ 8	+ 6	+ 2

Drill #4

13	10	12	14
- 4	- 5	- 8	- 6

16	15	11	13
- 9	- 7	- 2	- 7

13	10	12	10
- 5	- 6	- 5	- 9

11	18	11	12
-7	- 9	- 5	- 4

Write the next 3 numbers.

① 18 20 22 ___ ___ ___

② 34 36 38 ___ ___ ___

③ 70 72 74 ___ ___ ___

④ 156 158 160 ___ ___ ___

⑤ 5 7 9 ___ ___ ___

⑥ 49 51 53 ___ ___ ___

⑦ 71 73 75 ___ ___ ___

⑧ 147 149 151 ___ ___ ___

⑨ 2 5 8 ___ ___ ___

⑩ 5 8 11 ___ ___ ___

⑪ 7 10 13 ___ ___ ___

⑫ 9 12 15 ___ ___ ___

Drill #1

8	8	3	4
+ 2	+ 0	+ 8	+ 2

4	6	1	0
+ 7	+ 5	+ 2	+ 7

5	6	3	8
+ 6	+ 8	+ 1	+ 8

3	5	1	8
+ 6	+ 5	+ 9	+ 1

Drill #2

7	10	3	7
- 7	- 2	- 0	- 6

14	8	16	8
- 9	- 0	- 7	- 2

12	8	6	14
- 6	- 7	- 4	- 7

5	12	9	13
- 0	- 9	- 8	- 9

Drill #3

6	9	1	1
+ 9	+ 6	+ 6	+ 3

6	6	9	7
+ 0	+ 3	+ 8	+ 0

0	4	5	9
+ 4	+ 6	+ 7	+ 2

2	8	3	2
+ 7	+ 3	+ 3	+ 6

Drill #4

11	11	15	11
- 3	- 6	- 9	- 9

5	8	10	7
- 4	- 5	- 8	- 2

6	9	10	13
- 1	- 5	- 4	- 6

17	15	1	5
- 8	- 8	- 1	- 3

Cut on the solid lines only. Then fold on the dotted lines and glue to make a cube.

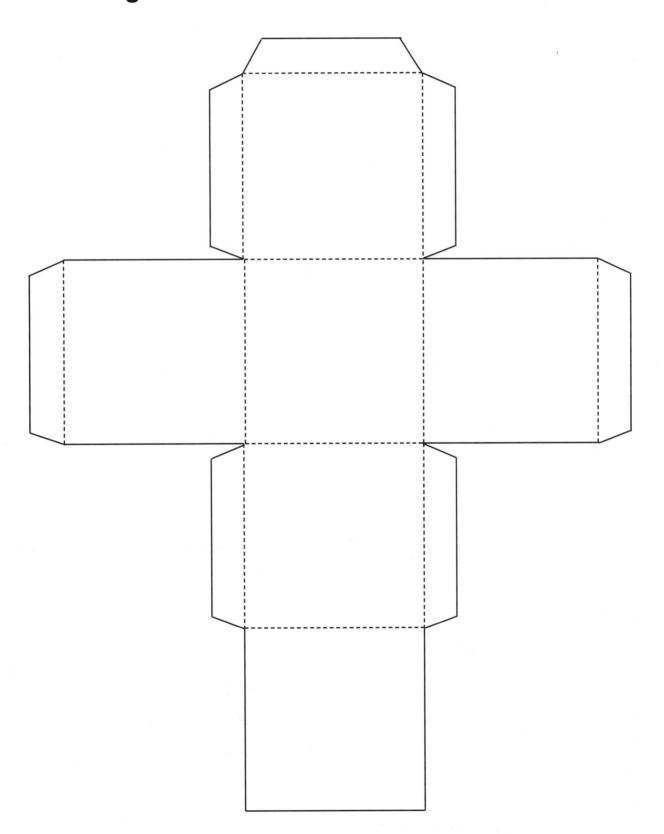

Add the money.

 = _____ ¢

 = _____ ¢

 = _____ ¢

Total _____ ¢

 = _____ ¢

 = _____ ¢

 = _____ ¢

Total _____ ¢

 = _____ ¢

 = _____ ¢

 = _____ ¢

Total _____ ¢

 = _____ ¢

 = _____ ¢

 = _____ ¢

Total _____ ¢

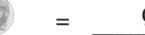 = _____ ¢

 = _____ ¢

 = _____ ¢

Total _____ ¢

 = _____ ¢

 = _____ ¢

 = _____ ¢

Total _____ ¢

Drill #1

5	5	8	6
+ 6	+ 0	+ 5	+ 6

1	4	5	5
+ 5	+ 8	+ 4	+ 2

7	9	6	3
+ 5	+ 9	+ 2	+ 9

2	8	3	7
+ 9	+ 7	+ 4	+ 9

Drill #2

10	7	6	10
- 8	- 4	- 4	- 4

8	9	10	11
- 2	- 8	- 2	- 6

6	13	5	15
- 1	- 6	- 5	- 8

14	12	3	10
- 7	- 6	- 2	- 1

Drill #3

3	9	1	9
+ 5	+ 4	+ 6	+ 5

8	1	5	8
+ 4	+ 0	+ 1	+ 3

2	5	8	5
+ 5	+ 8	+ 9	+7

8	4	4	7
+ 2	+ 7	+ 0	+ 0

Drill #4

8	13	4	11
- 7	- 9	- 2	- 3

17	7	8	14
- 8	- 3	- 4	- 9

11	16	12	6
- 9	- 7	- 9	- 0

5	9	9	15
- 1	- 7	- 0	- 9

Add.

42	75	31	16	43
+ 62	+ 71	+ 81	+ 90	+ 91

68	51	56	32	75
+ 61	+ 64	+ 91	+ 95	+ 94

94	52	45	71	23
+ 20	+ 86	+ 72	+ 58	+ 84

84	96	93	87	64
+ 81	+ 42	+ 76	+ 61	+ 73

67	24	84	45	99
+ 82	+ 95	+ 72	+ 83	+ 60

Drill #1

8	2	5	8
+ 3	+ 9	+ 2	+ 7

5	4	9	6
+ 7	+ 5	+ 9	+ 2

7	1	4	5
+ 0	+ 5	+ 8	+ 4

1	9	5	8
+ 6	+ 5	+ 0	+ 5

Drill #2

10	12	5	9
- 2	- 6	- 2	- 2

4	13	9	11
- 1	- 9	- 1	- 6

16	14	7	14
- 7	- 9	- 5	- 7

1	6	8	17
- 1	- 3	- 8	- 8

Drill #3

6	1	7	1
+ 5	+ 2	+ 3	+ 4

4	5	6	3
+ 1	+ 6	+ 8	+ 1

0	2	1	5
+ 9	+ 3	+ 9	+ 5

6	3	8	3
+ 1	+ 6	+ 0	+ 8

Drill #4

7	10	12	6
- 6	- 4	- 9	- 2

6	8	15	8
- 1	- 7	- 9	- 2

13	11	11	9
- 6	- 9	- 3	- 8

9	15	9	10
- 5	- 8	- 6	- 8

Make Up Your Own Word Problems

(1) **Story:** _____

_____

_____

_____

**Work the problem
from your story.
Label your answer.**

(2) **Story:** _____

_____

_____

**Work the problem
from your story.
Label your answer.**

(3) **Story:** _____

_____

_____

_____

**Work the problem
from your story.
Label your answer.**

① Add.

☐	☐	☐	☐	☐	☐
38	37	67	29	26	58
+ 2	+ 8	+ 3	+ 9	+ 9	+ 5

☐	☐	☐	☐	☐	☐
86	77	18	48	49	16
+ 5	+ 6	+ 9	+ 3	+ 3	+ 4

② Subtract.

69	53	85	67	93	48
-59	-12	-74	-33	-80	-26

27	87	49	95	74	81
-14	-30	-42	-15	-70	-21

Drill #1

1	2	1	8
+ 7	+ 4	+ 0	+ 4

4	2	7	2
+ 2	+ 2	+ 4	+ 8

7	1	5	2
+ 5	+ 1	+ 7	+ 3

3	7	0	1
+ 3	+ 6	+ 8	+ 8

Drill #2

12	15	11	6
- 3	- 6	- 8	- 1

14	9	10	14
- 5	- 5	- 7	- 8

4	16	8	11
- 2	- 8	- 3	- 4

10	13	12	17
- 3	- 8	- 7	- 9

Drill #3

3	9	9	7
+ 7	+ 8	+ 2	+ 2

8	4	4	6
+ 8	+ 5	+ 7	+ 6

7	9	6	7
+ 3	+ 5	+ 2	+8

2	8	6	5
+ 6	+ 5	+ 4	+ 5

Drill #4

14	13	10	12
- 6	- 7	- 9	- 4

12	11	12	11
- 8	- 2	- 5	- 5

10	15	10	18
- 5	- 7	- 6	- 9

13	16	13	11
- 4	- 9	- 5	- 7

Add the money.

  = _____ ¢

 = _____ ¢

 = _____ ¢

 = _____ ¢

 = _____ ¢

 = _____ ¢

Total _____ ¢

Total _____ ¢

  = _____ ¢

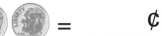 = _____ ¢

 = _____ ¢

 = _____ ¢

 = _____ ¢

     = _____ ¢

  = _____ ¢

 = _____ ¢

Total _____ ¢

Total _____ ¢

  = _____ ¢

 = _____ ¢

  = _____ ¢

 = _____ ¢

   = _____ ¢

  = _____ ¢

Total _____ ¢

Total _____ ¢

Drill #1

4	0	8	8
+ 2	+ 7	+ 8	+ 1

3	1	3	1
+ 8	+ 2	+ 1	+ 9

8	6	6	5
+ 0	+ 5	+ 8	+ 5

8	4	5	3
+ 2	+ 7	+ 6	+ 6

Drill #2

7	10	6	4
- 6	- 1	- 6	- 1

3	7	17	13
- 0	- 5	- 8	- 6

11	16	10	9
- 3	- 7	- 4	- 1

7	15	6	14
- 7	- 9	- 3	- 7

Drill #3

1	7	9	2
+ 3	+ 0	+ 2	+ 6

1	9	5	3
+ 6	+ 8	+ 7	+ 3

9	6	4	8
+ 6	+ 3	+ 6	+3

6	6	0	2
+ 9	+ 0	+ 4	+ 7

Drill #4

9	15	8	11
- 0	- 8	- 1	- 9

12	10	6	1
- 6	- 2	- 0	- 1

7	11	13	14
- 3	- 6	- 9	- 9

10	5	6	12
- 8	- 4	- 1	- 9

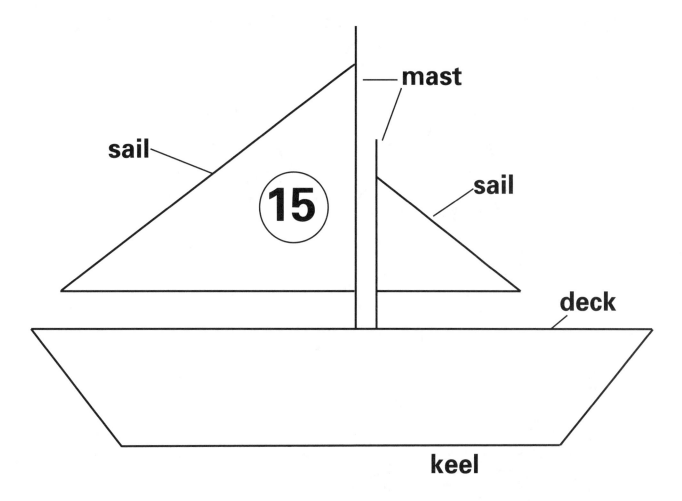

Measure the boat using a centimeter ruler. Color the picture.

1. The keel of the boat is _____ centimeters long.

2. The deck of the boat is _____ centimeters long.

3. The taller mast is _____ centimeters long.

4. The shorter mast is _____ centimeters long.

5. The horizontal length of the large sail is _____ centimeters long.

6. The horizontal length of the small sail is _____ centimeters long.

Connect the numbers starting at 100 and color the picture.

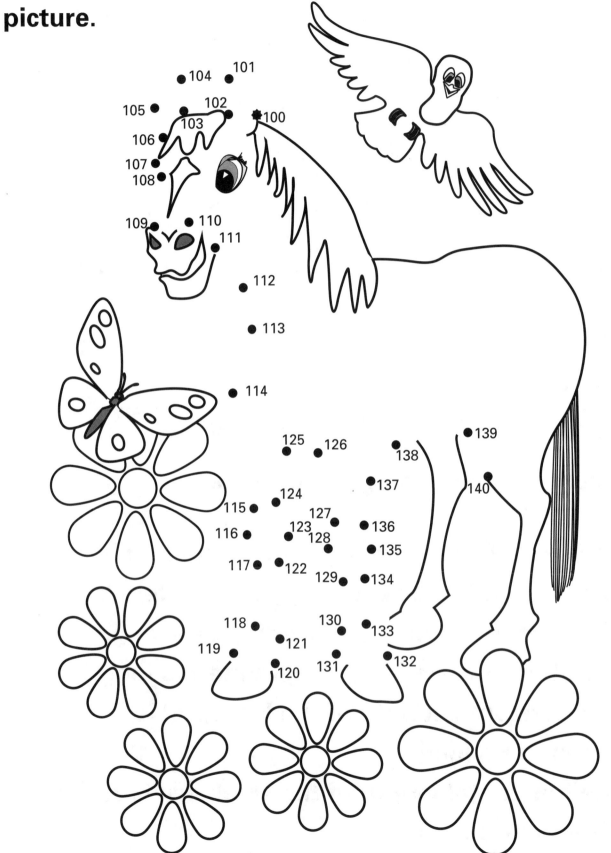

Fill in the missing numbers on the number chart.

100					105				
								118	
			123						
							137		
	142								
			154						
							167		
	172								
						186			
			193						

Drill #1

6	5	9	2
+ 6	+ 4	+ 9	+ 9

8	4	7	7
+ 5	+ 8	+ 5	+ 9

5	1	3	3
+ 0	+ 5	+ 9	+ 4

5	5	6	8
+ 6	+ 2	+ 2	+ 7

Drill #2

10	4	12	10
- 1	- 3	- 6	- 6

6	9	11	9
- 4	- 8	- 6	- 6

12	16	8	3
- 4	- 7	- 1	- 2

5	14	15	8
- 2	- 5	- 8	- 3

Drill #3

9	5	5	8
+ 5	+ 1	+ 8	+ 2

1	1	2	7
+ 6	+ 0	+ 5	+ 0

9	8	5	4
+ 4	+ 4	+ 7	+0

3	8	8	4
+ 5	+ 3	+ 9	+ 7

Drill #4

13	8	10	5
- 9	- 4	- 8	- 1

4	15	11	3
- 2	- 7	- 3	- 1

12	14	16	9
- 8	- 7	- 8	- 7

8	6	6	18
-7	- 5	- 2	- 9

1	1	2	8	5	3	8	7	1
+1	+9	+7	+9	+5	+5	+1	+3	+8

9	7	2	2	4	8	6	5	3
+5	+4	+1	+8	+4	+2	+2	+7	+4

4	6	7	6	2	2	1	8	1
+8	+1	+1	+9	+6	+9	+7	+8	+5

9	4	1	7	4	3	5	9	8
+6	+6	+4	+9	+5	+6	+6	+4	+7

2	8	1	3	4	1	7	6	5
+2	+3	+2	+2	+7	+3	+5	+8	+4

5	9	6	8	7	7	3	1	9
+3	+3	+7	+6	+7	+2	+8	+6	+9

7	4	6	9	5	6	3	9	6
+8	+2	+5	+2	+2	+6	+3	+7	+3

2	5	4	9	3	2	8	5	4
+3	+8	+3	+8	+7	+5	+4	+1	+9

6	8	2	5	3	9	3	4	7
+4	+5	+4	+9	+1	+1	+9	+1	+6

Drill #1

8	9	1	1
+7	+9	+5	+6

5	4	7	8
+2	+5	+0	+5

2	5	5	5
+9	+7	+4	+0

8	6	4	9
+3	+2	+8	+5

Drill #2

9	10	8	14
-2	-4	-5	-7

17	13	7	3
-8	-6	-7	-0

7	11	5	15
-2	-6	-4	-9

8	7	14	10
-3	-1	-9	-2

Drill #3

1	6	2	6
+4	+8	+3	+1

7	5	0	3
+3	+6	+9	+8

1	4	5	8
+2	+1	+5	+0

6	3	1	3
+5	+1	+9	+6

Drill #4

12	7	5	11
-6	-4	-3	-9

3	15	5	10
-1	-8	-0	-8

7	16	12	8
-0	-7	-9	-0

13	11	4	6
-9	-3	-3	-4

Subtract.

18	13	4	7	10	9	12	8	15
- 9	- 6	- 1	- 3	- 1	- 9	- 3	- 1	- 6

15	9	11	8	13	7	10	6	12
- 8	- 8	- 9	- 2	- 7	- 4	- 2	- 5	- 4

13	7	10	6	12	9	15	11	8
- 8	- 5	- 3	- 6	- 5	- 7	- 7	- 8	- 3

11	8	13	9	10	7	15	12	5
- 7	- 4	- 9	- 6	- 4	- 6	- 9	- 6	- 1

5	12	7	16	11	8	14	10	9
- 3	- 7	- 7	- 7	- 6	- 5	- 5	- 5	- 5

14	8	10	6	12	9	11	8	16
- 6	- 6	- 6	- 1	- 8	- 4	- 5	- 7	- 8

6	11	5	16	10	8	14	12	9
- 2	- 4	- 2	- 9	- 7	- 8	- 7	- 9	- 3

10	5	14	9	13	7	17	11	6
- 8	- 4	- 8	- 2	- 4	- 1	- 8	- 3	- 3

13	17	11	7	14	6	10	5	9
- 5	- 9	- 2	- 2	- 9	- 4	- 9	- 5	- 1

Drill #1

1	2	2	8
+ 8	+ 3	+ 8	+ 4

0	5	7	1
+ 8	+ 7	+ 4	+ 0

5	7	6	7
+ 5	+ 8	+ 6	+ 2

6	6	4	9
+ 4	+ 2	+ 7	+ 2

Drill #2

17	11	14	6
- 9	- 4	- 8	- 1

12	8	10	11
- 7	- 3	- 7	- 8

11	18	11	12
- 7	- 9	- 5	- 4

13	10	12	10
- 5	- 6	- 5	- 9

Drill #3

7	1	2	2
+ 6	+ 1	+ 2	+ 4

3	7	4	1
+ 3	+ 5	+ 2	+ 7

8	9	4	9
+ 5	+ 5	+ 5	+8

2	7	8	3
+ 6	+ 3	+ 8	+ 7

Drill #4

13	16	9	15
- 8	- 8	- 5	- 6

10	4	14	12
- 3	- 2	- 5	- 3

16	15	11	13
- 9	- 7	- 2	- 7

13	10	12	14
- 4	- 5	- 8	- 6

①　Write the answer.

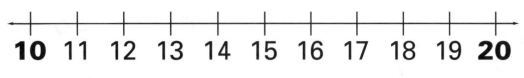

10　11　12　13　14　15　16　17　18　19　20

Is 13 closer to 10 or 20? ____

Is 18 closer to 10 or 20? ____

Is 17 closer to 10 or 20? ____

Is 12 closer to 10 or 20? ____

Is 14 closer to 10 or 20? ____

②　Circle the animal that is about 30 inches tall.

Circle the animal that is about 15 inches long.

③　Measure the line with an inch ruler.
Circle the correct answer.

about **3** or **4** inches

about **4** or **5** inches

about **2** or **3** inches

about **3** or **4** inches

Add.

$$
\begin{array}{r} 12 \\ + 37 \\ \hline \end{array} \qquad
\begin{array}{r} 63 \\ + 30 \\ \hline \end{array} \qquad
\begin{array}{r} 83 \\ + 12 \\ \hline \end{array} \qquad
\begin{array}{r} 46 \\ + 32 \\ \hline \end{array} \qquad
\begin{array}{r} 42 \\ + 51 \\ \hline \end{array} \qquad
\begin{array}{r} 21 \\ + 56 \\ \hline \end{array}
$$

$$
\begin{array}{r} 51 \\ + 57 \\ \hline \end{array} \qquad
\begin{array}{r} 32 \\ + 76 \\ \hline \end{array} \qquad
\begin{array}{r} 95 \\ + 12 \\ \hline \end{array} \qquad
\begin{array}{r} 57 \\ + 62 \\ \hline \end{array} \qquad
\begin{array}{r} 73 \\ + 80 \\ \hline \end{array} \qquad
\begin{array}{r} 93 \\ + 56 \\ \hline \end{array}
$$

$$
\begin{array}{r} 38 \\ + 54 \\ \hline \end{array} \qquad
\begin{array}{r} 27 \\ + 27 \\ \hline \end{array} \qquad
\begin{array}{r} 36 \\ + 48 \\ \hline \end{array} \qquad
\begin{array}{r} 15 \\ + 58 \\ \hline \end{array} \qquad
\begin{array}{r} 24 \\ + 47 \\ \hline \end{array} \qquad
\begin{array}{r} 49 \\ + 48 \\ \hline \end{array}
$$

$$
\begin{array}{r} 78 \\ + 99 \\ \hline \end{array} \qquad
\begin{array}{r} 56 \\ + 74 \\ \hline \end{array} \qquad
\begin{array}{r} 68 \\ + 62 \\ \hline \end{array} \qquad
\begin{array}{r} 82 \\ + 69 \\ \hline \end{array} \qquad
\begin{array}{r} 63 \\ + 89 \\ \hline \end{array} \qquad
\begin{array}{r} 89 \\ + 34 \\ \hline \end{array}
$$

$$
\begin{array}{r} 28 \\ + 34 \\ \hline \end{array} \qquad
\begin{array}{r} 76 \\ + 55 \\ \hline \end{array} \qquad
\begin{array}{r} 64 \\ + 23 \\ \hline \end{array} \qquad
\begin{array}{r} 79 \\ + 30 \\ \hline \end{array} \qquad
\begin{array}{r} 28 \\ + 6 \\ \hline \end{array} \qquad
\begin{array}{r} 50 \\ + 74 \\ \hline \end{array}
$$

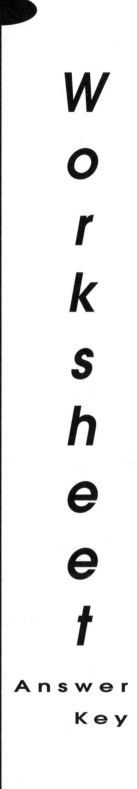

Worksheet

Answer
Key

(1) **Trace the numbers.**

0 1 2 3 4 5 6 7 8 9

(2) **Practice writing your numbers.**

Circle the first child to get a sailboat. Put an X on the sixth child. Color the pants of the ninth child blue. Then color the rest of the picture.

This child's pants should be colored blue.

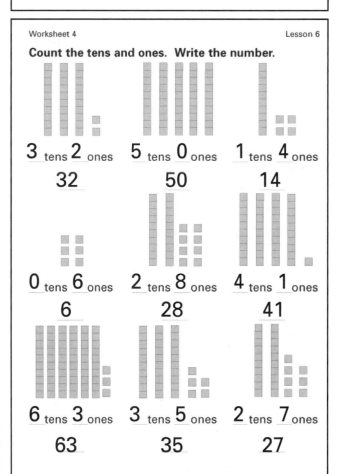

---

(1) **Circle the seventh lollipop.**
Put an X on the second lollipop.
Put a box around the fourth lollipop.

(2) **Write in the missing numbers by 10's.**

10   20   30   40   50   60   70

30   40   50   60   70   80   90

20   30   40   50   60   70   90

(3) **Write the numbers in order.**

10 8 7 9	4 7 6 5
7 8 9 10	4 5 6 7

Count the tens and ones. Write the number.

3 tens 2 ones   5 tens 0 ones   1 tens 4 ones

32   50   14

0 tens 6 ones   2 tens 8 ones   4 tens 1 ones

6   28   41

6 tens 3 ones   3 tens 5 ones   2 tens 7 ones

63   35   27

0	1	2	3	4	5	6	7	8	9
10	11	12	13	14	15	16	17	18	19
20	21	22	23	24	25	26	27	28	29
30	31	32	33	34	35	36	37	38	39
40	41	42	43	44	45	46	47	48	49
50	51	52	53	54	55	56	57	58	59
60	61	62	63	64	65	66	67	68	69
70	71	72	73	74	75	76	77	78	79
80	81	82	83	84	85	86	87	88	89
90	91	92	93	94	95	96	97	98	99

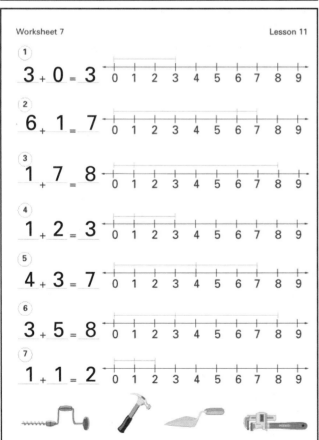

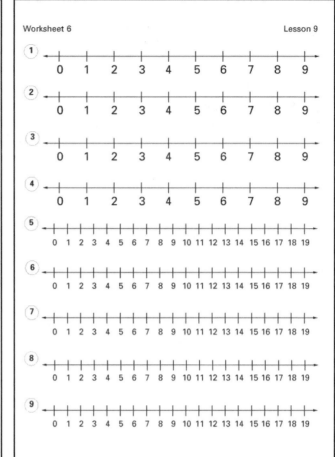

(1) 0 1 2 3 4 5 6 7 8 9

(2) 0 1 2 3 4 5 6 7 8 9

(3) 0 1 2 3 4 5 6 7 8 9

(4) 0 1 2 3 4 5 6 7 8 9

(5) 0 1 2 3 4 5 6 7 8 9 10 11 12 13 14 15 16 17 18 19

(6) 0 1 2 3 4 5 6 7 8 9 10 11 12 13 14 15 16 17 18 19

(7) 0 1 2 3 4 5 6 7 8 9 10 11 12 13 14 15 16 17 18 19

(8) 0 1 2 3 4 5 6 7 8 9 10 11 12 13 14 15 16 17 18 19

(9) 0 1 2 3 4 5 6 7 8 9 10 11 12 13 14 15 16 17 18 19

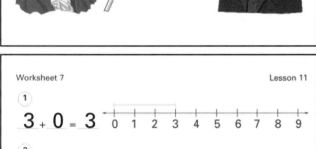

(1) $3 + 0 = 3$　0 1 2 3 4 5 6 7 8 9

(2) $6 + 1 = 7$　0 1 2 3 4 5 6 7 8 9

(3) $1 + 7 = 8$　0 1 2 3 4 5 6 7 8 9

(4) $1 + 2 = 3$　0 1 2 3 4 5 6 7 8 9

(5) $4 + 3 = 7$　0 1 2 3 4 5 6 7 8 9

(6) $3 + 5 = 8$　0 1 2 3 4 5 6 7 8 9

(7) $1 + 1 = 2$　0 1 2 3 4 5 6 7 8 9

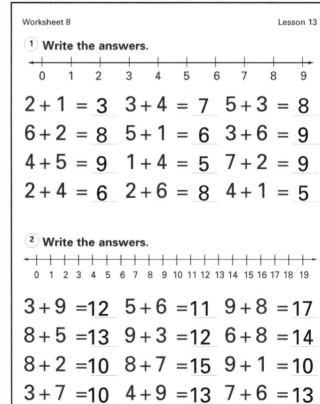

(1) **Write the answers.**

0 1 2 3 4 5 6 7 8 9

$2 + 1 = \underline{3}$　$3 + 4 = \underline{7}$　$5 + 3 = \underline{8}$
$6 + 2 = \underline{8}$　$5 + 1 = \underline{6}$　$3 + 6 = \underline{9}$
$4 + 5 = \underline{9}$　$1 + 4 = \underline{5}$　$7 + 2 = \underline{9}$
$2 + 4 = \underline{6}$　$2 + 6 = \underline{8}$　$4 + 1 = \underline{5}$

(2) **Write the answers.**

0 1 2 3 4 5 6 7 8 9 10 11 12 13 14 15 16 17 18 19

$3 + 9 = \underline{12}$　$5 + 6 = \underline{11}$　$9 + 8 = \underline{17}$
$8 + 5 = \underline{13}$　$9 + 3 = \underline{12}$　$6 + 8 = \underline{14}$
$8 + 2 = \underline{10}$　$8 + 7 = \underline{15}$　$9 + 1 = \underline{10}$
$3 + 7 = \underline{10}$　$4 + 9 = \underline{13}$　$7 + 6 = \underline{13}$

Number line: 0 1 2 3 4 5 6 7 8 9 10 11 12 13 14 15 16 17 18 19

(1)	1	2	3	4	5	2
	+4	+7	+6	+0	+1	+9
	5	9	9	4	6	11
(2)	4	6	5	7	8	5
	+7	+7	+6	+9	+4	+9
	11	13	11	16	12	14
(3)	8	6	9	8	7	9
	+2	+6	+8	+5	+3	+4
	10	12	17	13	10	13
(4)	0	1	5	1	9	6
	+5	+9	+5	+3	+5	+4
	5	10	10	4	14	10
(5)	2	4	2	0	8	1
	+1	+3	+8	+9	+8	+7
	3	7	10	9	16	8

(1) **Make a tally mark for each object.**

(balloons)	(objects)	(drums)
LΉ III	LΉ LΉ	IIII

(2) **Write the number for each word number.**

six **6**   four **4**   two **2**

ten **10**   seven **7**   nine **9**

(3) **Write < or > between each set.**

24 **<** 38   91 **>** 89   60 **>** 54

69 **<** 96   12 **<** 70   74 **>** 49

(4) **When counting by 2's, write the number that comes between.**

16 **18** 20   30 **32** 34   78 **80** 82

54 **56** 58   92 **94** 96   60 **62** 64

Number line: 0 1 2 3 4 5 6 7 8 9 10 11 12 13 14 15 16 17 18 19

(1)	3	4	8	1	9	1
	+0	+8	+7	+5	+6	+7
	3	12	15	6	15	8
(2)	7	3	5	3	8	0
	+7	+6	+9	+1	+3	+2
	14	9	14	4	11	2
(3)	2	9	0	8	4	8
	+4	+9	+6	+9	+3	+1
	6	18	6	17	7	9
(4)	6	7	4	8	7	4
	+1	+0	+1	+4	+3	+7
	7	7	5	12	10	11
(5)	4	8	9	5	1	6
	+5	+8	+2	+3	+1	+0
	9	16	11	8	2	6

CALENDAR

We use a calendar to help us remember the days and months in a year. It helps us know the time of the year.

(1) Write the name of today's month and year.

(2) Use a current calendar to write the numbers that stand for the days in the current month.

(3) Circle today's date on the calendar on this page.

(4) Put an X on the second Saturday of the month.

month				year		
Sunday	Monday	Tuesday	Wednesday	Thursday	Friday	Saturday

Teacher check using the current month's calendar.

Write the missing numbers on the number chart.

0	1	2	3	4	5	6	7	8	9
10	11	12	13	14	15	16	17	18	19
20	21	22	23	24	25	26	27	28	29
30	31	32	33	34	35	36	37	38	39
40	41	42	43	44	45	46	47	48	49
50	51	52	53	54	55	56	57	58	59
60	61	62	63	64	65	66	67	68	69
70	71	72	73	74	75	76	77	78	79
80	81	82	83	84	85	86	87	88	89
90	91	92	93	94	95	96	97	98	99

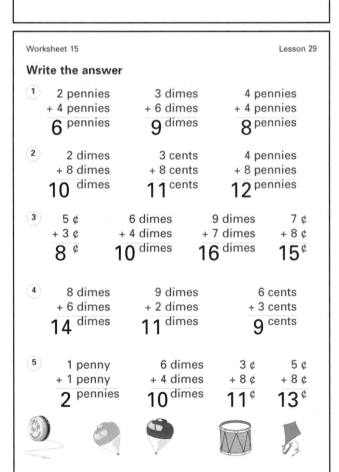

---

0 1 2 3 4 5 6 7 8 9 10 11 12 13 14 15 16 17 18 19

1.
$$3 + 7 = 10 \quad 2 + 0 = 2 \quad 2 + 9 = 11 \quad 8 + 3 = 11 \quad 9 + 1 = 10 \quad 3 + 8 = 11$$

2.
$$5 + 8 = 13 \quad 3 + 6 = 9 \qquad\qquad 8 + 0 = 8 \quad 4 + 9 = 13$$

3.
$$6 + 4 = 10 \quad 5 + 1 = 6 \qquad\qquad 3 + 2 = 5 \quad 5 + 6 = 11$$

4.
$$4 + 0 = 4 \quad 6 + 3 = 9 \quad 8 + 5 = 13 \quad 7 + 3 = 10 \quad 2 + 3 = 5 \quad 6 + 6 = 12$$

5.
$$2 + 7 = 9 \quad 3 + 9 = 12 \quad 1 + 9 = 10 \quad 9 + 7 = 16 \quad 5 + 3 = 8 \quad 7 + 5 = 12$$

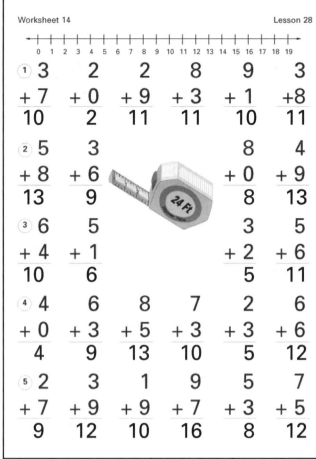

Write the answer

1.
2 pennies + 4 pennies = 6 pennies   3 dimes + 6 dimes = 9 dimes   4 pennies + 4 pennies = 8 pennies

2.
2 dimes + 8 dimes = 10 dimes   3 cents + 8 cents = 11 cents   4 pennies + 8 pennies = 12 pennies

3.
5 ¢ + 3 ¢ = 8 ¢   6 dimes + 4 dimes = 10 dimes   9 dimes + 7 dimes = 16 dimes   7 ¢ + 8 ¢ = 15 ¢

4.
8 dimes + 6 dimes = 14 dimes   9 dimes + 2 dimes = 11 dimes   6 cents + 3 cents = 9 cents

5.
1 penny + 1 penny = 2 pennies   6 dimes + 4 dimes = 10 dimes   3 ¢ + 8 ¢ = 11 ¢   5 ¢ + 8 ¢ = 13 ¢

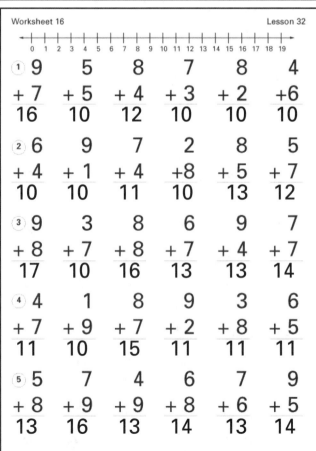

---

0 1 2 3 4 5 6 7 8 9 10 11 12 13 14 15 16 17 18 19

1.
$$9 + 7 = 16 \quad 5 + 5 = 10 \quad 8 + 4 = 12 \quad 7 + 3 = 10 \quad 8 + 2 = 10 \quad 4 + 6 = 10$$

2.
$$6 + 4 = 10 \quad 9 + 1 = 10 \quad 7 + 4 = 11 \quad 2 + 8 = 10 \quad 8 + 5 = 13 \quad 5 + 7 = 12$$

3.
$$9 + 8 = 17 \quad 3 + 7 = 10 \quad 8 + 8 = 16 \quad 6 + 7 = 13 \quad 9 + 4 = 13 \quad 7 + 7 = 14$$

4.
$$4 + 7 = 11 \quad 1 + 9 = 10 \quad 8 + 7 = 15 \quad 9 + 2 = 11 \quad 3 + 8 = 11 \quad 6 + 5 = 11$$

5.
$$5 + 8 = 13 \quad 7 + 9 = 16 \quad 4 + 9 = 13 \quad 6 + 8 = 14 \quad 7 + 6 = 13 \quad 9 + 5 = 14$$

| 0 1 2 3 4 5 6 7 8 9 10 11 12 13 14 15 16 17 18 19 |

① 2   4   6   7   8   3
+9   +8   +6   +5   +3   +7
11   12   12   12   11   10

② 9   1   5   3   4   6
+9   +9   +6   +9   +6   +7
18   10   11   12   10   13

③ 5   6   5   6   4   8
+9   +4   +7   +9   +9   +6
14   10   12   15   13   14

④ 7   9   8   8   9   7
+8   +1   +9   +4   +3   +6
15   10   17   12   12   13

⑤ 9   9   7   8   7   9
+7   +6   +3   +7   +9   +4
16   15   10   15   16   13

Draw a line from the word addition facts to the word number answer.

① five   + six   =   sixteen
   eight + five =   fourteen
   nine   + seven =   eleven
   six   + eight =   thirteen
   nine   + eight =   twelve
   seven + five =   seventeen
   nine   + six   =   eighteen
   nine   + nine =   fifteen

② seven + four =   fifteen
   five   + nine =   eleven
   ten   + five =   sixteen
   eight + eight =   fourteen
   four   + eight =   thirteen
   eight + nine =   twelve
   six   + seven =   seventeen

DOT-TO DOT
COUNTING BY SIXES

Drill #1

1	1	2	3
+ 0	+ 3	+ 4	+ 6

1	4	6	9
2	5	2	0
+ 1	+ 3	+ 3	+ 2

3	8	5	2
1	3	0	1
+ 4	+ 2	+ 4	+ 7

5	5	4	8
2	3	4	8
+ 5	+ 3	+ 2	+ 0
7	6	6	8

Drill #2

3	2	1	4
+ 5	+ 6	+ 8	+ 4

8	8	9	8
5	6	0	4
+ 4	+ 3	+ 6	+ 3

9	9	6	7
5	4	6	4
+ 2	+ 1	+ 2	+ 0

7	5	8	4
3	2	4	7
+ 4	+ 7	+ 5	+ 0
7	9	9	7

Drill #3

1	2	0	3
+ 5	+ 7	+ 7	+ 4

6	9	7	7
2	0	6	4
+ 2	+ 8	+ 1	+ 3

4	8	7	7
6	7	8	1
+ 2	+ 2	+ 1	+ 1

8	9	9	2
6	3	1	4
+ 3	+ 0	+ 2	+ 4
9	3	3	8

Drill #4

5	1	3	4
+ 0	+ 6	+ 1	+ 5

5	7	4	9
5	6	3	7
+ 2	+ 0	+ 6	+ 1

7	6	9	8
2	5	5	0
+ 4	+ 1	+ 4	+ 3

6	6	9	3
2	9	3	0
+ 3	+ 0	+ 5	+ 5
5	9	8	5

Write the answers in the blanks.

1 dime	5 dimes	9 dimes
4 pennies	6 pennies	9 pennies
14 ¢ total	56 ¢ total	99 ¢ total
4 dimes	8 dimes	2 dimes
6 pennies	7 pennies	8 pennies
46 ¢ total	87 ¢ total	28 ¢ total
3 dimes	1 dime	0 dimes
5 pennies	2 pennies	8 pennies
35 ¢ total	12 ¢ total	8 ¢ total

Add the numbers.

$\begin{array}{c}1\\2\\+7\\\hline 10\end{array}$ add 1+2=3 ------► $\begin{array}{c}3\\+7\\\hline 10\end{array}$ $\begin{array}{c}2\\4\\+5\\\hline 11\end{array}$ add 2+4= 6 ------► $\begin{array}{c}6\\+5\\\hline 11\end{array}$

①
6 7	8 9	5 8	2 8	6 9	7 9
1	1	3	6	3	2
+2	+2	+6	+3	+4	+6
9	11	14	11	13	15

②
1 7	4 6	7 8	3 7	5 6	3 5
6	2	1	4	1	2
+2	+7	+5	+5	+4	+6
9	13	13	12	10	11

③
3 4	5 7	8 9	4 9	6 8	5 8
1	2	1	5	2	3
+7	+2	+8	+9	+5	+2
11	9	17	18	13	10

Drill #1

5	1	8	6
+ 1	+ 6	+ 0	+ 1
6	7	8	7
2	3	1	9
+ 7	+ 1	+ 2	+ 0
9	4	3	9
7	2	6	3
+ 1	+ 3	+ 0	+ 2
8	5	6	5
4	3	0	4
+ 0	+ 4	+ 2	+ 1
4	7	2	5

Drill #2

3	3	0	1
+ 2	+ 0	+ 8	+ 1
5	3	8	2
5	2	2	2
+ 4	+ 1	+ 6	+ 2
9	3	8	4
2	0	2	6
+ 5	+ 9	+ 3	+ 2
7	9	5	8
5	1	4	1
+ 3	+ 4	+ 3	+ 0
8	5	7	1

Drill #3

3	4	5	1
+ 3	+ 5	+ 3	+ 3
6	9	8	4
4	0	7	2
+ 2	+ 4	+ 2	+ 4
6	4	9	6
5	1	0	3
+ 2	+ 7	+ 6	+ 6
7	8	6	9
2	4	5	3
+ 0	+ 3	+ 4	+ 5
2	7	9	8

Drill #4

4	8	6	3
+ 2	+ 1	+ 3	+ 3
6	9	9	6
2	1	7	3
+ 6	+ 8	+ 0	+ 4
8	9	7	7
7	2	4	5
+ 2	+ 5	+ 4	+ 3
9	7	8	8
1	3	6	4
+ 5	+ 5	+ 2	+ 5
6	8	8	9

Write the answers to the addition facts. Then color the harvest picture.

7	4	4	8	8	6	10
+ 5	+ 8	+ 7	+ 3	+ 7	+ 9	+ 5
12	12	11	11	15	15	15
				2	1	6
12	13	23	32	4	3	2
+ 3	+ 6	+ 45	+ 67	+ 7	+ 5	+ 9
15	19	68	99	13	9	17

Drill #1

3	7	0	2
+ 3	+ 2	+ 4	+ 7
6	9	4	9
6	8	1	0
+ 2	+ 1	+ 5	+ 7
8	9	6	7
7	8	4	3
+ 1	+ 0	+ 3	+ 4
8	8	7	7
2	1	5	5
+ 4	+ 7	+ 2	+ 0
6	8	7	5

Drill #2

3	3	6	1
+ 3	+ 4	+ 0	+ 6
6	7	6	7
6	0	5	3
+ 1	+ 3	+ 3	+ 1
7	3	8	4
4	7	1	4
+ 4	+ 0	+ 2	+ 5
8	7	3	9
4	2	3	4
+ 1	+ 5	+ 2	+ 0
5	7	5	4

Drill #3

3	6	2	7
+ 2	+ 3	+ 3	+ 1
5	9	5	8
9	1	5	2
+ 0	+ 2	+ 1	+ 6
9	3	6	8
6	8	4	5
+ 1	+ 0	+ 2	+ 4
7	8	6	9
1	3	1	3
+ 0	+ 3	+ 4	+ 5
1	6	5	8

Drill #4

6	1	0	2
+ 3	+ 8	+ 9	+ 5
9	9	9	7
2	4	2	1
+ 2	+ 4	+ 1	+ 3
4	8	3	4
1	0	3	3
+ 1	+ 8	+ 0	+ 2
2	8	3	5
3	5	2	2
+ 5	+ 4	+ 0	+ 3
8	9	2	5

Connect the numbers and color the picture.

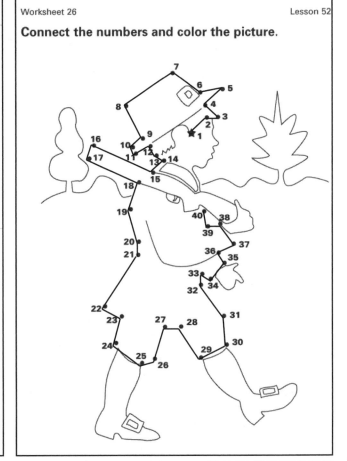

Write the answers in the blanks.

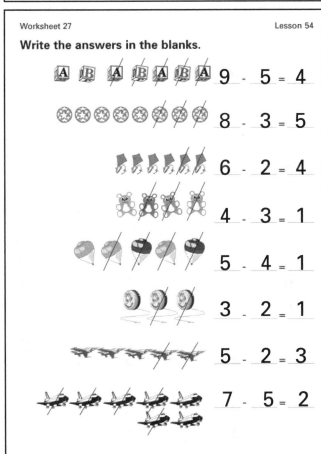

9 - 5 = 4

8 - 3 = 5

6 - 2 = 4

4 - 3 = 1

5 - 4 = 1

3 - 2 = 1

5 - 2 = 3

7 - 5 = 2

Drill #1

3	2	1	3
+ 6	+ 3	+ 7	+ 5
9	5	8	8
2	2	0	4
+ 4	+ 2	+ 4	+ 2
6	4	4	6
1	5	3	3
+ 3	+ 3	+ 0	+ 3
4	8	3	6
6	6	0	1
+ 1	+ 2	+ 9	+ 5
7	8	9	6

Drill #2

8	4	5	6
+ 0	+ 4	+ 1	+ 2
8	8	6	8
4	7	1	2
+ 3	+ 0	+ 8	+ 6
7	7	9	8
5	6	0	2
+ 4	+ 3	+ 6	+ 5
9	9	6	7
5	5	1	7
+ 0	+ 2	+ 3	+ 1
5	7	4	8

Drill #3

3	4	9	2
+ 4	+ 3	+ 0	+ 1
7	7	9	3
0	5	8	2
+ 7	+ 4	+ 1	+ 0
7	9	9	2
2	1	7	0
+ 7	+ 1	+ 2	+ 5
9	2	9	5
0	3	2	4
+ 4	+ 2	+ 5	+ 1
4	5	7	5

Drill #4

4	2	1	2
+ 5	+ 7	+ 5	+ 6
9	9	6	8
3	1	4	5
+ 1	+ 2	+ 4	+ 3
4	3	8	8
1	6	3	2
+ 6	+ 0	+ 3	+ 2
7	6	6	4
5	1	2	1
+ 2	+ 4	+ 4	+ 0
7	5	6	1

MEASURING WITH INCHES

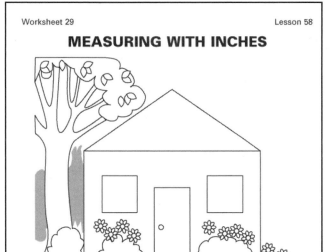

Measure the house using an inch ruler.

1. The house is _5_ inches wide.
2. The walls of the house are _3_ inches high.
3. The door is _2_ inches high.
4. The door is _1_ inches wide.
5. The windows are _1_ inches wide.
6. Each side of the roof is _3_ inches.
7. The doornob is _1_ inches from the ground.

Drill #1

1	5	7	2
+ 8	+ 4	+ 1	+ 3
9	9	8	5
5	4	8	1
+ 2	+ 4	+ 0	+ 2
7	8	8	3
0	3	9	6
+ 1	+ 2	+ 0	+ 1
1	5	9	7
1	6	2	2
+ 4	+ 3	+ 0	+ 5
5	9	2	7

Drill #2

0	2	3	2
+ 9	+ 1	+ 0	+ 7
9	3	3	9
5	0	4	0
+ 4	+ 8	+ 5	+ 5
9	8	9	5
3	2	1	3
+ 2	+ 2	+ 1	+ 5
5	4	2	8
3	2	1	6
+ 6	+ 4	+ 3	+ 0
9	6	4	6

Drill #3

6	5	0	5
+ 2	+ 3	+ 6	+ 1
8	8	6	6
1	0	2	2
+ 7	+ 4	+ 6	+ 4
8	4	8	6
1	3	4	7
+ 5	+ 3	+ 2	+ 0
6	6	6	7
0	2	0	3
+ 3	+ 7	+ 7	+ 4
3	9	7	7

Drill #4

4	5	3	5
+ 3	+ 2	+ 3	+ 0
7	7	6	5
5	7	8	3
+ 3	+ 2	+ 1	+ 6
8	9	9	9
2	4	3	4
+ 5	+ 2	+ 5	+ 1
7	6	8	5
0	1	3	4
+ 2	+ 6	+ 1	+ 5
2	7	4	9

Help the wise man find his way to the manger. The correct answer to each subtraction problem tells the correct path to take.

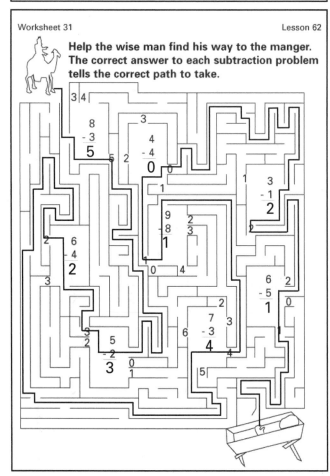

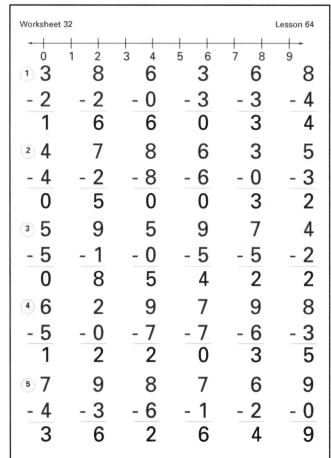

Drill #1

```
  1     4     1     2
+ 4   + 4   + 0   + 6
  5     8     1     8
  3     6     5     1
+ 1   + 0   + 2   + 6
  4     6     7     7
  4     1     4     3
+ 1   + 8   + 3   + 5
  5     9     7     8
  4     1     0     2
+ 0   + 2   + 8   + 1
  4     3     8     3
```

Drill #2

```
  1     2     5     0
+ 3   + 2   + 4   + 9
  4     4     9     9
  2     1     3     3
+ 4   + 1   + 6   + 5
  6     2     9     8
  5     3     2     2
+ 1   + 0   + 3   + 0
  6     3     5     2
  2     9     8     4
+ 5   + 0   + 1   + 2
  7     9     9     6
```

Drill #3

```
  0     3     7     5
+ 5   + 2   + 2   + 3
  5     5     9     8
  4     0     6     8
+ 5   + 0   + 1   + 0
  9     0     7     8
  7     6     1     2
+ 1   + 3   + 2   + 3
  8     9     3     5
  3     4     0     6
+ 4   + 2   + 4   + 2
  7     6     4     8
```

Drill #4

```
  0     3     1     2
+ 7   + 3   + 7   + 7
  7     6     8     9
  1     0     2     3
+ 5   + 4   + 5   + 6
  6     4     7     9
  5     7     6     4
+ 3   + 0   + 3   + 2
  8     7     9     6
  4     3     7     4
+ 5   + 4   + 2   + 3
  9     7     9     7
```

Write the numbers in the boxes when:

counting by fives: **counting by sevens:**

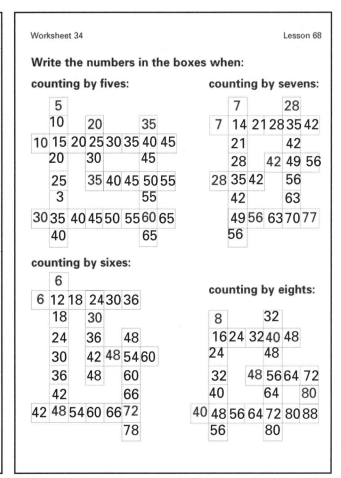

counting by sixes:

counting by eights:

Drill #1

```
  1     3     7     9
+ 8   + 8   + 6   + 7
  9    11    13    16
  3     2     7     2
+ 1   + 8   + 8   + 4
  4    10    15     6
  6     8     0     4
+ 9   + 8   + 4   + 2
 15    16     4     6
  0     5     8     6
+ 7   + 5   + 1   + 5
  7    10     9    11
```

Drill #2

```
  2     6     9     1
+ 6   + 3   + 2   + 3
  8     9    11     4
  5     6     9     3
+ 3   + 7   + 8   + 3
  8    13    17     6
  9     7     4     2
+ 6   + 2   + 6   + 7
 15     9    10     9
  1     6     5     9
+ 6   + 0   + 7   + 1
  7     6    12    10
```

Drill #3

```
  5     3     7     1
+ 6   + 6   + 5   + 7
 11     9    12     8
  4     7     4     8
+ 4   + 0   + 9   + 3
  8     7    13    11
  7     9     3     4
+ 9   + 3   + 4   + 3
 16    12     7     7
  9     3     4     6
+ 5   + 9   + 5   + 6
 14    12     9    12
```

Drill #4

```
  5     4     9     5
+ 0   + 8   + 9   + 2
  5    12    18     7
  8     1     6     2
+ 5   + 5   + 2   + 9
 13     6     8    11
  8     4     2     1
+ 2   + 7   + 5   + 0
 10    11     7     1
  3     5     5     8
+ 5   + 4   + 8   + 7
  8     9    13    15
```

Add and color the picture.

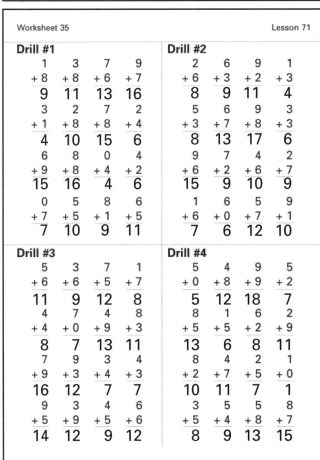
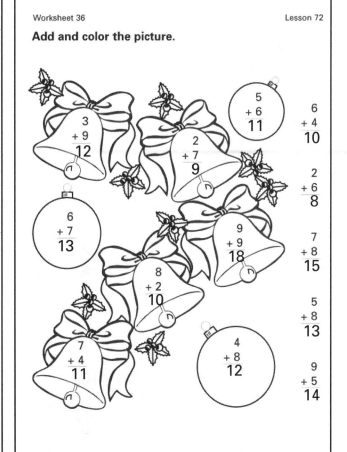

Al has 5 tomatoes on a plant in his garden. He picked 1 tomato from the plant. How many tomatoes were left on the plant? Label the answer.

5 - 1 = 4 tomatoes

There are 4 trumpet players in the band. 2 of them are sick today. How many trumpet players are left to play in the band today? Label the answer.

4 - 2 = 2 players

Hal had 8 cupcakes. He gave 4 to his friends. How many cupcakes did Hal have left? Label the answer.

8 - 4 = 4 cupcakes

Drill #1

9	7	8	2
+ 4	+ 7	+ 9	+ 5
13	**14**	**17**	**7**
7	4	6	5
+ 1	+ 0	+ 4	+ 1
8	**4**	**10**	**6**
1	5	6	2
+ 6	+ 3	+ 7	+ 7
7	**8**	**13**	**9**
3	9	4	0
+ 3	+ 8	+ 3	+ 5
6	**17**	**7**	**5**

Drill #2

3	7	5	1
+ 6	+ 5	+ 6	+ 7
9	**12**	**11**	**8**
3	2	7	8
+ 7	+ 3	+ 3	+ 4
10	**5**	**10**	**12**
3	0	2	1
+ 0	+ 9	+ 1	+ 4
3	**9**	**3**	**5**
6	3	4	9
+ 1	+ 2	+ 1	+ 0
7	**5**	**5**	**9**

Drill #3

8	5	1	6
+ 0	+ 9	+ 2	+ 8
8	**14**	**3**	**14**
1	1	2	1
+ 1	+ 9	+ 2	+ 0
2	**10**	**4**	**1**
0	8	7	4
+ 8	+ 2	+ 4	+7
8	**10**	**11**	**11**
1	7	2	2
+ 8	+ 6	+ 8	+ 4
9	**13**	**10**	**6**

Drill #4

3	9	3	7
+ 8	+ 7	+ 1	+ 8
11	**16**	**4**	**15**
6	5	0	6
+ 9	+ 5	+ 4	+ 5
15	**10**	**4**	**11**
0	8	8	4
+ 7	+ 8	+ 1	+ 2
7	**16**	**9**	**6**
2	9	6	1
+ 6	+ 2	+ 3	+ 3
8	**11**	**9**	**4**

①10	11	13	17	12	14
- 1	- 2	- 5	- 9	- 4	- 5
9	**9**	**8**	**8**	**8**	**9**
②11	15	10	16	14	10
- 3	- 8	- 2	- 7	- 6	- 3
8	**7**	**8**	**9**	**8**	**7**
③16	13	10	11	10	12
- 8	- 4	- 6	- 6	- 4	- 5
8	**9**	**4**	**5**	**6**	**7**
④10	14	11	13	12	10
- 5	- 8	- 5	- 8	- 7	- 9
5	**6**	**6**	**5**	**5**	**1**
⑤11	15	10	17	14	11
- 8	- 7	- 7	- 8	- 9	- 4
3	**8**	**3**	**9**	**5**	**7**

Drill #1

5	9	6	3
+ 3	+ 8	+ 7	+ 3
8	**17**	**13**	**6**
9	6	4	2
+ 6	+ 0	+ 6	+ 7
15	**6**	**10**	**9**
1	7	5	3
+ 6	+ 2	+ 7	+ 7
7	**9**	**12**	**10**
5	7	7	8
+ 6	+ 0	+ 5	+ 3
11	**7**	**12**	**11**

Drill #2

9	4	8	6
- 1	- 3	- 2	- 4
8	**1**	**6**	**2**
9	5	7	8
- 3	- 0	- 4	- 5
6	**5**	**3**	**3**
9	8	6	7
- 8	- 7	- 1	- 2
1	**1**	**5**	**5**
9	5	8	7
- 6	- 2	- 3	- 5
3	**3**	**5**	**2**

Drill #3

9	9	4	4
+ 5	+ 3	+ 5	+ 3
14	**12**	**9**	**7**
5	1	9	2
+ 0	+ 5	+ 9	+ 9
5	**6**	**18**	**11**
8	4	6	5
+ 5	+ 8	+ 2	+2
13	**12**	**8**	**7**
4	3	4	1
+ 4	+ 6	+ 9	+ 7
8	**9**	**13**	**8**

Drill #4

5	1	6	9
- 5	- 1	- 2	- 9
0	**0**	**4**	**0**
2	8	9	8
- 0	- 6	- 7	- 8
2	**2**	**2**	**0**
7	3	2	9
- 7	- 1	- 1	- 2
0	**2**	**1**	**7**
5	9	7	3
- 1	- 4	- 0	- 3
4	**5**	**7**	**0**

0 1 2 3 4 5 6 7 8 9 10 11 12 13 14 15 16 17 18 19

(1)
10	12	11	15	10	13
- 1	- 3	- 5	- 9	- 3	- 6
9	9	6	6	7	7

(2)
12	16	10	13	11	17
- 7	- 7	- 9	- 4	- 8	- 8
5	9	1	9	3	9

(3)
10	14	12	11	15	14
- 5	- 5	- 9	- 2	- 6	- 8
5	9	3	9	9	6

(4)
10	11	13	10	12	14
- 7	- 3	- 7	- 2	- 4	- 7
3	8	6	8	8	7

(5)
14	13	10	12	11	13
- 9	- 5	- 6	- 6	- 6	- 9
5	8	4	6	5	4

100	101	102	103	104	105	106	107	108	109
110	111	112	113	114	115	116	117	118	119
120	121	122	123	124	125	126	127	128	129
130	131	132	133	134	135	136	137	138	139
140	141	142	143	144	145	146	147	148	149
150	151	152	153	154	155	156	157	158	159
160	161	162	163	164	165	166	167	168	169
170	171	172	173	174	175	176	177	178	179
180	181	182	183	184	185	186	187	188	189
190	191	192	193	194	195	196	197	198	199

Drill #1

7	7	6	5
+ 1	+ 7	+ 4	+ 1
8	14	10	6
1	9	6	0
+ 3	+ 8	+ 9	+ 4
4	17	15	4
3	5	4	2
+ 3	+ 3	+ 2	+ 4
6	8	6	6
3	7	7	1
+ 7	+ 5	+ 3	+ 7
10	12	10	8

Drill #2

2	3	5	6
- 1	- 3	- 4	- 2
1	0	1	4
9	4	8	6
- 7	- 2	- 4	- 5
2	2	4	1
2	4	8	1
- 0	- 3	- 8	- 1
2	1	0	0
6	7	9	8
- 6	- 3	- 5	- 6
0	4	4	2

Drill #3

1	5	2	1
+ 1	+ 9	+ 2	+ 0
2	14	4	1
0	7	7	2
+ 8	+ 6	+ 4	+ 5
8	13	11	7
1	8	2	4
+ 8	+ 2	+ 8	+7
9	10	10	11
3	3	2	9
+ 0	+ 2	+ 1	+ 0
3	5	3	9

Drill #4

6	5	9	8
- 1	- 0	- 8	- 2
5	5	1	6
9	7	8	6
- 6	- 7	- 5	- 3
3	0	3	3
8	5	9	7
- 1	- 2	- 3	- 0
7	3	6	7
6	3	4	5
- 0	- 1	- 4	- 3
6	2	0	2

Color each area. The shapes below will tell you which color to use.

■ Yellow
▲ Blue
● Purple
— Black

▲ Orange
❘ Red
❱ Green

Teacher check

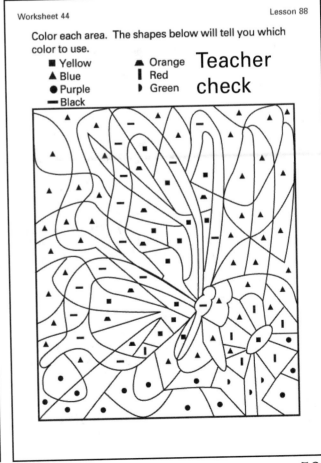

Worksheet 45 — Lesson 91

Drill #1

6	9	0	7
+ 9	+ 7	+ 4	+ 8
15	16	4	15
0	9	8	1
+ 7	+ 2	+ 1	+ 3
7	11	9	4
2	8	6	4
+ 6	+ 8	+ 3	+ 2
8	16	9	6
5	6	2	6
+ 3	+ 0	+ 7	+ 7
8	6	9	13

Drill #2

1	3	6	7
- 1	- 0	- 3	- 7
0	3	3	0
5	9	8	2
- 1	- 2	- 0	- 2
4	7	8	0
1	6	8	9
- 0	- 4	- 7	- 9
1	2	1	0
4	7	5	7
- 1	- 6	- 5	- 1
3	1	0	6

Drill #3

5	3	7	1
+ 6	+ 6	+ 5	+ 7
11	9	12	8
4	3	4	6
+ 4	+ 9	+ 9	+ 6
8	12	13	12
7	9	3	4
+ 9	+ 3	+ 4	+3
16	12	7	7
9	9	4	3
+ 6	+ 8	+ 6	+ 3
15	17	10	6

Drill #4

9	8	5	7
- 1	- 3	- 3	- 5
8	5	2	2
3	4	7	5
- 3	- 0	- 2	- 4
0	4	5	1
9	7	8	4
- 5	- 4	- 6	- 4
4	3	2	0
3	9	9	8
- 2	- 0	- 4	- 1
1	9	5	7

Worksheet 46 — Lesson 92

0 1 2 3 4 5 6 7 8 9 10 11 12 13 14 15 16 17 18 19

(1) 18	10	11	13	14	12
- 9	- 1	- 3	- 4	- 8	- 9
9	9	8	9	6	3
(2) 15	10	16	12	11	10
- 8	- 5	- 9	- 4	- 5	- 2
7	5	7	8	6	8
(3) 12	17	16	10	15	13
- 6	- 9	- 7	- 6	- 9	- 5
6	8	9	4	6	8
(4) 15	14	10	14	11	14
- 6	- 6	- 4	- 7	- 2	- 5
9	8	6	7	9	9
(5) 10	13	16	11	13	12
- 3	- 9	- 8	- 6	- 6	- 5
7	4	8	5	7	7

Worksheet 47 — Lesson 94

(1) Donna has 25 stamps. Joan gave 30 more stamps to Donna. How many stamps does Donna have in all?

25 + 30 =

$$25$$
$$+\ 30$$
$$55 \text{ stamps}$$

(2) Tim had 15 problems on his math paper on Monday. He had 12 problems on his math paper on Tuesday. How many problems did Tim have on Monday and Tuesday?

15 + 12 =

$$15$$
$$+\ 12$$
$$27 \text{ problems}$$

(3) Sarah's father had 13 baseball caps. He gave 4 of them to Joyce's father. How many caps did Sarah's father have left?

13 - 4 = 9 caps

(4) Jerry had a stack of 16 blocks. 8 of the blocks fell off. How may blocks did Jerry have left in his stack?

16 - 8 = 8 blocks

Worksheet 48 — Lesson 96

Drill #1

8	4	2	1
+ 2	+ 7	+ 5	+ 0
10	11	7	1
3	4	5	5
+ 5	+ 0	+ 8	+ 1
8	4	13	6
9	7	8	2
+ 4	+ 2	+ 9	+ 7
13	9	17	9
7	9	6	0
+ 1	+ 8	+ 4	+ 4
8	17	10	4

Drill #2

2	4	6	3
- 1	- 4	- 2	- 1
1	0	4	2
7	9	8	5
- 5	- 6	- 3	- 4
2	3	5	1
9	3	7	8
- 4	- 3	- 2	- 5
5	0	5	3
9	2	6	8
- 9	- 0	- 3	- 2
0	2	3	6

Drill #3

3	5	7	2
+ 7	+ 3	+ 3	+ 4
10	8	10	6
3	0	2	1
+ 0	+ 9	+ 1	+ 4
3	9	3	5
6	3	4	8
+ 1	+ 2	+ 1	+0
7	5	5	8
1	7	6	5
+ 3	+ 7	+ 9	+ 4
4	14	15	9

Drill #4

1	8	4	5
- 0	- 8	- 3	- 2
1	0	1	3
6	4	2	7
- 5	- 0	- 2	- 1
1	4	0	6
4	6	8	9
- 2	- 1	- 4	- 5
2	5	4	4
7	7	8	9
- 4	- 0	- 6	- 3
3	7	2	6

0 1 2 3 4 5 6 7 8 9 10 11 12 13 14 15 16 17 18 19

(1)
```
 10    12    14    11    13    10
- 3   - 8   - 6   - 4   - 6   - 1
  7     4     8     7     7     9
```

(2)
```
 13    10    15    13    11    12
- 5   - 5   - 6   - 9   - 6   - 3
  8     5     9     4     5     9
```

(3)
```
 11    15    14    10    12    18
- 8   - 7   - 8   - 7   - 7   - 9
  3     8     6     3     5     9
```

(4)
```
 13    11    10    13    12    15
- 7   - 5   - 9   - 4   - 4   - 9
  6     6     1     9     8     6
```

(5)
```
 11    16    12    14    17    10
- 2   - 8   - 6   - 9   - 8   - 4
  9     8     6     5     9     6
```

Drill #1
```
  8     3     5     4
+ 2   + 6   + 6   + 7
 10     9    11    11
  8     5     6     6
+ 0   + 5   + 8   + 5
  8    10    14    11
  3     1     3     1
+ 8   + 9   + 1   + 2
 11    10     4     3
  4     8     8     0
+ 2   + 1   + 8   + 7
  6     9    16     7
```

Drill #2
```
  5     6     9     7
- 0   - 3   - 2   - 7
  5     3     7     0
  9     8     8     5
- 1   - 7   - 0   - 1
  8     1     8     4
  9     6     7     3
- 8   - 4   - 5   - 0
  1     2     2     3
  4     6     8     7
- 1   - 6   - 2   - 6
  3     0     6     1
```

Drill #3
```
  2     0     6     6
+ 7   + 4   + 0   + 9
  9     4     6    15
  8     4     7     9
+ 3   + 6   + 0   + 6
 11    10     7    15
  3     5     9     1
+ 3   + 7   + 8   + 6
  6    12    17     7
  1     6     9     2
+ 3   + 3   + 2   + 6
  4     9    11     8
```

Drill #4
```
  3     5     6     8
- 2   - 4   - 1   - 4
  1     1     5     4
  7     8     6     4
- 3   - 5   - 0   - 2
  4     3     6     2
  9     5     8     1
- 7   - 5   - 1   - 1
  2     0     7     0
  9     7     9     5
- 0   - 2   - 5   - 3
  9     5     4     2
```

Write the subtraction facts.

(1)
$$3+7=10 \qquad 4+5=9 \qquad 8+3=11$$
$$10-7=3 \qquad 9-5=4 \qquad 11-3=8$$
$$10-3=7 \qquad 9-4=5 \qquad 11-8=3$$

(2)
$$2+6=8 \qquad 4+8=12 \qquad 3+4=7$$
$$8-6=2 \qquad 12-8=4 \qquad 7-4=3$$
$$8-2=6 \qquad 12-4=8 \qquad 7-3=4$$

(3)
$$5+7=12 \qquad 8+6=14 \qquad 7+8=15$$
$$12-7=5 \qquad 14-6=8 \qquad 15-8=7$$
$$12-5=7 \qquad 14-8=6 \qquad 15-7=8$$

(4)
$$7+6=13 \qquad 7+9=16 \qquad 5+9=14$$
$$13-6=7 \qquad 16-9=7 \qquad 14-9=5$$
$$13-7=6 \qquad 16-7=9 \qquad 14-5=9$$

Color the numbers > 150 brown.
Color the numbers < 150 yellow.
Color the nose and blocks.

Teacher check

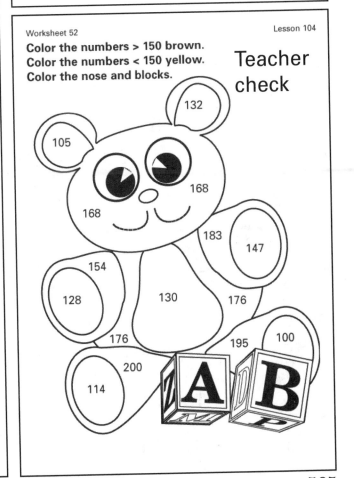

132, 105, 168, 168, 183, 147, 154, 128, 130, 176, 176, 195, 100, 200, 114

565

Worksheet 53 — Lesson 105

```
 0  1  2  3  4  5  6  7  8  9  10 11 12 13 14 15 16 17 18 19

1)  12      15      11      10      14      16
   - 3     - 7     - 5     - 4     - 8     - 9
   ----    ----    ----    ----    ----    ----
     9       8       6       6       6       7

2)  10      15      13      11      17      12
   - 1     - 9     - 6     - 4     - 8     - 5
   ----    ----    ----    ----    ----    ----
     9       6       7       7       9       7

3)  11      18      12      10      13      15
   - 3     - 9     - 7     - 9     - 4     - 6
   ----    ----    ----    ----    ----    ----
     8       9       5       1       9       9

4)  10      13      15      11      16      14
   - 7     - 5     - 8     - 2     - 8     - 6
   ----    ----    ----    ----    ----    ----
     3       8       7       9       8       8

5)  11      14      16      12      10      13
   - 6     - 5     - 7     - 4     - 3     - 8
   ----    ----    ----    ----    ----    ----
     5       9       9       8       7       5
```

Worksheet 54 — Lesson 106

Drill #1
```
  2     7     1     5
+ 9   + 5   + 5   + 6
---   ---   ---   ---
 11    12     6    11

  8     9     4     5
+ 7   + 9   + 8   + 0
---   ---   ---   ---
 15    18    12     5

  3     6     5     8
+ 4   + 2   + 4   + 5
---   ---   ---   ---
  7     8     9    13

  7     3     5     6
+ 9   + 9   + 2   + 6
---   ---   ---   ---
 16    12     7    12
```

Drill #2
```
  9     6     8     5
- 4   - 1   - 2   - 2
---   ---   ---   ---
  5     5     6     3

  8     1     9     7
- 3   - 0   - 8   - 4
---   ---   ---   ---
  5     1     1     3

  3     5     4     6
- 2   - 5   - 3   - 4
---   ---   ---   ---
  1     0     1     2

  9     8     7     2
- 6   - 1   - 6   - 2
---   ---   ---   ---
  3     7     1     0
```

Drill #3
```
  8     2     8     3
+ 2   + 5   + 4   + 5
---   ---   ---   ---
 10     7    12     8

  4     5     1     9
+ 7   + 8   + 0   + 4
---   ---   ---   ---
 11    13     1    13

  4     8     5     1
+ 0   + 9   + 1   + 6
---   ---   ---   ---
  4    17     6     7

  7     5     8     9
+ 0   + 7   + 3   + 5
---   ---   ---   ---
  7    12    11    14
```

Drill #4
```
  5     9     4     8
- 1   - 3   - 0   - 7
---   ---   ---   ---
  4     6     4     1

  9     2     7     6
- 7   - 1   - 3   - 6
---   ---   ---   ---
  2     1     4     0

  9     6     8     4
- 0   - 2   - 4   - 2
---   ---   ---   ---
  9     4     4     2

  3     6     6     9
- 1   - 0   - 5   - 9
---   ---   ---   ---
  2     6     1     0
```

Worksheet 55 — Lesson 108

```
1)   82      21      50      31      52
     11      35      42      12      31
   + 34    + 90    + 86    + 76    + 24
   ----    ----    ----    ----    ----
    127     146     178     119     107

2)  249     643     154     384     743
  + 540   + 125   + 823   + 405   + 216
   ----    ----    ----    ----    ----
    789     768     977     789     959
```

```
3)  12      13       2      13       8      12
   - 5     - 5     - 2     - 4     - 4     - 7
   ----    ----    ----    ----    ----    ----
     7       8       0       9       4       5

4)  15       9      10       5      17       7
   - 6     - 7     - 7     - 3     - 8     - 5
   ----    ----    ----    ----    ----    ----
     9       2       3       2       9       2

5)   6      11      16       9      11      18
   - 1     - 4     - 8     - 3     - 7     - 9
   ----    ----    ----    ----    ----    ----
     5       7       8       6       4       9
```

Worksheet 56 — Lesson 111

Drill #1
```
  1     7     5     8
+ 6   + 0   + 7   + 3
---   ---   ---   ---
  7     7    12    11

  9     1     4     2
+ 5   + 5   + 5   + 9
---   ---   ---   ---
 14     6     9    11

  5     4     9     5
+ 0   + 8   + 9   + 2
---   ---   ---   ---
  5    12    18     7

  8     5     6     8
+ 5   + 4   + 2   + 7
---   ---   ---   ---
 13     9     8    15
```

Drill #2
```
  1     7     4     8
- 1   - 7   - 1   - 3
---   ---   ---   ---
  0     0     3     5

  6     8     2     7
- 3   - 5   - 0   - 2
---   ---   ---   ---
  3     3     2     5

  8     7     9     5
- 8   - 5   - 1   - 2
---   ---   ---   ---
  0     2     8     3

  3     5     7     9
- 0   - 4   - 1   - 2
---   ---   ---   ---
  3     1     6     7
```

Drill #3
```
  6     0     4     1
+ 1   + 9   + 1   + 4
---   ---   ---   ---
  7     9     5     5

  3     2     5     7
+ 6   + 3   + 6   + 3
---   ---   ---   ---
  9     5    11    10

  8     1     6     1
+ 0   + 9   + 8   + 2
---   ---   ---   ---
  8    10    14     3

  3     5     3     6
+ 8   + 5   + 1   + 5
---   ---   ---   ---
 11    10     4    11
```

Drill #4
```
  9     5     6     7
- 5   - 0   - 1   - 6
---   ---   ---   ---
  4     5     5     1

  5     8     9     7
- 3   - 7   - 3   - 0
---   ---   ---   ---
  2     1     6     7

  9     4     7     3
- 6   - 3   - 4   - 1
---   ---   ---   ---
  3     1     3     2

  8     9     8     6
- 0   - 8   - 2   - 2
---   ---   ---   ---
  8     1     6     4
```

566

Worksheet 57 — Lesson 114

Color the first, third, fifth, seventh, ninth, eleventh, and thirteenth stripe red.

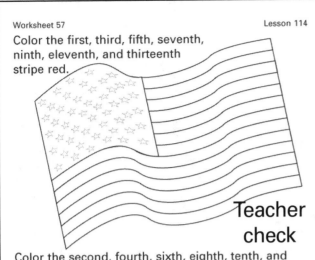

Teacher check

Color the second, fourth, sixth, eighth, tenth, and twelfth stripe white.

Color the box that the stars are in blue.

Color Washington's birth date green on the calendar.

Color Lincoln's birth date red on the calendar.

Feb. 22

February						
Sunday	Monday	Tuesday	Wednesday	Thursday	Friday	Saturday
			1	2	3	4
5	6	7	8	9	10	11
12	13	14	15	16	17	18
19	20	21	22	23	24	25
26	27	28				

Feb. 12

Worksheet 58 — Lesson 116

Drill #1
```
  3     7     4     1
+ 3   + 5   + 2   + 7
  6    12     6     8

  1     7     2     2
+ 1   + 6   + 2   + 4
  2    13     4     6

  0     5     7     1
+ 8   + 7   + 4   + 0
  8    12    11     1

  1     2     2     8
+ 8   + 3   + 8   + 4
  9     5    10    12
```

Drill #2
```
 10     4    14    12
- 3   - 2   - 5   - 3
  7     2     9     9

 13    16     9    15
- 8   - 8   - 5   - 6
  5     8     4     9

 12     8    10    11
- 7   - 3   - 7   - 8
  5     5     3     3

 17    11    14     6
- 9   - 4   - 8   - 1
  8     7     6     5
```

Drill #3
```
  2     7     8     3
+ 6   + 3   + 8   + 7
  8    10    16    10

  8     9     4     9
+ 5   + 5   + 5   + 8
 13    14     9    17

  6     6     4     9
+ 4   + 2   + 7   + 2
 10     8    11    11

  5     7     6     7
+ 5   + 8   + 6   + 2
 10    15    12     9
```

Drill #4
```
 13    10    12    14
- 4   - 5   - 8   - 6
  9     5     4     8

 16    15    11    13
- 9   - 7   - 2   - 7
  7     8     9     6

 13    10    12    10
- 5   - 6   - 5   - 9
  8     4     7     1

 11    18    11    12
- 7   - 9   - 5   - 4
  4     9     6     8
```

Worksheet 59 — Lesson 118

Write the next 3 numbers.

1. 18 20 22 24 26 28
2. 34 36 38 40 42 44
3. 70 72 74 76 78 80
4. 156 158 160 162 164 166
5. 5 7 9 11 13 15
6. 49 51 53 55 57 59
7. 71 73 75 77 79 81
8. 147 149 151 153 155 157
9. 2 5 8 11 14 17
10. 5 8 11 14 17 20
11. 7 10 13 16 19 22
12. 9 12 15 18 21 24

Worksheet 60 — Lesson 121

Drill #1
```
  8     8     3     4
+ 2   + 0   + 8   + 2
 10     8    11     6

  4     6     1     0
+ 7   + 5   + 2   + 7
 11    11     3     7

  5     6     3     8
+ 6   + 8   + 1   + 8
 11    14     4    16

  3     5     1     8
+ 6   + 5   + 9   + 1
  9    10    10     9
```

Drill #2
```
  7    10     3     7
- 7   - 2   - 0   - 6
  0     8     3     1

 14     8    16     8
- 9   - 0   - 7   - 2
  5     8     9     6

 12     8     6    14
- 6   - 7   - 4   - 7
  6     1     2     7

  5    12     9    13
- 0   - 9   - 8   - 9
  5     3     1     4
```

Drill #3
```
  6     9     1     1
+ 9   + 6   + 6   + 3
 15    15     7     4

  6     6     9     7
+ 0   + 3   + 8   + 0
  6     9    17     7

  0     4     5     9
+ 4   + 6   + 7   + 2
  4    10    12    11

  2     8     3     2
+ 7   + 3   + 3   + 6
  9    11     6     8
```

Drill #4
```
 11    11    15    11
- 3   - 6   - 9   - 9
  8     5     6     2

  5     8    10     7
- 4   - 5   - 8   - 2
  1     3     2     5

  6     9    10    13
- 1   - 5   - 4   - 6
  5     4     6     7

 17    15     1     5
- 8   - 8   - 1   - 3
  9     7     0     2
```

Cut on the solid lines only. Then fold on the dotted lines and glue to make a cube.

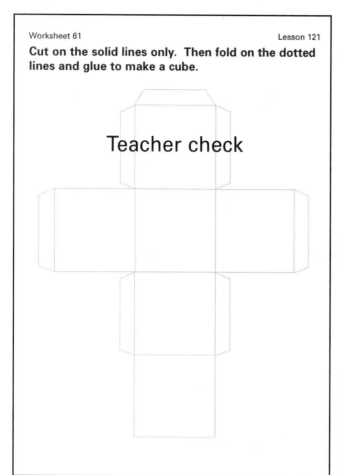

Teacher check

Add the money.

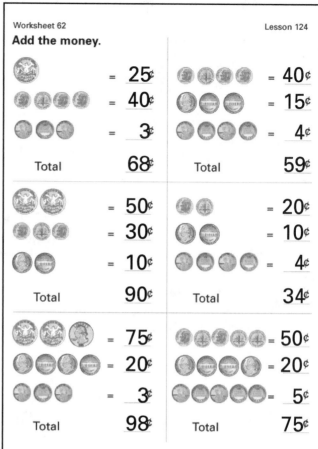

= 25¢	= 40¢
= 40¢	= 15¢
= 3¢	= 4¢
Total　68¢	Total　59¢
= 50¢	= 20¢
= 30¢	= 10¢
= 10¢	= 4¢
Total　90¢	Total　34¢
= 75¢	= 50¢
= 20¢	= 20¢
= 3¢	= 5¢
Total　98¢	Total　75¢

Drill #1

```
  5    5    8    6
+ 6  + 0  + 5  + 6
 11    5   13   12

  1    4    5    5
+ 5  + 8  + 4  + 2
  6   12    9    7

  7    9    6    3
+ 5  + 9  + 2  + 9
 12   18    8   12

  2    8    3    7
+ 9  + 7  + 4  + 9
 11   15    7   16
```

Drill #2

```
 10    7    6   10
- 8  - 4  - 4  - 4
  2    3    2    6

  8    9   10   11
- 2  - 8  - 2  - 6
  6    1    8    5

  6   13    5   15
- 1  - 6  - 5  - 8
  5    7    0    7

 14   12    3   10
- 7  - 6  - 2  - 1
  7    6    1    9
```

Drill #3

```
  3    9    1    9
+ 5  + 4  + 6  + 5
  8   13    7   14

  8    1    5    8
+ 4  + 0  + 1  + 3
 12    1    6   11

  2    5    8    5
+ 5  + 8  + 9  + 7
  7   13   17   12

  8    4    4    7
+ 2  + 7  + 0  + 0
 10   11    4    7
```

Drill #4

```
  8   13    4   11
- 7  - 9  - 2  - 3
  1    4    2    8

 17    7    8   14
- 8  - 3  - 4  - 9
  9    4    4    5

 11   16   12    6
- 9  - 7  - 9  - 0
  2    9    3    6

  5    9    9   15
- 1  - 7  - 0  - 9
  4    2    9    6
```

Add.

```
  42    75    31    16    43
+ 62  + 71  + 81  + 90  + 91
 104   146   112   106   134

  68    51    56    32    75
+ 61  + 64  + 91  + 95  + 94
 129   115   147   127   169

  94    52    45    71    23
+ 20  + 86  + 72  + 58  + 84
 114   138   117   129   107

  84    96    93    87    64
+ 81  + 42  + 76  + 61  + 73
 165   138   169   148   137

  67    24    84    45    99
+ 82  + 95  + 72  + 83  + 60
 149   119   156   128   159
```

Drill #1

8	2	5	8
+ 3	+ 9	+ 2	+ 7
11	11	7	15
5	4	9	6
+ 7	+ 5	+ 9	+ 2
12	9	18	8
7	1	4	5
+ 0	+ 5	+ 8	+ 4
7	6	12	9
1	9	5	8
+ 6	+ 5	+ 0	+ 5
7	14	5	13

Drill #2

10	12	5	9
- 2	- 6	- 2	- 2
8	6	3	7
4	13	9	11
- 1	- 9	- 1	- 6
3	4	8	5
16	14	7	14
- 7	- 9	- 5	- 7
9	5	2	7
1	6	8	17
- 1	- 3	- 8	- 8
0	3	0	9

Drill #3

6	1	7	1
+ 5	+ 2	+ 3	+ 4
11	3	10	5
4	5	6	3
+ 1	+ 6	+ 8	+ 1
5	11	14	4
0	2	1	5
+ 9	+ 3	+ 9	+ 5
9	5	10	10
6	3	8	3
+ 1	+ 6	+ 0	+ 8
7	9	8	11

Drill #4

7	10	12	6
- 6	- 4	- 9	- 2
1	6	3	4
6	8	15	8
- 1	- 7	- 9	- 2
5	1	6	6
13	11	11	9
- 6	- 9	- 3	- 8
7	2	8	1
9	15	9	10
- 5	- 8	- 6	- 8
4	7	3	2

Make Up Your Own Word Problems

1. Story: _____
   Teacher check

Work the problem from your story. Label your answer.

2. Story: _____
   Teacher check

Work the problem from your story. Label your answer.

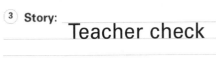

3. Story: _____
   Teacher check

Work the problem from your story. Label your answer.

1. Add.

38	37	67	29	26	58
+ 2	+ 8	+ 3	+ 9	+ 9	+ 5
40	45	70	38	35	63

86	77	18	48	49	16
+ 5	+ 6	+ 9	+ 3	+ 3	+ 4
91	83	27	51	52	20

2. Subtract.

69	53	85	67	93	48
-59	-12	-74	-33	-80	-26
10	41	11	34	13	22

27	87	49	95	74	81
-14	-30	-42	-15	-70	-21
13	57	7	80	4	60

Drill #1

1	2	1	8
+ 7	+ 4	+ 0	+ 4
8	6	1	12
4	2	7	2
+ 2	+ 2	+ 4	+ 8
6	4	11	10
7	1	5	2
+ 5	+ 1	+ 7	+ 3
12	2	12	5
3	7	0	1
+ 3	+ 6	+ 8	+ 8
6	13	8	9

Drill #2

12	15	11	6
- 3	- 6	- 8	- 1
9	9	3	5
14	9	10	14
- 5	- 5	- 7	- 8
9	4	3	6
4	16	8	11
- 2	- 8	- 3	- 4
2	8	5	7
10	13	12	17
- 3	- 8	- 7	- 9
7	5	5	8

Drill #3

3	9	9	7
+ 7	+ 8	+ 2	+ 2
10	17	11	9
8	4	4	6
+ 8	+ 5	+ 7	+ 6
16	9	11	12
7	9	6	7
+ 3	+ 5	+ 2	+ 8
10	14	8	15
2	8	6	5
+ 6	+ 5	+ 4	+ 5
8	13	10	10

Drill #4

14	13	10	12
- 6	- 7	- 9	- 4
8	6	1	8
12	11	12	11
- 8	- 2	- 5	- 5
4	9	7	6
10	15	10	18
- 5	- 7	- 6	- 9
5	8	4	9
13	16	13	11
- 4	- 9	- 5	- 7
9	7	8	4

Worksheet 69 — Lesson 138

Add the money.

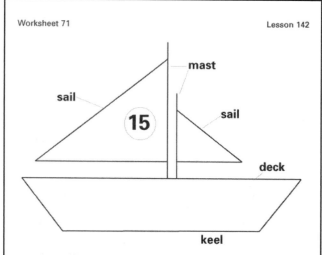

(coins)	= 50¢	(coin)	= 25¢
(coins)	= 15¢	(coins)	= 50¢
(coins)	= 4¢	(coins)	= 10¢
Total	**69¢**	**Total**	**85¢**
(coins)	= 40¢	(coins)	= 50¢
(coins)	= 40¢	(coins)	= 30¢
(coins)	= 7¢	(coins)	= 8¢
Total	**87¢**	**Total**	**88¢**
(coins)	= 50¢	(coins)	= 75¢
(coins)	= 30¢	(coin)	= 10¢
(coins)	= 15¢	(coins)	= 3¢
Total	**95¢**	**Total**	**88¢**

Worksheet 70 — Lesson 141

Drill #1

```
  4     0     8     8
+ 2   + 7   + 8   + 1
  6     7    16     9
  3     1     3     1
+ 8   + 2   + 1   + 9
 11     3     4    10
  8     6     6     5
+ 0   + 5   + 8   + 5
  8    11    14    10
  8     4     5     3
+ 2   + 7   + 6   + 6
 10    11    11     9
```

Drill #2

```
  7    10     6     4
- 6   - 1   - 6   - 1
  1     9     0     3
  3     7    17    13
- 0   - 5   - 8   - 6
  3     2     9     7
 11    16    10     9
- 3   - 7   - 4   - 1
  8     9     6     8
  7    15     6    14
- 7   - 9   - 3   - 7
  0     6     3     7
```

Drill #3

```
  1     7     9     2
+ 3   + 0   + 2   + 6
  4     7    11     8
  1     9     5     3
+ 6   + 8   + 7   + 3
  7    17    12     6
  9     6     4     8
+ 6   + 3   + 6   +3
 15     9    10    11
  6     6     0     2
+ 9   + 0   + 4   + 7
 15     6     4     9
```

Drill #4

```
  9    15     8    11
- 0   - 8   - 1   - 9
  9     7     7     2
 12    10     6     1
- 6   - 2   - 0   - 1
  6     8     6     0
  7    11    13    14
- 3   - 6   - 9   - 9
  4     5     4     5
 10     5     6    12
- 8   - 4   - 1   - 9
  2     1     5     3
```

Worksheet 71 — Lesson 142

(boat diagram with labels: mast, sail, sail, deck, keel, and **15** in the sail)

Measure the boat using a centimeter ruler. Color the picture.

1. The keel of the boat is **12** centimeters long.
2. The deck of the boat is **17** centimeters long.
3. The taller mast is **8** centimeters long.
4. The shorter mast is **5** centimeters long.
5. The horizontal length of the large sail is **8** centimeters long.
6. The horizontal length of the small sail is **4** centimeters long.

Worksheet 72 — Lesson 144

Connect the numbers starting at 100 and color the picture.

Fill in the missing numbers on the number chart.

100	101	102	103	104	105	106	107	108	109
110	111	112	113	114	115	116	117	118	119
120	121	122	123	124	125	126	127	128	129
130	131	132	133	134	135	136	137	138	139
140	141	142	143	144	145	146	147	148	149
150	151	152	153	154	155	156	157	158	159
160	161	162	163	164	165	166	167	168	169
170	171	172	173	174	175	176	177	178	179
180	181	182	183	184	185	186	187	188	189
190	191	192	193	194	195	196	197	198	199

Drill #1

```
 6    5    9    2
+6   +4   +9   +9
12    9   18   11

 8    4    7    7
+5   +8   +5   +9
13   12   12   16

 5    1    3    3
+0   +5   +9   +4
 5    6   12    7

 5    5    6    8
+6   +2   +2   +7
11    7    8   15
```

Drill #2

```
10    4   12   10
-1   -3   -6   -6
 9    1    6    4

 6    9   11    9
-4   -8   -6   -6
 2    1    5    3

12   16    8    3
-4   -7   -1   -2
 8    9    7    1

 5   14   15    8
-2   -5   -8   -3
 3    9    7    5
```

Drill #3

```
 9    5    5    8
+5   +1   +8   +2
14    6   13   10

 1    1    2    7
+6   +0   +5   +0
 7    1    7    7

 9    8    5    4
+4   +4   +7   +0
13   12   12    4

 3    8    8    4
+5   +3   +9   +7
 8   11   17   11
```

Drill #4

```
13    8   10    5
-9   -4   -8   -1
 4    4    2    4

 4   15   11    3
-2   -7   -3   -1
 2    8    8    2

12   14   16    9
-8   -7   -8   -7
 4    7    8    2

 8    6    6   18
-7   -5   -2   -9
 1    1    4    9
```

```
 1    1    2    8    5    3    8    7    1
+1   +9   +7   +9   +5   +5   +1   +3   +8
 2   10    9   17   10    8    9   10    9

 9    7    2    2    4    8    6    5    3
+5   +4   +1   +8   +4   +2   +2   +7   +4
14   11    3   10    8   10    8   12    7

 4    6    7    6    2    2    1    8    1
+8   +1   +1   +9   +6   +9   +7   +8   +5
12    7    8   15    8   11    8   16    6

 9    4    1    7    4    3    5    9    8
+6   +6   +4   +9   +5   +6   +6   +4   +7
15   10    5   16    9    9   11   13   15

 2    8    1    3    4    1    7    6    5
+2   +3   +2   +2   +7   +3   +5   +8   +4
 4   11    3    5   11    4   12   14    9

 5    9    6    6    8    7    7    3    1
+3   +3   +7   +6   +7   +2   +8   +6   +9
 8   12   13   14   14    9   11    7   18

 7    4    6    9    5    6    3    9    6
+8   +2   +5   +2   +2   +6   +3   +7   +3
15    6   11   11    7   12    6   16    9

 2    5    4    9    3    2    8    5    4
+3   +8   +3   +8   +7   +5   +4   +1   +9
 5   13    7   17   10    7   12    6   13

 6    8    2    5    3    9    3    6    7
+4   +5   +4   +9   +1   +1   +9   +1   +6
10   13    6   14    4   10   12    5   13
```

Drill #1

```
 8    9    1    1
+7   +9   +5   +6
15   18    6    7

 5    4    7    8
+2   +5   +0   +5
 7    9    7   13

 2    5    5    5
+9   +7   +4   +0
11   12    9    5

 8    6    4    9
+3   +2   +8   +5
11    8   12   14
```

Drill #2

```
 9   10    8   14
-2   -4   -5   -7
 7    6    3    7

17   13    7    3
-8   -6   -7   -0
 9    7    0    3

 7   11    5   15
-2   -6   -4   -9
 5    5    1    6

 8    7   14   10
-3   -1   -9   -2
 5    6    5    8
```

Drill #3

```
 1    6    2    6
+4   +8   +3   +1
 5   14    5    7

 7    5    0    3
+3   +6   +9   +8
10   11    9   11

 1    4    5    8
+2   +1   +5   +0
 3    5   10    8

 6    3    1    3
+5   +1   +9   +6
11    4   10    9
```

Drill #4

```
12    7    5   11
-6   -4   -3   -9
 6    3    2    2

 3   15    5   10
-1   -8   -0   -8
 2    7    5    2

 7   16   12    8
-0   -7   -9   -0
 7    9    3    8

13   11    4    6
-9   -3   -3   -4
 4    8    1    2
```

Worksheet 77 — Lesson 154

Subtract.

18	13	4	7	10	9	12	8	15
− 9	− 6	− 1	− 3	− 1	− 9	− 3	− 1	− 6
9	**7**	**3**	**4**	**9**	**0**	**9**	**7**	**9**
15	9	11	8	13	7	10	6	12
− 8	− 8	− 9	− 2	− 7	− 4	− 2	− 5	− 4
7	**1**	**2**	**6**	**6**	**3**	**8**	**1**	**8**
13	7	10	6	12	9	15	11	8
− 8	− 5	− 3	− 6	− 5	− 7	− 7	− 8	− 3
5	**2**	**7**	**0**	**7**	**2**	**8**	**3**	**5**
11	8	13	9	10	7	15	12	5
− 7	− 4	− 9	− 6	− 4	− 6	− 9	− 6	− 1
4	**4**	**4**	**3**	**6**	**1**	**6**	**6**	**4**
5	12	7	16	11	8	14	10	9
− 3	− 7	− 7	− 7	− 6	− 5	− 5	− 5	− 5
2	**5**	**0**	**9**	**5**	**3**	**9**	**5**	**4**
14	8	10	6	12	9	11	8	16
− 6	− 6	− 6	− 1	− 8	− 4	− 5	− 7	− 8
8	**2**	**4**	**5**	**4**	**5**	**6**	**1**	**8**
6	11	5	16	10	8	14	12	9
− 2	− 4	− 2	− 9	− 7	− 8	− 7	− 9	− 3
4	**7**	**3**	**7**	**3**	**0**	**7**	**3**	**6**
10	5	14	9	13	7	17	11	6
− 8	− 4	− 8	− 2	− 4	− 1	− 8	− 3	− 3
2	**1**	**6**	**7**	**9**	**6**	**9**	**8**	**3**
13	17	11	7	14	6	10	5	9
− 5	− 9	− 2	− 2	− 9	− 4	− 9	− 5	− 1
8	**8**	**9**	**5**	**5**	**2**	**1**	**0**	**8**

Worksheet 78 — Lesson 156

Drill #1

1	2	2	8
+ 8	+ 3	+ 8	+ 4
9	**5**	**10**	**12**
0	5	7	1
+ 8	+ 7	+ 4	+ 0
8	**12**	**11**	**1**
5	7	6	7
+ 5	+ 8	+ 6	+ 2
10	**15**	**12**	**9**
6	6	4	9
+ 4	+ 2	+ 7	+ 2
10	**8**	**11**	**11**

Drill #2

17	11	14	6
− 9	− 4	− 8	− 1
8	**7**	**6**	**5**
12	8	10	11
− 7	− 3	− 7	− 8
5	**5**	**3**	**3**
11	18	11	12
− 7	− 9	− 5	− 4
4	**9**	**6**	**8**
13	10	12	10
− 5	− 6	− 5	− 9
8	**4**	**7**	**1**

Drill #3

7	1	2	2
+ 6	+ 1	+ 2	+ 4
13	**2**	**4**	**6**
3	7	4	1
+ 3	+ 5	+ 2	+ 7
6	**12**	**6**	**8**
8	9	4	9
+ 5	+ 5	+ 5	+ 8
13	**14**	**9**	**17**
2	7	8	3
+ 6	+ 3	+ 8	+ 7
8	**10**	**16**	**10**

Drill #4

13	16	9	15
− 8	− 8	− 5	− 6
5	**8**	**4**	**9**
10	4	14	12
− 3	− 2	− 5	− 3
7	**2**	**9**	**9**
16	15	11	13
− 9	− 7	− 2	− 7
7	**8**	**9**	**6**
13	10	12	14
− 4	− 5	− 8	− 6
9	**5**	**4**	**8**

Worksheet 79 — Lesson 158

1 Write the answer.

10 11 12 13 14 15 16 17 18 19 **20**

Is 13 closer to 10 or 20? **10**
Is 18 closer to 10 or 20? **20**
Is 17 closer to 10 or 20? **20**
Is 12 closer to 10 or 20? **10**
Is 14 closer to 10 or 20? **10**

2 Circle the animal that is about 30 inches tall.

Circle the animal that is about 15 inches long.

3 Measure the line with an inch ruler. Circle the correct answer.

about ③ or **4** inches
about ④ or **5** inches
about **2** or ③ inches
about **3** or ④ inches

Worksheet 80 — Lesson 159

Add.

12	63	83	46	42	21
+ 37	+ 30	+ 12	+ 32	+ 51	+ 56
49	**93**	**95**	**78**	**93**	**77**
51	32	95	57	73	93
+ 57	+ 76	+ 12	+ 62	+ 80	+ 56
108	**108**	**107**	**119**	**153**	**149**
38	27	36	15	24	49
+ 54	+ 27	+ 48	+ 58	+ 47	+ 48
92	**54**	**84**	**73**	**71**	**97**
78	56	68	82	63	89
+ 99	+ 74	+ 62	+ 69	+ 89	+ 34
177	**130**	**130**	**151**	**152**	**123**
28	76	64	79	28	50
+ 34	+ 55	+ 23	+ 30	+ 6	+ 74
62	**131**	**87**	**109**	**34**	**124**

7